FOREIGN ACQUISITION OF U.S. BANKS

FOREIGN ACQUISITION OF U.S. BANKS

Staff of the Office
of the Comptroller
of the Currency

ROBERT F. DAME, INC.
1905 Huguenot Road
Richmond, Virginia 23235

ISBN 0-936-328-06-1
Library of Congress Catalog No. 81-66814

PRINTED IN THE UNITED STATES OF AMERICA

Designed and typeset by Publications Development Co. of
Crockett, Texas, Developmental Editor: Nancy Marcus Land,
Production Editor: Bessie Graham

CONTRIBUTORS

Research on the issues surrounding foreign acquisition of U.S. banks was initiated at the Office of the Comptroller of the Currency in the summer of 1979 under the aegis of C. F. Muckenfuss, III, Senior Deputy Comptroller for Policy, who contributed valuable insights in the conceptualization of the project and in careful review of many drafts. Management and oversight of the work was the responsibility of Judith A. Walter and Steven J. Weiss of the Strategic Analysis Division. As the following list of contributors shows, authors from other divisions also contributed to the series.

WILLIAM A. GLIDDEN
Special Assistant to the Chief Counsel

STEWART GODDIN
Senior International Economic Advisor
Banking Research and Economic Analysis Division

ELLEN S. GOLDBERG
Financial Analyst
Strategic Analysis Division

BLAIR B. HODGKINS
Financial Analyst
Strategic Analysis Division

THOMAS A. LOEFFLER
Financial Analyst
Strategic Analysis Division

WILLIAM A. LONGBRAKE
Deputy Comptroller
Research and Economic Programs

DIANE PAGE
Financial Analyst
Strategic Analysis Division

MELANIE R. QUINN
Financial Analyst
Strategic Analysis Division

JOHN E. SHOCKEY
Chief Counsel, Law Department

WM. PAUL SMITH
Economist
Banking Research and Economic Analysis Division

NEAL M. SOSS
Director
Banking Research and Economic Analysis Division

JUDITH A. WALTER
Deputy Director
Strategic Analysis Division

STEVEN J. WEISS
Director
Strategic Analysis Division

OFFICE OF THE COMPTROLLER OF THE CURRENCY

FOREWORD

Foreign banks and other investors owned banks in the United States more than a century ago, but foreign acquisitions of significant U.S. banks are a relatively recent phenomenon. Public awareness of foreign bank acquisitions and debate on the issues surrounding them began in the mid-1970s, but it was not until 1978, when proposals for foreign acquisitions of four major banks were announced, that there was a clear call for the development of national policy. In seeking to contribute to evaluation of the issue, the staff of the Office of the Comptroller of the Currency (OCC) discovered that there had been virtually no systematic collection of the facts. Accordingly, an effort was begun to develop a base of information that could be used to better understand the phenomenon and to assess the various concerns that it had prompted.

The 16 papers in this volume are the result of a year-long effort. They represent the first fully documented, comprehensive study of the acquisitions of U.S. banks by foreign investors. As such they will continue to provide essential factual underpinning for the thoughtful development of U.S. policy in this important area.

John G. Heimann
Comptroller of the Currency
May, 1981

CONTENTS

AN EVALUATION OF THE FOREIGN ACQUISITION ISSUE

JUDITH A. WALTER

STEVEN J. WEISS

Foreign acquisitions of existing U.S. banks are largely a phenomenon of the 1970s, particularly the latter half of the decade. From 1970 through the first half of 1980, there have been 96 foreign acquisitions of U.S. banks, 41 by foreign banking institutions and 59 by individuals or shell companies. In terms of assets acquired, 1979 and 1980 are the peak years, with $12.6 billion and $19.2 billion respectively, due chiefly to the acquisitions of three banks ranked among the largest 40 in the United States. The proposed acquisition of Crocket National, the twelfth largest U.S. bank, by Britain's Midland Bank would by itself nearly equal the 1980 figure if consummated. However, most of the acquired banks have been relatively small; their median asset size is less than $50 million. About 70 percent of foreign-acquired banks are located in California, New York, and Florida. Acquisitions by foreign individuals have been more widely dispersed than those by foreign banks, which are concentrated almost exclusively in money center states.

Foreign-owned banks, including those established *de novo* as well as acquired, represent about 5 percent of United States commercial bank assets. Through subsidiaries, branches, agencies, and other banking operations, foreign banks now control almost 15 percent of U.S. commercial bank assets. The large bank acquisitions consummated since 1979, which attracted so much attention and stimulated a lively debate about the pros and cons of foreign acquisitions and present U.S. policy, contributed less than 2 percent to the 15 percent total. Approximately 80 percent of the foreign bank assets held in this country is attributable to *de novo* activity and growth rather than acquisition.

Foreign acquisitions reflect primarily the long-run strategic interests of bank acquirers as well as economic and political features of the U.S. market that are attractive to foreign investors. Weak or failed U.S. banks are disproportionately represented among foreign acquisitions. Depressed bank stock prices and a weak dollar may also have been factors facilitating foreign acquisitions, but their significance is unclear.

Special considerations with regard to timing may also have contributed to acquisition activity at the end of the 1970s. First, the December 31, 1980 deadline was fast approaching for a number of large domestic one bank holding companies to divest either their banks or their unauthorized activities under the provisions of the Bank Holding Company Act Amendments of 1970. Second, some foreign banks with acquisition plans may have been spurred to action by fears that the intensified public debate would result in legislation restricting or prohibiting such purchases.

Another factor reflected in foreign acquisitions of U.S. banks is a historical trend toward an increasing transnational banking presence, including interest on the part of foreign banks in retail and "middle market" banking activities mirroring United States banks' growing interest in such "nontraditional" banking markets overseas.

The United States maintains a policy of openness toward foreign investment generally, including bank acquisitions. U.S. law and policy do not discriminate between foreign and domestic acquirers. The International Banking Act (IBA) incorporated a national treatment policy and, apart from "home state" limitations, the IBA did not affect acquisitions directly. By eliminating advantages of foreign branches or agencies relative to subsidiaries, the IBA appears to have given some impetus to foreign acquisition of U.S. bank subsidiaries.

During the past year, U.S. government agencies have documented the record of foreign acquisitions of U.S. banks, analyzed the possible effects of foreign ownership, and examined the various implications of the phenomenon for U.S. policy. Most important dimensions of the subject are examined in detail in this book and significant studies have been released by the Federal Reserve Board and the United States General Accounting Office (GAO).[1] The factual record and analysis contained in those studies constitute a substantial body of evidence which suggests, in our view, that the fears and concerns voiced by opponents of foreign takeovers are exaggerated or unjustified.[2] In the remainder of this paper, we will summarize the studies' findings bearing on major concerns that have been expressed with regard to supervisory, community and business credit, competitive, and national interest implications of foreign acquisitions and ownership of U.S. banks. We conclude that none of those concerns justifies a change in U.S. policy or a moratorium on foreign acquisitions of U.S. banks.

FINDINGS WITH RESPECT TO MAJOR CONCERNS

Performance of U.S. Banks Acquired by Foreigners

One of the concerns raised about foreign acquisitions of U.S. banks is that foreign owners may operate U.S. banks in an unsafe and unsound manner. However, evidence indicates that foreign owners have generally strengthened the acquired banks that were weak, in many cases by significant infusion of capital, and have maintained the pre-existing, good condition of others. Acquisitions by foreign banks have produced performance that generally is well rated by bank supervisors; the record of individual acquirers has been mixed, but, on the whole, foreign acquisitions have posed no special supervisory concerns for United States institutions.

In addition, the financial performance of acquired banks has been satisfactory. No unfavorable comparisons vis-a-vis domestically owned banks appear attributable to foreign ownership. Weaknesses in some foreign-acquired banks most often reflect continuation of pre-existing trends rather than changes that can be attributed to foreign ownership

U.S. Supervisor's Ability to Obtain Information on Foreign Owners and Transactions with Related Interests

Another concern is that U.S. regulators may be unable to obtain sufficient information about foreign acquirers or to exercise adequate control over relationships between a foreign-acquired bank and its foreign owner and related interests.

Although foreign ownership does pose some special problems of information and control, existing procedures are considered adequate and will be strengthened further by measures currently under consideration. Office of the Comptroller of the Currency (OCC) and Federal Reserve arrangements regarding the Hongkong and Shanghai Banking Corporation acquisition of Marine Midland Bank[3] demonstrate the adequacy of present supervisory authority. The issues are complex, but they have been addressed. The full panoply of United States statutes, regulations, and enforcement mechanisms apply directly to the United States subsidiary, of course, and information on foreign bank parents can be obtained through reports as well as contacts with foreign government authorities or even on-site visits, when necessary.

Reorientation of Acquired Bank Activities

An additional potential problem that has been raised is that foreign owners may reorient the activities of acquired banks and neglect the needs of communities served by the acquired banks or favor home country industry at the expense of U.S. companies. The record to date shows no evidence of foreign acquirers neglecting consumer or community interests; any such neglect would run counter to acquirer's long-run investment and practical business interests. Some foreign banks may tend to favor home country borrowers and indeed have as an objective the fostering of financial links between the United States and their home country. However, they do not need U.S. subsidiary banks for that purpose and, given competitive financial markets, there is no reason to expect that U.S. industry would be disadvantaged in any event. In fact, foreign banks here have generally competed aggressively for the accounts of U.S. companies.

U.S. Banks' Competitive Disadvantages in Acquisitions

Concerns have been expressed that U.S. banks suffer competitive disadvantages due to foreign acquisitions because (1) foreign banks enhance their relative global rank and competitive abilities by acquiring U.S. banks; (2) U.S. banks lack comparable opportunities to acquire overseas; (3) U.S. regulatory policy unfairly favors foreign versus domestic bank acquirers; and (4) foreign banks can acquire U.S. banks that are foreclosed in practice to domestic acquirers.

The evidence indicates that foreign banks' ability to acquire large U.S. banks has helped maintain or enhance the competitive position or world rank of some individual acquirers but has not had a significant effect on the overall global standing or competitive abilities of the U.S. banks. Although U.S. banks lack opportunities to acquire large banks overseas, that fact is largely attributable to structural characteristics of foreign banking markets or to foreign governments' socio-economic policy considerations that have not been a part of traditional U.S.

policies. A U.S. policy of requiring reciprocity in foreign acquisitions would be unlikely to promote new opportunities or to advance U.S. interests generally. Despite obstacles to large bank acquisitions in foreign markets, U.S. banks have developed a significant presence abroad which has enhanced their global standing and competitiveness.

Allegations that U.S. regulators unfairly favor foreign vis-a-vis domestic acquirers are invalid. U.S. regulators apply statutory criteria even-handedly to foreign and domestic acquirers. Many foreign bank acquisitions have been judged to have procompetitive effects on U.S. banking markets through the strengthening of acquired banks' capital or management or through the provision of new services or specialized expertise, which enable the acquired institution more effectively to challenge larger rivals. Although similar benefits could be obtained through domestic acquisitions, such transactions are often precluded by present federal and state laws or policy. Because of interstate banking prohibitions, state branching and bank holding company restrictions, and antitrust laws, foreign banks are able to acquire large U.S. banks that are foreclosed in practice to domestic acquirers.

Foreign-owned Banks' Competitive Advantages in the United States

Other competitive advantages that foreign-owned banks are alleged to enjoy in the United States relate to cost of funds, multistate operations, and involvement with nonbanking activities.

The IBA eliminated previously existing cost of funds advantages of foreign bank branches and agencies by authorizing the Federal Reserve to impose reserve requirements on those direct foreign bank operations and, further, requiring federal deposit insurance for foreign branches engaged in significant retail banking activity. In some cases, foreign branches may still benefit from relatively low capital requirements or other advantages enjoyed by the parent bank. However, even before the IBA changes, no cost of funds advantage was apparent for *subsidiaries* of foreign banks.

Foreign banking organizations do retain limited advantages in multistate operations, though substantially less than existed pre-IBA. Foreign banks' involvement with nonbanking enterprise is more extensive than that permitted U.S. institutions and may result in more diversification, lower risk, and greater growth potential on a global level; however, no significant competitive advantages in the United States accrue to foreign banks by virtue of their nonbanking investments and activities.

Interests of Shareholders of Acquired Banks

Concerns have been raised that U.S. shareholders may not receive an adequate return on purchases involving a foreign buyer. However, it appears that in fact shareholders have received attractive terms from foreign buyers. Shareholder interests are promoted by permitting foreign acquisitions, especially when capital is needed by a U.S. bank, and domestic bank acquirers are ruled out by U.S. law or policy. Shareholder interest does not justify any concern for unfriendly takeovers except to the same extent that any unfriendly takeover—whether foreign or domestic—may jeopardize the position of minority shareholders.

Impact of Foreign Bank Presence on U.S. Monetary Policy

Another potential problem that has been mentioned is that the presence of foreign banks may complicate implementation of monetary policy.

With the changes effected by the IBA, the Federal Reserve Board now has adequate control over foreign bank operations for monetary policy purposes. The record to date indicates no basis for concern that foreign banks will be unresponsive to moral suasion aspects of Fed policy.

Possible Influence of Foreign Government Policies

The concern has been expressed that foreign-owned banks may be subject to home country pressures running counter to U.S. national interests.

Although it is possible for the home government policies of foreign-owned banks to conflict with the U.S. national interest, to date there is no evidence of any problems arising as a result. Foreign banks have good reasons to see that their U.S. subsidiaries behave as good corporate citizens. U.S. regulators can use supervisory tools, and strong sanctions, if necessary, to counter any possible adverse effect. The most powerful sanction to any investor, foreign or domestic, is the potential loss of his investment. In an extreme situation, U.S. authorities could resort to a variety of measures to effectively achieve that result.

Unacceptable Level of Foreign Control Over
U.S. Banking

Finally, the fear has been expressed that unless acquisitions (or large acquisitions at least) are stopped, foreigners will soon control an unacceptably high percentage of U.S. bank assets.

Whether any level of foreign ownership of U.S. banks is "unacceptable" is a national policy question involving social, political, and foreign policy considerations. There is no clear basis for identifying any particular aggregate foreign share of U.S. banking resources as a threshold level to trigger policy concern. Although it would seem unrealistic to conclude, for example, that disparate foreign owners would or could act in concert against U.S. interests, even sympathetic observers concede that at some level of overall foreign control they would begin to feel uncomfortable. U.S. government authorities agree that that point has not been reached. The banking agencies have systems in place for monitoring current developments, and any new applications for acquisitions will receive close scrutiny on their merits and in the light of overall trends.

POLICY IMPLICATIONS

The foregoing review suggests that no strong case for a moratorium on foreign bank acquisitions can be made on the basis of the various concerns and fears that have been expressed. Federal bank supervisors have not found any serious or unmanageable difficulties or adverse consequences in the experience of foreign acquisition and ownership of U.S. banks to date. The GAO report supports that conclusion but recommends that a moratorium be imposed solely on the grounds of unfairness to domestic banks stemming from U.S. laws and policies that effectively foreclose large bank acquisition opportunities to domestic but not foreign bank buyers. That result is indeed anomalous and unfair to U.S. banking organizations.

It must be recognized, however, that the prospective number of foreign large bank acquisitions dependent on exploiting that unfair advantage is likely to be limited by several factors. The IBA's "home state" requirements limit the ability of foreign banks to expand their U.S. banking operations on a multistate basis. A very substantial number of large foreign bank buyers are thus now constrained by rules essentially similar to those limiting U.S. banks' acquisition opportunities. Even for those foreign banks without existing banking operations in the United States (and therefore unrestricted in the geographical scope of their potential acquisitions), the number of U.S. banks likely to be available for acquisition in key money center locations strongly favored by foreign bank entrants is probably rather limited.

Most importantly, any consideration of even a limited moratorium (e.g., one, such as GAO recommends, that would exempt small or failing banks) should include a careful assessment of the possible adverse effects. Any moratorium would be counter to the general U.S. policy of neutrality with respect to international investment flows and could damage the interests of U.S. banks abroad and perhaps those of other U.S. investors as well. Even a limited moratorium would rule out transactions that would enhance the health of our financial system through capital injections or other moves to strengthen the competitive abilities of U.S. banks other than those actually failing.

Thus a preferable alternative would be to maintain our policy of openness to foreign investment while at the same time moving expeditiously to remove the unfairness to U.S. banking organizations. The IBA called for a review of old limits on domestic institutions—limits that now are often circumvented by a variety of legal but inefficient means (LPO's, Edge Act facilities, nonbank affiliates) and are rendered increasingly obsolete by technological advances. By keeping the door open to foreign acquisitions while gradually eliminating interstate restrictions on United States bank expansion, we would have not only the continuing potential for benefit from foreign investment but also new possibilities for procompetitive domestic bank acquisitions and combinations.

FOOTNOTES

[1] See "Foreign Acquisitions of United States Banks," A Study by the Staff of the Federal Reserve Board, June 30, 1980; James V. Houpt, "The Effect of Foreign-Acquisitions on the Performance of U. S. Banks," Federal Reserve Board Staff Study, March 25, 1980, (summarized in *Federal Reserve Bulletin*, July 1980); and Report by the Comptroller General, *Despite Positive Effects, Further Foreign Acquistion of U. S. Banks Should be Limited Until Policy Conflicts are Fully Addressed*, (U. S. General Accounting Office), August 26, 1980.

[2] For statements of various concerns about foreign acquisitions, see Carol S. Greenwald, "Let's Put a Hold on Foreign Takeovers of Our Banks," *The Bankers Magazine*, November/December 1979, pp. 49-54; Sen. John Heinz III, "Foreign Takeovers of U. S. Banking—A Real Danger?" *The Journal of the Institute of Socioeconomic Studies*, Vol. 3, No. 4, Autumn 1979,

pp. 1-9; Rep. Benjamin Rosenthal, "Foreign Bank Takeovers Study Act," Statement on H. R. 5937, *Congressional Record*, November 27, 1979, pp. H11217-19; and Muriel Siebert, Letter to Rep. Henry S. Reuss, in Hearings before the Senate Committee on Banking, Housing and Urban Affairs on *Edge Corporation Branching; Foreign Bank Takeovers; and International Banking Facilities*, 96th cong., 1st sess., July 16 and 20, 1979, pp. 58-62.

[3] Statement of John G. Heimann, Comptroller of the Currency, in hearings before the Subcommittee on Commerce, Consumer, and Monetary Affairs of the Committee on Government Operations on *Foreign Acquisitions of U. S. Banks and the Non-Banking Activities of Foreign Bank Holding Companies*, 96th Cong., 2nd sess., June 25, 1980, Appendix A.

## 2

FOREIGN OWNERSHIP OF U.S. BANKS: FACTS AND PATTERNS

WILLIAM A. LONGBRAKE

MELANIE R. QUINN

JUDITH A. WALTER

SUMMARY

This paper contains a history and analysis of the foreign ownership of U.S. banks as well as a survey of existing and pending foreign ownership as of December 31, 1980. An appendix includes a comprehensive listing of foreign owned banks.

The history treats separately the establishment of *de novo* banks and the acquisition of existing banks. *De novo* entry developed momentum in the 1950s and 1960s, reaching a high in the 1970s, and has been concentrated in the money center states of New York and California where laws did not favor the establishment of branching by foreign banks. Nationality of owner, whether bank or individual, and location of the U.S. bank is analyzed by decade of establishment.

Foreign entry by acquisition began somewhat later and did not draw attention until the 1972-1973 acquisitions of Franklin National Bank and the Bank of California, N.A. From the beginning of 1970 through 1980, there were 100 foreign acquisitions of U.S. banks, including 41 by foreign banking institutions and 59 by individual investors. Over three quarters of those acquisitions have occurred since the mid-1970s.

A majority of the post-1970 acquisitions have involved banks with less than $50 million in assets. Although there are several prominent exceptions, foreign individuals have generally purchased smaller U.S. institutions than foreign banks. The largest acquisitions by foreign banks include four in 1979-1980 which together accounted for $26 billion in assets.

The paper describes many other patterns of the acquisition phenomenon. Most foreign-acquired banks are located in California, New York and Florida. There are some apparent relationships between the acquirer's nationality and choice of location. Purchases by Asian banks and individuals have been heavily concentrated in California, and Florida has been the major focus of Latin American acquirers. Acquisitions by individuals have been much more widely dispersed than acquisitions by foreign banks.

Banks from the United Kingdom, Canada, Japan and Spain account for about three quarters of acquisitions by foreign banking institutions. Individual acquirers, by contrast, have been predominantly from countries with less developed banking and financial structures.

The survey of existing foreign ownership of U.S. banks notes the following facts among many others:

- Foreign-owned banks account for 27 of the largest 300 U.S. banks.
- There are 111 U.S. banking organizations as of December 31, 1980 with a minimum ownership of 10 percent by a single foreign investor.
- These 111 are less than one percent of all U.S. commercial banks but have $79.4 billion, or about 4.7 percent, of all insured U.S. commercial bank assets.
- Banks acquired or established by foreigners have a median size in the $100-499 million asset range, compared to a median size for all U.S. banks of less than $50 million in assets.

There are nine known pending foreign acquisitions of U.S. banks and they mirror existing foreign ownership patterns. The total assets of those nine U.S. banks as of December 31, 1979, was $17.8 billion.

INTRODUCTION AND OVERVIEW

Although there is evidence of foreign ownership of a U.S.-chartered bank as early as 1854,[1] significant foreign involvement in U.S. banks is a relatively recent phenomenon. In the 1950s and 1960s establishment of U.S. subsidiaries was one of several means by which a few foreign banks began to expand into this country.[2] However, it was not until the 1970s that there was rapid and marked increase in the number of U.S. banks owned by foreign interests, including both newly established (*de novo*) banks and those acquired from domestic owners.

As of December 31, 1980, 27 of the 300 largest U.S. banks and 7 of the 50 largest were foreign owned. Overall, foreign-owned U.S. banks now account for about 0.8 percent of insured U.S. commercial banks and about 4.7 percent of all insured U.S. commercial bank domestic and foreign assets.

More than half of the existing 45 foreign owned *de novo* U.S. banks were established in the 1970s, and acquisitions of U.S. banks by foreigners were concentrated in that decade, particularly the latter half. Of 100 identified acquisitions since 1970,[3] nearly 80 percent have occurred since 1975.

Both foreign banks, primarily the largest foreign multinationals headquartered in industrialized countries, and foreign individuals, over 60 percent from non-OECD countries,[4] now own U.S. banks. Acquisition and chartering activity by foreign banks has been predominantly in the money centers—New York and California. The U.S. banks owned by foreign banks tend to be relatively large, with a median asset size in the $100 to $499 million range. Acquisition and chartering activity by foreign individuals has occurred in 14 states, the District of Columbia and Puerto Rico, with some concentration in the money center states of California and New York, and in Florida.[5] The U.S. banks owned by foreign individuals are generally smaller; the median is in the $50-99 million asset range.

Public awareness of foreign ownership of U.S. banks, particularly the acquisitions phenomenon, was raised in 1972-73 with the first foreign purchase of significant interest in sizable U.S. banks—Franklin National Bank and The Bank of California, N.A. This touched off a policy debate that simmered through the mid-1970s and intensified in the spring and summer of 1978 when, within three months, there were announcements of three major foreign acquisition proposals: Marine Midland Bank (N.Y.), National Bank of North America (N.Y.), and Union Bank (California). For the first time, controlling interest in banks among the largest 40 in the country was to be acquired, under non-emergency circumstances, by foreign banks.[6]

In the debate that ensued, it became evident that there was limited public information about the extent and nature of foreign ownership of U.S. banks. The purpose of this paper, one of a series on the issue, is to present the facts and examine salient features, patterns and trends of foreign ownership of U.S. banks.

METHODOLOGY

An alphabetized list of known foreign acquisitions of U.S. banks as of December 31, 1980 is contained in Appendix I (sections a and b). A similar list of existing foreign owned *de novo* banks is in Appendix II. Those appendices include every case of foreign ownership that could be identified from available data. However, because official systematic monitoring efforts are relatively new, particularly with regard to non-bank foreign investors, the compilation cannot be regarded as definitive.[7]

The Federal Reserve Board, which began publishing information on foreign bank activity in 1972, was the primary source of data on control of U.S. banks by foreign bank holding companies.[8] Prior to implementation of federal change of control legislation in 1979, recordkeeping on foreign individual purchases of U.S. banks was sporadic. Therefore, acquisitions by foreign individuals before the Change in Bank Control Act required supplementation of official records by press accounts. Those accounts were, in turn, verified by checking individual bank files, when possible. Such acquisitions before 1979 are, therefore, extremely difficult to ascertain. The problem is compounded when shell companies are used as investment vehicles. Complicated webs of control created for tax purposes, for instance, can sometimes obscure the identities and nationalities of the individuals who are beneficial owners.[9]

To make Appendices I and II broadly inclusive of cases of significant foreign ownership, they contain all instances of 10 percent or more ownership by a single foreign interest that could be identified with reasonable confidence.[10] That is a somewhat conservative threshold, generally following the regulatory concept of control used in administering the Change in Bank Control Act of 1978.[11]

The discussion in this paper is based on the lists in Appendices I and II and the detailed tables derived from those lists which appear in Appendices III through XI. The text tables have deliberately been kept simple. For example, ownership has been classified as either bank or individual, although finer distinctions could be made.[12] For more detail, consult the appendices.

Each case of foreign ownership of a U.S. bank has unique characteristics that arise from a combination of individual investor objectives, the parameters set by statutory and political environments, and, in the case of acquisitions, attributes of the U.S. bank which is purchased. Nevertheless, a number of patterns are evident, many of them apparently related to whether the foreign owners are banks or individuals.

This paper first looks at the history of foreign ownership of U.S. banks, considering *de novo* establishment and acquisition separately. The status of foreign ownership as of December 31, 1980 is then examined. Finally, pending acquisitions are described.

HISTORY OF FOREIGN OWNERSHIP

Banks Established De Novo

As Table 1 indicates, although a few existing foreign-owned U.S. banks date back to the 1920s, establishment of U.S. subsidiaries by foreign interests did not develop on any scale until the 1950s and 1960s, when such activity was part of a wider foreign bank expansion into U.S. markets in a variety of forms.[13] According to a report submitted to the Joint Economic Committee of the U.S. Congress in 1966: "Most foreign banks prefer to establish branches rather than subsidiaries. . . .

Table 1
Foreign-Owned *De Novo* U.S. Banks (December 31, 1980)
Classified by Geographic Location of De Novo Bank and Decade Established

Year Established	Location of De Novo				Total
	New York	California	Illinois	Other	
1920-1929	4	–	–	–	–
1930-1939	–	1 (1)	–	–	1 (4)
1940-1949	–	–	–	–	–
1950-1959	5	2	–	1	8
1960-1969	4 (1)	4	1 (1)	–	9 (2)
1970-1980	9(2)	11(5)	2	1(1)	23(8)
	22(3)	18(6)	3(1)	2(1)	45(11)

Notes: Previously established foreign *de novo* banks that were not in existence on December 31, 1980 do not appear in this table. The table excludes, for example, Chartered Bank of London-San Francisco, which was merged into Union Bank in January 1980; French Bank of California, which was merged into Bank of the West in March 1980; and the Hongkong Bank of California, which was divested in February 1979.

Numbers in parentheses indicate the number of *de novo* banks established by foreign individual(s) or nonbank companies. Numbers without parentheses are totals, including banks established by foreign banks and by foreign individual(s)/ nonbanks.

One bank established *de novo* by a foreign bank was subsequently acquired by foreign individuals.

[Those] which have elected the subsidiary form have done so because the alternative of branching has not been made available."[14]

Establishment of *de novo* subsidiaries was initially centered in California and New York, where the impetus for such activity was largely provided by state laws.[15] In California, state law encouraged foreign banks to enter by establishing subsidiaries. California law did not permit foreign bank branches to accept domestic deposits unless they were insured by the FDIC.[16] Until the passage of the International Banking Act, that insurance was not available to U.S. branches of foreign banks.

Two New York laws operated to make the subsidiary form more attractive to foreign banks. The first one was a reciprocity requirement, which precluded the establishment of branches by foreign banks whose home country did not permit New York banks to open branches. The second was a limitation that permitted operation of an agency or a branch, but not both, while permitting operation of both an agency and a subsidiary. Because agencies enjoyed greater operating freedom than branches, a number of banks preferred the combination of agency-plus-subsidiary to relying solely on a branch.[17] As chartering by foreigners increased in the 1970s, the focus on the California and New York money centers continued. At the same time, foreign individuals became a significant owner group, accounting for nearly 35 percent of existing foreign owned *de novo* banks established in the last 10 years.

Table 2 shows the nationalities of the foreign owners of U.S. *de novo* banks. Japanese and Canadian banks have established nearly 50 percent of existing U.S. *de novo* subsidiaries. Investors from a number of Asian countries, such as Hong Kong, Taiwan, and the Philippines, have comprised the bulk of foreign individuals establishing U.S. *de novo* banks, especially in the 1970s.

As Table 3 shows, there has been some correlation between the type and nationality of owners and the states in which *de novo* banks are chartered. New York, the nation's major money center, has attracted the most banks and the broadest range of owner nationalities. Of the 18 foreign banks that currently own New York *de novo* subsidiaries, 12 also operate agencies, probably reflecting the preference for the combination, as discussed earlier.[18] The five Canadian banks that have established New York subsidiaries had no choice. Because Canada excluded U.S. bank branches, Canadian branches were precluded by New York's reciprocity requirement. In California, Japanese banks and individuals from other Asian countries comprise nearly 70 percent of the foreign ownership of *de novo* banks, reflecting trans-Pacific trade flows as well as the state's ethnic composition.[19]

Table 2
Foreign-Owned *De Novo* U.S. Banks (December 31, 1980)
Classified by Nationality of Owner and Decade Established

Year Established	Nationality of Owner						Total
	Japan	Other Asia	Canada	U.K.	Europe	Other	
1920-1929	–	–	1	1	1	1	4
1930-1939	–	1 (1)	–	–	–	–	1 (1)
1940-1949	–	–	–	–	–	–	–
1950-1959	4	–	3	–	1	–	8
1960-1969	2 (1)	1	3	1	–	2 (1)	9 (2)
1970-1980	9 (1)	7 (6)	2 (1)	1	2	2	23(8)
	15 (2)	9 (7)	9 (1)	3	4	5(1)	45(11)

Notes: Previously established foreign *de novo* banks that were not in existence on December 31, 1980 do not appear on this table.

Numbers in parentheses indicate the number of *de novo* banks established by foreign individual(s) or non-bank companies. Numbers without parentheses are totals, including banks established by foreign banks and foreign individual(s)/nonbanks.

One bank established *de novo* by a foreign bank was subsequently acquired by foreign individuals.

Foreign Acquisitions of U.S. Banks 1970-1980[20]

Table 4 shows the number of U.S. banks and aggregate assets acquired by both foreign banks and foreign individuals for the years 1970 through 1980. In terms of the number of U.S. banks acquired, activity began to

Table 3
Foreign-Owned *De Novo* U.S. Banks (December 31, 1980)
Classified by Location and Nationality of Owner

Location	Nationality of Owner						Total
	Japan	Other Asia	Canada	U.K.	Europe	Other	
New York	4	3 (2)	5	2	3	5 (1)	22 (3)
California	8 (1)	6 (5)	3	1	–	–	18 (6)
Illinois	2 (1)	–	–	–	1	–	3 (1)
Other	1	–	1 (1)	–	–	–	2 (1)
	15 (2)	9 (7)	9 (1)	3	4	5 (1)	45 (11)

Notes: Previously established foreign *de novo* banks that were not in existence on December 31, 1980 do not appear on this table.

Numbers in parentheses indicate the number of *de novo* banks established by foreign individual(s) or non-bank companies. Numbers without parentheses are totals, including banks established by foreign banks and by foreign individual(s)/nonbanks.

One bank established *de novo* by a foreign bank was subsequently acquired by foreign individuals.

accelerate in the mid-1970s and reached a peak in 1978. Acquisitions by foreign individuals have accounted for at least half the acquisitions in six of the years shown and comprised more than two-thirds in each of the five years—1972, 1973, 1975, 1978, and 1979.

The first substantial acquisition in terms of total assets occurred in 1972, when Michele Sindona acquired a 21.6 percent interest in Franklin National Bank which had assets of $3.5 billion. After that it was not until 1979 and 1980 that total assets acquired in any one year exceeded $3.5 billion. In 1979, Union Bank (assets $5.2 billion) was acquired by the Standard and Chartered Banking Group and National Bank of North America (assets $4.3 billion) by National Westminster Bank, Ltd. The acquisition of Marine Midland Bank, N.A. (assets $15.7 billion) by the Hongkong and Shanghai Banking Corp. accounted for nearly the entire total of assets acquired in 1980. If consummated, the proposed acquisition of Crocker National Bank (assets $16.1 billion) by Midland Bank, Ltd. will be the largest foreign acquisition of a U.S. bank to date.

For the entire period shown in Table 4, foreign banks have accounted for nearly three-quarters of the total assets acquired.

Size of U.S. Banks at Time of Acquisition

As Table 5 indicates, the majority of acquisitions since the beginning of 1970 have involved banks that had less than $50 million in total assets when they were acquired. Acquisitions by foreign individuals are especially numerous in the smaller size categories. Three-quarters of the acquisitions by individuals have been of banks with less than $100 million in total assets; nearly two-thirds have had less than $50 million in total assets. Acquisitions by foreign banks have spanned a broader size range and been somewhat less concentrated in any size range. Foreign banks have made the very largest of the acquisitions, Union Bank and Marine Midland Bank, N.A., the only banks with more than $5 billion in assets when they were acquired. At the other end of the spectrum, only slightly more than two-fifths of acquisitions by foreign banks have involved U.S. banks with less than $50 million in assets.

Geographic Location of Acquired Banks

Acquisitions activity has been centered mainly in California, New York, and Florida, as Table 6 shows. Foreign purchases of banks began occurring somewhat earlier in New York and California (50 percent of

Table 4
Foreign Acquisitions of U.S. Banking Organizations (1970-1980)

	NUMBER OF BANKS Acquirer			TOTAL ASSETS PRIOR TO ACQUISITION (millions) Acquirer			Adjusted Total[a]
	Bank	Individual(s)	Total	Bank	Individual(s)	Total	
1970	2	1	3	$ 74.7	$ 22.3	$ 97.0	$ 106.1
1971	–	–	–	–	–	–	–
1972	1	2[b]	3	51.1	3,546.5	3,597.6	3,597.6
1973	1	5[c]	6	32.3	3,140.9	3,173.2	3,002.4
1974	5[b]	4[d,e]	9	3,271.3	554.6	3,825.9	3,329.2
1975	3	7[f,g]	10	1,019.6	1,185.2	2,204.8	1,756.0
1976	8[h]	3	11	398.7	287.3	686.0	519.3
1977	7[f]	7[i]	14	483.0	436.9	919.9	657.9
1978	3	14[j]	17	781.8	2,678.9	3,460.7	2,306.4
1979	4	11[d]	15	12,332.9	305.1	12,638.0	7,764.3
1980	7[c]	5[g,i]	12	18,725.5	465.7	19,191.2	10,815.0
	41	59	100				
Pending	6	3[e]	9	17,270.8	589.4	17,860.2	

[a] Adjusted using the GNP implicit price deflator; 1972 = 100.

[b] Franklin National Bank (FNB) is included in counts for 1972 (FNB assets = $3,373.3 million) when Michele Sindona acquired 21.6 percent of the bank's outstanding shares and 1974 when European-American Bank & Trust Co. acquired $1,579.0 million of the assets of the failed bank.

[c] Underwriters Bank & Trust Co. is included in counts for 1973 (UBTC assets = $53.2 million), when Spanish investors acquired 53.2 percent of the bank's outstanding shares, and 1980 (UBTC assets = $43.2 million) when it was acquired by Banco Central de Madrid.

[d] Alamosa National Bank is included in counts for 1974 (ANB assets = $18.1 million) when Adnan Khashoggi acquired 14.4 percent of the bank's outstanding stock through Triad Holding Corp. and 1979 (ANB assets = $28.3 million) when Robert Elliot acquired 96 percent of the bank's outstanding shares.

[e] Great Western B&TC is included in counts for 1974 (GWBTC assets = $284.4 million) when Count Ferdinand Graf Von Galen acquired roughly 18% of the bank through Westphalian American Association, and pending acquisitions (GWBTC assets = $479.7 million) due to an intended acquisition of the bank by a group of Kuwaiti investors.

[f] Century National Bank (CNB) was acquired by David Graiver in 1975 (CNB assets = $48.3 million) and was subsequently purchased by Banco Exterior de Espana in 1977 (CNB assets = $43.0 million).

[g] Totalbank is included in counts for 1975 (Tb assets = $11.4 million) when it was acquired by Francisco E. Blanco, and 1980 (Tb assets = $89.3 million) when a portion of Blanco's bank stock was purchased by a Spanish group headed by Ignacio Herrero.

[h] The count for 1976 includes the Bank Leumi Trust Co. acquisition of American Bank and Trust Co. (ABT assets = $177.4 million), although ABT was originally acquired by foreign interests in 1963.

[i] Central National Bank of Miami is included in counts for 1977 (CNBM assets = $38.1 million) when two Colombian investors acquired 76 percent of the bank's outstanding shares and 1980 (CNBM assets = $58.2 million) when Colombian investors acquired the bank through their holding companies.

[j] The 12 member banks of Financial General Bankshares, Inc. are counted as one banking organization.

Table 5
Foreign Acquisitions of U.S. Banking Organizations (1970-1980)
By Asset Size at Acquisition

Total Assets Prior to Acquisition	NUMBER OF BANKS ACQUIRED		
	Acquired by Foreign Bank	Acquired by Foreign Individual(s)	Total
Over $5 billion	2	–	2
$1-$5 billion	5	4	9[a]
$500-$999 million	4	–	4
$100-$499 million	6	11	17
$50-$99 million	7	7	14[b]
Less than $50 million	17	37	54[b,c]
	41	59	100

[a]Franklin National Bank is counted twice—for acquisitions by Michele Sindona in 1972 and by European-American Bank and Trust Co. in 1974.

The 12 member banks of Financial General Bankshares, Inc. are counted as one banking organization.

[b]Central National Bank of Miami is counted twice—for acquisitions by Colombian investors in 1977 and 1980.

Totalbank is counted twice—for acquisitions by Spanish investors in 1975 and 1980.

Underwriters Bank & Trust Co. is counted twice—for acquisitions by Spanish investors in 1973 and Banco Central de Madrid in 1980.

[c]Alamosa National Bank is counted twice—for acquisitions by Adnan Khashoggi/Triad Holding Corp. in 1974 and by Robert Elliot in 1979.

Century National Bank is counted twice—for acquisitions by David Graiver in 1975 and by Banco Exterior de Espana in 1977.

the acquisitions were made before 1976) than in Florida (only 20 percent of the acquisitions were made before 1976).

By far the greatest number of acquisitions by foreign banks has occurred in California. More than half of these acquisitions were undertaken by foreign bank-owned *de novo* subsidiaries, all but one of which followed a pattern begun in the 1960s when a number of the larger California banks, both foreign and domestically owned, began to expand their branch networks by acquiring smaller community banks outside the San Francisco and Los Angeles money centers.[21] Such expansion by foreign *de novo* subsidiaries generally involve the acquisition of banks with less than $100 million in assets.[22]

The other primary locations of acquisitions by foreign banks are New York and Florida. Among the acquisitions by foreign banks in New York are several cases of foreign bank *de novo* subsidiary expansion somewhat like those in California, but they involve larger U.S. banks and are not nearly so numerous. The earliest example was the 1974 merger of the First Westchester National Bank (assets $214 million)

Table 6
Foreign Acquisitions of U.S. Banking Organizations (1970-1980)
Classified by Geographic Location of Acquired Bank and Ownership Category

Location	Ownership Categories		Total
	Bank	Individual(s)	
Arizona	–	2	2
California	16 (15)	12(8)	28(23)
Colorado	–	3(2)	3 (2)
District of Columbia	–	2[a]	2
Florida	7	21(16)	28(23)
Georgia	–	1	1
Hawaii	–	1	1
Illinois	2	1	3
Louisiana	–	1	1
Massachusetts	–	1	1
Michigan	–	1	1
New Hampshire	–	1	1
New Jersey	–	2	2
New York	10	4(1)	14(10)
Puerto Rico	5	2	7
Texas	–	4	4
Virginia	1	–	1
TOTAL	41(40)	59(46)	100(86)

Note: Numbers in parentheses result from adjusting the count for subsequent divestitures.

[a]The 12 member banks of Financial General Bankshares, Inc. (FGB) have been counted as one banking organization and listed as an acquisition in the District of Columbia, where the holding company and one bank are located. Other FGB banks are located in Maryland, Virginia, Tennessee, and New York.

into Barclays Bank of New York. The acquisition of Franklin National Bank by European-American Bank and Trust Co. and of American Bank and Trust Co. by Bank Leumi Trust Co., a direct result of the failures of the U.S. banks, provided the two foreign *de novo* banks the opportunity to expand their New York operations.[23]

The seven cases of acquisition by a foreign financial institution in Florida all involve the same owner, The Royal Trust Co. of Canada, which in 1972 began a series of acquisitions that continued through 1977.[24]

Unlike acquisitions by foreign banks, those by foreign individuals are quite widespread, scattered through 14 states, the District of Columbia, and Puerto Rico. More acquisitions have occurred in sunbelt states than in other regions, primarily because of concentrations in California and, even more, in Florida. Acquisitions by foreign individuals in Florida alone have accounted for 36 percent of all such acquisitions of U.S. banks.

Nationalities of Acquirers of U.S. Banks

The figures in Table 7 show that banks from four countries—the United Kingdom, Canada, Japan, and Spain—have accounted for 73 percent of the acquisitions made by foreign banks. Except for the Spanish banks, those banks began to make acquisitions of U.S. banks in the late 1960s and early 1970s. The Spanish banks are relative newcomers, with all seven of their acquisitions made after 1975. All acquisitions by Japanese banks involved expansion of previously established *de novo* subsidiaries.[25]

Of the acquisitions by foreign banks from other nations in the 1970s, all but two[26] occurred after 1975 and involved banks from Israel, Venezuela, Mexico, the Philippines, the Netherlands, Hong Kong,[27] France, Chile, and West Germany.

Among the foreign individual investors, those from the United King-

Table 7
Foreign Acquisitions of U.S. Banking Organizations (1970-1980)
Classified by Nationality of Acquirer and Ownership Category

Nationality of Acquirer	Ownership Categories		
	Bank	Individual(s)	Total
NORTH & SOUTH AMERICA			
Canada	9	4	13
Latin America	2	16 (11)	18 (13)
EUROPE			
United Kingdom	9	1	10
Spain	7	8 (7)	15 (14)
Other Europe	4[a]	5 (4)	9 (8)
MIDDLE EAST			
Israel	1	–	1
Other Middle East	–	11 (9)[b]	11 (9)
ASIA			
Japan	5	–	5
Other Asia	3 (2)	10 (7)	13 (9)
MISCELLANEOUS			
Chile/W. Germany	1	–	1
Netherlands/Canada	–	1	1
Switzerland/Canada	–	1	1
Spain/Latin America	–	2 (1)	2 (1)
	41 (40)	59 (46)	100 (86)

Notes: Numbers in parentheses result from adjusting the count for subsequent divestitures.

[a] Includes one bank acquired by a banking group composed of a British bank and five European banks.

[b] The 12 member banks of Financial General Bankshares, Inc. have been counted as one banking organization.

dom, Canada, Japan, and Spain—home countries of most of the acquiring banks—account for less than one-quarter of the acquisitions. Nationalities of approximately two-thirds of the foreign individual acquirers can be traced to three areas of the world—Latin America, the Middle East, and Asia (excluding Japan).[28] Latin American investors have focused almost exclusively on Florida (Miami) banks. Middle Eastern investments in U.S. banks have been in six states and the District of Columbia, with some concentration in Texas where four acquisitions have been made.[29] All acquisitions by Asian investors have been in California except one, which is in Hawaii.

In general, the nationalities of foreign bank and foreign individual acquirers divide between industrialized and developing countries. Foreign bank acquirers overwhelmingly are major multinational banks from developed countries with mature banking structures.[30] Individual acquirers tend to come predominantly from countries with less developed banking and financial structures. Investors involved in about one-third of the acquisitions made by foreign individuals come from OPEC countries: Middle Eastern OPEC members (9); Venezuela (5); Indonesia (2); and Ecuador (1).

Other Acquisition Patterns

Just as with banks established *de novo* by foreign investors, there are some noteworthy relationships between acquirer nationality and the states in which acquisitions have been made. The relationships are evident in Table 8.

California has a concentration of Japanese and other Asian acquirers. As for *de novo* banks, this again reflects the countries that are California's major trading partners and the Asian ethnic groups in the state.

Florida (specifically, Miami) has been the almost exclusive focus of bank acquisitions by individual investors from Latin America, Spain and Portugal.[31] Only one Florida bank has been sold to foreign individual investors not from one of those areas. Banks involved in these acquisitions have been small—all had less than $150 million in assets at the time of acquisition, and more than three-quarters had less than $50 million in assets.

Five of the seven Puerto Rican banks acquired by foreign interests were purchased by Spanish banks and individuals.[32] Because of Puerto Rico's Hispanic heritage, this pattern is not surprising. Three of those acquisitions involved failing banks; one involved a bank in less than satisfactory condition.

Table 8
Foreign Acquisitions of U.S. Banking Organizations (1970-1980)
Classified by Geographic Location and Nationality of Acquirer

Location	Japan	Other Asia	Latin America	Canada	Middle East	United Kingdom	Spain	Other Europe	Multiple Regions	Total
California	5	11	1	–	2	7	–	2	–	28
Florida	–	–	12	8	–	–	6	1	1	28
New York	–	1	3	–	1	2	3	2[a]	2	14
Puerto Rico	–	–	–	2	–	–	5	–	–	7
Texas	–	–	–	–	4	–	–	–	–	4
Other	–	1	2	3	5[b]	1	1	4	2	19
	5	13	18	13	12	10	15	9	5	100

[a]Includes the acquisition of Franklin National Bank by European-American Bank, whose owner are one British bank and five continental European banks.

[b]The 12 member banks of Financial General Bankshares, Inc. have been counted as one banking organization.

Table 9
Existing Foreign-Owned U.S. Banking Organizations (December 31, 1980)
Number and Aggregate Assets

	Number of Foreign-Owned U.S. Banking Organizations	Aggregate Assets Total Assets 12-31-79[a] ($ million)
Acquired by U.S. Banks		
Acquired by Foreign Banks[b]	24	37,763.4
Acquired by Foreign Individual(s)[c]	42[d]	11,744.2
	66	49,507.6
De Novo U.S. Banks		
Established by Foreign Banks	25	11,929.5[e]
Established by Foreign Individual(s)	10	965.9
	35	12,895.4
Foreign Owned De Novo U.S. Banks That Subsequently Acquired U.S. Banks[f]	10	17,021.1
Total Foreign-Owned U.S. Banks	111	79,424.1
All Insured U.S. Banks	14,364	1,692,078.0

Note: Foreign controlled banks that have ceased to exist due to divestiture or merger do not appear on this table.

[a]Total assets (consolidated foreign and domestic) in millions of dollars as of the December 1979 Call Report, except where indicated.

[b]Includes four foreign-acquired U.S. banks that subsequently acquired another U.S. bank.

[c]Includes two foreign-acquired U.S. banks that subsequently acquired another U.S. bank.

[d]The 12 member banks of Financial General Bankshares, Inc. are counted as one banking organization.

[e]Figure includes the December 1979 total assets reported to *Polk's World Bank Directory* by one foreign *de novo* bank.

[f]Includes one foreign *de novo* bank acquirer established by a foreign individual/shell company (total assets = $4,415.3 million).

Individuals from the Middle East are the only known foreign investors in Texas banks. At least three of the four acquisitions there have been accomplished through investor groups whose partners include U.S. citizens.[33]

CURRENT STATUS OF FOREIGN OWNERSHIP OF U.S. BANKS

Table 9 shows that 111 U.S. banks were identified as having a minimum of 10 percent ownership by a single foreign investor as of December 31, 1980. Those banks represent less than 1 percent of the 14,364 insured U.S. commercial banks, and have assets of $79,424 million, approximately 4.7 percent of the assets (domestic and foreign) of all insured U.S. commercial banks. U.S. banks with foreign *bank* ownership— including banks acquired directly and those established *de novo* (a number of which grew by acquisition)—account for about 50 percent of the number of foreign owned U.S. banks and 75 percent of foreign owned U.S. bank assets.[34]

Altogether 76, or two-thirds, of the U.S. banks currently owned by foreign interests have involved acquisition.[35] They account for 84 percent of the assets of foreign-owned U.S. banks.

Table 10 classifies the 109 currently foreign owned banks according to asset size class, ownership category, and acquired vs. *de novo* banks. As of December 31, 1979, nearly half had total assets of $100 million or less. They represent 0.4 percent of the 12,821 commercial banks in that size range. The size classes that have the largest proportion of banks with foreign ownership are the $1-$5 billion and over $5 billion size classes, where banks with foreign ownership represent 10.4 percent and 7.1 percent, respectively. Thus, although foreign parties have significant equity interests in a substantial number of small banks, banks acquired or established by foreigners have a median size in the $100-$499 million asset range, compared to a median size for all U.S. banks of less than $50 million in assets.

Foreign-owned banks account for 27 of the 300 largest U.S. banks.[36] As shown in Table 11, 15 of the 27 are *de novo* bank subsidiaries, 14 of which were established by foreign banks and one by a foreign individual. Included among the 15 are nine whose sizes reflect the acquisition of one or more U.S. banks and four that acquired branches from U.S.

Table 10

Existing Foreign-Owned U.S. Banking Organizations by Asset Size (December 31, 1980)

Total Assets	Acquired U.S. Banks		De Novo U.S. Banks		Foreign-Owned De Novo U.S. Banks That Subsequently Acquired A U.S. Bank	Total Foreign-Owned U.S. Banks	All Insured U.S. Banks	Foreign Ownership as a % of Total
	Acquired by Foreign Bank	Acquired by Foreign Individual(s)	Established by Foreign Bank	Established by Foreign Individual(s)				
Over $5 billion	2	–	–	–	–	2	28	7.1%
$1-$5 billion	5[a]	3[b]	3	–	4[c]	15	144	10.4%
$500-$999 million	1	–	3	–	4	8	149	5.4%
$100-$499 million	6[a]	15[a]	10	3	2	36	1,222	2.9%
$50-$99 million	3	5	3	1	–	12	1,764	0.7%
Less than $50 million	7	19	6	6	–	38	11,057	0.3%
	24	42	25	10	10	111	14,364	0.8%

Note: Foreign-controlled banks which have ceased to exist due to divestiture or merger do not appear on this table.

[a]Includes two foreign acquired U.S. banks that subsequently acquired another U.S. bank.

[b]The 12 member banks of Financial General Bankshares, Inc. are counted as one banking organization.

[c]Includes one foreign *de novo* bank acquirer established by a foreign individual/shell company.

Table 11
Existing Foreign-Owned U.S. Banks (December 31, 1980)
Banks Among the Top 300 U.S. Banks

Deposit Rank 12-31-79	Bank Name	Type[a]	State
13	Marine Midland Bank, NA	Acq	NY
26	Union Bank	Acq #	CA
34	European-American Bank & Trust Co.	De Novo +	NY
36	National Bank of North America	Acq	NY
41	Republic NB of New York	De Novo +	NY
47	California First Bank	De Novo +	CA
48	Bank of Tokyo Trust Co.	De Novo	NY
53	The Bank of California, NA	Acq	CA
61	Lloyds Bank California	Acq +	CA
85	Bank of Virginia	Acq	VA
90	Sumitomo Bank of California	De Novo	CA
94	Bank Leumi Trust Co. of New York	De Novo +	NY
95	U.S. Trust Co.	Acq	NY
116	J. Henry Schroder Bank & Trust Co.	De Novo	NY
163	Bank of the Commonwealth	Acq	MI
170	Fuji Bank & Trust Co.	De Novo	NY
172	LaSalle NB	Acq +	IL
179	First American Bank, NA (member, Financial General Bankshares, Inc.)	Acq	DC
181	Industrial Bank of Japan Trust Co.	De Novo	NY
187	First American Bank of Virginia (member, Financial General Bankshares, Inc.)	Acq	VA
195	Chartered Bank of London, SF (subsequently merged with Union Bank)	De Novo +	CA
207	UBAF Arab-American Bank	De Novo	NY
217	Golden State Sanwa Bank	De Novo +	CA
223	Barclays Bank of California	De Novo +	CA
260	Bank of the West (subsequently merged with French Bank of California)	Acq #	CA
263	California Canadian Bank	De Novo +	CA
266	Barclays Bank of New York	De Novo +	NY

Note: Deposit ranks are taken from the *American Banker* 1979 year-end rankings of the 5,000 largest U.S. commercial banks (March 28, 1980).

[a]Types are:

ACQ: a U.S. bank acquired by foreign investor(s);

ACQ +:   a U.S. bank acquired by foreign investor(s) that has subsequently acquired another U.S. bank;

ACQ #:   a U.S. bank acquired by foreign investor(s) that has subsequently merged with a foreign-owned *de novo* U.S. bank;

De Novo: foreign-owned *de novo* U.S. bank;

De Novo +:   foreign-owned *de novo* U.S. bank that has acquired other U.S. bank(s) through merger or bank holding company affiliations.

banks. Only 12 of the foreign owned banks among the largest 300 in the U.S. were the result primarily of acquisition. Of the 12, eight were acquired by foreign banks[37] and four by foreign individuals.

Table 12

Existing Foreign-Owned U.S. Banking Organizations by Geographic Location (December 31, 1980)

Location	Acquired U.S. Banks		De Novo U.S. Banks		Foreign-Owned De Novo U.S. Banks That Subsequently Acquired A U.S. Bank	Total Foreign-Owned U.S. Banks
	Acquired by Foreign Bank	Acquired by Foreign Individual(s)	Established by Foreign Bank	Established by Foreign Individual(s)		
Arizona	—	2	—	—	—	2
California	5	7	6	6	6	30
Colorado	—	2	—	—	—	2
D.C.	—	2[a]	—	—	—	2
Florida	7	15	—	—	—	22
Georgia	—	1	1	—	—	2
Hawaii	—	1	—	—	—	1
Illinois	1	1	2	—	—	5
Louisiana	—	1	—	1	—	1
Massachusetts	—	1	—	—	—	1
Michigan	—	1	—	—	—	1
New Hampshire	—	1	—	—	—	1
New Jersey	—	2	—	—	—	2
New York	6	—	16	2	4	28
Puerto Rico	4	1	—	—	—	5
Texas	—	4	—	—	—	4
Vermont	—	—	—	1	—	1
Virginia	1	—	—	1	—	1
Total	24	42	25	10	10	111

Note: Foreign-controlled banks which have ceased to exist due to divestiture or merger do not appear on this table.
[a]The 12 member banks of Financial General Bankshares, Inc. are counted as one banking organization located in Washington, D.C.

Table 12 shows that 72 percent of the U.S. banks currently identified as having significant foreign ownership are in California, New York, and Florida. Altogether, 17 states plus the District of Columbia and Puerto Rico have one or more banks with at least 10 percent foreign ownership by single or related foreign interests. With only two exceptions,[38] foreign banks have acquired or established banks in only four states—California, Florida, Illinois, and New York—and Puerto Rico. Since foreign bank-owned U.S. banks tend to be larger than those owned by foreign individuals, there is a parallel geographic concentration of assets of foreign-owned U.S. banks: 82.8 percent in California and New York; 4.5 percent in Florida and Illinois, with the remaining 12.7 percent scattered through 13 other states, the District of Columbia, and Puerto Rico.

Figures in Table 13 show the nationalities of owners in the various ownership categories. The most significant countries of ownership are Canada, the U.K., Spain, and Japan, which account for nearly half of the U.S. banks with foreign ownership. Foreign owners from Japan and Israel have, in all cases, first entered the U.S. banking markets by establishing a *de novo* subsidiary. Those from Spain and Middle Eastern countries (except Israel) have entered only through acquisitions.

PENDING ACQUISITIONS

There are nine known acquisitions of U.S. banking organizations by foreign interests pending, six by banks and three by individuals.[39] They are listed in Table 14.

The geographic patterns for those acquisitions mirror, for the most part, existing foreign ownership. Five of the six proposed acquisitions by foreign banks are in California. Most significant among these is the pending acquisition of Crocker National Bank (assets $16.1 billion) by Midland Bank, Ltd. If consummated, it will be the largest foreign acquisition of a U.S. bank. The remaining transaction by a foreign bank involves the purchase of Miami National Bank by Banco Zaragozano of Spain. With the exception of the Royal Trust Company whose Florida acquisitions have been grandfathered, this will be the first acquisition of an existing Florida bank by a foreign financial institution. Similar transactions will now be possible as a result of an April 1980 U.S. Supreme Court decision voiding portions of Florida's 1972 law prohibit-

Table 13

Existing Foreign Owned U.S. Banking Organizations by Nationality of Owner (December 31, 1980)

Nationality of Owner	Acquired U.S. Banks		De Novo U.S. Banks		Foreign-Owned De Novo U.S. Banks That Subsequently Acquired A U.S. Bank	Total Foreign-Owned U.S. Banks
	Acquired by Foreign Bank	Acquired by Foreign Individual(s)	Established by Foreign Bank	Established by Foreign Individual(s)		
NORTH & SOUTH AMERICA						
Canada	9	4	7	1	1	22
Latin America	2	10	1	–	1	14
EUROPE						
United Kingdom	3	1	1	–	2	7
Spain	5	5	–	–	–	10
Other Europe	2	4	3[a]	–	1[b]	10
MIDDLE EAST						
Israel	–	–	2	–	1	3
Other Middle East	–	9[c]	–	–	–	9
ASIA						
Japan	–	–	9	2	4	15
Other Asia	2	6	2	7	–	17
MULTIPLE NATIONALITIES						
Chile/W. Germany	1	–	–	–	–	1
Neth./Canada	–	1	–	–	–	1
Switz./Canada	–	1	–	–	–	1
Spain/L. America	–	1	–	–	–	1
	24	42	25	10	10	111

Notes: Foreign-controlled banks which have ceased to exist due to divestiture or merger do not appear on this table.

[a] One foreign *de novo* bank is owned by a French-Middle Eastern banking consortium based in France.

[b] Foreign *de novo* bank is owned by a banking group composed of a British bank and five European banks.

[c] The 12 member banks of Financial General Bankshares, Inc. are counted as one banking organization.

Table 14
Pending Acquisitions of U.S. Banks by Foreign Interests

Name of Bank	Total Assets December 31, 1979 (millions)[a]	Percentage of Equity to be Purchased	Type of Acquirer[b]	Nationality of Acquirer	Location
Crocker National Bank	$16,087.5	51	ACQ-B	United Kingdom	California
Manufacturers Bank	705.7	100	MER-B	Japan	California
First National Bank of San Diego County	155.8	100	MER-B	Japan	California
First City Bank	145.7	100	MER-B	Japan	California
Westlands Bank	121.2	40	ACQ-B	Canada	California
Miami National Bank	54.9	84.5	ACQ-B	Spain	Florida
Great Western Bank & Trust Co.[c]	479.7	100	ACQ-I	Kuwait	Arizona
Central State Bank	71.5	100	ACQ-I	S. America	New York
Bank of Perrine	38.2	100	ACQ-I	Colombia	Florida
	$17,860.2				

[a]Total assets (consolidated foreign and domestic) in millions of dollars as of the December 1979 Call Report.
[b]ACQ-B = U.S. bank with a pending acquisition by a foreign bank/BHC;
ACQ-I = U.S. bank with a pending acquisition by a foreign individual(s)/shell company;
MER-B = U.S. bank with a pending merger into an existing U.S. bank controlled by a foreign bank/BHC.
[c]A West German investor currently controls roughly 18% of Great Western Bank & Trust Co.

ing control of a Florida bank by foreign corporations.[40] The three pending acquisitions by foreign individuals are in Florida, New York, and Arizona.

Similarly, ownership nationalities fit the established patterns. Japanese banks account for three of the six proposed acquisitions by banks; the other three are banks from Canada, Spain, and the United Kingdom. Investors from Latin America (2) and the Middle East (1) are the principals in the three acquisitions by foreign individuals.

In summary, the characteristics of pending acquisitions do not differ appreciably from existing patterns. If all of these proposed transactions were consummated (and if there were no divestitures of currently foreign-owned U.S. banks), the total number of identified U.S. banking organizations with significant foreign ownership would be 116.[41] Total assets of the 116 banks would represent 5.7 percent of total insured U.S. commercial bank assets (based on December 31, 1979 data).

CONCLUSION

Although foreign ownership of U.S. banks increased rather markedly in the last decade, the portion of the U.S. commercial banking system controlled by foreign interests is relatively low in terms of both numbers of banks (0.8 percent) and total assets (4.7 percent). Foreign bank owners are among the world's largest multinationals and have concentrated their efforts in the major U.S. money centers in California, Illinois and New York. Ownership by foreign individuals appears most often to reflect patterns of international trade and commerce. For example, Asian owners are concentrated in California and Latin Americans in Florida. Thus, for the most part, the patterns of foreign ownership appear to be based on rational business and trade considerations.

Acknowledgments

Nancy Lowther assisted in the research for this paper. Valuable comments on earlier drafts were made by C. F. Muckenfuss, III and Steven J. Weiss.

FOOTNOTES

[1] In 1854 the Darmstadter bank of Germany acquired an interest in a New York City bank. (Clyde Williams Phelps, *The Foreign Expansion of American Banks*, 1927, p. 28.)

[2] Diane Page and Neal M. Soss, *Some Evidence on Transnational Banking Structure*, OCC Paper, this book.

[3] Only five foreign acquisitions occurring before 1970 have been identified—one each in 1963, 1966, 1968, and two in 1969. Four of these involved acquisition by foreign banks and one by foreign individuals; the largest of the acquired banks had assets of $76.3 million at the time of acquisition.

[4] Members of the Organization for Economic Cooperation and Development (OECD) are Australia, Austria, Belgium, Canada, Denmark, Finland, France, West Germany, Greece, Iceland, Ireland, Italy, Japan, Luxembourg, the Netherlands, New Zealand, Norway, Portugal, Spain, Sweden, Switzerland, Turkey, the United Kingdom, and the United States.

[5] Foreign acquisition activity has probably both benefited from and contributed to Miami's emerging role as a Latin American financial center. By year-end 1980, Miami had 16 foreign bank agencies, 2 foreign bank representative offices, and 23 U.S. bank Edge Act Corporations, in addition to 16 banks owned by foreign interests—13 of them owned by individuals from Spain and Latin America.

[6] The acquisition proposals announced in 1978 were:

Month	U.S. Bank	1978 Rank (deposits)	Proposed Acquirer
April	Marine Midland Bank	12	Hongkong and Shanghai Banking Corp.
May	National Bank of North America	37	National Westminster Bank, Ltd.
June	Union Bank	25	Standard Chartered Bank, Ltd.

Franklin National Bank was the country's 20th largest bank when Michele Sindona acquired 21.6 percent ownership. Following Franklin's failure in 1974, European-American Bank submitted the highest bid to the FDIC to purchase the assets and assume the liabilities of Franklin.

[7] The Office of Foreign Investment in the United States (OFIUS), established in 1976 within the Department of Commerce, sought the cooperation of bank regulators to establish a more comprehensive and up-to-date reporting system for foreign ownership in the banking sector. In November of 1979, the Interagency Coordinating Committee recommended that the individual bank agencies participate in the maintenance of a list of institutions having 10 percent or more ownership by foreign interests. The list, which is maintained by the Federal Reserve Board, was first produced in its present form in December of 1980 and contained June 30, 1980 data. It is entitled "Foreign Investment in U.S. Banking Institutions" and is updated quarterly.

Also, under Section 13(d) of the Securities Exchange Act, holders of more than 5 percent of classes of securities registered under federal securities laws are required to provide citizenship information to the Securities and Exchange Commission. (See *Report of the Securities and Exchange Commission on Beneficial Ownership Reporting Requirements Pursuant to Section 13(h) of the Securities Exchange Act of 1934*, June 27, 1980.)

[8] Under the Bank Holding Company Act, the Federal Reserve Board classifies as a bank holding company any company that owns at least 25 percent of a U.S. bank, a level of interest presumed to be controlling. Additionally, in some instances the Board may determine effective control at less than 25 percent ownership, which would also result in classification as a bank holding company.

[9] An example of a complicated shell company structure is the one used by the Venezuelan family of Jose Alvarez Stelling for their investment in the First National Bank of Hialeah. In a

reorganization designed to take advantage of a tax treaty between the United States and the Netherlands, the family contributed their stock to a Curacao corporation, Marsh Investments, N.V., which they owned. Marsh Investments, N.V. exchanged the bank stock for stock in Marsh Investments, B.V. (a Netherlands corporation), which then exchanged the bank stock for the stock of M.F.G. Investments, Inc., (based in Hialeah, Fla.). Thus, although the owner of record of the Hialeah bank is a Florida corporation, the beneficial owners, found by tracing the ownership of the Florida, Netherlands, and Curacao companies, are Venezuelan individuals.

[10] This excludes, for example, recent reported foreign investments in Long Island Trust Co., where three apparently unrelated foreign purchasers each independently acquired less than a 10 percent interest. U.S. Trust Co. of New York is, however, included due to the acquisition of a 9.997% interest (rounded to 10%) by Banco de Chile and an additional 9% interest held by Schroder, Munchmeyer, Hengst, & Co. (W. Germany).

[11] The statutory definition of "control" under the Change in Bank Control Act, like that of the Bank Holding Company Act, is ownership of 25 percent or more of voting stock. In addition, regulators use 10 percent ownership as a "control" level if the institution has issued registered securities or if the acquiring person will be the institution's largest shareholder. (John E. Shockey and William B. Glidden, *Foreign-Controlled U.S. Banks: The Legal and Regulatory Environment*, OCC Paper, this book.)

The 10 percent ownership level is also the threshold used by the Department of Commerce in monitoring foreign direct investment in the United States. Other thresholds might have been selected. The U.S. Department of Agriculture, for example, uses a 5 percent level to monitor cases of ownership by a single foreign individual or groups of individuals closely related by blood or business and a 20 percent aggregate level for foreign ownership scattered among unrelated individuals. Lloyd's of London adopted a threshold of 20 percent in 1978 as the maximum allowable for foreign investment in its brokers, on the grounds that 20 percent was "the most that could represent an 'investment,' rather than a position of control." (Robert D. Hershey, Jr., "Lloyd's May Drop Rules on Foreign Takeovers," *New York Times*, January 1980.)

By using the 10 percent definition, several important cases of foreign acquisition of between 10 percent and 25 percent, such as Financial General Bankshares, Inc. (18.6 percent) and Bank of Virginia (15 percent), are included on the list. (See Appendix XI.)

[12] For instance, although the majority of foreign non-bank acquisitions have been undertaken by individuals, in a few cases acquisitions have been made by foreign non-bank enterprises or jointly-acting groups comprised predominately of individuals and/or non-bank companies but also including foreign banks. Also, it is not uncommon for individuals to use wholly owned offshore shell financial companies as investment vehicles.

[13] Page and Soss, *op. cit.*

[14] Dr. Jack Zwick, *Foreign Banking in the United States*, Paper No. 9 for J.E.C., 19th Cong., 2nd Session, pp. 5-6. The branch form was seen to provide a less complicated organizational structure, be more amenable to effective control from the head office, require less capital, afford substantial tax advantages, and allow the parent bank to trade on the prestige of its own name.

[15] All *de novo* subsidiary banks were state-chartered. Provisions of the National Banking Act required that all directors of national banks be U.S. citizens and local residents. Furthermore, all national banks, as members of the Federal Reserve System, were required to hold non-interest earning reserves. Therefore, formation of a national bank was not attractive.

[16] New York did not require FDIC coverage.

[17] Zwick, *op. cit.* pp. 7-8.

[18] Until 1972, when it sold its subsidiary, the International Commercial Bank of China was another foreign bank that operated a subsidiary-plus-agency combination in New York.

[19] According to the California State Office of International Trade, 63 percent of California's external trade in 1979 was with Asia. A state survey conducted in July 1976 indicated that approximately 4 percent of California's population is Oriental, and the concentration is higher in

the San Francisco-Oakland SMSA where seven of the 12 Asian *de novo* banks in California have been founded.

[20] In this section, the "foreign bank" acquirer category includes acquisitions made directly by foreign banks as well as those made by U.S. *de novo* subsidiaries of foreign banks. (In the following section, which examines the current status of foreign ownership, the two types are broken out separately.) The "foreign individual" category subsumes all nonbank acquirers; these are mostly individuals but a handful of acquisitions has been made by non-bank foreign companies.

[21] Acquisition of branches from one of the larger banks sometimes achieved the same expansion goal. For example, in 1977 when the Bank of California put 33 of its 74 branches up for sale, Wells Fargo Bank bought eight and Sumitomo Bank of California bought 19. (Six widely dispersed offices were sold independently.)

[22] The one foreign bank acquisition that clearly deviated from this pattern was the merger in 1975 of the weak Southern California First National Bank (San Diego), which had $890 million in assets, into the Bank of Tokyo of California. The resulting bank was remaned California First Bank.

[23] Also, as in California, the sale of branches by one of the larger New York banks provided a means for foreign *de novo* bank expansion. The Bank of Montreal appeared on the verge of buying 89 Bankers Trust branches in 1978. Ultimately, those sales were made in smaller groups: 31 were purchased by Barclays Bank of New York, 16 by National Bank of North America, 13 by Bank Leumi Trust Co., and 12 by Republic National Bank of New York.

[24] Florida's 1972 law prohibiting control of a Florida bank by foreign (non-Florida) corporations made an exception for institutions that already controlled a Florida bank on December 20, 1972. Thus, Royal Trust Co. was grandfathered, although, ironically, "it's initial entry prompted that legislation." (Mira Wilkins, *Foreign Enterprise in Florida*, 1979, p. 91.)

[25] Refer to the previous section on "Banks Established *De Novo*."

[26] (1) In 1970, Hongkong and Shanghai Banking Corp. of California (a *de novo* subsidiary) acquired Republic National Bank and Trust Co. The subsidiary was divested in 1979. (2) In 1974, European-American Bank (owned by a consortium of European banks) acquired the failed Franklin National Bank through a purchase and assumption agreement.

[27] Hongkong and Shanghai Banking Corp. has been listed under Hong Kong where it is headquartered, although it is chartered in the U.K. and managed principally by U.K. citizens.

[28] The nationality of some foreign investors is difficult to ascertain. For example, Edmond Safra (Republic National Bank) is a Lebanese-born Brazilian living in Switzerland. Ismael Dudhia, described as a "British investor," lives in Switzerland.

[29] If Financial General's member banks are counted separately, the number of states in which Middle Eastern individuals have acquired an interest in banks increases to 10 states and the District of Columbia.

[30] The few exceptions are Banco Union (Venezuela) Banco de Chile, Banco Nacional de Mexico, and Metropolitan Bank & Trust (Philippines). Of the 25 foreign banks that have acquired U.S. banks since 1970, 15 are listed among the world's 100 largest banks. It should be noted that the Swiss, German, Belgian, and large French banks (except Banque Nationale de Paris) have not made acquisitions, probably because they are unwilling to make the required divestiture of their U.S. securities affiliates to purchase a subsidiary.

[31] Until recently, Florida permitted foreign bank presence only in agency or representative office form. The law that barred full service foreign bank branches and acquisitions by foreign banks but not individuals may have been partly responsible for several acquisitions by foreign individuals who own or are closely related to banks in Spain and Latin American countries. Reported examples are Jose Alvarez Stelling, president of Banco de Centro Consolidado, Venezuela; Humberto Vagalara Rojas and Eduardo Espina Fernandez, close to management of Banco de Colombia; and Jaime Castell Lastortras, president of Banco Catalan de Desarrollo, Spain.

Revisions to the Florida State banking rules and regulations adopted in 1979 and 1980 expanded the list of permissable activities for foreign financial institutions. The new banking rules should encourage the presence of more foreign banks in Florida.

Venezuelan law may encourage Venezuelan bankers wishing to own U.S. banks to acquire rather than form a bank *de novo* because it does not require approval of acquisitions but does require that *de novo* operations be approved by Venezuelan banking authorities and meet minimum capital requirements. (Thomas P. Eldred, III, Comptroller, Banco Industrial de Venezuela, New York, "Foreign Retail Banking: Experiences Slow Growth in U.S.," *American Banker*, March 23, 1979.)

[32] The two not purchased by Spanish interests were acquired by Canadian banks—The Bank of Nova Scotia acquired Banco Mercantile de Puerto Rico and the Royal Bank of Canada acquired Banco de San Juan. Canadian banks, with a long history in the Caribbean, have had branches in Puerto Rico for some time.

[33] For example, Main Bank of Houston was acquired by an investor group that included two Saudi Arabian businessmen, former Texas Governor John Connally, and Texas banker Fredrick Erck.

The 1978 purchases of Western Bank, the third acquisition involving a Middle Easterner in less than a year, prompted state banking officials to state publicly they were watching such acquisitions closely. Archie P. Clayton, counsel to the State Department of Banking, suggested that when Texas received an application from an *all*-foreign group, it would cause regulatory problems for the state. See, "Texas Regulators Study Closely Bank Acquisition Bids Involving Foreigners," *American Banker*, July 11, 1978.

[34] Individuals own 12 (27 percent) of foreign-owned *de novo* banks and $5,460.5 million (nearly 20 percent) of the assets of those banks. Only one *de novo* bank owned by a foreign individual has expanded by acquisition.

[35] Some foreign banks have made multiple acquisitions, most frequently by merger into existing U.S. *de novo* subsidiaries. Thus, the number of foreign acquisitions of U.S. banks accounted for by these 76 existing banks is 93.

[36] In addition, 43 U.S. branches of foreign banks have asset bases greater than the 300th largest U.S. bank.

[37] Union Bank, acquired in 1979 by Standard Chartered Bank Ltd., has recently absorbed its parent bank's *de novo* U.S. subsidiary, Chartered Bank of London—SF, through merger. Similarly, French Bank of California, Banque Nationale de Paris' *de novo* subsidiary, has been absorbed by BNP's recently acquired Bank of the West.)

[38] Banca March (Spain) has a 15 percent interest in the Bank of Virginia. Sumitomo Bank (Japan) owns 13.7 percent of Central Pacific Bank in Hawaii, which was founded *de novo* in 1954.

[39] These nine include one that has regulatory approval, seven that have filed notice or application with regulatory agencies and one that has only been reported as pending in the press.

[40] Mira Wilkins, *New Foreign Enterprise in Florida*, p. 88.

[41] Three of the proposed transactions involve merger with a U.S. bank already foreign owned, and one is an acquisition of a bank already foreign owned.

Appendix

Appendix I(a)

Known and Pending Foreign Acquisitions of U.S. Commercial Banks (December 31, 1980)

Acquired U.S. Bank (Present Name)	Location (Year Estab.)	Type of Trans.[1] (Date of Trans.)	% o/s Shares Acquired[2]	Acquirer Category[3]	Name of Acquirer (Foreign Bank Parent) [Beneficial Owner]	Nationality of Acquirer	Total Assets ($ million)[4]	
							Acquired Bank Prior to Trans. (Reference Date)	Resultant Bank as of 12-31-79
1. Ahmanson Bank (California Overseas Bank)[5]	Los Angeles, CA (1957)	ACQ (11-08-76)	99.9	FI/SC	Philippine Investors	Philippines	25.9 (12-31-75)	150.0
2. Alamosa National Bank	Alamosa, CO (1907)	ACQ (04-74)	14.4	FI/SC	Triad Holding Corp. [Adnan Khashoggi]	Saudi Arabia	18.1 (12-31-73)	
		ACQ (12-31-79)	96.0	FI/SC	Robert Elliot[6]	Canada	28.3 (09-30-79)	29.5
3. American Bank & Trust Co.	New York, NY (1914)	ACQ (10-63)	75.0	FBHC	Swiss-Israel Trade Bank	Switzerland	41.5 (12-31-62)	
(Bank Leumi Trust Co. of New York)[7]		MERGER Emer. Trans.[8] (09-15-76)	100	FBHC	Bank Leumi Trust Co. of New York (Bank Leumi Ie-Israel B.M.)	Israel	177.4[9] (09-15-76)	1,625.1
4. American Bank of Commerce	Phoenix, AZ (1974)	ACQ (03-09-79)	100	FI/SC	Charles Allard	Canada	8.0 (12-31-78)	10.3
5. American Bank of Orange County (Royal Trust Bank of Orlando)	Orlando, FL (1973)	ACQ (05-30-78)	98.0	FBHC	The Royal Trust Co.	Canada	7.6 (03-31-78)	19.2
6. American Security Bank	Honolulu, HI (1935)	ACQ (09-16-76)	23.0	FI/SC	John M. K. Lee	Indonesia	235.1 (06-30-76)	346.1

No.	Bank (parent)	Location (year)	Transaction	%	Category	Acquirer	Country	Value (date)	Final
7.	Banco de Ahorro de Puerto Rico (Banco Commercial de Mayaguez)	Puerto Rico (1966)	MERGER Emer. Trans.[8] (09-06-78)	100	FI/SC	Banco Commercial de Mayaguez[10] [Gregorio Diego]	Spain	11.7[9] (09-06-78)	128.0
8.	Banco Commercial de Mayaguez	Puerto Rico (1969)	ACQ (12-29-77)	69.8	FI/SC	Gregorio Deigo[10] ^	Spain	74.3 (09-30-77)	128.0
9.	Banco Credito y Ahorro Ponceno (Banco de Santander, PR & Banco Popular de Puerto Rico)	Puerto Rico (1895)	MERGER (04-03-78)	N/A[11]	FBHC	Banco de Santander, Puerto Rico (Banco de Santander, SA)	Spain	701.7 (12-31-77)	383.8
10.	Banco de San Juan	Puerto Rico (1927)	ACQ (09-80)	100	FBHC	Royal Bank of Canada	Canada	296.8 (12-31-79)	296.8
11.	Banco Economias (Banco Central y Economias)	Puerto Rico (1881)	ACQ Emer. Trans.[8] (09-02-77)	100	FBHC	Banco Central de Madrid	Spain	179.4 (06-30-77)	458.2
12.	Banco Mercantile de Puerto Rico (Scotiabank de Puerto Rico)	Puerto Rico (1966)	ACQ (06-09-75)	80.3	FBHC	The Bank of Nova Scotia	Canada	99.2 (04-16-75)	461.3[12]
13.	The Bank of California, NA	San Francisco, (1910)	ACQ (1973)	14.0	FI/SC	Baron Edmond de Rothschild	France	2,655.9 (12-31-72)	3,446.4
			Add'l Purchases (Total as of 07-79)	32.2					
14.	Bank of Commerce[13]	New York, NY (1914)	ACQ (01-78)	18.6	FI/SC	Middle Eastern Investors	Saudi Arabia, Kuwait, and Abu Dhabi	261.3 (12-31-77)	301.1

Appendix I(a) (continued)

Acquired U.S. Bank (Present Name)	Location (Year Estab.)	Type of Trans.[1] (Date of Trans.)	% o/s Shares Acquired[2]	Acquirer Category[3]	Name of Acquirer (Foreign Bank Parent) [Beneficial Owner]	Nationality of Acquirer	Total Assets ($ million)[4]	
							Acquired Bank Prior to Trans. (Reference Date)	Resultant Bank as of 12-31-79
15. Bank of the Commonwealth	Detroit, MI (1916)	ACQ (02-75)	31.0 (Common) 54.0 (Preferred)	FI/SC	Ghaith Pharaon	Saudi Arabia	1,034.4 (12-31-74)	
		ACQ (01-25-77)	76.6	FI/SC[14]	First Arabian Corp. [Ghaith Pharaon][15]	Saudi Arabia	925.0 (12-31-76)	1,084.4
16. Bank of Cutler Ridge (Creditbank)	Cutler Ridge, FL (1964)	ACQ (03-31-78)	100	FI/SC	Jose Luis Calonge	Spain	13.0 (12-31-77)	23.7
17. Bank of Miami Beach[16] (Intercontinental Bank)	Miami, FL (1954)	ACQ (06-22-73) Add'l Purchases (Total as of 09-77)	61.5 85.2	FI/SC	Jaime Castell Lastortras & Family	Spain	40.5 (12-31-72)	306.1
18. Bank of Perrine	Perrine, FL (1959)	ACQ (Pending)	100	FI/SC	Felix Corea Maya & Fabio Hurtado Saldarriaga	Colombia	38.2 (12-31-79)	38.2
19. Bank of Suffolk County (Extebank)	Stony Brook, NY (1907)	MERGER (06-30-80)	100	FBHC	Century National Bank (Banco Exterior de Espana)[17]	Spain	90.6 (12-31-79)	90.6
20. Bank of Virginia	Richmond, VA (1922)	ACQ (11-29-79)	15.0	FBHC	Banca March, SA	Spain	1,898.1 (09-30-79)	1,986.2
21. Bank of the West	San Jose, CA (1874)	Merger (03-18-80)	100	FBHC	French Bank of California (Banque Nationale de Paris)[18]	France	589.3 (12-31-79)	589.3

No.	Bank	Transaction (Date)	%	Type	Acquirer	Country	Value (Date)	Total
22.	Baymeadows Bank (Royal Trust Bank of Jacksonville) Jacksonville, FL (1975)	ACQ (06-22-77)	99.7	FBHC	The Royal Trust Co.	Canada	9.6 (03-31-77)	14.2
23.	Biscayne Bank Miami, FL (1973)	ACQ (06-78 & 11-78)[19]	50.0	FI/SC	Manuel R. P. Espirito Santo Silva	Portugal	13.1 (03-31-78)	48.6
24.	Camino-California Bank (America California Bank) Palo Alto, CA (1972)	ACQ (04-75 & 07-75) Add'l Purchases (Total as of 03-79)	67.2 / 69.0	FI/SC	Y. T. Chou	Hong Kong	21.5 (12-31-74)	7.7[20]
25.	Centinela Bank (Tokai Bank of California) Inglewood, CA (1963)	Merger (07-11-75)	100	FBHC	Tokai Bank of California (Tokai Bank, Ltd.)	Japan	31.2 (06-30-75)	158.9
26.	Central National Bank of Miami Miami, FL (1957)	ACQ (08-10-77)	76.0	FI/SC	Eduardo Espina Fernandez & Humberto Vagalara Rojas	Colombia	38.1 (06-30-77)	
		ACQ (02-22-80)	87.9[21]	FI/SC	Sabrina Properties/ Eagle National Holding Co. [Humberto Vagalara Rojas & Jaime Michaelson Urive]	Colombia	58.2 (12-31-79)	58.2
27.	Central State Bank New York, NY (1919)	ACQ (Pending)	100	FI/SC	South American Investors	South America	71.5 (12-31-79)	71.5

Appendix I(a) (continued)

Acquired U.S. Bank (Present Name)	Location (Year Estab.)	Type of Trans.[1] (Date of Trans.)	% o/s Shares Acquired[2]	Acquirer Category[3]	Name of Acquirer (Foreign Bank Parent) [Beneficial Owner]	Nationality of Acquirer	Total Assets ($ million)[4]	
							Acquired Bank Prior to Trans. (Reference Date)	Resultant Bank as of 12-31-79
28. Century National Bank & Trust Co. (Extebank)	New York, NY (1964)	ACQ (05-20-75)	98.0	FI/SC	John Graiver	Argentina	48.3 (04-16-75)	
		ACQ (12-09-77)	98.0	FBHC	Banco Exterior de España[17]	Spain	43.0 (09-30-77)	116.6
29. Charter Bank (Golden State Sanwa Bank)[22]	Culver City, CA (1963)	Merger (11-29-73)	100	FBHC	The Sanwa Bank of California (The Sanwa Bank, Ltd.)	Japan	32.3 (12-31-72)	675.2
30. Chelsea National Bank (Union Chelsea National Bank)	New York, NY (1964)	ACQ Emer. Trans.[8] (12-31-76)	100	FBHC	Banco Union, SA	Venezuela	31.2 (12-31-76)	76.6
31. City Bank of San Diego (California Canadian Bank)	San Diego, CA (1962)	Merger (07-07-69)	100	FBHC	California Canadian Bank[23] (Canadian Imperial Bank of Commerce)	Canada	21.5[24] (12-31-68)	618.3
32. Commercial and Farmers Bank of Oxnard (The Chartered Bank of London-SF → Union Bank)[25]	Oxnard, CA (1965)	Merger (12-16-77)	100	FBHC	The Chartered Bank of London-SF (Standard-Chartered Banking Group)	United Kingdom	79.6 (09-30-77)	840.0
33. Community Bank of San Jose (California Commerce Bank)	San Jose, CA (1963)	ACQ (06-30-78)	95.0	FBHC	Banco Nacional de Mexico[26]	Mexico	72.5 (03-31-78)	76.3

#	Bank, City (year)	Type (date)	%	Code	Acquirer	Country	Value (date)	Value
34.	Community State Bank[13], Albany, NY (1915)	ACQ (01-78)	18.6	FI/SC	Middle Eastern Investors	Saudi Arabia, Kuwait, and Abu Dhabi	78.7 (12-31-77)	71.8
35.	Coolidge Bank & Trust Co., Watertown, MA (1960)	ACQ (11-09-78)	60.2	FI/SC[14]	Bellevue Holding Corp. & Colonial General, Inc. [Ismael Dudhia][27]	United Kingdom	140.0 (09-30-78)	139.0
36.	County Bank of Santa Barbara (Barclays Bank of California), Santa Barbara, CA (1968)	Merger (10-01-74)	100	FBHC	Barclays Bank of California[28] (Barclays Group)	United Kingdom	43.1 (10-15-74)	698.1
37.	Crocker National Bank, San Francisco, CA (1870)	ACQ (Pending)	51.0	FBHC	Midland Bank, Ltd.	United Kingdom	16,087.5 (12-31-79)	16,087.5
38.	Dale Mabry State Bank (Royal Trust Bank of Tampa), Tampa, FL (1973)	ACQ (02-25-76)	100	FBHC	The Royal Trust Co.	Canada	7.3 (12-31-75)	13.1
39.	Dania Bank, Dania, FL (1926)	ACQ (04-11-78)	74.0	FI/SC	J.J. Gonzalez Gorrondona,Jr.[29]	Venezuela	126.3 (03-31-78)	119.8
40.	Deerfield Beach State Bank, Deerfield Beach, FL (1971)	ACQ (12-15-80)	31.0	FI/SC	MFG Investments,Inc. (José Alvarez Stelling)[30]	Venezuela	37.2 (12-31-79)	37.2
41.	Du Quoin State Bank, Du Quoin, IL (1915)	ACQ (03-79)	86.6	FI/SC	Saleh S. Jabr	Middle East	40.4 (12-31-78)	46.3
42.	Eastern Shore National Bank[13], Pocomoke City, MD (1934)	ACQ (01-78)	18.6	FI/SC	Middle Eastern Investors	Saudi Arabia, Kuwait, and Abu Dhabi	38.8 (12-31-77)	42.0

Appendix I(a) (continued)

Acquired U.S. Bank (Present Name)	Location (Year Estab.)	Type of Trans.[1] (Date of Trans.)	% o/s Shares Acquired[2]	Acquirer Category[3]	Name of Acquirer (Foreign Bank Parent) [Beneficial Owner]	Nationality of Acquirer	Total Assets ($ million)[4]	
							Acquired Bank Prior to Trans. (Reference Date)	Resultant Bank as of 12-31-79
43. Fidelity National Bank of S. Miami (International Bank of Miami, NA)	S. Miami, FL (1964)	ACQ (01-69)	70.0	FI/SC	Roberto Alejos & Carlos Hegel	Guatemala	15.0 (12-31-68)	
		ACQ (09-30-73)	98.6	U.S. BHC	First Bancshares of Florida, Inc.	U.S.	37.0 (12-31-72)	
		ACQ (09-27-79)	100	FI/SC	3 Groups of Spanish Investors including Banco Internacional de Comercio	Spain	33.0 (06-30-79)	41.1
44. First American Bank of Maryland[13]	Silver Spring, MD (12-31-78)[31]	ACQ (01-78)	18.6	FI/SC	Middle Eastern Investors	Saudi Arabia, Kuwait, and Abu Dhabi	207.8 (12-31-77)	300.1
45. First American Bank of Virginia[13]	McLean, VA (03-31-78)[32]	ACQ (01-78)	18.6	FI/SC	Middle Eastern Investors	Saudi Arabia, Kuwait, and Abu Dhabi	286.3 (12-31-77)	811.1
46. First Bank of Gulfport (Royal Trust Bank of St. Petersburg)	Gulfport, FL (1964)	ACQ (07-22-76)	100	FBHC	The Royal Trust Co.	Canada	24.3 (06-30-76)	35.8
47. First Bank of Pembroke Pines (Royal Trust Bank of Broward City)	Pembroke Pines, FL (1973)	ACQ (05-07-77)	99.7	FBHC	The Royal Trust Co.	Canada	19.8 (03-31-77)	37.6
48. First City Bank	Rosemead, CA (1929)	Merger (Pending)	100	FBHC	Golden State Sanwa Bank[22] (The Sanwa Bank,Ltd.)	Japan	145.7 (12-31-79)	145.7

No.	Bank	Location (Year)	Transaction (Date)	%	Type	Acquirer	Country	Value (Date)	Total
49.	First City National Bank of Jacksonville	Jacksonville, FL (1975)	ACQ (02-14-79)	64.0	FI/SC	Canadian and Dutch Investors[6]	Canada (32%) Netherlands (32%)	8.2 (12-31-78)	10.4
50.	First National Bank of Hialeah (First National Bank of Greater Miami)	Hialeah, FL (1963)	ACQ (12-18-77)	80.0	FI/SC[14]	José Alvarez Stelling → MFG Investments, Inc.[30]	Venezuela	138.9 (09-30-77)	236.5
51.	First National Bank of Lexington[13]	Lexington, VA (1890)	ACQ (07-28-78)	18.6	FI/SC	Middle Eastern Investors	Saudi Arabia, Kuwait, and Abu Dhabi	11.3 (06-30-78)	13.0
52.	First National Bank of Puerto Rico (Banco de Santander, Puerto Rico)	Puerto Rico (1972)	ACQ (09-03-76) Add'l Purchases (Total as of 12-77)	67.7 93.8	FBHC	Banco de Santander, SA[11]	Spain	22.9 (06-30-76)	383.8
53.	First National Bank of San Diego County	Escondido, CA (1964)	Merger (Pending)	100	FBHC	The Mitsubishi Bank of California[33] (The Mitsubishi Bank, Ltd.)	Japan	155.8 (12-31-79)	155.8
54.	First State Bank of Northern California (Lloyds Bank California)	San Leandro, CA (1962)	Merger Emer. Trans.[8] (05-22-76)	100	FBHC	Lloyds Bank California[34] (Lloyds Group)	United Kingdom	52.3[9] (05-22-76)	2,472.8
55.	First Valley Bank (Barclays Bank of California)	San Jose, CA (1955)	Merger (01-16-70)	100	FBHC	Barclays Bank of California[28] (Barclays Group)	United Kingdom	50.2[24] (06-30-69)	697.1
56.	First Westchester National Bank (Barclays Bank of New York)	New Rochelle, NY (1934)	Merger (06-01-74)	100	FBHC	Barclays Bank of New York (Barclays Group)	United Kingdom	214.2 (12-31-73)	600.5

Appendix I(a) (continued)

Acquired U.S. Bank (Present Name)	Location (Year Estab.)	Type of Trans.[1] (Date of Trans.)	% o/s Shares Acquired[2]	Acquirer Category[3]	Name of Acquirer (Foreign Bank Parent) [Beneficial Owner]	Nationality of Acquirer	Total Assets ($ million)[4] Acquired Bank Prior to Trans. (Reference Date)	Resultant Bank as of 12-31-79
57. First Western Bank & Trust Co. (Lloyds Bank California)	Los Angeles, CA (1961)	ACQ (01-16-74)	99.5	FBHC	Lloyds Group[34]	United Kingdom	1,333.6 (12-31-72)	2,472.8
58. Flagler Bank (Intercontinental Bank)[16]	Miami, FL. (1969)	ACQ (06-25-75)	92.9	FI/SC	Castell Family	Spain	19.0 (12-31-74)	306.1
59. Flagship Bank of Adventura (SafraBank)	N. Miami Beach, FL (1974)	ACQ (08-07-78)	100	FI/SC[14]	Edmond Safra → SafraCorp.[35]	Brazil	13.3 (06-30-78)	95.9
60. Flagship National Bank of Dadeland (Dadeland National Bank)	Miami, FL (1969)	ACQ (03-15-77)	95.0	FI/SC	Spanish & South American Investors	Colombia Costa Rica El Salvador Spain Panama Guatemala	37.9 (12-31-76)	38.3
61. Franklin National Bank (European-American Bank & Trust Co.)	New York,NY (1926)	ACQ (07-12-72)	21.6	FI/SC	Michele Sindona	Italy	3,537.5 (12-31-71)	
		Merger Emer. Trans.[8] (10-08-74)	100	FBHC	European-American Bank & Trust Co.: Amsterdam-Rotterdam Bank, NV (17.0%)	Netherlands	1,579.0[9] (10-08-74)	4,675.5

#	Bank (Location/Year)	Transaction	%	Type	Acquirer	Country	Assets (Date)	Total
					Creditanstalt-Bankverein (2.5%)	Austria		
					Deutsche Bank A.G. (20.125%)	W. Germany		
					Midland Bank,Ltd. (20.125%)	United Kingdom		
					Société Générale de Banque, S.A. (20.125%)	Belgium		
					Société Générale (20.125%)	France		
62.	Golden State Bank (Golden State Sanwa Bank) Downey, CA (1974)	Merger (12-27-77)	100	FBHC	The Sanwa Bank of California[22] (The Sanwa Bank, Ltd.)	Japan	144.7 (09-30-77)	675.2
63.	Great Western Bank & Trust Co. Phoenix, AZ (1906)	ACQ (1974-1978) Slow Market Purchase	17.9[36]	FI/SC	Westphalian American Association [Count Ferdinand Graf Von Galen]	W. Germany	284.4 (12-31-73)	
		ACQ (Pending)	100	FI/SC	GWB Holding,B.V. [Kuwaiti Investors]	Kuwait	479.7 (12-31-79)	479.7
64.	Guaranty Bank of Stapleton (Dominion Bank of Denver) Denver, CO (1966)	ACQ (03-09-79)	67.0	FI/SC	Robert Elliot[6]	Canada	11.2 (12-31-78)	12.7
65.	Hacienda Bank (The Mitsubishi Bank of California) La Habra, CA (1969)	Merger (02-09-76)	100	FBHC	The Mitsubishi Bank of California[33] (The Mitsubishi Bank, Ltd.)	Japan	55.6 (12-31-75)	286.7
66.	Hartford Plaza Bank (LaSalle NB) Chicago, IL (1963)	Merger (04-21-80)	100	FBHC	LaSalle National Bank (Algemene Bank Nederland)[37]	Netherlands	38.1 (12-31-79)	38.1
67.	Hemisphere National Bank Washington, D.C. (1974)	ACQ (12-05-79)	21.4	FI/SC	Nestor Julio Garcia	Argentina	21.0 (09-30-79)	23.4

Appendix I(a) (continued)

Acquired U.S. Bank (Present Name)	Location (Year Estab.)	Type of Trans.[1] (Date of Trans.)	% o/s Shares Acquired[2]	Acquirer Category[3]	Name of Acquirer (Foreign Bank Parent) [Beneficial Owner]	Nationality of Acquirer	Total Assets ($ million)[4]	
							Acquired Bank Prior to Trans. (Reference Date)	Resultant Bank as of 12-31-79
68. Independence Bank	Encino, CA (1963)	ACQ (01-08-80)	100	FI/SC	Halifax Financial Holdings, Inc. [Huang Tiong Chan]	Hong Kong	145.5 (12-31-79)	145.5
69. International Bank of California	Los Angeles, CA (1962)	ACQ (12-15-77) Add'l Purchases (Total as of 09-78)	34.2 44.9	FBHC	Metropolitan Bank & Trust Co.	Philippines	6.9 (09-30-77)	8.4
70. International Bank of Miami (Royal Trust Bank of Miami, NA)	Miami, FL (1963)	ACQ (09-02-72)	99.5	FBHC	The Royal Trust Co.	Canada	51.1 (12-31-71)	169.0
71. Kings Lafayette Bank & Trust Co. (Republic National Bank of New York)[25]	Brooklyn, NY (1889)	ACQ (06-30-74)	100	FI/SC	Edmond Safra → Republic National Bank of New York[35]	Brazil	226.5 (12-31-73)	4,415.3
72. LaSalle National Bank	Chicago, IL (1927)	ACQ (08-14-79)	99.8	FBHC	Algemene Bank Nederland[37]	Netherlands	925.7 (06-30-79)	1,053.9
73. Liberty National Bank (The Chartered Bank of London-SF→ Union Bank)[25]	San Francisco, CA (1928)	Merger (07-01-74)	100	FBHC	The Chartered Bank of London-SF (Standard - Chartered Banking Group)	United Kingdom	101.4 (12-31-73)	840.0
74. Main Bank of Houston	Houston, TX (1962)	ACQ (09-06-77)	69.1	FI/SC	Ghaith Pharaon (19.7%) & Khaled Bin Mahfouz (49.3%)[38]	Saudi Arabia	93.3 (06-30-77)	

No.	Bank Name	Location (Year)	Ownership Reorganization (07-21-78)		Type	Owner	Country		
			Ownership Reorganization (07-21-78)	69.1	FI/SC	Khaled Bin Mahfouz (acquired Pharoan's 19.7%)	Saudi Arabia	68.4 (06-30-78)	72.3
75.	Manufacturers Bank	Los Angeles, CA (1962)	Merger (Pending)	100	FBHC	Mitsui Bank of California (The Mitsui Bank, Ltd.)	Japan	705.7 (12-31-79)	705.7
76.	Marine Midland Bank, NA	Buffalo, NY (1812)	ACQ (03-04-80) Add'l Purchases (Total as of 10-80)	41.0 51.0	FBHC	The Hongkong and Shanghai Banking Corp.	Hong Kong	15,690.9 (12-31-79)	15,690.9
77.	Meadowlands National Bank	N. Bergen, NJ (1925)	ACQ (01-79 & 04-79)	80.0 (Approx.)	FI/SC	Jacobo Finkielstain & several associates	Argentina	32.2 (12-31-78)	35.0
78.	Metropolitan National Bank	Houston, TX (1972)	ACQ (01-03-79)	77.3	FI/SC	Atef Daniel	Syria	20.8 (12-31-78)	23.3
79.	Miami National Bank	Miami, FL. (1956)	ACQ (Pending)	84.5	FBHC	Banco Zarogozano	Spain	54.9 (12-31-79)	54.9
80.	National American Bank of New Orleans	N. Orleans, LA (1917)	ACQ (08-73 to 07-74)	42.7	FI/SC	Arturo Ferruzzi → Artfer, Inc. & Inter Financing Exchange[39]	Italy	294.0 (12-31-72)	351.0
81.	National Bank of Georgia	Atlanta, GA (1911)	ACQ (01-78 & 06-78) Add'l Purchases (Total as of 03-80)	60.5 98.3	FI/SC	Ghaith Pharaon[38]	Saudi Arabia	388.9 (12-31-77)	417.9
82.	National Bank of North America	New York, NY (1905)	ACQ (04-16-79)	100	FBHC	National Westminster Bank, Ltd.	United Kingdom	4,326.0 (03-31-79)	4,849.0

Appendix I(a) (continued)

Acquired U.S. Bank (Present Name)	Location (Year Estab.)	Type of Trans.[1] (Date of Trans.)	% o/s Shares Acquired[2]	Acquirer Category[3]	Name of Acquirer (Foreign Bank Parent) [Beneficial Owner]	Nationality of Acquirer	Total Assets ($ million)[4]	
							Acquired Bank Prior to Trans. (Reference Date)	Resultant Bank as of 12-31-79
83. Northern California National Bank of San Mateo (California Canadian Bank)	San Mateo, CA (1964)	Merger (08-22-66)	100	FBHC	California Canadian Bank[23] (Canadian Imperial Bank of Commerce)	Canada	8.4[24] (06-30-66)	618.3
84. Pan American Bank of Coral Gables, NA (Caribank, N.A.)	Coral Gables, FL (1963)	ACQ (05-12-77)	88.9	FI/SC	J. J. Gonzalez Gorrondona, Jr.[29]	Venezuela	27.9 (03-31-77)	26.9
85. Pan American National Bank of East Los Angeles (Pan American National Bank of Los Angeles)	Los Angeles, CA (1965)	ACQ (04-20-78)	96.8	FI/SC	Oen Yin Choy	Indonesia	30.4 (03-31-78)	56.1
86. Peoples Bank	Houston, TX (1970)	ACQ (07-21-78)	51.7	FI/SC	Ali Fayed	Saudi Arabia	33.6 (06-30-78)	49.3
87. Peoples National Bank of Leesburg[13]	Leesburg, VA (1888)	ACQ (01-78)	18.6	FI/SC	Middle Eastern Investors	Saudi Arabia, Kuwait, and Abu Dhabi	39.4 (12-31-77)	42.3
88. Peoples National Bank of Littleton	Littleton, NH (1966)	ACQ (05-01-78)	65.0	FI/SC	J. Kent McKinlay & Don Cutts	Canada	4.3 (03-31-78)	6.7
89. Redwood Bank	San Francisco, CA (1963)	ACQ (03-03-80)	100	FI/SC	Empire Holdings, Inc.[Ramon L.Siy and others]	Philippines	135.5 (12-31-79)	135.5
90. Republic National Bank of Miami	Miami, FL (1965)	ACQ (10-30-70)	61.5	FI/SC[14]	Rebank Corp. [Isaias family][40]	Ecuador	22.3 (12-31-69)	297.0

No.	Bank	Location	Transaction	%	Type	Owner/Investor	Country	Date	Amount
91.	Round Hill National Bank[13]	Round Hill, VA (1920)	ACQ (01-78)	18.6	FI/SC	Middle Eastern Investors	Saudi Arabia, Kuwait, and Abu Dhabi	17.0 (12-31-77)	18.1
92.	Security National Bank	Walnut Creek, CA (1963)	ACQ (01-10-73)	95.1	FI/SC	Adnan Khashoggi[41]	Saudi Arabia	97.3 (12-31-72)	226.3
93.	Security National Bank of New Jersey	Newark, NJ (1965)	ACQ (07-15-76)	56.3	FI/SC[14]	Fiduciary Investment Co. of New Jersey[42]	Switzerland & Canada	26.3 (06-30-76)	49.2
94.	Shenandoah Valley National Bank[13]	Winchester, VA (1866)	ACQ (01-78)	18.6	FI/SC	Middle Eastern Investors	Saudi Arabia, Kuwait, and Abu Dhabi	71.5 (12-31-77)	75.9
95.	Southern California First National Bank, San Diego (California First Bank)	San Diego, CA (1883)	Merger (10-01-75)	100	FBHC	The Bank of Tokyo of California (The Bank of Tokyo, Ltd.)	Japan	889.2 (06-30-75)	3,267.5
96.	Sunshine State Bank	S. Miami, FL (1972)	ACQ (05-78 & 08-78)	77.0	FI/SC	Alma Robles Chiari & José Andonie Fernandez	Panama & Honduras	11.9 (06-30-78)	28.1
97.	Surety National Bank (California Overseas Bank)	Encino, CA (1964)	Merger (11-08-79)	100	FI/SC	California Overseas Bank[5]	Philippines	46.6 (09-30-79)	150.0
98.	Totalbank	Miami, FL (1974)	ACQ (06-30-75)	24.6	FI/SC	Francisco E. Blanco	Spain	11.4 (04-16-75)	
			Add'l Purchases (Total as of 12-78)	89.4					
			ACQ (07-80)	50.0	FI/SC	Ignacio Herrero Group[43]	Spain	89.3 (12-31-79)	89.3

Appendix I(a) (continued)

Acquired U.S. Bank (Present Name)	Location (Year Estab.)	Type of Trans.[1] (Date of Trans.)	% o/s Shares Acquired[2]	Acquirer Category[3]	Name of Acquirer (Foreign Bank Parent) [Beneficial Owner]	Nationality of Acquirer	Total Assets ($ million)[4]	
							Acquired Bank Prior to Trans. (Reference Date)	Resultant Bank as of 12-31-79
99. Underwriters Bank & Trust Co. (Banco Central of New York)	New York, NY (1929)	ACQ (11-08-73)	53.2	FI/SC	Spanish & Latin American Investors	Spain & Latin America	53.2 (12-31-72)	
		ACQ (08-21-80)	100	FBHC	Banco Central de Madrid	Spain	43.2 (12-31-79)	43.2
100. U. S. Trust Co.	New York, NY (1853)	ACQ (01-23-80)	9.997	FBHC	Banco de Chile	Chile	1,976.6 (12-31-79)	
		ACQ (06-80)	9.0	FBHC	Schroder, Munchmeyer, Hengst, & Co.[36]	W. Germany	1,976.6 (12-31-79)	1,976.6
101. Union Bank	Los Angeles, CA (1914)	ACQ (04-17-79)	100	FBHC	Standard-Chartered Banking Group[25]	United Kingdom	5,183.1 (03-31-79)	5,761.5
102. Union First National Bank of Washington[13] (First American Bank, NA)	Washington, DC (1872)	ACQ (01-78)	18.6	FI/SC	Middle Eastern Investors	Saudi Arabia, Kuwait, and Abu Dhabi	587.0 (12-31-77)	673.0
103. Valley Fidelity Bank & Trust Co.[13]	Knoxville, TN (1914)	ACQ (01-78)	18.6	FI/SC	Middle Eastern Investors	Saudi Arabia, Kuwait, and Abu Dhabi	145.8 (12-31-77)	173.0
104. Valley National Bank[13]	Harrisonburg, VA (1908)	ACQ (01-78)	18.6	FI/SC	Middle Eastern Investors	Saudi Arabia, Kuwait, and Abu Dhabi	51.9 (12-31-77)	53.2

105.	Western Bank	Houston, TX (1958)	ACQ (07-24-78)	96.0	FI/SC	Syria	O. R. Lababedi		152.6 (06-30-78)	240.8
106.	Westlands Bank	Santa Ana, CA (1970)	ACQ (Pending)	40.0	FBHC	Canada	Canadian Commercial and Industrial Bank of Edmonton		121.2 (12-31-79)	121.2
107.	Worth Avenue National Bank (Royal Trust Bank of Palm Beach, NA)	Palm Beach, FL (1971)	ACQ (11-29-76)	95.2	FBHC	Canada	The Royal Trust Co.		27.7 (09-30-76)	52.3

[1] Acquisitions have been divided into two basic types of transactions: direct acquisition; and merger, which is defined as an acquisition of a U.S. bank by an existing foreign-owned U.S. bank.

[2] 100% is used throughout to indicate the acquisition of 100% of the bank's outstanding shares, less directors' qualifying shares.

[3] FI/SC = Foreign individual(s) or a shell company controlled by foreign beneficial owner(s); FBHC = Foreign bank or foreign near-bank.

[4] Total assets (consolidated foreign and domestic) in $ million as of the referenced Call Report date, except where indicated.

[5] California Overseas Bank was established to accomplish the purchase of the assets and liabilities of Ahmanson Bank and Trust Co. (except for the trust business). COB subsequently acquired Surety National Bank (Encino, California) on November 08, 1979.

[6] Robert Elliot (Canada) acquired Alamosa National Bank (12-31-79), Guaranty Bank of Stapleton (03-09-79), and is one of the investors who acquired First City National Bank of Jacksonville (02-14-79).

[7] The Graiver family signed a purchase agreement to buy American Bank & Trust Co. in 1975. However, the purchase was never consummated. ABT was placed in receivership on September 15, 1976 and subsequently merged with Bank Leumi Trust Co. of New York.

[8] Emer. Trans. = Emergency transaction; FDIC assisted in the transaction by serving as liquidating agent for the bank.

[9] Assets purchased by the acquiring bank.

[10] Gregorio Diego acquired Banco Commercial de Mayaguez through several holding companies that he controls. BCM subsequently merged with Banco de Ahorro de Puerto Rico.

[11] Banco de Santander, SA acquired the First National Bank of Puerto Rico in 1976 forming Banco de Santander, PR. It subsequently acquired approximately one-third of Banco Credito y Ahorro Ponceno's branches in 1978.

[12] Banco Mercantile de Puerto Rico and three Bank of Nova Scotia branches were incorporated in September 1979 to form Scotiabank de Puerto Rico.

[13] Subsidiary of Financial General Bankshares, Inc. (Purchase of additional shares is pending.)

[14] Shell holding company is considered to be a bank holding company by the Federal Reserve Board.

[15] Under a 1977 recapitalization plan, new Bank of the Commonwealth shares were issued. Existing shareholders were given the first opportunity to buy the new stock; remaining shares were purchased by First Arabian Corp. First Arabian Corp. also bought all of BC's stock owned by Ghaith Pharaon. After the recapitalization, Pharaon no longer owned any BC stock directly. He is, however, an indirect owner since he is a major investor in First Arabian Corp.

[16] Jaime Castell Lastortras and family acquired the Bank of Miami Beach in 1973 and Flagler Bank in 1975. The two banks were merged on December 16, 1977, with the resulting bank becoming "Intercontinental Bank." In March 1978, 11.8% of the newly merged Intercontinental Bank was acquired by Banco Catalan de Desarrollo (Spain), of which Jaime Castell Lastortras is president.

[17] American Bank and Trust Co., held 98% of the outstanding shares of Century National Bank and Trust Co. as collateral on loans to John Graiver. When American Bank and Trust Co. failed in September 1976, the FDIC acquired and auctioned off the 98% holding in Century National Bank and Trust Co. Banco Exterior de Espana submitted the highest bid and took control of the bank. Century NB & TC subsequently acquired Bank of Suffolk County (06-30-80) to form Extebank.

[18] Banque Nationale de Paris acquired Banc West Corp. (holding company parent of Bank of the West) in March 1980. Bank of the West then absorbed BNP's U.S. subsidiary, the French Bank of California.

[19] Manual R. P. Espirito Santo Silva acquired 24.9% of the outstanding shares of Biscayne Bank in June 1978 and an additional 25.1% in November 1978.

[20] Two branches of Camino-California Bank were sold to Imperial Bank (Los Angeles) in 1978, thus accounting for the decrease in total assets between 1974 and 1979.

[21] Eduardo Espina Fernandez and Humberto Vagalara Rojas acquired 76% of Central National Bank of Miami's stock in 1977. Under a February 1980 reorganization, Espina sold his interest in the bank. Vagalara and Jaime Michaelson Urive formed Sabrina Properties (Netherlands Antilles) which entirely owns Eagle National Holding Co. (Miami). Eagle exchanged its shares for 81.2% of CNBM's 132,000 outstanding shares. Following the exchange, an additional stock issue and purchase brought Eagle's holding in CNBM to roughly 88%.

[22] The Sanwa Bank of California absorbed Charter Bank in 1973. SBC subsequently merged with Golden State Bank in 1977 to form Golden State Sanwa Bank. GSSB now plans to acquire First City Bank (Rosemead, California).

[23] California Canadian Bank merged with Northern California National Bank of San Mateo in 1966 and City Bank of San Diego in 1969.

[24] Total assets reported by the bank to Polk's World Bank Directory. (Call Report data unavailable.)

[25] The Chartered Bank of London-SF merged with Liberty National Bank in 1974 and Commercial and Farmers Bank of Oxnard in 1977. CBL-SF was subsequently absorbed by Union Bank (January 1980) after Union Bank was acquired by the Standard-Chartered Banking Group.

[26] Banco Nacional de Mexico's Los Angeles-based subsidiary, Amex Holding Company, acquired 95% of the outstanding shares of Community Bank of San Jose. CBSJ merged with Mexican American National Bank (foreign de novo U.S. bank) in June 1980, to form California Commerce Bank.

[27] The Federal Reserve Board approved an application by Bellevue Holding Corp. (Geneva, Switzerland) and Colonial General, Inc. (New York) to purchase controlling interest in First Coolidge Corp., parent holding company of Coolidge Bank and Trust Company. Both companies were created for the purpose of acquiring Coolidge Bank and Trust Co. by Ismael Dudhia.

[28] Barclays Bank of California merged with First Valley Bank (San Jose, California) in 1970 and County Bank of Santa Barbara in 1974.

[29] J. J. Gonzalez Gorrondona, Jr. acquired Pan American Bank of Coral Gables, N.A. in 1977 and Dania Bank in 1978.

[30] Jose Alvarez Stelling and family acquired the First National Bank of Hialeah in 1977. Despite an apparent divestiture in February 1979, they continue to maintain controlling interest through foreign firms owned by the family. Under an arrangement approved by the Federal Reserve, the family's interest is held by MFG Investments, Inc. (Hialeah, Florida) which in turn is held by Marsh Investments NV (Curacao) a subsidiary of Marsh Investments NV (Rotterdam). MFG Investments, Inc. subsequently acquired approximately 31% of the outstanding common stock of Deerfield Beach State Bank in December 1980.

[31] First American Bank of Maryland resulted from the 12-31-78 merger of American Bank of Maryland (Silver Spring, Maryland) and Chesapeake National Bank (Towson, Maryland).

[32] First American Bank of Virginia resulted from the 03-31-78 merger of Alexandria National Bank of Northern Virginia; Arlington Trust Co., Inc.; and Clarendon Bank and Trust.

[33] The Mitsubishi Bank of California absorbed Hacienda Bank in 1976. MBC has subsequently applied for regulatory approval to acquire First National Bank of San Diego County.

[34] Lloyds Group acquired First Western Bank and Trust in 1974 and changed the bank's name to Lloyds Bank California. LBC subsequently acquired First State Bank of Northern California in 1976.

[35] Edmond Safra acquired Kings Lafayette Bank and Trust Co. in 1974 and Flagship Bank of Adventura in 1978. KLBTC was absorbed by Republic National Bank of New York (Safra's *de novo* bank) in 1974. Safra's stock in FBA was purchased by SafraCorp in April 1979.

[36] All of the voting shares of Great Western Bank & Trust Co. are owned by Patagonia Corp. Slightly more than 17% of the common shares plus some convertible debentures (roughly 26%, if all were converted) of Patagonia Corp. are owned by Westphalian American Association. Count Ferdinand Graf Von Galen owns Westphalian American Association through a limited partnership which he controls.

Count Von Galen is Senior Partner of Schroder, Munchmeyer, Hengst & Co. (W. Germany's second largest bank). SMHC acquired 9% of U.S. Trust Co. (June 1980) and Von Galen was subsequently elected to U.S. Trust's Board of Directors.

[37] Algemene Bank Nederland acquired LaSalle National Bank in 1979. LaSalle National Bank subsequently absorbed Hartford Plaza Bank (April 1980).

[38] Ghaith Pharaon is known to have held an equity interest in two American banks. In 1977, Pharaon and Shiek Khaled Bin Mahfouz acquired 69.1% of the outstanding shares of the Main Bank of Houston. Pharaon sold his stock in MBH to Mahfouz the following year. In the interim, Pharaon began acquiring shares in the National Bank of Georgia. He controlled 98.3% of NBG by March 1980.

[39] Arturo Ferruzzi (Italy) acquired 42.6% of the outstanding shares of National American Bank of New Orleans during 1973 and 1974. This stock was then resold in July 1974 to Artfer, Inc. (24.99%) and Inter Financing Exchange, S.A. (17.58%). Both companies are, however, controlled by the Ferruzzi family.

[40] On November 2, 1980, the controlling ownership of Republic National Bank of Miami was sold to Rebank Corp., a Florida corporation. Rebank Corp. was organized to hold the stock interest and is wholly owned by Nahim Isaias (Ecuador).

[41] Adnan Khashoggi acquired the Bank of Contra Costa in 1972 and Security National Bank in 1973. BCC was subsequently divested in 1980. A San Francisco bank has tentatively agreed to purchase SNB from Khashoggi.

[42] Control of Security National Bank of New Jersey is held by Fiduciary Investment Company (New Jersey). Banco di Roma per la Svizzera (Switzerland); St. Paul's Benevolent, Educational & Missionary Institute, Inc.; and Canada Permanent Mortgage Corp. hold a majority of the bank holding company's non-voting stock. The voting stock is held by U.S. citizens.

[43] A group of Spaniards headed by Ignacio Herrero acquired 50% of the ownership of Totalbank Corp. of Florida (bank holding company that controls the shares of Totalbank) from Francisco Blanco. Aggregate foreign ownership remains constant at approximately 90%.

Appendix I(b)

U.S. Commercial Banks Known to Have Been Acquired and Later Divested by Foreign Investors (December 31, 1980)

Acquired U.S. Bank (Present Name)	Location (Year Estab.)	Type of Trans.[1] (Date of Trans.)	% o/s Shares Acquired[2]	Acquirer Category[1]	Name of Acquirer (Foreign Bank Parent) [Beneficial Owner]	Nationality of Acquirer	Total Assets ($ million)[4]	
							Acquired Bank Prior to Trans. (Reference Date)	Resultant Bank as of 12-31-79
1. Bank of Contra Costa	Walnut Creek, (1970)	ACQ (03-01-72)	66.0	FI/SC	Adnan Khashoggi[5]	Saudi Arabia	9.0 (12-31-71)	
		Add'l Purchases (Total as of 12-79)	99.6					
		Divested (01-07-80)	99.6	U.S. I/SC	Paul W. Learner	U.S.	37.9 (12-31-79)	37.9
2. Continental National Bank of Miami	Miami, FL (1974)	ACQ (09-79)	25.8	FI/SC	Armando de Armas Melendez	Venezuela	54.4 (06-30-79)	
		Divested (06-02-80)	25.2	U.S. I/SC	Charles Dascal, et al.	U.S.	54.3 (12-31-79)	54.3
3. First National Bank of Fresno (Central Bank, Oakland)[6]	Fresno, CA (1962)	ACQ (07-10-75)	99.0	FI/SC	Amos W. Dawe[7]	Malaysia	38.1 (06-30-75)	
		Default on Sale (03-01-76)	99.0	U.S. BHC	Central Banking System, Inc.	U.S.	39.9 (12-31-75)	524.9
4. Laidlaw and Co.[8] (Manufacturers & Traders Trust Co.)	New York, NY (1842)	ACQ (11-01-68)	100	FBHC	Hambros Bank, Ltd.	United Kingdom	76.3[9] (03-31-68)	
		Merger (01-01-76)	100	U.S. Bank	Manufacturers & Traders Trust Co.	U.S.	106.2 (12-31-75)	1,698.0

Appendix I(b) (continued)

Acquired U.S. Bank (Present Name)	Location (Year Estab.)	Type of Trans.[1] (Date of Trans.)	% o/s Shares Acquired[2]	Acquirer Category[1]	Name of Acquirer (Foreign Bank Parent) [Beneficial Owner]	Nationality of Acquirer	Total Assets ($ million)[4]	
							Acquired Bank Prior to Trans. (Reference Date)	Resultant Bank as of 12-31-79
5. National Bank of South Florida (Manufacturers National Bank)	Miami, FL (1964)	ACQ (09-02-77)	99.7	FI/SC	Juan Evelio Pou & Gustavo Villoldo	Colombia	26.5 (06-30-77)	
		Divested (03-17-78)	99.7	U.S. I/SC	Gustavo E. Mustelier	U.S.	15.6 (12-31-77)	19.8
6. Northside Bank of Miami	Miami, Fl (1964)	ACQ (02-21-78)	56.9	FI/SC	Andres F. Rodrequez	Cuba	11.4 (12-31-77)	
		Default on Loan (03-10-79)	56.9	U.S. Bank	The Bank of Miami[10]	U.S.	15.5 (12-31-78)	11.3
7. Peninsula National Bank (Central Bank, Oakland)	Burlingame, CA (1964)	ACQ (12-16-74)	97.6	FI/SC	Amos W. Dawe[7]	Malaysia	25.6 (12-31-73)	
		Default on Sale[11] (11-25-75)	76.8	FBHC	Pacific Atlantic Bank, Inc.	Panama	24.1	
			20.8	U.S. BHC	Central Banking System, Inc.	U.S.	(09-30-75)	
		Divested (03-31-77)	76.8	U.S. Bank	Central Bank, Oakland (Acquired stock from Pacific Atlantic Bank, Inc.)	U.S.	19.9 (12-31-76)	524.9

No. Bank (Location, Founded)	Acquiring Bank	Transaction (Date)	%	FBHC	Beneficial Owner	Nationality	Total Assets (Date)	
8. Republic National Bank & Trust Co. (Central Bank, Oakland)	Beverly Hills, CA (1964)	Merger (12-15-70)	100	FBHC	Hongkong and Shang- hai Banking Corp. of California	Hong Kong	24.5[9] (12-31-69)	
		Merger (02-23-79)	100	U.S. Bank	Central Bank, Oakland	U.S.	117.7 (12-31-78)	524.9
9. Tahoe National Bank (Central Bank, Oakland)[6]	S. Lake Tahoe, CA (1963)	ACQ (07-01-75)	93.0	FI/SC	Amos W. Dawe[7]	Malaysia	12.5 (04-16-75)	
		Default on Sale (03-01-76)	88.3[12]	U.S. BHC	Central Banking System, Inc.	U.S.	14.7 (12-31-75)	524.9

[1] Acquisitions have been divided into two basic types of transactions: direct acquisition; and merger, which is defined as an acquisition of a U.S. bank by an existing foreign owned U.S. bank.

[2] 100% is used throughout to indicate the acquisition of 100% of the bank's outstanding shares, less directors' qualifying shares.

[3] FI/SC = Foreign individual(s) or a shell company controlled by foreign beneficial owner(s); FBHC = foreign bank or foreign near-bank.

[4] Total assets (consolidated foreign and domestic) in $ million as of the referenced Call Report date, except where indicated.

[5] Adnan Khashoggi acquired the Bank of Contra Costa in 1972 and Security National Bank in 1973.

[6] Central Bank, Oakland (owned by Central Banking System, Inc.) absorbed the First National Bank of Fresno and Tahoe National Bank in October 1979.

[7] Amos W. Dawe acquired First National Bank of Fresno, Peninsula National Bank, and Tahoe National Bank from Central Banking System, Inc. He subsequently defaulted on the terms of each sale and forfeited control of all three banks.

[8] Laidlaw and Co. was a stock brokerage firm that engaged in private commercial bank activities. It was acquired by Hambros Bank, Ltd. in 1968, becoming Hambros American Bank and Trust Co. HABTC was later renamed "First Empire Bank-New York" and eventually merged with Manufacturers and Traders Trust Co. in 1976.

[9] Total assets reported by the bank to Polk's World Bank Directory. (Call Report data unavailable.)

[10] Northside Bank of Miami was purchased in 1978 by nine investors (including Andres F. Rodriguez) with a $1.35 million loan from The Bank of Miami, with Northside stock as collateral. The Bank of Miami took control when several of the noteholders defaulted on their payments.

[11] From 1969 until 1974, Peninsula National Bank was owned by Central Banking System, Inc., then CBS sold its interest in PNB to Amos Dawe. As a result of Dawe's default on the purchase of PNB, Pacific Atlantic Bank, Inc., as a guarantor of Dawe's loan, succeeded to Dawe's 78% interest in PNB. 20% of PNB's stock was not transferred from CBS to Dawe and CBS continued to retain that interest in PNB as a consequence of the default PNB's assets in the bank were then purchased and its liabilities assumed by Central Bank in 1977.

[12] After ownership of Tahoe National Bank reverted back to Central Banking System, Inc., CBS held approximately 88% of the bank's outstanding shares and an additional 1.5% was issued to the bank's newly appointed directors. Dawe retained approximately 3% of the bank's stock.

Appendix II
Foreign-Owned *De Novo* U.S. Banks (December 31, 1980)

	De Novo U.S. Bank Name	Location	Year Established	Foreign Owner	Owner's Nationality	T. Assets (12-31-79)[1] $ million[1]
1.	American Asian Bank	San Francisco, CA	1974	C. Y. Tung	Hong Kong	45.0
2.	Asian International Bank	New York, NY	1980	Jointly-Acting Group[2]	Philippines	N/A
3.	Atlantic Bank of New York	New York, NY	1926	National Bank of Greece	Greece	385.6
4.	Banco de Bogota Trust Co.	New York, NY	1977	Banco de Bogota	Colombia	95.2
5.	Banco di Roma	Chicago, IL	1973	Banco di Roma	Italy	177.6
6.	Bank Leumi Trust Co. of New York[3]	New York, NY	1968	Bank Leumi Le-Israel B.M.	Israel	1,625.1
7.	Bank of Canton of California[4]	San Francisco, CA	1937	Cheng Wai Wang & others	Taiwan	318.8
8.	Bank of Montreal-California	San Francisco, CA	1864	Bank of Montreal	Canada	88.2
9.	Bank of Montreal Trust Co.	New York, NY	1923	Bank of Montreal	Canada	38.9
10.	Bank of Nova Scotia Trust Co.	New York, NY	1959	Scotiabank	Canada	7.0
11.	Bank of the Orient	San Francisco, CA	1971	Ernesto Lee Go	Philippines	125.1
12.	Bank of Tokyo Trust Co.	New York, NY	1955	Bank of Tokyo	Japan	3,366.9
13.	Barclays Bank of California[5]	San Francisco, CA	1965	Barclays Group	U.K.	698.1
14.	Barclays Bank of New York[6]	New York, NY	1971	Barclays Group	U.K.	600.5
15.	California Canadian Bank[7]	San Francisco, CA	1864	Canadian Imperial Bank of Commerce	Canada	618.3
16.	California First Bank[8] (formerly: The Bank of Tokyo of California)	San Francisco, CA	1953	Bank of Tokyo	Japan	3,267.5
17.	California Korea Bank	Los Angeles, CA	1974	Korea Exchange Bank	Korea	88.1
18.	Canadian Bank of Commerce Trust Co.	New York, NY	1951	Canadian Imperial Bank of Commerce	Canada	24.4
19.	Central Pacific Bank	Honolulu, HI	1954	Sumitomo Bank, Ltd.	Japan	410.7
20.	Chicago-Tokyo Bank	Chicago, IL	1964	Jointly-Acting Group[9]	Japan	293.4
21.	Chinese American Bank	New York, NY	1967	Bank of China (later called International Commercial Bank of China)[10]	Taiwan	79.3
22.	Daiwa Bank Trust Co.	New York, NY	1977	Daiwa Bank	Japan	408.3

	Parent Bank	De Novo U.S. Bank location	Year	Group	Country	Amount
23.	European-American Bank & Trust Co.[11]	New York, NY	1953	European-American 'Group'[12]	6 European countries	4,675.5
24.	First Pacific Bank of Chicago	Chicago, IL	1972	Dai-Ichi Kangyo Bank	Japan	158.5
25.	Fuji Bank & Trust Co.	New York, NY	1974	Fuji Bank	Japan	895.6
26.	Global Union Bank	New York, NY	1979	Asian Investors	Asia	15.6
27.	Golden State Sanwa Bank[13] (formerly: The Sanwa Bank of California)	San Francisco, CA	1972	The Sanwa Bank, Ltd.	Japan	675.2
28.	Industrial Bank of Japan	New York, NY	1974	Industrial Bank of Japan	Japan	818.3
29.	Israel Discount Trust Co.	New York, NY	1922	Israel Discount Bank	Israel	49.0
30.	Japan California Bank	Los Angeles, CA	1974	Jointly-Acting Group[14]	Japan	108.5
31.	Kyowa Bank of California	Los Angeles, CA	1978	Kyowa Bank	Japan	39.7
32.	The Mitsubishi Bank of California	Los Angeles, CA	1972	Mitsubishi Bank	Japan	286.7
33.	Mitsui Bank of California	Los Angeles, CA	1974	Mitsui Bank	Japan	264.4
34.	Mountain Trust Co.	Stowe, VT	1977	M. Gamerhoff & Lionel Schwartz	Canada	7.1
35.	Pacific Union Bank & Trust Co.[15]	Menlo Park, CA	1975	Payson Cha & family	Singapore & Hong Kong	15.9
36.	Philippine Bank of California	San Francisco, CA	1977	Jointly-Acting Group[16]	Philippines	36.5
37.	Republic National Bank of New York[17]	New York, NY	1966	Edmond J. Safra/Trade Development Bank	Brazil	4,415.3
38.	Royal Bank & Trust Co.	New York, NY	1951	Royal Bank of Canada	Canada	255.0
39.	J. Henry Schroder Bank & Trust Co.	New York, NY	1929	Schroder Group	U.K.	1,545.4
40.	Sumitomo Bank of California	San Francisco, CA	1952	Sumitomo Bank	Japan	1,662.2
41.	Tokai Bank of California[18]	Los Angeles, CA	1963	Tokai Bank	Japan	158.9
42.	Toronto Dominion Bank of California	San Francisco, CA	1971	Toronto Dominion Bank	Canada	126.4
43.	Toronto Dominion Bank Trust Co.	New York, NY	1960	Toronto Dominion Bank	Canada	10.1[19]
44.	U.B.A.F. Arab-American Bank	New York, NY	1976	Union de Banques Arabes et Francaises	Franco-Arab consortium	819.9
45.	UMB Bank & Trust Co.	New York, NY	1978	United Mizrahi Bank	Israel	114.8

Note: Previously established foreign de novo banks that are not currently in existence do not appear on this table. For example, the following de novo banks have subsequently been absorbed by banks acquired by the parent bank.

Parent Bank	De Novo U.S. Bank	Acquired U.S. Bank	Merger Date
The Royal Trust Co.	Royal Trust Bank of S. Dade	Royal Trust Bank of Miami, N.A.	April 1979
Standard-Chartered Group	Chartered Bank of London-SF	Union Bank	January 1980
Banque Nationale de Paris	French Bank of California	Bank of the West	March 1980

Appendix II (continued)

[1] Total Assets (consolidated foreign and domestic) in $ million as of the December 1979 Call Report, except where indicated.

[2] Asian International Bank is owned by a jointly-acting group which includes the Bank of Philippine Islands, Far East Bank & Trust Co., China Banking Corp., Pacific Banking Corp., and Consolidated Bank & Trust Co.

[3] Bank Leumi Trust Co. of New York merged with American Bank & Trust Company (New York) on September 15, 1976.

[4] Bank of Canton of California is currently owned by Vei-Chih Wang and 11 others from Taiwan.

[5] Barclay's Bank of California merged with First Valley Bank (San Jose, California) on January 16, 1970 and County Bank of Santa Barbara (Santa Barbara, California) on October 1, 1974.

[6] Barclay's Bank of New York merged with First Westchester National Bank (New Rochelle, New York) on June 1, 1974.

[7] California Canadian Bank merged with Northern California National Bank of San Mateo (San Mateo, California) on August 22, 1966 and City Bank of San Diego (San Diego, California) on July 7, 1969.

[8] Bank of Tokyo of California merged with Southern California First National Bank (San Diego, California) on October 1, 1975 to form California First Bank.

[9] Chicago-Tokyo Bank is owned by a jointly-acting group comprised of 104 individuals and 52 Japanese corporations, one of which is the Bank of Tokyo, Ltd. which owns 4.9%.

[10] Chinese American Bank was acquired by 11 Taiwanese businessmen on March 3, 1972.

[11] European-American Bank and Trust Co. merged with Franklin National Bank on October 8, 1974.

[12] European American 'Group' is composed of:

Amsterdam-Rotterdam Bank, NV	Netherlands
Creditanstalt-Bankverein	Austria
Deutsche Bank A.G.	W. Germany
Midland Bank, Ltd.	United Kingdom
Société Générale de Banque, S.A.	Belgium
Société Générale	France

[13] Sanwa Bank of California merged with Charter Bank (Culver City, California) on December 29, 1973 and Golden State Bank (Downey, California) on December 27, 1977 to become Golden State Sanwa Bank.

[14] Japan California Bank is owned by a jointly-acting group comprised of 37 corporations, including the Dai-Ichi Kangyo Bank, Ltd. and the Long-Term Credit Bank of Japan.

[15] Pacific Union Bank & Trust Co. was acquired by Purisima Katiqbak Tan (Philippines) in 1979.

[16] Philippine Bank of California is owned by a jointly-acting group which includes the Government Service Insurance System, the Land Bank of the Philippines, the Social Security System, the Philippines National Bank, and the Development Bank of the Philippines.

[17] Republic National Bank of New York merged with Kings Lafayette Bank and Trust Co. (Brooklyn, New York) on June 30, 1974.

[18] Tokai Bank of California merged with Centinela Bank (Inglewood, California) on July 11, 1975.

[19] Total Assets for Toronto Dominion Bank Trust Co. were $4.8 million as of 12-31-79, as reported in *Polk's World Bank Directory*.

Appendix III

Existing Foreign-Owned *De Novo* U.S. Banks (December 31, 1980), by Year of Establishment, Asset Size, and Type of Parent

Year Established	U.S. Bank Name	Total Assets 12-31-79 ($ million)[1]	Establisher Category[2]	Name of Establisher
1922	Israel Discount Trust Co.	49.0	B/BHC	Israel Discount Bank
1923	Bank of Montreal Trust Co.	38.9	B/BHC	Bank of Montreal
1926	Atlantic Bank of New York	385.6	B/BHC	National Bank of Greece
1929	J. Henry Schroder Bank and Trust Co.	1,545.4	B/BHC	Schroder Group
1937	Bank of Canton of California	318.8	I/SC	Cheng Wai Wang family
1951	Canadian Bank of Commerce Trust Co.	24.4	B/BHC	Canadian Imperial Bank of Commerce
1952	Sumitomo Bank of California	1,662.2	B/BHC	Sumitomo Bank
1953	European-American Bank & Trust Company[3]	4,675.5	B/BHC	European-American Group[4]
1953	California First Bank[3] (formerly: The Bank of Tokyo of California)	3,267.5	B/BHC	Bank of Tokyo
	Total for 1953:	7,943.0		
1954	Central Pacific Bank	410.7	B/BHC	Sumitomo Bank, Ltd.
1954	Royal Bank & Trust Co.	255.0	B/BHC	Royal Bank of Canada
	Total for 1954:	665.7		
1955	Bank of Tokyo Trust Co.	3,366.9	B/BHC	Bank of Tokyo
1959	Bank of Nova Scotia Trust Co.	7.0	B/BHC	Scotiabank
1960	Toronto Dominion Bank Trust Co.	10.1[5]	B/BHC	Toronto Dominion Bank
1963	Tokai Bank of California[3]	158.9	B/BHC	Tokai Bank
1964	California Canadian Bank[3]	618.3	I/SC	Canadian Imperial Bank of Commerce
1964	Chicago-Tokyo Bank	293.4	I/SC	Jointly-Acting Group[6]
1964	Bank of Montreal-California	88.2	B/BHC	Bank of Montreal
	Total for 1964:	999.9		
1965	Barclays Bank of California[3]	698.1	B/BHC	Barclays Group
1966	Republic National Bank of New York[3]	4,415.3	I/SC	Edmond J. Safra/Trade Development Bank
1967	Chinese American Bank	79.3	B/BHC	Bank of China[7]
1968	Bank Leumi Trust Co.[3]	1,625.1	B/BHC	Bank Leumi Le-Israel
1971	Barclays Bank of New York[3]	600.5	B/BHC	Barclays Group
1971	Toronto Dominion Bank of California	126.4	B/BHC	Toronto Dominion Bank
1971	Bank of the Orient	125.1	I/SC	Ernesto Lee Go
	Total for 1971:	852.0		

Appendix III (continued)

Year Established	U.S. Bank Name	Total Assets 12-31-79 ($ million)[1]	Establisher Category[2]	Name of Establisher
1972	Golden State Sanwa Bank[3] (formerly: The Sanwa Bank of California)	675.2	B/BHC	Sanwa Bank
	The Mitsubishi Bank of California[3]	286.7	B/BHC	Mitsubishi Bank
	First Pacific Bank of Chicago	158.5	B/BHC	Dai-Ichi Kangyo Bank
	Total for 1972:	1,120.4		
1973	Banco di Roma	177.6	B/BHC	Banco di Roma
1974	Fuji Bank & Trust Co.	895.6	B/BHC	Fuji Bank
	Industrial Bank of Japan Trust Co.	818.3	B/BHC	Industrial Bank of Japan
	Mitsui Bank of California	264.4	B/BHC	Mitsui Bank
	Japan California Bank	108.5	I/SC	Jointly-Acting Group[6]
	California Korea Bank	88.1	B/BHC	Korea Exchange Bank
	American Asian Bank	45.0	I/SC	C. Y. Tung
	Total for 1974:	2,219.9		
1975	Pacific Union Bank & Trust Co.	15.9	I/SC	Payson Cha & Family[8]
1976	U.B.A.F. Arab-American Bank	819.9	B/BHC	Union de Banques Arabes et Francaises
1977	Daiwa Bank Trust Co.	408.3	B/BHC	Daiwa Bank
	Banco de Bogota Trust Co.	95.2	B/BHC	Banco de Bogota
	Philippine Bank of California	36.5	I/SC	Jointly-Acting Group[6]
	Mountain Trust Co.	7.1	I/SC	M. Gamerhoff & L. Schwartz
	Total for 1977:	547.1		
1978	UMB Bank & Trust Co.	114.8	B/BHC	United Mizrahi Bank
	Kyowa Bank of California	39.7	B/BHC	Kyowa Bank
	Total for 1978:	154.5		
1979	Global Union Bank	15.6	I/SC	Asian Investors
1980	Asian International Bank	N/A	I/SC	Jointly-Acting Group[6]
Total All Years	N = 45	29,916.5		

Note: Previously established foreign *de novo* banks that are not currently in existence do not appear on this table. For example, the following *de novo* banks have subsequently been absorbed by banks acquired by the parent bank.

Parent Bank	De Novo U.S. Bank	Acquired U.S. Bank	Merger Date
The Royal Trust Co.	Royal Trust Bank of S. Dade	Royal Trust Bank of Miami, N.A.	April 1979
Standard-Chartered Group	Chartered Bank of London, SF	Union Bank	January 1980
Banque Nationale de Paris	French Bank of California	Bank of the West	March 1980

[1] Total assets (consolidated foreign and domestic) in $ million as of the December 1979 Call Report, except where indicated.

[2] B/BHC = Bank or holding company (bank or non-bank); I/SC = Individual(s) or shell companies.

[3] Foreign de novo bank subsequently acquired another U.S. bank.

[4] European-American Group is composed of: Amsterdam-Rotterdam Bank, NV; Creditanstalt-Bankverein; Deutsche Bank A.G.; Midland Bank, Ltd; Société Générale de Banque S.A.; and Société Générale (France).

[5] Toronto Dominion Bank Trust Co. is a non-insured commercial bank. Total assets for the bank were $10.1 million as of December 1979, as reported in Polk's World Bank Directory.

[6] Bank is controlled by a jointly-acting group that includes a bank and non-bank companies. Participants are exempt from registering as bank holding companies.

[7] Chinese American Bank was acquired by 11 Taiwanese businessmen in March 1972.

[8] Pacific Union Bank & Trust Co. was acquired by Purisima Katiqbak Tan (Philippines) in 1979.

65

Existing Foreign-Owned *De Novo* U.S. Banks (December 31, 1980), by Year of

Year Established	Nationality of Establisher								
	U.K.			Europe			Japan		
	Location	No.	Assets[1]	Location	No.	Assets	Location	No.	Assets
1922		–			–			–	
1923		–			–			–	
1926		–		NY	(1)	385.6		–	
1929	NY	(1)	1,545.4		–			–	
1937		–			–			–	
1951		–			–			–	
1952		–			–		CA	(1)	1,662.2
1953		–		NY	(1)	4,675.5[2]	CA	(1)	3,267.5
1954		–			–		HI	(1)	410.7
1955		–			–		NY	(1)	3,366.9
1959		–			–			–	
1960		–			–			–	
1963		–			–		CA	(1)	158.9
1964		–			–		IL	(1)	293.4
1965	CA	(1)	698.1		–			–	
1966		–			–			–	
1967		–			–			–	
1968		–			–			–	
1971	NY	(1)	600.5		–			–	
1972		–			–		CA	(2)	961.9
							IL	(1)	158.5
							Total	(3)	1,120.4
1973		–		IL	(1)	177.6		–	
1974		–			–		CA	(2)	372.9
							NY	(2)	1,713.9
							Total	(4)	2,086.8
1975		–			–			–	
1976		–		NY	(1)	819.9[4]		–	
1977		–			–		NY	(1)	408.3
1978		–			–		CA	(1)	39.7
1979		–			–			–	
1980		–			–			–	
Total All Years	CA	(1)	698.1	IL	(1)	177.6	CA	(8)	6,463.1
	NY	(2)	2,145.9	NY	(3)	5,881.0	HI	(1)	410.7
							IL	(2)	451.9
							NY	(4)	5,489.1
		(3)	2,844.0		(4)	6,058.6		(15)	12,814.8

Note: Previously established foreign *de novo* banks that are not currently in existence do not appear on this table.

[1] Total Assets (consolidated foreign and domestic) in $ million as of the December 1979 Call Report, except where indicated.

[2] Bank was established by a consortium composed of a British bank and five European banks.

Establishment, Asset Size, Nationality of Establisher, and Location

Other Asia			Canada			Latin America			Middle East		
Location	No.	Assets	Location	No.	Assets	Location	No.	Assets	Location	No.	Assets
–	–		–			–			NY	(1)	49.0
–			NY	(1)	38.9	–			–		
–			–			–			–		
–			–			–			–		
CA	(1)	318.8	–			–			–		
–			NY	(1)	24.4	–			–		
–			–			–			–		
–			–			–			–		
–			NY	(1)	255.0	–			–		
–			–			–			–		
–			NY	(1)	7.0	–			–		
–			NY	(1)	10.1³	–			–		
–			–			–			–		
–			CA	(2)	706.5	–			–		
–			–			–			–		
–			–			NY	(1)	4,415.3	–		
NY	(1)	79.3	–			–					
–			–			–			NY	(1)	1,625.1
CA	(1)	125.1	CA	(1)	126.4	–			–		
–			–			–			–		
–			–			–			–		
CA	(2)	133.1	–			–			–		
CA	(1)	15.9	–			–			–		
–			–			–			–		
CA	(1)	36.5	VT	(1)	7.1	NY	(1)	95.2	–		
–			–			–			NY	(1)	114.8
NY	(1)	15.6	–			–			–		
NY	(1)	N/A	–			–			–		
CA	(6)	629.4	CA	(3)	832.9						
NY	(3)	94.9	NY	(5)	335.4						
			VT	(1)	7.1						
	(9)	724.3		(9)	1,175.4		(2)	4,510.5		(3)	1,788.9

³ Total assets for the bank were $10.1 million as of December 1979, as reported in *Polk's World Bank Directory*.

⁴ Bank was established by a consortium composed of French and Middle Eastern banks.

Appendix V

Known and Pending Foreign Acquisitions of U.S. Banking Organizations (December 31, 1980), by Year of Acquisition, Asset Size, and Type of Acquirer

Year Acquired	Bank Name at Time of Acquisition	Total Assets ($ millions)[1]	Acquirer Category[2]	Acquirer	Control Relinquished
1963	American Bank & Trust Co.[3]	41.5	B/BHC	Swiss-Israel Trade Bank	1976
1966	Northern California National Bank of San Mateo	8.4	B/BHC	California Canadian Bank	
1968	Laidlaw & Co.	76.3[4]	B/BHC	Hambros Bank, Ltd.	1976
1969	City Bank of San Diego	21.5[4]	B/BHC	California Canadian Bank	
	Fidelity National Bank of South Miami[3]	15.0	I/SC	Roberto Alejos & Carlos Hegel	1973
	Total for 1969:	36.5			
1970	First Valley Bank	50.2[4]	B/BHC	Barclays Bank of California	
	Republic National Bank & Trust Co.	24.5[4]	B/BHC	Hongkong & Shanghai Banking Corp. of California	1979
	Republic National Bank of Miami	22.3	I/SC	Rebank Corp.	
	Total for 1970:	97.0			
1972	Franklin National Bank[3]	3,537.5	I/SC	Michele Sindona	1974
	Inter National Bank of Miami	51.1	B/BHC	The Royal Trust Co.	1980
	Bank of Contra Costa	9.0	I/SC	Adnan Khashoggi	1980
	Total for 1972:	3,597.6			
1973	The Bank of California, NA	2,655.9	I/SC	Baron Edmond de Rothschild	
	National American Bank of New Orleans	294.0	I/SC	Arturo Ferruzzi → Artfer, Inc. & Inter Financing Exchange	
	Security National Bank	97.3	I/SC	Adnan Khashoggi	Pending
	Underwriters Bank & Trust Co.[3]	53.2	I/SC	Spanish & Latin American Investors	1980
	Bank of Miami Beach	40.5	I/SC	Castell Family	
	Charter Bank	32.3	B/BHC	The Sanwa Bank of California	
	Total for 1973:	3,173.2			
1974	Franklin National Bank[3]	1,579.0[5]	B/BHC	European-American Bank & Trust Co.	
	First Western Bank & Trust	1,333.6	B/BHC	Lloyds Group	
	Great Western Bank & Trust Co.[3]	284.4	I/SC	Westphalian American Assoc. [Von Galen]	Pending

Year	Bank	Type	Amount	Acquirer	Date
	Kings Lafayette Bank & Trust Co.	I/SC	226.5	Edmond Safra → Republic National Bank of New York	
	First Westchester National Bank	B/BHC	214.2	Barclays Bank of New York	
	Liberty National Bank	B/BHC	101.4	The Chartered Bank of London, SF	
	County Bank of Santa Barbara	B/BHC	43.1	Barclays Bank of California	
	Peninsula National Bank	I/SC	25.6	Amos W. Dawe	1975 & 1977[6]
	Alamosa National Bank[3]	I/SC	18.1	Triad Holding Corp. [Khashoggi]	1979
	Total for 1974:		3,825.9		
1975	Bank of the Commonwealth	I/SC	1,034.4	Ghaith Pharaon → First Arabian Corp.	
	Southern California First National Bank, San Diego	B/BHC	889.2	The Bank of Tokyo of California	
	Banco Mercantile de Puerto Rico	B/BHC	99.2	The Bank of Nova Scotia	1977
	Century National Bank & Trust Co.[3]	I/SC	48.3	John Graiver	1976
	First National Bank of Fresno	I/SC	38.1	Amos W. Dawe	
	Centinela Bank	B/BHC	31.2	Tokai Bank of California	
	Camino-California Bank	I/SC	21.5	Y. T. Chou	
	Flagler Bank	I/SC	19.0	Castell Family	
	Tahoe National Bank	I/SC	12.5	Amos W. Dawe	1976
	Totalbank[3]	I/SC	11.4	Francisco E. Blanco	
	Total for 1975:		2,204.8		
1976	American Security Bank	I/SC	235.1	John M. K. Lee	
	American Bank & Trust Co.[3]	B/BHC	177.4[5]	Bank Leumi Trust Co. of New York	
	Hacienda Bank	B/BHC	55.6	The Mitsubishi Bank of California	
	First State Bank of Northern California	B/BHC	52.3[5]	Lloyds Bank California	
	Chelsea National Bank	B/BHC	31.2	Banco Union, SA	
	Worth Avenue National Bank	B/BHC	27.7	The Royal Trust Co.	
	Security National Bank of New Jersey	I/SC	26.3	Fiduciary Investment Co. of New Jersey	
	Ahmanson Bank	I/SC	25.9	Philippine Investors	
	First Bank of Gulfport	B/BHC	24.3	The Royal Trust Co.	
	First National Bank of Puerto Rico	B/BHC	22.9	Banco de Santander, SA	
	Dale Mabry State Bank	B/BHC	7.3	The Royal Trust Co.	
	Total for 1976:		686.0		

Appendix V (continued)

Year Acquired	Bank Name at Time of Acquisition	Total Assets ($ millions)[1]	Acquirer Category[2]	Acquirer	Control Relinquished
1977	Banco Economias	179.4	B/BHC	Banco Central de Madrid	
	Golden State Bank	144.7	B/BHC	The Sanwa Bank of California	
	First National Bank of Hialeah	138.9	I/SC	José Álvarez Stelling → MFG Investments, Inc.	
	Main Bank of Houston	93.3	I/SC	Ghaith Pharaon & Sheik Khaled Bin Mahfouz	
	Commercial and Farmers Bank of Oxnard	79.6	B/BHC	The Chartered Bank of London, SF	
	Banco Commercial de Mayaguez	74.3	I/SC	Gregorio Diego	
	Century National Bank & Trust Co.[3]	43.0	B/BHC	Banco Exterior de Espana	
	Central National Bank of Miami[3]	38.1	I/SC	Eduardo Espina Fernandez & Humberto Vagalara Rojas	
	Flagship National Bank of Dadeland	37.9	I/SC	Spanish & Latin American Investors	
	Pan American Bank of Coral Gables, NA	27.9	I/SC	J. J. G. Gorrondona, Jr.	
	National Bank of South Florida	26.5	I/SC	Juan Evelio Pou & Gustavo Villoldo	1978
	First Bank of Pembroke Pines	19.8	B/BHC	The Royal Trust Co.	
	Baymeadows Bank	9.6	B/BHC	The Royal Trust Co.	
	International Bank of California	6.9	B/BHC	Metropolitan Bank & Trust Co.	
	Total for 1977:	919.9			
1978	Financial General Bankshares, Inc.[7]	1,728.4	I/SC	Middle Eastern Investors	
	Banco Credito y Ahorro Ponceno	701.7	B/BHC	Banco de Santander, P. R.	
	National Bank of Georgia	388.9	I/SC	Ghaith Pharaon	
	Western Bank	152.6	I/SC	O. R. Lababedi	
	Coolidge Bank & Trust Co	140.0	I/SC	Bellevue Holding Co. & Colonial General, Inc. [Ismael Dudhia]	
	Dania Bank	126.3	I/SC	J. J. Gonzalez Gorrondona, Jr.	
	Community Bank of San Jose	72.5	B/BHC	Banco Nacional de Mexico	
	Peoples Bank	33.6	I/SC	Ali Fayed	
	Pan American National Bank of E. Los Angeles	30.4	I/SC	Oen Yin Choy	
	Flagship Bank of Adventura	13.3	I/SC	Edmond Safra → Safra Corp.	
	Biscayne Bank	13.1	I/SC	M. R. P. Espirito Santo Silva	
	Bank of Cutler Ridge	13.0	I/SC	Jose Luis Calonge	

Year	Bank	Type	Acquiring Party	
	Sunshine State Bank	I/SC	Alma Robles Chiari & Jose Andonie Fernandez	
	Banco de Ahorro de Puerto Rico	I/SC	Banco Commercial de Mayaguez [G. Diego]	1979
	Northwide Bank of Miami	I/SC	Andres F. Rodriguez	
	American Bank of Orange County	B/BHC	The Royal Trust Co.	
	Peoples National Bank of Littleton	I/SC	J. McKinlay & Don Cutts	
	Total for 1978: 3,460.7			
1979	Union Bank	B/BHC	Standard & Chartered Banking Group	
	National Bank of North America	B/BHC	National Westminster Bank, Ltd.	
	Bank of Virginia	B/BHC	Banca March, SA	
	LaSalle National Bank	B/BHC	Algemene Bank Nederland	1980
	Continental National Bank of Miami	I/SC	Armando de Armas Melendez	
	Surety National Bank	I/SC	California Overseas Bank	
	Du Quoin State Bank	I/SC	Saleh S. Jabr	
	Meadowlands National Bank	I/SC	Jacobo Finkielstain & Others	
	Fidelity National Bank of South Miami[3]	I/SC	Spanish Investors	
	Alamosa National Bank[3]	I/SC	Robert Elliot	
	Hemisphere National Bank	I/SC	Nestor Julio Garcia	
	Metropolitan National Bank	I/SC	Atef Daniel	
	Guaranty Bank of Stapleton	I/SC	Robert Elliot	
	First City National Bank of Jacksonville	I/SC	Canadian & Dutch Investors	
	American Bank of Commerce	I/SC		
	Total for 1979: 12,638.0			
1980	Marine Midland Bank, NA	B/BHC	The Hongkong & Shanghai Banking Corp.	
	U.S. Trust Co.	B/BHC	Banco de Chile & Schroder, Munchmayer, Hengst & Co.	
	Bank of the West	B/BHC	French Bank of California/Banque Nationale de Paris	
	Banco de San Juan	B/BHC	Royal Bank of Canada	
	Bank of Suffolk County	B/BHC	Century NB & TC/Banco Exterior de Espana	
	United Americas Bank[3]	B/BHC	Banco Central de Madrid	
	Hartford Plaza Bank	B/BHC	LaSalle NB/Algemene Bank Nederland	

Amounts column:
- Sunshine State Bank — 11.9
- Banco de Ahorro de Puerto Rico — 11.7[5]
- Northwide Bank of Miami — 11.4
- American Bank of Orange County — 7.6
- Peoples National Bank of Littleton — 4.3
- Union Bank — 5,183.1
- National Bank of North America — 4,326.0
- Bank of Virginia — 1,898.1
- LaSalle National Bank — 925.7
- Continental National Bank of Miami — 54.4
- Surety National Bank — 46.6
- Du Quoin State Bank — 40.4
- Meadowlands National Bank — 33.2
- Fidelity National Bank of South Miami[3] — 33.0
- Alamosa National Bank[3] — 28.3
- Hemisphere National Bank — 21.0
- Metropolitan National Bank — 20.8
- Guaranty Bank of Stapleton — 11.2
- First City National Bank of Jacksonville — 8.2
- American Bank of Commerce — 8.2
- Marine Midland Bank, NA — 15,690.9
- U.S. Trust Co. — 1,976.6
- Bank of the West — 589.3
- Banco de San Juan — 296.8
- Bank of Suffolk County — 90.6
- United Americas Bank[3] — 43.2
- Hartford Plaza Bank — 38.1

Appendix V (continued)

Year Acquired	Bank Name at Time of Acquisition	Total Assets ($ millions)[1]	Acquirer Category[2]	Acquirer	Control Relinquished
	Independence Bank	145.5	I/SC	Halifax Financial Holdings, Inc. [Huang Tiong Chan]	
	Redwood Bank	135.5	I/SC	Empire Holdings, Inc. [Ramon L. Siy, et. al.]	
	Totalbank	89.3	I/SC	Herrero Group	
	Central National Bank of Miami[3]	58.2	I/SC	Sabrina Properties/Eagle National Holding Co. [Vagalara & Michaelson]	
	Deerfield Beach State Bank	37.2	I/SC	MFG Investments, Inc. [Alvarez Stelling]	
	Total for 1980:	19,191.2			
Pending	Crocker National Bank	16,087.5	B/BHC	Midland Bank, Ltd.	
	Manufacturers Bank	705.7	B/BHC	Mitsui Bank of California	
	First National Bank of San Diego County	155.8	B/BHC	Mitsubishi Bank of California	
	First City Bank	145.7	B/BHC	Golden State Sanwa Bank	
	Westlands Bank	121.2	B/BHC	Canadian Commercial & Industrial Bank of Edmonton	
	Miami National Bank	54.9	B/BHC	Banco Zarogozano	
	Great Western Bank & Trust Co.[3]	479.7	I/SC	GWB Holding BV	
	Central State Bank	71.5	I/SC	South American Investors	
	Bank of Perrine	38.2	I/SC	Felix Corea Maya & Fabia Hurtado Saldarriago	
	Total Pending:	17,860.2			

[1] Total assets (consolidated foreign and domestic) in $ million as of the closest available Call Report prior to the acquisition, except where indicated.
[2] B/BHC = bank or holding company (bank or non-bank); I/SC = individual(s) or shell companies.
[3] Bank appears twice due to successive acquisitions (pending or consummated) by unrelated foreign investor(s).
[4] Total asset figures for the bank were taken from *Polk's World Bank Directory*.
[5] Total assets purchased by the acquiring bank.
[6] Peninsula National Bank was acquired by Amos Dawe in 1975. As a result of Dawe's default on the purchase, Pacific Atlantic Bank of Panama (as guarantor of Dawe's loan) succeeded to Dawe's interest in the bank. Pacific Atlantic Bank sold its interest in Peninsula to Central Bank of Oakland in 1977

[7] A Middle Eastern investing group acquired 18.6% of Financial General Bankshares, Inc. in January 1978. The multibank holding company includes the following member banks: Bank of Commerce; Community State Bank; Eastern Shore National Bank; First American Bank, NA; First American Bank of Maryland; First American Bank of Virginia; First National Bank of Lexington; Peoples National Bank of Leesburg; Round Hill National Bank; Shenandoah National Bank; Valley Fidelity Bank and Trust Co.; and Valley National Bank.

Known and Pending Foreign Acquisitions of U.S. Banking Organizations

Year Acquired	U.K.			Europe			Japan		
	Location	No.	Assets[1]	Location	No.	Assets	Location	No.	Assets
1963		–		NY	(1)	41.5[2]		–	
1966		–			–			–	
1968	NY	(1)	76.3		–			–	
1969		–			–			–	
1970	CA	(1)	50.2		–			–	
1972		–		NY	(1)	3,537.5[2]		–	
1973		–		CA	(1)	2,655.9	CA	(1)	32.3
				FL	(1)	40.5			
				LA	(1)	294.0			
				Total	(3)	2,990.4			
1974	CA	(3)	1,478.1	AZ	(1)	284.4		–	
	NY	(1)	214.2	NY	(1)	1,579.02[2,3]			
	Total	(4)	1,692.3	Total	(2)	1,863.4			
1975		–		FL	(2)	30.4	CA	(2)	920.4
1976	CA	(1)	52.3	PR	(1)	22.9	CA	(1)	55.6
				NJ	(1)	26.3[4]			
				Total	(2)	49.2			
1977	CA	(1)	79.6	NY	(1)	43.0[2]	CA	(1)	144.7
				PR	(2)	253.7			
				Total	(3)	296.7			
1978	MA	(1)	140.0	FL	(2)	26.1		–	
				PR	(2)	713.4			
				Total	(4)	739.5			
1979	CA	(1)	5,183.1	FL	(1)	33.0[2]		–	
	NY	(1)	4,326.0	IL	(1)	925.7			
				VA	(1)	1,898.1			
	Total	(2)	9,509.1	Total	(3)	2,856.8			
1980		–		CA	(1)	589.3		–	
				FL	(1)	89.3[2]			
				IL	(1)	38.1			
				NY	(2)	133.8[2]			
				Total	(5)	850.5			
Pending	CA	(1)	16,087.5	FL	(1)	54.9	CA	(3)	1,007.2

[1] Total assets (consolidated foreign and domestic) in $ million. Data sources, as in Appendix I, are predominantly from the closest available Call Report prior to acquisition. Where necessary, asset figures were taken from *Polk's World Bank Directory* and FDIC purchase releases.

[2] Asset figures for one bank appear twice due to successive acquisition (pending or consummated) by unrelated foreign investors.

(December 31, 1980), by Year of Acquisition, Asset Size, Nationality of Acquirer, and Location

Other Asia			Canada			Latin America			Middle East		
Location	No.	Assets	Location	No.	Assets	Location	No.	Assets	Location	No.	Assets
	–		CA	(1)	8.4		–			–	
	–			–			–			–	
	–		CA	(1)	21.5	FL	(1)	15.0[2]		–	
CA	(1)	24.5		–		FL	(1)	22.3		–	
	–		FL	(1)	51.1		–		CA	(1)	9.0
	–			–		NY	(1)	53.2[2]	CA	(1)	97.3
CA	(1)	25.6		–		NY	(1)	226.5	CO	(1)	18.1[2]
CA	(3)	72.1	PR	(1)	99.2	NY	(1)	48.3[2]	MI	(1)	1,034.4
CA	(1)	25.9	FL	(3)	59.3	NY	(1)	31.2	NY	(1)	177.4[2]
HI	(1)	235.1									
Total	(2)	261.0									
CA	(1)	6.9	FL	(2)	29.4	FL	(5)	269.3[2,5]	TX	(1)	93.3
CA	(1)	30.4	NH	(1)	4.3	CA	(1)	72.5	DC	(1)	1,728.4
			FL	(1)	7.6	FL	(4)	162.9	GA	(1)	388.9
									TX	(2)	186.2
			Total	(2)	11.9	Total	(5)	235.4	Total	(4)	2,303.5
CA	(1)	46.6	AZ	(1)	8.0[2]	DC	(1)	21.0	IL	(1)	40.4
CA	(1)	46.6	CO	(2)	39.5[2,6]	FL	(1)	54.4	TX	(1)	20.8
			FL	(1)	8.2	NJ	(1)	33.2			
			Total	(4)	55.7	Total	(3)	108.6	Total	(2)	61.2
CA	(2)	281.0	PR	(1)	296.8	FL	(2)	95.4[2]			
NY	(1)	15,690.9				NY	(1)	1,976.6[7]		–	
Total	(3)	15,971.9				Total	(3)	2,072.0			
	–		CA	(1)	121.2	FL	(1)	38.2	AZ	(1)	479.7[2]
						NY	(1)	71.5			
						Total	(2)	109.7			

[3] Bank was acquired by a banking group composed of one British bank and five European banks.

[4] Bank was acquired by Swiss and Canadian investors.

[5] One bank was acquired by Spanish and Latin American investors.

[6] One bank was acquired by Canadian and Dutch investors.

[7] One bank was acquired by a Chilean bank and a West German bank.

Appendix VII

Existing Foreign-Owned U.S. Banking Organizations (December 31, 1980), by Location, Method of Entry, and Owner Category

Location	Foreign Acquisitions				Foreign De Novo Institutions			
	B/BHC Acquisitions[1]		I/SC Acquisitions[2]		De Novo Institutions		De Novo Institutions with Subsequent Acquisitions	
	No.	Total Assets 12-31-79 ($ million)[3]	No.	Total Assets 12-31-79 ($ million)	No.	Total Assets 12-31-79 ($ million)	No.	Total Assets 12-31-79 ($ million)
Arizona	–	–	2	490.0	–	–	–	–
California	5	9,900.4[4]	7	4,167.5	12	2,918.8	6	5,704.7
Colorado	–	–	2	42.2	–	–	–	–
District of Columbia	–	–	2[5]	2,598.1	–	–	–	–
Florida	7	341.2	15	1,457.1	–	–	–	–
Georgia	–	–	1	417.9	–	–	–	–
Hawaii	–	–	1	346.1	1	410.7	–	–
Illinois	1	1,092.0[6]	1	46.3	3	629.5	–	–
Louisiana	–	–	1	351.0	–	–	–	–
Massachusetts	–	–	1	139.0	–	–	–	–
Michigan	–	–	1	1,084.4	–	–	–	–
New Hampshire	–	–	1	6.7	–	–	–	–
New Jersey	–	–	2	84.2	–	–	–	–
New York	6	22,843.5[6]	–	–	18	8,929.3[7]	4	11,316.4
Puerto Rico	4	1,600.1	1	128.0	–	–	–	–
Texas	–	–	4	385.7	–	–	–	–
Vermont	–	–	–	–	1	7.1	–	–
Virginia	1	1,986.2	–	–	–	–	–	–
Total	24	37,763.4	42	11,744.2	35	12,895.4	10	17,021.1

Note: Foreign-owned banks which have ceased to exist due to divestitute or merger do not appear on this table.

[1] B/BHC = bank or holding company (bank or non-bank).

[2] I/SC = individual(s) or shell companies.

[3] Total assets (consolidated foreign and domestic) in $ million as of the December 1979 Call Report, except where indicated.

[4] California acquisition figures include three instances in which a foreign *de novo* U.S. bank was absorbed in 1980 by another U.S. bank acquired by the foreign parent. On this table, the merged banks are counted as one banking organization with assets equal to the combined year-end assets of the merger partners.

[5] The 12 member banks of Financial General Bankshares, Inc. are counted as one banking organization located in Washington, D.C.

[6] State acquisition figures include one instance in which a foreign-acquired U.S. bank acquired another U.S. bank in 1980. On this table, the merged banks are counted as one banking organization with assets equal to the combined year-end assets of the merger partners.

[7] Figure includes the December 1979 total assets reported to *Polk's World Bank Directory* by one foreign *de novo* bank.

Appendix VIII

Existing and Pending Foreign-Owned U.S. Banking Organizations (December 31, 1980), by Location and Nationality of Owner

Location	Regional Origin of Owner	Nationality of Owner	Foreign De Novo U.S. Banks No.	T. Assets 12-31-79[1] ($ millions)	Foreign-Acquired U.S. Banks No.	T. Assets 12-31-79 ($ millions)	Total Foreign-Owned U.S. Banks No.	T. Assets 12-31-79 ($ millions)	Pending Foreign Acquisitions of U.S. Banks No.	T. Assets 12-31-79 ($ millions)
Arizona	Europe	W. Germany	—	—	1	479.7	1	479.7	—	—
	Canada	Canada	—	—	1	10.3	1	10.3	—	—
	Middle East	Kuwait	—	—	—	—	—	—	1	479.7[2]
			—	—	2	490.0	2	490.0	1	479.7
California	U.K.	U.K.	1	698.1	2[3]	9,074.3[3]	3	9,772.4	1	16,087.5
	Europe	France	—	—	2[4]	4,164.9[4]	2	4,164.9	—	—
	Japan	Japan	8	6,463.1	—	—	8	6,463.1	3	1,007.2
	Other Asia	Hong Kong	1	45.0	2	153.2	3	198.2	—	—
		Indonesia	—	—	1	56.1	1	56.1	—	—
		Korea	1	88.1	—	—	1	88.1	—	—
		Philippines	3	177.5	3	293.9	6	471.4	—	—
		Taiwan	1	318.8	—	—	1	318.8	—	—
	Canada	Canada	3	832.9	—	—	3	832.9	1	121.2
	L. America	Mexico	—	—	1	99.2[5]	1	99.2	—	—
	Middle East	S. Arabia	—	—	1	226.3	1	226.3	—	—
			18	8,623.5	12	14,067.9	30	22,691.4	5	17,215.9
Colorado	Canada	Canada	—	—	2	42.2	2	42.2	—	—
District of Columbia	L. America	Argentina	—	—	1	23.4	1	23.4	—	—
	S. America									
	Middle East	S. Arabia, Kuwait, & Abu Dhabi	—	—	1[6]	2,574.7	1	2,574.7	—	—
			—	—	2	2,598.1	2	2,598.1	—	—
Florida	Europe	Portugal	—	—	1	48.6	1	48.6	—	—
		Spain	—	—	4	460.2	4	460.2	1	54.9
	Canada	Canada	—	—	7	341.2	7	341.2	—	—

State	Category	Country	No.	Amount	No.	Amount	No.	Amount	No.	Amount
	L. America	Brazil	–	–	1	95.9	1	95.9	–	–
		Colombia	–	–	1	58.2	1	58.2	1	38.2
		Ecuador	–	–	1	297.0	1	297.0	–	–
		Panama	–	–	1	28.1	1	28.1	–	–
		Venezuela	–	–	4	420.4	4	420.4	–	–
		Spain/L. Amer.	–	–	1	38.3	1	38.3	–	–
		Neth./Canada	–	–	1	10.4	1	10.4	–	–
	Multiple Nationalities		–	–	22	1,798.3	22	1,798.3	2	93.1
Georgia	Middle East	S. Arabia	–	–	1	417.9	1	417.9	–	–
Hawaii	Japan		1	410.7	–	–	1	410.7	–	–
	Other Asia	Indonesia	–	–	1	346.1	1	346.1	–	–
			1	410.7	1	346.1	2	756.8	–	–
Illinois	Europe	Italy	1	177.6	–	–	1	177.6	–	–
		Netherlands	–	–	1	1,092.0[7]	1	1,092.0	–	–
	Japan	Japan	2	451.9	–	–	2	451.9	–	–
	Middle East	Middle East	–	–	1	46.3	1	46.3	–	–
			3	629.5	2	1,138.3	5	1,767.8	–	–
Louisiana	Europe	Italy	–	–	1	351.0	1	351.0	–	–
Massachusetts	U.K.	U.K.	–	–	1	139.0	1	139.0	–	–
Michigan	Middle East	S. Arabia	–	–	1	1,084.4	1	1,1084.4	–	–
New Hampshire	Canada	Canada	–	–	1	6.7	1	6.7	–	–
New Jersey	L. America	Argentina	–	–	1	35.0	1	35.0	–	–
	Multiple Nationalities	Switz./Canada	–	–	1	49.2	1	49.2	–	–
			–	–	2	84.2	2	84.2	–	–
New York	U.K.	U.K.	2	2,145.9	1	4,849.0	3	6,994.9	–	–
	Europe	France	1[8]	819.9	–	–	1	819.9	–	–
		Greece	1	385.6	–	–	1	385.6	–	–
		Spain	–	–	2	250.4[9]	2	250.4	–	–
		Var. Europe	1[10]	4,675.5	–	–	1	4,675.5	–	–
	Japan	Japan	4	5,489.1	–	–	4	5,489.1	–	–

Appendix VIII (continued)

Location	Regional Origin of Owner	Nationality of Owner	Foreign De Novo U.S. Banks		Foreign-Acquired U.S. Banks		Total Foreign-Owned U.S. Banks		Pending Foreign Acquisitions of U.S. Banks	
			No.	T. Assets 12-31-79[1] ($ millions)	No.	T. Assets 12-31-79 ($ millions)	No.	T. Assets 12-31-79 ($ millions)	No.	T. Assets 12-31-79 ($ millions)
	Other Asia	Hong Kong	—	—	1	15,690.9	1	15,690.9	—	—
		Taiwan	1	79.3	—	—	1	79.3	—	—
		Var. Asia	2	15.6	—	—	2	15.6	—	—
	Canada	Canada	5	335.4[11]	—	—	5	335.4	—	—
	L. America	Brazil	1	4,415.3	—	—	1	4,415.3	—	—
		Colombia	1	95.2	—	—	1	95.2	—	—
		Venezuela	—	—	1	76.6	1	76.6	—	—
		Var. S. America	—	—	—	—	—	–	1	71.5
	Middle East	Israel	3	1,788.9	—	—	3	1,788.9	—	—
	Multiple Nationalities	Chile/W. Germany	—	—	1	1,976.6	1	1,976.6	—	—
			22	20,245.7	6	22,843.5	28	43,089.2	1	71.5
Puerto Rico	Europe	Spain	—	—	3	970.0	3	970.0	—	—
	Canada	Canada	—	—	2	758.1	2	758.1	—	—
					5	1,728.1	5	1,728.1		
Texas	Middle East	S. Arabia	—	—	2	121.6	2	121.6	—	—
		Syria	—	—	2	264.1	2	264.1	—	—
					4	385.7	4	385.7		

| Vermont | Canada | | 1 | 7.1 | — | 1 | — | 1 | 7.1 | — | — |
| Virginia | Spain | Europe | — | 1,986.2 | 1 | 1,986.2 | 1 | — | 1,986.2 | — | — |

Note: Foreign-owned banks which have ceased to exist due to divestiture or merger do not appear on this table.

[1] Total Assets (consolidated foreign and domestic) in $ million as of the December 1979 Call Report, except where indicated.

[2] One acquired bank appears twice due to a subsequent pending foreign acquisition.

[3] Standard & Chartered Banking Group (U.K.) acquired Union Bank (Los Angeles) in April 1979. Union Bank then absorbed the British bank's *de novo* subsidiary in California, effective January 1980. On this table, the merged banks are counted as one banking organization with assets equal to the combined year-end assets of the acquired and the *de novo* bank.

[4] Banque Nationale de Paris (France) acquired Bank of the West (San Jose, California) in March 1980. Bank of the West then absorbed the French bank's *de novo* subsidiary in California. On this table, the merged banks are counted as one banking organization with assets equal to the combined year-end assets of the acquired and the *de novo* bank.

[5] Banco Nacional de Mexico (Mexico) acquired Community Bank of San Jose in June 1978. CBSJ then absorbed Mexican American National Bank (foreign *de novo* bank) in June 1980. On this table, the merged banks are counted as one banking organization with assets equal to the combined year-end assets of the acquired and the *de novo* bank.

[6] The 12 member banks of Financial General Bankshares, Inc. are counted as one banking organization located in Washington, D.C.

[7] Algemene Bank Nederland (Netherlands) acquired LaSalle NB in August 1979. LNB then absorbed Hartford Plaza Bank in April 1980. On this table, the merged banks are counted as one banking organization with assets equal to the combined year-end assets of the acquired banks.

[8] UBAF Arab-American Bank (New York) is owned by a French-Middle Eastern banking consortium based in France.

[9] Banco Exterior de Espana (Spain) acquired Century National Bank & Trust Co. in December 1977. CNBTC then absorbed the Bank of Suffolk County in June 1980. On this table, the merged banks are counted as one banking organization with assets equal to the combined year-end assets of the acquired banks.

[10] European-American Bank & Trust Co. is owned by a banking group composed of a British bank and five European banks.

[11] Figure includes the December 1979 total assets reported to *Polk's World Bank Directory* by one foreign *de novo* bank.

Appendix IX

Existing and Pending Foreign-Owned U.S. Banking Organizations (December 31, 1980) by Nationality of Owner

Regional Origin of Owner	Nationality of Owner	Foreign De Novo U.S. Banks		Foreign-Acquired U.S. Banks		Total Foreign-Owned U.S. Banks		Pending Foreign Acquisitions of U.S. Banks	
		No.	T. Assets 12-31-79 ($ millions)	No.	T. Assets 12-31-79 ($ millions)	No.	T. Assets 12-31-79 ($ millions)	No.	T. Assets 12-31-79 ($ millions)
U.K.	U.K.	3	2,844.0	4[2]	14,062.3	7	16,906.3	1	16,087.5
Europe	France	1	819.9[3]	2	4,164.9[4]	3	4,984.8	—	—
	Greece	1	385.6	—	—	1	385.6	—	—
	Italy	1	177.6	1	351.0	2	528.6	—	—
	Netherlands	—	—	1	1,092.0[5]	1	1,092.0	—	—
	Spain	—	—	10	3,666.8[6]	10	3,666.8	1	54.9
	Portugal	—	—	1	48.6	1	48.6	—	—
	W. Germany	—	—	1	479.7[7]	1	479.7	—	—
	Var. Europe	1	4,675.5[8]	—	—	1	4,675.5	—	—
	Total	4	6,058.6	16	9,803.0	20	15,861.6	1	54.9
Japan	Japan	15	12,814.8	—	—	15	12,814.8	3	1,007.2
Other Asia	Hong Kong	1	45.0	3	15,844.1	4	15,889.1	—	—
	Indonesia	—	—	2	402.2	2	402.2	—	—
	Korea	1	88.1	1	—	1	88.1	—	—
	Philippines	4	177.5	3	293.9	7	471.4	—	—
	Taiwan	2	398.1	—	—	2	398.1	—	—
	Var. Asia	1	15.6	—	—	1	15.6	—	—
	Total	9	724.3	8	16,540.2	17	17,264.5	—	—
Canada	Canada	9[9]	1,175.4	13	1,158.5	22	2,333.9	1	121.2
L. America	Argentina	—	—	2	58.4	2	58.4	—	—
	Brazil	1	4,415.3	2	95.9	2	4,511.2	—	—
	Colombia	1	95.2	1	58.2	2	153.4	1	38.2
	Ecuador	—	—	1	297.0	1	297.0	—	—
	Mexico	—	—	1	99.2[10]	1	99.2	—	—
	Panama	—	—	1	28.1	1	28.1	—	—
	Venezuela	—	—	5	497.0	5	497.0	—	—

							1	71.5
							2	109.7
Var. S. America								
Total	2	4,510.5	12	1,133.8	14	5,644.3	2	109.7
Middle East								
Israel	3	1,788.9	—	—	3	1,788.9	—	—
Kuwait	—	—	—	—	—	—	1	479.7[7]
S. Arabia	—	—	5	1,850.2	5	1,850.2	—	—
Syria	—	—	2	264.1	2	264.1	—	—
Var. Middle East	—	—	2[11]	2,621.0	2	2,621.0	—	—
Total	3	1,788.9	9	4,735.3	12	6,524.2	1	479.7
Multiple Nationalities								
Chile/W. Germany	—	—	1	1,976.6	1	1,976.6	—	—
Neth./Canada	—	—	1	10.4	1	10.4	—	—
Spain/L. America	—	—	1	38.3	1	38.3	—	—
Switz./Canada	—	—	1	49.2	1	49.2	—	—
Total	—	—	4	2,074.5	4	2,074.5	—	—
Total All Countries	45	29,916.5	66	49,507.6	111	79,424.1	9	17,860.2

Note: Foreign owned U.S. banks which have ceased to exist due to divestiture or merger do not appear on this table.

[1] Total assets (consolidated foreign and domestic) in $ million as of the December 1979 Call Report, except where indicated.

[2] Standard & Chartered Banking Group (U.K.) acquired Union Bank (Los Angeles) in April 1979, Union Bank then absorbed the British bank's *de novo* subsidiary in California, effective January 1980. On this table, the merged banks are counted as one banking organization with assets equal to the combined year-end assets of the acquired and the *de novo* bank.

[3] UBAF Arab-American Bank (New York) is owned by a French-Middle Eastern banking consortium based in France.

[4] Banque Nationale de Paris (France) acquired Bank of the West (San Jose, California) in March 1980. Bank of the West then absorbed the French bank's *de novo* subsidiary in California. On this table, the merged banks are counted as one banking organization with assets equal to the combined year-end assets of the acquired and the *de novo* bank.

[5] Algemene Bank Nederland (Netherlands) acquired LaSalle National Bank in August 1979. LBN then absorbed Hartford Plaza Bank in April 1980. On this table, the merged banks are counted as one banking organization with assets equal to the combined year-end assets of the acquired banks.

[6] Banco Exterior de Espana (Spain) acquired Century National Bank & Trust Co. in December 1977. CNBTC then absorbed the Bank of Suffolk County in June 1980. On this table, the merged banks are counted as one banking organization with assets equal to the combined year-end assets of the acquired banks.

[7] One acquired bank appears twice due to a subsequent pending foreign acquisition.

[8] European-American Bank & Trust Co. is owned by a banking group composed of a British bank and five European banks.

[9] Figure includes the December 1979 total assets reported to *Polk's World Bank Directory* by one foreign *de novo* bank.

[10] Banco Nacional de Mexico (Mexico) acquired Community Bank of San Jose in June 1978. CBSJ then absorbed Mexican American National Bank (foreign *de novo* bank) in June 1980. On this table, the merged banks are counted as one banking organization with assets equal to the combined year-end assets of the acquired and the *de novo* bank.

[11] The 12 member banks of Financial General Bankshares, Inc. are counted as one banking organization located in Washington, D.C.

Appendix X
Existing Foreign-Owned U.S. Banks (December 31, 1980), by Deposit Ranking in the 5,000 Largest U.S. Banks[1]

12/31/79 Deposit Rank[2]	U.S. Bank Name	Location	Nationality of Owner	Method of Entry[3]
13	Marine Midland Bank, NA	NY	Hong Kong	Acq
26	Union Bank	CA	U.K.	Acq #
34	European-American Bank & Trust Co.	NY	Europe	De Novo +
36	National Bank of North America	NY	U.K.	Acq
41	Republic NB of New York	NY	Brazil	De Novo +
47	California First Bank	CA	Japan	De Novo +
48	Bank of Tokyo Trust Co.	NY	Japan	De Novo
53	The Bank of California, NA	CA	France	Acq
61	Lloyds Bank California	CA	U.K.	Acq +
85	Bank of Virginia	VA	Spain	Acq
90	Sumitomo Bank of California	CA	Japan	De Novo
94	Bank Leumi Trust Co. of New York	NY	Israel	De Novo +
95	U.S. Trust Co.	NY	Chile & W. Germany	Acq
116	J. Henry Schroder Bank & Trust Co.	NY	U.K.	De Novo
163	Bank of the Commonwealth	MI	Saudi Arabia	Acq
170	Fuji Bank & Trust Co.	NY	Japan	De Novo
172	LaSalle National Bank	IL	Netherlands	Acq +
179	First American Bank, NA[4]	DC	S. Arabia/Kuwait	Acq
181	Industrial Bank of Japan Trust Co.	NY	Japan	De Novo
187	First American Bank of Virginia[4]	VA	Middle East	Acq
195	Chartered Bank of London, SF (subsequently merged with Union Bank)	CA	U.K.	De Novo +
207	UBAF Arab-American Bank	NY	France/Middle East	De Novo
217	Golden State Sanwa Bank	CA	Japan	De Novo +
223	Barclays Bank of California	CA	U.K.	De Novo +
260	Bank of the West (subsequently merged with French Bank of California)	CA	France	Acq #
263	California Canadian Bank	CA	Canada	De Novo +
266	Barclays Bank of New York	NY	U.K.	De Novo +
319	Scotiabank de Puerto Rico	PR	Canada	Acq
320	Great Western Bank & Trust Co.	AZ	W. Germany	Acq

366	Central Pacific Bank	HI	Japan	De Novo
370	Banco De Santander, Puerto Rico	PR	Spain	Acq +
379	Atlantic Bank of New York	NY	Greece	De Novo
386	National Bank of Georgia	GA	Saudi Arabia	Acq
397	Daiwa Bank Trust Co.	NY	Japan	De Novo
403	Banco Central y Economias	PR	Spain	Acq
427	American Security Bank	HI	Indonesia	Acq
436	National American Bank of New Orleans	LA	Italy	Acq
462	Bank of Canton	CA	Taiwan	De Novo
476	Bank of Commerce[4]	NY	Middle East	Acq
479	Intercontinental Bank	FL	Spain	Acq
481	First American Bank of Maryland[4]	MD	Middle East	Acq
493	Banco de San Juan	PR	Canada	Acq
498	Mitsui Bank of California	CA	Japan	De Novo
510	Republic NB of Miami	FL	Ecuador	Acq
534	Mitsubishi Bank of California	CA	Japan	De Novo +
545	Chicago Tokyo Bank	IL	Japan	De Novo
634	FNB of Greater Miami	FL	Venezuela	Acq
657	Security National Bank	CA	Saudi Arabia	Acq
673	Royal Bank & Trust Co.	NY	Canada	De Novo
695	Western Bank	TX	Syria	Acq
810	Valley Fidelity Bank & Trust Co.[4]	TN	Middle East	Acq
864	Banco de Roma	IL	Italy	De Novo
866	Royal Trust Bank of Miami, NA	FL	Canada	Acq #
930	Tokai Bank of California	CA	Japan	De Novo +
934	Independence Bank	CA	Hong Kong	Acq
940	California Overseas Bank	CA	Philippines	Acq +
975	First Pacific Bank of Chicago	IL	Japan	De Novo
985	Coolidge Bank & Trust Co.	MA	U.K.	Acq
1010	Redwood Bank	CA	Philippines	Acq
1099	Bank of the Orient	CA	Philippines	De Novo
1152	Banco Commercial De Mayaguez	PR	Spain	Acq +
1196	French Bank of California (subsequently merged with Bank of the West)			
1202	Dania Bank	CA	France	De Novo
1226	Toronto Dominion Bank of California	FL	Venezuela	Acq
1363	UMB Bank & Trust Co.	CA	Canada	De Novo
1395	Century NB & Trust Co.	NY	Israel	De Novo
		NY	Spain	Acq +

Appendix X (continued)

12/31/79 Deposit Rank[2]	U.S. Bank Name	Location	Nationality of Owner	Method of Entry[3]
1525	Japan California Bank	CA	Japan	De Novo
1647	Safra Bank	FL	Brazil	Acq
1672	Totalbank	FL	Spain	Acq
1916	Chinese American Bank	NY	Taiwan	De Novo
1958	California Korea Bank	CA	Korea	De Novo
2120	Shenandoah Valley NB[4]	VA	Middle East	Acq
2154	Community State Bank[4]	NY	Middle East	Acq
2174	Community Bank of San Jose	CA	Mexico	Acq #
2437	Union Chelsea NB	NY	Venezuela	Acq
2482	Main Bank of Houston	TX	Saudi Arabia	Acq
2509	Bank of Montreal-California	CA	Canada	De Novo
2747	Pan American NB of Los Angeles	CA	Indonesia	Acq
2967	Valley NB[4]	VA	Middle East	Acq
3135	Central NB of Miami	FL	Colombia	Acq
3167	Royal Trust Bank of Palm Beach, NA	FL	Canada	Acq
3358	Peoples Bank	TX	Saudi Arabia	Acq
3392	Security NB of New Jersey	NJ	Switz./Canada	Acq
3534	Biscayne Bank	FL	Portugal	Acq
3602	Du Quoin State Bank	IL	Middle East	Acq
3604	United Americas Bank	NY	Spain/L. America	Acq
3922	Peoples NB of Leesburg[4]	VA	Middle East	Acq
3964	Eastern Shore NB[4]	MD	Middle East	Acq
4014	American Asian Bank	CA	Hong Kong	De Novo
4205	Dadeland National Bank	FL	Spain/L. America	Acq
4396	Deerfield Beach State Bank	FL	Venezuela	Acq
4558	Royal Trust Bank of Broward City	FL	Canada	Acq
4667	Royal Trust Bank of St. Petersburg	FL	Canada	Acq
5000	Kyowa Bank of California	CA	Japan	De Novo

Foreign-Owned U.S. Banks Smaller Than the Largest 5000, Sorted Alphabetically

| | Alamosa National Bank | CO | Canada | Acq |
| | American Bank of Commerce | AZ | Canada | Acq |

Asian International Bank	NY	Philippines	De Novo
Banco de Bogota Trust co.	NY	Colombia	De Novo
Bank of Cutler Ridge	FL	Spain	Acq
Bank of Montreal Trust Co.	NY	Canada	De Novo
Bank of Nova Scotia Trust Co.	NY	Canada	De Novo
Camino-California Bank	CA	Hong Kong	Acq
Canadian Bank of Commerce Trust Co.	NY	Canada	De Novo
Fidelity NB of S. Miami	FL	Spain	Acq
First City NB of Jacksonville	FL	Netherlands/Canada	Acq
FNB of Lexington[4]	VA	Middle East	Acq
Global Union Bank	NY	Asia	De Novo
Guaranty Bank of Stapleton	CO	Canada	Acq
Hemisphere National Bank	DC	Argentina	Acq
International Bank of California	CA	Philippines	Acq
Israel Discount Trust Co.	NY	Israel	De Novo
Meadowlands National Bank	NJ	Argentina	Acq
Metropolitan National Bank	TX	Syria	Acq
Pan American Bank of Coral Gables, NA	FL	Venezuela	Acq
Peoples NB of Littleton	NH	Canada	Acq
Philippine Bank of California	CA	Philippines	De Novo
Round Hill National Bank[4]	VA	Middle East	Acq
Royal Trust Bank of Broward City	FL	Canada	Acq
Royal Trust Bank of Jacksonville	FL	Canada	Acq
Royal Trust Bank of Orlando	FL	Canada	Acq
Royal Trust Bank of Tampa	FL	Canada	Acq
Sunshine State Bank	FL	Panama	Acq
Toronto Dominion Bank Trust Co.	NY	Canada	De Novo

Pending Acquisitions

12	Crocker NB	CA	U.K.	Acq
222	Manufacturers Bank	CA	Japan	Merger
928	FNB of San Diego County	CA	Japan	Merger
958	First City Bank	CA	Japan	Merger
1155	Westlands Bank	CA	Canada	Acq
2216	Central State Bank	NY	S. America	Acq
3059	Miami National Bank	FL	Spain	Acq
4520	Bank of Perrine	FL	Colombia	Acq

Note: Foreign-owned banks which have ceased to exist due to divestitute or merger do not appear on this table.

87

Appendix X (continued)

[1] Banks with 10% foreign ownership and above are included in this table. (10% ownership may or may not imply effective control, depending on the stock distribution.)

[2] Deposit ranks are taken from the *American Banker* year-end rankings of the 5,000 largest U.S. commercial banks (March 28, 1980).

[3] Acq = a U.S. bank acquired by foreign investor(s);

Acq + = a U.S. bank acquired by foreign investor(s) that has subsequently acquired another U.S. bank;

Acq # = a U.S. bank acquired by foreign investor(s) that has subsequently merged with a foreign-owned *de novo* U.S. bank;

De Novo = foreign-owned *de novo* U.S. bank;

De Novo + = foreign-owned *de novo* U.S. bank that has acquired other U.S. bank(s) through merger or bank holding company affiliations.

Merger = pending merger of a U.S. bank with a foreign-owned *de novo* U.S. bank.

[4] Member of Financial General Bankshares, Inc.

Appendix XI
Foreign Ownership of U.S. Banking Organizations (December 31, 1980)

Percentage of Bank's Equity Controlled	Percentage of Total Equity Controlled					
	Number of Acquired U.S. Banks		Number of De Novo U.S. Banks		Total Number of Foreign-Owned U.S. Banks
	Foreign Bank Owner	Foreign Individual Owner	Foreign Bank Owner	Foreign Individual Owner	
98-100	16	8	28	4	56
50- 97.9	5	27	4	7	43
25- 49.9	1	3	0	1	5
10- 24.9	2	4	1	0	7
	24	42	33	12	111

Notes: Foreign-controlled banks which have ceased to exist due to divestiture or merger do not appear on this table.

The 12 member banks of Financial General Bankshares, Inc. are counted as one banking organization.

## 3

FOREIGN-CONTROLLED U.S. BANKS: THE LEGAL AND REGULATORY ENVIRONMENT

WILLIAM A. GLIDDEN

JOHN E. SHOCKEY

SUMMARY

This paper discusses the broad outlines of United States bank regulation and supervision, highlighting certain aspects of the regulatory system that are relevant to foreign acquisition and control of United States banking organizations. The major banking statutes and regulations are reviewed in terms of entry controls, expansion controls, geographic market and product segmentation, bank safety and soundness, and community service and investor protection. Then follows a description of the supervisory process by which compliance with this body of law and regulation is monitored. The paper concludes with a discussion of enforcement powers and sanctions. Salient facts about foreign entry and subsequent control of United States banking organizations are interwoven throughout the paper, both in the text and, in more detailed fashion, in the footnotes.

A number of general observations emerge from the discussion. The United States system of bank supervision and regulation is comprehensive and pervasive. A foreign control party's United States banking organization fits within that framework. By and large, United States laws and regulations are facially neutral with respect to the nationality of a United States banking organization's controlling owner. The United States approach, most recently embodied in the International Banking Act of 1978, has been one of national treatment. Foreign banks are permitted to engage in activities in the United States generally under the same ground rules as United States banks with the exception that the foreign country involved will allow United States banks to engage in the foreign country in activities permitted to the foreign country's banks.

INTRODUCTION

Banks in the United States are subject to a comprehensive scheme of regulation and supervision principally administered by three federal banking agencies and by supervisory authorities in each of the fifty states. United States banks that are established *de novo* or acquired by foreign individuals or companies (including foreign banks) are subject to this regulatory framework. This is the crucial fact to remember in any analysis of foreign control of United States banking organizations; such organizations fit within the entire supervisory structure that applies to domestically owned institutions. Some features of United States law and regulation do impact in a special way or have particular relevance in the context of foreign control of United States banks. However, United States banking laws and supervisory functions generally seek to encompass overseas personnel, activities and transactions of foreign banking organizations and individuals controlling United States banks only to a limited extent: the extraterritorial thrust of bank supervision focuses on those events and relationships that relate to and have a substantial effect on banks and banking transactions in the United States.

The most important features of United States banking law, regulation and supervision will be discussed in this paper. Special attention will be given to those provisions and practices which have differential impact because the control party or potential control party is foreign. For descriptive convenience, the applicable body of law is divided into the following conceptual segments which focus upon different purposes of bank supervision and regulation:

1. entry controls;
2. expansion controls and geographic market segmentation;
3. product market segmentation;
4. safety and soundness in bank operations;
5. bank investors, bank customers, and service to communities.

We then briefly explore the principal supervisory processes through which compliance with this body of law and regulation is administered.

Finally, we note the formal sanctions available to address individual and institutional noncompliance.

ENTRY CONTROLS

Persons and companies may establish a bank *de novo* or may purchase control of an existing bank or bank holding company. Entry by means of a new bank requires the approval of the Office of the Comptroller of the Currency (OCC) in the case of a national bank, or the appropriate state banking department in the case of a state bank. For state banks that wish to be members of the Federal Reserve System, approval of the Federal Reserve Board (FRB) is also needed. Similarly, the Federal Deposit Insurance Corporation (FDIC) must approve applications for nonmember insured banks.[1] Under the Federal Deposit Insurance Act, the federal regulators, before authorizing a new bank to commence business, must consider the adequacy of the institution's capital structure and its future earnings prospects, the general character of its proposed management, the convenience and needs of the community to be served, and whether its corporate powers are consistent with the purposes of the Federal Deposit Insurance Act.[2] Most states require the state bank supervisor to consider similar factors in deciding whether to issue a state bank charter to an applicant.[3] Any bank that is established *de novo* by a company must also be approved by the FRB under criteria and procedures embodied in the Bank Holding Company Act.[4]

Acquisition of an existing bank or bank holding company is governed by the Bank Holding Company Act or the Change in Bank Control Act.[5] Under section 3 of the Bank Holding Company Act, written permission of the FRB is required before any company can directly or indirectly obtain ownership or control of 25 percent of the voting stock of a bank or control in any manner the election of a majority of the directors.[6] "Company" is defined to mean any corporation, business trust, association, "or similar organization" and includes a foreign bank.[7] The FRB must deny any acquisition whose effect "in any section of the country" would substantially lessen competition unless it finds the anticompetitive effects of the proposed transaction are outweighed in the public interest by the probable effect in meeting the "convenience and needs of the community" to be served. The FRB must, in every case, consider the financial and managerial resources and future prospects of the company and the bank concerned and the convenience and needs of the community to be served.[8]

In acting upon an application by a foreign bank or other foreign company to acquire a United States bank, the FRB considers the same statutory factors that apply to United States bank acquisitions by domestic companies.[9] The appropriate supervisory authority (the OCC in the case of a national bank acquisition or the state supervisor in the case of a state bank acquisition) ordinarily submits to the FRB a recommendation on the proposed acquisition. If a denial is recommended, the FRB notifies the applicant of this fact and holds a hearing. Based upon the findings of the hearing, the FRB approves or denies the application. In an emergency or failing bank situation, the FRB may grant or deny an application without a hearing notwithstanding any recommended disapproval by the appropriate supervisory authority.[10]

The Change in Bank Control Act of 1978 applies to any acquisition of control that is not otherwise governed by the Bank Holding Company Act or the Bank Merger Act.[11] Under this law, no person, broadly defined to include an individual or group or any form of entity, can acquire control of any insured bank (defined to include a bank holding company having an insured bank) through a purchase, assignment, transfer, pledge, or other disposition of voting stock of such bank unless the appropriate federal banking agency has been given sixty days prior notification of the proposed acquisition and allows the transaction to be consummated.[12] "Control" is defined to mean the power, directly or indirectly, to direct the management or policies of an insured bank or to vote 25 percent or more of any class of voting stock of such bank.[13]

An acquiring person must in the prior notice to the federal regulator provide extensive information concerning such person's background, activities and affiliations, assets and liabilities, management, source of funds to carry out the intended acquisition, any plans for change in the business or management of the bank and any additional relevant information that the agency may require by general rule or specific request.[14] Grounds for disapproval of an acquisition include the following:[15]

1. The proposed acquisition of control would result in a monopoly or an attempt to monopolize the business of banking in any part of the United States;
2. the effect of the proposed acquisition in any section of the country may be substantially to lessen competition, and the anticompetitive effects are not clearly outweighed in the public interest

by the probable effect of the transaction in meeing the convenience and needs of the community to be served;

3. the financial condition of any acquiring person is such as might jeopardize the financial stability of the bank or prejudice the interests of depositors;

4. the competence, experience or integrity of any acquiring person or any of the proposed new management indicates it would not be in the interest of bank depositors or in the public interest to permit such person to control the bank, or

5. any acquiring person does not furnish to the appropriate banking agency all information required by that agency.

A willful violation of the statute, such as failure to provide prior notice, is punishable by a fine of up to $10,000 per day for each day during which the violation continues.[16]

A majority of the states have enacted legislation to regulate the acquisition of control in banks by persons or companies.[17] Some require the approval of the state supervisory authorities before a controlling interest in a bank may be acquired or exercised. Others merely require notice to be given that a change has taken place.[18] State takeover statutes will be discussed later in connection with protections afforded bank shareholders.

While being subject to this matrix of federal and state laws and procedures that govern entry into the commercial banking system, *foreign* acquisitions are affected by a few additional statutes as well. In at least a dozen states the acquisition of stock of a domestic bank by an out-of-state company is restricted.[19] It is unclear to what extent companies outside the United States fall within the intended scope of these provisions.[20] South Carolina does specifically prohibit the acquisition of more than 25 percent of the voting stock of a bank located within its borders by a "holding company" organized under the laws of a "foreign state, kingdom or government . . ."[21] The State of Washington forbids a bank whose primary place of business is in a foreign country from acquiring a domestic bank or trust company within its borders.[22] According to the literal terms of this statute, it would seem that the prohibition does not extend to foreign individuals or nonbank companies.

Finally, the National Bank Act requires that ordinarily all the directors of a national bank be United States citizens and two-thirds of the directors be local residents.[23] At least 34 states require that somewhere between a majority and all of the directors of a state bank be American citizens and/or local residents.[24]

EXPANSION CONTROLS AND GEOGRAPHIC
MARKET SEGMENTATION

Once foreign investors have established or acquired a United States bank or bank holding company, they face the same restrictions as domestic owners with respect to further geographic expansion within the United States. These restrictions are imposed by a combination of the McFadden Act, the Douglas Amendment embodied in the Bank Holding Company Act, and state laws. Generally, the United States bank can establish branch offices only when and to the extent that the statute law of the state where it is situated permits such additional offices. In any event, a United States bank cannot branch across state lines.[25] By and large and apart from certain grandfathered systems, a bank holding company and its subsidiaries are forbidden from owning banks in more than one state.[26] A bank cannot merge or consolidate with another bank in a different state.[27]

To the extent that bank expansion is possible—whether in the form of branching, holding company acquisition of an additional bank, or the merger or consolidation of two or more banks or bank holding companies—it is subject to statutory decision factors and to the approval of one or more banking regulators. Branching statutes vary substantially from state to state.[28] The FRB must approve any bank holding company acquisition of an additional bank or merger with another bank holding company in the same state under the procedures and decision criteria discussed earlier in connection with bank holding company formations.[29] The Bank Merger Act similarly requires the appropriate federal regulator, in deciding whether to approve a merger of two or more banks, to weigh any anticompetitive effects against the convenience and needs of the community to be served and to consider the financial and managerial resources and future prospects of the banks.[30] Many states have laws that specify whether and under what conditions banks may merge or bank holding companies may acquire an additional bank.[31]

Prior to the passage of the International Banking Act of 1978, foreign banks that owned no domestic bank subsidiary in the United States could establish deposit-taking branches in any state that permitted such entry.[32] The new law requires that a foreign bank operating at any combination of branches, agencies or subsidiary banks select a "home state."[33] Outside its home state, the foreign bank is restricted to establishing agencies, which cannot accept deposits from United States citizens or residents, or branches that, pursuant to an agreement entered into with the FRB, can accept only such deposits as are permissible to Edge Corporations.[34]

Despite the prohibitions against branching or acquiring banks across state lines, United States banks are able to conduct business on a multistate basis. Some banks have established loan production offices outside their home jurisdiction.[35] Some banks own Edge Corporations, which are licensed by the FRB to engage in international or foreign financing and banking activities. The FRB has recently revised its regulations to permit Edge Corporations to establish financial offices on a nationwide basis.[36] Finally, and most importantly, bank holding companies can operate on a multistate basis certain types of business that the FRB has determined are "closely related to banking."[37] Examples include mortgage companies, consumer and business finance companies, real estate trusts, leasing, insurance and data processing.[38]

In sum, except for Edge Corporations and permissible nonbanking subsidiaries, banks operating in the United States are largely restricted to the state where they are situated. In many cases, state law prohibits branches, mergers, or bank holding company acquisitions, or restricts such types of expansion to one region within the state. Without delving into the complexities of the federal and state body of law that affects bank expansion, it is fair to say that there is substantial geographic market segmentation of the banking business within the United States. Of course, national banks and many state banks may operate branches or acquire banking organizations under varying rules in countries around the world.[39]

PRODUCT MARKET SEGMENTATION

Commercial banks in the United States are restricted not only in geographical terms, but also in the types of business in which they may engage domestically. Generally, commercial banks are confined to doing the business of commercial banking. They cannot engage, to any significant extent, in investment banking, the securities business, or in commercial activity that is not related to banking. On the other hand, United States banks, with a few qualifications, compete with foreign banks overseas to the full extent permitted by the laws and practices of the host countries. These basic principles will be illustrated and expanded upon in the following discussion.

National banks can exercise certain express powers and "all such incidental powers as shall be necessary to carry on the business of banking. . . ." Specific enumerated powers include the discounting and the
negotiating of promissory notes, drafts, bills of exchange and other evi-
dences of debt, the receiving of deposits, the buying and selling of exchange, the loaning of money on proofs of security, and the issuing and
circulating of notes according to the provisions of the National Bank
Act.[40] State laws enumerate the permissible banking powers of state-
chartered institutions. The majority of states also make use of an "incidental powers" clause.[41] There has, however, never been a clear division
between the business which is properly incidental to banking and that
which is not.

The Banking Act of 1933, popularly known as the Glass-Steagall
Act, makes it illegal for any person or company engaged in the business of issuing, underwriting, selling or distributing securities to engage
at the same time in the business of receiving deposits.[42] There is a pro-
viso that commercial banks can deal in, underwrite, purchase and sell
investment securities or issue securities to the extent permitted to national banks under 12 USC § 24.[43] This section of the National Bank
Act authorizes national banks (1) to purchase and sell securities upon
the order and for the account of their customers; (2) to purchase for
their own account a specified amount of investment securities, defined
to mean marketable obligations of any person or company in the form
of bonds, notes or debentures; and, (3) to deal in, underwrite and purchase for their own account, without regard to capital and surplus limitations or other restrictions, United States Government obligations,
general obligations of state and local governments, and certain other
types of obligations specified in the statute. National banks generally
cannot invest in corporate stock.[44] The Banking Act of 1933 also
amended the Federal Reserve Act to prohibit affiliation or interlocking
management or employment between member banks and securities
companies.[45]

The Bank Holding Company Act mandates a general separation between banking and commerce.[46] The statute provides for certain
exemptions from the nonbanking prohibitions. Thus, a bank holding
company can own up to 5 percent of the voting stock of any company.[47] A bank holding company can control any company whose
activities the FRB determines by order or regulation "to be so closely
related to banking or managing or controlling banks as to be a proper
incident thereto."[48] A bank holding company can control any company which does no business in the United States except as "incidental

to its international or foreign business" if the FRB determines that under the circumstances the exemption would not be substantially at variance with the purposes of the Act and would be in the public interest.[49]

There are two additional exemptions available to foreign bank holding companies. First, a foreign bank holding company can control any foreign company "the greater part of whose business is conducted outside the United States" if the FRB by general regulation or specific order grants its approval.[50] Second, section 2(h) of the Bank Holding Company Act allows a foreign bank holding company that is "principally engaged in the banking business outside the United States" to own a foreign company principally engaged in business outside the United States, which company can in turn own a United States company that is engaged in the same general line of business or in a business related to that of the investor company.[51] Some qualifications are imposed on this section 2(h) exemption. The foreign bank holding company cannot own shares of a foreign company that engages in the securities business in the United States. The foreign bank holding company may engage in the United States in operations or activities permitted to domestic bank holding companies under section 4(c)(8) of the Act—activities that the FRB has determined are "closely related to banking"—only with the FRB's general or specific approval under such section. In other words, the section 2(h) special exemption for foreign bank holding companies is not available for United States operations or activities arguably permissible under section 4(c)(8). Finally, no United States office or subsidiary of the foreign bank holding company can extend credit to a United States office or subsidiary of the exempt company on terms more favorable than those afforded similar borrowers in this country.[52]

The Bank Holding Company Act thus regulates conduct by banks and related nonbanking institutions in the United States and largely excludes from its prohibitions the overseas operations of both domestic and foreign bank holding companies. To a large extent, other laws enable United States banks to compete abroad on terms dictated by the rules and policies of the host country. Federal law defines the permissible activities of national banks, and state law defines such powers for state banks. In addition, national and state member banks are subject to regulations promulgated by the FRB, and state nonmember banks are subject to rules adopted by the FDIC.

Under the Federal Reserve Act, for example, any national bank with a capital and surplus of one million dollars or more may, upon approval of the FRB and subject to such terms and conditions as the FRB may impose, (1) establish branches in foreign countries; (2) invest up to 10 percent of its paid-in capital and surplus in one or more Edge Corporations or Agreement Corporations that principally engage in international or foreign banking either directly or through the ownership or control of local institutions in foreign countries; and (3) own one or more foreign banks that do not engage in any activity in the United States except that which the FRB determines is incidental to their international or foreign business.[53]

The Federal Reserve Act authorizes the FRB to promulgate regulations that permit a United States bank's foreign branch to exercise powers usual in the host country where it is doing business, except that such foreign branch cannot engage in the general business of producing, distributing, buying or selling goods or merchandise and cannot, except for obligations of the government in the country where the branch is located, underwrite, sell or distribute securities.[54] The permissible overseas activities and investments of member banks, bank holding companies, and Edge and Agreement Corporations are set forth in greater detail in the FRB's Regulation K, now entitled International Banking Operations.[55] It should be noted that a United States banking organization cannot control a foreign bank that engages in the securities business in the United States.[56]

Section 101 of the Financial Institutions Regulatory and Interest Rate Control Act of 1978 amends section 18 of the Federal Deposit Insurance Act so that, when authorized by state law, a state nonmember insured bank can, with the consent of the FDIC and upon such conditions and under such regulations as the FDIC may prescribe, establish foreign branches or acquire ownership in one or more foreign banks or other foreign entities.[57] The acquired foreign bank or entity cannot engage in any activity in the United States except as the FDIC judges to be incidental to its international or foreign business.[58]

SAFETY AND SOUNDNESS IN BANK OPERATIONS

Most banking laws and regulations seek in some manner to promote the safety and soundness of the individual banks and the banking system as a whole. Generally, this is done in the context of furthering other broad public policies, such as the strengthening of competition, service to communities, fair dealing with bank customers, and the achievement of an efficient allocation of credit. However, the primary purpose of some laws is the protection of banks.

Thus, a national bank can invest only in government obligations and in certain other types of "investment securities" that, by definition, are marketable and nonspeculative in nature.[59] As already mentioned, a national bank cannot generally own corporate stock.[60] The directors of the bank may periodically declare dividends out of net profits, but only if there is an adequate surplus fund.[61] A national bank is restricted in the amount of money it may borrow, in the types and amount of real estate loans it may make, in the amount of credit that it may extend to a single borrower, and in the type and amount of drafts and bills of exchange it may accept.[62] Generally, the limitations are based upon a specified percentage of the bank's unimpaired capital and surplus. Some of these prudential rules are applied to state banks by the Federal Reserve Act or the Federal Deposit Insurance Act. In addition, the states regulate the borrowing, lending and investment activities of state banks to the extent that such regulation is compatible with federal law.

Laws governing affiliate transactions, designed to protect a bank from abuse by insiders or related companies in a position to influence the bank's policies or practices, perhaps assume particular significance when a bank is controlled by foreign interests. A United States bank cannot lend to or make investments in any affiliated institution, including its parent bank holding company, in excess of 10 percent of the bank's capital stock and surplus.[63] A 20 percent lending limit is imposed on all affiliate transactions in the aggregate. The term "affiliate" includes any corporation, business trust, association or similar organization which is controlled by the bank or by controlling shareholders of the bank, or any organization which itself owns or controls a majority of the stock of the bank or can elect a majority of the bank's directors. Any extension of credit by the bank to its affiliate must ordinarily be secured by specified collateral having a market value in excess of such extension of credit. Loans to individuals associated with an affiliate may be deemed to be extensions of credit to the affiliate.[64] Any foreign person or organization, regardless of location, falls within the coverage of these provisions. Section 2(h) of the Bank Holding Company Act specifically states that the application of this law "shall not be affected by the fact that the transaction takes place wholly or partly outside the United States or that a company is organized or operates outside the United States."[65]

Extensions of credit to insiders—officers, directors, shareholders who

own more than 10 percent of a class of securities, and their related interests—are limited as to type, cannot exceed specified individual and
aggregate amounts, cannot be preferential in any way, and may require
the prior approval of a disinterested majority of the bank's entire board
of directors.[66] The executive officers and principal shareholders of a
bank must file an annual report with the board of directors concerning
any indebtedness they may have with a correspondent bank.[67] A bank
must file annually a publicly available report with the appropriate federal banking agency listing its principal shareholders, all of its officers
and directors who are indebted, or whose related interests are indebted,
to the bank or one of its correspondents, and the aggregate amount of
indebtedness.[68]

BANK INVESTORS, BANK CUSTOMERS, AND SERVICE TO COMMUNITIES

   In a broad sense, any law or administrative practice that protects
the safety and soundness of banks may be assumed to have a beneficial
impact on bank investors and customers and to strengthen the economy.
But some laws are designed specifically with one or more of these bank
relationships in mind. Individual deposits are protected up to $100,000
by FDIC deposit insurance.[69] Borrowers are afforded many protections
in their dealings with banks. A bank's community service record is reviewed during examinations and may affect its potential for expansion.
Securities laws, some state takeover statutes, shareholder rights embodied in the National Bank Act and some state merger statutes, and
disclosure rules issued by the Securities and Exchange Commission
(SEC) and the banking agencies directly or indirectly seek to promote
the interests of investors. Aspects of these laws and procedures will be
highlighted in the following discussion.[70]
   Disclosure rules adopted by the OCC provide that, unless an exemption is applicable, a national bank cannot make a public offering of its
securities unless it makes use of an offering circular that has been filed
with and declared effective by the OCC.[71] The OCC regulation encompasses banks in organization as well as existing banks selling equity or
subordinated notes to raise additional capital. For a bank in organization, pertinent information must be provided to potential investors concerning such matters as the nature of the offering, the intended use of
proceeds, the proposed business of the bank, the organizers and pro-

posed management, the principal security holders, and any proposed material transactions between the bank and such parties. More detailed bank information is mandated for existing institutions raising new capital.

The federal securities laws generally seek to protect investors by assuring full and accurate disclosure of material information concerning the shares of covered companies that are being offered for sale to the public or that are being traded. The banking agencies have a general responsibility to issue rules similar to those adopted by the SEC for other types of business enterprises.[72] Banks whose shares are traded on a national exchange or with 500 shareholders of record and more than one million dollars in assets must register with the appropriate federal banking agency.[73] The registration statement filed with the agency is available to the public and discloses pertinent information concerning the bank, its affiliated companies, officers and directors, and any shareholders that have beneficial ownership of more than 5 percent of a class of securities.[74] Registered banks must also file quarterly and annual reports and certain other reports to provide fully current material information to the bank regulator and to investors.[75]

Securities transactions involving registered banks are subject to a variety of additional disclosure rules. Any person making a tender offer or otherwise soliciting shares of a registered bank that would result in more than 5 percent ownership must file a report with the appropriate federal banking agency.[76] The report form requires that the acquiring party disclose extensive background and financial information, sources of funds, and intentions relating to change in the bank. The banking agencies have amended their forms effective January 1, 1980, to obtain information on the acquiror's citizenship or place of incorporation.[77] Within 10 days after acquiring more than 5 percent ownership of a registered bank, by whatever means, a shareholder must provide certain information, including citizenship or place of incorporation information, to the bank regulator.[78] Proxy solicitations in connection with annual shareholder meetings must comply with disclosure standards spelled out in regulations of the federal banking agencies.[79] Insiders—officers, directors, and 10 percent shareholders—must report any changes in their beneficial ownership of the bank's shares and disgorge any short-swing profits.[80]

Banks whose shares are not registered are not subject to the above rules. However, the anti-fraud and civil liability provisions of the Securities Act of 1933 and the Securities Exchange Act of 1934 apply to the purchase and sale of securities of all banks.[81] State securities laws and state takeover statutes afford additional investor protections.[82] All takeover statutes that apply to banks require extensive disclosure and a waiting period between the filing of the required information and the effective date of the tender offer.[83]

In addition to deposit insurance, a substantial body of law seeks to protect persons in their dealings with banks. In the past decade, federal consumer protection laws have been developed to supplement state laws on the subject. The Truth in Lending Act, for example, requires that banks fully and accurately disclose the cost of credit in consumer transactions so that persons can more easily "shop" for credit.[84] State usury laws limit the amount of interest that banks may charge on various categories of loans. The Equal Credit Opportunity Act forbids discrimination in any aspect of a credit transaction on the basis of race, religion, sex, national origin or similar prohibited bases.[85] Other federal and state legislation regulates the dealings between banks and their customers.

The licensing-type procedures previously discussed in connection with the entry and expansion controls on banks mandate that the federal regulatory authorities consider, as one element in their decisions, the convenience and needs of the communities to be served by the new or expanded bank.[86] State statutes frequently require that the state supervisory officials consider public benefits or local needs in their determinations on bank charters and branch approvals.[87] These strands of public policy have most recently been codified in the Community Reinvestment Act of 1977.[88] This law directs the federal banking agencies to use their authority when examining banks to encourage the banks to help meet the convenience and needs, including the credit needs, of their local communities. The agencies must assess the records of the institutions they supervise in meeting the credit needs of the entire community, including low and moderate income neighborhoods, consistent with safe and sound banking practices. The community reinvestment record must be taken into account in any application by a financial institution (including a holding company) for a bank charter, deposit insurance, a branch office, relocation of a home or branch office, or any bank acquisition, merger or consolidation.

THE EXAMINATION AND SUPERVISORY PROCESS

As is apparent from the preceding discussion, the legal and regulatory environment which shapes and conditions the establishment and operation of banking organizations in the United States is pervasive. At the heart of bank supervision is the examination process, which utilizes both remote and on-site inspections. Remote inspections have traditionally relied on the receipt and analysis of regular and special reports from banks and bank holding companies. The information derived from these reports directs or assists on-site examinations. In this way, the regulatory agencies monitor developments in individual banks and in the banking system at large. Intensified supervisory attention is devoted to institutions experiencing particular difficulties.

The exercise of examination and visitorial power with respect to United States banking organizations, including those owned by foreign persons or companies, is without parallel elsewhere in the American economy.[89] This section summarizes the main features of the examination process, especially as applied to multinational banks and bank holding company organizations. We also note the evolving institutional mechanisms designed to improve the effectiveness of bank regulation in an international setting.

The federal banking agencies have broad examination authority to determine that the institutions they supervise are conducting their banking business in a prudent manner and in conformity with all applicable laws, regulations and orders. Under the Federal Deposit Insurance Act, for example, the appropriate agency or its designated representatives, "are authorized to administer oaths and affirmations, and to examine and take and preserve testimony under oath as to any matter in respect to the affairs or ownership of any [insured] bank or institution or affiliate thereof."[90] The attendance of witnesses and the production of documents "may be required from any place in any State or in any territory or other place subject to the jurisdiction of the United States. . . ."[91] The National Bank Act provides that refusal to give the OCC "any information required" in the course of examination of any affiliate of a national bank subjects the bank to forfeiture of its "rights, privileges, and franchises. . . ."[92] Each of the banking agencies has authority to demand information in the form of regular or special reports, sworn to be accurate and complete by the appropriate bank officials.[93] Failure to submit complete, timely reports exposes a bank to civil penalties.[94] Submission of false statements to examiners, falsification of bank records, or false reports to the regulator constitute felonies punishable by a fine and imprisonment.[95]

Each of the federal bank regulators utilizes a variety of supervisory tools in implementing its comprehensive examination authority. The OCC's programs and procedures will be highlighted here because the authors are most familiar with that agency's approach. It should be noted, however, that the examination process administered by the OCC does not differ conceptually from the process administered by the FRB and FDIC in connection with the institutions they supervise.

National banks submit a variety of regular and special reports to the OCC. These include the regular quarterly report of condition and annual report of income and dividends, quarterly reports on affiliates (including holding company affiliates) as required by the OCC, annual trust department reports, reports of international operations and foreign exchange activities, reports on ownership of the reporting bank and on indebtedness of executive officers and principal shareholders to the reporting bank and its correspondent banks, quarterly past due loan reports, reports filed under the federal securities laws, semi-annual country exposure reports, and any additional reports that the OCC may request.[96] The analysis of reported information is supplemented by OCC communications with bankers, other United States bank supervisors, foreign bank supervisors, and other United States and foreign government authorities.

The OCC's National Bank Surveillance System, Special Projects Division, and Multinational Banking Division are examples of programs developed in recent years in an effort to increase the effectiveness of the remote examination process in bank supervision.[97] The National Bank Surveillance System is a computer-based information system primarily designed for the early detection of banks requiring special supervisory attention and, more generally, to reveal adverse trends that may affect the banking industry regionally or nationwide.[98] Follow-up corrective measures at individual institutions are monitored as well.

The Special Projects Division consolidates a number of agency functions applicable to banks identified as deserving special supervisory attention. The program encompasses all banks in excess of $2 billion in assets and, in addition, any other bank that is experiencing difficulties. The problems may relate to such matters as quality and depth of bank management, quality of assets, sufficiency of earnings and capital, liquidity, and similar items that undermine the strength and viability of an institution.[99] The Washington and regional offices of the OCC coordinate their activities. Within the Washington office, the Special Projects Division draws upon persons responsible for reviewing bank reports submitted to the OCC or filed under the securities laws, examination reports, National Bank Surveillance System analyses, formal enforcement and administrative actions, and corporate activities in order to assure a pooling of all available information and the broadest possible consideration of supervisory approaches.[100]

The OCC created the Multinational Banking Division in 1979 to assume centralized responsibility for examination, analysis and supervision of "multinational banks," initially defined as banks with assets in excess of $10 billion. The Multinational Banking Division also encompasses the international activities of all national banks with overseas branches.[101] The OCC recognized that the ten or fifteen largest United States banks have little in common with most banking organizations that are supervised primarily by regional offices located in various parts of the country. Obtaining an overview of a large banking organization's national and international operations was becoming increasingly difficult to achieve at the local level. Furthermore, the more than 100 national banks that have significant activities in foreign countries pose special problems to the regulator, including the difficulty of obtaining full access to and understanding of information and transactions on an international scale and the need to coordinate supervisory programs with authorities in those other countries.[102]

The reporting systems and centralized data analysis provide a general framework for on-site bank examinations in the United States. These examinations in turn enable the agency to obtain an in-depth review of a bank's current status at the time of visitation. The *Comptroller's Handbook for National Bank Examiners* summarizes the mission and responsibilities of examiners as follows:

> The Office of the Comptroller of the Currency (OCC) is responsible for promoting and assuring the soundness of the country's system of national banks. The bank examination process is the OCC's fact-finding arm in discharging that responsibility. The essential objectives of an examination are:
>
> 1. to provide an objective evaluation of a bank's soundness;
> 2. to permit the OCC to appraise the quality of management and directors; and
> 3. to identify those areas where corrective action is required to strengthen the bank, to improve the quality of its performance, and to enable it to comply with applicable laws, rulings and regulations. The evaluation of the prudency of practices, adherence to laws and regulations, adequacy of liquidity and capital, quality of assets and earnings, nature of operations, and adequacy of internal control and internal audit are among the procedures utilized to accomplish those objectives.[103]

On-site examination consists of an ongoing and dynamic process through which the bank regulatory agencies seek to assure compliance with laws and regulations, verify the accuracy of all submitted reports, and informally influence bank managers to achieve acceptable norms of safe and sound operation of their banks.[104] Examiners utilize questionnaires to test whether a bank's internal controls are adequate to provide institutional protection and assure adherence to management's policies. Sampling techniques are applied to loan files and other bank records to review the effectiveness of bank audit systems, the appropriateness of loan classification procedures in use at the bank, compliance with laws and regulations, and numerous other matters.[105] Examiners interview bank personnel and observe practices on a spot basis.

A disciplined evaluation of bank activities, based on the performance of examiner work programs, is embodied in a comprehensive examination report which is then reviewed in the appropriate regional office and in Washington.[106] Examiner teams meet with bank management to discuss any problems that may have been uncovered. Examiners meet periodically with the bank's board of directors to present their criticisms, recommendations, and, in some cases, directives for change. Thus, the examination process combines reporting by the supervised institutions, on-site examinations and verification, analysis of records, interviews with bank personnel, formal criticisms as appropriate, and recommendations that may escalate into formal sanctions against a recalcitrant institution.[107]

As noted earlier, United States banking organizations that maintain branches or own banking subsidiaries overseas are generally allowed to conduct banking business at such overseas locations in conformity with the local laws and practices.[108] The United States supervisory authorities do insist upon obtaining all information necessary to effectively monitor the foreign operations of these institutions.[109] The OCC's examination of a national bank's international division does not differ conceptually from the regular commercial exam. Nevertheless, it is often necessary to give special attention to additional types of bank assets and liabilities not found domestically and to different accounting procedures and laws and regulations that may be applicable to the foreign activities.[110] The OCC conducts on-site examinations in about 20 countries each year to determine the current and ongoing impact that selected offices, branches and foreign affiliates are having on their parent United States institutions.[111]

Bank supervision through remote and on-site examination is rendered more complicated by the dispersal of authority and responsibility among three federal and fifty state regulatory agencies. National banks are examined and supervised by the OCC, state member banks by the

FRB, and state non-member insured banks by the FDIC. In addition, state banks are examined and supervised by the state banking authorities. The FRB has general supervisory responsibility for domestic and foreign bank holding companies.[112] This dispersal of authority has required special efforts to coordinate a comprehensive system of supervision at an acceptable cost and with minimum duplication. This effort is reflected in a variety of institutions and arrangements.

The Federal Financial Institutions Examination Council (Council), created by Title X of the Financial Institutions Regulatory and Interest Rate Control Act of 1978, is charged with establishing uniform principles and standards and report forms for the examination of banks and bank holding companies to be applied by the three federal banking agencies.[113] The Council also makes recommendations for uniformity and greater effectiveness in other supervisory matters, including the classification of loans subject to country risk and the evaluation of tools for determining the impact of bank holding companies on their subsidiary banks.[114] To further encourage the application of uniform exam principles and standards by state and federal supervisory agencies, the Council maintains a liaison committee composed of five representatives of the state agencies.

The fact that the FRB examines and supervises the holding companies, and the OCC or FDIC examines the banking subsidiaries except for those that are state member banks, has for some time been the subject of congressional concern and of discussion among the regulators.[115] As of December 1978, 2,115 bank holding companies (excluding multi-tiered companies) controlled 4,101 commercial banks out of the 14,602 commercial banks in the United States and accounted for more than 73 percent of all banking assets.[116] The supervisory challenge is essentially one of achieving coordination among the agencies so that holding company networks are supervised in a manner that ensures the banks are protected in their affiliate transactions and relationships. The Council has recently recommended, and the agencies have implemented, a series of steps designed to better harmonize federal supervision of bank holding companies.[117] The General Accounting Office has reported to Congress its belief that these new initiatives, if properly applied, will significantly improve bank holding company supervision.[118]

With specific reference to foreign bank holding companies, the FRB is undertaking several initiatives in order to promote two broad goals: first, to assure that the United States subsidiary bank is operated in a safe and sound manner, and second, to assure that the foreign parent is a source of strength to the United States bank.[119] These initiatives include requiring additional financial information at the time a foreign company (usually a foreign bank) applies to acquire control of a United States bank, soliciting the views of foreign bank regulatory authorities with regard to foreign banks subject to their jurisdiction, improving the ongoing financial information on foreign bank holding companies, instituting a quarterly report on the transactions between the United States subsidiary bank and its foreign parent, increasing examiner surveillance of intercompany transactions and common customer credits, and proposing to amend Regulation Y so that only foreign companies principally engaged in banking abroad qualify for exemption from certain of the nonbanking prohibitions of the Bank Holding Company Act.[120]

The various United States supervisory and examination initiatives, particularly with respect to the international operations of domestic and foreign bank holding companies, are taking place in the context of increasing cooperation among authorities in the developed nations of the world. Events of the mid-1970s, including the failure of the Franklin National Bank in New York and the Herrstadt Bank in West Germany, highlighted the growing interdependence of multinational banking organizations and the need for improved cooperation among the regulators.[121] The most important international forum is the Committee on Banking Regulations and Supervisory Practices, known informally as the Cooke Committee after its incumbent chairman.[122] Established in 1974, this committee consists of representatives from the supervisory authorities and central banks of the countries of the Group of Ten plus Switzerland and Luxembourg.[123] It has a secretariat provided by the Bank for International Settlements at Basle and meets three times a year.

The committee's main focus has been to establish broad principles upon which the supervisors could agree, notwithstanding significant differences in banking laws and regulatory practices among the countries represented. For example, a 1975 Concordat recognized that parent banking institutions have a moral commitment to serve as a source of strength to their overseas offices and subsidiaries and that parent and host country supervisors should facilitate the remote and on-site examination process in their respective jurisdictions.[124] The committee also serves as a clearinghouse wherein supervisors identify gaps in the regulatory coverage of international banking, compare supervisory approaches, exchange information of a sensitive nature derived from a variety of sources and suggesting potential banking problems, and develop further guidelines to demarcate the responsibilities of host and parent authorities.[125]

ENFORCEMENT POWERS AND SANCTIONS

Titles I and VIII of the Financial Institutions Regulatory and Interest Rate Control Act of 1978 amended section 8 of the Federal Deposit Insurance Act and certain other provisions of law to broaden the enforcement powers available to the federal banking agencies.[126] Under the law, the appropriate regulator can issue a cease and desist order against a bank or any director, officer, employee, agent or person participating in the conduct of affairs of the bank that the agency finds has committed a violation of law or has engaged in an unsafe and unsound practice. The order may require the bank or person to take "affirmative action" to correct the conditions resulting from any such violation or practice.[127] In addition, the banking agency may impose civil money penalties on a bank and bank-related individuals for violation of various banking statutes and regulations or for noncompliance with any final cease-and-desist order that has been issued by the agency.[128] An officer, director, or other person participating in the affairs of a bank may be suspended or removed from office and prevented from further participation if indicted or convicted of a felony or if found to have engaged in violations or practices that threaten the interest of the bank or depositors, or that involve personal dishonesty or a breach of fiduciary duty.[129]

In addition to these formal banking agency enforcement powers and remedies, there are civil and criminal sanctions of various kinds. If the directors of a national bank knowingly permit the management or employees of the bank to violate any of the provisions of the National Bank Act, all the "rights, privileges, and franchises of the association" may be terminated in a lawsuit brought by the OCC. Every director who participates in or consents to a violation is personally liable "for all damages which the association, its shareholders, or any other person" may sustain as a result.[130] The insured status of any national or state bank may be terminated under the Federal Deposit Insurance Act upon a finding that it has engaged in violations of law or unsafe or unsound practices.[131]

Individuals—bank employees, shareholders, or customers—may be referred by the bank regulators to the Justice Department for prosecution whenever an apparent violation of a criminal statute is uncovered.[132] Most relevant to bank supervision are the criminal penalties imposed under Title 18 of the United States Code for embezzlement or misapplication of funds and for false entries or statements by any person associated with a bank.[133]

CONCLUSION

This paper has not attempted to catalog the full panoply of laws, regulations, and supervisory powers and approaches that apply to banks in the United States. Instead, we have tried to convey the broad outlines of bank supervision and to highlight certain aspects of the regulatory system which are particularly relevant to foreign acquisition and control of United States banking organizations. Developments in the 1970s have accelerated the growing interdependence of national economies and the impact of multinational banking institutions. The United States authorities have undertaken and are still in the process of implementing new programs and strategies designed to deal more effectively with banking in an international setting.

While providing a more thorough and sophisticated framework within which to attempt to ensure that foreign interests (individuals and organizations) are a source of strength to the United States bank or banks that they control, the evolving structure of laws, regulations and administrative practices that comprises United States bank supervision obviously offers no guarantee against abuse in every instance. This is also true in the case of a domestically owned bank. As the federal banking agencies continue to work on supervisory strategies, standards and procedures, and continue to study issues and monitor developments associated with foreign ownership of banks and banking facilities in the United States, the relevant question which the preceding discussion should help answer is whether the current and evolving supervisory structure can reasonably be expected to minimize the risks and maximize the benefits of such ownership to the United States banking system.

FOOTNOTES

[1] 12 USC § 21 *et seq.*; American Bankers Association, *State Banking Law Service*, ch. 10, 273-75 (1978 revision). We are discussing the regulation and supervision of commercial banks in the United States. It should be noted, however, that in addition to their regulatory and supervisory responsibilities in connection with state member banks and state nonmember insured banks respectively, the FRB and the FDIC exercise important functions designed to enhance the effectiveness and stability of the banking system generally. Thus, as a central bank, the FRB influences the availability of money and credit in the economy. It attempts to ensure that money and credit growth over the longer run is sufficient to provide a rising standard of living. In the short run it adapts its policies to combat deflationary or inflationary pressures as they may arise. FRB monetary policy is exercised principally through three related and complimentary instruments affecting the reserve position of the banking system. These are open market operations in domestic securities (mainly U.S. Government securities), discount operations, and changes in reserve requirements. *See, e.g., The Federal Reserve System: Purpose and Functions*, by Board of Governors of Federal Reserve System (5th ed. 1963); *Id.* (6th ed. 1974); B. Beckhart, *Federal Reserve System* (1972). The FDIC was created in 1933 to help restore public confidence in the banking system and to safeguard bank depositors through deposit insurance. Deposit insurance not only protects individual deposits but serves as a stabilizing influence in the economy through its role in strengthening public confidence in banks generally. The FDIC also assumes the task of liquidating assets of failed or failing banks that are not "bankable." In the past, the adverse repercussions of individual bank failures or crises tended to "snowball" and spread to otherwise healthy financial institutions. The FDIC role is to confine the impact to the affected bank alone. *See generally* Randall, *The Federal Deposit Insurance Corporation: Regulatory Functions and Philosophy*, Current Issues in Banking: A Symposium 64-80 (1969); FDIC *Annual Report* 4-22 (1978).

[2] 12 USC § § 1814, 1816. In addition, the National Bank Act provides that persons uniting to form a national banking association shall submit an organization certificate to the OCC which specifies, among other things, the names and places of residence of the shareholders. The OCC must examine into the condition of the association being organized, ascertain the amount of capital paid in, the name and place of residence of each of its directors, and generally whether the association has complied with the National Bank Act required to entitle it to engage in the business of banking. 12 USC § § 21, 22, 26, 27.

[3] State bank chartering requirements typically involve the following considerations: (1) capital adequacy; (2) deposit insurance; (3) public convenience and necessity; (4) character and fitness of the organizers and proposed management or directors; (5) the likelihood of success; and (6) competitive effect. *See* American Bankers Association, *State Banking Law Service*, ch. 10 app., at 297-303 (1978).

[4] 12 USC § § 1841, 1842. In addition to the criteria embodied in the Bank Holding Company Act, when the application involves a company seeking to establish a new bank, the FRB can investigate and consider the factors that the bank chartering authority—the OCC or the state bank supervisor—would consider. *See Bank of Boulder* v. *Board of Governors of Federal Reserve System*, 535 F.2d 1221 (10th Cir. 1976). Section 3 of the Bank Holding Company Act, 12 USC § 1842, provides a detailed federal statutory framework for considering bank holding company formations and acquisitions, whether the company is seeking a *de novo* bank charter or is acquiring an existing bank. Thus, "(a) It shall be unlawful except with the prior approval of the Board, (1) for any action to be taken that causes any company to become a bank holding company; (2) for any action to be taken that causes a bank to become a subsidiary of a bank holding company; (3) for any bank holding company to acquire any direct or indirect ownership or control of any voting shares of any bank if, after such acquisition, such company will directly or indirectly own or control more than 5 percent of the voting shares of

such bank; (4) for any bank holding company or subsidiary thereof, other than a bank, to acquire all or substantially all of the assets of a bank; or (5) for any bank holding company to merge or consolidate with any other bank holding company. ... (b) Upon receiving from a company any application for approval under this section, the Board shall give notice to the Comptroller of the Currency, if the applicant company or any other bank the voting shares or assets of which are sought to be acquired is a national banking association or a District bank, or to the appropriate supervisory authority of the interested State if the applicant company or any bank the voting share or assets of which are sought to be acquired is a State bank, in order to provide for the submission of the views and recommendations of the Comptroller of the Currency or the State supervisory authority, as the case may be." See the text and accompanying footnotes on holding company acquisitions of existing banks for a discussion of the criteria embodied in 12 USC § 1842(c).

⁵ 12 USC § 1841 *et seq*.; 12 USC § 1817(j). The Change in Bank Control Act of 1978 was enacted as Title VI of the Financial Institutions Regulatory and Interest Rate Control Act of 1978, Public Law 95-630, § § 601 and 602, and is incorporated as an amendment to section 7(j) of the Federal Deposit Insurance Act, 12 USC § 1817(j). Originally enacted in 1966, 12 USC § 1817(j)(1) provided that whenever a change occurred in the voting stock of an insured bank which would result in control or in a change in control of the bank, the president or other chief executive officer had to promptly report the transaction to the appropriate federal banking agency. Under 12 USC § 1817(j)(2), whenever an insured bank made a loan secured by 25 percent or more of the voting stock of another insured bank, the president or other chief executive officer of the lending bank had to promptly report such fact to the federal banking agency that supervised the bank whose stock secured the loan. The International Banking Act of 1978, Public Law 95-369, signed into law September 17, generally provides for the federal supervision of foreign banks operating directly through a branch or agency in the United States. Section 6(c)(12) of the IBA amended section 7(j) of the Federal Deposit Insurance Act so that the FDIC could exempt from the reporting requirements of 7(j)(1) any transaction in the stock of a foreign bank to the extent that the making of such a report would be prohibited by law or rendered impracticable by the "customs and usages" of the foreign bank's home country. The section 7(j)(2) reporting requirements would not apply in the case of a loan secured by the stock of a foreign bank if the lending bank was a foreign bank under the laws of whose domicile the report would be prohibited. Less than two months later, the President signed into law the Financial Institutions Regulatory and Interest Rate Control Act of 1978, including the Change in Bank Control Title which completely revised section 7(j) of the Federal Deposit Insurance Act, 12 USC § 1817(j). In this process, the IBA language relating to foreign bank reporting requirements—involving changes in control and loans secured by the stock of foreign banks—was dropped. The federal banking agencies, in their regulations issued to implement the Change in Bank Control Act, have exempted foreign banks and foreign bank holding companies from the prior notice requirement but not from the reporting provisions of 12 USC § 1817(j)(9), (10), and (12). *See* 44 Fed. Reg. 7119 *et seq*. (1979). Most importantly for the present discussion, the Change in Bank Control Act does convert 12 USC § 1817(j) from a subsequent reporting statute to a screening mechanism, whereby the federal banking agencies are authorized to prohibit transfer of control in appropriate circumstances.

⁶ 12 USC § 1842. "Control" *may* be found to exist, in specified circumstances, when a company owns, controls or has power to vote more than 5 percent of any class of voting securities of a bank or other company. Regulation Y, 12 CFR 225.2(b). Of course, a company that is already a bank holding company because it controls a U.S. bank needs FRB approval to acquire more than 5 percent of the stock or substantially all of the assets of an additional bank in the U.S., or to merge or consolidate with another bank holding company. Under the statutory formulation, the FRB must give its approval before two foreign bank holding companies could merge or consolidate. However, "bank" is defined in section 2 of the Act, 12 USC § 1841(c), to be an institution "organized under the laws of the United States, any State of the United States, the District of Columbia, any territory of the United States, Puerto Rico, Guam, Ameri-

can Samoa, or the Virgin Islands which (1) accepts deposits that the depositor has a legal right to withdraw on demand, and (2) engages in the business of making commercial loans. Such term does not include . . . any organization which does not do business within the United States." This means that a foreign bank holding company could acquire control of a foreign bank overseas without seeking approval of the FRB.

[7] 12 USC § 1841(b). Most of the foreign bank holding companies are indeed foreign banks or organizations primarily engaged in banking overseas. Domestic banks are forbidden from owning the stock of other U.S. banks and therefore are not encompassed within the Bank Holding Company Act definition of "company." This distinction is more apparent than real, however, since a domestic bank can organize into a holding company framework and then acquire additional banks in the same state where it is situated through its holding company.

[8] 12 USC § 1842(c). The FRB apparently has considerable flexibility and discretion in applying the statutory criteria embodied in 12 USC § 1842(c). For example, in *Board of Governors of Federal Reserve System* v. *First Lincoln Corp.*, 439 U.S. 234 (1978), the Supreme Court held that the FRB has authority under § 3(c) to disapprove formation of a bank holding company solely on grounds of financial or managerial unsoundness. The FRB's authority is not limited to instances in which the financial or managerial unsoundness would be caused or exacerbated by the proposed transaction. The Court concluded that the FRB's denial was supported by "substantial evidence" that the applicant "would not be a sufficient source of financial and managerial strength to its subsidiary bank." However, it *would* seem that the FRB's decision in any particular case might be overturned as "arbitrary and capricious and not in accord with law" if its disapproval was not in some reasonable way related to one of the factors set forth in the statute. *See, e.g., Western Bancshares, Inc.*, v. *Board of Governors Federal Reserve System*, 480 F.2d 749 (10th Cir. 1973). (The FRB was granted neither express nor implied authority to regulate, control, fix, supervise, or otherwise interfere with the price or consideration which the bank holding company proposed to pay to shareholders for stock in the bank unless the condemnations contained in the statute are established in relation to the disparate acquisitions, and where such was not the case the FRB had no authority to order divestiture of an acquired bank merely because the minority stockholders' interest had been purchased for approximately 2/3 less than the majority interest without disclosure of the disparity.) Furthermore, the Bank Holding Company Act does not encompass all transactions involving control of a bank. Thus, an individual or individuals acting in concert are not a "company" and can buy a bank without seeking approval of the FRB under this law. Companies acting in concert may also avoid the statutory scheme so long as none of them purchases 25 percent of the acquiree bank's stock or can individually be found to " control" the bank. For these reasons, the Change in Bank Control Act assumes particular importance: the decision criteria embodied therein are somewhat broader and give the appropriate federal regulator considerable flexibility to deny a particular transaction; an individual or individuals acting in concert to purchase control are subject to the Act; and companies acting in concert to obtain controlling influence of a bank are also encompassed in the Act.

[9] The statute does not list nationality of an acquiring party as one of the factors to be considered by the FRB. 12 USC § 1842(b) and (c). Of course, a foreign banking organization may have a practical advantage, particularly when the U.S. bank to be acquired is large, because the anti-competitive effect of a merger or bank acquisition involving two U.S. banking organizations in the same state is likely to be substantial. In contrast, a foreign company that has no subsidiary bank in the U.S. is unlikely to be thwarted on competitive grounds.

[10] 12 USC § 1842(b). In view of the elaborate and detailed nature of the federal law on holding company acquisitions—including the authority conferred on the FRB to overrule the OCC or a state supervisory authority on any application—it is unclear to what extent state legislation of conferring decision-making authority on a state bank regulator with respect to specific holding company applications would be preempted. There is no question that the states can legislate general rules regarding holding company entry and expansion and establish general policies and standards with respect to such activities. Section 7 of the Bank Holding Company Act,

12 USC § 1846, indicates that the Act "shall not be construed as preventing any State from exercising such powers and jurisdiction which it now has or may hereafter have with respect to banks, bank holding companies, and subsidiaries thereof." The difficulty arises when the state law seeks to grant the state supervisor power to approve or deny a particular acquisition. Such discretion may be incompatible and inconsistent with the FRB's right to approve or deny an application regardless of what recommendation it receives from the supervisory authority, and further, in an emergency or failing bank circumstance, to do so without even holding a hearing. For a summary classification of state laws affecting the corporate acquisition of bank stock, *see* Association of Bank Holding Companies, *Bank Holding Companies: A Practical Guide to Bank Acquisitions and Mergers*, ch. VI (revised to January 1, 1979).

[11] Specifically, the Act does not apply to a "transaction subject to section 3 of the Bank Holding Company Act of 1956 (12 USC 1842) or section 18 of [the Federal Deposit Insurance Act, 12 USC 1828]." A merger or consolidation of two or more U.S. banks is treated under the Bank Merger Act. A merger or consolidation of bank holding companies is subject to approval of the FRB under the Bank Holding Company Act. Under the Bank Merger Act, 12 USC § 1828(c), an "insured bank" needs the prior approval of the FDIC before it can "(A) merge or consolidate with any noninsured bank or institution; (B) assume liability to pay any deposits . . . made in, or similar liabilities of, any noninsured bank or institution in consideration of the assumption of liabilities for any portion of the deposits made in such insured bank." Under 12 USC § 1828(c)(2), no insured bank can merge or consolidate with any other insured bank or acquire the assets of or assume liability to pay any deposits made in any other insured bank, unless the appropriate regulator approves the transaction. The appropriate agency is the OCC if the acquiring, assuming or resulting bank is a national bank, the FRB if the acquiring, assuming or resulting bank is a state member bank, and the FDIC if the acquiring, assuming or resulting bank is a nonmember insured bank. Ordinarily, the Bank Merger Act is triggered by a merger, consolidation, purchase of assets or assumption of liabilities involving two or more U.S. banks. In the context of foreign acquisitions, therefore, this law would seem relevant primarily to subsequent expansion of operations by a foreign person or company that already controls a U.S. bank. The Bank Holding Company Act or the Change in Bank Control Act would normally govern an initial entry by a foreign acquiring party.

[12] The appropriate federal banking agency is the OCC if the bank being acquired is a national bank, the FRB in the case of a bank holding company or a state member bank, and the FDIC in the case of a nonmember bank. Unlike the bank chartering statutes, the Bank Holding Company Act and the Bank Merger Act, the Change in Bank Control Act does not require an affirmative administrative approval. Instead, the law confers discretion on the federal regulator to obtain as much information about the potential control party as seems necessary to make a judgment in the matter. The regulator may deny consummation, based upon one or more of the statutory criteria—quite broad in nature—but no affirmative action of the regulator is necessary in order for the acquisition of control to take place. The Change in Bank Control Act is essentially a screening mechanism. Note also that the law only covers acquisitions of control through a transfer of voting stock; it does not cover a purchase of bank assets or an assumption of bank liabilities. However, since a purchase of bank assets or assumption of bank liabilities constitutes a "merger," it would be subject to regulatory approval under the Bank Merger Act or, if part of a bank holding company transaction, under the Bank Holding Company Act. *See* 12 USC § 1828(c)(1) and (2); 12 USC § 1842(a).

[13] Each of the federal banking agencies has issued regulations to implement the Change in Bank Control Act. *See* 12 CFR Part 15 (OCC), Part 225 (FRB), and Part 303 (FDIC), published at 44 Fed. Reg. 7119 *et seq.* (1979). Persons whose proposed acquisitions are disapproved are notified of the reason for the decision and have an opportunity to receive a hearing before the agency. There is also opportunity for a judicial review following the hearing. The regulations elaborate upon the concept of "control." Under the statute, acquisition of 25 percent or more of a class of voting stock is always a control transaction. In addition, a purchase, assignment, transfer, pledge or other disposition of voting stock through which any person will acquire

ownership, control or the power to vote 10 percent or more of a class of voting securities of an insured bank is deemed by the regulators to be an acquisition of power to direct the institution's management or policies if (1) the institution has issued any class of security subject to registration under the Securities Exchange Act of 1934 or (2) if the acquiring person will be the institution's largest shareholder. The presumptions relating to 10 percent ownership may be challenged before the agency. *Id.*

[14] 12 USC § 1817(j)(6).

[15] 12 USC § 1817(j)(7).

[16] 12 USC § 1817(j)(15).

[17] *See, e.g.,* Association of Bank Holding Companies, *Bank Holding Company Facts*, "Classification of State Laws Affecting the Corporate Acquisition of Bank Stock" 30-31 (Spring 1979); American Bankers Association, *State Banking Law Service*, ch. 10, "Chartering and Transfer of Control" 273-310 (1978). According to the holding company list, twelve states require the approval of the state supervisory authority for some or all corporate acquisitions of bank stock. An additional sixteen states impose various other types of restrictions or limitations upon corporate acquisition of bank stock. The ABA Chapter deals with acquisition of control by individuals and specifically excludes from its scope acquisitions by bank holding companies. According to the summary, thirty-three states and Puerto Rico regulate transfers of control by statute or regulation. Four of these states require any transfers in bank stock to be reported to the state supervisor. Sixteen states require notice of any transfer of "control." This concept, when defined, usually means somewhere between 10 to 25 percent of voting stock. Thirteen states and Puerto Rico empower the state supervisor to disapprove a sale to any control person who does not meet statutory standards. About half of these jurisdictions require prior approval of the regulator, and the other half confer veto authority. Many of the commercially prominent states—California, Florida, Illinois, New York, Pennsylvania, Texas—have such a screening mechanism. The statutory standards vary. The most commonly found criteria relate to the character, background and financial responsibility of the proposed new owner. Convenience and needs, the public interest, and protection of other shareholders, depositors, and creditors are other themes commonly found in these state laws. Any plans for change in the nature of business of the bank being acquired must sometimes be disclosed. Pennsylvania and Connecticut mandate that the prospective investor satisfy the standards required of an applicant for a new bank charter. Most of the states that confer disapproval power on the state regulator, and some of the "notice" states, provide for civil and criminal penalties in the event of noncompliance. All of the above state transfer of control laws were passed prior to the 1978 Change in Bank Control Act. Those laws that purport to authorize a state regulator to approve or deny specific transfers of control in bank stock may be preempted by the federal law, which confers such authority on the appropriate federal banking agency acting pursuant to statutory decision factors. The OCC has concluded that such state legislation, with respect to national banks at least, would be incompatible and inconsistent with, and therefore preempted by, the Change in Bank Control Act. The 1979 mid-year report of the American Bankers Association's Office of the State Legislative Counsel, entitled *State Banking, Credit Union, and Savings and Loan Legislation*, at page 6 indicates that North Dakota should be added to the list of states that regulate transfer of control. A new law, S.B. 2071, requires that anyone selling or purchasing control of a banking institution notify the state banking board. If the board deems a hearing necessary, notice of this fact must be given within 30 days of the notification. If no order is issued within 10 business days following the hearing, the transaction is deemed approved. "Control" means the direct or indirect ownership, control of, or power to vote 25 percent or more of any class of voting shares at the election of directors of the bank or bank holding company, whether by individuals, corporations, partnerships or trusts.

[18] *Id.* See the discussion in the previous footnote.

[19] Association of Bank Holding Companies, *Bank Holding Company Facts, supra* at 30; D. Van Praag Marks, "State Law Restrictions on the Acquisition of U.S. Banks by Foreign Parties, and on Other Modes of Foreign Entry into the American Banking Industry," Contract No. OM

(Nov. 1979). *Bank Holding Company Facts* classifies a dozen states—Florida, Iowa, Kansas, Maine, Maryland, Michigan, Mississippi, Missouri, New Jersey, New Hampshire, Oregon, and South Carolina—as jurisdictions where "acquisition of the stock of a domestic bank by an out-of-state corporation is restricted." The restrictions on acquisition of bank stock by out-of-state corporations should be distinguished from the regulation of acquisitions of bank stock by bank holding companies. A domestic or foreign bank holding company—thus, a company wherever organized, that controls a U.S. bank—is subject to the Douglas Amendment in the Bank Holding Company Act (12 USC § 1842(d)) which prohibits a bank holding company from acquiring any voting shares in any additional U.S. bank located outside the state in which the U.S. banking business of the holding company is principally conducted unless the acquisition of such shares is specifically authorized by the statute law of the state where such additional bank is located. The state law restrictions presently being discussed relate to out-of-state companies, as opposed to out-of-state bank holding companies.

[20] The Marks study, *supra* at 7, lists five states—Iowa, Maine, Michigan, New Hampshire, and Oregon—as jurisdictions which forbid or restrict acquisition of bank stock by out-of-state entities without specifying whether such provisions apply to companies organized under the laws of a foreign country or only to companies organized under the laws of another state in the U.S.

[21] Code Laws S. Car. 1976 Ann., title 34, Banking, Financial Institutions and Money, ch. 23, Bank Holding Companies, § 34-23-30(B) declares it unlawful for any "foreign holding company, whether a bank holding company or otherwise," to acquire ownership or control of more than 25 percent of the voting shares of a bank situated in South Carolina." A "foreign holding company" is defined as a "corporation, partnership, business trust, voting trust, incorporate [*sic*] associations, joint stock association or similar organization created by or organized under the laws of the U.S. and not having its principal place of business in South Carolina or under the laws of any foreign state, kingdom or government or under the laws of any state of the United States other than South Carolina." The ambiguity here arises from the fact that although the terms "company," "foreign holding company" and "bank holding company" are defined in the statute, the distinction between a holding company and a bank holding company is not spelled out. In other words, it is unclear whether a holding company that is not a bank holding company must own some shares of a U.S. bank (though not a controlling share) or shares of some finance related entity. Thus, even in those states that specify whether "foreign" refers to other states in the U.S. or encompasses other countries as well, there may be remaining questions concerning transactions that are permitted or prohibited to foreign (overseas) investors.

[22] An "alien" bank—defined as a "bank organized under the laws of a foreign country and having its principal place of business in that country, the majority of the beneficial ownership and control of which is vested in citizens of countries other than the United States"—cannot "take over or acquire an existing federal or state chartered bank, trust company, mutual savings bank, savings and loan association, or credit union or any branch of such [entity] . . .". R.C.W.A. § 30.42.010 (1978 Supp.). It is unlikely that such a law could withstand constitutional challenge, certainly as it purports to apply to federally chartered financial institutions. The authors have not found any state statute which prohibits or restricts the ownership of bank stock by foreign individuals.

[23] 12 USC § 72. Residence and citizenship qualifications for bank directors have a long history. Organic statutes creating the first and second Bank of the United States in 1791 and 1816, respectively, barred the election of aliens as directors and the giving of proxies by non-residents of the U.S. *See* Committee to Study Foreign Investment in the United States of the Section of Corporation, Banking and Business Law of the American Bar Association, *A Guide to Foreign Investment Under United States Law* 6 (1979). Section 2 of the International Banking Act of 1978, Public Law 95-369, amends 12 USC § 72 so that the OCC has discretion to waive the citizenship requirement in the case of not more than a minority of the directors of a national bank which is a subsidiary or affiliate of a foreign bank. The Senate Banking Committee explained that the waiver of citizenship provision "will facilitate foreign bank chartering and

acquisition of national bank subsidiaries, without unduly compromising the principle of local ownership and control." *See* S. Rep. No. 95-1073, 95th Cong., 2d Sess. 3 (1978). The citizenship waiver, because it is limited to a national bank that is a "subsidiary or affiliate of a foreign bank," is not available in the case of a national bank controlled by foreign individuals or by a foreign company that does not qualify under the definition of "foreign bank" contained in section 1 of the IBA. The two principal policy objectives of the IBA are to provide a system of federal regulation of foreign banking activities and establish equal treatment for foreign and domestic banks operating in the U.S. *See* H. R. Rep. No. 95-910, 95th Cong., 2d Sess. 5 (1978). Besides the citizenship waiver possibility, Congress in section 3 of the IBA amended section 25(a) of the Federal Reserve Act, 12 USC § 619, so that one or more foreign banks, with permission of the FRB, can own 50 percent or more of the stock of an Edge Corporation. Previously, majority ownership of an Edge Corporation was restricted to U.S. citizens or to companies controlled by U.S. citizens.

Most of the other changes effected by the IBA were designed to promote competitive equality between domestic and foreign banks operating in the U.S. by removing or minimizing certain advantages enjoyed by the foreign banks. Thus, a foreign bank operating at a branch or agency now faces restrictions with respect to interstate branching and nonbanking activities and is subject to reserve requirements and mandatory FDIC deposit insurance at its U.S. offices in specified circumstances. *See* IBA § § 3 (ownership in Edge Corporations), 5 (interstate branching), 8 (nonbanking activities), 7 (reserve requirements), and 6 (depositor insurance). Various provisions of the IBA, and of implementing regulations issued by the federal banking agencies, are discussed in more detail in the remainder of this paper under appropriate headings. A basic point to keep in mind is the distinction between a foreign bank and a foreign bank holding company. A foreign bank holding company may or may not be a foreign bank. It *does* "control" a U.S. bank. A foreign bank, by contrast, in the sense used in this discussion of the IBA, does not have a U.S. banking subsidiary but operates directly at a branch, agency, or commercial lending company subsidiary in the U.S. It was these foreign banks that, prior to IBA, escaped the interstate and nonbanking restrictions imposed on domestic banks and on domestic and foreign bank holding companies. About 90 percent of the branches and agencies of foreign banks were located in New York, California, and Chicago at the time the IBA passed. *See International Banking Act of 1978: Hearing on H. R. 10899 Before the Subcommittee on Financial Institutions of the Senate Committee on Banking, Housing and Urban Affairs*, 95th Cong., 2d Sess. 50 (1978).

[24] Marks, *supra* at 9 and footnotes 29-31. More specifically, 33 states require that some percentage of the directors of a state bank—usually between a majority and three-fourths—be residents of the state or a contiguous state. Sixteen of these states, plus Kentucky, require that some percentage of state bank directors—usually from three-fourths to all—be U.S. citizens. New York gives the superintendent of banking discretion to permit up to one-half of the directors to serve even though they are not U.S. citizens or residents of New York or a continguous state. *See* N.Y. Banking Law § 7001(2)(a) (McKinney 1971).

[25] The McFadden Act, as amended, 12 USC § 36(c), provides that a national bank may, with the approval of the OCC, establish and operate branches "at any point within the State in which said association is situated, if such establishment and operation are at the time authorized to State banks by the statute law of the State in question. . . ." The term "branch" is defined in 12 USC § 36(f) to include any office at which "deposits are received, or checks paid, or money lent." No state has as yet adopted legislation that permits out-of-state banks to establish branches therein. Even were this to happen, the language of 12 USC § 36(c) that authorizes a national bank to branch "within the State in which said association is situated" would apparently operate to prohibit a national bank from taking advantage of such a state statute. As of mid-1978, according to a list compiled by the American Bankers Association, 21 states permitted statewide branching, 17 states permitted limited branching, and 11 prohibited branching. Wyoming had no branching statute. Most of the prohibitive states allowed one or more "facilities" to be established, usually in the same community as the bank's main office. The

limited branching states frequently provided home-office protection by stating that a bank could not establish branches in locations close to where an existing bank has its main office. ABA, *State Banking Law Service*, ch. 4 (1978).

[26] As already discussed, this result is achieved by 12 USC § 1842(d), which provides that no application under the Bank Holding Company Act can be approved by the FRB which would permit any bank holding company or its subsidiary to acquire a bank outside the state in which its principal banking business is conducted unless "the acquisition . . . of a state bank by an out-of-state bank holding company is specifically authorized by the statute laws of the State in which such bank is located. . . ." As of February 1981, only Maine, South Dakota, and Delaware had passed laws permitting out-of-state bank holding company acquisitions in specified, limited circumstances. Seven domestic and five foreign bank holding companies that controlled banks in two or more states at the time the Bank Holding Company Act passed in 1956 were grandfathered by the Act. Association of Registered Bank Holding Companies, *The Bank Holding Company: Its History and Significance in Modern America* 27-29 (1968). Some state laws prohibit multibank holding companies within the same state. *Bank Holding Company Facts, supra* at 30-32.

[27] Under 12 USC § 215, "any national association or any bank incorporated under the laws of any State may, with the approval of the Comptroller, be consolidated with one or more national banking associations *located in the same State* under the charter of a national banking association. . . ." Under 12 USC § 215a, "one or more national banking associations or one or more State banks, with the approval of the Comptroller, . . . may merge into a national banking associations *located within the same State* . . . ." (emphasis added) Although the Bank Merger Act, 12 USC § 1828(c), does not specifically address the issue of whether two state banks may merge across state lines, the branching statutes explicitly or implicitly prohibit such a result. Ordinarily, offices of merged institutions continue to operate as branches of the surviving bank.

[28] ABA, *State Banking Law Service*, ch. 4 *supra. See also* A. S. Pratt and Sons, Inc., *Fed. Bkg. Law Serv.*, para. 438.3; CCH, *Fed. Bkg. Law Rpts.*, para. 3106 (1978).

[29] 12 USC § 1842.

[30] 12 USC § 1828(c).

[31] *See generally Bank Holding Companies: A Practical Guide to Bank Acquisitions and Mergers, supra.*

[32] This was because such foreign bank was not a foreign bank holding company subject to the Douglas Amendment in the Bank Holding Company Act. Furthermore, it was not a "bank" subject to the McFadden Act or the state branching laws in the states where the branches operated. As a practical matter, most branches of foreign banks were located in Chicago and New York. Only a handful of these engaged in the retail deposit taking business. Most "agencies" of foreign banks—defined under state law as offices not able to accept deposits, or not able to accept deposits from residents or citizens of the United States—were located in New York and California. According to figures supplied by the FRB and summarized in the Senate hearings that accompanied the International Banking Act, as of April 1978, there were 48 agencies and 59 branches in New York, 27 branches in Chicago, and 66 agencies in California. The breakdown in branches and agencies of foreign banks in other jurisdictions was as follows: two branches in Puerto Rico, two branches in Guam, three branches in the Virgin Islands, two agencies in Florida, four agencies in Georgia, one agency in Hawaii, three branches in Massachusetts, two branches in Oregon, and eight branches in the State of Washington. *International Banking Act of 1978: Hearing on H.R. 10899 Before the Subcomm. on Financial Institutions of the Senate Comm. on Banking, Housing, and Urban Affairs*, 95th Cong., 2d Sess. 50 (1978).

[33] 12 USC § 3103.

[34] Generally, an Edge Corporation may receive in the United States demand, savings and time deposits from foreign governments and their instrumentalities, persons (individuals and organizations) conducting business principally at offices or establishments abroad, and individuals residing abroad. An Edge Corporation may also receive domestic deposits in certain other defined circumstances. *See* 12 CFR 211.4(e), as amended in final form by the FRB June 20, 1979,

44 Fed. Reg. 36009. Under the grandfather provisions in § 5b of the International Banking Act of 1978, 12 USC § 3103(b), a foreign bank can establish and operate, outside its home state, any branch, agency, or bank or commercial lending company subsidiary which commenced business or for which an application had been lawfully filed on or before July 27, 1978. The FRB's implementation of this home state rule contains the following elements:

(1) A foreign bank with no deposit taking offices in the United States, even though it may have offices in more than one state that do not take deposits, is not required to select a home state.

(2) The home state of a foreign bank with one branch or subsidiary bank, and no other offices, in the United States, is the state in which that branch or subsidiary bank is located.

(3) A foreign bank can change its home state once, such change to be conditioned upon the foreign bank either closing branches opened in reliance on its original home state designation, or converting such branches to agency or limited branch status of the Edge Act variety, and divesting any interest acquired in banks in reliance upon its original home state designation.

(4) Under § 5(a) of the IBA and § 3(d) of the Bank Holding Company Act, a foreign bank with a subsidiary bank in one state (state X) and a branch in another state (state Y) that declares state Y as its home state is prohibited from acquiring more than five percent of the shares of an additional bank in state Y (by the provisions of § 3(d) of the Bank Holding Company Act) or from acquiring more than five percent of the shares of an additional bank in state X (by the provision of § 5(a)(5) of the IBA). The FRB is concerned that a foreign bank might be able to acquire an additional bank *by merger* in state X and at the same time continue to expand its deposit taking capabilities in state Y by further branching. It therefore requires that a foreign bank with a subsidiary bank (or banks) and branches located in different states that chooses as its home state a state other than where its subsidiary bank is located be required to give the FRB 60 days' notice prior to acquiring all or substantially all of the assets of a larger bank outside its home state. The FRB would then make a determination as to whether the foreign bank should be required to show cause as to why its home state should not be changed to the state where its subsidiary bank is located. *See* 45 Fed. Reg. 67056 (1980), to be codified at 12 CFR 211.21-22.

[35] These offices have traditionally been treated as exempt, at least at the federal level, from the McFadden Act and state law branching restrictions because they are not "branches" at which "deposits are received, or checks paid, or money lent." They are essentially representative offices that perform a customer relations and promotion function for the parent bank. According to a summary in the *Legal Times of Washington*, April 9, 1979, at 31, loan production offices are permitted in 16 states, not permitted in 19 states, and in six states there is no statutory ruling on the subject. The Independent Bankers Association of American estimates that there are 360 LPO's throughout the country. The legality of the OCC's Interpretive Ruling 7.7380, 12 CFR 7.7380, which authorized national banks to establish LPO's, has recently been upheld by the U.S. Circuit Court of Appeals in the District of Columbia. *See Independent Bankers Association of America* v. *John G. Heimann*, (Civ. Action No. 79-1696) (June 11, 1980 opinion), reversing a lower court decision.

[36] 12 CFR 211.4(c), as amended in final form at 44 Fed. Reg. 36005 (1979). The FRB's liberalization of rules pertaining to Edge Corporations, including the new branching rule, is being done pursuant to a congressional mandate expressed in § 3 of the International Banking Act of 1978 that such corporations should not be unduly restricted or limited in their operations.

[37] 12 USC § 1843(c)(8).

[38] P. Heller, *Handbook of Federal Bank Holding Company Law* 229-59 (1976).

[39] 12 USC § 601 *et seq.*; 12 USC § 1828(*I*); Regulation K, 12 CFR Part 211, now encompassing former Regulation M (Foreign Activities of National Banks, 12 CFR Part 213) and por-

tions of former Regulation Y (12 CFR Part 225). Under 12 CFR 211.3, a national or state member bank that has branches in two or more foreign countries may establish initial branches in additional foreign countries after 60 days' notice to the FRB, and, without prior approval or prior notice, a national or state member bank may establish additional branches in any foreign country in which it operates one or more foreign branches. *See* 44 Fed. Reg. 36008 (1979). See the text and accompanying footnotes on product market segmentation in this paper for more details on foreign activities of national and state banks.

[40] 12 USC § 24(7).

[41] American Bankers Association, *State Banking Law Service*, ch. 5 "Banking Powers and 'Wild Card' Statutes" (1978 revision).

[42] Glass-Steagall § § 16, 20, 21, 32, codified at 12 USC § § 24(7), 78, 377, 378.

[43] 12 USC § 378.

[44] 12 USC § 24(7).

[45] 12 USC § 377.

[46] Section 4 of the Bank Holding Company Act, 12 USC § 1843.

[47] 12 USC § 1843(c)(6).

[48] 12 USC § 1843(c)(8).

[49] 12 USC § 1843(c)(13).

[50] 12 USC § 1843(c)(9). The exemption provided by § 4(c)(9) is implemented by Regulation Y, 12 CFR 225.4(g). The § 4(c)(9) exemption is somewhat more liberal than the § 4(c) (13) exemption, available to domestic bank holding companies, because the controlled foreign company merely must conduct the "greater part" of its business outside the U.S. A policy issue reflected in the FRB's actions under § 4(c)(9) is the national interest in assuring a healthy environment for the operations of U.S. banks abroad and in avoiding discouragement of foreign investment in this country. A relevant consideration is whether it is better to allow foreign banks to engage in activities in the U.S. that the foreign country involved permits to U.S. banks (reciprocity), or better to permit foreign banks to engage in activities in the United States that U.S. banks are permitted in the U.S. with the understanding that the foreign country will allow U.S. banks to engage in the foreign country in activities permitted to the foreign country's banks (national treatment). The Board has generally administered the Bank Holding Company Act, and the § 4(c)(9) exemption specifically, on the basis of national treatment, seeking to promote competitive equality between foreign and domestic banks, whether they are operating in the U.S. under U.S. rules or abroad under the laws of the foreign country involved. *See* Heller, *supra* at 283; 36 Fed. Reg. 11944 (1971); *Cf. Bank of Tokyo, Ltd*/Tokyo Bancorp. International (Houston), 61 Fed. Res. Bull. 449 (1975). *See also* n. 120 *supra*, which discusses the FRB's recently proposed redefinition of "foreign bank holding company" for purposes of the section 4(c)(9) exemption.

[51] Note that this Bank Holding Company Act § 2(h) exemption, 12 USC § 1841(h), is only available to those foreign bank holding companies whose principal business overseas is banking. The § 2(h) exemption was added to the Bank Holding Company Act in 1966 by Pub. Law 89-485, § 6. It originally exempted from the nonbanking prohibitions "shares of any company organized under the laws of a foreign country that does not do any business within the United States, if such shares are held or acquired by a bank holding company that is principally engaged in the banking business outside the United States." Section 8(e) of the International Banking Act of 1978 broadened the exemption to its present form.

[52] IBA § 8(e), amending 12 USC § 1841(h).

[53] Sections 25 and 25(a) of the Federal Reserve Act, 12 USC § § 601-604a, 611-632. The FRB's Regulation K, 12 CFR Part 211, which implements these sections of the law, has recently been revised and expanded at 44 Fed. Reg. 36005 (1979) to encompass rescinded Regulation M (12 CFR Part 213, Foreign Activities of National Banks) and § 225.4(f) of Regulation Y (12 CFR Part 225.4(f), Foreign Activities of Domestic Bank Holding Companies). It is stated in § 211.1 of revised Regulation K that the Part is in furtherance of the purposes of the Federal Reserve Act, the Bank Holding Company Act and the International Banking Act. The regula-

tion applies to Edge and Agreement Corporations, to member banks with respect to their foreign branches and investments in foreign banks under § 25 of the Federal Reserve Act (12 USC §§ 601-604a), and to bank holding companies with respect to the § 4(c)(13) exemption from the nonbanking prohibitions of the Bank Holding Company Act (12 USC § 1843(c)(13). Footnote one to Regulation K explains that § 25 of the Federal Reserve Act, which refers to national banking associations, "also applies to State member banks of the Federal Reserve System by virtue of § 9 of the FRA (12 USC 321)." *See* 44 Fed. Reg. 36007 (1979).

[54] 12 USC § 604a; 12 CFR 211.3, as revised at 44 Fed. Reg. 36008 (1979).

[55] 12 CFR Part 211, 44 Fed. Reg. 36007 (1979). The regulation at § 211.7(c)(2) provides that "Edge Corporations, member banks, and bank holding companies shall file such reports on their foreign activities as the Board may require." The OCC's regulations at 12 CFR 20.1(b) indicate that the notifications and reports which national banks must furnish to the OCC in connection with their foreign branches, or their interests in any Edge Corporation, Agreement Corporation or foreign bank, "will provide the basis, where needed, for special examination by [the OCC], and for the issuance of appropriate instructions."

[56] 12 CFR 211.5(b)(5). A U.S. "investor" must also, unless the FRB authorizes retention, dispose of an investment that engages in the general business of buying or selling goods, wares, merchandise, or commodities in the United States or transacts any business in the United States that is not incidental to its international or foreign business. *Id.*

[57] 12 USC § 1828(*l*). As of mid-1978, at least 13 states, including many of the commercially prominent ones, specifically authorized state banks to establish branches abroad. *See* American Bankers Association, *State Banking Law Service*, ch. 4, "Branching," Appendix C (July 1978 revision).

[58] 12 USC § 1828(*l*). The FDIC has amended certain portions of its regulations—12 CFR Parts 303, 304, and 332—and adopted a new regulation—12 CFR Part 347 (Foreign Activities of Insured State Nonmember Bank)—to implement the new law. The guidelines established in the new regulation generally parallel those adopted by the FRB for member banks. *See* 44 Fed. Reg. 25193, 25195 (1979).

[59] 12 USC § 24(7); 12 CFR Part 1.

[60] *Id.* There are a number of narrowly defined exceptions to this general prohibition. *See, e.g.*, 12 USC §§ 1861-1865 (bank service corporations); 12 CFR 7.7376 (operating subsidiaries).

[61] 12 USC §§ 51-51c, 56, 60, and relevant interpretive rulings of the OCC published at 12 CFR Part 7.

[62] *See respectively* 12 USC §§ 82 (borrowing), 371 (real estate loans), 84 (lending limits), 372 and 373 (bankers' acceptances).

[63] Section 23A of the Federal Reserve Act, 12 USC § 371c, applied to nonmember insured banks by § 18(j) of the Federal Deposit Insurance Act, 12 USC § 1828(j). The International Banking Act of 1978 has amended the definitional section of the Federal Deposit Insurance Act so that the term "insured bank" includes "a foreign bank having an insured branch." Some interpretive problems flow from this amendment. Dozens of federal statutory provisions apply to "insured banks." Is the parent foreign bank considered the insured bank, or is the definition limited in most contexts to the insured branch or branches within the United States? A related problem stems from the fact that branches and agencies, unlike domestic subsidiary banks, are really extensions of the parent institution and any separate corporate identity is largely artificial in nature. The Congress and the federal banking agencies have, in a variety of ways, taken steps to regulate the U.S. branches and agencies and at the same time to avoid undue intrusiveness into the affairs of the parent foreign institutions. With reference to the affiliate transactions statute, section 6(c)(28) of the IBA specifically addresses the definitional problem by adding a final sentence to 12 USC § 1828(j)(1):

> The provisions of this subsection [applying the 12 USC § 371c affiliate transactions statute to nonmember insured banks] shall not apply to any foreign bank having an insured branch with respect to dealings between such bank and any affiliate thereof.

By logical deduction, it becomes evident that the affiliate transactions statute also does not apply to dealings between a foreign bank and its *uninsured* branches and agencies in the United States.

[64] 12 USC § § 371c, 1828(j).

[65] 12 USC § 1841(h).

[66] *See* Financial Institutions Regulatory and Interest Rate Control Act of 1978, Pub. L. No. 95-630, § 104, codified at 12 USC § § 375a and 375b. The provisions of 12 USC § 375b relating to limitations on extensions of credit to executive officers, directors and shareholders are applied to nonmember insured banks by 12 USC § 1828(j)(2). This section was added to the Federal Deposit Insurance Act by FIRIRCA § 108. For more details on insider transactions, including reports that must be filed by banks and insiders, *see* the FRB's implementing Regulation O, 12 CFR Part 215, revised in final form at 44 Fed. Reg. 67973 (1979).

[67] Financial Institutions Regulatory and Interest Rate Control Act of 1978, Pub. L. No. 95-630, § 801 (correspondent accounts), codified at 12 USC § 1972.

[68] Financial Institutions Regulatory and Interest Rate Control Act of 1978, Pub. L. No. 95-630, § 901 (disclosure of material facts), codified at 12 USC § 1817(k). Title 8 of FIRIRCA prohibits banks that maintain correspondent account relationships with other banks from extending credit on preferential terms to one another's executive officers, directors and principal shareholders. This statutory prohibition is self explanatory and therefore not elaborated upon in any implementing regulations. Regulation O does cover the reporting requirements established by Titles 8 and 9 of FIRIRCA. Under these titles, a bank that controls another bank could be viewed as a principal shareholder and subject to the reporting requirements. This situation would arise mainly in the case of foreign banks, since U.S. banks are generally prohibited from holding the shares of another bank. Regulation O as adopted in final form excludes banks (including foreign banks) from the definition of principal shareholder for purposes of the Title 8 and 9 reporting requirements. Individuals and nonbank companies that control such banks, however, *are* principal shareholders and have to file reports. The federal banking agencies have adopted this approach in the belief that the reporting burdens would be substantial and achieve no real purpose in the case of normal and routine inter-bank transactions. The exclusion of bank principal shareholders from the reporting requirements of Titles 8 and 9 is consistent with the lending restrictions of § 22(h) of the Federal Reserve Act (Title 1 of FIRIRCA, 12 USC § 375b, which excludes insured banks as principal shareholders, the exemption from the affiliate lending restrictions of § 23A of the Federal Reserve Act (12 USC § 371c) for loans by a member bank to an insured bank, where the member bank owns 50 percent of the insured bank's voting shares, and the intent by Congress not to disrupt transactions between a bank and its correspondents. The FRB also observed in a footnote to the final Regulation O that because foreign banks and U.S. bank subsidiaries deal with many of the same correspondent banks, the inclusion of the foreign bank as a principal shareholder would restrict or even prohibit normal transactions between the foreign bank and its own correspondent banks. For similar reasons, banks (including foreign banks) are excluded from the definition of "related interest" in the final regulations. *See generally* 44 Fed. Reg. 67973 *et seq.* (1979).

[69] 12 USC § 1813(m), 1817(i), 1821(a)(1), 1821(i), as amended by the Depository Institutions Deregulation and Monetary Control Act of 1980, Pub. L. No. 96-221, § 308(a); 12 CFR Part 305.

[70] In addition to the laws that will be discussed in this section of the paper, it should be noted that Congress has in the past few years enacted several statutes designed to collect data or achieve disclosure on foreign investment in commercial enterprises in this country. Although not singled out for special attention, U.S. banks and bank holding companies are obviously affected by such developments. Thus, in 1974 Congress directed the Commerce and the Treasury Departments to conduct studies of foreign direct (more than 10 percent ownership) and portfolio (less than 10 percent ownership) investment and report back. The reports were submitted to Congress in 1976. Both departments concluded that there was no cause for alarm but did recommend that data collected on foreign investments be improved on an ongoing basis. Con-

gress enacted the International Investment Survey Act of 1976 to authorize the President to collect information on international investment and to provide analyses of such information to the Congress, the executive agencies, and the general public. The Act expressly declared that it was not intended "to restrain or deter foreign investment in the United States or United States investment abroad." *Guide to Foreign Investment Under United States Law, supra* 12-19, 16. Another disclosure requirement was added to the Foreign Corrupt Practices Act of 1977 by the Domestic and Foreign Investment Improved Disclosure Act of 1977. *See* Title II of Pub. L. No. 95-213, 91 Stat. 1498 (1977). Among other things, this law amended the reporting requirements of § 13(d) of the Securities Exchange Act of 1934 to add citizenship and residence to the facts that must be disclosed by beneficial owners of 5 percent of the registered equity securities of U.S. issuers. While reporting and disclosure have been the main themes of legislation enacted in recent years in response to the rise in foreign investment in the United States, there has also been some concern about foreign government commercial activities in this country. In 1976 Congress passed the Foreign Sovereign Immunities Act, Pub. L. No. 94-583, 90 Stat. 2891, which codified the evolving judicial doctrine that a foreign government is not immune from the jurisdiction of U.S. courts with respect to its commercial activities or property. Sovereign immunity is automatically waived in such circumstances. *Id.* 19-20.

[71] 12 CFR Part 16. The FRB and the FDIC have no regulations on offering circulars by state banks. Instead, state authorities are relied upon to regulate such activities. The Securities Act of 1933 (the 1933 Act) provides for disclosure, primarily through the mechanism of a registration statement and a prospectus, of all pertinent information concerning securities being publicly offered and sold in interstate commerce or through the mails. Banks are exempt from the registration and prospectus provisions pursuant to § 3(a)(2) of the 1933 Act. Bank holding company stock, however, is subject to registration with the SEC and to that Agency's general enforcement jurisdiction under the 1933 Act and under the Securities Exchange Act of 1934 (the 1934 Act).

[72] Section 12(i) of the 1934 Act confers on the federal banking agencies authority to administer and enforce, with respect to the banks they supervise, the 1934 Act sections relating to registration requirements for securities being traded (§ 12), reports (§ 13), proxies (§ 14), and insider trading activities (§ 16). However, as already mentioned, bank holding companies are subject to the 1933 and 1934 Acts as administered by the SEC. This is an important fact to remember because most of the large U.S. banks are subsidiaries of holding companies. A foreign acquirer of holding company stock would thus be subject to the reporting, disclosure and other rules and procedures of the SEC. Acquisition of banks is discussed in the text, so holding companies will be the focus here. Essentially, there are five different ways that the acquisition of a domestic bank holding company by a foreign investor may be effectuated: the foreign investor may buy assets for cash, exchange assets, carry out a merger, exchange its securities for securities of the U.S. target company, or buy the U.S. target company's shares for cash. Each of these approaches will be summarized very briefly. For further details, consult Chapter 4 of the *Guide to Foreign Investment Under United States Law, supra* and the source material cited therein. (1) A purchase of assets for cash enables the purchaser to avoid SEC registration (with its costs and delays) which is usually required when securities are exchanged for assets. But most state corporation statutes require shareholder approval for the sale of substantially all of a corporation's assets, which means that the selling U.S. holding company may have to hold a shareholders meeting and solicit proxies. If the seller's securities are registered pursuant to section 12 of the 1934 Act, the SEC's proxy rules would apply. (2) If instead of purchasing assets for cash, the foreign investor acquires the assets in exchange for securities, the domestic holding company encounters basically the same questions of state law with respect to shareholder approval, dissenting shareholder rights, bulk sales law protections for creditors, and sales taxes on the transfer, and the same need to comply with SEC proxy rules when shareholder approval is sought. In addition, the purchaser will have to satisfy the registration requirements of the federal and state securities laws for the securities exchanged for the assets. (3) A merger may take one of three forms: a straight merger, a triangular merger, or a reverse triangular merger. A

straight merger is a merger of the acquired company into a U.S. subsidiary of the foreign investor. The U.S. subsidiary issues its stock to the shareholders of the acquired company. A triangular merger involves a merger of the acquired company into a U.S. subsidiary of the foreign investor pursuant to which the shareholders of the acquired company receive stock of the foreign investor. A reverse triangular merger is a merger of a domestic subsidiary of the foreign investor into the acquired corporation. In such a transaction, the shareholders of the acquired corporation receive stock of the foreign investor and the foreign investor acquires all the stock of the acquired corporation. Regardless of the consideration used in a merger—securities or cash—state corporation statutes typically require shareholder approval of the merger, and proxy materials are therefore required. Shareholders typically have dissenters' rights. (4) The acquisition of stock in exchange for securities is the least popular means of acquisition employed by foreign investors generally, according to the 1976 Commerce Department report to Congress. This may be due to the cost and delays entailed in registration procedures under federal and state securities laws and, more particularly, to the fact that the securities of a foreign issuer may not be attractive to the holders of U.S. shares because the securities are unfamiliar. (5) Acquisition of the voting shares of the target company for cash generally entails a tender offer of some kind, with the attendant securities laws requirements. In addition to the SEC reporting requirements, including the disclosure of citizenship or place of incorporation of 5 percent equity shareholders, both the Treasury and the Commerce Departments require reports of shareholder ownership by foreign persons in connection with their delegated duties under the International Investment Survey Act of 1976. Acquisition of a bank holding company would ordinarily fall within the scope of these more general statutes.

[73] Sections 12(b) and (g) of the 1934 Act.

[74] 12 CFR Part 11 (OCC), Part 206 (FRB), and Part 335 (FDIC).

[75] *Id.*

[76] Section 14(b) of the 1934 Act.

[77] *See e.g.*, 12 CFR 11.54, 44 Fed. Reg. 69614 (1979).

[78] Section 13(d) of the 1934 Act.

[79] *See* 12 CFR Parts 11, 206, 335.

[80] *Id.*; § 16 of the 1934 Act.

[81] § § 12(2) and 17 of the 1933 Act; § 10 and Rule 10 b-5, 1934 Act.

[82] For details concerning state securities laws—popularly known as blue sky laws—*see* CCH, *Blue Sky L. Rep.*; Gray, *Blue Sky Practice—A Morass?* 15 Wayne L. Rev. 1519 (1969). More generally, *Guide to Foreign Investment Under United States Law, supra*, particularly ch. 4, has a good discussion of the impact of the securities laws on foreign acquisitions. Bank holding companies, as already mentioned, fit into the general securities law scheme as administered by the SEC. According to Marks, *supra* 9 and footnote 34, ten states have enacted legislation that regulates takeovers when a bank is the target. Other states regulate takeovers of companies generally albeit not banks specifically. It is noted in *Guide to Foreign Investment Under United States Law, supra* 105-06, that since 1968, when the Williams Act amendments to the 1934 Act were passed, an increasing number of states have adopted legislation regulating corporate takeovers by tender offer. Many of these laws impose restrictions and requirements different from those imposed by the 1934 Act. In general, the state takeover statutes require advance notice of a tender offer and a longer offering period than the Williams Act, the filing of disclosure documents with the state agency, and administrative hearings (in some cases at the instance of the target company and in others at the discretion of the agency) on the adequacy of disclosure and, in some cases, "fairness." Most state statutes do not apply to "friendly" tender offers—those favored by the target company's management.

[83] Marks, *supra* 9-10. Of course, state takeover laws may offer more protection to existing management than to shareholders in any particular instance. Furthermore, it is unclear to what extent such laws can withstand constitutional challenge. *Great Western United* v. *Kidwell*, 439 F. Supp. 420 (N. D. Tex), *aff'd.* 577 F .2d 1256 (5th Cir. 1978), *rev'd. on other grounds*, 99 S. Ct. 2710 (1979), held the Idaho takeover statute unconstitutional on preemption and burden on interstate commerce grounds. The preemption stems from inconsistency with the federal

securities laws regulation of tender offers and takeovers generally. The Idaho law did not cover banks specifically but the rationale of the *Kidwell* case would seem to be relevant in a banking context. The Maryland law, which forbids "unfriendly" takeovers, is currently being challenged in connection with the proposed acquisition of Financial General Bancshares, Inc. by certain foreign investors. *See* Brief for Petitioners, in the D. C. Cir. Court of Appeals, No. 79-1294 (1979).

[84] 15 USC § 1601 *et. seq.*; 12 CFR Part 226.

[85] 12 USC § 1691; 12 CFR Part 202.

[86] 12 USC § § 1814, 1816, 1828(c), 1842(c).

[87] ABA, *State Banking Law Service, supra* at ch. 10, Appendix, "Chartering Requirements" (1978).

[88] Pub. L. No. 95-128, codified at 12 USC § 2901 *et. seq.*

[89] K. Davis, *Administrative Law Treatise*, vol. 1, § 4.04 (1958) comments on bank supervision as follows: "Probably the outstanding example in the federal government of regulation of an entire industry through methods of supervision, and almost entirely without formal adjudication, is the regulation of national banks. The regulation of banking may be more extensive than the regulation of any other industry, and it is the oldest system of economic regulation. The system may be one of the most successful, if not the most successful. . . . The substantive systems of regulation by such nonbanking agencies as the ICC, FPC, and FCC are much the same as one portion of the system of regulation by the banking agencies, the portion having to do with the requirement of licenses and approvals. The major substantive difference in the systems of regulation is that the banking agencies have and the nonbanking agencies lack the power of close supervision of day to day operations." The statement remains true today. It should be noted that Mr. Davis, in more recent publications, has raised some objections to the far-reaching powers exercised by the federal banking agencies on procedural fairness or due process grounds. *See, e.g.*, Davis, *Administrative Procedure in the Regulation of Banking*, Law and Contemporary Problems, v. 31 at 713 *et seq.* (Autumn 1966).

[90] 12 USC § 1820(c).

[91] 12 USC § 1818(n).

[92] 12 USC § 481.

[93] 12 USC § § 161(a), 161(c), 324, 334, 1817(a).

[94] 12 USC § § 164, 324, 334, 1817(a).

[95] 18 USC § § 1001, 1005, 1006.

[96] See, *e.g.*, 12 USC § § 161, 1817(j) & (k), and 31 USC § § 1051-1122; 12 CFR Parts 4.11(b), 4.13, 9, 11, 15, 16, 20, 215, and 31 CFR Part 128. A convenient summary of the types of reports commonly required of national banks is contained in *Comptroller's Handbook for National Bank Examiners* § 408 (Feb. 1980).

[97] *See generally*, C. Stirnweis, A Review of the National Bank Surveillance System (Manuscript, Pacific Coast Banking School, April 1977); U.S. Treasury Department, OCC, *The NBSS Bank Performance Report: A User's Guide for Bankers and Examiners* (1978); S. Stratton, Early Warning Systems: Identification of Future Problem Banks (Manuscript, Pacific Coast Banking School, Aug. 1979); Information concerning the national banking system, prepared by the OCC, printed in *Third Meeting on the Condition of the Financial System: Hearing Before Sen. Comm. on Banking, Housing, and Urban Affairs*, 96th Cong., 1st Sess. 264-330 (1979); Examining Circular No. 160, Banks Requiring Special Supervisory Attention: Composite Rated 3, 4, and 5 Banks (Aug. 12, 1977); Supp. No. I to Examining Circular No. 160 (May 9, 1980); Examining Circular No. 159 (Revised), Uniform Financial Institutions Rating System (Dec. 10, 1979); Statement of John G. Heimann, Comptroller of the Currency, Before the Senate Committee on Banking, Housing, and Urban Affairs, May 21, 1980 at 19-20 (OCC press release) (hereafter, "Heimann May 21, 1980 statement.")

[98] Stirnweis, *supra*; Stratton, *supra* at 26-44. As currently operated, NBSS consists of the following elements:

(1) The Bank Performance Report (BPR). BPRs are produced from a data base obtained

from official reports of condition and income and other reports submitted by banks and some separate reports submitted by bank examiners. As a reflection of the bank's official financial reports in a form which can be readily analyzed, the BPR is utilized as a bank supervisory, examination and management tool showing the effect of management's decisions and economic conditions on the bank's performance and composition. The reports contain several years of data, updated quarterly, displayed in a variety of ratios, percentages, and dollar figures. Each report also contains corresponding ratios for the bank's peer group and percentage rankings of some ratios. Special peer groups may be identified for the purposes of displaying areas of vulnerability arising from a variety of economic occurrences.

(2) An Anomaly Severity Ranking System (ASRS). ASRS is a computerized scoring system which allocates the highest numerical score to those banks having the most abnormal positions, changes, and trends in performance or composition. The performance ASRS measures the current positions, the short-term changes, and the long-term trends of significant performance ratios. The composition ASRS measures the short-term changes in the components of certain groups of assets and liabilities. Those banks receiving the highest scores are selected for special review. The overall purpose of ASRS is to function as a computerized early warning system.

(3) Analysis by NBSS Specialists. A specially trained national bank examiner reviews and analyzes the BPRs and other available information on each bank selected by ASRS. The NBSS specialist's conclusions and recommendations are presented in writing to a regional administrator. Identification of serious conditions of potential concern result in examination, investigation, or discussions with bank management.

(4) Action Control System (ACS). A separate element of the NBSS provides status, progress, and summary reports at preselected intervals to regional administrators and other senior OCC officials on those banks selected for primary review.

(5) A bank holding company performance report (BHCPR) was introduced into the NBSS during 1979. This report is designed to produce data similar to that produced by the BPR but on an integrated holding company basis in order to permit similar timely analysis of overall trends in holding company performance and the relationship of those trends to the condition of individual banks within the holding company system. The NBSS video display system provides terminal access in each OCC regional office to the NBSS data base and statistical data derived from examination reports.

[99] Examining Circular No. 159 (Revised), 160, Supp. No. I to 160 and 161 *supra*.

[100] *Id.*

[101] Heimann May 21, 1980 statement, *supra* 19-20.

[102] *See, e.g.*, Fact Sheet on Multinational Banking Division (undated OCC news release); Heimann, *Supervision of International Bank Lending*, International Conference of Banking Supervisors, London July 5-6, 1979 at 12-16.

[103] *Comptroller's Handbook for National Bank Examiners*, Introduction, § 1.1 (Feb. 1980).

[104] Historically, on-site examinations tended to focus on past bank performance. There was no systematic attempt to evaluate current trends in bank policies, procedures and standards which might serve as a useful early warning system and predictor of future performance. As a result of certain studies undertaken and changes implemented in the mid-1970s, the OCC's approach now emphasizes the development and analysis of information with predictive value for bank performance and risk. *See, e.g.*, OCC Haskins and Sells Study 1974-1975, § § A, B-3 through 19, C; Comptroller General of the United States, *Federal Supervision of State and National Banks*, ch. 4-5, 7 (Jan. 31, 1977).

[105] *See generally Comptroller's Handbook for National Bank Examiners* (Feb. 1980); *Comptroller's Handbook for Consumer Examinations (1979); Comptroller's Handbook for National Trust Examiners* (1979).

[106] *Id.*

[107] *Id.*

[108] *Id.*

[109] *See* 12 CFR Parts 20, 211, and 347.

[110] *Comptroller's Handbook for National Bank Examiners*, International, § § 800 *et seq.* (Feb. 1980). *See also* Annual Report of the Comptroller of the Currency, International Banking and Finance at 39 (1978), which highlights the international examinations area as follows:

> Examinations of international divisions, foreign branches and foreign affiliates are especially tailored to the organizational, geographical and reporting structure of the banks under examination. Examiners evaluate the quality of international loan and investment portfolios and analyze foreign exchange activities, reporting procedures, accounting and bookkeeping systems, and the adequacy of internal controls and audit programs. During 1978, approximately 175 national bank examiners participated in examinations of international banking divisions in the 14 regions. Over the same period, 142 examiners traveled to 19 countries to examine 61 foreign branches. The assets of the other foreign branches, including 'shell' branches, were examined using records maintained at the banks' head offices or elsewhere. Three foreign subsidiaries and 10 electronic data processing centers were examined on-site. The Office maintains a permanent staff of six examiners in London who are responsible for continuously supervising the activities of the branches of 26 national banks located there.

In late 1978, the OCC, the FRB and the FDIC adopted uniform procedures for evaluating and commenting on "country risk" factors in international lending by U.S. banks. Under the new system, implemented during 1979, examiners in the three agencies segregate country risk factors from the evaluation of other lending risks, and deal with this special category of lending risk in a separate section of their examination reports. The commercial credit risk in the bank's international portfolios continue to be assessed on an individual loan basis according to "traditional" standards of credit analysis. A key element in the new procedures is the assessment of bank managers' ability to analyze and monitor country risk in banks' international lending. *See, e.g.*, Heimann May 21, 1980 statement at 19-20.

[111] OCC, Annual Report at 39 (1978).

[112] *See, e.g.*, 12 USC § § 325, 481, 1813(q), 1820(b) and (c), 1844.

[113] 12 USC § § 3301, 3305(a).

[114] 12 USC § § 3301, 3305(b).

[115] *Oversight Hearing Into the Effectiveness of Federal Bank Regulation (Regulation of Problem Banks) Before a Subcomm. of the House Comm. on Government Operations*, 94th Cong., 2nd Sess. (1976); *Problem Banks: Hearings Before Sen. Comm. on Banking, Housing and Urban Affairs*, 94th Cong., 2nd Sess. (1976); Comptroller General of the United States, *Federal Supervision of State and National Banks*, ch. 11 (Jan. 31, 1977); Comptroller General of the United States, *Report to Congress: Federal Supervision of Bank Holding Companies Needs Better, More Formalized Coordination* (Feb. 12, 1980) (hereafter, "GAO Feb. 12, 1980 report").

[116] GAO Feb. 12, 1980 report at 1.

[117] The Council in December, 1979 recommended, and the bank regulatory agencies adopted, two policy statements that summarize the major steps being taken to achieve better supervision of bank holding companies. The first policy statement requires coordinated inspections and examinations of a holding company and its lead bank in the case of (1) bank holding companies with consolidated assets of $10 billion; (2) any holding company or lead bank rated 4 or 5 in the 5-category uniform rating system applied by the regulators to banks and holding companies; and (3) any holding company or lead bank that is rated 3 if the institution's financial condition has worsened significantly since the last examination. To the extent possible, other banks in multibank holding company systems will be examined on a coordinated basis as well. State supervisory authorities will be kept informed and encouraged to participate where state banks are concerned. The second policy statement requires a federal banking agency that is contemplating a formal enforcement action against an institution that it supervises to notify and con-

sult with the other two federal bank regulators before instituting the action. If there is disagreement among the agencies concerning the appropriateness of some proposed supervisory action, the matter may be referred to the Council for consideration. State supervisory authorities will be notified when a holding company or state bank is involved. *See*, letter of Dec. 7, 1979, from John G. Heimann, Chairman of the Council, to Allen R. Voss, of the General Accounting Office, with attachments, reprinted in GAO Feb. 12, 1980 report, Appendix IV.

[118] GAO Feb. 12, 1980 report at iii-iv, 17-22.

[119] FRB Press Release dated Feb. 23, 1979, accompanied by statement of policy on supervision and regulation of foreign bank holding companies, reprinted in Practicing Law Institute, *International Banking Operations in the U.S.: An Update* 97-103 (1979).

[120] *Id*. Proposed Report of Intercompany Transactions for Foreign Bank Holding Companies and Their U.S. Bank Subsidiaries (F.R. Y-8f), 44 Fed. Reg. 6294 (1979); Proposed Report Requirement: Annual Report of Foreign Bank Holding Companies, Foreign Banks and Foreign Parent Companies (F.R. Y-7), 44 Fed. Reg. 64906 (1979). The Board issued final report forms on February 9, 1981. *See also*, revision of Regulation K, 45 Fed. Reg. 81537 (1980) which, among other things, limits the Bank Holding Company Act § 4(c) (9) exemption for nonbanking activities to only those foreign banking organizations that are primarily engaged in the banking business abroad. The rationale for such a change relates in part to the fact that foreign banks are ordinarily more carefully supervised and regulated than nonbank companies. The U.S. supervisory authorities can therefore more easily cooperate with foreign supervisory authorities in the regulation of international activities and operations when the foreign parent is a banking organization. A foreign parent that is not primarily a banking organization abroad will have to divest its nonbank subsidiaries or qualify under the more stringent test imposed by § § 4(c) (8) or 4(c) (13) of the Bank Holding Company Act.

[121] One commentator has described a number of these events as follows:

> Beginning with the collapse of Herstatt Bank in West Germany, a succession of rumors and crises hit bank after bank in Europe, the United States and elsewhere. In Great Britain there was a liquidity crisis in the secondary banking sector, brought on by a collapse of real estate values; in Switzerland, Italy, Belgium and the United States there were losses attributable to unwise or unauthorized foreign-exchange operations; and in several countries there were chain-reactions to collapses rumored or announced in other countries. Confidence in the stability of the banks was disturbed, to put it mildly, by the apparent inability of bank managements to correct unauthorized dealing, and of the regulatory authorities to head off trouble before it could spill over to the markets of other countries.

Hutton, "The Regulation of Foreign Banks—A European Viewpoint," *Columbia Journal of World Business*, p. 109 (Winter 1975).

[122] *See generally* Blunden, *International Cooperation in Banking Supervision*, Bank of England Quarterly Bulletin, June 1977; "Supervising the Euromarket Dinosaur," *The Banker* at 77 *et seq*. (August 1978); International Conference of Banking Supervisors London July 5-6, 1979, *Record of Proceedings* (hereafter, "London Proceedings 1979").

[123] *Id*. The Group of 10 countries are the United States, Canada, Japan, Belgium, France, West Germany, Italy, the Netherlands, the United Kingdom, and Sweden. The FRB, and since 1978 the OCC, represent the United States at Cooke committee meetings.

[124] Muller, *The Concordat: A Model for International Cooperation*, London Proceedings 1979 at 63. Muller summarizes the major elements of the Concordat as follows:

1. the supervision of foreign banking establishments is the joint responsibility of parent and host authorities.
2. no foreign banking establishment may escape supervision, so that each country must ensure that foreign banking establishments are supervised. In the case of joint-ventures, the host authority is practically the only authority able to exercise supervision.
3. the supervision of *liquidity* rests first of all with the *host* authorities, with perhaps a

more limited supervisory role where foreign currencies or the currency of a parent authority are concerned.

4. the supervision of *solvency* rests first of all with *parent* authorities with a more important role for host authorities in the case of subsidiaries and in particular in the case of joint-ventures.

5. practical cooperation should be promoted on a reciprocal basis in three ways—

    a. by the direct transfer of information between host and parent authorities.

    b. by direct inspections by parent authorities on the territory of the host authority.

    c. by indirect inspections by host authorities at the request of parent authorities.

Where legal constraints—particularly in the field of professional secrecy or national sovereignty—would hamper these forms of cooperation, every effort should be made to remove these constraints.

[125] Blunden, *supra*; London Proceedings 1979.

[126] Pub. L. No. 95-630, § § 101, 103, 107, and 801, amending § 8 of the Federal Deposit Insurance Act, 12 USC § 1818; sections 22 and 23A of the Federal Reserve Act (12 USC § § 371c, 375, 375a, 376); 12 USC § 1972. This section of the paper deals with civil and criminal enforcement authority of the federal banking agencies and the courts with respect to U.S. banks and persons and companies associated therewith. It is interesting to note, however, that Congress has recently considered the matter of the extraterritorial reach of the U.S. banking laws—and specifically the Federal Deposit Insurance Act Section 8 administrative proceeding— as applied to foreign banks operating at a branch or agency in this country. Section 6(c)(15) of the International Banking Act of 1978 amends 12 USC § 1818 by adding a new subsection (r): ". . . (2) An act or practice outside the United States on the part of a foreign bank or any officer, director, employee, or agent thereof may not constitute the basis for any action by any officer or agency of the United States under this section, unless—(A) such officer of agency alleges a belief that such act or practice has been, is, or is likely to be a cause of or carried on in connection with or in furtherance of an act or practice within any one or more States which, in and of itself, would constitute an appropriate basis for action by a Federal officer or agency under this section; (B) the alleged act or practice is one which, if proven, would, in the judgment of the Board of Directors, adversely affect the insurance risk assumed by the Corporation [the FDIC]. (3) In any case in which any action or proceeding is brought pursuant to an allegation under paragraph (2) of this subsection for the suspension or removal of any officer, director, or other person associated with a foreign bank, and such person fails to appear promptly as a party to such action or proceeding and to comply with any effective order or judgment therein, any failure by the foreign bank to secure his removal from any office he holds in such bank and from any further participation in its affairs shall, in and of itself, constitute grounds for termination of the insurance of the deposits of any branch of the bank." The venue of any judicial or administrative proceeding under 12 USC § 1818 is wherever the branch or agency of the foreign bank is located. Service of process may be accomplished at any such location. The International Banking Act also states, in § 6(c)(5), that the FDIC may obtain an injunction in any U.S. district court to compel a foreign bank that has an insured branch or any officer, employee, or agent of such foreign bank to deliver such assets to the FDIC as that agency may deem necessary or appropriate to protect the insurance fund. This pledge of assets provision— supportable by an injunction—was enacted in recognition of the "risks entailed in insuring the domestic deposits of a foreign bank whose activities, assets, and personnel are in large part outside the jurisdiction of the United States." *See* IBA § 6(c)(7), adding subsection (b)(4) to 12 USC § 1815. Section 11 of the IBA further provides that a foreign bank having a branch or agency in the United States is subject to 12 USC § 1818(b), (c), (d), (h), (k), (l), (m), and (n). The exact import of this is unclear. For example, by its terms the reach of the amendment subjects a foreign bank or associated person resident abroad to the cease-and-desist enforcement powers including the subpoena provisions ancillary thereto. But 12 USC § 1818(n) seems to compel the attendance of witnesses or production of documents, pursuant to subpoena, only

from places subject to U.S. jurisdiction. It is unlikely that a foreign bank or associated person, located overseas, could be considered subject to the jurisdiction of the United States in ordinary civil enforcement circumstances.

[127] 12 USC § 1818(b). A temporary cease-and-desist order may be imposed at the commencement of proceedings. Such order remains in effect pending completion of the adjudication unless it is overturned in a court of law or is withdrawn by the agency. 12 USC § 1818(c).

[128] 12 USC §§ 93, 371c, 375, 375a, 376, 1818, 1972.

[129] 12 USC § 1818(e) and (g). In connection with a cease-and-desist proceeding, or indeed any regular examination or special investigation of any insured bank or affiliate thereof, it is clear that the U.S. bank and any bank-related individual or institution falls within the scope of the law. A question does arise, however, concerning the reach of the subpoena power and the banking agencies' ability generally to obtain access to persons and records overseas. It is stated in 12 USC § 1818(n) that the banking agency conducting an adjudicatory proceeding under 12 USC § 1818, or an examination or investigation of an insured bank and "affiliates thereof" under 12 USC § 1820(c), has the power through any of its representatives to administer oaths and affirmations, take or cause to be taken depositions, or issue subpoenas and subpoenas duces tecum, and to make rules and regulations with respect to proceedings, examinations or investigations. The attendance of witnesses and the production of documents "may be required from any place in any State or in any territory or other place subject to the jurisdiction of the United States . . .," at any place where an administrative proceeding is being conducted. Under 12 USC § 1820(c), the appropriate federal agency is authorized to "administer oaths and affirmations, and to examine and to take and preserve testimony under oath as to any matter in respect to the affairs or ownership of any such [insured] bank or institution or affiliate thereof. . . ." While the examination and investigation authority encompasses any matter in respect to the "affairs or ownership" of a U.S. bank, presumably wherever the relevant person or institution may be located, it is doubtful that the banking agency could compel the attendance of foreign nationals or the production of documents from abroad. This is true even in the case of a formal cease-and-desist or removal adjudication. Of course, as explained elsewhere, there are dramatic and thorough measures that could be taken with respect to the U.S. bank and any of its officers, directors, employees, agents or other participating persons located within the U.S., to make the institution safe from abuse by a foreign investor. Indeed, the investment could be rendered unattractive or useless to a recalcitrant control party.

[130] 12 USC § 93.

[131] 12 USC § 1818(a).

[132] For example, the Bank Secrecy Act, 12 USC § 1829b, requires insured banks to maintain records and other appropriate evidence concerning the identity of persons having a checking or savings account. This Act reaches businesses as well as natural persons who are bank customers. The bank must also keep a microfilm or other reproduction of checks, drafts or similar instruments drawn on it and presented for payment and a record of checks, drafts or similar instruments received by it for deposit or collection. The purpose of the Act is to prevent the use of bank accounts to conceal tax fraud, gambling operations, and other activities typical of organized crime. *In re Grand Jury No. 76-3 (MIA) Subpoena Duces Tecum*, 555 F.2d 1306 (8th Cir. 1977). Rules promulgated by the Treasury Department implement the statute. *See* 31 CFR Part 103 (Financial Recordkeeping and Reporting of Currency and Foreign Transactions). The International Banking Act of 1978 amended 12 USC § 1829b so that the Bank Secrecy Act does not apply to any foreign bank except with respect to the transactions and records of an insured branch of such a bank. In other words, a foreign bank operating at an agency or uninsured branch in the United States need not comply with the recordkeeping requirements of this Act. *See* 12 USC § 1829b(i). The same Treasury Department regulations, 31 CFR Part 103, also implement the Currency and Foreign Transactions Reporting Act, 31 USC §§ 1051-1122. This law does apply to foreign banks operating at a branch or agency in the United States. It also covers American banks doing business overseas and various other specified entities that deal in or transfer funds or "monetary instruments" to or from the U.S. The stated purpose of

the Currency and Foreign Transactions Reporting Act is to require "certain reports or records where such reports or records have a high degree of usefulness in criminal, tax, or regulatory investigations or proceedings." 31 USC § 1051. The Secretary of the Treasury has broad discretion to establish appropriate recordkeeping and reporting rules and procedures for affected institutions. Under 31 USC § 1081, for example, "transactions involving any domestic financial institution shall be reported to the Secretary at such time, in such manner and in such detail as the Secretary may require if they involve the payment, receipt, or transfer of the United States currency, or such other monetary instruments as the Secretary may specify, in such amounts, denominations, or both, or under such circumstances, as the Secretary shall by regulation prescribe." The Treasury Department regulations at 31 CFR § 103.22(a) require financial institutions to "file a report of each deposit, withdrawal, exchange of currency or other payment or transfer, by, through, or to such financial institution, which involves a transaction in currency of more than $10,000." "Financial institution" is defined in the regulations to include each agency, branch, or office within the United States of any person doing business in a banking capacity. *See* 31 CFR § 103.11. Under 31 CFR § 103.23(a), "each person who physically transports, mails, or ships or causes to be physically transported, mailed, or shipped, currency or other monetary instruments in an aggregate amount exceeding $5,000 on any one occasion from the United States to any place outside the United States, or into the United States, shall make a report thereof." There are some exemptions and various other reporting and record-keeping provisions detailed in the regulations. For example, 31 CFR § 103.22(b)(2) exempts from the currency transaction reporting requirements "transactions solely with, or originated by, financial institutions or foreign banks." The law contains both civil and criminal penalty provisions. *See* 31 USC § § 1054, 1056, 1058, 1059.

[133] 18 USC § § 651, 1001. It is generally true that the United States can exercise jurisdiction and attach legal consequences to conduct that occurs outside its territory so long as the conduct has a substantial effect within its territory. *See United States* v. *Aluminum Co. of America*, 148 F.2d 416, 443-44 (2d Cir. 1945); *Restatement Second of Foreign Relations Law of the United States* § 18 (1965). Even assuming the Congress has chosen to exercise such authority in a particular statute, other practical and legal problems are attendant upon reaching persons and records overseas when voluntary compliance with a banking agency request is not forthcoming. *See* discussion notes 126 and 129 *supra*. In connection with a civil lawsuit before a U.S. court, similar difficulties with respect to the issuance and enforcement of subpoenas are present. Of course, if the court assumes jurisdiction over an absent defendant, any assets located in the United States could be executed upon to satisfy an ensuing judgment. The cooperation of a foreign sovereign would be needed in order to execute upon assets located abroad. *See generally* Wright and Miller, *Federal Practice and Procedure: Civil* § 2460 (1971); *Restatement Second of Foreign Relation Law of the United States* § 20 (165); *International Shoe Co.* v. *Washington*, 326 U.S. 310 (1945) and progeny. *See Shaffer* v. *Heitner*, 433 U.S. 186 (1977). When it is alleged that a person has committed a crime, the situation is different. Assume, for example, that a foreign control party acting overseas has caused a misapplication of funds in the United States or has falsified documents relating to its U.S. bank, in violation of Title 18 of the U.S. Code. Criminal conduct may trigger an extradition request. *See generally* H. Steiner and D. Vagts, *Transnational Legal Problems*, particularly ch. 7. It is much more likely that a U.S. court will obtain the physical presence of a person residing overseas when there is a criminal prosecution involved.

## 4

SOME EVIDENCE ON TRANSNATIONAL BANKING STRUCTURE

DIANE PAGE

NEAL M. SOSS

SUMMARY

This paper presents some historical and contemporary data on the activities of banking institutions outside of their home countries through branches agencies, banking affiliates, and banking subsidiaries.

A bank may establish a foreign presence for a variety of reasons and in a variety of forms, based upon the resources and preferences of the bank and the regulations and policies of the host country. The establishment of bank offices in foreign nations dates from antiquity as a complement to international trade.

The post World War II transnational banking network reflects colonial history, improvements in communications and other technologies, and increased global economic interdependence and economic development, including the growth of multinational corporations. The network is characterized by growing numbers of branches, agencies, affiliates, and subsidiaries, and the global presence of banks from a handful of developed countries, most notably the United States and the United Kingdom.

Throughout the world, there are over 4000 branches and agencies which are directly owned by a foreign banking institution and over 400 banking subsidiaries which are majority-owned by a foreign banking institution.

Time series data show distinct patterns of growth and change in the foreign branch and agency networks of the world's banks over the past two decades. Since 1961, the number of branches and agencies maintained by British, French, and other European banks in the former colonial areas of Africa, Asia, and Australia has decreased significantly. However, British and French banks have expanded their branch and agency presence in other areas and, along with United States banks, have large global networks of branches and agencies.

Banks from other countries have concentrated their foreign branch and agency networks regionally in geographic proximity to their home countries, but have increasingly begun to establish offices in the international banking centers of London and New York. The presence of branches and agencies in the offshore booking centers in the Caribbean, Panama, Singapore, Malaysia, and Bahrain still reflects geographic and historical factors. For example, Canadian and United States banks account for much of the branch and agency growth in the Caribbean.

When foreign banking subsidiaries and affiliates are considered, Germany Japan, Canada, and the Netherlands also appear as countries whose banking systems maintain a global presence, while banks of the United Kingdom and United States still appear as the major sources of banking presence outside the home country. These two countries also host large numbers of foreign banks.

Although the larger internationally active United States banks have foreign office networks comparable in size to those of United Kingdom banks, the state-restricted, local market structure of the United States banking system is seen in the low average number of foreign offices per United States bank compared to averages for banks in other countries which have international presence. Many United States banks have only one foreign branch in the Caribbean offshore booking center.

151 United States banks maintain 800 branches and agencies, over 100 banking subsidiaries and over 200 affiliate banking relationships in other countries. New York, California, and Illinois banks have the largest share of this foreign presence. In turn, non-United States banks maintain most of their United States agencies, branches, affiliates, and subsidiaries in those states and in Florida.

INTRODUCTION

Banking organizations have established banking offices outside their home jurisdictions throughout recorded financial history. The current patterns of transnational banking presence are highly developed and complex. This paper presents some evidence on the structure of transnational banking presence. Much of this evidence has not previously been available to researchers in a convenient form, and it is the authors' hope that the publication of this evidence will be useful in research relating to a great many hypotheses about banking and international finance.

To provide some perspective on the subject of transnational banking we first discuss the motivations for establishing a banking presence outside the home country market and the organizational forms for doing so. We then present some anecdotal historical evidence on the development of the transnational banking structure through the early twentieth century.

We then present time series data on the development of the transnational banking structure from 1961 to 1978. These data focus on the use of the branch and agency organizational form and depict the presence of banking institutions from ten home countries and six home regions in nine host country markets and seven host region markets.[1]

The last section of this chapter updates and elaborates on the 1978 pattern by including subsidiary and affiliate organizational forms and utilizing the most recently available data, covering the period 1978-1979. Finally, this pattern is further expanded by presenting data for the United States as a country of origin and as a host country, recognizing the separate state-by-state banking structure which exists in this country. The chapter ends with brief summary comments.

Data sources and the counting rules used in developing this material are discussed in the appendix. We should note at the outset that the data presented here were prepared from several sources. The use of multiple sources resulted in inconsistent tabulation in certain instances of the presence of banks from some countries in some foreign jurisdictions. We believe our data are accurate to an order of magnitude but would caution the reader against placing excessive reliance on the data at a very fine level of detail. It is advisable that users of these data pay careful attention to the appendix, which describes the procedures used.

MOTIVATIONS AND ORGANIZATIONAL FORMS

Since their development as a form of financial intermediary, banks have been involved in extending credit to bridge gaps in time and space. Broadly speaking, banks may bridge geographic gaps in two ways.

The first is by the establishment of relationships between separate banks in different locales. Such relationships, which constitute an essential element of correspondent banking, are used by buyers and sellers to bridge the geographic gap between them as ultimate payers and payees. Alternatively, a bank may bridge the geographic gap by establishing its own banking presence in different locales. In this case the banking company internalizes the geographic separation between the ultimate payer and payee.[2]

The motivations for banks to establish a banking presence in a foreign jurisdiction may include a number of considerations such as: servicing the international financial transactions needs of customers from the home country; servicing the international or host country financial transactions needs of multinational customers based in the home country; exploiting opportunities for asset or profit growth in the local host country market; and achieving greater currency or trade area diversification of risk.[3] Of course, several of these motivations may coexist in a particular bank s decisions with respect to entering a specific market outside its home country.[4]

In establishing its own banking presence in a different locale from its home office, a banking company may choose one or more of a variety of organizational forms. Which forms are *available* in a specific situation is usually determined by legal and regulatory constraints. Which forms are *chosen* in a specific instance depends on considerations of operating efficiency and profitability within those constraints. The following discussion, therefore, is couched in terms of logical possibility rather than actual practice in a specific jurisdiction.

At the most general level, a banking organization may establish a presence in a foreign market through a traveling representative or a local representative office. This organizational form is generally a mechanism for soliciting business and customer relationships to be serviced elsewhere. Representative offices do not constitute the establishment of a true banking presence in the jurisdiction, since the banking business is not actually conducted there.

In order to establish a true banking presence in a new locale, a bank may open a branch or agency. A branch is an integral part of the bank and is generally permitted to exercise all the powers of the bank itself. An agency is also an integral part of the bank, but it is generally restricted in terms of the powers which may be exercised from its premises. Agencies commonly are prohibited from taking certain types of deposits.

A banking company may also establish a presence in a foreign locale through a separately incorporated subsidiary or affiliate bank. The possibilities here include chartering a new bank on a wholly- or partially-owned basis or acquiring a whole or partial interest in an existing bank in the foreign locale. The bank's partners in a partial interest situation may be indigenous banks, other banks from its own home jurisdiction, or banks from still other foreign jurisdictions. Depending upon the legal and business circumstances, the bank's partners may also be entitities which are not primarily engaged in banking.

HISTORIC OVERVIEW OF TRANSNATIONAL BANKING

As long as there has been international trade there has been a need for international banking activities to finance it. Even in ancient times banks established themselves in different countries to serve the needs of their commercial customers. Klaas Peter Jacobs comments on the international banking scene of ancient Egypt and Sumer thus:

> When private business entered into competition with the state-run import and export monopolies of the Pharoahs and priest-kings, the silver and gold the merchants brought with them to pay for grain or finished goods became too cumbersome and too vulnerable to theft to be transported over the trade routes of the Fertile Crescent. It was easier to open branches and subsidiaries in the alien countries, and to pay with letters of credit and checks issued by the bankers who had accompanied the traders to the foreign settlements and there opened their own offices.[5]

Martin Mayer, in discussing the development of banking to service international trade in the Middle Ages and Renaissance periods, notes that:

> To make an international banking system work required a bank at each end of the transaction, and in the early years it was considered best for the same family to own both, establishing a son or a nephew or an in-law as at least a partner in the remote enterprise. Banking being predominately Italian, the early banking houses all over Europe were Italian. The place where the money market grew up in London was called Lombard Street, and even today a secured loan is known in Germany as a "Lombard loan."[6]

In the post-Renaissance period, technological improvements (especially in transportation and communications), the emergence of colonial and industrial powers, and international political rationalization furthered the need for international banking activities and for transnational banking presence. By the middle of the nineteenth century some of the essential characteristics of modern banking had evolved, including the use of deposits as a source of funding and the acceptance of demand deposits as a substitute for bank notes. The Industrial Revolution was fully underway, and a prolonged period of relative international peace provided a great impetus for international trade and economic growth. The existing economic power of England and the emerging economic power of the United States seem to have served as focal points for an expansion in international banking activities and transnational banking presence.[7]

By 1880, foreign banks had established a significant presence in California, for example, holding 15 percent of all deposits in the state and accounting for the third and fourth largest California banks.[8] Those two banks were British-owned, but both Canadian- and Asian-based banks were also present in California well before the turn of the century. California Canadian Bank was established in San Francisco by the Canadian Imperial Bank of Commerce in 1864. In the latter half of the nineteenth century, the Hongkong and Shanghai Banking Corporation established an agency in California and the Bank of Tokyo conducted business through a California chartered subsidiary.[9]

Similarly, foreign banking agencies began to appear in New York State shortly after the Civil War. In 1911, the New York banking law was amended to allow freer foreign establishment of agency operations in that state and 19 foreign banks were licensed the following year.[10] By 1925 there were 33 agencies of 32 foreign banks in New York.[11] Furthermore, while New York law at that time prohibited foreign branching, it did permit foreign banks to charter subsidiary trust company banking operations, and six foreign banks had done so by 1925—three Italian, one British, one Greek, and one Portuguese.[12]

An organizational form used especially by German banks in the nineteenth and early twentieth centuries to gain entry into foreign markets was the purchase of a controlling interest in an existing local bank. The Darmstadter Bank of Germany acquired a controlling interest in a New York bank in 1854. Deutsche Bank acquired controlling interests in existing banks in New York (1872), Paris (1873), Vienna (1877 and 1895), and Madrid (1895).[13] The method was also used occasionally by banks from other countries. National City Bank of New York, for example, held a controlling interest in the Banque Nationale de la Republique d'Haiti from 1922 until 1925, when it purchased the remaining capital stock of the institution and transformed it into a wholly owned subsidiary.[14]

London, as the premier international financial center, acted as a magnet for foreign banking presence from many countries, including the United States. Although private American banking houses appear to have had London operations earlier, by 1887 there is evidence of a London branch of the incorporated Jarvis Conklin Mortgage Trust Co., New York. Tamagna and Willis recount the transnational presence of United States banks in this early period thus:

> In 1887 Guaranty Trust Company of New York opened its London office, which it still maintains. In 1901 International Banking Corporation was organized under Connecticut law and soon established branches in London, Asia, and other parts of the world. Various banks and insurance companies held interests in this corporation from time to time before it was acquired by the National City Bank of New York in 1915. Branches in London and Paris were established in 1906 by Farmers Loan and Trust Company, New York, and in 1912 by Equitable Trust Company, New York . . . Another branch in London was opened in 1913 by Empire Trust Company, New York. A foreign banking corporation, Continental Banking and Trust Company, was organized in 1913 under the laws of West Virginia and conducted business through offices in New York and Panama until dissolved in 1922.[15]

Even in this early period banks' presence in foreign markets took different forms: some through direct branches or agencies, some through subsidiaries or branches of subsidiaries, and some through ownership interests in consortium banks with foreign offices.

A legal bar on direct branching by national banks abroad slowed the development of transnational presence by United States banks during this period.[16] Some states had similar statutory provisions covering their state-chartered banks.[17]

Nationally chartered banks were freed from that constraint by the 1913 passage of the Federal Reserve Act, which empowered them to branch abroad. In 1916, amendments to Section 25 of the Federal Reserve Act broadened the powers of national banks to invest in state-chartered corporations engaged in foreign banking operations under an agreement with the Federal Reserve Board specifying their permitted activities—so-called "agreement corporations." Three years later, passage of the Edge Act, Section 25(a) of the Federal Reserve Act, permitted federally chartered corporations to be established for the purpose of engaging in international finance and foreign banking. Edge Act subsidiaries were permitted to establish offices outside the home market of the parent banks.

With those broadened powers, several major United States banks established overseas branches to capitalize on the great increase in the volume of world commerce which occurred during and after World War I. By 1926, 12 United States banks had established 154 foreign branches around the globe.[18] This movement slowed in the latter half of the 1920s, however, and substantial retrenchment occurred during the 1930s as economic activity slowed worldwide. The disruptions of World War II were accompanied by still further contraction in the foreign presence of United States banks.[19] In 1955, ten years after the end of the war, only seven United States banks had foreign branches. The total foreign branch network of these seven banks numbered 111 branches.[20] The tremendous growth in the United States network during the 1960s and 1970s is thus one part of the recent history of worldwide branch banking expansion.

THE BRANCH AND AGENCY NETWORK IN THE POSTWAR PERIOD

As we have seen, the origins of transnational banking are ancient. Nonetheless, transnational banking presence in the period since the end of World War II seems qualitatively different from anything that came before because it is so much more extensive. The postwar expansion of the transnational network is a part of the more general global integration and interdependence associated with advances in transportation and communications technology as well as with explicit efforts at multilateral political cooperation that have taken place in this period.

This section presents some time series evidence on the development of transnational banking presence in the postwar period. It concentrates on the branch and agency forms of banking presence and presents the global patterns at intervals of roughly a decade: 1961, 1970, and 1978. The detailed data are presented in Tables 1 through 3 for each of these periods respectively. Summary data are presented in Tables 4 through 7.

On Tables 1 through 3, the rows show the countries or regions of origin of banks which maintain branches and/or agencies in a foreign juris-

Table 1
Global Network of Overseas Branches and Agencies, 1961

Country of Origin	Banks	Host Area															
		U.S.	U.K.	Fra.	Ger.	Switz.	Neth.	Other Eur.	Other Lat. A.	Jap.	H.K.	Other Far F.E.	Mid- East	Africa	Carib.	Pan.	Sing./Mal.
U.S.	[8]	N.A.	11	3	3	0	0	4	52	14	2	11	4	7	4	8	5
U.K.	[17]	2	N.A.	24	2	1	0	30	64	7	6	1693	49	2182	81	0	43
France	[16]	0	2	N.A.	5	1	0	44	45	0	2	11	14	232	5	0	0
Germany	[2]	0	0	0	N.A.	0	0	0	1	0	0	1	0	0	0	0	0
Switzerland	[3]	2	0	0	0	N.A.	0	0	1	0	0	0	0	0	0	0	0
Netherlands	[2]	0	0	0	0	0	N.A.	1	9	3	1	8	8	4	3	0	2
Italy	[5]	2	0	0	0	1	0	7	2	0	0	0	3	11	0	0	0
Other Europe	[13]	0	6	9	3	1	0	19	12	0	2	0	18	33	0	0	0
Canada	[5]	14	10	1	1	2	0	11	31	0	0	0	0	0	84	0	0
Latin America	[2]	2	0	1	0	0	0	1	1	0	0	0	0	0	0	0	3
Japan	[6]	8	3	0	2	0	0	0	4	N.A.	1	4	2	0	0	0	3
Australia	[4]	0	4	0	0	0	0	0	0	0	0	12	0	0	0	0	0
Other Far East	[17]	2	4	0	0	0	1	5	0	10	7	73	4	12	0	0	28
Mid-East	[6]	2	0	1	0	0	0	0	0	0	0	0	23	11	0	0	0
Africa	[6]	0	0	0	0	0	0	0	0	0	0	0	9	38	0	0	0
Caribbean	[1]	0	0	0	0	0	0	0	7	0	0	0	0	0	2	0	0

Source: *The Bankers' Almanac and Yearbook*, 1961-62.

Table 2

Global Network of Overseas Branches and Agencies, 1970

Country of Origin	Banks	Host Area															
		U.S.	U.K.	Fra.	Ger.	Switz.	Neth.	Other Eur.	Other Lat. A.	Jap.	H.K.	Other Far. E.	Mid-East	Africa	Carib.	Pan	Sing/Mal.
U.S.	[68]	N.A.	37	15	21	11	9	32	109	14	10	57	10	13	89	26	14
U.K.	[13]	10	N.A.	15	3	5	2	47	100	6	32	2027a	110	1634	128	0	73
France	[19]	2	5	N.A.	7	3	0	18	62	1	3	30	10	33	3	0	2
Germany	[2]	0	0	0	N.A.	0	0	0	1	0	1	2	0	0	0	0	1
Switzerland	[6]	2	9	0	1	N.A.	1	0	1	0	3	0	0	0	1	0	0
Netherlands	[3]	2	1	0	1	0	N.A.	1	14	3	3	4	6	2	0	0	3
Italy	[4]	3	0	0	0	0	0	7	5	0	0	0	4	0	0	0	0
Other Europe	[12]	0	6	26	2	0	0	9	18	0	5	0	0	0	0	6	0
Canada	[5]	11	13	0	0	0	1	4	34	0	0	0	1	0	171	0	0
Latin America	[11]	4	1	10	3	0	0	0	21	0	0	0	0	0	0	2	0
Japan	[11]	16	9	0	4	0	0	1	11	N.A.	4	15	0	0	0	0	4
Australia	[8]	0	14	0	0	0	0	0	0	0	0	301	0	0	0	0	2
Other Far East	[31]	8	28	1	2	0	0	0	2	14	34	52	13	14	0	0	121
Mid-East	[10]	5	3	2	2	0	0	0	0	0	0	0	36	6	1	0	0
Africa	[8]	0	1	2	0	0	0	0	0	0	0	0	4	65	0	0	0
Caribbean	[1]	0	0	0	0	0	0	0	47	0	0	0	0	0	3	2	0

[a]Growth between 1961 and 1970 entirely represented by Australia and New Zealand Bank, Ltd., which listed 897 branches and agencies in Australia, New Zealand and Oceania in 1961, and 1657 branches, sub-branches, agencies and offices in 1970.

Source: *The Bankers' Almanac and Yearbook*, 1970-71.

Table 3
Global Network of Overseas Branches and Agencies, 1978

Country of Origin	Banks	Host Area															
		U.S.	U.K.	Fra.	Ger.	Switz.	Neth.	Other Eur.	Other Lat. A.	Jap.	H.K.	Other Far E.	Mid-East	Africa	Carib.	Pan.	Sing/Mal.
U.S.	[136]	N.A.	56	21	22	8	7	60	85	32	31	69	30	16	188	19	26
U.K.	[20]	19	N.A.	21	8	8	6	66	102	8	87	357ᵃ	142	148	78	5	59
France	[24]	11	13	N.A.	16	10	2	46	30	7	10	18	23	30	4	3	3
Germany	[12]	13	6	2	N.A.	0	0	1	1	5	4	5	0	0	2	5	3
Switzerland	[12]	8	8	0	0	N.A.	1	3	0	3	0	0	1	0	7	0	2
Netherlands	[7]	8	5	0	2	0	N.A.	8	28	3	2	5	10	2	9	1	3
Italy	[6]	11	4	0	0	0	0	6	6	1	0	0	5	1	0	0	1
Other Europe	[32]	18	158	79	7	1	1	20	22	0	3	0	6	1	1	0	0
Canada	[7]	28	15	2	6	0	2	5	26	0	2	3	7	1	138	2	6
Latin America	[15]	16	4	2	1	0	1	3	39	0	0	0	1	1	7	11	1
Japan	[23]	47	23	1	11	0	0	6	9	N.A.	7	16	0	0	1	0	10
Australia	[9]	7	17	0	0	0	0	0	0	0	0	528ᵃ	0	0	0	0	0
Other Far East	[47]	36	130	4	5	0	1	2	1	18	43	76	81	24	5	1	138
Mid-East	[21]	17	20	6	8	0	0	3	0	0	0	4	106	10	3	0	0
Africa	[15]	0	8	4	0	0	0	0	0	0	0	0	13	15	0	0	0
Caribbean	[1]	0	0	0	0	0	0	0	13	0	0	0	0	0	0	0	0

ᵃThe Australia and New Zealand Bank moved its head office to Australia and is therefore counted as an Australian bank. Its branches, agencies, sub-branches and offices no longer appear as British-owned. Branches, agencies, sub-branches and offices of the bank located outside of Australia are included in the Australia row, Other Far-East column.

Source: *The Bankers' Almanac and Yearbook, 1978-79*.

diction and the columns show the host countries or regions in which these transnational branches and/or agencies are located. The figure in brackets to the right of the name of the country or region of origin is the number of banking organizations from that country or region which have branches or agencies outside the home country.

The entries in the matrix represent the number of branches and/or agencies maintained by banks *from* the country or region along the row *in* the foreign country or region down the column. The entries along the portion of the diagonal of the matrix where the same *country* is the origin and the host are, of course, meaningless and are designated NA. The entries along the portion of the diagonal where the same *region* is both origin and host are not necessarily meaningless; entries in these

Table 4
Global Network of Branches and Agencies
Totals by Country of Origin

Country of Origin	1961	1970	1978
United States	128	467	670
United Kingdom	4184^a	4192^b	1114^c
France	361	179	226
Germany	2	5	47
Switzerland	3	15	33
Netherlands	39	40	86
Italy	26	19	35
Other Europe	103	72	317
Canada	154	235	243
Latin America	5	41	89
Japan	27	65	131
Australia	16	317	552^d
Other Far East	146	289	565
Mid-East	37	55	177
Africa	47	72	40
Caribbean	9	52	13
Grand Total	5287	6115	4338

^{a}Figures include sub-branches of the Australia and New Zealand Bank, Ltd.; the Bank of London and South America, Ltd.; Barclays Bank D.C.O.; National Grindlays Bank, Ltd.; and the Standard Bank of South Africa, Ltd.

^{b}Figures include offices and sub-branches of the Australia and New Zealand Bank, Ltd.; and sub-branches of The Bank of London and South America, Ltd.; The National Bank of New Zealand; and The Standard Bank.

^{c}Figures include sub-branches of Barclays Bank and The Bank of London and South America, Ltd.

^{d}Figures include sub-branches and offices of the Australia and New Zealand Banking Group.

Table 5
Global Network of Branches and Agencies
Totals by Host Country

Host Country	1961	1970	1978
United States	34	63	239
United Kingdom	40	127	467
France	39	72	142
Germany	16	46	86
Switzerland	6	19	27
Netherlands	1	13	21
Other Europe	122	119	229
Other Latin America	229	425	362
Japan	34	38	79
Hong Kong	21	92	189
Other Far East	1813	2488	1081
Mid-East	134	194	425
Africa	2530	1767	249
Caribbean	179	396	443
Panama	8	36	47
Singapore/Malaysia	81	220	252
Grand Total	5287	6115	4338

Table 6
Number of Originating Banks by Country of Origin

Country of Origin	1961	1970	1978
United States	8	68	136
United Kingdom	17	13	20
France	16	19	24
Germany	2	2	12
Switzerland	3	6	12
Netherlands	2	3	7
Italy	5	4	6
Other Europe	13	12	32
Canada	5	5	7
Latin America	2	11	15
Japan	6	11	23
Australia	4	8	9
Other Far East	17	31	47
Mid-East	6	10	21
Africa	6	8	15
Caribbean	1	1	1
Total	113	212	387

positions represent the number of branches and/or agencies maintained by banks *from* a country in that region *in* another country within the *same* region.

In Table 1, for example, the entry in the second column of the first row shows that United States banks maintained a total of 11 branches/ agencies in the United Kingdom in 1961. The entry in the third column of the second row shows 24 branches/agencies maintained by United Kingdom banks in France. The entry in the 14th (Mid-East) row, 12th (Mid-East) column shows that banks from various Middle Eastern countries maintained 23 branches/agencies in other Middle Eastern countries. A branch of a Lebanese bank in Jordan, for instance, would appear in this entry.

Tables 2 and 3 show the same information for 1970 and 1978, respectively.

Tables 4 and 5 are summary tables showing branch/agency totals over time. Table 4 shows *row* totals for 1961, 1970, and 1978, i.e., the number of branch/agencies maintained by banks from each country or region of origin in *all* other countries and regions. Table 5 shows *column* totals for 1961, 1970, and 1978, i.e., the number of branches/ agencies from all other countries and regions hosted in each country or region.

The top line in Table 4, for example, shows that the number of United States banks' branches/agencies in other countries grew from 128 in 1961 to 467 in 1970 and then to 670 in 1978. The top line of Table 5 shows that the number of branches/agencies from banks headquartered in other countries hosted by the United States grew from 34 in 1961 to 63 in 1970 and to 239 in 1978.

The growth of the United States as both host and originator of foreign branches/agencies is suggestive of accelerating growth of international banking as a whole in the years following World War II. However, the total *global* branch/agency network described by Tables 4 and 5 portrays a seemingly different picture. The grand total rows on Tables 4 and 5 show the number of foreign branches/agencies maintained by banks from all countries and regions of the world. Between 1961 and 1970 this global branch/agency network increased by 16 percent, from 5287 to 6115, but between 1970 and 1978 the global network decreased by 29 percent, from 6115 to 4338.

Careful examination of the individual foreign branch/agency originators and hosts reveals some trends which explain the pattern of expansion followed by contraction. The broad-based expansion of the international branch/agency network is offset between 1960 and 1978 by the shrinking branch/agency network of colonial powers in former colonies. The most striking illustration of this trend is the United Kingdom.

Table 4 shows that the United Kingdom banks' branch/agency network declined from 4192 to 1114 between 1970 and 1978, a loss of over 3000 branches/agencies. That decline alone more than explains the shrinking of the global network as a whole by 1777 branches/agencies during that decade. Tables 2 and 3 indicate that this reduction occurred almost entirely in the Africa and Other Far East host regions.[21]

A comparison of Tables 1 and 2 shows that United Kingdom branch presence in Africa also declined, though not as rapidly, during the 1960s. By contrast, the numbers of African branches/agencies maintained by French, Italian, and the Other European banks dropped precipitously during that decade and changed little during the 1970s.

Table 6 shows the number of originating banks from each country and region of origin over time, and demonstrates that the total number of banks throughout the world with at least one foreign branch or agency has grown. In fact, banks from the United Kingdom, Italy, and Other Europe (mentioned above as having declining branch networks in former colonial areas) are the only ones which also show a decline in number of banks active in transnational branching. Such a decline could be explained by a number of factors besides the loss of foreign branches, such as closing of a bank, relocation of the head office to another country, or a merger. In the case of the United Kingdom, two United Kingdom-chartered banks which had foreign branches/agencies in 1961, and hence are included in Table 1, are not included in Table 2 because by 1970 they no longer had branch/agency networks in Africa and the Far East.[22]

A comparison of Tables 4 and 6 shows that, except for the United Kingdom and France, the magnitude and timing of the increase in numbers of originating banks in a particular country roughly parallels the magnitude and timing of the increase in foreign branches/agencies. Indeed, the growth of the branch/agency network is more the result of the increase in the number of banks involved in this type of transnational activity than the result of expansion in the average number of foreign branches.

This effect can be seen more graphically in Table 7 which shows the grand totals of foreign branches/agencies and parent banks for the three periods, separating out the banks from the United Kingdom and France. United Kingdom and French banks excluded, the number of banks engaged in transnational branching expanded by 90 percent between 1970 and 1978 while the number of branches/agencies they maintained expanded by 72 percent. The same phenomenon can also be seen in the decline of the average size of foreign networks of such banks from 9.7 branches in 1970 to 8.7 in 1978. Incidentally, the table also illustrates the decline of the United Kingdom and French banks as a dominant part of the total transnational banking picture. In 1960, United Kingdom and French banks accounted for 29 percent of all banks with foreign branches, and their branches accounted for 86 percent of the total. By 1978, these figures had declined to 11 percent and 31 percent, respectively.

The explanation for the shrinking colonial branch/agency network described above is not simply nationalization or exclusion of foreign banking operations by the newly independent former colonies, although those are factors. An important reason for the observed decline in the branch/agency network is that many newly independent African and Asian nations have adopted policies which restrict the type of foreign banking presence to subsidiaries or affiliates, no longer permitting direct branch operations.[23] Thus, branches which apparently disappeared over the last two decades may have instead changed in form. For example, at least two United Kingdom banks—Barclays Bank and to a lesser extent Grindlays Bank—formed subsidiary companies to take over their branches in several African countries during the 1970s. Societe Generale of France did the same a decade earlier, while Credit Lyonnais maintains a minority interest in banks formed from its former African branches.

Although the foreign branch/agency decline is specific to former European colonial powers, the trend of branch/agency expansion over time is a generalized one. In a discussion of expansion, originating countries fall roughly into two categories, those which maintain global branch/agency networks and those which maintain branches/agencies mostly in neighboring countries and the international financial centers of London and New York.

There is an approximate correlation between the extent of a country's or region's industrial development and the scope and size of its branch/agency networks, although Japan and Germany are notable exceptions. By glancing across the rows of Tables 1 through 3, it can be seen that the United States, the United Kingdom, and Franch have large global branch/agency networks. While French and United Kingdom bank presence has declined in former colonial areas, it has generally expanded in other parts of the world. Excluding Africa and the Far East, the foreign branch/agency network of United Kingdom banks expanded by 97 percent from 1961 to 1978 and that of France by over 50 percent.

United States banks experienced spectacular growth between 1961 and 1970, with a 265 percent increase in the number of their foreign branches/agencies, followed by a further expansion of 43 percent from 1970 to 1978. During the 1960s, United States banks began establishing large numbers of branches in the offshore booking centers of the Caribbean. Indeed, 30 percent of the total expansion of the United States foreign branch/agency network during the 1960s took place in the Caribbean and Panama, and almost half of the expansion between 1970 and 1978 took place in the Caribbean.

Canadian banks grew steadily worldwide over the past two decades, but maintained the bulk of their branch/agency network in nearby areas—in the Caribbean, United States, and Latin America. The German banks' network, although not large in numbers, jumped between 1970 and 1978 as German banks entered the United States and other markets. Thirty percent of the expansion of the German banks' foreign branch/agency network in this period occurred in the United States, starting from no recorded presence in 1970.

Japanese banks approximately doubled their networks in each of the periods covered by the tables, developing their presence primarily in the United States, the United Kingdom, and Asian countries. The same pattern was exhibited by banks from the Other Far East region. Australian and Middle Eastern banks' branches/agencies grew in a similar manner—in the United States and United Kingdom and within their own geographic areas. Latin American banks grew in the United States and in other Latin American countries; African banks established branches/agencies in the United Kingdom, Africa and the Middle East.

The discussion so far has centered upon the originating countries with some mention of the host countries. Certain host country trends merit further exploration.

Table 5 shows that the total number of branches/agencies hosted in formerly colonial Africa and Other Far East have indeed dropped over the past two decades, by 90 percent and 40 percent, respectively.

As mentioned earlier, foreign branch/agency presence in the United States and the United Kingdom has grown greatly over the last ten years, reflecting the increasing attractiveness of the international financial centers of London and New York. The United States and the United Kingdom are not only global originators but also global hosts. The worlds' booking centers—Panama, the Caribbean, and Singapore and Malaysia (Bahrain is included in the Middle East region in the tables)—have also recently become global hosts, as can be seen by a comparison of the columns for these countries in Tables 1 through 3. Geographic and colonial ties, however, still play a large role in the patterns of foreign presence in the offshore booking centers. The preponderance of United States, Canadian and United Kingdom bank presence in the Caribbean, United Kingdom bank presence in the Far East and United States bank presence in Panama are examples.

The evidence presented in Tables 1 through 7 shows several trends in the composition of the international branch/agency network. Banking systems based on the colonial presence of the United Kingdom, France and other European nations in Africa and the Far East appear to have diminished. The banking systems of the United States, the United Kingdom and, to a lesser extent, France, are clearly global in their branching patterns. The banking systems of some other European countries and Japan have also been increasing the worldwide scope of their branch/agency networks. Banks from the developing nations of Africa, the Middle East, Asia, and Latin America concentrate much of their networks in neighboring countries. They, however, have increasingly established branches/agencies in New York and London, which has produced the recent large growth of the United States and the United Kingdom as global hosts. In another recent trend, offshore booking centers, once the province of their industrialized neighbors and former colonizers, have begun to host banks from all over the world.

The international branch/agency network presents a useful but far from complete picture of the foreign banking presence in various parts of the world. The tables do not show, for example, the extensive participation of German banks in affiliate relationships with banks in other European countries. More generally, the evidence presented in this section does not consider or account for two very significant organization-

Table 7
Average Transnational Branches/Agencies Per Bank

All Banks	1961	1970	1978
U.K. and French Banks			
Number of Banks	33	32	44
Number of Branches/Agencies	4545	4371	1340
Average per Bank	137.7	136.6	30.5
Other Banks			
Number of Banks	80	180	343
Number of Branches/Agencies	742	1744	2998
Average per Bank	9.3	9.7	8.7
Total Banks			
Number of Banks	113	212	387
Number of Branches/Agencies	5287	6115	4338
Average per Bank	46.8	28.8	11.2

al forms of foreign bank presence—subsidiaries and affiliates. As noted earlier, the choice of organizational form is determined by the preferences of originating banks as well as the policies of host country governments. To provide a fuller description of current patterns, the next section presents evidence on transnational banking through subsidiaries and affiliates as well as more complete data on branches and agencies.

THE GLOBAL PATTERN IN 1978-1979

To present the broadest picture of the current patterns of bank presence outside the home country market, we have compiled in Tables 8-25 the number of banking subsidiaries, banking affiliates, and branches (and/or agencies) maintained by banking organizations from 11 countries and seven regions of the world in 26 different foreign locales. The data are from most recently available sources covering the period 1978-1979.

Each table represents a country or region of origin and shows the number of subsidiaries, affiliates, and branches/agencies that banks from that place maintain in each of the foreign host locales. Table 8, for example, shows the numbers for United States banks in each foreign area. Table 9 shows the corresponding information for United Kingdom banks, and so forth. Where the volume of transnational banking presence did not warrant presenting the data on a country-by-country basis, countries were consolidated into geographic regions.

The data presented in these tables portray a rich, varied, and complex pattern of transnational presence. For the reader's convenience, these data are summarized in Tables 26 and 27. Table 26 shows the total number of foreign subsidiaries, affiliates, and branches/agencies maintained by banks from each country or region of origin, irrespective of the locations of the foreign host jurisdictions. Table 27 shows the number of foreign banks' subsidiaries, affiliates, and branches/agencies in each host locale irrespective of the locations of the bank's origins.

Looking first at the total row of Table 26, we see that of the many thousands of banking organizations around the world only 520 have an identified banking presence outside their home country. Of these, the largest concentration from a single country is from the United States, which accounts for 151, or 29 percent, of all the banking organizations with a transnational presence. By contrast, measured by average transnational presence per bank, the United States banking system

Table 8
United States Foreign Banking Presence (151 Banks) 1978-1979

Host Country	Subs	Affl	Brch
United Kingdom	17	26	60
France	6	12	19
Germany	7	3	25
Switzerland	7	4	9
Netherlands	1	2	7
Belgium	4	2	12
Italy	2	1	14
Spain/Portugal	2	4	4
Other Europe	11	13	42
Canada	1	1	0
Brazil	1	11	20
Other Latin America	3	14	99
Japan	0	0	30
Korea	0	0	11
Hong Kong	12	2	51
Other Asia	2	9	61
Middle East	4	9	22
Africa	7	39	20
Australia/New Zealand	1	8	0
Oceania	0	5	15
Caribbean	15	45	207
Panama	3	3	32
Singapore/Malaysia	1	8	29
Bahrain	0	2	8
Channel Islands	6	21	3
Total	113	244	800

is apparently the least transnational of the banking systems in the major countries. This is accounted for by the unusual banking structure in the United States in which there are very large numbers of relatively small banks serving relatively restricted domestic geographic markets.

The world's 520 transnational banks have a total of 440 subsidiaries, 1,232 affiliate relationships, and 4,375 branches/agencies outside their home countries. On average, therefore, the transnational presence of these banks includes just under one subsidiary, relationships with over two affiliates, and maintenance of over eight branches outside the home country market.

A word of explanation is necessary on the interpretation of affiliates. The data show a total of 1,232 instances of banks' having partial-ownership interests in other banks in foreign jurisdictions. This is not to say that there are 1,232 separate such banks in the world. The number of affiliates counted here is an inflated estimate of the number of such banks, because a single banking institution may be an affiliate of several participating banks and hence be counted more than once. Thus, the

Table 9
United Kingdom Foreign Banking Presence (25 Banks) 1978-1979

Host Country	Subs	Affl	Brch
United States	7	2	22
France	4	6	19
Germany	2	3	5
Switzerland	7	1	7
Netherlands	1	1	4
Belgium	3	4	4
Italy	1	0	0
Spain/Portugal	0	1	14
Other Europe	3	2	49
Canada	1	0	0
Brazil	0	1	14
Other Latin America	1	1	88
Japan	0	0	9
Korea	0	1	4
Hong Kong	4	3	84
Other Asia	0	3	144
Middle East	2	3	51
Africa	27	6	99
Australia/New Zealand	3	6	207
Oceania	0	0	5
Caribbean	4	2	78
Panama	0	0	4
Singapore/Malaysia	2	7	40
Bahrain	1	0	8
Channel Islands	13	1	2
Total	86	54	961

figure 1,232 is accurate from the point of view of the owning institution's networks of foreign presence through affiliate relationships, but cannot be interpreted as the number of distinct banks in any jurisdiction which are partially owned by foreign banking organizations.

The data presented in the tables demonstrates that the ownership of the network of transnational banking presence is relatively concentrated. Over two-thirds of the subsidiaries are owned by banks from just five countries: the United States, the United Kingdom, France, Canada, and Japan. Over one-half of the affiliate relationships are by banks from five countries, in this case a different list: the United States, France, Germany, Japan, and Italy. Finally, over 40 percent of all foreign branches/agencies are maintained by banks from just 2 countries: the United States and the United Kingdom.

Although United States banks loom large in a description of transnational presence in absolute terms, they do not maintain as much foreign presence *on average* as the banks from certain other countries. For example, the 151 transnational United States banks have an average of

Table 10
France Foreign Banking Presence (19 Banks) 1978-1979

Host Country	Subs	Affl	Brch
United States	2	4	17
United Kingdom	2	15	12
Germany	0	8	18
Switzerland	4	3	13
Netherlands	1	1	2
Belgium	3	5	14
Italy	1	0	3
Spain/Portugal	0	0	7
Other Europe	6	6	7
Canada	1	0	0
Brazil	1	3	0
Other Latin America	2	9	32
Japan	0	0	5
Korea	0	0	4
Hong Kong	1	0	11
Other Asia	0	1	5
Middle East	3	13	10
Africa	5	46	19
Australia/New Zealand	0	2	5
Oceania	3	2	28
Caribbean	1	4	4
Panama	1	2	3
Singapore/Malaysia	0	1	5
Bahrain	0	1	4
Channel Islands	0	0	0
Total	37	126	228

5.3 foreign branches/agencies while the corresponding averages for banks from some other countries are: United Kingdom banks, 38.4; Canadian banks, 27.8; Dutch banks, 18.2; and French banks, 12.0. The same observation pertains to subsidiaries and affiliates. Transnational banks from the United Kingdom, the Netherlands, Canada, and France average well over twice as many foreign subsidiaries as transnational United States banks. Belgian, French, Italian, and German transnational banks average over three times as many foreign affiliates as their United States counterparts, because many United States banks with a transnational presence maintain very small foreign networks. Indeed, 76 of the 151 transnational United States banks have one branch in an offshore booking center in the Caribbean as their entire transnational network.

The discussion so far has concentrated on the countries of origin of the transnational banks. Table 27 reverses the focus and looks at the foreign jurisdictions which play host to them.

The United Kingdom is the most active individual host country, ac-

Table 11
Germany Foreign Banking Presence (21 Banks) 1978-1979

Host Country	Subs	Affl	Brch
United States	0	2	16
United Kingdom	0	15	8
France	0	11	2
Switzerland	1	5	0
Netherlands	0	3	0
Belgium	0	4	3
Italy	0	1	0
Spain/Portugal	0	5	1
Other Europe	13	12	0
Canada	0	1	0
Brazil	0	4	1
Other Latin America	0	2	2
Japan	0	0	5
Korea	0	1	0
Hong Kong	0	0	2
Other Asia	0	1	0
Middle East	0	6	0
Africa	0	35	0
Australia	0	1	0
Oceania	0	0	0
Caribbean	0	2	4
Panama	1	0	10
Singapore/Malaysia	1	3	1
Bahrain	0	0	0
Channel Islands	0	1	0
Total	16	115	55

counting for over 9 percent of all the foreign branches in the world, over 15 percent of all the affiliate relationships, and 8 percent of all the subsidiaries. The United States is a close second in terms of hosting large numbers of foreign banking presences. The offshore booking centers in the Caribbean, Panama, the Channel Islands and Bahrain account for 13 percent of the world's branches, 11 percent of the affiliate relationships, and 19 percent of the subsidiaries.

Analysis of the data in Tables 8-25 indicates that banks from relatively few countries are truly global in that they are present in a large number of foreign jurisdictions and in a multiplicity of organizational forms. As demonstrated by Tables 8 and 19, there is a United States banking presence in every host country or region, whereas there is no identified Brazilian bank presence in 12 host countries or regions.[24] Moreover, note that the United States bank presence consists of all the organizational forms in each jurisdiction,[25] whereas the Brazilian presence in a country or region is often restricted to only one organizational form.

A review of the data using these criteria of global presence indicates

Table 12
Switzerland Foreign Banking Presence (13 Banks) 1978-1979

Host Country	Subs	Affl	Brch
United States	2	1	9
United Kingdom	1	6	7
France	1	4	0
Germany	0	2	0
Netherlands	0	0	1
Belgium	1	2	0
Italy	0	0	0
Spain/Portugal	0	0	0
Other Europe	4	2	2
Canada	1	0	0
Brazil	0	3	0
Other Latin America	0	0	0
Japan	0	0	3
Korea	0	0	0
Hong Kong	0	0	0
Other Asia	0	0	0
Middle East	1	2	0
Africa	0	6	1
Australia/New Zealand	0	0	0
Oceania	0	0	0
Caribbean	4	1	6
Panama	3	0	0
Singapore/Malaysia	0	1	2
Bahrain	0	0	1
Channel Islands	0	0	0
Total	18	30	32

that the banking systems from the United States, the United Kingdom, France, the Netherlands, Japan, Canada, and, only slightly less so, Germany are global. The transnational presence of the banks from other countries or regions of origin tends to be concentrated in the international banking centers of New York and London, the offshore booking centers, and selected other host jurisdictions, often within the same region of the world as the home country of the bank.

Tables 28-30 show the numbers of foreign bank subsidiaries, affiliates, and branches/agencies, respectively, hosted in very broad geographic areas broken out by the origin of the parent banks. The tables classify the origins of the parent banks into three categories: the global banking system countries (United States, United Kingdom, France, Netherlands, Japan, Canada, and Germany); the non-global countries which are within the same region as the host (e.g., a Spanish bank's affiliate in another European country or a Saudi Arabian bank's branch in another Middle Eastern country; and finally, the remainder, which represents banks from countries outside the host country's region which are not global banking system countries.

Table 13
Netherlands Foreign Banking Presence (6 Banks) 1978-1979

Host Country	Subs	Affl	Brch
United States	1	3	7
United Kingdom	1	6	5
France	1	4	5
Germany	3	2	4
Switzerland	3	0	0
Belgium	3	4	3
Italy	0	0	1
Spain/Portugal	0	1	0
Other Europe	2	1	6
Canada	1	0	1
Brazil	1	1	7
Other Latin America	0	0	26
Japan	0	0	3
Korea	0	0	1
Hong Kong	0	0	3
Other Asia	0	0	5
Middle East	0	1	10
Africa	1	0	7
Australia/New Zealand	0	1	0
Oceania	0	0	0
Caribbean	3	1	9
Panama	0	0	1
Singapore/Malaysia	0	0	3
Bahrain	0	0	1
Channel Islands	0	0	1
Total	20	25	109

The general conclusion that emerges from these tables is that banks from the seven countries we have identified as having global networks account for the preponderance of transnational banking. Extraterritorial, intra-regional banking accounts for a great proportion of the rest. The remainder of the observed pattern is accounted for by the attraction of banks to the major international banking centers of the United Kingdom and the United States and the offshore booking centers, as well as pairings of country of origin and host country related to patterns of international trade and commerce and extra-regional geographic proximity.

Table 14
Belgium Foreign Banking Presence (6 Banks) 1978-1979

Host Country	Subs	Affl	Brch
United States	0	3	1
United Kingdom	1	5	0
France	0	6	0
Germany	2	2	0
Switzerland	2	2	0
Netherlands	0	0	0
Italy	0	0	0
Spain/Portugal	0	0	0
Other Europe	2	4	0
Canada	0	0	0
Brazil	0	0	0
Other Latin America	0	0	0
Japan	0	0	1
Korea	0	0	0
Hong Kong	0	0	6
Other Asia	0	0	0
Middle East	0	1	1
Africa	0	25	0
Australia/New Zealand	0	1	0
Oceania	0	0	0
Caribbean	0	0	0
Panama	0	0	0
Singapore/Malaysia	0	0	0
Bahrain	0	0	1
Channel Islands	0	0	0
Total	5	49	10

Table 15
Italy Foreign Banking Presence (13 Banks) 1978-1979

Host Country	Subs	Affl	Brch
United States	1	2	13
United Kingdom	0	13	4
France	2	6	0
Germany	0	3	1
Switzerland	2	6	0
Netherlands	0	1	0
Italy	0	5	0
Spain/Portugal	0	2	2
Other Europe	2	7	4
Canada	0	0	0
Brazil	0	1	1
Other Latin America	0	1	1
Japan	0	0	1
Korea	0	0	0
Hong Kong	0	0	0
Other Asia	0	0	0
Middle East	0	2	5
Africa	1	23	1
Australia/New Zealand	0	0	0
Oceania	0	0	0
Caribbean	3	6	0
Panama	0	0	0
Singapore/Malaysia	0	0	1
Bahrain	0	0	0
Channel Islands	0	6	0
Total	11	84	34

Table 16

Spain/Portugal Foreign Banking Presence (20 Banks) 1978-1979

Host Country	Subs	Affl	Brch
United States	1	3	12
United Kingdom	3	5	11
France	1	5	39
Germany	1	2	1
Switzerland	0	1	0
Netherlands	1	1	0
Belgium	1	1	0
Italy	0	0	0
Other Europe	0	2	0
Canada	0	0	0
Brazil	0	1	0
Other Latin America	4	10	0
Japan	0	0	0
Korea	0	0	0
Hong Kong	0	0	0
Other Asia	1	1	1
Middle East	0	0	1
Africa	0	4	50
Australia/New Zealand	0	0	0
Oceania	0	0	0
Caribbean	2	2	0
Panama	1	1	0
Singapore/Malaysia	0	0	0
Bahrain	0	0	0
Channel Islands	0	0	0
Total	16	39	115

Table 17

Other Europe Foreign Banking Presence (47 Banks) 1978-1979

Host Country	Subs	Affl	Brch
United States	2	2	6
United Kingdom	3	23	94
France	0	14	2
Germany	0	10	4
Switzerland	1	20	2
Netherlands	1	2	1
Belgium	0	2	0
Italy	0	0	0
Spain/Portugal	0	1	0
Other Europe	10	8	15
Canada	0	0	1
Brazil	0	2	0
Other Latin America	0	1	0
Japan	0	0	0
Korea	0	0	1
Hong Kong	0	0	2
Other Asia	0	0	7
Middle East	2	3	86
Africa	2	11	21
Australia/New Zealand	0	1	0
Oceania	0	0	0
Caribbean	1	6	5
Panama	0	0	0
Singapore/Malaysia	0	3	0
Bahrain	0	1	1
Channel Islands	0	0	0
Total	22	110	248

Table 18
Canada Foreign Banking Presence (8 Banks) 1978-1979

Host Country	Subs	Affl	Brch
United States	9	1	22
United Kingdom	1	6	12
France	3	3	3
Germany	0	2	2
Switzerland	0	0	0
Netherlands	1	0	1
Belgium	0	1	1
Italy	0	0	0
Spain/Portugal	0	0	0
Other Europe	1	1	4
Canada	0	1[a]	0
Brazil	0	2	1
Other Latin America	0	2	18
Japan	0	0	0
Korea	0	0	1
Hong Kong	2	1	1
Other Asia	0	1	2
Middle East	1	1	5
Africa	0	0	1
Australia/New Zealand	0	2	1
Oceania	0	0	0
Caribbean	12	12	0
Panama	2	0	138
Singapore/Malaysia	0	2	2
Bahrain	0	0	5
Channel Islands	2	1	1
Total	34	39	222

Table 19
Brazil Foreign Banking Presence (8 Banks) 1978-1979

Host Country	Subs	Affl	Brch
United States	0	0	15
United Kingdom	0	4	3
France	0	2	2
Germany	0	0	1
Switzerland	0	0	0
Netherlands	0	0	1
Belgium	0	0	0
Italy	0	0	1
Spain/Portugal	0	0	1
Other Europe	0	0	0
Canada	0	0	0
Other Latin America	0	4	9
Japan	0	0	2
Korea	0	0	0
Hong Kong	0	0	0
Other Asia	0	0	0
Middle East	0	0	0
Africa	0	0	1
Australia/New Zealand	0	0	0
Oceania	0	0	0
Caribbean	0	1	9
Panama	0	1	3
Singapore/Malaysia	0	0	0
Bahrain	0	0	1
Channel Islands	0	0	0
Total	0	12	49

[a] An affiliate of a Canadian bank located on St. Pierre-Miquelon, a French-owned island off the east coast of Canada.

Table 20
Other Latin America Foreign Banking Presence (26 Banks) 1978-1979

Host Country	Subs	Affl	Brch
United States	3	4	36
United Kingdom	1	10	1
France	0	0	0
Germany	0	0	0
Switzerland	0	0	0
Netherlands	0	0	0
Belgium	0	0	0
Italy	0	0	0
Spain/Portugal	0	0	1
Other Europe	0	0	0
Canada	0	0	0
Brazil	0	0	3
Other Latin America	0	0	30
Japan	0	0	0
Korea	0	0	0
Hong Kong	0	0	0
Other Asia	0	0	0
Middle East	0	0	0
Africa	0	0	0
Australia/New Zealand	0	0	0
Oceania	0	0	0
Caribbean	0	1	0
Panama	0	0	5
Singapore/Malaysia	0	0	0
Bahrain	0	0	0
Channel Islands	0	0	0
Total	4	15	76

Table 21
Japan Foreign Banking Presence (23 Banks) 1978-1979

Host Country	Subs	Affl	Brch
United States	13	7	50
United Kingdom	1	19	21
France	0	11	1
Germany	0	2	11
Switzerland	3	2	0
Netherlands	3	0	0
Belgium	1	4	5
Italy	0	0	1
Spain/Portugal	0	0	0
Other Europe	1	2	0
Canada	0	0	0
Brazil	3	7	0
Other Latin America	0	0	9
Korea	0	1	3
Hong Kong	2	6	4
Other Asia	0	6	11
Middle East	0	6	0
Africa	0	3	0
Australia/New Zealand	0	7	0
Oceania	0	0	0
Caribbean	1	1	0
Panama	1	0	1
Singapore/Malaysia	0	8	10
Bahrain	0	0	0
Channel Islands	0	1	0
Total	29	93	127

Table 22
Other Asia Foreign Banking Presence (52 Banks) 1978-1979

Host Country	Subs	Afl	Brch
United States	2	3	50
United Kingdom	3	1	127
France	0	0	4
Germany	0	0	5
Switzerland	0	0	0
Netherlands	0	0	1
Belgium	0	0	2
Italy	0	0	0
Spain/Portugal	0	0	0
Other Europe	0	1	0
Canada	0	0	0
Brazil	0	0	0
Other Latin America	0	0	2
Japan	0	0	16
Korea	0	0	1
Hong Kong	0	0	50
Other Asia	0	0	77
Middle East	1	2	68
Africa	2	1	32
Australia/New Zealand	0	0	0
Oceania	0	0	16
Caribbean	0	0	4
Panama	0	0	1
Singapore/Malaysia	0	2	124
Bahrain	0	0	9
Channel Islands	1	0	0
Total	9	10	589

Table 23
Middle East Foreign Banking Presence (43 Banks) 1978-1979

Host Country	Subs	Afl	Brch
United States	3	14	19
United Kingdom	1	26	19
France	3	18	8
Germany	0	20	8
Switzerland	2	2	0
Netherlands	0	0	0
Belgium	0	6	0
Italy	0	13	1
Spain/Portugal	0	0	0
Other Europe	0	1	3
Canada	0	0	0
Brazil	0	0	0
Other Latin America	1	0	0
Japan	0	0	1
Korea	0	0	0
Hong Kong	0	0	0
Other Asia	0	0	2
Middle East	0	2	71
Africa	1	3	7
Australia/New Zealand	0	0	0
Oceania	0	0	0
Caribbean	2	0	2
Panama	0	0	0
Singapore/Malaysia	0	0	0
Bahrain	0	6	12
Channel Islands	0	0	0
Total	13	111	153

Table 24
Africa Foreign Banking Presence (31 Banks) 1978-1979

Host Country	Subs	Affl	Brch
United States	0	8	0
United Kingdom	0	14	7
France	0	14	4
Germany	0	14	0
Switzerland	0	0	0
Netherlands	0	0	0
Belgium	0	6	0
Italy	0	8	0
Spain/Portugal	0	0	0
Other Europe	0	1	0
Canada	0	0	0
Brazil	0	0	0
Other Latin America	0	0	0
Japan	0	0	0
Korea	0	0	0
Hong Kong	0	0	0
Other Asia	0	0	0
Middle East	0	1	1
Africa	0	0	5
Australia/New Zealand	0	0	0
Oceania	0	0	0
Caribbean	0	0	0
Panama	0	0	0
Singapore/Malaysia	0	0	0
Bahrain	0	0	0
Channel Islands	0	0	0
Total	0	66	17

Table 25
Australia/New Zealand Foreign Banking Presence (8 Banks) 1978-1979

Host Country	Subs	Affl	Brch
United States	0	0	9
United Kingdom	0	1	15
France	0	0	0
Germany	0	0	0
Switzerland	0	0	0
Netherlands	0	0	0
Belgium	0	2	0
Italy	0	0	0
Spain/Portugal	0	0	0
Other Europe	0	0	0
Canada	0	0	0
Brazil	0	0	0
Other Latin America	0	0	0
Japan	0	0	0
Korea	0	0	0
Hong Kong	0	2	1
Other Asia	0	1	0
Middle East	0	0	0
Africa	0	0	0
Australia/New Zealand	3	0	473
Oceania	3	2	52
Caribbean	0	1	0
Panama	0	0	0
Singapore/Malaysia	0	1	0
Bahrain	0	0	0
Channel Islands	1	0	0
Total	7	10	550

Table 26
Transnational Banking Presence Through Subsidiaries, Affiliates, and Branches

Country or Region of Origin	Number of Banking Institutions	Subsidiaries	Affiliates	Branches
United States	151	113	244	800
United Kingdom	25	86	54	961
France	19	37	126	228
Germany	21	16	115	55
Switzerland	13	18	30	32
Netherlands	6	20	25	109
Belgium	6	5	49	10
Italy	13	11	84	34
Spain/Portugal	20	16	39	115
Other Europe	47	22	110	248
Canada	8	34	39	222
Brazil	8	0	12	49
Other Latin America	26	4	15	76
Japan	23	29	93	127
Other Asia	52	9	10	589
Middle East	43	13	111	153
Africa	31	0	66	17
Australia/New Zealand	8	7	10	550
Grand Total	520	440	1232	4375

1978-1979

Table 27
Transnational Banking Presence Through Subsidiaries, Affiliates, and Branches

Host Country or Region	Subsidiaries	Affiliates	Branches
United States	46	59	304
United Kingdom	35	195	406
France	21	116	108
Germany	13	73	85
Switzerland	32	46	31
Netherlands	9	11	18
Belgium	16	48	44
Italy	4	23	21
Spain/Portugal	2	14	30
Other Europe	55	63	132
Canada	5	3	2
Brazil	6	36	47
Other Latin America	11	44	316
Japan	0	0	76
Korea	0	3	26
Hong Kong	21	14	215
Other Asia	3	23	315
Middle East	14	23	331
Africa	46	52	264
Australia/New Zealand	7	29	685
Oceania	6	9	116
Caribbean	48	85	466
Panama	12	7	62
Singapore/Malaysia	4	36	220
Bahrain	1	10	47
Channel Islands	23	31	8
Grand Total	440	1232	4375

1978-1979

Table 28
Transnational Subsidiaries by Host Area and Originating Area 1978-1979

Host Area	Originating Area			
	Total	Global Countries[a]	Intra-Regional	Remainder
North America	51	36	NA	15
Europe	187	137	40	10
Latin America	17	12	0	5
Africa	46	40	0	6
Middle East	14	10	0	4
Asia	24	23	0	1
Australia/New Zealand/ Oceania	13	7	6	0
Booking Centers[b]	88	70	NA	18

Table 29
Transnational Affiliates by Host Area and Originating Area 1978-1979

Host Area	Originating Area			
	Total	Global Countries[a]	Intra-Regional	Remainder
North America	62	22	NA	40
Europe	589	250	175	164
Latin America	80	57	4	19
Africa	202	129	0	73
Middle East	52	39	2	11
Asia	40	36	0	4
Australia/New Zealand/ Oceania	38	34	2	2
Booking Centers[b]	169	129	NA	40

Table 30
Transnational Branches, Agencies by Host Area and Originating Area 1978-1979

Host Area	Originating Area			
	Total	Global Countries[a]	Intra-Regional	Remainder
North America	306	135	NA	171
Europe	875	470	185	220
Latin America	363	317	42	4
Africa	264	146	5	113
Middle East	331	48	71	212
Asia	632	460	144	28
Australia/New Zealand/ Oceania	801	260	525	16
Booking Centers[b]	803	616	NA	187

[a]The United States, the United Kingdom, France, the Netherlands, Japan, Canada, Germany.

[b]The Caribbean, Panama, Singapore, Malaysia, Bahrain, Channel Islands.

TRANSNATIONAL BANKING AND THE
UNITED STATES

Aggregate data for United States banks' subsidiaries, affiliates, and branches/agencies in various foreign jurisdictions are presented in Table 8 and show that banks from the United States maintain a banking presence in all three organizational forms in virtually all of the host countries or regions. Appendix II of the *Report to Congress on Foreign Government Treatment of U.S. Commercial Banking Organizations* describes the policies regarding foreign bank entry and United States bank presence in 141 jurisdictions in 1979, including all countries recognized by the United States.[26] For each jurisdiction, Appendix II presents information on whether United States bank entry is permitted in the form of representative offices, branches, subsidiaries, and affiliates. It also describes the organizational form United States bank presence actually takes in each locale.

A summary judgment of the information presented in the Report is that there exists a positive correlation between a country's level of economic development and the ease of entry it permits United States banking organizations. Except for some of the very poorest countries, which are rather open to foreign bank entry, there is a general tendency for underdeveloped countries to be more restrictive and industrialized countries to be more permissive regarding entry. There are, however, important exceptions to this generalization and a great deal of variation concerning the regulatory terms and organizational forms through which entry is permitted.

In mid-1979, of the 141 jurisdictions surveyed, 104 permitted entry by United States banks in the form of representative offices; 59 permitted entry in the form of branches; 51 permitted entry in the form of subsidiaries; and 80 permitted entry in the form of affiliates. Some jurisdictions which did not permit United States bank entry in one or more forms at that time had done so in the past. The study showed that United States banks were extensively represented in jurisdictions which permitted entry or had done so in the past.

As noted previously, not all United States banks are active abroad. Out of over 14,300 United States commercial banks, only 151 have an identified banking presence in a foreign jurisdiction. The banks that are most active transnationally tend to be the largest in the country. Indeed, the five largest United States bank holding companies, owning banks which at year-end 1979 held 13 percent of the aggregate domestic assets of all United States commercial banks, have 51 percent of all the foreign branches/agencies of United States banks and 37 percent of all the foreign subsidiaries identified in Table 8.

In discussing the behavior of United States banks it is necessary to consider the existence of geopolitical restrictions on them. The United States banking system, unlike most others, is not nationwide but rather is restricted in important respects to a series of state banking systems. Tables 31-63, therefore, expand on the data presented in Table 8 for the presence of United States banks abroad by showing this pattern of presence classified by the home states of the banks.

The tables show the pattern of representation by 151 United States banks headquartered in 33 different states through banking subsidiaries, banking affiliates and branches/agencies in 15 specific foreign jurisdictions and 10 regions of the world. The sum of the detailed information by states presented in these tables equals the aggregate information presented in the previous section.

A review of the tables shows 800 foreign branches/agencies of United States banks in existence by 1979. Additionally, United States banks show a total of 113 (majority-owned) subsidiaries and 244 (minority-owned) affiliates engaged in commercial, merchant, and investment banking in foreign countries.[27]

The off-shore banking centers of the Caribbean account for the single largest concentration of United States banks' foreign presence—207 branches/agencies, 45 affiliates, and 15 subsidiaries. The most extensive and varied presence in a single country is in the United Kingdom, where United States banks have 60 branches, 26 affiliates, and 17 subsidiaries. In fact, significant concentrations of banking presence are found almost all over the world with those in Hong Kong, Japan, and France being particularly noteworthy.

Banks in New York State account for much of United States transnational presence. Sixteen banking organizations headquartered in New York have transnational operations. Texas has 13 banks which maintain a foreign banking presence; Pennsylvania has 11; and Illinois and California each have seven banks with such presence.

The 16 New York-based banks with identified foreign presence maintain 398 foreign branches, or 50 percent of United States banks' foreign branches. In addition, the New York banks have 87 foreign banking affiliates and 46 foreign subsidiaries, 36 percent and 41 percent of United States banks' presence in these forms. Comparable percentages for the seven California based banks with foreign operations are 17 percent of total United States banks' foreign branches/agencies, 21 percent of foreign affiliates, and 12 percent of foreign subsidiaries.

The seven Illinois-based banks with foreign operations maintain only 7 percent of United States banks' overseas branches/agencies, but 22 percent of the subsidiaries. Although there are a relatively large number of banks with foreign presence headquartered in Texas and Pennsylvania, they have small overseas networks. The 24 transnational banks from these two states together account for under 6 percent of United States banks' overseas branches/agencies and 4 percent of the subsidiaries.

The concentration of foreign banks in the United States roughly parallels this pattern. The Federal Reserve reports statistics on the presence of foreign banks in each United States state.[28] These data help to add texture to the information provided in Tables 31-48 concerning the foreign bank presence in the United States. March 1980 data indicate a total of at least 345 foreign bank presences in the United States representing at least 153 different parent banking organizations from over 34 foreign jurisdictions.[29] Of these 345 presences, 172 were located in New York, 97 in California and 35 in Illinois. Of the 153 foreign banking organizations represented in the United States, 23 are Japan-based, 8 are United Kingdom-based, 8 are Canada-based, 51 are Continental Europe-based and the remaining 63 are based in other countries. Foreign banking organizations operate 164 agencies, 134 branches, 47 subsidiary commercial banks, six investment companies, and two agreement corporations in the United States.[30]

While 68 foreign banking organizations operate in the United States through only one outlet, 14 operate through five or more. The Bank of Nova Scotia has the largest number of separately licensed or incorporated United States banking presences, with ten branches, agencies and

Table 31
Alabama Foreign Banking Presence (1 Bank)
1978-1979

Host Country	Subs	Affl	Brch
Caribbean	0	0	1
Total	0	0	1

Table 32
Arizona Foreign Banking Presence (3 Banks)
1978-1979

Host Country	Subs	Affl	Brch
Caribbean	0	2	3
Channel Islands	0	1	0
Total	0	3	3

Table 33
California Foreign Banking Presence (7 Banks) 1978-1979

Host Country	Subs	Affl	Brch
United Kingdom	3	6	9
France	1	2	1
Germany	0	1	5
Switzerland	0	2	1
Netherlands	0	0	2
Belgium	0	0	3
Italy	1	1	0
Spain/Portugal	1	1	0
Other Europe	1	4	7
Brazil	0	2	0
Other Latin America	1	2	27
Japan	0	0	9
Korea	0	0	3
Hong Kong	2	1	7
Other Asia	0	1	19
Middle East	0	3	0
Africa	0	22	2
Australia/New Zealand	1	1	0
Oceania	0	1	2
Caribbean	1	0	21
Panama	1	0	5
Singapore/Malaysia	0	2	7
Bahrain	0	0	2
Channel Islands	1	0	1
Total	14	52	133

Table 34
Colorado Foreign Banking Presence (2 Banks)
1978-1979

Host Country	Subs	Affl	Brch
Caribbean	0	2	2
Channel Islands	0	1	0
Total	0	3	2

Table 35
Connecticut Foreign Banking Presence (7 Banks)
1978-1979

Host Country	Subs	Affl	Brch
Caribbean	0	3	7
Channel Islands	0	1	0
Total	0	4	7

Table 36
**District of Columbia Foreign Banking Presence
(4 Banks) 1978-1979**

Host Country	Subs	Affl	Brch
Belgium	1	0	0
Other Europe	1	0	0
Hong Kong	1	0	0
Middle East	1	0	0
Africa	1	0	0
Caribbean	3	2	3
Channel Islands	0	1	0
Total	8	3	3

Table 37
Florida Foreign Banking Presence (1 Bank) 1978-1979

Host Country	Subs	Affl	Brch
Caribbean	0	0	1
Total	0	0	1

Table 38
**Georgia Foreign Banking Presence (4 Banks)
1978-1979**

Host Country	Subs	Affl	Brch
United Kingdom	0	1	0
Caribbean	2	2	4
Channel Islands	0	1	0
Total	2	4	4

Table 39
**Hawaii Foreign Banking Presence (2 Banks)
1978-1979**

Host Country	Subs	Affl	Brch
Oceania	0	4	12
Caribbean	0	2	0
Channel Islands	0	1	0
Total	0	7	12

Table 40
Illinois Foreign Banking Presence (7 Banks) 1978-1979

Host Country	Subs	Affl	Brch
United Kingdom	4	0	10
France	0	3	3
Germany	0	0	6
Switzerland	2	2	1
Netherlands	1	0	2
Belgium	1	0	2
Italy	0	0	3
Spain/Portugal	1	2	0
Other Europe	1	0	5
Brazil	0	2	0
Other Latin America	1	1	0
Japan	0	0	3
Korea	0	0	2
Hong Kong	2	1	2
Other Asia	1	2	1
Middle East	3	0	3
Africa	3	1	1
Australia/New Zealand	0	2	0
Caribbean	2	2	9
Panama	1	0	2
Singapore/Malaysia	1	2	2
Bahrain	0	1	0
Channel Islands	1	0	0
Total	25	21	57

Table 41
Indiana Foreign Banking Presence (3 Banks)
1978-1979

Host Country	Subs	Affl	Brch
United Kingdom	0	1	0
Switzerland	1	0	0
Other Europe	0	0	1
Caribbean	0	3	3
Channel Islands	0	1	0
Total	1	5	4

Table 42
Iowa Foreign Banking Presence (1 Bank) 1978-1979

Host Country	Subs	Affl	Brch
Caribbean	0	0	1
Total	0	0	1

Table 43
Kentucky Foreign Banking Presence (2 Banks)
1978-1979

Host Country	Subs	Affl	Brch
Caribbean	0	0	2
Total	0	0	2

Table 44
Louisiana Foreign Banking Presence (3 Banks)
1978-1979

Host Country	Subs	Affl	Brch
Caribbean	0	0	3
Total	0	0	3

Table 45
Maryland Foreign Banking Presence (4 Banks)
1978-1979

Host Country	Subs	Affl	Brch
United Kingdom	0	1	1
Caribbean	0	0	4
Total	0	1	5

Table 46
Massachusetts Foreign Banking Presence (4 Banks)
1978-1979

Host Country	Subs	Affl	Brch
United Kingdom	1	1	2
France	0	0	1
Germany	1	0	1
Other Europe	1	0	1
Brazil	0	0	9
Other Latin America	0	0	19
Japan	0	0	1
Hong Kong	1	0	0
Caribbean	0	2	6
Panama	1	0	1
Channel Islands	1	0	0
Total	6	3	41

Table 47
Michigan Foreign Banking Presence (5 Banks)
1978-1979

Host Country	Subs	Affl	Brch
United Kingdom	0	3	3
Germany	0	0	1
Japan	0	0	1
Caribbean	0	0	5
Total	0	3	10

Table 48
Minnesota Foreign Banking Presence (3 Banks)
1978-1979

Host Country	Subs	Affl	Brch
Other Europe	2	0	1
Caribbean	0	2	4
Channel Islands	0	1	0
Total	2	3	5

Table 49
Missouri Foreign Banking Presence (3 Banks)
1978-1979

Host Country	Subs	Affl	Brch
Caribbean	0	2	3
Channel Islands	0	1	0
Total	0	3	3

Table 50
New Jersey Foreign Banking Presence (7 Banks)
1978-1979

Host Country	Subs	Affl	Brch
Caribbean	0	2	7
Channel Islands	0	1	0
Total	0	3	7

Table 51
New York Foreign Banking Presence (16 Banks) 1978-1979

Host Country	Subs	Affl	Brch
United Kingdom	6	10	23
France	4	5	12
Germany	6	1	11
Switzerland	3	0	7
Netherlands	0	2	3
Belgium	2	2	7
Italy	1	0	11
Spain/Portugal	0	1	4
Other Europe	5	6	26
Canada	1	1	0
Brazil	1	5	11
Other Latin America	1	10	53
Japan	0	0	13
Korea	0	0	6
Hong Kong	6	0	33
Other Asia	1	6	40
Middle East	0	4	19
Africa	3	16	17
Australia/New Zealand	0	5	0
Oceania	0	0	1
Caribbean	3	4	52
Panama	0	1	24
Singapore/Malaysia	0	3	17
Bahrain	0	1	6
Channel Islands	3	4	2
Total	46	87	398

Table 52
North Carolina Foreign Banking Presence (4 Banks)
1978-1979

Host Country	Subs	Affl	Brch
United Kingdom	1	0	1
Hong Kong	0	0	1
Caribbean	1	0	4
Total	2	0	6

Table 53
Ohio Foreign Banking Presence (8 Banks) 1978-1979

Host Country	Subs	Affl	Brch
United Kingdom	0	1	0
Caribbean	0	1	8
Total	0	2	8

Table 54
Oklahoma Foreign Banking Presence (4 Banks)
1978-1979

Host Country	Subs	Affl	Brch
Caribbean	0	2	4
Channel Islands	0	1	0
Total	0	3	4

Table 55
Oregon Foreign Banking Presence (2 Banks)
1978-1979

Host Country	Subs	Affl	Brch
Caribbean	0	2	2
Channel Islands	0	1	0
Total	0	3	2

Table 56
Pennsylvania Foreign Banking Presence (11 Banks)
1978-1979

Host Country	Subs	Affl	Brch
United Kingdom	0	1	4
France	1	2	1
Germany	0	1	1
Other Europe	0	3	1
Brazil	0	2	0
Other Latin America	0	1	0
Japan	0	0	1
Hong Kong	0	0	1
Middle East	0	2	0
Caribbean	2	2	17
Panama	0	2	0
Singapore/Malaysia	0	1	0
Channel Islands	0	1	0
Total	3	18	26

Table 57
Rhode Island Foreign Banking Presence (2 Banks)
1978-1979

Host Country	Subs	Affl	Brch
Caribbean	0	0	2
Total	0	0	2

Table 58
South Carolina Foreign Banking Presence (2 Banks)
1978-1979

Host Country	Subs	Affl	Brch
Caribbean	0	0	2
Total	0	0	2

Table 59
Tennessee Foreign Banking Presence (5 Banks)
1978-1979

Host Country	Subs	Affl	Brch
Caribbean	0	2	5
Channel Islands	0	1	0
Total	0	3	5

Table 60
Texas Foreign Banking Presence (13 Banks)
1978-1979

Host Country	Subs	Affl	Brch
United Kingdom	2	1	4
France	0	0	1
Caribbean	0	4	13
Singapore/Malaysia	0	0	2
Channel Islands	0	2	0
Total	2	7	20

Table 61
Virginia Foreign Banking Presence (5 Banks)
1978-1979

Host Country	Subs	Affl	Brch
Caribbean	1	2	5
Channel Islands	0	1	0
Total	1	3	5

Table 62
Washington (State) Foreign Banking Presence
(3 Banks) 1978-1979

Host Country	Subs	Affl	Brch
United Kingdom	0	0	2
Switzerland	1	0	0
Japan	0	0	2
Hong Kong	0	0	7
Other Asia	0	0	1
Caribbean	0	0	2
Singapore/Malaysia	0	0	1
Total	1	0	15

Table 63
Wisconsin Foreign Banking Presence (3 Banks)
1978-1979

Host Country	Subs	Affl	Brch
United Kingdom	0	0	1
Caribbean	0	0	2
Total	0	0	3

Table 64
Foreign Bank Presence in the United States
1972-1980

Agencies	November 1972	May 1977	March 1980
Japan	21	28	24
Canada	9	12	17
Europe	11	22	40
Other	9	23	83
Total	50	95	164
Branches	**November 1972**	**May 1977**	**March 1980**
Japan	1	14	28
Canada	4	6	9
Europe	13	44	66
Other	8	17	31
Total	26	81	134
Banking Subsidiaries[a]	**November 1972**	**May 1977**	**March 1980**
Japan	6	10	13
Canada	8	8	9
Europe	9	12	22
Other	2	4	11
Total	25	34	55

[a]Includes trust companies and investment corporations and agreement corporations established under Article XII of the New York Banking Law.

Source: Federal Reserve Board data. March 1980 data on subsidiaries adjusted to include seven banks not listed by the Federal Reserve Board. See note 28 to the text.

Table 65
Foreign Bank Presence by State
March 1980

	New York	California	Illinois	Florida	Other
Agencies	59	81	—	21	3
Branches	82	—	31	0	21
Banking Subsidiaries[a]	31	16	4	0	4

[a]Includes trust companies and investment corporations and agreement corporations established under Article XII of the New York Banking Law.

Source: Federal Reserve Board Data. March 1980 data on subsidiaries adjusted to include seven banks not listed by the Federal Reserve Board. See note 28 to the text.

subsidiaries. Of the 153 foreign banking organizations or groups operating in the United States, 73 have a banking presence in only one state, 39 are present in two states, and 28 are present in three states. The remaining handful operate in more than three states, with five foreign banks having a banking presence in as many as six states.

Foreign bank presence in the United States dates back to the nineteenth century, but much of the current pattern is accounted for by relatively recent developments.[31] Table 64 shows the pattern of banking presence in the United States by banks from Japan, Canada, Europe, and other foreign countries through three different organizational forms as of 1972, 1977, and March 1980. Between 1972 and 1980 the number of foreign bank agencies in the United States more than tripled, branches quintupled, and banking subsidiaries more than doubled. Banks from Japan substantially increased their presence through branches and to a lesser extent through subsidiaries while they remained relatively constant in the use of the agency form. Banks from regions other than Japan, Canada or Europe, by contrast, seem to have expanded their United States presence through extensive use of the agency form. The expansion in the use of subsidiaries by Europe-based banking organizations is particularly pronounced, accounting for almost half the expansion in these organizational forms of banking presence.

Assessment of the extent of foreign bank presence in the United States is complicated by the geopolitical separation of the United States banking market by states. Table 65, therefore, presents the pattern of foreign bank presence in the individual states as of March 1980. The general conclusion which may be drawn from the table is that the major world financial center of New York is clearly the most attractive location for foreign banks in the United States, accounting for almost half of the foreign branches and agencies in the United States.[32] The four states shown separately in the table—New York, California, Illinois, and Florida—account for 98 percent of all foreign banks' agencies in the United States, 84 percent of all branches and 93 percent of all banking subsidiaries.

It is interesting to note the rough balance between the various states as host markets for foreign banks and as points of origin of the United States banking presence abroad. The states of New York, California, and Illinois are particularly good examples of this balance.

CONCLUSION

The pattern of transnational banking presence is varied and complex. Although the practice of establishing banking offices in foreign locales dates back to the earliest recorded civilizations, the expansion of the transnational network since the end of World War II has been noteworthy.

This study contains evidence of a substantial broadening in the transnational branching network in the last two decades, even in the face of a contraction associated with the decline of colonialism. In addition to the branch and agency forms of transnational banking presence, banks from a great many countries use the subsidiary and affiliate forms. Nonetheless, transnational presence is not a uniform or common practice among the world's banks. It is restricted to a relatively small number of banks. Moreover, banks from only a handful of countries can be said to have truly global networks. Most banks which maintain a transnational presence are restricted in their geographic coverage to the major world financial centers, the offshore banking centers, and selected foreign countries, often within the same region as the parent bank's home market.

The United States has emerged as one of the major world financial centers and is host to a large volume of transnational presence. This presence is, however, concentrated in a few parts of the country. As originators, United States banks as a whole have attained a global presence, despite the fact that the vast majority of United States banks have no transnational operations at all and, among those that do, most cannot properly be described as global.

The purpose of this study has been to provide a readily accessible body of data relating to the structure of banking presence outside home country markets. These data can be useful in assisting researchers on a wide variety of topics related to banking, finance, and international economic and political relations. No study of this kind could be complete without suggesting the need for further research. The authors' experience in preparing this study strongly suggests the desirability of extending the structural measures of presence by compiling financial information about the volume and scope of banking business done in the transnational banking network.

Acknowledgments

Arnita Thurston and David Dale provided valuable research assistance.

APPENDIX

Tables 1-7

The source for the branch and agency information in Tables 1-7 was the *Bankers Almanac and Yearbook* for 1961-62, 1970-71 and 1978-79 (Sussex: Thomas Skinner Directories). Numbers of foreign branches and agencies, listed by country under each bank entry in the *Almanac*, were totalled to obtain the numbers in Tables 1-3.[33] Country of origin was determined by the country in which the bank was chartered.

For some banks, entries in the *Almanac* consolidated numbers of branches, agencies, sub-branches and offices. Individual instances in which numbers included offices other than branches and agencies are described in notes to the appropriate tables.

Tables 8-63

The banking institutions covered in Tables 8-63 are those which have branches, agencies, banking affiliates and/or subsidiaries in foreign countries. Subsidiaries, affiliates, and branches were defined as follows for the purpose of constructing the table:

Subsidiaries: Those banking institutions which are described as subsidiaries in the source compilations or in which the participating institutions hold a greater than 50 percent interest. Includes subsidiaries of the following: the participating institution's domestic subsidiaries, its foreign subsidiaries, and its parent bank holding company.

Affiliates: Those banking institutions which are described as affiliates in the source compilations or in which the participating institution holds a 50 percent or lesser interest. Includes affiliates of the participating institution's domestic subsidiaries, its foreign subsidiaries, and its parent bank holding company. A consortium bank and its subsidiaries are counted as affiliates of each participating bank. Subsidiaries and affiliates of international groups (such as Societe Financiere pour Les Pays D'Outre Mer, which has seven banking subsidiaries and eight banking affiliates in Africa) are counted as affiliates of each participating bank. Affiliate totals for rows and columns are therefore necessarily inflated relative to the actual number of such banks in the world, as one bank may be an affiliate of several participating institutions.

Branches: Branches and agencies of the parent institution and branches and agencies of its domestic subsidiaries.

Branches, agencies, affiliates and subsidiaries of a banking institution located in a territory or dependency of that institution's country of origin are considered foreign and included in the tables, because territories and dependencies often represent a distinct financial market and conduct independent banking policy.

The data used in constructing the tables spanned two years, 1978 and 1979. *Who Owns What in World Banking* 1979-80 (London: The Banker Research Unit) contains information from year-end 1978 and early 1979. *The Bankers Almanac and Yearbook* 1978-79 (Sussex. Thomas Skinner Directories) contains data as of mid-year 1978. The *Almanac* is more comprehensive in terms of numbers of institutions listed and more specific in terms of numbers of branches listed for each institution, while *Who Owns What* contains detailed ownership information for banking and non-banking affiliates and subsidiaries of the world's largest banks as well as bank consortia. Data from the *Almanac* was used to supplement information found in *Who Owns What*.

The sources generally agreed, but minor discrepancies existed. Obviously, it is unreasonable to expect publications which list hundreds of banks to be free of minor inconsistencies. Where practicable, telephone contacts were made to resolve questions.

Federal Reserve Board year-end 1979 data on foreign bank subsidiaries, branches and agencies in the United States and United States bank branches in other countries served to correct and expand the United States rows and columns of the tables. Additional information was found in "1979 Director of Foreign Banking in America" (*Institutional Investor*, September 1979): "International Activities of U.S. Banks" for year-end 1978 (Anthony F. Mattera in the *American Banker*, March 23, 1979); and *Foreign Ownership of U.S. Banks: Facts and Patterns* (William A. Longbrake, Melanie R. Quinn and Judith A. Walter, OCC Paper, this book.)

In the United States, a clear distinction can be made between commercial banks, which accept demand deposits, and other financial institutions. We have restricted our attention to the United States commercial banks which, directly and through Edge Act subsidiaries and bank holding companies, establish branches and participate in ownership of subsidiary and affiliate banks in other countries. Banking structures in other countries differ. Publications such as the *Almanac* and *Who Owns What* include such diverse financial institutions as merchant banks, savings banks, mutual credit associations, trust companies, and leasing and underwriting firms. So that the large British merchant banks and other recognized major banking institutions such as Credit Agricole of France would not be excluded from the tables, the following criteria were observed:

All banks and deposit-accepting institutions and institutions engaged in banking activities according to balance sheet information or the capsule descriptions in the *Almanac* and *Who Owns What* are included in the tables if they have some type of foreign presence as described above. Trust companies, leasing, underwriting, and factoring firms were excluded, except for foreign bank owned trust companies in the United States, which have banking powers.

Tables 64-65

These tables were constructed using data compiled by the International Banking Division of the Federal Reserve Board on form FR 886, which lists all foreign-owned financial institutions in the United States.

As indicated in the footnotes to Tables 64-65, the Federal Reserve Board data has been corrected to include additional bank-owned institutions listed in *Foreign Ownership of U.S. Banks: Facts and Patterns.*

Comparison of the Tables

The source for Tables 1-7 is the *Bankers Almanac and Yearbook* (Sussex: Thomas Skinner Directories). As noted above, Tables 8-63 were constructed using additional sources, including Federal Reserve data, and contain, for example, more complete figures for United States banks.

Country of origin for each bank appearing in Tables 1-7 was determined by country of charter due to the difficulty involved in determining bank ownership as far back as 1960. In Tables 8-63, ownership of banking subsidiaries was traced back to the parent bank and its country of charter. Thus, the numbers of originating banks as well as the numbers of branches in Table 3 and Tables 8-63 may differ.

Tables 64-65 were constructed from Federal Reserve data, as noted above, and differ from the other tables in two respects. First, the Federal Reserve data categorizes territories and dependencies of the United States as part of the United States. Therefore, neither mainland branches of territorial banks nor territorial branches of mainland banks appear in Tables 64-65. Such offices are included in Tables 1-63. Secondly, Federal Reserve data categorizes consortium banks as being group-owned. Thus, while European American Banking Corporation in New York is included as an affiliate of its six participating banks in Tables 8-30, it appears as an agreement corporation owned by the European American "Group" on the Federal Reserve listing.

Geography

The countries included in each region in the tables are listed below. The lists serve merely to define regions and do *not* indicate that each country within a region necessarily contains banking institutions which have some type of foreign presence or hosts foreign banking institutions.

A.   Tables 8-63

1.   Host Regions

Other Europe

Andorra	Iceland
Austria	Lichtenstein
Bulgaria	Luxembourg
Cyprus	Monaco
Czechoslovakia	Norway
Denmark	Poland
Faero Islands	Romania
Finland	Sweden
German Democratic Republic	Turkey
Gibraltar	USSR
Greece	Yugoslavia
Hungary	

Other Latin

Argentina	Guyana
Belize	Honduras
Bolivia	Mexico
Chile	Nicaragua
Colombia	Paraguay
Costa Rica	Peru
Ecuador	Surinam
El Salvador	Uruguay
Guatemala	Venezuela

Other Asia

Afghanistan	Nepal
Bangladesh	Pakistan
Brunei	Peoples Republic of China
Burma	Philippines
India	Sri Lanka
Indonesia	Taiwan
Laos	Thailand
Macao	

Mid East

Iran
Iraq
Israel
Jordan
Kuwait
Lebanon
Oman

Qatar
Saudi Arabia
Syria
United Arab Emirates
Yemen
Yemen Arab Republic

Africa

Algeria
Angola
Azores
Benin
Botswana
Burundi
Cameroun
Canary Islands
Central African Empore
Chad
Comoro Islands
Egypt
Equatorial Guinea
Ethiopia
Gabon
Gambia
Ghana
Guinea
Guinea–Bissau
Ivory Coast
Kenya
Lesotho
Liberia
Libya
Madeira

Mauritius
Morocco
Mozambique
Namibia
Niger
Nigeria
Peoples Republic of Congo
Republic of Djibouti
Reunion
Rwanda
Senegal
Seychelles
Sierra Leone
Somalia
South Africa
Sudan
Swaziland
Tanzania
Togo
Tunisia
Uganda
Upper Volta
Zaire
Zambia
Zimbabwe

Oceania

Fiji
Guam
New Caledonia

New Hebrides
Papua New Guinea
Tonga

Caribbean

Anguilla
Antigua
Barbados

Bermuda
British Virgin Islands

British West Indies
   (includes Bahamas and Cayman
   Islands)
Cuba
Dominican Republic
French West Indies
Grenada

Haiti
Netherlands Antilles
Puerto Rico
U.S. Virgin Islands

2. Originating Regions—same as Host regions with the following exceptions:

Other Latin—Includes Caribbean, Panama
Other Asia—Includes Hong King, Korea, Malaysia, Singapore
Mid East—Includes Bahrain

B. Tables 1-7

1. Host Region—same as in Tables 8-63 with the following exceptions:

Other Europe—Includes Belgium, Italy, Spain, Portugal
Other Latin—Includes Brazil
Other Far East—Includes Korea, Other Asia, Australia, New Zealand, Oceania

2. Originating Region—Same as in Tables 8-30 with following exceptions:

Other Europe—Includes Belgium, Spain, Portugal
Latin America—Includes Brazil, does not include Caribbean
Other Far East—Includes Other Asia, New Zealand

FOOTNOTES

[1] See the Appendix for a listing of countries contained in originating and host regions.

[2] Correspondent banking remains a significant part of the current banking scene because of its cost effectiveness and because of the existence of jurisdictions which restrict non-local bank entry. It is likely to continue, even if entry restrictions are lifted, because it is impractical for any bank (let alone all banks) to maintain a physical presence in all the locales where pairs of payers and payees may choose to conduct business.

[3] The need for credit to bridge geographic separation and the capability of banks to do so through correspondent relationships or physical presence in more than one locale are conceptually no different where the geographic separation to be bridged is across town, across state lines, or across the ocean. The differences in degree are, of course, vitally important in practice, but are not really differences in kind. The same observation is equally pertinent with regard to establishing branch offices or subsidiary/affiliate relationships to exploit growth or profit opportunities or to reduce overall risk to the banking company through geographic diversification. The only inherent differences in the transnational context relate to currency and exchange rate considerations.

[4] For a discussion of motivating factors in foreign acquisitions of U.S. banks, see Judith A. Walter, *Foreign Acquisitions of U.S. Banks: Motives and Tactical Considerations*, OCC Paper, this book.

[5] Klaas Peter Jacobs, "The Development of International and Multinational Banking in Europe," *Columbia Journal of World Business*, Winter 1975, pp. 33-39.

[6] Martin Mayer, *The Bankers*, (New York: Weybright and Talley, 1974), p. 40. The very terms "bank" and "bankrupt" are further parts of the heritage of this era. The term "bankrupt" harks back to the symbolic breaking of the bank or bench when a moneychanger could not meet his obligations.

[7] There is some evidence to suggest that there was also considerable presence by banks from the major industrial and colonial powers in the less developed countries from at least the late nineteenth century on. See notes 11 and 16 below and accompanying text.

[8] As of year-end 1979, a century later, foreign banks through their agencies and subsidiaries accounted for just under 21 percent of the total commercial bank assets in California. Geoff Brouillette, "Foreign Subsidiaries are Fastest Growing Segment of California Banking," *American Banker*, July 30, 1975.

[9] *Report on Foreign Banking Matters of the Superintendent of Banks, State of California*, April 1974.

[10] *Annual Report of the Superintendent of Banks of the State of New York*, Albany, New York, January 1, 1913, pp. 29-30.

[11] Clyde William Phelps, *The Foreign Expansion of American Banks* (New York: Ronald Press Co., 1927), p. 200.

[12] Phelps, p. 201.

[13] Deutsche Bank also had branch offices in China and Japan during this period.

[14] Phelps, pp. 28-31.

[15] Frank M. Tamagna and Parker B. Willis, "United States Banking Organization Abroad," *Federal Reserve Bulletin*, December 1956, pp. 1284-1299.

[16] Prior to 1914, overseas banking branches and subsidiaries could legally be operated only by separately chartered foreign banking corporations, which existed solely for that purpose.

[17] Such provisions are not unique to the United States and have survived to the present time in some countries.

[18] Only three of those 12 banks survive today under their original names—First National Bank of Boston, Bankers Trust Co., and the American Express Co. The latter, of course, is not engaged in domestic banking. Perhaps reflecting the geographic distribution of U.S. commercial and trade relations in this period, the 107 branches of the 11 domestic banks were heavily concentrated in Latin America (61), and the remainder were distributed almost evenly throughout Europe (25) and the Far East (21). Martin Mayer reports that the Banco de Boston operation in Argentina made enough of an impression on the local scene to have a tango written about it. Mayer, p. 435.

[19] See Frederick R. Dahl, "International Operations of U.S. Banks: Growth and Public Policy Implications," *Law and Contemporary Problems*, Winter 1967, p. 103.

[20] Source: Board of Governors, Federal Reserve System, data include only Federal Reserve member banks.

[21] Other Far East includes Asian countries not listed separately as well as Australia and Oceania. See the Appendix for a list of countries included in each originating and host region. The increase in U.K. presence in the Far East between 1961 and 1970 is artificial because the format of the entry for the Australia and New Zealand Bank, Ltd. in *Bankers Almanac and Yearbook*, changed between 1961 and 1970. The 1960 entry included only branches and agencies, whereas the 1970 entry also included sub-branches and offices. The Australia and New Zealand Bank appears as an Australian bank in Table 3 since the headquarters moved from the United Kingdom to Australia between 1970 and 1978. This accounts for much of the decline in the number of U.K. bank branches in the Far East over this period. See the Notes to Tables 1-3.

[22] The two banks are: The British and French Bank, Ltd. and E. D. Sasoon Banking Company, Ltd.

[23] See *Report to Congress on Foreign Government Treatment of U.S. Commercial Banking Organizations*, Department of the Treasury, 1979, Table II-1 for a summary of foreign bank entry policies by country. Conversations with officials of two major British banks confirmed the decline in branch presence in Africa as new subsidiary banks were established to maintain the British banking presence there.

[24] Illustrative of the difficulty in obtaining current data is the fact that three new offices of Brazilian banks, located in Belgium and Africa, have been established subsequent to the period covered by our data sources. Although inclusion of these three offices would change the detailed picture portrayed in Table 19, they do not materially change our conclusion presented in the text. It is interesting to note that the Brazilian transnational banking network seems to encompass the major banking centers (such as New York), the booking centers (such as Bahrain), and the major coffee growing and trading regions of the world.

[25] This should not be misinterpreted to say that individual U.S. banks maintain a presence through subsidiaries, affiliates, and branches simultaneously in each foreign jurisdiction. While this is sometimes the case, it is by no means the general rule, and in any event the extent of this pattern is beyond the scope of our data.

[26] See Note 23 for complete citation.

[27] Within varying limitations set by the laws of their countries of origin and the foreign jurisdictions in which they conduct business, banking organizations are permitted to invest in companies engaged in activities other than banking. This study concentrates on foreign *banking* activities and thus excludes from the tabulations foreign *non-banking* subsidiaries and affiliates. Sources of data on foreign non-banking activities of banking organizations include *Who Owns What in World Banking*, (London: The Banker Research Unit) published annually and Anthony F. Mattera, "International Activities of U.S. Banks," *American Banker*, March 23, 1979.

[28] See the Appendix for a discussion of this data source. Federal Reserve Board data were supplemented by the inclusion of seven bank or multi-bank owned subsidiaries not listed by the Federal Reserve Board. They are:

Bank Name	State	Foreign Owner
LaSalle National Bank	IL	Algemene Bank Nederland
Bank of the West	CA	Banque Nationale de Paris
National Bank of North America	NY	National Westminster Bank, Ltd.
Union Bank	CA	Standard-Chartered Group
Union Chelsea National Bank	NY	Banco Union, S.A.
Philippine Bank of California	CA	Philippine National Bank & others
Marine Midland Bank, NA	NY	The Hongkong and Shanghai Banking Corporation

Source: William A. Longbrake, Melanie R. Quinn and Judith A. Walter, *Foreign Ownership of U.S. Banks: Facts and Patterns*, OCC Paper, this book.

[29] The Federal Reserve Board lists the ownership of a consortium bank as a "group" without identifying the participant banks. The 153 different parent organizations reported by the Federal Reserve Board, therefore, include more than 153 different banks.

[30] This summary does not present the complete picture because it concentrates on commercial banking activities and does not cover banking-related activities such as factoring which foreign bank holding companies may and do conduct in the United States. It also does not cover certain operations such as securities affiliates which foreign banks were permitted to establish before the adoption of the International Banking Act of 1978. The Act permits preexisting securities affiliates of foreign commercial banks to continue in operation, but no new ones may be established.

[31] Accompanying the structural expansion of the foreign bank presence in the United States in recent years has been a growth in assets. As of June 1979, the assets of branches, agencies, investment companies, agreement corporations, and subsidiary commercial banks established *de novo* by foreign banks in the United States amounted to $144.6 billion. Assets of foreign-acquired subsidiary commercial banks, including all known acquisitions pending at that time, amounted to $29.9 billion. In computing aggregate assets of *de novo* and acquired banks, assets as of June 1979 of banks which resulted from the subsequent merger of a *de novo* bank and a domestically-owned bank were pro-rated according to relative asset sizes of the two banks at the time of merger. Thus roughly 20 percent of the aggregate assets of foreign banks in this country are attributable to acquisition activity, while 80 percent of the assets are attributable to the business of *de novo* foreign bank entries in the domestic market.

[32] Combining branches and agencies is justified for this purpose because despite differences in powers between branches and agencies, the primary distinction in the choice of form is the state statutory and regulatory environment which in some instances requires reciprocity with the entrant's home country for one form but not the other or permits entry in only one of the two forms. See William B. Glidden and John E. Shockey, "U.S. Branches and Agencies of Foreign Banks: A Comparison of Federal and State Chartering Options," *The University of Illinois Law Forum*, April 1980, pp. 65-90.

[33] This method of tabulating information from the *Almanac* was used by Francis A. Lees in *International Banking and Finance* (New York: Wiley, 1974).

## 5

U.S. BANKS' LOSS OF GLOBAL STANDING

C. STEWART GODDIN

STEVEN J. WEISS

SUMMARY

The number of U.S. banks appearing among the rankings of the world's largest banks has declined substantially over the past twenty-five years, giving rise to concerns that U.S. banks' competitive position in the international market place may be weakening. This paper reviews that trend in depth, examines the validity of those concerns, and analyzes the effects of broad economic trends, exchange rate changes, differences in domestic market structures and banking policies, and foreign acquisitions of U.S. banks on the rankings of the world's largest banks.

In 1956, 44 U.S. banks ranked among the world's top 100; the number had dropped to only 27 in 1967 and steadily fell further to 15 by the end of 1979. In contrast, the number of Japanese banks appearing in the top 100 increased from 9 in 1956 to 24 in 1979, and German banks' presence among the world's largest grew from 3 to 14 over the same period. In absolute terms, however, U.S. banks have achieved substantial growth since 1956.

The potential growth of any nation's banking system, and individual banks within that system, is heavily dependent upon the overall growth in that nation's domestic economy and levels of international trade and investment. U.S. economic growth during the 1956-1979 period was significantly overshadowed by that of Europe and Japan, resulting in a steady decline of the relative worldwide importance of the U.S. economy, trade and investment. The predominance of American banks in the world rankings in the 1950s and the slippage in the 1960s and 1970s are found to closely parallel those fundamental changes in the balance of economic power between the United States and the rest of the world.

Comparisons of bank sizes are usually made in terms of the U.S. dollar, raising questions about whether exchange rates might not be a major factor in explaining the ascendancy of banks from countries, such as Japan and Germany, whose currencies have appreciated greatly against the dollar in recent years. Mechanical reranking of the world's top 100 banks by holding exchange rates constant is found to substantially overstate the apparent impact of currency realignments. Other evidence suggests that exchange rate movements may not have materially affected the rankings.

Government policies regarding domestic bank operations and expansion opportunities appear to have played an important role in the evolution of the top 100 bank rankings. U.S. banks are constrained in a number of ways in which banks in many foreign countries are not. Laws and regulations restrict the scope of banking activities U.S. commercial banks may conduct. Nationwide banking is prohibited and even statewide banking is proscribed or severely limited in some states. Few countries, if any, impose as stringent antitrust barriers to acquisitions as the U.S. does. Banks abroad are usually authorized to engage in both commercial and investment banking activities, and nationwide branching is generally permitted for major banks in foreign countries.

Substantial consolidation of banking systems has occurred in European nations and elsewhere during the postwar decades. Domestic market shares of the largest foreign banks tend to be very high. Whereas the ten largest U.S. banking organizations hold about one-third of total U.S. commercial bank deposits, the concentration of assets in other nations was found to be generally much higher, with a small number of large banks holding from 40 to over 80 percent of total assets.

The inclusion of institutions other than commercial banks has also reduced the relative ranking of U.S. banks. For example, France's Credit Agricole, which is made up of 94 fairly autonomous regional agricultural banks and over 3,000 co-operative banks, was first included in the rankings in 1975 as the world's third largest bank. Seven of the fourteen German banks appearing in the top 100 world bank list in 1979 are central giro institutions, only three of which are currently active in the international markets.

Finally, the paper demonstrates that foreign acquisitions of U.S. banks have had relatively little impact on the U.S. share of deposits held by the world's 100 largest banks. The increase in the foreign bank share of the top 100 banks attributable to their acquisitions of U.S. banks, including pending acquisitions as of December 31, 1980, is estimated to be approximately 0.9 percent.

INTRODUCTION

The number of U.S. banks appearing in the rankings of the world's largest banks has declined substantially over the past 25 years, giving rise to concern that U.S. banks' competitive position in the international market place may be weakening. This paper reviews that trend in depth, examines the validity of that concern, and analyzes the impact that broad economic factors, exchange rate changes, domestic market structures and banking policies, and foreign acquisitions of U.S. banks have had on the rankings of the world's largest banks.

DEVELOPMENTS IN THE "WORLD'S LARGEST" BANKING DERBY (1956-79)

Table 1 presents an overview of developments in the "world's largest" banking "derby" since 1956.[1] The preeminence of U.S. banks in the rankings has fallen consistently over this period. In 1956, 44 U.S. banks ranked among the world's top 100; the number had dropped to only 22 in 1970; and steadily declined to 15 by the end of 1979.[2]

Other trends are also apparent. At the beginning of the period, the world's largest banks were headquartered in a very small number of countries. Their distribution spread to a much greater number of nations in the next 23 years. Looking at the very largest banks—the top 10—France is seen to gain most prominently. Looking at the top 50 and 100, however, Japan and Germany emerge as the rapidly ascendent nations.

Regardless of the group examined, the United States appears throughout this period as the major loser in ranking.

Table 1
Nationality of World's Largest Banks[1]

Country[3]	No. of Banks in Top 10 by Deposit Size				No. of Banks in Top 50 by Deposit Size				No. of Banks in Top 100 by Deposit Size				% of Top 100 Deposits held by National Groups[2]			
	1956	1960	1970	1979	1956	1960	1970	1979	1956	1960	1970	1979	1956	1960	1970	1979
Japan	—	—	—	—	3	8	11	16	9	12	24	24	5.1	9.7	19.4	23.6
United States	5	6	4	2	25	19	13	6	44	37	22	15	52.4	44.8	29.1	14.4
Germany	—	—	1	2	—	3	4	7	3	7	11	14	1.3	5.0	10.0	16.8
Italy	—	—	1	—	3	5	4	2	6	7	9	9	3.8	5.4	8.7	6.6
Canada	2	1	1	—	6	5	5	4	7	7	5	6	9.5	8.7	6.8	5.2
United Kingdom	3	3	2	2	7	5	4	4	10	10	5	5	14.9	13.6	7.6	6.9
France	—	—	1	4	3	3	3	4	5	4	3	4	4.0	4.1	4.8	10.4
Netherlands	—	—	—	—	—	—	1	3	1	1	3	4	0.4	0.5	2.1	4.5
Spain	—	—	—	—	—	—	—	—	2	1	3	4	0.9	0.5	1.3	1.9
Switzerland	—	—	—	—	—	—	3	3	5	4	3	3	2.2	2.4	3.2	3.3
Belgium	—	—	—	—	—	—	—	1	1	3	4	3	0.5	1.3	2.1	2.1
Sweden	—	—	—	—	—	—	—	—	2	2	2	2	1.1	1.2	1.0	0.9
Australia	1	1	—	—	1	1	1	—	2	2	3	2	1.2	1.1	2.1	0.9
Other[4]	2	1	—	—	2	1	—	—	3	3	3	5	2.2	2.0	1.8	2.5

Source: American Banker, "500 Largest Banks in the Free World," annual listing, adjusted to eliminate double counting of subsidiary banks appearing separately on the list.

Notes:

[1] See Appendix A for a discussion of data and coverage in alternative rankings based on assets and reflecting more complete consolidation of bank groups and holding companies.

[2] May not total to 100% due to rounding.

[3] Countries listed in order of number of banks represented in the top 100 as of 12/79.

[4] "Other" includes Argentina, India, Brazil, Hong Kong, Israel, and Austria, none of which had more than one bank in the top 100 in any year covered.

CONCERN OVER THE DECLINE IN
U.S. BANKS' PREEMINENCE

The rapid decline in the number of U.S. banks appearing among the rankings of the world's largest banks has generated considerable political attention in this country during the past three years. It apparently had an impact on the debate which lead up to the moratorium on foreign acquisitions of domestic banks enacted on March 31, 1980 (Depository Institutions Deregulation and Monetary Control Act, Title IX). New York Bank Superintendent Muriel Siebert, for example, highlighted the decline in U.S. banks' preeminence in a letter to Representative Henry Reuss, Chairman of the House Banking Committee:

> In 1970, seven of the world's largest banks were American; by 1977 these figures had reversed and only three of the world's top ten banks were American.[3]

Senator Heinz, commenting on the same phenomenon, associated it with the growth of foreign bank presence in the U.S.:

> Since 1972, . . . foreign bank assets in the U.S. have more than quadrupled, from $16 billion to more than $74 billion . . . the pattern of expansion and growth behind these figures is striking. In 1972, there were 66 foreign banks operating in the U.S.; by the end of 1978 there were 189. . . . Over the same period, our post-war preeminent position in world banking declined dramatically. . . . Over the past five years, large U.S. banks have grown at a much slower rate than their foreign competitors. . . .[4]

During congressional hearings in July 1979, the chairman of a major Texas bank observed that "we are becoming less competitive because of size and stature in the world markets;"[5] and Senatory Moynihan opined, ". . . nowhere do I see the problem of our declining position in world banking markets being addressed."[6]

VALID CONCERNS?

It is generally accepted that the managerial, technological, and innovative capabilities of U.S. banks remain in the forefront and that the decline in U.S. bank rankings should not be blamed on the banks themselves. Some observers have blamed the decline on foreign acquisitions of U.S. banks and on differences in national banking policies and regulations. To the extent that those factors are valid, they raise a number of legitimate concerns and possible policy implications.

Concern about U.S. banking organizations' global position also undoubtedly reflects a large measure of national pride and a reluctance to accept a diminution in the relative worldwide importance and acceptance of any American institution, whether it is banking, the automobile, or the American way of life and political system in general.

Some diminution in the relative worldwide importance of U.S. banks since World War II was inevitable as Europe and Japan rebuilt their economies and as their financial institutions grew domestically and reestablished their positions in international finance. The predominance of American banks in the world rankings in the 1950s and the slippage in the 1960s and 1970s closely parallel fundamental changes in the balance of economic power between the United States and the rest of the world. That decline, to the extent it reflects the overall decline in the relative worldwide strength of the U.S. economy, stems from causes which are not unique to, and extend well beyond, the field of banking.

It is also important to bear in mind that the changes have been in the *relative* standing of U.S. banks. In absolute terms, U.S. banks have exhibited tremendous growth since 1956, both overall and in their international operations.

The total deposit size of the top 10 U.S. banks, for example, rose from $40 billion at the end of 1956 to over $388 billion at the end of 1979.[7] Similarly, international operations of U.S. banks have grown in total size and importance. Total assets of overseas branches of U.S. banks have mushroomed from a miniscule $2 billion in 1956 to over $312 billion at the end of 1979,[8] considerably more than the $171.6 billion in total assets held by foreign banks in the United States.[9] International operations also play a significant role in the earnings of many of our largest banks.[10]

THE RANKINGS—BROAD ECONOMIC FACTORS

The potential growth of any nation's banking system, and individual banks within that system, is heavily dependent upon the overall rate of growth in that nation's economy and money supply and underlying factors, such as household savings and private capital formation, which influence economic growth.[11] Similarly, a number of studies have indicated that a bank's international operations typically are directed at serving the financial needs generated by international trade and investment activities of home country industries.[12]

As shown in Table 2, the industrialized nations experienced significant economic growth between 1956 and 1979, in both nominal and real terms. Although the United States' Gross Domestic Product (GDP) grew 456 percent in nominal terms and 113 percent in real terms over that period, that growth was significantly overshadowed in both Europe and Japan. In nominal terms, most industrialized nations grew substantially faster. In real terms, European growth generally outpaced that of the U.S. by half. Japan registered a 553 percent increase in her GDP over the period considered, nearly five times the U.S. increase.[13] Thus, the opportunity for domestic growth was considerably more constrained for U.S. banks than for their European and Japanese competitors.

The rapid internationalization of banking also paralleled international trade and investment flows which blossomed during the postwar period.

The level of international trade, for example, increased more than fifteen-fold from just under $100 billion in 1956 to over $1.5 trillion in 1979. In 1956, the United States accounted for 17.1 percent of total world trade flows; 14.8 percent in 1970; and only 13.1 percent in 1979.[14] International direct investment flows from the major industrial countries, increased from an estimated annual level of $4 billion in 1958-62 to over $30 billion in 1978. United States predominance in foreign direct investment activity ebbed, however, in the 1960s and 1970s as Europe and Japan increased their direct investment activities.

The decline in the relative rankings of U.S. banks among the world's largest banks, and the emergence of Japanese and European banks in the rankings have reflected these national and international developments. This can be seen in Figure I, which compares trends in national preeminence among the world's top 100 banks[15] with the relative international importance of each nation's gross domestic product[16] and volume of international trade.[17]

The relative worldwide importance of the U.S. economy fell substantially from 1960 to 1979, as can be seen in the decline from 54 percent to 34 percent of the U.S.'s portion of the total gross domestic product of all OECD countries. U.S. banking preeminence over this period fell even more precipitously, from 45 percent to 14 percent, and now is approximately equal to the relative importance of U.S. trade flows.

Table 2

Gross Domestic Product in Purchasers' Values (In billions of domestic currency units)

Country	In Nominal Terms			In 1975 Prices		
	1956	1979	Percent Increase	1956	1979	Percent Increase
United States	422.62	2,349.92	456	849.80	1,813.18	113
Japan	9,706.00	221,507.00	2,182	28,706.00	187,401.00	553
Germany	213.67[1]	1,400.16	555	461.00[1,4]	1,210.56	163
United Kingdom	20.73	189.28	813	63.88	114.52	79
Italy	17,455.13[1]	268,868.00	1,440	51,073.99[1,4]	145,615.00	185
Canada	32.25	265.91	722	70.19	192.76	175
France	188.34[2]	2,430.62	1,191	575.90[2,4]	1,678.26	191
Netherlands	31.88[1]	299.01	838	93.11[1,4]	236.46	154
Spain	476.75[3]	13,226.60	2,675	2,071.13[3,4]	6,631.00	220
Switzerland	29.25	157.97	440	73.33	145.16	98
Belgium	473.66[1]	3,175.01	570	1,067.91[1,4]	2,540.00	138
Sweden	55.24	456.01	726	146.10	312.54	114
Australia	11.32	113.82	905	30.15	79.90	165

[1] The accounting system for gross domestic product was changed in 1960; 1956 GDP has been adjusted to reflect the change.
[2] The accounting system for gross domestic product was changed in 1959; 1956 GDP has been adjusted to reflect the change.
[3] The accounting system for gross domestic product was changed in 1964; 1956 GDP has been adjusted to reflect the change.
[4] OECD reports the 1956 GDP in terms of 1970 prices only; restated to approximate value in terms of 1975 prices.

Source: National Accounts of OECD Countries, 1950-1979 (Organization for Economic Cooperation and Development, 1981).

The relationship between banking preeminence and general economic developments is also apparent for other nations. The share of U.K. banks in the top 100 virtually halved over the 1960-1979 period, corresponding to a relative decline of about one-third in GDP and trade. On the other side of the ledger, the relative preeminence of Japanese banks more than doubled as did the relative importance of Japanese trade and GDP. The relative increase in German GDP and trade helped reinforce the dramatic jump in German bank preeminence from 5.0 percent in 1960 to 16.8 percent in 1979. Similar patterns may be observed for most of the other nations represented in the top 100 banks list. Thus, the foregoing would strongly suggest that the world bank rankings are heavily influenced by changes in the basic economic relationships among the nations. However, the relationships are not perfect, indicating that other factors also have an influence.

EXCHANGE RATE TRENDS

Comparisons of bank size, whether by assets or deposits, are usually made in terms of the U.S. dollar. That fact has raised questions about whether the apparent ascendancy of banks from countries such as Japan and Germany, whose currencies have appreciated greatly against the dollar over recent years, is due in some major part to the statistical enlargement of their dollar equivalent assets and liabilities caused by exchange rate movements.[18]

Table 3 presents a simplistic mechanical reranking of the number of banks by nation in the world's top 50, calculated by applying constant 1960 and constant 1970 dollar exchange rates to the 1970 and 1979 rankings, respectively. Not surprisingly, given relatively stable exchange rates over the 1960's, there is little change in the 1970 rankings. In 1979, however, the number of banks in the top 50 after this mechanical exchange rate adjustment shows a substantial change for the United States (9 banks instead of 6) and Japan (12 banks instead of 16). The U.K., Canada, and Italy, whose currencies depreciated against the dollar during the 1970s, also increased their numbers after the foreign exchange adjustment. Germany, Switzerland, and Belgium, whose currencies appreciated against the dollar, lost ground. Thus, on the surface, exchange rate changes would appear to have played a material role in the ranking movements in the 1970s. Such a conclusion, however, would

Figure II   Bank Deposits, GDP and Trade.

Key: ■■■■■ % of top 100 banks' deposits (American Banker, adjusted);
      □□□□□ % of OECD nations' GDP (OECD, see footnote 16) ;
      ▨▨▨▨▨ % of OECD nations' trade (OECD, see footnote 17).

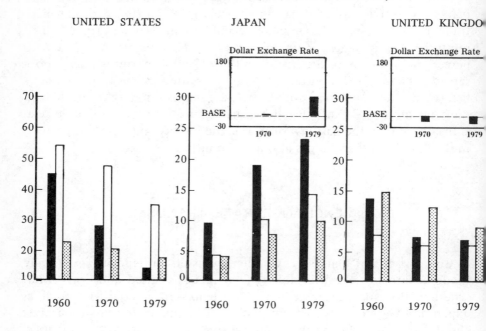

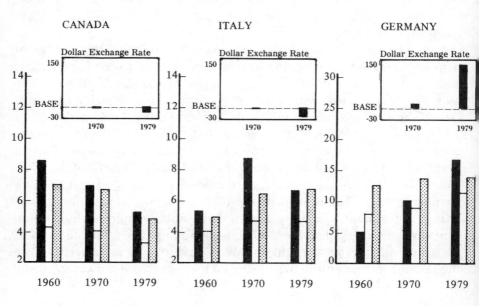

Figure II   Continued.

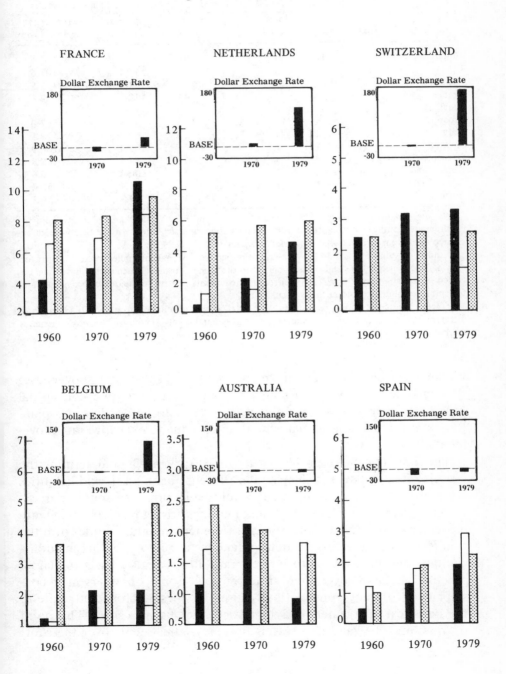

Table 3
Reranking of World's Top Fifty Banks Adjusting For Exchange Rate Movements

	Number of Banks in World Top 50				Index of U.S. Dollar Exchange Rates[1]	
	1960	1970	1970 Adj.	1979	1979 Adj.	1960-1970 (1960 = 100)	1970-1979 (1970 = 100)
United States	19	13	14	6	9	–	–
U.K.	5	4	4	4	5	117.1	107.6
Canada	5	5	5	4	5	101.5	115.5
France	3	3	3	4	4	112.6	72.8
Brazil	1	1	0	0	0	[2]	[2]
Japan	8	11	11	16	12	99.8	67.0
Italy	5	4	4	2	6	100.4	129.1
Australia	1	1	1	0	0	100.4	100.9
Germany	3	4	4	7	6	87.5	47.5
Switzerland	0	3	3	3	0	100.3	36.6
Netherlands	0	1	1	3	3	95.4	53.0
Belgium	0	0	0	1	0	99.9	56.5

Source: American Banker, "500 Largest Banks in the Free World," annual listing, adjusted to eliminate double counting of subsidiary banks appearing separately on the list. Foreign exchange rates from *International Financial Statistics.*

[1] Index of value of U.S. dollar vis-a-vis the respective national currencies, used to adjust foreign bank deposits at the end of each period to the U.S. equivalent which would have been obtained in the absence of any foreign currency movements relative to the dollar. Exchange rates for end December are used in these calculations.

[2] Over part of the period considered, the Brazilian cruzeiro has been subject to a number of different official exchange rates and was not in general freely traded on the world currency markets.

be incorrect because the adjustment in Table 3 substantially overstates the possible impact of currency realignment due to two conceptual problems described below. In fact, it is virtually impossible to isolate the extent of statistical enlargement, if any, due to exchange rate movements.[19]

The first conceptual problem arises from factors which determine the movements in relative exchange rates. Because bank assets and liabilities are reported in nominal terms, it would be incorrect to consider as statistical enlargement changes in bank rankings arising from exchange rate movements that reflect underlying differences in national rates of inflation.[20] Exchange rates are determined by a host of factors including capital flows in response to interest rate differentials, "leads and lags," speculation, and government intervention. Some observers may consider that currency appreciations caused by these factors contribute to the statistical enlargement of a domestic bank's balance sheet. This point of view may be valid in assessing currency adjustments over the short term; however, it is less valid for an examination of trends spanning a decade.

The second conceptual problem arises from the methods used to compute the bank rankings. Many banks have a significant proportion of nondomestic currency assets and liabilities. However, bank rankings are based on consolidated balance sheets reported in terms of domestic currency only. Those figures are converted to dollars using the current domestic currency/U.S. dollar exchange rate. Unfortunately, details on the currency composition of assets and liabilities are not made available, thus resulting in an overadjustment for exchange rates whenever calculations such as those used in Table 3 are attempted.[21]

Changes in underlying economic factors or possible effects of exchange rate movements are not the only factors affecting national preeminence in the world banking derby. The next section examines the impact of differences in domestic market structure and bank regulatory policies.

DOMESTIC MARKET STRUCTURE AND BANKING POLICIES

Because a bank's size depends on its growth in both domestic and international activities, developments in domestic markets may also significantly affect the world rankings. As shown earlier, the more rapid growth of the European and Japanese economies has undoubtedly had a major impact, but government policies regarding domestic bank operations and expansion opportunities would also appear to have played an important role.

In terms of achieving sheer size, U.S. banks are constrained in a number of ways in which banks in many major foreign countries are not. Compared to domestic banking structures in other nations, the American system is highly atomistic, consisting of over 14,700 commercial banks, and thousands of other depository institutions such as savings and loan associations, mutual savings banks and credit unions of widely varying deposit size. Moreover, nonbank financial institutions such as money market mutual funds, finance companies, securities brokers and dealers, and even retail department stores have aggressively pursued activities once considered the traditional domain of banks.[22] The impact of these other depository and nonbank financial institutions is evident in the decline of the commercial banking sector's share of assets held by all private financial institutions in the U.S. from 57.3% in 1946 to 39.7% in 1977.[23]

U.S. banking laws and policies have promoted these structural characteristics and have tended to thwart banking consolidation. Federal and state laws and regulations restrict the types of banking activities U.S. commercial banks may conduct. The Glass-Steagall Act prohibits commercial banks from engaging in most investment banking functions. Nationwide banking is proscribed by the McFadden Act and the Douglas Amendment to the Bank Holding Company Act and, in many cases, even statewide banking is prohibited or severely limited by state law. Further, antitrust laws generally preclude mergers between banks of any significant size in their home markets.[24]

The result of these policies is that major U.S. commercial banks can achieve domestic growth only through internal growth or relatively minor acquisitions. This is generally not the case in other nations. Few countries, if any, impose antitrust barriers to mergers as stringent as the U.S. does. Banks usually are authorized to engage in both commercial and investment banking activities, and nationwide branching is generally permitted for major banks in foreign countries. Many nations, especially in Europe, have promoted "universal" banks, whose activities extend well beyond the scope of commercial banking.[25]

Unusual Banks in the List

The largest bank in the world in 1979,[26] Caisse Nationale de Credit Agricole, is a unique organization which has benefited under France's complex system of financial regulation. It has a near monopoly in agricultural lending and benefits from preferences in housing finance, and accounts for about 21 percent of total banking credits outstanding in France.[27] Credit Agricole, however, is not a bank in the strict sense of the word, but is made up of 94 fairly autonomous regional agricultural banks and over 3,000 local co-operative banks. Until 1975, neither the *Banker* nor the *American Banker* considered Credit Agricole as a "bank" for inclusion in their world rankings.[28]

The case of Credit Agricole highlights the danger of relying too heavily on the world's largest bank rankings as a measure of international competitive standing. Credit Agricole derives virtually all its strength domestically. Notwithstanding its size, it is generally not considered to be competitive force in the international marketplace, except for agricultural trade finance. Similarly, seven of the fourteen German banks appearing in the world's top 100 banks list in 1979[29] are central giro institutions which act as clearing centers for over 650 savings banks.[30] However, only three of these institutions are generally considered to be active in the international markets.[31]

Consolidation of Foreign Banking Markets

Most of the European nations have been moving toward greater consolidation of their banking systems.[32] Domestic market shares of the largest foreign banks tend to be very high. Whereas the ten largest U.S. banking organizations hold about one-third of total U.S. commercial bank deposits, concentration of assets in a smaller number of large institutions is generally much higher in other industrialized countries, ranging from around 40 percent to over 80 percent (see Table 4).

Consolidation of commercial banking has been significant in many countries during the postwar years. The French government encouraged mergers of two of the market-dominating nationalized banks in the 1960s, and has permitted large private bank mergers.[33] In Germany, the large banks, which were split into 30 smaller institutions after World War II, have regrouped and merged[34] to the point where a small number of large banks dominates the commercial and investment banking structure. The smaller banks have continued to consolidate with stronger institutions.[35] The 13 large city banks of Japan hold more than half of the assets of the Japanese banking system, and some hold influential positions in wide-ranging industrial groups as well. Two major mergers among the Japanese city banks have occurred in the last 10 years.[36] The Dai-Ichi Bank and the Nippon Kangyo Bank merged in 1971, resulting in the world's fifth largest bank, illustrating the possible impact of mergers on the world bank rankings. In 1970, they were ranked 40th and 46th, respectively.[37] In the U.K., the number of London clearing banks has declined from 11 to six through mergers and amalgamations.[38] Mergers and consolidations in Spain have served to reinforce the dominance of that country's "big seven" banks.[39] Major bank mergers have also occurred in Sweden[40] and Canada[41]. Perhaps the most spectacular concentration process occurred in the Netherlands, where the number of independent domestic banks declined from 114 in the early 1960s to only 20 at the end of 1979.[42] Several observers have noted that in some cases the consolidation movements among banks in other countries have been in reaction to the "competitive onslaught" by U.S. and other foreign banks in their markets.[43]

Table 4
Indicators of Banking Concentration in Major Foreign Countries

Large Banks	% of Commercial Banking Assets	% of Total Banking Assets
Australia		
7 Major Trading Banks	88	49
Belgium		
3 Largest Commercial Banks	80	32
Canada		
5 Largest Chartered Banks	90	60
France		
3 Largest Nationalized Banks	55	45-50
Germany		
3 Largest Commercial Banks	42	10
Italy		
Big 5 Banks	47	28
Japan		
13 City Banks	N.A.	53
The Netherlands		
3 Largest Commercial Banks	60	41
Spain		
"Big Seven" Commercial Banks	58*	34*
Switzerland		
5 Big Banks	N.A.	48
United Kingdom		
6 London Clearing Banks	70	N.A.
United States		
3 Largest Commercial Banks	18	12**
10 Largest Commercial Banks	34	23**

Sources: Report to Congress and OCC files for foreign countries; U.S. data from call reports and *Federal Reserve Bulletin*, Appendix Tables 1.24 and 1.38. Data are for various dates.
   Notes:
    *Share of Deposits
    **Includes savings and loan associations and mutual savings banks.

It should be noted that U.S. banks also gained or maintained ranks through large consolidations in earlier years before more stringent anti-trust standards were applied to banks in the early 1960s. In 1961, Manufacturers Hanover jumped to fourth compared to the merging banks' prior year ranks of 10 and 32. J. P. Morgan and Guaranty Trust, which ranked 70 and 16, respectively, in 1958, emerged as Morgan Guaranty ranked ninth in 1959. Wells Fargo and American Trust, both in San Francisco, merged in 1960 to rank 20, versus their 1959 ranks of 94 and 27, respectively. Chemical Bank, ranked 10 in 1958, acquired New York Trust Co., ranked 62, to boost its position to eighth. Such mergers in the top 100 partly account for the declining number of U.S. banks on the list through the early sixties.[44]

In foreign countries banks can grow rapidly to a very large size in a manner denied to banks in the U.S. because of our antitrust laws, the McFadden Act, and the Douglas Amendment. The liberal merger, acquisition and branching policies common to other nations help explain the trends in the top 10, 50 and 100 rankings. German, Japanese and French banks have grown quickly to achieve an impressive worldwide presence. U.S. banks, constrained by antitrust policy and domestic geographic limits, have lost ground.

In fact, as shown in Table 5, the largest U.S. banks and bank holding companies have actually lost ground to faster growing medium-sized and smaller banks, in terms of their shares of domestic deposits. The domestic shares held by the largest U.S. banking organizations dropped sharply after 1940, subsequently recovered a little and, more recently, have gradually eroded. This pattern stands in sharp contrast to consolidation that has occurred in other countries.

FOREIGN ACQUISITIONS OF U.S. BANKS

Some observers believe that the neutral policy of the United States toward foreign bank acquisitions of domestic banks, in contrast with the restrictive foreign bank acquisition policies followed by other na-

Table 5
Large U.S. Banks' Domestic Performance

Year	Percent Share of Domestic Deposits Held by Top 100 U.S. Banking Organizations	Percent Share of Domestic Deposits Held by Top 10 U.S. Banking Organizations
1940	59.4	26.9
1955	49.3	20.7
1960	49.5	21.2
1970	49.9	19.9
1977	45.0	18.3

Source: Cynthia A. Glassman and Robert A. Eisenbeis, "Bank Holding Companies and Concentration of Banking and Financial Resources," Table 1, p. 246 in *The Bank Holding Company Movement to 1978: A Compendium*, A Study by the Staff of the Board of Governors of the Federal Reserve System (Washington, 1978).

tions, has been an important factor in the decline of U.S. preeminence in the ranking of world banks. Although a few foreign banks have maintained or improved their relative positions via acquisition of large U.S. banks, growth by this means is not a major factor in the overall shift of world rankings.[45]

More importantly, as shown in Appendix B, foreign acquisitions of U.S. banks have had relatively little impact on the U.S. presence in the top 100 banks of the world.

The increase in the foreign bank share of total deposits of the world's top 100 world banks attributable to their acquisitions of U.S. banks consummated by the end of 1980 is only 0.48%. Even when pending acquisitions are taken into account, the impact rises to just 0.88%. The data presented above and in the Appendix A tables indicate clearly that the decline in U.S. banks' global standing began well before the first significant foreign acquisitions occurred in the 1970s.[46] Foreign banks' growth in the U.S. has been mostly *de novo*.[47] The largest banks in the world have not attained their positions through acquisitions of banks in the U.S. or other countries foreign to them.

CONCLUSION

The foregoing review of factors affecting changes in ranking of the world's largest banks suggests that real economic forces have played a predominant role. U.S. antitrust policies, the prohibition of nationwide banking, and the relatively narrow scope of permissible commercial banking activities in the U.S. compared to other nations have also been contributing factors. Foreign acquisitions of U.S. banks, however, have had relatively little impact.

World bank rankings are an imperfect measure of a nation's international banking competitiveness. Regardless of changes in its *relative* position, no strong U.S. bank is likely to suffer adverse consequences, e.g., in terms of access to first-tier interbank financing, particularly as the total volume of international banking activity continues to grow. In response to a congressional inquiry about possible federal laws or policies to enhance U.S. banks' positions, the Federal Reserve indicated that it "does not give weight in its decisions to the rankings of individual large U.S. banks among the leading banks of the world . . . So long as U.S. banks are soundly managed and adequately capitalized they will be able to compete effectively, domestically and internationally. . ."[48]

APPENDIX A

COMPARISON OF RANKINGS

Two annual rankings of the world's largest banking institutions are referred to at different points in this study: the comprehensive annual listings by the *American Banker* (AB), and those prepared by The Banker Research Unit (BRU) and published in *The Banker*. The purpose of the note is to describe differences between the two listings. The AB rankings (adjusted, as noted below) form the basis for tables in this paper and in the Appendix A tables which follow, showing rankings by country from 1956 to 1979. The BRU rankings are available only beginning with data for 1969.

Measure of Size

AB ranks according to deposits; BRU uses assets, adjusted for contra accounts,[49] *when available*. The BRU list also shows deposits and other balance sheet figures. BRU points out that assets are easier "to define and pinpoint than deposits and can, therefore, be more confidently referred to as an accurate guide to a bank's strength."[50] The assets versus deposits basis makes a large difference in only a limited number of cases. For example, for 1978 Banco do Brasil ranked 17 on BRU's list, with $49.0 billion in assets less contra accounts but ranked 51 on the AB list, with $22.7 billion in deposits.

Consolidation

Both lists consolidate foreign banks' subsidiaries when data are available to do so. AB, however, lists large subsidiaries individually for ranking purposes, even though their deposits are already reflected in the parent's figures. In our use of the AB rankings, we have eliminated this double counting.

The BRU shows U.S. banking organizations on a bank holding company basis, while AB shows only individual banks. Although this difference does not affect many institutions' relative standings, it has a significant impact on the position of some holding companies without a clearly dominant lead bank. Thus, First Bank System was 113 on BRU's 1978 list but its largest subsidiary appeared on AB's list at 402.[51] That difference favored U.S. companies, especially in earlier BRU rankings when a number of U.S. holding companies with more than one relatively large subsidiary were fairly high in the standings.

Coverage

AB includes consortium banks, but BRU does not, "on the grounds that their capital is owned by other banks and to include them would lead to a large measure of double-counting."[52]

Both lists include "central banks" for European cooperative and savings bank systems, many of which are quite large. Beginning with its 1978 list, BRU has included a number of savings and cooperative banks "which do a large amount of commercial and international lending."[53] Several appeared among the top 100 in 1978 but were not included in the AB ranking for that year. A large Japanese cooperative bank was first listed by BRU in 1978, ranked 27. In 1979, this bank was ranked 15th by BRU and appeared for the first time on the AB list.[54] In an even more dramatic entry, Credit Agricole made its first appearance on both lists in 1975, ranked third.[55]

Calendar Dates

Both sources use year-end data whenever possible. Exceptions apply most frequently to Japanese banks, whose reports are often for September. This may introduce significant distortions in periods of sharp exchange rates movements.

Other Notes

The BRU asset basis includes trust assets as well as banking assets for a number of Japanese banks. Neither list consolidates Japanese "Trust & Banking Companies" which may in fact be "related" to same-surnamed Japanese banks, although not through formal ties. Both lists contain footnotes indicating known data problems that could not be solved.

Acknowledging these and other problems inherent in drawing up a list encompassing such diverse institutions from so many nations, BRU noted with some understatement in 1972 that "there are several reasons why comparisons between banks must be treated with considerable caution."[56] In describing its method, BRU concluded with an apt cautionary note:

> The "Top 300" listing, while providing a ranking, is designed to be not so much a league table, but rather a convenient framework for showing in broad terms the relative size of the world's largest banks and how they have developed over a 12-month period.[57]

COMPARISON OF RESULTS

Notwithstanding the difficulties inherent in such rankings, and the differences in their coverage and method, the AB and BRU listings show broadly similar results. The following table shows the national distribution of the AB and BRU top 10 for 1969 and 1979, and the top 100 for 1979:

| | No. of Banks in Top 10 | | | | No. in Top 100 | | |
| | 1969 | | 1979 | | 1979 | | |
	BRU	AB	BRU	AB	BRU	AB	AB (adj)**
Australia	–	–	–	–	2	2	2
Belgium	–	–	–	–	5	3	3
Canada	–	1	–	–	5	6	6
France	–	–	4	4	8	4	4
Germany	–	1	2	2	11	14	14
Italy	1	1	–	–	8	8	9
Japan	–	–	1	–	24	24	24
Netherlands	–	–	–	–	4	4	4
Spain	–	–	–	–	3	4	4
Sweden	–	–	–	–	3	2	2
Switzerland	–	–	–	–	3	3	3
U.K.	2	2	1	2	5	8*	5
U.S.	7	5	2	2	15	13	15
Other	–	–	–	–	4	5	5

*Three U.K. subsidiaries double-counted.
**Adjusted to eliminate double-counting of U.K. subsidiaries.

Differences in the 1979 top 100 distributions are primarily due to BRU's inclusion of several European savings banks located in France, Belgium and Sweden, which the AB does not list. In earlier years, significant differences in the U.S. position occurred because the AB listing does not consolidate U.S. bank holding companies. For example, among BRU's 1969 top 10 was Western Bancorp, which was represented by its largest subsidiary bank, United California Bank, much lower on AB's 1969 list. By 1979, such differences in consolidation had disappeared from the top ranks.

Distribution of the top 100 in terms of assets and deposits in 1979 is shown in the following table:

	BRU % Assets	BRU % Deposits	AB (adj) % Deposits
Australia	0.9	0.8	0.9
Belgium	3.2	3.5	2.1
Canada	4.2	4.8	5.2
France	12.8	13.3	10.4
Germany	13.9	14.3	16.8
Italy	6.7	6.7	6.6
Japan	23.1	22.3	23.6
Netherlands	4.0	4.5	4.5
Spain	1.5	1.5	1.9
Sweden	1.4	1.2	0.9
Switzerland	3.2	3.3	3.3
U.K.	6.4	6.9	6.9
U.S.	16.1	14.7	14.4
Other	2.8	2.1	2.5

The most striking result shown in this table is that a broadly similar picture emerges in spite of the remaining differences in measure of size, coverage and consolidation. Comparing the two deposit columns, the most significant differences are apparently attributable to BRU's inclusion of large savings banks (in France, Belgium and Sweden) and AB's apparent different definition of German commercial bank deposits.[58] The differences in asset versus deposit measures between the two BRU columns are relatively minor. In the case of the U.S. the difference may reflect nonbank activities of the large bank holding companies. For "Other," the difference is explained by the previously noted remarkable asset/deposit difference for the Banco do Brasil.

Appendix A: Table 1
Countries Represented In a Listing of the 10 Largest Banks, by Deposit Size, in the Free World

Country	Number times country represented																							
	1956	'57	'58	'59	'60	'61	'62	'63	'64	'65	'66	'67	'68	'69	'70	'71	'72	'73	'74	'75	'76	'77	'78	'79
United States	5	5	5	6	6	6	6	6	6	6	6	6	6	5	4	3	3	3	3	3	3	3	3	2
United Kingdom	3	3	3	3	3	2	2	2	2	2	2	2	1	2	2	2	2	2	2	2	—	—	—	2
Canada	2	2	2	1	1	2	2	2	2	2	1	1	1	1	1	—	—	—	—	—	—	—	—	—
France	—	—	—	—	—	—	—	—	—	—	1	1	1	—	1	2	2	3	3	4	4	4	4	4
Italy	—	—	—	—	—	—	—	—	—	—	—	—	1	1	1	1	—	—	—	—	—	—	—	—
Germany	—	—	—	—	—	—	—	—	—	—	—	—	—	1	1	1	—	1	2	1	3	3	2	2
Japan	—	—	—	—	—	—	—	—	—	—	—	—	—	—	—	1	3	1	—	—	—	—	1	—

Source: American Banker, "500 Largest Banks in Free World."

Appendix A: Table 2

Countries Represented In a Listing of the 50 Largest Banks, by Deposit Size, in the Free World

Country	1956	'57	'58	'59	'60	'61	'62	'63	'64	'65	'66	'67	'68	'69	'70	'71	'72	'73	'74	'75	'76	'77	'78	'79
									Number times country represented															
United States	25	22	21	20	19	18	18	17	16	16	16	16	15	14	13	11	10	10	10	9	8	7	6	6
United Kingdom	7	7	5	5	5	5	5	5	5	5	5	5	5	4	4	4	4	4	4	4	4	4	6	4
Canada	6	5	5	5	5	5	5	5	5	5	5	5	5	5	5	4	4	3	4	4	5	4	4	4
France	3	4	2	3	3	3	3	3	3	3	3	3	3	3	3	3	3	3	3	4	4	4	3	4
Brazil	1	1	–	1	1	–	1	1	1	1	1	–	1	1	1	–	–	1	1	1	1	1	–	–
Japan	3	4	5	6	8	9	9	9	10	10	11	11	11	10	11	13	16	14	12	11	13	14	16	16
Italy	3	3	4	5	5	5	5	5	5	5	5	4	4	4	4	4	4	4	3	4	2	2	2	2
Australia	1	1	1	1	1	–	–	1	–	–	–	1	1	1	1	–	–	–	–	–	–	–	–	–
Argentina	1	–	–	–	–	–	–	–	–	–	–	–	–	–	–	–	–	–	–	–	–	–	–	–
Germany	–	2	4	3	3	4	4	4	5	5	4	4	4	4	4	7	6	8	8	8	7	8	8	7
Spain	–	1	1	–	–	–	–	–	–	–	–	–	–	–	–	–	–	–	–	–	–	–	–	–
India	–	–	1	1	–	1	–	–	–	–	–	–	–	–	–	–	–	–	–	–	–	–	–	–
Switzerland	–	–	1	–	–	1	–	–	–	–	–	–	2	3	3	3	2	2	2	2	2	3	3	3
Sweden	–	–	–	1	–	–	–	–	–	–	–	–	–	–	–	–	–	–	–	–	–	–	–	–
Netherlands	–	–	–	–	–	–	–	–	–	–	–	–	–	1	1	1	1	1	3	3	3	3	3	3
Belgium	–	–	–	–	–	–	–	–	–	–	–	–	–	–	–	–	–	–	–	–	1	–	1	3

Source: American Banker, "500 Largest Banks in Free World." Annual Listing adjusted to eliminate double counting of subsidiary banks appearing separately on the list.

Appendix A: Table 3
Countries Represented In a Listing of the 100 Largest Banks, by Deposit Size, in the Free World

Country	Number times country represented																							
	1956	'57	'58	'59	'60	'61	'62	'63	'64	'65	'66	'67	'68	'69	'70	'71	'72	'73	'74	'75	'76	'77	'78	'79
United States	44	41	39	38	37	35	32	30	28	29	29	27	24	23	22	21	21	18	18	18	16	16	15	15
United Kingdom	10	10	10	11	10	10	9	9	9	9	6	7	7	5	5	5	5	5	5	5	5	5	5	5
Canada	7	7	7	7	7	5	5	5	5	5	5	5	5	5	5	5	5	5	5	5	5	5	5	6
France	5	5	4	4	4	4	4	4	4	4	3	3	3	3	3	3	3	4	3	4	4	5	4	4
Brazil	1	1	1	1	1	1	1	1	1	1	1	1	1	1	1	1	1	1	1	1	1	1	1	1
Japan	9	10	11	12	12	14	16	17	18	19	20	20	22	24	24	23	24	23	22	22	22	22	24	24
Italy	6	6	6	7	7	8	9	9	9	9	10	10	10	10	9	8	8	8	8	9	8	7	8	9
Australia	2	2	3	3	2	2	1	1	1	1	2	3	3	3	3	3	3	4	4	3	3	3	2	2
Argentina	1	1	—	—	—	—	—	—	—	—	—	—	—	—	—	—	—	—	—	—	—	—	—	—
Germany	3	4	6	4	7	7	9	10	9	8	10	10	11	12	11	11	12	14	14	13	15	15	15	14
Spain	2	3	3	2	1	2	2	2	1	1	2	2	2	2	3	4	4	4	4	4	—	3	4	4
India	1	1	1	1	1	1	1	1	1	1	1	1	1	1	1	1	1	—	—	—	—	1	1	1
Switzerland	5	5	5	4	4	4	4	4	4	3	4	3	3	3	3	3	3	3	3	3	3	3	3	3
Sweden	2	2	—	2	2	2	1	2	2	2	2	2	3	2	3	2	2	2	3	3	3	3	3	2
Netherlands	1	1	—	1	1	1	1	1	3	3	3	3	3	3	3	4	3	4	4	4	4	4	4	4
Belgium	1	1	1	2	3	3	3	3	3	3	3	3	3	3	4	4	3	3	3	3	3	3	3	3
Turkey	—	1	—	1	1	1	1	1	1	1	—	1	1	1	1	1	1	1	1	1	1	1	1	1
Hong Kong	—	—	—	—	—	—	—	—	—	—	—	1	1	1	1	1	1	1	1	1	1	1	1	1
Israel	—	—	—	—	—	—	—	—	—	—	—	—	—	—	—	—	—	1	1	1	1	1	1	1
Austria	—	—	—	—	—	—	—	—	—	—	—	—	—	—	—	—	—	—	1	1	1	1	1	1
Iran	—	—	—	—	—	—	—	—	—	—	—	—	—	—	—	—	—	—	1	1	1	—	—	—

Source: American Banker, "500 Largest Banks in Free World." Annual Listing adjusted to eliminate double counting of subsidiary banks appearing separately on the list.

215

APPENDIX B*

IMPACT OF FOREIGN ACQUISITIONS OF U.S. BANKS ON NATIONAL SHARES OF WORLD BANKING

This appendix examines the extent to which foreign banks' acquisitions of U.S. banking organizations have or have not affected the relative world market share held by U.S. banks. Since the mid-1950s the number of U.S. banks appearing in the *American Banker's* annual listing of the top 100 commercial banks has steadily declined. (See Appendix A, Table 3.) This would seem to indicate an erosion of U.S. banks' market position relative to their world banking competitors. During the same period, but most notably since the early 1970s, several U.S. banks have been acquired by, or merged with, foreign banks that appear on the top 100 list, either directly or through mergers into their U.S. subsidiaries. Recently, some observers have been attempting to establish a causal relationship between these two series of events—namely, that the acquisition of U.S. banks by foreign banking concerns has precipitated the decline of U.S. banks' preeminence in the annual ranking of world banks. This Appendix has been constructed to determine the validity of that assertion.

Foreign Acquisitions of U.S. Banks: Description of Tables 1 and 2

Table 1 presents a list of U.S. banks which have been acquired directly by foreign banks that appeared in the 1979 listing of the top 100 banks. The table also identifies acquisitions that were pending as of year-end 1980.

The format for each entry is as follows: Columns (1) and (2) list the acquiring foreign bank and present its respective position within the *American Banker's* 1979 ranking of the Top 100. Column (3) gives the name of the corresponding acquired U.S. bank. Column (4) gives the total deposits of the acquired U.S. bank as of December 31, 1979.

Table 1 is divided into three sections. Section A lists U.S. banks acquired before December 31, 1979; they had total deposits of $11.4 billion as of year-end 1979. Section B lists U.S. banks acquired in 1980; they had total deposits of $12.8 billion as of yearend 1979. Section C lists U.S. banks whose acquisitions were pending on December 31, 1980; they had total deposits of $12.6 billion as of year-end 1979. Deposits for all U.S. banks acquired directly by foreign banks or pending totalled $36.8 billion.

Table 2 lists U.S. banks which have been merged with *de novo* U.S. subsidiaries of foreign banks that appeared in the 1979 ranking of the top 100. Table 2 is also divided into three sections; part A for mergers completed by year-end 1979; part B for mergers completed in 1980; and part C for mergers pending as of December 31, 1980. Although the column format corresponds in general to that used in Table 1, most deposit figures in part A of Table 2 had to be estimated since the merged banks lost their separate accounting identities. These estimates are predicted on the assumption that the deposits attributable to the *de novo* subsidiary and the merged U.S. bank grew at the same rate after the merger. Total deposits attributable to pending and completed mergers amounted to $7.6 billion as of year-end 1979.

Foreign Acquisition Effect on U.S. Bank's Relative World Market Share: Description of Summary Table 3

The results of Appendix B Tables 1 and 2 have been used to determine the effect of these acquisitions and mergers on the relative share of the total deposits of the world's 100 largest banks held by foreign and U.S. banks, respectively. The adjustments made to the *American Banker's* 1979 Top 100 deposit totals are presented in Appendix B Table 3.

Column A gives the total level of deposits held by the world Top 100 banks. Column B gives the total deposits held by foreign banks in the Top 100. Column C gives the share of total deposits (Column A) held by foreign banks (Column B) and equals B/A. The share held by U.S. banks in the Top 100 is given in parentheses. The actual, unadjusted deposit figures for year-end 1979 are given on Line 1. Foreign banks' unadjusted share of total deposits held by banks in the Top 100 was 85.65% (U.S. banks' share equals 14.35%).

These deposit figures include, however, deposits of U.S. banks acquired by foreign banks prior to year-end 1979 (Table 1, Section A), and also the deposits attributable to U.S. banks merged with *de novo* U.S. subsidiaries of foreign banks in the Top 100 prior to year-end 1979 (Table 2, Section A). To arrive at adjusted deposit totals which would exclude the impact of these acquisitions or mergers, the deposit

(1)	(2)	(3)	(4)
Acquiring Foreign Bank (Country)	World Rank of Foreign Bank 12/31/79[2]	Acquired U.S. Bank (Present Name if Applicable)	Total Deposits U.S. Bank as of 12/31/79 (In $U.S. Mill.)
A. U.S. Banks Acquired Prior to Year-end 1979			
Standard Chartered Bank, Ltd. (U.K.)	54	Union Bank	4,503.7
Nat'l Westminster Bank, Ltd. (U.K.)	9	Nat'l Bank of North America	3,634.3
Lloyds Bank, Ltd. (U.K.)	33	First Western B&TC First State Bank of Northern Cal. (Lloyds Bank, CA)	2,146.0
Algemene Bank Nederland (Netherlands)	25	LaSalle Nat'l Bank	781.2
Banco Central de Madrid (Spain)	75	Banco Economias (Banco Central y Economias)	333.3
		Subtotal:	($11,398.5)
B. U.S. Banks Acquired in 1980			
Hongkong & Shanghai Banking Corp. (Hongkong)	71	Marine Midland Bank, N.A.	$12,537.2
Royal Bank of Canada (Canada)	28	Banco de San Juan	256.8
Algemene Bank Nederland LaSalle Nat'l Bank (Netherlands)	25	Hartford Plaza Bank	34.4
		Subtotal:	($12,828.4)
C. U.S. Bank Acquisitions Pending as of 12/31/80			
Midland Bank, Ltd. (U.K.)	26	Crocker National Bank	$12,539.6
Banco Central de Madrid (Spain)	75	United Americas Bank	40.9
		Subtotal:	($12,580.5)
		Total:	$36,807.4

Notes:

[1] This table reflects acquisitions consummated or pending as of 12/31/80.

[2] Based on the *American Banker* Listing of the "500 Largest Banks in the World," July 25, 1980.

[3] Total deposits (consolidated foreign and domestic) as of the December 1979 Call Report.

Notes to Table 2:

[1] This table reflects transactions completed before or pending as of 12/31/80.

[2] Based on the *American Banker* Listing of the "500 Largest Banks in the World," July 25, 1980.

[3] Deposits (consolidated foreign and domestic) based on December 1979 Call Reports; deposits estimated under assumption that existing *de novo* and U.S. bank deposits before merger continued to grow proportionately after merger.

[4] Banco Mercantile was consolidated with existing branches of Bank of Nova Scotia to create Scotiabank of Puerto Rico.

U.S. Banks Merged with *De Novo* Subsidiaries in the U.S. of Foreign Banks in the Top 100[1]

Foreign Parent Bank (U.S. Bank Subsidiary)	World Rank of Foreign Parent Bank 12/31/79[2]	Merged U.S. Bank(s)	Deposits Attributable to Merged U.S. Banks As of 12/31/79 ($U.S. Mill.)[3]
A. Bank Mergers Prior to Year-end 1979			
Amsterdam Rotterdam Bank	29	Franklin National Bank	$2,707.3
Creditanstalt-Bankverein	80		
Deutsche Bank	4		
Midland Bank, Ltd.	26		
Societe Generale de Banque	41		
Societe Generale (France)	6		
(European-American B&T Co.)			
Bank of Tokyo, Ltd.			
(California First Bank)	37	Southern California FNB	1,321.5
Standard Chartered Bank, Ltd.		Liberty Nat'l Bank	
(Chartered Bank of London)	54	Commercial & Farmers Bank of Oxnard	483.8
Barclays Bank, Ltd.		First Westchester	
(Barclays Bank of New York)	10	National Bank	400.3
Bank Leumi of Israel		American Bank and	
(Bank Leumi Trust Co. of New York)	99	Trust Co.	356.5
Sanwa Bank, Ltd.		Charter Bank	
(Golden State Sanwa Bank)	21	Golden State Bank	336.8
Barclays Bank, Ltd.		First Valley Bank	
(Barclays Bank of CA)	10	County Bank of Santa Barbara	221.4
Canadian Imperial Bank of of Commerce		Northern CA Nat'l Bank of San Mateo	
(California Canadian Bank)	34	City Bank of San Diego	129.6
Bank of Nova Scotia (Scotiabank of Puerto Rico)[4]	50	Banco Mercantile de Puerto Rico	128.2
Mitsubishi Bank, Ltd. (Mitsubishi Bank of California)	20	Hacienda Bank	73.5
Tokai Bank, Ltd. (Tokai Bank of CA)	38	Centinela Bank	47.7
		Subtotal:	($6,206.6)
B. Bank Mergers in 1980			
Banque Nationale de Paris (French Bank of California)	2	Bank of the West	516.7
C. Pending Bank Mergers as of 12/31/80			
Mitsui Bank, Ltd. (Mitsui Bank of California)	42	Manufacturers Bank	605.0
Mitsubishi Bank, Ltd. (Mitsubishi Bank of California)	20	First National Bank of San Diego County	136.5
Sanwa Bank, Ltd. (Golden State Sanwa Bank	21	First City Bank	131.6
		Subtotal:	($873.1)
		Total:	$7,596.4

Appendix B: Table 3
Impact of Foreign Acquisitions on Foreign and U.S. Banks' Share of Top 100 Banks' Deposits*

	Column A Total Deposits of World's 100 Largest Banks as of 12/31/79 (in $ U.S. Mill.)	Column B Total Deposits Held by Foreign Banks in the Top 100 as of 12/31/79 (in $ U.S. Mill.)	Column C (B)/(A) % Share of Total Deposits Held by Foreign Banks in Top 100 (U.S. Banks' Share)
1. Deposits, end 1979, Actual	$3,158,502.4	$2,705,148.9	85.65% (14.35%)
Less:			
2a. Total Deposits of U.S.Banks acquired by foreign banks in the Top 100 prior to end-1979	11,398.5	11,398.5	
2b. Total deposits attributed to U.S. banks merged with *de novo* subsidiaries in the U.S. of foreign banks in the Top 100 prior to end-1979	6,206.6	6,206.6	
Equals:			
3. Total deposits excluding effect of acquisitions of U.S. Banks by foreign banks in the Top 100, or of mergers of U.S. banks with *de novo* subsidiaries in the U.S. of foreign banks in the Top 100 prior to end-1979	3,140,897.3	2,687,543.8	85.57% (14.43%)
Add to Line 1:			
4a. Total deposits of U.S. banks acquired in 1980 (excluding Marine Midland Bank) by foreign banks in the Top 100	291.2	291.2	
4b. Total deposits of Marine Midland Bank (Acquired by Hongkong and Shanghai Banking Corporation)	—	12,537.2	
4c. Total deposits attributed to U.S. Banks merged with *de novo* subsidiaries in the U.S. of Foreign Banks in the Top 100 in 1980	516.7	516.7	

Equals

5. Total deposits including   3,159,310.3   2,718,494.0   86.05%
   - All U.S. Banks acquired by foreign banks in the Top 100, including 1980.
   - All mergers of U.S. banks with *de novo* subsidiaries in the U.S. of foreign banks in the Top 100, including 1980.   (13.95%)

Add to Line 5:

6a. Total deposits of pending U.S. bank acquisitions by foreign banks in the Top 100, (excluding the proposed acquisition of Crocker National Bank by Midland Banks, Ltd.)   40.9   40.9

6b. Total deposits of Crocker National Bank   —   12,539.6

6c. Total deposits of pending U.S. bank mergers with *de novo* subsidiaries in the U.S. of Foreign Banks in the Top 100   873.1   873.1

Equals:

7. Total deposits including; All actual or pending: 3,160,224.3   2,731,947.6   86.45%
   - Acquisitions of U.S. Banks by foreign banks in the Top 100.
   - Mergers of U.S. banks with *de novo* subsidiaries in the U.S. of foreign banks in the Top 100.   (13.55%)

*Ranking of the Top 100 banks is based on the *American Banker* listing (adjusted) and deposit figures from that source.

totals of the acquired or merged U.S. banks ($11,398.5 million and $6,206.6 million, respectively) must be subtracted from the Line 1 deposit figures. Lines 2a and 2b display these adjustments.

Line 3 thus represents the adjusted total deposit figures. Column C shows that the foreign banks' share of total deposits held by banks in the Top 100 at end 1979 would have been 85.57% if the acquisitions or mergers of U.S. banks did not take place. This adjusted share is only 0.08% lower than the actual, unadjusted share reported on line 1. The U.S. banks' share would have been 14.43% as opposed to the actual level of 14.35%.

1980 was also an important year for foreign bank acquisition activity in the United States, especially due to the purchase of Marine Midland Bank by the Hongkong and Shanghai Banking Corporation. The *American Banker's* ranking for 1980 was not available at the time of this writing. In order to determine .what impact 1980 acquistions or mergers *would* have had on the *1979* Top 100 deposit shares, another series of adjustments has been made. Those adjustments are contained in lines 4a-4c and must be added to the totals given on line 1.

Line 4a adjusts for the acquisitions of U.S. banks actually consummated in 1980, excluding the acquisition of Marine Midland. Banks' consolidated deposits are used as the basis for the Top 100 ranking and, because the deposits of the U.S. banks acquired by foreign banks in 1980 have not been included in the *American Banker's* 1979 deposit totals, they must be added to line 1. The deposit figure of $291.2 million presented on line 4a is derived from Appendix B Table 1, Section B.

Because Marine Midland Bank ranked 97th on the 1979 *American Banker* list, its deposits are already included in Line 1, Column A. However, Marine Midland's 1979 deposit figure of $12,537.2 million must be added to Line 1, Column B to account for its transfer to foreign ownership. That adjustment is contained in line 4b.

The adjustment made by line 4c is similar in nature to that of 4a. The addition of $516.7 million to line 1 adjusts for mergers of U.S. banks with *de novo* subsidiaries of foreign banks appearing in the Top 100 list which were consummated in 1980. This deposit figure comes from Appendix B Table 2, Section C.

Line 5 yields the total estimated impact on the 1979 Top 100 ranking of all actual acquisitions or mergers of U.S. banks by foreign banks in the Top 100 prior to year-end 1980. As can be observed in Column C on Line 5, the inclusion of acquired or merged U.S. banks' deposits in the share of total deposits held by foreign banks in the Top 100 would result in an adjusted foreign banks' share of 86.05% for year-end 1979.

That share is 0.48% higher than it would have been if there were no foreign acquisitions or mergers of U.S. banks.

Lines 6a, 6b, and 6c make similar adjustments for all acquisitions or mergers that were pending as of December 31, 1980. As was the case for line 4, deposit totals need to be added to the total deposit levels given in the 1979 *American Banker* rankings. Since Crocker National Bank ranked 96th in 1979, the adjustment procedure must be analogous to that used for Marine Midland Bank in Line 4b.

Line 7 yields the total estimated impact on the 1979 Top 100 ranking of all actual or pending acquisitions or mergers as of end 1980 of U.S. banks by foreign banks in the Top 100 ranking. As can be seen in Column C, the share of total deposits held by foreign banks in the top 100 *would* have been 86.45%, 0.88% higher than if there had been no actual or pending acquisitions or mergers of U.S. banks.

Therefore, it is apparent from the results contained in Appendix B Table 3 that foreign acquisitions or mergers of U.S. banks have had relatively little impact on the U.S.'s world market share compared to its foreign banking competitors.

Acknowledgments

The authors were ably assisted by J. Philip Hinson in early drafting of the paper, and by Nancy Lowther, Diane Page, Stephen Wood, Betty Callaghan and Mark Au, in work on the statistical base. Valuable comments on earlier drafts of this paper were given by Robert R. Bench and C. F. Muckenfuss III.

FOOTNOTES

[1] Both the *American Banker* and *The Banker* publish comprehensive annual listings of the world's largest banks, ranked by deposits and assets, respectively. The *American Banker* listing is used here because it dates back to 1956. *The Banker* began publishing its "Top 300" listing with 1969 data. (Beginning in 1979, *The Banker* expanded its list to the Top 500.) Yearly data showing the geographical distribution of the world's top 10, 50, and 100 banks (based on deposits) for the period 1956-79 are presented in Appendix A tables 1, 2, and 3. Also see Appendix A for a full technical discussion of the differences between the rankings.

[2] The rankings do not change substantially when determined on the basis of consolidated assets for banking groups and bank holding companies (see Appendix A).

[3] Muriel Siebert, letter of March 1, 1979, to Representative Reuss concerning the proposed acquisition of the Marine Midland Banks, Inc. by the Hongkong and Shanghai Banking Corporation. This statement apparently refers to 1969 asset data for bank groups and bank holding companies rather than *banks*. On this basis, the U.S. had seven banking organizations in the world's top 10 in 1969, six in 1970, and three in 1977. Counting U.S. banks rather than holding companies and ranking in terms of deposits, there were five U.S. institutions in the top in 1969, four in 1970, and three in 1977. See Appendix A for a discussion of the differences in the compilation of rankings.

[4] Senator John Heinz III, "Foreign Takeovers of U.S. Banking—A Real Danger?," *The Journal of the Institute for Socioeconomic Studies*, vol. 3 (Autumn 1979), p. 2.

[5] Elvis L. Mason, Chairman of the Board, First National Bank in Dallas, Testimony Before the Senate Committee on Banking, Housing and Urban Affairs, in Hearings on *Edge Corporation Branching; Foreign Bank Takeovers; and International Banking Facilities*, 96th Cong., 1st Sess., July 20, 1979, p. 341.

[6] *Ibid*. p. 328.

[7]

Deposits of Top 10 U.S. Banks
($ billion)

1956	1960	1965	1970	1975	1979
39.7	49.2	75.4	126.2	256.1	388.5

Source: The American Banker, annual listings.

[8]

Overseas Branches of U.S. Banks, Selected Dates Since 1955
(dollars in billions)

	12/55	12/60	12/65	12/70	12/75	12/79
Number of banks	7	8	13	79	137	139
Number of overseas branches	111	124	211	532	762	789
Assets of overseas branches*	$2.0	$3.5	$9.1	$47.4	$176.5	$312.9

*Includes claims on other foreign branches of parent banks.

Note: Includes Federal Reserve member banks only; does not include assets of foreign bank and nonbank subsidiaries of U.S. banks (estimated at $40 billion and $12 billion, respectively, at the end of 1977. See U.S. Department of the Treasury, *Report to Congress on Foreign Government Treatment of U.S. Commercial Banking Organizations*, 1979, Ch. 2.).

Source: Federal Reserve Board

[9]

Assets of U.S. Offices of Foreign Banks
(Dollars in Billions)

May 1973	May 1976	May 1980
$30.5	$60.5	$171.6

Source: Federal Reserve Board

10

International Earnings as a Percent of Total Earnings					
	1975	1976	1977	1978	1979
Citicorp	70.6	72.4	82.2	71.8	64.7
Chase Manhattan	64.5	78.0	64.9	53.2	46.9
Bank America Corp.	54.7	46.7	41.8	34.6	37.7
Manufacturers Hanover Corp.	49.1	59.3	60.2	51.2	48.8
J. P. Morgan & Co.	60.2	46.1	48.1	51.0	52.0
Chemical N.Y. Corp.	41.6	41.1	38.8	42.0	35.1
Bankers Trust N.Y.	58.6	60.4	82.8	67.9	51.5
First Chicago Corp.	34.0	17.0	21.0	16.0	3.5
Continental Ill. Corp.	13.4	23.0	16.6	17.8	18.5
Security Pacific Corp.	12.6	6.9	11.6	15.1	10.4
Composite	52.5	50.8	50.5	45.5	42.6

Source: Salomon Brothers, "Lending to LDCs: Mounting Problems," April 2, 1980, Table 19, p. 24.

[11] As can be seen from the following table, the rate of household savings and gross fixed capital formation in the United States has consistently lagged behind the other major industrialized nations. These factors would indicate that the relative demand for financial (and banking) services has been higher outside of the United States.

	Household Savings as % of Gross Domestic Product[1]			Gross Fixed Capital Formation as % of Gross Domestic Product[2]		
	1961	1970	1978	1960	1970	1979
Belgium	8.2	12.4	11.8	19.3	22.7	21.0
Canada	2.3	3.7	6.9	21.9	20.8	22.5
France	7.5	9.3	10.7	20.1	23.4	21.3
Germany	10.8	11.8	8.7*	24.3	25.6	22.7
Japan	NA	11.7	14.7	30.1	35.4	31.7
Italy	18.7	17.1	19.1	22.6	21.4	18.7
Spain	8.3+	9.5	7.5*	19.4	23.2	19.0
Switzerland	NA	NA	NA	24.8	27.5	21.9
U.K.	4.2	3.7	7.7	16.4	18.6	17.8
U.S.	4.3	5.6	3.8	17.6	17.3	18.1

Notes: +/1964; */1977; −/old series; NA−not available.
Source:
[1] Organization for Economic Co-operation and Development, *National Accounts of OECD Countries 1961-1978*, Volume II, Paris 1980.
[2] Organization for Economic Co-operation and Development, *National Accounts of OECD Countries 1950-1979*, Volume I, Paris 1981.

[12] See, for example: Jurgen Reimnitz, "German Banks Follow German Investment," *Euromoney*, June 1978, p. 91; "Japanese Banks Move for Internationalization," *Oriental Economist*, November 1976, p. 6; Fred H. Klopstock, "A New Stage in the Evolution of International Banking," *International Review of the History of Banking* No. 6, 1973. p. 1; E. N. Roussakis, "The Internationalization of U.S. Commercial Banks," *The Magazine of Bank Administration*, October-November 1979, p. 24; Henry S. Terrell and Sydney J. Key, *Growth of Foreign Banking in the United States: An Analytical Survey*, Board of Governors of the Federal Reserve System, 1977.

[13] Organization for Economic Co-operation and Development, *National Accounts of OECD Countries, 1950-79* (Paris, 1981).

[14] *International Financial Statistics* (International Monetary Fund, Washington, D.C.).

[15] Measured as a percent of total deposits held by the world's top 100 banks, based on *American Banker* lists, adjusted (see Appendix A). This measure is superior to using only the number of banks in the top 100 as it also reflects movements towards the top and bottom of the top 100 rankings.

[16] Nominal gross domestic product converted into dollars at current exchange rates as percent of the total gross domestic product of all members of the Organization for Economic Co-operation and Development (OECD). Source: *National Accounts of OECD Countries, 1950-1979* (Organization for Economic Co-operation and Development, Paris, 1981).

[17] As the importance of a nation's international trade increases, it can be expected that its banks will also increase their international activities. Figures used in the chart are nominal value of exports plus imports converted into dollars at current exchange rates as a percent of the total value of international trade for all members of the OECD. (Source: Organization for Economic Co-operation and Development, *National Accounts of OECD Countries, 1950-1979* (Paris, 1981).

The use of other economic measures, such as domestic consumption or domestic investment as a percent of overall OECD activity, results in relationships similar to those indicated in Figure II.

OECD comparisons are appropriate in this context because U.S. banks are mainly in competition with banks from other OECD nations (Australia, Austria, Belgium, Canada, Denmark, Finland, France, Germany, Greece, Iceland, Ireland, Italy, Japan, Luxembourg, the Netherlands, New Zealand, Norway, Portugal, Spain, Sweden, Switzerland, Turkey, United Kingdom, and Yugoslavia [Special Status]).

[18] Foreign exchange values have changed dramatically since 1976. At the end of 1973, the dollar commanded 1.7 Deutschmarks as compared to 4.2 at the end of 1956; 240 yen compared to 360 yen; 1.9 Dutch guilders as compared to 3.8, and 1.6 Swiss francs compared to 4.3. The British pound, worth $2.78 in 1956, had fallen as low as $1.56 during 1976, and was worth $2.22 at the end of 1979. *International Financial Statistics* (International Monetary Fund, Washington, D.C.).

[19] This frustration is perhaps best exemplified by *The Banker's* comments on the 1972 world rankings contained in its June 1973 issue: "again the German and French banks show better in the listing as a result of the revaluation of the D-mark and the franc against the dollar. The effects of these factors are difficult to quantify and as a consequence it is almost impossible to estimate how much of the remarkable growth of the Continental European banks was due to growth in their domestic economies" (*The Banker*, June 1973, p. 647).

[20] As an example, assume Bank A from the United States had total assets of $2 billion in 1970, and $2.2 billion in 1971. With an inflation rate of 10%, the value of Bank A's assets in real terms in 1971 is the same as 1970. Similarly, assume Bank B from Germany had assets of DM 4 billion in 1970 and DM 4 billion in 1971, with inflation at 0% for 1971. Therefore, its assets in "real" terms have remained the same. Clearly, the relative "real" size of Bank A and Bank B remained the same in 1970 and 1971. In terms of nominal dollar value of assets, however, the relative ranking of Bank B would decline unless the DM appreciated by 10% or more in 1971.

[21] For example, assume a German bank in Period I has DM 10 billion in domestic deposits and $4 billion in dollar deposits; in Period II, DM 15 billion in domestic deposits and $7 billion in dollar deposits. The exchange rate in Period I is DM 4 = $1; in Period II, DM 2 = $1. The only information reported by the German bank, however, is its consolidated assets in terms of $ U.S., converted from DM using the current exchange rate. Thus the German bank would report assets of $6.5 billion in Period I and $14.5 billion in Period II.

Period I: DM 10 billion + ($4 billion) (4) = DM 26 billion = $6.5 billion
Period II: DM 15 billion + ($7 billion) (2) = DM 29 billion = $14.5 billion.

These figures would be used to determine the unadjusted rankings in Table 3. Since only the consolidated $ U.S. assets of the German bank are known, the adjustment used in Table 3 is predicted upon the (false) assumption that all of a German bank's assets are in DM and is made by applying the Period I exchange rate (i.e., DM 4 = $1) to Period II assets. Thus the German bank's assets adjusted for constant exchange rantes would be calculated at $6.5 billion in Period I and $7.25 billion in Period II.

Period I = $6.5 billion, which represents DM 26 billion at DM 4 = $1, converted back to dollars at DM 4 = $1 = $6.5 billion.
Period II = $14.5 billion which represents DM 29 billion at DM 2 = $1, which then is converted back to dollars at Period I rate (DM 4 = $1) = $7.25 billion.

However, the true adjustment should have been to $10.75 billion in Period II if one had information on the currency breakdown of the German bank's deposits.

Period II = DM 15 billion (at DM 4 = $1) + $7 billion = $10.75 billion

Thus the mechanical adjustment method used in Table 3 overadjusts for exchange rate changes (in the example above by $3.5 billion), dictating great care in its interpretation.

[22] See, for example, John G. Heimann, "Incursions by Nonbanking Institutions–Who Will Provide Private Banking Services in 1985?" (Remarks delivered March 10, 1980, to the Government Research Corporation, Second Policy Forum on American Banking, London, England).

[23] See data, based on Federal Reserve flow of funds accounts, in Will R. Sparks, "Financial Competition and the Public Interest," reprinted in Senate Committee on Banking, Housing, and Urban Affairs Hearings on *Edge Corporation Branching, Foreign Bank Takeovers, and International Bank Facilities*, 96th Cong., 1st Sess., July 16 and 20, 1979, pp. 368-9. Data on financial market trends in other nations are collected using different methods and definitions, precluding any meaningful comparison of these trends with those in other nations.

[24] Both the Bank Merger Act and the Bank Holding Company Act contain antitrust provisions which require disapproval of any acquisition, consolidation or merger involving an FDIC-insured bank that would result in a monopoly, or substantially lessen competition unless public interest considerations outweighed such antitrust considerations. See John E. Shockey and William B. Glidden, *Foreign-Controlled U.S. Banks: The Legal and Regulatory Environment*, OCC Staff Paper, 1980.

[25] For descriptions of bank structure and regulation in foreign markets, see U.S. Department of the Treasury, *Report to Congress on Foreign Government Treatment of U.S. Commercial Banking Organizations*, 1979, Chs. 8-28, and Dimitri Vittas, ed., *Banking Systems Abroad*, Inter-Bank Research Organisation, April 1978.

[26] Based on assets (*The Banker*, June 1980); Credit Agricole ranked third on the *American Banker's* list (based on deposits).

[27] David White, "France's Credit Agricole," *Financial Times*, May 27, 1980, pp. xxx; and Vivian Lewis, "Credit Agricole–French Bankers' 'bete noir'," *The Banker*, May 1979, pp. 25. See also, Jacques Melitz, "The French Financial System, Mechanisms and Propositions for Reform," (Paper prepared for the conference on the Political Economy of France, American Enterprise Institute, Washington, D.C., May 29-31, 1980) for an informative discussion of France's financial system.

[28] Credit Agricole was included in the world bank rankings compiled by *The Banker* and *The American Banker* in 1975 as the world's third largest bank. (See *The Banker*, June 1976, and the *American Banker*, July 30, 1976, p. 200). The *American Banker* commented at the time: "Although not recognized as a commercial bank under French regulations, the bank [Credit Agricole], which is the central organization for co-operative associations mainly in the agricultural sector, was added because it offers the same types of services as commercial banks." See further discussion in Appendix A regarding coverage of various types of institutions in the rankings.

[29] *The American Banker*, July 25, 1980.

[30] Vittas, *op. cit.*, pp. 60-64.

[31] Westdeutsche Landesbank Girozentrale, Bayerische Landesbank Girozentrale, and Hessische Landesbank Gironzentrale.

[32] A summary of consolidation trends in foreign markets appears in Ian Morrison and Dimitri Vittas, "The Structure of Banking Systems Abroad," *The Magazine of Bank Administration*, August 1979, pp. 42-46.

[33] See David A. Alhadeff, *Competition and Controls in Banking: A Study of the Regulation of Bank Competition in Italy, France and England* (University of California Press, Berkeley, CA, 1968), pp. 112-117 and 124-34; and Morrison and Vittas, p. 46.

[34] Morrison and Vittas, *op. cit.*, p. 46.

[35] "Bigger and Fewer," *The Economist*, February 14, 1976, p. 34.

[36] Morrison and Vittas, *loc. cit*. Rumors of additional mergers among large Japanese banks have been reported (see "There *are* happy marriages," *Euromoney*, March 1980, p. 72).

[37] *The Banker*, June 1972, p. 810.

[38] Jack Revell, *The British Financial System*, Harper and Row, 1973, p. 121; and Morrison and Vittas, *loc. cit.*, p. 46.

[39] *Report to Congress . . .*, p. 91.

[40] See Morrison and Vittas, *loc. cit.*

[41] For a list of bank mergers and amalgamations in Canada since 1867, see *The Canadian Banker & ICB Review*, Vol. 85, No. 5, October 1978. The list depicts the movement toward a small number of dominant nationwide banks. The impact of domestic consolidation on world ranking is illustrated in one case: The Canadian Bank of Commerce and the Imperial Bank of Canada were ranked 15th and 70th, respectively, among the world's largest banks before their merger in 1961 which produced the world's 9th largest bank.

[42] H. Peter Dreyer, "Dutch Welcome Foreign Banks," *Journal of Commerce*, March 14, 1980, p. 11.

[43] See Klopstock, *op. cit.*, p. 21, and Morrison and Vittas, *loc. cit.*; Dreyer reported that the number of foreign banks operating in the Netherlands increased from four to 37 during the period of domestic bank consolidation (*loc. cit.*).

[44] These selected examples are based on *American Banker* annual listings and do not include large earlier consolidations such as that forming Chase Manhattan, nor Continental Illinois' and other banks' mergers with institutions below the top 100.

[45] On a pro forma basis, the largest recent (actual or proposed) foreign acquisitions of U.S. banks increased (or would have increased) the acquiring banks' 1979 world rankings as follows:

Acquiring Bank	U.S. Acquisition	Acquirer's World Rank	
		Before	After
Hongkong and Shanghai	Marine Midland	76	41#
Midland Bank	Crocker National	26	13#
NatWest	NBNA	15*	11
Standard Chartered	Union Bank	74*	59

Notes: Acquiring banks' ranks are based on adjusted assets compiled by The Banker Research Unit, *The Banker* (June 1980).

*Acquisition consummated before year-end 1979; pro forma rank derived by subtracting acquired bank assets as of 12/31/79.

#Acquisition not consummated by year-end 1979; pro forma rank derived by adding U.S. bank assets as of 12/31/79.

[46] For a comprehensive description of the magnitude and timing of foreign acquisitions, see William A. Longbrake, Melanie Quinn, and Judith A. Walter, *Foreign Ownership of U.S. Banks: Facts and Patterns*, OCC Staff Paper, 1980.

[47] See Diane Page and Neal M. Soss, *Some Evidence on Transnational Banking Structure*, OCC Staff Paper, 1980.

[48] Henry C. Wallich, Governor, Federal Reserve Board, Written responses to questions of Senator John Heinz III during testimony before the Senate Committee on Banking, Housing and Urban Affairs, in Hearings on *Edge Corporation Branching; Foreign Bank Takeovers; and International Banking Facilities*, 96th Cong., 1st Sess., July 16, 1979, p. 49.

[49] "Acceptances, letters of credit, securities on behalf of customers, etc." BRU notes that these items cannot always be identified from balance sheets. Although in most cases they are not large in relation to total balance sheet items, "the size of a number of institutions would be grossly exaggerated by their inclusion." *The Banker*, June 1979, p. 87.

[50] *Ibid*. Illustrating the difficulty of "pinpointing" deposits, there is a difference of over $20 billion in the December 1978 deposit figures shown by AB and BRU for Deutsche Bank (both shown on a consolidated basis).

[51] Similarly, Marine Midland ranked 77 on BRU's 1975 list (consolidated); the company's largest bank ranked 100 on AB's list, but the organization would have ranked 67 if its 10 subsidiary banks were consolidated (as actually occurred on January 1, 1976).

[52] *The Banker*, June 1979, p. 87.

[53] *Ibid*.

[54] See *The Banker*, June 1978, p. 103, and *American Banker*, July 25, 1980, p. 13.

[55] *The Banker*, June 1976 and *American Banker*, July 30, 1976, p. 200.

[56] *The Banker*, June 1972, p. 807.

[57] *The Banker*, June 1979, p. 87.

[58] See footnote 49.

## 6

FOREIGN ACQUISITIONS OF U.S. BANKS: MOTIVES AND TACTICAL CONSIDERATIONS

JUDITH A. WALTER

SUMMARY

This paper identifies factors motivating foreign acquirers of U.S. banks during the 1970s when there was a dramatic upsurge in acquisition activity. Strategic needs identified are opportunities for profitable growth, diversification, and access to a dollar base. The effect on acquirers of tactical considerations—depressed U.S. bank stock prices, a declining dollar, and maintenance of prestige or position among competing banks, as well as prospects in the late 1970s for new legislative restrictions on foreign ownership of U.S. banks—are also considered.

Three major influences on the receptivity of U.S. bank to acquisition bids are the impact of a U.S. bank's earnings and/or capital problems, divestiture requirements of the 1970 Bank Holding Company Act Amendments, and, for larger U.S. banks, legislative impediments to potential U.S.-based acquirers.

The overall findings of the paper are that the U.S. banking markets in their size and growth potential as well as the political and economic stability of the United States have been strong attractions to foreign acquirers.

The paper does not support the notion that depressed U.S. bank stock prices during the 1970s have induced foreign acquisitions, because foreign acquirers have paid premiums over both book and market values substantially greater than domestic acquirers and have purchased a disproportionate number of relatively weak banks. The paper also suggests that the influence of the dollar's decline on the acquisition upsurge has been overestimated. However, two additional factors are believed to have had an influence even though they cannot be quantified. One is the effect that acquisition initiatives taken by some banks may have had on their competitors, who may have countered with acquisitions of their own in order to maintain prestige or position with customers. The other is the fear that Congressional debates in the mid and late 1970s would result in new restrictions on foreign participation in U.S. banking markets.

In the analysis of U.S. bank receptivity to acquisition bids, the paper develops support for the hypothesis that foreigners have concentrated on less successful U.S. banks that would be strengthened by the acquisition. Nearly 24 percent of U.S. banks acquired by foreign banks in the last decade were either failing or in serious condition at the time they were acquired and an additional 24 percent of the acquisitions involved a commitment of new capital by the acquirer. A sample of banks acquired by foreign individuals also shows a disproportionate number of relatively weak banks were acquired.

The paper concludes that, for the most part, foreign acquisitions of U.S. banks appear to have been transactions that offered benefits to both partners.

INTRODUCTION

Foreign acquisitions of U.S. banks have been a phenomenon chiefly of the 1970s, particularly the latter half.[1] Because the upsurge in acquisition activity was dramatic and appeared to signal not only a shift in the form of foreign bank expansion in the U.S. but also unprecedented interest by foreign individuals, many analysts have attempted to identify motives or other special factors that may have had an impact on the magnitude or the timing.

Motives and other influencing factors, which are discussed in this paper, were drawn from written commentary and inferred from acquisition patterns. They were confirmed, supplemented, and refined or refuted by questioning some key participants—primarily investment and foreign bankers. In some cases it was not possible to collect much evidence beyond that available in anecdotal form. Nevertheless, even in the absence of substantive quantifiable data, it was possible to make some evaluations of the relative influence of various factors by weighing the opinions of participants, industry analysts, and academic experts along with the available evidence.

The paper first examines motives and factors believed to influence acquirers. These are divided into longer term strategic motives and other more tactical considerations. The sections dealing with longer term motivations focus primarily on foreign banks, about which there is a fair amount of written commentary and anecdotal evidence. The first two sections which discuss tactical considerations that may influence acquirers—depressed U.S. bank stock prices and the decline in the value of the dollar—apply to both foreign bank and foreign individual acquirers. The third—"fashion" or maintenance of prestige—appears to relate mostly to foreign bank acquirers. The fourth—the U.S. legislative and political environment—applies to both types of acquirers.

The paper then looks at three factors that may influence the receptivity of U.S. banks to acquisition bids or even induce U.S. banks to seek foreign acquirers. These tactical influences, which appear to figure prominently in the process of pairing specific acquirers and acquisition candidates, are the failure or weakened condition of some U.S. banks, divestiture requirements of the Bank Holding Company Act, and the restriction of acquisition options for U.S. banks resulting from U.S. law and policy.

LONGER TERM STRATEGIC MOTIVES OF FOREIGN ACQUIRERS

Chief among the factors widely considered to motivate foreign bank purchasers of U.S. banks are the strategic needs to expand and diversify. Acquisition of a U.S. bank affords purchasers the immediate opportunity to participate in what is perceived to be a prosperous, growing market and to deploy assets in a stable investment environment. The other fundamental motivation, judged to be important for many foreign bank acquirers, is desire for the broader dollar base that a U.S. bank provides. Analysts, academicians, the business press, investment bankers, foreign bankers, as well as all available evidence, point to these longer term strategic considerations as the original impetus for recent foreign acquisitions of U.S. banks.

Although the sections that follow deal with foreign bank acquirers, many of the points probably could be extended, with only slight modification, to foreign individual acquirers. Very little has been written about foreign individuals who acquire U.S. banks. However, logic and patterns of acquisition suggest that they are also motivated to some degree by long term needs for profitable investment opportunities and asset diversification. Thus, it is likely that a number of the attractions that the United States has for foreign bank acquirers, e.g., economic growth potential and a stable investment climate, have also appealed to foreign individuals who have acquired banks.

Growth Opportunities

The latter half of the 1970s saw reduced growth opportunities in a number of foreign domestic markets. Serge Bellanger, chairman of the Institute of Foreign Bankers, is reported to have expressed the opinion that a number of foreign banks have looked abroad for expansion opportunities as a result of home market growth constraints (e.g., credit controls) imposed on banks for domestic economic reasons.[2] In a number of countries domestic growth potential has been further undercut by intensified competition from foreign banks. *The Economist* reported in 1979, for instance, that "a quarter of all bank loans to British companies and consumers are now accounted for by foreign cuckoos in the nest and over 30 percent of loans to British manufacturing corporations."[3]

Moreover, many believe that international markets in general have lost the potential for earnings growth that they had in the late 1960s and early 1970s. This also has led to a focus on the U.S. as David Cates, president of the consulting bank analyst firm Cates, Lyons & Co., Inc., pointed out:

> Worldwide private demand for credit has been lackluster, and lending spreads in big syndicates—an important profit determinant for big banks—had been coming down since 1976. This combination of available funds and shrinking margins, then, leads foreign banks to search for new volume and new markets, among which the U.S. is ideal.[4]

The U.S. market has been especially attractive because in the late 1970s perceptions have been that "America is still in the middle of its biggest ever banking boom. . . . . "[5]

Thus, the size of the U.S. economy and the perceived growth potential of U.S. banking markets have been major attractions. And acquisition is an expeditious means of achieving a presence in the U.S. market.

By making an acquisition a foreign bank gains, through the acquired bank's market position and recognition, instant access to a domestic market. Achieving such market presence might take years to accomplish with a branch or *de novo* bank.[6] Similarly, the acquirer obtains a ready-made operating infrastructure. This includes, most importantly, staff and systems—both of which would be costlier and much slower to build from scratch. It also removes an element of risk because there is not the same degree of uncertainty about the success of the venture that would be attached to a *de novo* operation.

Acquisition has become an especially advantageous means of entry as diminished opportunities for growth in U.S. wholesale banking have impelled some foreign as well as domestic banks to devote more energy to developing the U.S. "middle" (i.e., regional corporate) and consumer banking markets. Subsidiaries are a better organizational form for developing these markets than the more traditional foreign bank branches or agencies which have been better suited for trade financing and multinational corporate lending.

The purchase of technology may also be a major factor in some cases. U.S. banks have been global pioneers in such areas as computerized data processing, consumer services, cash management and other advanced corporate services, and in liability management. In interviews with OCC staff, several investment bankers suggested that such leading-edge products and management techniques may have been an additional attraction for some foreign bank purchasers of U.S. banks.[7]

Diversification

Linked to growth needs is the strategic desire to diversify risk in international holdings. For example, a *Financial Times* (London) analysis pointed out that the "strategic need to diversify earnings" was judged by some to be "the most important factor" underlying the acquisition plans of the British, whose branch networks in the former British colonial empire left them heavily dependent on some of the world's poorer and less stable areas.[8] During the time of the proposal and subsequent acquisition of Union Bancorporation, public statements of both the chairman and the chief executive officer of Standard Chartered Bank, Ltd. alluded to diversification benefits that would stem from the acquisition.[9]

For foreign investors seeking international diversification, the political and economic stability of the U.S. is felt by most analysts to exert a strong attraction.[10] Carter Golembe, a banking consultant, is among those who put considerable weight on this motivation:

> We think the most important single cause, applying to investment in banks as well as in other fields, is a basic faith in political and economic stability in the United States. Few foreign investors expect this country will experience heady prosperity in the years immediately ahead. Nevertheless, our own inquiries, conversation with informed observers, reading of the financial press, and common sense combine to tell us that for multinational financial institutions that feel a need to diversify, an indigenous presence in the U.S. is extremely attractive.[11]

For a number of foreign banks, the U.S. commitment to private enterprise is an important part of this attraction. The senior Barclays Bank official in the United States, A. Richard Carden, put it this way: "It may be a hackneyed phrase, but we view the United States as the last bastion of capitalism. We feel our money's safe here."[12]

Dollar Base

The desire for a dollar base is a long term strategic motivation related to growth and diversification that recurs in many discussions of foreign bank acquisitions of U.S. banks. The need for a dollar base stems, in the first instance, from the dominance the dollar has achieved as the world's major trading and reserve currency. Banks financing international trade and commerce need a means of access to (or a channel for investing) dollars.[13] U.S. offices of a foreign bank can participate in U.S. money markets, serve as depositories and clearing centers for the parent and, due to time zone differences, operate in foreign exchange markets when the head office of the parent is closed.[14]

In a discussion of international banking in general, Fred H. Klopstock some time ago pinpointed the reasons—cost and stability—that a bank subsidiary operation would typically be superior to a branch for purposes of securing a base in an indigenous currency:

> The primary weakness in the deposit structure of many [overseas] branches is their dependence on short-dated, relatively high priced and often volatile deposits bid for in highly competitive money markets. Unlike indigenous banks, branches with few exceptions have no far-flung network of offices in their countries of operation and thus find it difficult to obtain sizable and, in the aggregate, stable deposits in the form of transaction balances from businesses and individuals.[15]

The stability effect was stressed by Klaus Jacobs, president of European American Bank & Trust Co., who noted that the acquisition of Franklin National Bank ". . . gave us a very strong deposit presence in the U.S. . . . These [deposits] are less sensitive to the situation in the money markets and the economy than corporate balances."[16]

The quest for stability by acquiring U.S. banks may be given further impetus by uncertainties about the continuing supply of Eurodollars should there be successful governmental attempts to regulate the Eurocurrency market, a decrease in the U.S. balance of payments deficit, or an event with disruptive consequences. This has led some commentators to emphasize that ownership of a U.S. bank ". . . provides a significant dollar base which could prove useful in the unlikely event of serious disturbances in the Euromarkets."[17]

The cost aspect of securing a dollar base by purchasing a U.S. bank has two facets. First, a number of observers have commented that acquisition of a U.S. bank lowers the average cost of funds for a foreign bank operating in U.S. markets in large part because of the access to retail deposits. Paul Horvitz, a University of Houston professor and former director of research at the Federal Deposit Insurance Corporation, stated his view that:

> Acquisition of a bank in the U.S. offers the unique opportunity to take advantage of American bank depositors and to obtain deposit funds at low cost. Only in America does the Government prohibit the payment of interest on demand deposits and set a ceiling as low as 5-¼ percent on time deposits, while the rate on prime business loans exceeds 11 percent.[18]

However, U.S. retail bank operations are not universally perceived to have cost advantages. Some foreign bank officers, such as Robert F. Cassidy, executive vice president of the New York branch of Union Bank of Bavaria, note the high overhead costs and extensive regulation that go hand-in-hand with retail banking in the U.S.[19] David L. Rothstein, president of the New York branch of the Argentine Banking Corporation, expressed his opinion that "only the largest foreign institutions will be willing to confront the costs and risks associated with the major investment in U.S. retail banking."[20] Thomas P. Eldred, comptroller of Banco Industrial de Venezuela states:

> Certainly one of the more significant factors against retail banking is the comparative openness of the operation as opposed to wholesale banking. The retail exposure through governmental review by agencies

such as the FDIC, and regulatory compliance with numerous Federal
Reserve statutes [sic], such as Truth in Lending, Fair Credit Reporting,
and anti-redlining regulations, to name only a few.[21]

Furthermore, according to Eldred

> Retail banking requires high commitments in capital for fixed assets,
> and historically has earned a low return on assets, and requires a high
> degree of close internal supervision of its operations. These costs do
> not compare favorably to a comparable wholesale operation which can
> be highly leveraged and have a small staff.[22]

On the wholesale side, there seems to be no disagreement that U.S.
(i.e., dollar-based) banks enjoy cost advantages. According to C. Edward
McConnell, vice president of Keefe, Bruyette, and Woods, it will take
"considerable time before a non-American bank, regardless of its size,
is able to access the domestic money markets at rates that are exactly
comparable to such major money center banks as Morgan, City [sic],
Chase or Bank of America."[23]

Branches and agencies of foreign banks usually are required to pay
"at least one-quarter percent premium" over the rate paid by U.S.
banks.[24] The amount of the premium usually reflects the length of time
a foreign bank has been established in the U.S. market, and newer, less
familiar banks pay a higher premium.[25] The consequence in some cases
has been that foreign banks expend extra effort (by trading in U.S.
money markets beyond their essential needs) to develop a name and
reputation in order to reduce the premium.[26] Acquisition of a U.S.
bank can thus be a shortcut. Immediate access to money markets at the
domestic bank rate is obtained without paying the penalty of a differential for being foreign.

TACTICAL CONSIDERATIONS THAT MAY
AFFECT FOREIGN ACQUIRERS

Beyond the underlying strategic motivations for expanding into the
U.S. bank market, foreign acquirers have also been thought to be influenced by several tactical considerations. Four factors are generally believed to have had either a facilitating or propelling effect on acquisitions

during the latter half of the 1970s: depressed bank stock prices, the declining value of the dollar, the maintenance of prestige, and the legislative/political environment.

The actual influence of stock prices and of the value of the dollar has been a subject of some disagreement among participants and analysts. Available evidence tends not to support the notion that bank stock price levels have been an inducement for acquirers, and the evidence of the impact of the dollar's decline is inconclusive. Competitive pressure to maintain prestige may have been an influence in some cases of acquisitions by foreign banks although its importance is not easily measured. Finally, those with acquisition plans may have been spurred to swifter action by the threat that restrictive legislation was imminent.

Depressed U.S. Bank Stock Prices

The relatively depressed levels of U.S. bank stock values since the 1973-1974 recession have been judged by many to provide an important economic incentive for foreign acquisition of U.S. banks.[27] According to one bank stock index, price/earnings ratios dropped from a 1970s peak of 14.2 in 1972 to 5.5 in 1974, rose only as high as 9.6 in 1976, and then fell pretty much continuously for the next four years, hitting a new low of 5.0 in the first quarter of 1980.[28] Moreover, during the 1970s the level of bank stock price/earnings ratios was consistently lower than that of the index for Standard and Poors' (S & P) 400 Industrials. In 1975 the bank stock index price/earnings ratio reached a low of less than 60 percent of the price/earnings ratio of the S&P 400 and has not been above 82.1 percent since that time.[29] Low valuations have also been evident in the relationship of stock price to book value. In the years 1978-1980, for example, the bank stock index was about 20 percent below book value and for some of the weaker banks the discount was as much as 50 percent.[30]

Quite a few observers have inferred a causal link between the phenomena of historically low stock prices and heightened foreign demand for U.S. banks. According to a statement attributed to Harry Keefe "the key to the foreign interest . . . is that American bank stocks are continuing to sell at near record lows."[31] Senator H. John Heinz, III has expressed concern that "the depressed level of bank stocks . . . [has] enabled foreigners to acquire American banks at bargain prices."[32] David Cates has opined further that foreign investors believe that at current prices bank stocks may be undervalued:

"[foreign banks] are betting that both the dollar and the U.S. market for bank stocks are low today relative to their future prospects. If either or both recover, they think, they're in for an investment profit."[33]

However, Donald Jacobs takes issue with the notion that foreign investors are attracted because bank stocks are undervalued:

[Another] hypothesis is that banking equities in the U.S. have been oversold. This would imply that buyers are speculating on American equities in an industry in which the buyers are especially knowledgeable. This argument is not convincing since the buyers are purchasing relatively weak institutions and/or are paying a relatively high price.[34]

The same argument is advanced by Crane, Marshall, and Lanham in a study of 15 large U.S. banks acquired or pending acquisition by foreign banks. The authors conclude that

foreign buyers did not pay bargain prices due to the substantial premiums paid over market. . . . Given the premiums paid for target banks, it would thus seem unreasonable to conclude that a depressed market is responsible for recent acquisitions.[35]

Research conducted by Office of the Comptroller of the Currency staff also casts doubt on the view that foreigners have been induced to make acquisitions because undervalued stock prices offer the opportunity for a bargain. The premiums over book value (and hence over any market value that is at a discount to book) paid by foreigners to acquire U.S. banks have been substantially greater than those paid by domestic acquirers.[36] Moreover, foreigners have acquired a disproportionate number of relatively weak banks.[37]

In at least one instance the high premium paid for a U.S. bank was noted with disapproval in the acquirer's home country. British critics of National Westminster's acquisition of National Bank of North America pointed out that the purchase price was 23 times 1978 earnings while stocks of the largest U.S. banks were selling in the market at five-to-six times earnings at the same time.[38] Furthermore, in interviews with investment and foreign bankers it was suggested that most foreign banks pay substantial prices to acquire a U.S. bank not with plans to sell, but because the acquisition is seen as an investment satisfying strategic needs and having prospects for favorable operating returns over the long run.

Nevertheless, whatever the merits of depressed bank stock prices as an incentive for foreign investors to buy, it is undoubtedly true that at a time when market prices are low and there is no immediate prospect for improvement, shareholders may have an incentive to sell. Moreover, banks with a weak capital position may find it advantageous to avoid the equity markets and bolster capital by finding an acquisition partner.[39]

Decline in Value of the Dollar

The increase in acquisitions activity also coincided with the decline in the value of the dollar, particularly the sharp plunge in 1977 and 1978. From 1976 to the end of 1978, the dollar dropped 25 percent against the German deutschemark, 41 percent against the Swiss franc, and 42 percent against the Japanese yen.[40] This decline has what is termed a "wealth effect." It makes the holders of strong currencies wealthier in the sense that they are able to purchase greater amounts of assets denominated in dollars for a fixed amount of their own currency. Put another way, it enables some foreigners to purchase larger U.S. banks without paying more in terms of their home currency.

There is fairly widespread belief that this slippage of the dollar, which has made U.S. banks relatively cheap internationally, has at least facilitated, if not actually stimulated, acquisitions by foreigners.[41] Despite its intuitive appeal, this notion is not uniformly supported by evidence or opinion.

In a study of eight large U.S. banks acquired since 1976, exchange rate data show that the countries of the acquiring banks are mostly weak currency countries or countries whose currency is not strong relative to the dollar The only exception is the Netherlands.[42] Because strong currency countries have not been represented to any significant degree in recent acquisitions, this suggests that the decline in the value of the dollar has not been a strong motivating factor. At the same time, home country may not be the only relevant consideration; some large multinational banks from weak currency countries are believed to have accumulated substantial inventories of strong international currencies (deutschemarks or Swiss francs) which would be available to make acquisitions.

Some have expressed the opinion that foreign acquisitions may be prompted by a belief that the dollar is undervalued and that there will be an investment appreciation when the value of the dollar adjusts upward.[43] However, Donald Jacobs has questioned the significance of this factor:

> It has been argued that the relative decline in the value of the dollar makes a purchase of United States equities increasingly attractive, especially for banks that denominate their accounts in strong currencies. This rationale is not compelling because a purchase is an income stream in dollars that must be converted to the strong currency. In effect, it assumes the managements of foreign banks believe the dollar was oversold and was, therefore, purchasing currently inexpensive dollars for future delivery. Since the income stream will continue for a long period into the future, this would imply speculation on the secular trend in the value of the dollar. This might explain some of the buying interest, especially among banks whose home offices are in countries with chronically weak currencies. But I don't believe, overall, this is an important rationale.[44]

Maintenance of Prestige

It has been suggested that a part of the increase in acquisition activity during the last half of the 1970s was a defensive response by some foreign banks to keep up with competitors or merely reflected a desire to maintain prestige by emulating others.

In surveying the acquisitions trend by foreign banks, Carter Golembe finds it "fashionable" for major foreign banks to have a U.S. retailing presence.

> Bankers are, perhaps to an unusual degree, preoccupied with comparisons between themselves and their "peers" .... The results of peer pressure in banking are not always fortunate ..., but just as often they are salutary. Movements that develop momentum generally have some rational foundation, however blind may be some of the followers. From what we can tell, it is distinctly fashionable these days for major international banks headquartered in the world's great trading nations to have a retail banking presence in the United States. One suspects that such investments are also considered chic in the world of sheiks.[45]

The same idea appeared in the 1979 *American Banker* article by Eldred, who commented that "the intangible factor of the foreign banker's prestige . . . is increased substantially through ownership of a domestic U.S. bank."[46]

The influence of a herd instinct on the bank buying proclivities of foreign interests is not easy to evaluate. Irving M. Geszel, bank analyst at Bear, Stearns and Company, was reported to have said "sales trigger additional sales. . . . If one buys, then others become interested for competitive and other reasons."[47] The announcements in 1979 of interest in the acquisition of U.S. banks by three Spanish banks are possible evidence of such an influence. Similar motivations have been ascribed to all five major London clearing banks.[48]

However difficult it may be to gauge the influence of fashion, such a motivation probably should not be dismissed as inconsequential.[49] Imitation of competitors is venerable practice in the banking industry, rooted in the competitive reality that banks generally must maintain prestige among peers so as not to lose valuable customers.[50]

Legislative and Political Environment

There appears to be a broad consensus among most observers of the acquisitions phenomenon that the debates leading to the passage of the International Banking Act of 1978, as well as the provisions of the Act itself, helped accelerate the pace of acquisitions in the second half of the 1970s.[51] It is also possible that concerns about foreign involvement in the U.S. banking system which were raised in several state legislatures at about the same time had a reinforcing effect.[52]

Legislative deliberations about foreign incursions in U.S. bank markets began in 1966 with a report submitted to the Joint Economic Committee of the Congress and the introduction of proposed legislation by Congressman Wright Patman and Senator Jacob Javits. However, serious attention to foreign bank activities in this country did not occur until 1973. In that year, two bills were filed which aimed at establishing federal jurisdiction over foreign banking activities in the U.S.—Congressman Wright Patman's Foreign Bank Control Act and Congressman Thomas Rees' Foreign Bank Regulatory Act. According to Francis Lees, both were prompted by the successful growth of foreign banking in this country and were shaped in part by moderately protectionist reaction to the 1971 and 1973 dollar devaluations, a depressed stock market which seemed to invite takeover bids and a continuing weak U.S. balance of payments position.[53]

Both bills proposed controls on foreign acquisitions of U.S. banks. Two years later the Federal Reserve's proposed Foreign Banking Act of 1975, specifying a policy of national treatment for foreign banks in the U.S., and the 1973 bills were consolidated into the International Banking Act of 1975.

The 1975 bill contained provisions for federal agency approval of acquisitions of domestic banks by foreign individuals—provisions similar to those that ultimately were incorporated in the Change of Bank Control Act of 1978.[54] As the International Banking Act (IBA) was modified in 1976, 1977 and 1978, the issue of acquisitions *per se* lost importance in deliberations that increasingly focused on broader issues of federal supervision and competitive parity for foreign banks' U.S. operations. Thus the question of foreign acquisitions of U.S. banks is "nowhere addressed specifically in the International Banking Act . . . ."[55]

However, the acquisitions issue was kept alive in the press, and congressional debate itself was not entirely insulated from concerns aroused by the major acquisition proposals (National Bank of North America, Union Bank, Marine Midland and LaSalle) announced in 1978. In his statement before the Senate Subcommittee on Financial Institutions during hearings on the IBA, G. William Miller, then Chairman of the Federal Reserve Board, cited the acquisition proposals as evidence of need for national policy on foreign banking activities in this country.[56] M. A. Schapiro and Company, Inc. submitted the May 1978 issue of their publication *The Bank Stock Quarterly* to the Committee to point out that U.S. law and regulation resulted in inequality of acquisition opportunity between domestic and foreign-owned banks.[57] Foreshadowing legislative initiatives in 1979, the U.S. Labor Party's statement to the Subcommittee urged a moratorium on foreign takeovers of American financial institutions.[58]

The effect the political atmosphere may have had on the pace of acquisitions was articulated by a British financial journalist just before the IBA was passed:

> Three big United States banks, in as many months, have moved or are moving into British control. The hurry is significant: British bankers are anticipating the day when the rules for competing in the U.S. are changed. When that day comes, they want to be on the inside looking out. They know, too, that their actions must bring the day closer.[59]

Moreover, apart from the general concern about future restrictions raised by the IBA debates, the specific provisions of the Act may also have influenced foreign banks' thinking about alternative modes of participating in the U.S. market. The probability that regulations implementing the IBA instituting reserve requirements for foreign bank branches would significantly reduce their cost advantages has led some to conclude that there could be a corresponding increase in the desirability of acquiring a U.S. bank subsidiary. C. Edward McConnell has expressed this view:

> ... Foreign banks' [branches] will not be able to continue to garner large share of market increments at the expense of the American banks once the element of price competitiveness is lost. That advantages has already been lost with the passage of the International Banking Act. . . . If the "name of the game" is to secure the lowest cost of funds, a privilege almost exclusively reserved for dollar-based banks, then perhaps it would make sense for a non-dollar based bank to become dollar-based, that is, acquire an existing U.S. banking operation.[60]

Serge Bellanger takes the position that "the deliberate effect of the IBA has been to encourage foreign bank entry through subsidiaries."[61]

TACTICAL CONSIDERATIONS IN THE PAIRING PROCESS: WHY SOME U.S. BANKS MAY BE MORE LIKELY ACQUISITION PARTNERS THAN OTHERS

Once a foreign bank has made the strategic decision to purchase a U.S. bank, potential partners are searched out with a careful eye to "fit." Investment bankers say that, in most cases, their foreign bank clients have required that U.S. acquisition candidates be in one of the money center states—New York, California, or Illinois. The would-be acquirers then take into account their own strengths and weaknesses in developing other selection criteria. The goal of this tailoring process is to be able to put together combinations that will result in enhanced profitability for the acquired bank and, hence, a greater investment return for the foreign parent bank.

In disclosing plans for newly acquired National Bank of North America (NBNA), for example, the chairman of National Westminster emphasized the U.K. bank's long experience in retail banking in its home market, where it has the country's largest branch network: "We are probably as good as anyone in the world at running a retail network. We feel sure we can introduce improvements in the [NBNA] network and increase its business."[62]

Similarly, Standard Chartered Bank reportedly hopes to be able to use its ownership of Union Bank to exploit the need perceived among medium-sized California companies for better banking services over-seas.[63] Other matches have included those in which complementarity of the foreign bank and U.S. bank overseas branch networks was a major factor and others in which foreign banks sought U.S. partners geograph-ically situated to participate in the U.S. end of trade financing with their home country.

Much less is known about the selection criteria used by foreign indi-vidual acquirers. However, there are some correlations between acquir-er's nationalities and the locations of acquired banks that suggest that business connections and/or ethnic populations in certain U.S. cities or states are important.[64] For instance, Miami, which is rapidly becoming a center of U.S.-Latin America trade and finance, accounts for 11 of the 15 acquisitions by individuals from Latin American countries. Sim-ilarly, eight of the nine acquisitions made by individuals from Asian countries have been in California and four of the 11 acquisitions made by Middle Eastern individuals have been in Houston.

For both types of acquirers, calculations as to how receptive poten-tial U.S. partners may be to an acquisition bid figure importantly in the selection process. Henry Keefe has commented that, unlike the situa-tion with industrial companies, a transaction to purchase a bank "has to be friendly. If the board leaves, [the buyer] might lose a third of [the bank's] deposit base."[65] Investment bankers generally advise their for-eign bank clients to avoid situations in which the purchase attempt is likely to be contested by the acquisition candidate.[66] Thus, U.S. banks that anticipate net benefits from being acquired are more likely to be willing partners. And those that *need* to be acquired may welcome ac-quisition bids, if they are not already actively seeking them.[67]

The following sections examine three factors that appear to have made certain U.S. banks particularly susceptible to foreign acquisition bids—weakened condition, divestiture forced by law, and legal impedi-ments to some domestic acquisitions.

Failed or Weak Banks

David Cates has asserted that "the plain truth is that successful large banks are not for sale, and those banks that are on the block tend to be troubled."[68] The available evidence does indicate a strong connection between bank performance and acquisition by foreigners.

The possibility of such a connection is suggested by the coincidence of the surge in number of bank acquisitions by foreign interests and the increase in number of troubled U.S. banks in the latter half of the 1970s. Of the 100 foreign acquisitions of U.S. banks since the beginning of 1970, 69 occurred in the years 1976-1980.[69] Tables 1 and 2 show that during the same period the number of troubled U.S. banks increased substantially.

Analysis of the condition of the banks that foreigners acquired reveals a high incidence of institutions that were in a weakened financial condition, making them particularly susceptible to takeover bids. Table 3 shows that 24 percent of the U.S. banks purchased by foreign banks in the last decade were either failing or in serious condition at the time they were acquired. An additional 24 percent were accompanied by a commitment of new capital by the acquirer, implying that the acquisition candidate's financial position needed strengthening.

The summary of condition at acquisition of a sample of 24 U.S. banks acquired by foreign individuals displayed in Table 4 also shows a large

Table 1
U.S. Banks with Serious Problems (1970-1979)

Year	Serious Problem Banks[a]	All Insured U.S. Banks	%
1970	251	13,840	1.81
1971	239	13,939	1.71
1972	190	14,059	1.35
1973	155	14,298	1.08
1974	183	14,550	1.26
1975	349	14,714	2.37
1976	379	14,740	2.57
1977	368	14,741	2.50
1978	342	14,716	2.32
1979	287	14,365	2.00

[a]Banks rated "4" or "5" (serious problem) or the equivalent by federal bank regulators.

Table 2
Weak and Serious Problem National Banks (1975-1979)

Year	Weak and Serious Problem National Banks[a]	All National Banks	%
1975	85	4,797	1.77
1976	147	4,791	3.07
1977	259	4,652	5.57
1978	306	4,557	6.71
1979	266	4,445	5.98

[a]Banks rated "3" (weak), "4" or "5" (serious problem) by OCC examiners. Comparable data are not available for state-chartered banks or for earlier years.

Table 3
**Summary of 37 Federal Reserve, FDIC or OCC Approval Orders for Foreign Banks to
Acquire U.S. Banks or for Mergers of Domestic U.S. Banks with
Foreign-owned U.S. Banks (1969-1980)**

	Number of Banks	Percentage of Banks
No problem noted	20	52.6
No problem noted; increase in capital committed	9*	23.7
Serious problem	2	5.3
Serious problem; increase in capital committed	1	2.6
Emergency acquisition	4	10.5
Emergency acquisition	2	5.3
	38	100.0

*Three of these banks were divested pursuant to the Bank Holding Company Amendment of 1970.

proportion of troubled banks.[70] Two of the 24, slightly more than eight percent of the sample, were failed banks acquired under emergency arrangements. Nearly 60 percent were rated by examiners as "weak" or "serious problem" banks.

To look at this aspect of the acquisition phenomenon from a slightly different perspective, an audit was performed on the 138 notices for changes in control filed with the OCC between March 10, 1979, when the Change in Control Act became effective, and December 31, 1980. These notices included intended acquisitions by both U.S. and foreign individuals. Only 31 of the 138 notices (23 percent) involved banks in the "weak" or "serious problem" categories. Thus it appears that a disproportionate number of the purchasers of weak banks have been foreign rather than domestic.

Other data developed in recent OCC research yield a final bit of evidence that the U.S. banks acquired by foreigners have been relatively weak: A sample of 20 foreign-acquired banks showed returns on both equity and assets significantly lower than those of their non-acquired peer banks for the two years immediately preceding acquisition.[71]

The evidence, then, supports the hypothesis that to help assure favorable responses to acquisition bids, would-be foreign acquirers have concentrated on less successful U.S. banks, i.e., those that would be likely to perceive benefits in the affiliation, either from an injection of fresh capital, added international expertise, or some other strength the foreign purchaser would bring.

Table 4
Summary of the Condition at Acquisition of 24 Banks
Acquired by Foreign Individuals

	Number of Banks	Percentage of Sample
Failure	2	8.3
Serious problem	3	12.5
Weak	11	45.8
No problem	8	33.3
	24	100.0

Divestitures Under the Bank Holding Company Act

The Bank Holding Company Act Amendments of 1970 extended the coverage of the Act to one-bank holding companies which were previously unregulated. One-bank holding companies that controlled both banks and other business enterprises engaged in unauthorized activities under provisions of the Act were required to divest the banks or unauthorized activities by December 31, 1980. Because of the McFadden Act, the Douglas Amendment to the Bank Holding Company Act and U.S. antitrust laws, holding companies with large bank affiliates which decided to divest their bank affiliates found it difficult to find eligible U.S. acquirers with the capacity to absorb these large banks.

This was directly responsible for the foreign acquisition of three large banks—National Bank of North America, LaSalle National Bank, and First Western Bank and Trust Company. The smallest of these three banks was LaSalle National Bank with $900 million in total assets. However, because LaSalle is located in Illinois, which prohibits both branching and multi-bank holding companies, there were essentially no U.S. buyers to purchase the bank. The other two banks, although located in statewide branching states, were large enough that the number of banks with the capacity to purchase them and that would not have been in violation of the antitrust statutes was small.[72]

McFadden Act, Douglas Amendment, and Antitrust Laws as Impediments to the Acquisition of U.S. Banks by Other U.S. Banks[73]

M. A. Schapiro and Company pointed out in the *Bank Stock Quarterly* that major opportunities in U.S. banking are effectively reserved *for foreign banks only*, since they are free to make acquisitions of banks in the United States that are foreclosed to domestic banking.[74]

State laws govern branching within the state and generally prohibit branches of banks from outside the state. In 1927 the U.S. Congress enacted the McFadden Act which applied these state laws to nationally chartered banks—affirmatively permitting branching, but generally limiting branch locations to those permitted to state banks. Thus, branching across state lines by banks is generally prohibited. Because of the increased importance of multibank holding companies, Congress chose to apply the principle of the McFadden Act to bank holding companies by passing the Douglas Amendment to the Bank Holding Company Act. This amendment prohibits acquisition of a bank in any state other than that in which it has its principal operations unless specifically authorized by the state in which the bank is located. The effect, then, of current banking laws is to preclude interstate acquisitions by U.S. banks and bank holding companies.

Within a state, acquisition possibilities are defined by state banking structure laws. A number of states limit or prohibit branching or multibank holding companies. For larger banks, within-state acquisition options may be further restricted by antitrust standards.

At the same time, the laws do permit acquisition by foreign banks.[75] Paul A. Volcker, when president of the New York Federal Reserve Bank, pointed out that

> The implication is that a sizable domestic bank seeking sale or merger (or perhaps a large injection of capital in a depressed stock market) may be almost forced to look abroad for a partner.[76]

CONCLUSION

Foreign acquisitions of U.S. banks appear to be fundamentally motivated by the purchasers' strategic considerations. Unanimity of opinion exists among participants and observers that the long term needs to expand profitably, to diversify assets, and to secure a dollar base have been the major forces behind the acquisitions by foreign banks. Foreign individuals appear to have long term investment motives that are somewhat similar.

With regard to profitable expansion or investment opportunities, the size and growth prospects of U.S. banking markets appear to have been a strong attraction, particularly when there have been reduced opportunities at home and in international markets. For some foreign acquirers the U.S. retail and "middle" markets have exerted a special pull, and for some the advanced state of U.S. bank technology and management techniques may have provided an added appeal.

For foreign acquirers whose strategic priorities include diversification of assets, the economic and political stability of the U.S., as well as this country's commitment to private enterprise and a free flow of capital, have been asserted by most analysts and a good number of acquirers to be key elements in the attraction. Because a significant portion of the business of all multinational banks is done in the major international currencies, their perceived need for a secure dollar base over the long haul has figured importantly in the complex of strategic motivations.

Although in theory any or all of these strategic goals could be satisfied by entering the U.S. through a *de novo* subsidiary or a branch, only by acquisition can a foreign owner accomplish these purposes almost instantly, without having to engage in the long, costly, and possibly risky process of building recognition, market position, and infrastructure.

Acquisition of a subsidiary seems to have several other features which make it an especially attractive means for a foreign bank to enter U.S. markets. Since a subsidiary operation typically has a larger proportion of nonvolatile (i.e., retail) deposits than a branch, it is likely to have a more stable liability structure. An *acquired* subsidiary, with an established name and reputation in U.S. money markets, has the additional advantage of avoiding the premium in purchasing funds that is usually required of foreign bank branches and *de novo* subsidiaries. Moreover, an offsetting cost advantage formerly enjoyed by U.S. branches of foreign banks—freedom from reserve requirements—has been removed by regulations implementing the International Banking Act of 1978. In the view of most analysts and bankers, the relative attraction of acquiring a subsidiary is thereby further enhanced.

Beyond strategic motivations, it has appeared to many that considerations of a tactical nature have provided extra impetus for the recent upsurge in foreign acquisitions of U.S. banks. The four factors most often cited in this context are the U.S. political/legislative environment in the 1970s with respect to foreign participation in U.S. banking markets; the dictates of "fashion," or maintenance of prestige, among competing banks; the sharp drop in the value of the dollar, especially in 1977-78; and the depressed prices of U.S. bank stocks since 1973. However, evidence and informed opinion do not give equal support to all four factors. In particular, the influence of the dollar's decline and of low stock prices have been judged by some analysts to be more apparent than real.

There is some evidence that the intensifying public debate on foreign participation in U.S. banking markets contributed to a quickening of the pace of acquisitions. There seems to be fairly wide agreement that a number of banks with acquisition plans may have been galvanized into action by fears that the door was about to close, that Congressional debates would result in restrictions on foreign bank activity in this country.

In light of the increase in acquisition activity in the last half of the 1970s, it is also not unreasonable to suppose that some foreign banks were prodded into making an acquisition as a defensive act, to keep up with their competitors. Thus, a number of knowledgeable commentators seem to believe that the maintenance of prestige among peers has been an influencing factor for some acquiring banks, whose rationale is to prevent customers from straying to their competitor banks. There is some evidence, albeit not conclusive, to suggest that, for some banks, "fashion," or competitive considerations may indeed have been a factor.

The notion that the plunge of the dollar provided an economic incentive and hence stimulated foreign acquisitions of U.S. banks pervades much of the commentary on this subject, but the real influence of this factor is not clear. It is true that the dollar's decline would facilitate purchases made with stronger currencies, but banks from strong currency countries generally have not made acquisitions. At the same time, many of the banks that *have* made acquisitions are believed to have substantial inventories of strong currencies on hand, and the same may be true of foreign individual acquirers. Nevertheless, the idea that foreign acquisitions were prompted by a belief that the dollar was undervalued and there was an investment gain to be made has been disputed persuasively by several analysts.

Although a link between depressed stock prices and foreign acquisitions of banks has been alleged, it seems to have been misperceived. The high premiums paid and the weak condition of many of the banks acquired tend to undercut the view that acquirers have been attracted by the ability to obtain a bargain. However, it is surely the case that when bids from foreign acquirers were high relative to stock prices, stockholders had an incentive to sell.

In fact, the foreign acquisitions phenomenon appears to have been marked by a disproportionate number of purchases in which the U.S. bank had some incentive to sell. Because bank acquisitions are seldom unilateral transactions, it is not surprising that in the case of recent foreign acquisitions there seem to be factors operating on both sides to promote the partnerships.

On one side are strategic considerations that seem almost to impel some foreign banks (and perhaps some foreign individuals) to look for U.S. acquisitions. On the other side are factors that serve to "pre-select" the most likely U.S. partners and that incline some U.S. banks to find acquisition desirable or even, in some cases, imperative. Most often the available (i.e., potentially willing) U.S. acquisition candidates have been banks that were weak or in a situation of forced divestiture under the Bank Holding Company Act. The last critical element acting to make certain sizable U.S. banks even more susceptible to foreign acquisitions bids is the effective foreclosure of domestic bank acquisition options for many of the larger U.S. banks that stems from antitrust and bank structure laws. As a result, large U.S. banks with a need to be acquired are virtually pushed into affiliation with a foreign partner.

In conclusion, acquisitions of U.S. banks by foreign banks appear primarily motivated because they are the most effective means of satisfying long-term strategic needs for profitable growth, diversification in a stable investment environment, and a base in the home country of the dollar—the world's major trading and commercial currency. Tactical considerations that may have contributed to heightened foreign acquisition activity in the latter 1970s include the fear that Congress was about to pass laws restricting foreign participation in U.S. banking markets and, possibly, a "bandwagon effect" as some banks reacted to the acquisition initiatives taken by their competitors. The real influence of economic incentives provided by the decline in the value of the dollar and the depression of bank stock prices seems to have been overestimated by many observers. As for the U.S. banks that are acquired, they generally appear to have had an incentive to sell. By design or necessity, foreign acquirers have concentrated either on U.S. banks that were relatively weak and would stand to gain by being acquired or on those that *had* to be acquired. For the most part, then, these transactions appear to have been marriages of convenience, offering benefits to both partners.

Acknowledgments

William A. Longbrake provided valuable guidance throughout the drafting process. Diane Page assisted in the research, and Robert R. Bench, Steven J. Weiss, and Cantwell F. Muckenfuss, III made helpful comments on earlier drafts.

FOOTNOTES

[1] William A. Longbrake, Melanie R. Quinn, and Judith A. Walter, *Foreign Ownership of U.S. Banks: Facts and Patterns*, OCC Staff Paper, 1980.

[2] Cited in "Spaniards Look at Chi. Bank; Foreign Bids Seen Continuing," C. Frederic Wiegold, *American Banker*, July 3, 1979.

In the U.K., for example, the Bank of England in mid-1978 instituted restrictions on growth of interest bearing liabilities in order to restrain lending. This so-called "corset" was not loosened until June, 1980. In France, stringent lending ceilings were already in place earlier in the 1970s and were made progressively even more restrictive beginning in 1979.

[3] "Competing Onshore. International Banking: A Survey," *The Economist*, March 31, 1979, p. 12.

[4] "Foreign Banks are Cracking the Facade of U.S. Banking," David C. Cates, *Fortune*, August 28, 1978, p. 95. Also, in a speech delivered before the twelfth International Banking Meeting in Esteponz, Spain, in June 1979, Harry Taylor, vice chairman of Manufacturers Hanover Trust, emphasized the same motivating factor:

> Perhaps the most compelling reason [for foreign bank expansion into the U.S.] is that international markets simply do not hold the promise of rapid incremental earnings growth they once did, a factor I might add, that has caused American Banks to re-examine their own strategies.

[5] *Economist*, p. 15.

[6] Donald P. Jacobs, Banking Professor and Dean of Graduate School of Management, Northwestern University, *Proposed Public Policy on the Purchase of American Banks* (unpublished paper 1979), p. 8. Jacobus T. Severiens, Associate Professor of Finance, Cleveland State University, "Assessing Foreign Bank Acquisitions," *Burroughs Clearing House*, February 1980.

[7] Noel Delaney, in analyzing differences between U.S. bank expansion abroad and foreign bank influx into the U.S., went a step further to reason that the overseas colonial networks of some European banks actually retarded growth along contemporary global lines because the older systems "lacked the modern capabilities for loan syndications, funds management, and integrated worldwide financial services." "Foreign Banks in the United States," *Memorandum*, L. F. Rothschild, Untenberg, Towbin, January 1, 1979, p. 4.

[8] "The Reasons for Going In," William Hall and Michael Lafferty, *Financial Times* (London), March 19, 1979.

[9] Lord Barber, chairman, noted the acquisition would "improve the strength and the balance of [Standard Chartered Bank's] worldwide banking operations." (Quoted in *Wall Street Journal*, June 9, 1978.) Peter Graham, chief executive officer, spoke of "the better geographical spread" achieved by the acquisition. (Quoted in *Financial Times*, March 19, 1979.)

[10] One French banker called the U.S. "a zone of refuge for European banks, . . . free of the anarchy and violence of Europe." ("Here Come Foreign Banks Again," *Business Week*, June 26, 1978, p. 80.)

See also Hall and Lafferty; David L. Rothstein, "Deterrents to Retail Involvement for Foreign Branches," *American Banker*, March 23, 1979; Anthony F. Mattera, "Spanish Bank Seeks Second NYS Acquisition," *American Banker*, July 13, 1979; Cates, p. 96.

[11] Carter Golembe, "Memorandum Re: Foreign Banking Activities in the United States," Golembe Associates, Inc., Vol. 1979-6, p. 8.

[12] Quoted in Neil Osborn, "Will Foreign Takeovers of U.S. Banks Be Stopped," *Institutional Investor*, September 1979, p. 157.

[13] Same banks, e.g., the Swiss, often have *excess* dollars to *place* in U.S. markets. Moreover, as Clifton Hudgins, New York agent for Banco Nacional de Mexico, has noted, even for those banks primarily seeking funding "it's important to be in the money market on both sides. . . . If a bank comes to New York just to tap the market, it doesn't do much for its name." Quoted in Peter Field, "Biting into the Big Apple," *Euromoney*, June 1978.

[14] Francis A. Lees, *Foreign Banking and Investment in the United States*, (N.Y. Wiley, 1976) pp. 20-21.

[15] Fred H. Klopstock, "A New Stage in the Evolution of International Banking," excerpt from *International Review of the History of Banking*, no. 6, 1973, p. 3.

[16] *Euromoney*, June 1978, p. 57. The desire for stability was apparently a factor as well in the expansion plans of Hongkong Shanghai Banking Corporation (HSBC). Ian MacDonald, the manager for overseas operations, was reported in 1976 to say that HSBC "would like to develop a substantial nonvolatile deposit base in the U.S. and Europe," Louis Kraar, "Hong Kong's Beleaguered Financial Fortress," *Fortune*, May 1976.

[17] Hall and Lafferty, See also, "Here Come Foreign Banks Again," p. 81; Delaney, pp. 2 and 7; *Economist*, p. 21.

[18] Paul Horvitz, "How to Discourage Foreign Takeovers," *American Banker*, 1979.

Actually, such interest restrictions on bank deposits are not unique to the U.S. British, French, and German banks usually do not pay interest on demand deposits, and there are controls on time deposit interest rates in France and Japan. (See, for example, Dimitri Vittas, ed., *Banking Systems Abroad*, InterBank Research Organisation, London: April 1978.)

[19] "The International Banking Act's Cost Impact on Foreign Banks," *American Banker*, March 23, 1979, p. 12.

[20] Rothstein.

[21] Thomas P. Eldred, III, "Foreign Retail Banking Experiences Slow Growth in the U.S.," *American Banker*, March 23, 1979.

[22] *Ibid.*

[23] C. Edward McConnell, vice president of Keefe, Bruyette, Woods, "The Impact of International Banking Activities on Bank Performance," in an address before the American Bankers Association, January 19, 1979.

[24] *Ibid.*

[25] A corporate treasurer noted the premium is often required of foreign banks "not because they are less reliable than their American counterparts, but just because they have funny names and that can worry some corporate officials." "Foreign Banking's U.S. Invasion," *Dun's Review*, February, 1978, p. 78; Field p. 53.

[26] OCC staff interviews with foreign bankers, October 1979.

[27] See, for example,

Muriel Siebert, New York Superintendent of Banks, in a February 16, 1979 letter to Congressman Henry S. Reuss, submitted in House Banking and Urban Affairs Committee hearings on Edge Corporation Branching; Foreign Bank Takeovers; and International Banking Facilities, 96th Cong., 1st sess. 1979, p. 58;

John S. Cummings, Jr. and James L. Kamment, testimony on behalf of the American Bankers Association before the House Banking Committee in hearings on Edge Corporation Branching, p. 485;

H. John Heinz, III, "Foreign Takeovers of U.S. Banking—A Real Danger?" *The Journal of the Institute for Socioeconomic Studies*, vol IV, No. 3, Autumn 1979, p. 4;

Robert Metz, "Banks as Lure to Foreign Bids," *New York Times*, April 16, 1979, p. D-4.

Carol S. Greenwald, testimony before a Subcommittee of the House Committee on Government Operations on the Operations of Federal Agencies in Monitoring, Reporting on, and Analyzing Foreign Investments in the United States, pt. 4, 96th Cong., 1st sess. 1979, p. 25;

Golembe, pp. 6-7.

[28] Salomon Brothers, "Price/Earnings Multiple for Selected Banks, By Quarters 1970 through 1980," February 19, 1981.

[29] *Ibid.*

[30] Salomon Brothers, *Bank Weekly*, December 26, 1980.

[31] Wiegold.

[32] Heinz, p. 4.

[33] Cates, p. 96.

[34] Jacobs, p. 8.

[35] "Foreign Bank Acquisition of American Banks," Dwight B. Crane, Paul W. Marshall and Kenneth E. Lanham, Report to the Office of the Comptroller of the Currency, November 1979, p. I-6.

[36] Thomas A. Loeffler and William A. Longbrake, *Prices Paid by Foreign Interests to Acquire U.S. Banks*, OCC Staff Paper, 1981.

Investment bankers say, in fact, that because acquisition bids are generally keyed to book value, market values are largely irrelevant to potential acquirers. When stocks are selling at a discount to book value, it follows that an acquisition bid above book value will be at an even higher premium relative to market value.

[37] See pp. 246-249 in this paper.

[38] *Journal of Commerce*, April 25, 1979. National Westminster's chairman Robin Leigh-Pemberton is said to have responded at the bank's annual general meeting that "these critics were not comparing like with like . . . . that the Natwest's purchase price for NBNA falls neatly into the middle of the range of prices being paid by overseas buyers for American banks." (Midland's proposed bid for the Walter Heller group was also reportedly considered by some to be too high. *Journal of Commerce*, July 13, 1979.)

[39] See pp. 246-249 in this paper.

[40] These percentages are based on average exchange rates for the year taken from Board of Governors of the Federal Reserve System, *Annual Statistical Digest* 1973-1977 and 1974-1978.

[41] See, for example, "U.S. Acquisitions–Springboard for Growth," *Financial Times* (London), September 19, 1978; "Why British Banks are Storming Us!" *American Banker*, March 29, 1979; p. 4; Siebert letter to Reuss; Henry C. Wallich, statement, House Committee on Government Operations, hearings on the Operations of Federal Agencies, p. 73; Gerald H. Anderson, "Current Developments in the Regulation of International Banking," Federal Reserve Bank of Cleveland *Economic Review*, January 1980.

[42] Crane, Marshall & Lanham, p. I-6. Another exception, not among the group of banks considered in the study, is the 1977 purchase of Golden State Bank, which was merged with Sanwa Bank of California, a Japanese-owned bank established *de novo* in 1972. Golden State Bank was not large at the time of acquisition ($144.7 million in total assets), and because it fits a pattern established by the Japanese banks prior to the sharp drop in the value of the dollar, it is not a strong exception.

[43] See, for example, Cates, p. 96.

[44] Jacobs, p. 7. Crane, Marshall and Lanham have also disputed the notion that acquisition is motivated by belief the dollar is undervalued:

> It is possible that foreign banks believe that the dollar is undervalued and that an investment in an American bank will appreciate in the future. However, there are simpler ways to invest in the dollar in which substantial premiums are not required. (p. I-8).

[45] Golembe pp. 7-8.

[46] Eldred.

[47] "Some Foreign Banks Weighing U.S. Bank Purchases," *American Banker*, May 10, 1978.

[48] Barclays Bank Limited, having established *de novo* subsidiaries early in both New York and California, subsequently acquired existing U.S. banks by merger into those *de novo* subsidiaries. National Westminster Bank Limited acquired National Bank of North America in 1979. Midland Bank Limited is a 20 percent partner in European-American Bank, which acquired Franklin National Bank in 1974, and has indirect ownership through its stake in Standard Chartered Bank and Standard's *de novo* subsidiary Chartered Bank of London, of San Francisco, in Union Bank, acquired in 1979. Lloyd's Bank Limited purchased First Western Bank in 1972. It should be added that Midland, in addition to its indirect U.S. entry, proposed a direct entry in June 1979 when it attempted to purchase the Walter Heller group, owners of American National Bank in Chicago. (Discussions were terminated a few months later.)

[49] In a recent publication, Payment Systems, Inc. (PSI) averred:

> Some analysts have suggested that it is fashionable in some foreign circles to establish a presence in the U.S. banking industry. PSI would prefer to believe that foreign-investment decisions are based on more substantial considerations. While some examples may exist, little weight can be given this trivial a justification.

Foreign Banks: A New Competitive Force in the U.S.., Payment Systems Research Program White Paper, October, 1979, p. 5.

[50] Klopstock, in a review of the remarkable growth of the banking market in London in the late 1960s and early 1970s observed an earlier example of peer pressure in international banking. After acknowledging "the City's pivotal role in the Eurodollar market" as a "principal factor" for the presence of more than 100 foreign banks in London, he went on to list other significant reasons including the fear of many banks that without a London branch "their . . . prestige would suffer." Among the benefits of a London branch, Klopstock states, was that it "serve[d] to enhance the parent bank's name, image, and stature. . ., thus helping to keep clients in the fold." (p. 17)

The maintenance of national prestige also may be an ingredient in the mix of peer pressure among the multinationals. Delaney has discerned a different reactive component in foreign bank expansion into the U.S.: "Inroads by Americans into [foreign banks'] traditional [home] markets" present, "an unacceptable . . . political cost," providing an incentive for similar invasions of U.S. Domestic markets. (p. 4).

[51] See, for example, Golembe; "Statement of Richard Thomas, President, First Chicago Corp., before the Senate Committee on Banking, Housing, and Urban Affairs," July 16, 1979; and Lord O'Brien, "United States Sets the Boundaries for Foreign Banks," *The Banker*, December 1978.

[52] For example, in New York, a takeover bill was introduced in the state legislature in July, 1978; in Texas, in the same year, the Texas House Financial Institutions Committee was asked to look into the issue of foreign investment in the state's banks. A year earlier, the Florida legislature had passed a law prohibiting foreign bank control of a Florida bank.

[53] Lees, p. 110.

[54] For a full exposition of the entry controls in the Change of Bank Control Act see John E. Shockey and William B. Glidden, *Foreign-Controlled U.S. Banks: The Legal and Regulatory Environment*, OCC Staff Paper, 1980.

[55] Paul A. Volcker, "Treatment of Foreign Banks in the United States: Dilemmas and Opportunities," *FRBNY Quarterly Review*, Summer 1979, p. 3.

[56] U.S. Senate U.S., Congress, International Banking Act of 1978, Hearings Before the Subcommittee on Financial Institutions of the Committee on Banking, Housing and Urban Affairs. 95th Congr. 2nd Session, H.R. 10899, June 21, 1978.

[57] "Unequal Opportunity: Growth of Domestic Banks Constricted," *Bank Stock Quarterly*, M. A. Schapiro & Co., Inc., May 1978.

[58] House IBA Hearings, June 21, 1978, pp. 384-89.

[59] London Letter, *Finance Magazine*, July/August 1978, p. 65. Quoted in "Confinement of Domestic Banking in the United States: The Coming of Nationwide Banking," *Bank Stock Quarterly*, M.A. Schapiro and Co., Inc., October 1978, p. 8.

[60] C. Edward McConnel, vice president of Keefe, Bruyette, Woods, in an address before the American Bankers Association on January 19, 1979. See also Jacobs; Patricia Skigen and John D. Fitzsimmons, "The Impact of the International Banking Act of 1978 on Foreign Banks and Their Domestic and Foreign Affiliates," *The Business Lawyer*, vol. 35, November 1979, p. 82; and Serge Bellanger, "The Operational Implications of the International Banking Act of 1978, or the New Rules," remarks to the International Banking Conference of the American Bankers' Association, January 28, 1980.

[61] Letter submitted to the Senate Committee on Banking, Housing, and Urban Affairs for the *Hearing on Edge Corporation Branching; Foreign Bank Takeovers; and International Banking Facilities*, July 16 and 21, 1979, p. 210.

[62] Tom Herman, "National Westminster Sets Big Expansion For Its National Bank of North America," *The Wall Street Journal*, April 25, 1979.

[63] *Economist*, p. 18.

[64] Longbrake, Quinn, and Walter, pp. 24-26.

[65] C. Frederick Wiegold, "Some Big Foreign Banks Weighing U.S. Bank Purchase," *American Banker*, May 10, 1978.

The case of Financial General Bankshares, Inc. is a noteworthy exception to the general avoidance of unfriendly situations.

[66] OCC staff interviews. In fact, one investment banker who was interviewed described a case in which the foreign bank immediately dropped consideration of a particular acquisition candidate upon learning the U.S. bank was not interested. (See also Robert J. Cole, "Talking Business with Robert F. Greenhill of Morgan Stanley—Unfriendly Takeovers," *New York Times*, February 28, 1980, p. D-4.)

[67] Two banks alleged to be on the auction block were named in a 1978 *Business Week* article. Chicago's Central National Bank, which "needed $15 million capital," was reported to have hired Warburg Paribas Becker to find a buyer. Coolidge Bank and Trust (Massachusetts), ultimately found a foreign purchaser after it "searched for two years but could not find an American investor" to help increase capital. ("Here Come Foreign Banks Again," p. 82.)

Buyers are not always readily found for banks seeking to be acquired. One investment banking firm hired by a midwestern bank was unsuccessful in its efforts to locate a foreign buyer, at least in part because the client was not a money center bank. (OCC Staff interviews.)

[68] Cates, p. 96.

[69] Longbrake, Quinn and Walter, p. 14.

[70] Reports of examination for a sample of banks acquired by foreign individuals were reviewed. (Judith A. Walter, *Supervisory Performance of Foreign-Owned Banking Organizations*, OCC Staff Paper, 1980.) Table 4 summarizes composite ratings (or their precursor equivalents) just prior to acquisition, with banks rated "3" characterized as "weak" and those rated "4" or "5" characterized as "serious problem."

[71] Blair B. Hodgkins and Ellen S. Goldberg, *Effect of Foreign Acquisition on the Balance Sheet Structure and Earnings Performance of American Banks*, OCC Staff Paper, 1980.

[72] According to Federal Reserve data as of May 31, 1980, only 12 banks remain subject to required divestiture and most are quite small. Only two are in the $500 million-1 billion range, another two are in the $100-300 million range, and the rest are smaller. Few are in money center locations.

[73] This subject is treated in depth in Wm. Paul Smith and Steven J. Weiss, *Potential Acquisition Partners for Large U.S. Banks: The Discriminatory Effect of Law and Policy*, OCC Staff Paper, 1980.

[74] "Unequal Opportunity: Growth of Domestic Banks Constricted," p. 1.

[75] Subject to geographic restrictions imposed by IBA "home state" regulations.

[76] "Treatment of Foreign Banks in the U.S.," p. 4.

Federal Reserve Board governor Andrew Brimmer observed the same dilemma in a specific case: ". . . Marine Midland needs a substantial investment of capital. There is no way in the present system in the United States for any large domestic bank to make that kind of investment. . . . No bank in New York can do it. No bank across state lines in this country can do it. So where is Marine Midland to get the capital?" Quoted in Richard B. Miller, "Brimmer on Banking—Moving into the Eighties," *The Banker's Magazine*, (Boston) vol. 162 no. 5, September-October 1979, p. 33.

See also Smith and Weiss, *Potential Acquisition Partners for Large U.S. Banks.*

## 7

A CRITICAL EVALUATION OF RECIPROCITY IN FOREIGN BANK ACQUISITIONS

STEVEN J. WEISS

SUMMARY

This paper addresses the conflict between the current U.S. policy regarding foreign entry into U.S. banking markets, a policy of non-discrimination known as "national treatment" and the policy sometimes advocated by critics called "reciprocity" which would treat foreign entry into the U.S. *quid pro quo* as U.S. entry abroad is treated.

The paper's specific purpose is to evaluate whether U.S. policy interests would be advanced by applying reciprocity to foreign bank applications for U.S. bank acquisition. It concludes that such an action would be unlikely to promote U.S. banks' foreign acquisition opportunities and would be inimical to other, broader U.S. States policy interests.

In arriving at that conclusion, the paper reviews the entry policies of other nations, the structural differences between banking markets in the United States and those in other countries, the actual record of U.S. entry and expansion abroad and finally alternative reciprocity policies. In this review, the paper assembles important facts.

- Seven of the 15 nations whose banks appear in the current list of the top 100 banks worldwide prohibit foreign acquisition of controlling interest in their indigenous commercial banks by law or official policy.
- While U.S. interstate prohibitions and intrastate branching laws have reduced banking concentration at the national level, they have also provided potential foreign acquirers of U.S. banks with many more significant acquisition opportunities. There are, for instance, 169 commercial banks with over $1 billion in assets in the United States.

- Even if U.S. banks were totally unrestrained in making foreign bank acquisitions, the number of available, large foreign banking organizations is quite small by U.S. comparison. The reason is the striking structural difference between the U.S. and foreign banking markets. In most other industrialized nations, a top tier of three to seven banks control 40 to 80 percent of total commercial banking assets. Further narrowing the field is the fact that some of these banks are government-owned.

- U.S. entry to foreign banking markets, even if permitted by foreign governmental policy or structural availability, might take the other routes it already has—branching and *de novo* subsidiaries—for reasons of flexibility, control and relatively low cost. Not only are the overwhelming majority of U.S. banking assets abroad in direct branches, but branching has been the primary form of foreign bank entry into the United States where the policy of national treatment has presented to foreign banks no real barriers to expansion via acquisition.

After a review of existing and proposed reciprocity-based policies, the paper concludes that any U.S. attempt at a strict reciprocity policy would be doomed to fail because of the structural differences of foreign banking markets. Benefits to the U.S. economy from enhancing domestic competition and capital infusion into the banking systems would be reduced as well. Most important, such a policy might jeopardize overall U.S. foreign trade and investment policy. Instead, the paper recommends that the current policy of national treatment continue to be offered by the U.S. to foreign banking institutions and continue to be encouraged and expected from foreign governments for U.S. banks abroad. More systematic coordination of foreign developments affecting U.S. banks and U.S. diplomatic efforts is also recommended for more effective remedial action when necessary.

INTRODUCTION

Foreign acquisitions of large banks in the United States have led many U.S. bankers to espouse the view that "it doesn't make sense to allow foreigners to acquire big U.S. banks when foreigners won't allow outsiders to buy their large banks."[1]

Several observers of the recent foreign acquisitions in this country have cited a lack of similar opportunities for U.S. banks to purchase banks overseas. New York Superintendent of Banks, Muriel Siebert, stated that:

> On the basis of discussions with my counterparts in other countries, no developed country other than the U.S. would permit any significant local bank to be acquired by a nondomestic bank. [2]

The U.S. banking system is indeed open to foreign acquisitions, in keeping with our government's strong commitment to free flow of capital among nations. The traditional U.S. policy, enunciated as early as 1791 by Alexander Hamilton, has prevailed throughout most of our history,[3] and was recently reaffirmed in a 1977 Treasury policy statement:

> The fundamental policy of the U.S. Government toward international investment is to neither promote nor discourage inward or outward investment flows or activities . . . [Therefore, the Government] should normally avoid measures which would give special incentives or disincentives to investment flows or activities and should not normally intervene in the activities of individual companies regarding international investment. Whenever such measures are under consideration, the burden of proof is on those advocating intervention to demonstrate that it would be beneficial to the national interest.[4]

With regard to establishment and operations of foreign banks in the United States and the acquisition of existing institutions by foreign banks, the federal government has embraced the principle of national treatment, a policy of nondiscrimination that attempts to accord essential equality of competitive opportunity to foreign and domestic banks. The Federal Reserve Board has followed a national treatment approach with regard to foreign acquisitions and supervision of foreign bank holding companies.[5] Congress incorporated the national treatment principle into the International Banking Act of 1978 (IBA), which created the first federal regulatory framework for foreign banks in this country.[6]

The U.S. government undertakes efforts to secure competitive opportunities for U.S. banks in foreign markets, including the ability to acquire foreign banks.[7] This thrust of U.S. policy was endorsed by the Senate Banking Committee which affirmed, in its report on the IBA, that the U.S. government, "in light of the substantial privileges enjoyed by foreign banks in the United States, should seek to secure national treatment for our banks abroad as well."[8]

Present U.S. policy on foreign bank acquisitions has been criticized as ineffective with regard to the interests of U.S. banks. For example, Superintendent Siebert expressed the view that "opening the U.S. banking system to foreign acquisitions probably will not create equivalent acquisition opportunities for our banks abroad."[9] A spokesman for a leading U.S. international bank commented as follows:

> as we read existing [U.S.] law foreign and domestic bank acquisitions must generally be judged under the same banking, competitive and public interest standards. We would, however, in the case of foreign bank acquisitions of large U.S. banks, like to see formal consideration given to the issue of reciprocity—whether U.S. banks are able to acquire indigenous banks of comparable size in the country of the acquiring foreign bank. It seems to us that the U.S. should be willing to use its leverage on behalf of its banks.[10]

Similarly, other critics have suggested that United States banks' opportunities to acquire foreign banks could be promoted more effectively if reciprocity were taken into account.

Some host governments impose reciprocity requirements in connection with foreign bank applications as a means of applying pressure on foreign countries to open their markets to competition by banks from the host jurisdiction. The U.S. government has chosen instead to apply pressure for national treatment through diplomatic and other channels. A reciprocity approach would be at odds with the policies of national treatment and open capital markets because it would selectively restrict investment from certain countries, and for other reasons which are discussed later in this paper.

This paper evaluates whether U.S. policy interests would be advanced by considering reciprocity in connection with foreign bank applications to acquire U.S. banks. Policies of other nations with regard to foreign acquisition of domestic banks are reviewed. To put U.S. banks' foreign acquisition opportunities in perspective, the paper describes the salient structural differences between the U.S. banking market and those in other countries and cites the actual record of overseas bank acquisitions by U.S. banking organizations and their expansion in foreign markets by other means. Reciprocity-based policies are reviewed, and the present U.S. government approach is described in contrast to those policies. Alternative policies based on reciprocity are presented in the final part of the paper and evaluated in comparison to the present U.S. policy. Finally, it is concluded that a reciprocity-based policy would be unlikely to promote U.S. banks' foreign acquisition opportunities and would be inimical to other, broader U.S. policy interests.

OTHER NATIONS' POLICIES ON
FOREIGN BANK ACQUISITIONS

U.S. institutions' ability to make significant bank acquisitions abroad is limited by foreign laws, policies and official practices.[11] Seven of the 15 nations whose banks are among the world's 100 largest[12] prohibit foreign acquisition of controlling interest in indigenous commercial banks by law or official policy. India, Brazil and Sweden flatly prohibit any foreign purchases of ownership interests. Others set maximum foreign ownership percentages, as follows: Australia (10%), Canada (10%), Japan (5%), and the Netherlands (49%).[13] Although the Bank of England maintains a flexible approach, it announced in an unusual policy statement in 1972 that it is not, in general, willing to permit any bank registered outside the EEC to acquire a participation of more than 15% in a major U.K. bank.[14]

Similar rules also exist in many other countries.[15] Moreover, restrictions on foreign acquisition of equity interests in indigenous banks appear to exist commonly as a matter of unwritten policy in many foreign nations, even when there are no specific laws on the matter.

> A large number of countries, including many with otherwise liberal entry policies, such as permitting foreign branch and *de novo* bank subsidiaries, take a more restrictive approach to foreign acquisition of domestic banks ... [sometimes] ... by unwritten policy. Such policies have not often been clearly enunciated or tested, at least within the realm of public knowledge, particularly with regard to acquisitions of large banks. Although evidence of impediments to foreign (including U.S.) acquisition of very large indigenous banks is largely impressionistic, decisions regarding any given acquisition would be heavily influenced by the particular circumstances surrounding the proposed acquisition. Informed judgments suggest that, as a general matter, such acquisitions would be discouraged by most governments.[16]

U. S. BANKING ORGANIZATIONS' ACQUISITIONS
OF FOREIGN BANKS

Although restrictive laws or policies of foreign governments clearly deter overseas acquisitions by U.S. banks and bank holding companies, two other factors must be considered. First, other means of international expansion may be relatively more attractive. Second, the structure of most foreign banking markets severely limits acquisition opportunities. These factors are discussed briefly below and some new data on overseas bank acquisitions by U.S. banking organizations are presented.

ALTERNATIVE MEANS OF INTERNATIONAL EXPANSION

U.S. institutions have expanded their overseas banking operations primarily by branching. Branches and *de novo* subsidiaries, which are in many ways the functional equivalent of branches, are attractive organizational forms for multinational banks because of flexibility, control and relatively low cost.[17] Most U.S. banking assets held overseas are in direct branches rather than bank subsidiaries or affiliates.[18] The international expansion of the largest multinational banks from other countries has generally been similar. In its discussion of the progress of the world's largest banks in 1972, *The Banker* noted that international branching has been "a traditionally successful route to great size in banking."[19] Foreign bank presence in the United States, which constitutes over 10 percent of total U.S. commercial banking assets, has been achieved mostly via *de novo* entry. Even after taking into account recent foreign acquisitions of large U.S. banks, only about 20 percent of U.S. commercial bank assets controlled by foreign banks is attributable to acquisitions.[20]

When large acquisitions are permitted and available, they are clearly an attractive way for banks to establish an immediate, significant presence in a foreign market. Availability of large banks for acquisition in foreign markets is limited, however, as Fred Klopstock has observed:

> For the most part, the largest banks abroad have not been for sale. Many of them are owned by foreign governments. U.S. acquisitions have usually been directed to the smaller private banks and specialized banks such as development corporations.[21]

Thus, acquisition opportunities for U.S. banking organizations would be limited, even if foreign governments were completely open to foreign acquisitions, because of the structure of foreign banking markets.

FOREIGN BANKING MARKET STRUCTURE

Any suggestion that U.S. banking organizations are denied reciprocity in making acquisitions abroad, i.e., that they are unfairly denied acquisition opportunities in foreign countries comparable to those available to foreign banks here, ignores salient structural differences between the U.S. and other nations' banking systems. In other industrialized nations, banking markets are typically very highly concentrated. In most cases, a top tier of three to seven banks controls 40 to 80 percent of total commercial banking assets (see Table 1). A foreign bank that acquired any one of the top tier banks would immediately hold a substantial share of the country's domestic banking assets and a nationwide network of offices. Below the small number of top tier banks, most foreign banking markets are fragmented and comprised of considerably smaller institutions, many of which have specialized or locally oriented operations. There is generally a paucity of medium-sized banks that would constitute logical targets for foreign takeover.

The U.S. structure presents a striking contrast. Concentration is much lower at the national level; the top three banking organizations hold 18 percent of total commercial bank assets and the top ten hold 34 percent.[22] More importantly, in terms of significant acquisition opportunities for foreign banks, of the approximately 14,700 commercial banks in this country, 169 have over $1 billion in assets. Moreover, because U.S. law confines full service banking operations of banks and bank holding companies to a single state, acquisition of even a leading U.S. banking organization would not yield a nationwide presence equivalent to the positions of leading banks in foreign markets.[23]

FOREIGN BANK ACQUISITIONS BY U.S. BANKING ORGANIZATIONS

Acquisitions of foreign banks by U.S. banks and bank holding companies are limited by foreign government restrictions and by the structural factors discussed above. Because very little information on the subject is readily available, some U.S. observers may have exaggerated notions about the inability of U.S. institutions to acquire foreign

Table 1
Indicators of Banking Concentration in Major Foreign Countries

Large Banks	% of Commercial Banking Assets	% of Total Banking Assets
AUSTRALIA 7 Major Trading Banks	88%	49%
BELGIUM 3 Largest Commercial Banks	80%	32%
CANADA 5 Largest Chartered Banks	90%	60%
FRANCE 3 Largest Nationalized Banks	55%	45-50%
GERMANY 3 Largest Commercial Banks	42%	10%
ITALY Big 5 Banks	47%	28%
JAPAN 13 City Banks	N.A.	53%
THE NETHERLANDS 3 Largest Commercial Banks	60%	41%
SPAIN "Big Seven" Commercial Banks	58%[a]	34%[a]
SWITZERLAND 5 Big Banks	N.A.	48%
UNITED KINGDOM 6 London Clearing Banks	70%	N.A.
UNITED STATES 3 Largest Commercial Banks	18%	12%[b]
10 Largest Commercial Banks	34%	23%[b]

Sources: Report to Congress, and OCC files for foreign countries; U.S. data from call reports and *Federal Reserve Bulletin*, Appendix Tables 1.24 and 1.38. Data are for various dates.
Notes: [a] Share of deposits
[b] Includes savings and loan associations and mutual savings banks.

banks. Available data on such acquisitions in the postwar period are summarized in Table 2. The information in the table was compiled mostly through an OCC telephone survey of major U.S. banking organizations[24] and is neither complete nor definitive.[25]

The available information reveals that 22 U.S. banking organizations have acquired 107 subsidiary or affiliate banks in 48 foreign countries (excluding purely offshore banking operations). Nearly half of these foreign banks are majority-owned or effectively controlled by U.S. institutions.[26] They engage in commercial, merchant, development and

Table 2
Foreign Banks Acquired by U.S. Banking Organizations

A.   *Size, Distribution*

Foreign Banks Controlled by U.S. Banking Institutions,
by Asset Size, 1977[a]

	Number of Banks	Percent Distribution
Over $1 billion	3	6
$500.1 million to $1 billion	8	16
$100.1 to $500 million	15	29
$50.1 to $100 million	3	6
$10.1 to $50 million	12	23
Less than $10 million	6	12
Data not available	4	8
TOTAL	51	100%

B.   *Geographic Distribution*

Region	No. of Banks Acquired[b]	No. of Acquired Banks Controlled[a] by U.S. Insts.	Median Asset Size of Controlled Banks, 1977 ($ million)
Europe	36	21	$377.9
Asia[c]	27	11	48.9
South America	12	5	200.0
Oceania	12 }	4	34.6
Africa	11 }		
North & Central America[d]	9	6	21.1
TOTAL	107	47[e]	$142.3

[a]Includes cases of majority ownership or effective control determined by the Federal Reserve Board. The latest detailed data available are for 1977.

[b]Includes cases of at least 10% ownership.

[c]Includes Middle East.

[d]Includes Caribbean.

[e]Data are not available for 4 of the 51 controlled banks.

Note: See text and accompanying footnotes for explanation of derivation and limitations of the data.

consumer-oriented banking activities. The asset size of the acquired banks ranged widely from less than $500,000 to approximately $4.0 billion at the time of acquisition. Based on available data, total assets of the foreign banks identified as acquired and controlled by U.S. banking organizations were $17.7 billion as of year-end 1977. The median asset size as of the same date[27] for all cases where data were obtained was $142.3 million. The table reveals that U.S. banking organizations have acquired control of a number of banks in all regions of the free world.[28] The relatively small size of U.S.-controlled foreign banks reflects both the dearth of midsized banks available for acquisition in those countries and probable discouragement of larger acquisitions by host governments.

As indicated above, the structural differences between the U.S. and the typical foreign banking markets are important to bear in mind in considering whether a requirement of reciprocity in foreign acquisition opportunities would be a reasonable basis for U.S. policy. In the following sections, reciprocity-based policies are reviewed and contrasted with the U.S. national treatment approach.

POLICIES BASED ON RECIPROCITY

A review of policies based on reciprocity, as practiced in various foreign countries and some states of the U.S. indicates that various jurisdictions implement reciprocity-based policies in quite different ways. The Swiss approach, for example, is to allow banks from country or state "A" to enter and operate in Switzerland only to the extent that Swiss banks are accorded comparable privileges in "A." Reciprocity requirements take different forms elsewhere and may be subject to alternative interpretations.

In this discussion, the term "reciprocity" is used to denote the imposition of conditions or requirements by a host jurisdiction. It should be noted that the term may be used, alternatively, to denote a mutual interchange of privileges. It was in that sense that some European bankers, in their comments on the IBA, urged the Congress to consider "reciprocity" as preferable to national treatment. In their view, reciprocity would mean that their banks could do the same kinds of business in the U.S. that U.S. banks can do in their country.[29] Because foreign banks, and U.S. banks, generally enjoy broader operating privileges in Europe than in the U.S., that approach, from a European perspective, has obvious advantages over national treatment, which subjects foreign entrants to U.S. limitations on the scope of permissible banking activities here. Rep. St Germain, after a dialogue on reciprocity with some foreign bankers, aptly observed that whether anyone likes the word "reciprocity" . . . "all depends on which dictionary you use to define [it]."[30]

RECIPROCITY REQUIREMENTS IN OTHER COUNTRIES

Many countries require, as a condition of foreign bank entry, that similar opportunities be available to their own banks in the home country of the applicant.[31] Reciprocity tests may be applied in a variety of ways, formally or informally, very rigidly or in a quite flexible manner. The test may entail a comparison of allowable *forms* of bank entry (i.e., via branch, subsidiary, affiliate or otherwise) or a detailed enumeration of powers available to foreign banks. Alternatively, reciprocity requirements may extend more generally to consideration of whether the host country's banks are afforded a reasonable opportunity to conduct business in the applicant's home country.

A narrow, rigid application of reciprocity is illustrated by the policy of the Brazilian central bank, which invokes

> a one-for-one interpretation of the reciprocity concept. That is, Brazil should approve one foreign bank branch for each branch a Brazilian bank operates in the foreign bank's home country. Brazil's authorities argue that because there are many more U.S. banks in Brazil than Brazilian banks in the U.S., the current balance favors U.S. banks.[32]

Switzerland, which has generally followed a very open policy toward foreign bank entry,[33] including entry by acquisition of established Swiss banks, enacted a reciprocity provision in 1971 with the intent of ensuring that Swiss banks not be subjected to materially more limiting provisions in a foreign country than Switzerland imposes on banks from that country. The Swiss policy specifically addresses the *form* of foreign bank entry and considers, with respect to applications by U.S. banks, the effects of both federal and state law. Because of the reciprocity policy, Swiss authorities were reported to be reluctant:

> to issue branch permits to U.S. banks chartered in states that prohibit branch banking unless the U.S. bank's home state would expressly guarantee that a Swiss branch banking operation would be exempt from any such prohibition. In 1970, the Swiss authorities decided that the opportunity for Swiss banks to establish subsidiaries in Illinois (a state which does not permit branching) constituted adequate reciprocity to justify approval of a Chicago-based bank's branch in Switzerland. The Swiss banking community and financial press criticized this policy on grounds that it did not ensure identically reciprocal treatment for Swiss banks and, as a result, the Swiss authorities began applying a stricter interpre-

tation of reciprocity, permitting Chicago-based banks to enter through subsidiaries, but not branch operations.[34]

U.S. banks seeking permission to establish branches in Switzerland have encountered some difficulties in satisfying the reciprocity test since the Swiss authorities consider both U.S. federal law, which effectively prohibits interstate branching, and the laws of U.S. applicants' home states, some of which prohibit branching generally or prohibit or place severe restrictions on foreign banks. In contrast, Swiss banking law does not limit branching by commercial banks. Thus, Swiss authorities may refuse to issue branch permits to U.S. banks chartered in states that prohibit branch banking or that do not allow foreign bank branches. In some cases where the home state allows branching but subjects applications to an economic needs test, Swiss authorities have sought and obtained assurances from the state bank supervisor that such requirements would not preclude approval of branch applications by qualified Swiss banks. After enactment of the International Banking Act, which effectively limited new full service foreign bank presence in the U.S. to a single "home state," the Swiss considered, but rejected, reciprocal limitation of U.S. bank expansion to a single canton.[35]

Although the Swiss attention to detail is unusual, other countries apply reciprocity tests in a similar manner, including consideration of state laws. For example, although Japanese banks operate several representative offices and one agreement corporation in Texas, Japan has denied requests by two Texas-based banks to establish branches because Texas does not permit the operation of foreign bank branches.[36]

Among the industrialized nations, reciprocity considerations are most commonly applied in a reasonably flexible way. Among the member nations of the EEC, reciprocity is at least taken into account in actions on foreign bank applications for entry by authorities in Italy, Denmark, and the Netherlands.[37] The relevant laws or policies are usually couched in general terms and do not refer to acquisitions of local banks as opposed to other forms of entry. An exception appears in the stated policy of the Bank of England:

> In considering proposals for participations by EEC banks [the Bank of England] will also take account of the authorities' attitudes elsewhere in the community to participations by British banks.[38]

Reciprocity in acquisition opportunities is undoubtedly taken into account in the deliberations of other foreign supervisory authorities as an element of unwritten policy.

RECIPROCITY REQUIRED BY STATES
IN THE UNITED STATES

Reciprocity has played a part in some state governments' policies regarding licensing of foreign banks, most prominently New York.[39] Under state law, a foreign bank may establish and maintain *branch* operations in New York state only if a New York bank or trust company may be authorized either to maintain a branch or agency in the bank's home country or to own all of the shares of a banking organization organized under the laws of that country. Under that law, New York would not approve branch applications from countries that restrict U.S. entry, e.g., Mexico or Australia. Establishment and operation of agencies or subsidiary banks by foreign banking organizations is permitted, however, without regard to reciprocity. Foreign banks, therefore, enjoy opportunities for operating in New York even when their home countries deny reciprocal branching privileges to New York banks.[40] Moreover, New York law does not require reciprocal opportunities for acquisition of established banks.[41] Similar requirements are imposed in Illinois and other states.

As in foreign countries, reciprocity requirements may be a matter of state law *or policy*. For example, in Massachusetts, the Board of Bank Incorporation denied a Canadian bank's branch application in the early 1970s, reportedly because of Massachusetts banks' inability to establish branches in Canada under Canadian law. After a policy change in 1977, a Canadian branch application was approved by the Board.

U. S. GOVERNMENT POLICY: RECIPROCITY SOUGHT
BUT NOT REQUIRED

Reciprocity is not a factor in U.S. federal law or policy on foreign acquisitions of U.S. banks, nor is reciprocity considered with regard to foreign bank applications for federal branches or agencies.[42] Foreign banks' acquisitions of domestic institutions are governed by the Bank Holding Company Act, which is implemented by the Federal Reserve Board. The Act does not include reciprocity among the factors to be weighed by the Board in its decisions on foreign bank applications to acquire U.S. banks.[43] Any U.S. regulatory requirement of reciprocity in acquisitions would apparently require statutory changes.

The present U.S. government approach is indicated in the following exchange between Senator Heinz and Federal Reserve Governor Wallich:

> **Senator Heinz.** Does the Federal Reserve use reciprocity as a criteria [*sic*.] for allowing foreign investment in the U.S. banking industry?
>
> **Mr. Wallich.** We seek reciprocity in the ability to operate abroad, but we use national treatment. That is, we treat foreign banks the same as ours, but when it involves U.S. acquisitions abroad we would like to be treated the same way we treat others here.
>
> **Senator Heinz.** But if a foreign bank or if a group of investors that may or may not be a foreign bank from a country that would not let a U.S. bank acquire a bank in that country comes here, we don't consider that a factor in whether or not we should let that bank acquire one of our banks or that group of investors acquire one of our banks?
>
> **Mr. Wallich.** We don't insist on strict reciprocity. We do work at establishing general conditions under which we would have reciprocity, but we don't tie it to any particular transaction.[44]

The key point in Governor Wallich's statement is that reciprocity is not a factor in the Board's decision on any particular transaction. Federal regulators consider foreign applications to acquire U.S. banks on their merits, on a case-by-case basis, and the nationality of the acquirer does not enter into their decisions.[45] Nonetheless, as indicated earlier, the U.S. government endeavors on a continuing basis to promote competitive opportunities for U.S. banks in foreign countries. This is done in the context of our overall relationships with foreign governments, through official meetings, contacts among bank supervisors, diplomatic efforts and encouragement of adherence to the principle of national treatment by all available means.[46] In the IBA, the Congress provided for a regulatory framework according equality of competitive opportunity, or national treatment, to foreign banks operating or desiring to operate here. U.S. government efforts to obtain similar treatment for our banks in foreign markets are in accordance with a U.S. policy *goal*, which may be expressed as reciprocity of national treatment. It is only in this implicit and very positive sense that U.S. policy on banking can be said to involve reciprocity.[47]

Reciprocity in the negative sense of conditions or requirements was rejected as an alternative to national treatment in the IBA for a number of reasons:

(1) Most importantly, requiring reciprocity would raise barriers against banking investments from certain countries, in conflict

with the U.S. policy of neutrality toward international capital flows. In testimony on bank acquisitions, Deputy Secretary of the Treasury, Robert Carswell, remarked that new limits ". . . could undermine foreign confidence in our open-door investment policy . . . [and] could be viewed as a forerunner of restrictions on acquisitions first in banking and then in other industries."[48]

(2) Reciprocity represents a reactive rather than a positive approach. National treatment is a flexible approach that enables the host country to adopt a policy that best serves its interests, irrespective of other governments' views. Governor Wallich described how a reciprocity-based policy would produce a very different result from the present policy which seeks to establish a balance of competitive equality between domestic and foreign banks in the United States:

> Given the wide disparities of legal treatment to which American banks are exposed in the foreign countries in which they operate, reciprocity would lead to a crazy quilt of divergent rules. Banks from a country with liberal banking legislation would receive corresponsingly liberal treatment in the United States. Banks from a country with more confining legislation would be treated correspondingly severely. Both treatments very likely would differ also from the treatment given to U.S. banks in the United States and create competitive inequities.[49]

(3) Reciprocity requirements would create an administrative nightmare, entailing detailed information of regulation on a country-by-country basis.[50]

(4) Experience in international relations has demonstrated that reciprocal arrangements generally tend to narrow opportunities available to affected parties, to their mutual disadvantage.[51] The Treasury Department testified in 1977 that

> While reciprocity has a superficial appeal, it would not be desirable for us to adopt it. Such a policy would reduce permissible international banking activities to the lowest common denominator, as countries tighten regulations to achieve strict reciprocity.[52]

POSSIBLE EFFECTS OF A UNITED STATES RECIPROCITY-BASED POLICY ON FOREIGN BANK ACQUISITIONS

In spite of the general drawbacks of a reciprocity-based policy, responsible observers have suggested that reciprocity might be considered by federal regulators at least with regard to foreign acquisitions of large U.S. banks.[53] To justify altering the present U.S. policy, it could be argued that large banks play such a pivotal role in the economy that an exception to the traditional U.S. opendoor policy is warranted; that foreign governments would generally understand such a move, since it would put U.S. policy more or less in line with their own practices; and that administrative and other problems could be surmounted.

If federal regulators were required to take account of reciprocity in acquisitions, they could adopt any one of a variety of regulatory approaches. While proponents of reciprocity have not made specific recommendations for implementation, two variants of a reciprocity-based approach can be identified for the sake of discussion, namely "strict" and "moderate" reciprocity. Strict reciprocity implies rigid application of specific requirements or conditions. Moderate reciprocity would encompass any more flexible, judgmental approach.

Strict reciprocity requirements could take any number of forms which could range widely in severity. For example, perhaps the least restrictive requirement would be a rule permitting a foreign bank to acquire a U.S. bank only if U.S. banks would be eligible to acquire a bank in the applicant's home country, not only by law but also in actual practice. More stringent conditions could be set in order to address an apparent imbalance in opportunities for foreign takeovers of *large* banks. Conceivably, conditions could be set in terms of absolute size, national rank, or market share of the bank to be acquired. More generally, the U.S. regulator could be required to obtain assurances from the applicant's home country authorities indicating that an acquisition proposal by a U.S. institution would be evaluated on the same terms as a domestic applicant's.

A moderate reciprocity approach could also be implemented in a variety of ways. Such an approach rests on the idea that it might be appropriate and indeed constructive for the U.S. to take into account, in broader terms, the access of U.S. banks to foreign banking markets, as an additional factor in evaluating foreign acquisition proposals. A determination could be made, for example, as to whether the applicant's home country affords U.S. banks "reasonably equivalent access" to its domestic market.[54] Thus, if an applicant's home country denies U.S. banks even limited branching opportunity, that would weight against approval of a proposed acquisition. Any such consideration would entail careful review of the home country's financial and regulatory structure to assure that a test of reasonableness is applied fairly. A substantial measure of regulatory judgment would clearly be required.

It is uncertain, at best, whether a strict or moderate reciprocity approach would induce significant changes in foreign government policies toward U.S. acquisitions of their domestic banks, particularly large banks. Pressure for change could come as a result of increasing interest in international expansion by foreign banks whose acquisition opportunities in the U.S. would be directly affected. Such pressure would seem most likely to be effective under a moderate reciprocity approach, in which some liberalization, to provide greater competitive opportunities to U.S. banks, short of permitting acquisition of a large domestic bank, might be acceptable to the foreign government and banking sector.[55] However, a strict reciprocity approach, particularly one intended to produce new opportunities for U.S. acquisitions of large banks overseas, would probably be foredoomed to failure. Because of the vastly different structures of U.S. and foreign banking markets and close relationships between governments and the largest banks in some countries, it appears unreasonable to expect opportunities for U.S. banks to acquire established banks abroad on a basis that is even approximately equivalent with options available for foreign acquisitions here.

Although the possible benefits to U.S. banks of leverage applied by the government through a reciprocity-based policy are quite uncertain, the potential costs to the U.S. financial system and the economy in general are readily apparent. A strict reciprocity requirement would preclude many, if not most, foreign acquisition proposals. The more rigid the test and the more specific its focus on large bank acquisitions the more complete such foreclosure would be. Benefits to the U.S. economy from foreign acquisitions' enhancing of domestic competition and infusion of capital into the banking system would be reduced correspondingly, with no assurance of offsetting benefits to U.S. interests. Most importantly, as stated earlier, application of a reciprocity test would represent a fundamental break with long-standing U.S. policy, raising concerns abroad about possible restrictions in other areas and generally jeopardizing the U.S. position on foreign trade and investment.

Rather than adopting a policy based on reciprocity in either a strict or moderate form, the U.S. government could maintain and perhaps strengthen its present approach based on national treatment. This policy was adopted by the Congress as desirable for our country and preferable to an approach incorporating reciprocity. Our present approach leaves room for flexibility, based on recognition of unique circumstances and legitimate policy objectives in other nations with regard to their treatment of foreign banks.

If acquisition opportunities for U.S. banks were a serious concern in a particular country, U.S. diplomatic efforts should seek more equivalence of treatment. Monitoring of the treatment of U.S. banks abroad could be intensified. Remedial actions would be more effective if there were a means established for more systematic coordination of efforts undertaken by the different agencies involved. Regular review and study of current regulatory and legislative developments affecting United States banks abroad would help ensure that remedial efforts are undertaken in accordance with clear priorities and on a consistent basis. At the same time, new avenues may become available.[56] There is no reason to expect, however, that large bank takeover opportunities would be a principal focus of such efforts.

Acknowledgments

Nancy Lowther assisted in the research for this paper. Valuable comments on earlier drafts were given by C. F. Muckenfuss, III, Robert R. Bench, Charles E. Lord, and Neal M. Soss.

FOOTNOTES

[1] "Outcome of Foreign Bids for U.S. Banks Put In Doubt by New Interest In Congress," *The Wall Street Journal*, March 5, 1979, p. 13.

[2] Letter of February 6, 1979, from Muriel Siebert to Congressman Henry S. Reuss submitted in Hearings before the Senate Banking, Housing and Urban Affairs Committee on *Edge Corporation Branching; Foreign Bank Takeovers; and International Banking Facilities*, 96th Cong., 1st sess., July 16 and 20, 1979, p. 59.

[3] See discussion in Testimony of John G. Heimann, Comptroller of the Currency, and other witnesses in Hearings before the Subcommittee of the House Committee on *Government Operations on the Operations of Federal Agencies in Monitoring, Reporting on, and Analyzing Foreign Investments in the United States*, 96th Cong., 1st sess., July 31 and August 1, 1979, pt. 4, p. 55.

[4] U. S. Department of the Treasury, "U.S. Government Policy on Direct International Investment," July 6, 1977.

[5] "Statement of Policy on Supervision and Regulation of Foreign Bank Holding Companies," Federal Reserve Board Release, February 23, 1979.

[6] See U.S. Congress, Senate, Committee on Banking, Housing and Urban Affairs, *International Banking Act of 1978*, Rept. No. 95-1073 to accompany H.R. 10899, 95th Cong., 2nd sess., 1978, and discussion in U.S. Department of the Treasury, *Report to Congress on Foreign Government Treatment of U.S. Commercial Banking Organizations*, 1979, Ch. 1. (Cited hereafter as *Report to Congress*.)

[7] See *Report to Congress*, Ch. 36, for a description of U.S. government remedial efforts to secure equal competitive opportunity for U.S. banks abroad.

[8] U.S. Senate, Committee on Banking, Housing and Urban Affairs, Report on *International Banking Act of 1978*, p. 9.

[9] Siebert letter to Congressman Reuss, submitted in Senate Banking Housing and Urban Affairs Committee Hearings on *Edge Corporation Branching* . . . .

[10] Statement of Richard Thomas, President, First Chicago Corp., in Hearings before the Senate Committee on Banking, Housing and Urban Affairs on *Edge Corporation Branching* . . ., p. 307.

[11] See, generally, *Report to Congress*, Ch. 5, individual country studies in Chs. 8-34, and summary information for 141 countries in Appendix II. That source focuses on *commercial banking* opportunities available to nondomestic banking institutions and this paper does likewise. In some countries (e.g., Australia) commercial bank entry is prohibited to foreign institutions but foreign participation is allowed in closely related activities (e.g., merchant banking).

[12] Reference is to the 1978 *American Banker* list, "500 Largest Banks in the World," July 25, 1979. Other lists of the world's largest banking organizations (e.g., the "Top 300" published each June in *The Banker*) are constructed on a different basis, but the representation and relative position of individual nations' banking organizations is little changed (See C. Stewart Goddin and Steven J. Weiss, *U.S. Banks' Loss of Global Standing*, OCC Staff Paper, 1980, (Appendix A).

[13] The Netherlands policy is unclear; foreign ownership in excess of 50 percent might be possible in some circumstances. See *Report to Congress*, p. 88.

[14] "Banking Mergers and Participations" (Text of Bank of England Press Notice issued on November 16, 1972), *Bank of England Quarterly Bulletin*, December 1972, p. 452.

[15] See *Report to Congress*, Table 5.8, pp. 25-7.

[16] *Ibid.*, pp. 135-6.

[17] For a discussion of factors influencing choice of organizational form and some evidence on U.S. institutions' choice of alternative forms, see *Report to Congress*, pp. 6-9, and 19-20.

[18] As of year-end 1979, U.S. banking organizations had $287 billion in assets at major foreign branches. (Federal Reserve Board Statistical Release E.11, March 1980). Latest available asset figures for U.S. foreign banking subsidiaries are as of year-end 1977 and total $40.4 billion. Total assets of foreign affiliates (including "near banks" and nonbanking companies) in which U.S. banks and bank holding companies held minority shares has been estimated at "on the order of $25 billion" in 1976, the only year for which data are presently available (see *Report to Congress*, p. 9).

[19] "Top 300 Survey," *The Banker*, June 1973, p. 611.

[20] See Diane M. Page and Neal M. Soss, *Some Evidence on Transnational Banking Structure*, OCC Staff Paper, 1980. The estimate of assets attributable to acquisitions takes account of mergers of U.S. banks into foreign subsidiaries that were established *de novo*.

[21] Fred H. Klopstock, "A New Stage in the Evolution of International Banking," *International Review of the History of Banking*, (no. 6, 1973) p. 14.

[22] The top ten U.S. commercial banking organizations held 18% of *domestic* commercial bank deposits in 1977 and their share of domestic deposits has diminished over time (see Cynthia A. Glassman and Robert A. Eisenbeis, "Bank Holding Companies and Concentration of Banking and Financial Resources," Table 1, p. 246 in *The Bank Holding Company Movement to 1978: A Compendium*, A Study by the Staff of the Board of Governors of the Federal Reserve System, Washington, 1978.)

[23] As noted elsewhere, legal restraints on geogrpahic expansion of U.S. banks create acquisition opportunities for foreign banks that are foreclosed, in practice, to domestic institutions. See M. A. Schapiro & Company, "Confinement of Domestic Banking in the United States," *Bank Stock Quarterly* (October 1978), pp. 1-12, and the analysis presented in Wm. Paul Smith and Steven J. Weiss, *Potential Acquisition Partners for Large U.S. Banks: Discriminatory Effects of Law and Policy*, OCC Staff Paper, 1980.

[24] Lists of U.S. institutions with overseas banking subsidiaries or affiliates were compiled from various sources, including OCC and Federal Reserve records; FINE Study (*Financial Insti-*

tutions and the Nation's Economy, Compendium of Papers Prepared for the FINE Study, Committee on Banking, Currency and Housing, House of Representatives, 94th Congress, Second Session, Part 4, Appendix 4); *Who Owns What in World Banking, 1977-8*, The Banker Research Unit, The Financial Times, Ltd., London, 1979; and the *American Banker* listing of "International Activities of U.S. Banks." The telephone survey, based on those lists, confirmed whether U.S.-owned banks were acquired or established *de novo* and determined their dates of purchase and size.

[25] The OCC telephone survey confirmed listings from the sources cited in footnote 24 and also produced some additions and deletions. A number of overseas bank subsidiaries or affiliates had been sold since their listing in the source documents. Some were determined to be non-banks and were therefore excluded. Others were merely corporate shells or were found to have been erroneously reported in the source materials.

The list used for present purposes *excludes* 17 subsidiaries and affiliates in exclusively offshore banking locations and excludes more than 50 cases where the U.S. institutions' ownership interest is less than 10%.

[26] Effective control in cases of less than majority ownership is based on Federal Reserve determinations (6 cases).

[27] In many cases, asset size at the time of acquisition is not readily available.

[28] Data for *de novo* subsidiaries, also obtained by the OCC telephone survey, is summarized in the following table (See Table 2 for explanatory notes).

Region	No. of Banks Established	No. of *De Novo* Banks Controlled by U.S. Bkg. Insts.	Median Asset Size, 1977 (Controlled Banks)
Europe	53	27	$145.8 million
Asia	31	9	61.2 million
South America	2	2	N.A.
Oceania	10	3	2.6 million
Africa	12	6	40.4 million
North & Central America	10	8	26.7 million
TOTAL	118	55	77.7 million

The acquired banks tend generally to be somewhat larger than the *de novo* banks. The total number is almost the same and the geographical distribution is broadly similar. Available data indicate total assets of the 55 controlled banks in excess of $10 billion (as of 12/31/77).

[29] Carter Golembe, "Foreign Banking Activities in the United States," (Golembe Associates, Inc., vol. 1976-9) pp. 10-11.

[30] Representative Fernand J. St Germain in Hearings before a subcommittee of the House Banking, Finance and Urban Affairs Committee on the *International Banking Act of 1977*, July 12, 13 and 19 1977, p. 545.

[31] See *Report to Congress*, pp. 20-21.

[32] *Report to Congress*, p. 20. Similarly, Pakistan may grant entry to a given foreign bank only at such time as a Pakistani bank has been authorized to enter the foreign bank's home country. (*Ibid.*)

[33] *Ibid.*, pp. 97-98.

[34] *Ibid.*, p. 21. Acquisition of a minority interest in a Swiss bank does not require official approval and is, therefore, not subject to any reciprocity test. However, reciprocity is considered in licensing representative offices; the test is whether Swiss banks are permitted to establish representative offices with the same functions in the applicant's home country (*Ibid.*, p. 98).

[35] *Ibid.* A policy of allowing U.S. banks to accept deposits only in the canton in which they were initially registered (an analog of the IBA's home state limitation) was not adopted, but the

Swiss authorities did use the occasion to announce that, in their view, U.S. banks are now treated more favorably in Switzerland than Swiss banks are in the U.S. (Letter of April 4, 1979, to Comptroller of the Currency John G. Heimann, from Bernhard Mueller, Director, Swiss Bank Commission cited in *Ibid.*)

The central bank of the Netherlands, also in a letter to the Comptroller of the Currency, indicated a strong "sympathy with the view that the McFadden Act should be reviewed at short notice" to complement the progressive nature of the IBA, particularly considering the relative freedom given to U.S. banks to establish branches in EEC countries (*Ibid.*, p. 88). A Canadian banker expressed a similar view, asking (with respect to proposed banking law changes in Canada) if "it's really fair that we give some bank in the state of Georgia access to all of Canada in return for our being allowed in Georgia?" (quoted in John Dizard, "The Bittersweet Future of Foreign Banks in Canada," *Institutional Investor*, February 1980, p. 130).

[36] *Ibid.*, p. 21.

[37] Inter-Bank Research Organisation, *The Regulation of Banks in the Member States of the EEC*, 1978 Summary Table (insert). In some instances, most notably Ireland, differential privileges are extended to fellow EEC members' banks (see *Report to Congress*, Ch. 32).

[38] ' Banking Mergers and Participations," *loc. cit.*

[39] New York Banking Law, Section 202-a. California, Florida, Georgia, Illinois, Pennsylvania and Washington also impose reciprocity conditions, requiring that a foreign bank applicant be able to demonstrate that the country under whose laws it was organized permits at least roughly equivalent access to U.S. banks. Only eight states expressly prohibit foreign banks or corporations from conducting banking business within their borders. The laws of over half the states are silent with regard to foreign bank operations. See William B. Glidden and John E. Shockey, "U.S. Branches and Agencies of Foreign Banks: A Comparison of the Federal and State Chartering Options," *Illinois Law Forum*, Vol. 1980, No. 1.

[40] A law enacted in Colombia in 1975 required that all banks operating there be at least 51% owned by Colombian nationals, thereby precluding U.S. bank branches (See *Report to Congress*, pp. 108-109) As a result of that law, a Colombian bank was informed by the New York Banking Department that it would have to close its New York branch. The bank subsequently reorganized its New York operations by establishing a subsidiary bank. See Federal Reserve Board Order approving the application of Banco de Bogota and Banbogota, Inc. (*Federal Reserve Bulletin*, July 1977, pp. 671-2).

[41] Thus for example, a Venezuelan bank acquired a bank in New York notwithstanding its home country's prohibition of establishment of branch or subsidiary banks by U.S. institutions. See Federal Reserve Board Order approving the application of Banco Union, C.A. (*Federal Reserve Bulletin*, January 1977, pp. 61-3) and *Report to Congress*, pp. 105-6.

[42] In its regulation of federal branches and agencies of foreign banks, the OCC has determined that it is not bound by state reciprocity requirements (see 12 CFR Part 28). That determination along with other portions of the Comptroller's regulation, has been challenged in *Conference of State Bank Supervisors, et al.* v. *John G. Heimann, Comptroller of the Currency of the United States* Civil Action No. 80-3284 (D.D.C., filed Dec. 30, 1980).

[43] For a discussion of the legal framework governing foreign acquisitions of U.S. banks, see John E. Shockey and William B. Glidden, *Foreign-Controlled U.S. Banks: The Legal and Regulatory Environment*, OCC Staff Paper, 1980.

[44] Hearings before the Senate Banking, Housing and Urban Affairs Committee on *Edge Corporation Branching . . .*, p. 38.

[45] This is true with regard to agency actions under the Change in Bank Control Act, which covers acquisitions by individuals, as well as Federal Reserve decisions under the Bank Holding Company Act. In foreign bank holding company applications, however, the Federal Reserve Board may consider the effectiveness of bank supervision in the applicant's home country. (See Shockey and Glidden, *op cit.*)

[46] See *Report to Congress*, Ch. 36.

[47] *Ibid.*, p. 3.

[48] Hearings before the Senate Committee on Banking, Housing and Urban Affairs on *Edge Corporation Branching. . .*, p. 20. Mr. Carswell's comments were directed toward a proposed temporary moratorium. His observations would apply *a fortiori* to a policy of reciprocity that would impose clear restrictions on acquisitions.

[49] Henry C. Wallich, "Developments in International Banking," an Address to the Association of Foreign Banks in Switzerland, Bern, Switzerland, June 15, 1979, p. 2.

[50] Anthony M. Solomon, Testimony in Hearings before a subcommittee of the House Banking, Finance and Urban Affairs Committee on the *International Banking Act of 1977*, p. 262.

[51] For an example of the negative working of reciprocal arrangements, see the discussion of U.S.-Canadian fisheries agreements and their history leading to a situation when, "In June 1978, reciprocal fisheries arrangements . . . broke down with each country ordering the other's trawlers out of its coastal waters," in Helen Sinclair and Martin Krossell, "Reciprocity: A Tough Game," *The Canadian Banker & ICB Review*, Vol. 85, No. 5 (October 1978), pp. 10-15.

[52] Solomon, *op. cit.*, p. 262.

[53] Muriel Siebert has argued that additional factors are relevant to regulatory evaluation of foreign—as opposed to domestic—acquisitions, including, first, "reciprocity, or the ability of our banks to make the same kind of acquisitions abroad . . ." (Siebert letter to Congressman Reuss, February 6, 1979); Paul A. Volcker, then president of the Federal Reserve Bank of New York, questioned "whether open entry on a basis of national treatment in instances where the home country does not provide reasonably equivalent access to American and other foreign banks is equitable to United States banking interests or fully responsive to the national policy of open markets" ("Treatment of Foreign Banks in the United States: Dilemmas and Opportunities," Federal Reserve Bank of New York *Quarterly Review*, Summer 1979, p. 5); Senator Stevenson, noting that federal regulators and foreign banking authorities treat acquisitions ". . . as a question separate and distinct from other foreign treatment issues . . . ," asked, "Does that not argue for applying the rule of reciprocity to acquisitions, recognizing that national treatment is unlikely to be attainable with respect to acquisitions?" (Senate Committee on Banking, Housing and Urban Affairs, Hearings before the Subcommittee on International Finance, 96th Cong., 1st sess., December 12-24, 1979, p. 68.); views of U.S. bankers were previously cited in footnotes 1 and 10.

[54] Volcker, *op. cit.*, p. 5.

[55] Foreign governments' liberalization of their treatment of nondomestic banks is sometimes motivated by a desire to promote international opportunities for their own banks. In Canada, proposals to allow foreign bank entry were intended to foster that objective (White Paper on the Revision of Canadian Banking Legislation, issued by Canadian Finance Minister in August 1976, p. 26). Similarly, recent Spanish reforms were intended to "ensure that Spanish banks can expand internationally without running into restrictions that could have been imposed abroad had existing Spanish legislation [prohibiting foreign bank entry] remained in force" ("Foreign Banks Law Delay Criticized," *Financial Times*, June 22, 1978, p. 2). There is no assurance that similar pressure will be exerted everywhere; for example, "The Australian government at this state sees no reason why it should consider issuing licenses to foreign banks," (Vincent W. Stove, "Australia Firm on Bank Policy," *Journal of Commerce*, June 5, 1979, p. 330.

[56] For example, the Office of the Special Representative for Trade Negotiations is participating in a project undertaken by the OECD Secretariat which will investigate impediments to trade in services. Banking is included among the industries for initial pilot studies. See "New Focus on International Services," *The Morgan Guaranty Survey*, May 1980, pp. 10-14.

8

POTENTIAL ACQUISITION PARTNERS FOR LARGE U.S. BANKS: THE DISCRIMINATORY EFFECTS OF LAW AND POLICY

WM. PAUL SMITH

STEVEN J. WEISS

> . . . The silliness of a situation in which U.S. bankers' fears of ownership
> of neighboring banks by other American institutions opens the door to
> foreign ownership of banks is just too much to ignore any more.

"Editorial: Thinking the Unthinkable," *The American Banker*, April 24, 1980, p. 4

United States laws and competitive policy severely restrict domestic acquisitions, particularly of large banks, and have therefore given some impetus to takeovers by foreign banking organizations. This paper describes the present restraints on domestic acquisitions and analyzes their effects in limiting the number of potential domestic acquirers of large United States banks.

The analysis takes account of laws restricting interstate and within-state acquisitions and antitrust policy. The number of potential domestic acquirers of the largest banks in each state is estimated, subject to legal restrictions, specific decision rules concerning the feasibility of particular combinations, and alternative assumptions regarding the likelihood of denial on antitrust grounds.

The analysis, which necessarily entails a fair amount of judgment, purports only to produce a rough picture of possible outcomes. It is assumed throughout that an acquisition of one of a state's largest banks is sought in order to strengthen the bank's competitive position or managerial or financial resources. Thus, a key decision rule for determining potential acquisition partners requires that the acquiring organization be twice the size of the bank to be acquired. Combinations among like-sized banks in a state's top 10 are not counted, even though they would be possible in some situations. In other respects the decision rules are quite conservative, i.e., they tend to overstate the number of feasible combinations. The decision rules and assumptions underlying the analysis are described in an appendix which also includes tables displaying the state-by-state results in detail.

The effects of existing domestic restrictions are found to be quite far-reaching. For example, subject to legal restrictions and feasibility constraints and assuming conventional antitrust standards, only 16 of the three largest banks in each of the 50 states, D.C. and Puerto Rico would have potential domestic acquisition partners, short of an emergency (failing bank) situation; and no domestic partner would be available for any of the four largest banks in 36 states, nor for any of the top 10 banks in eight states. The numbers of large banks without potential domestic acquirers would be slightly higher under an assumption of antitrust policy based on the potential competition and entrenchment doctrines.

Further analysis indicates that the importance of antitrust considerations in determining the results should not be exaggerated. Taking into account only the decision rules specifying feasible combinations and state law restrictions, i.e., assuming no concern whatever for antitrust considerations, it is shown that in 33 states two or more of the four largest banks would still have no domestic acquisition partner.

The analysis also shows that in a number of states the only feasible domestic acquirers of some of the largest banks are subsidiaries of out-of-state bank holding companies. Moreover, even if interstate acquisitions were permitted for banks with deposits in excess of $500 million, no domestic bank acquirers would be available for 28 leading banks in 11 states, most of them in less affluent states.

In some states, not even a foreign bank could rescue a troubled large bank, because of prohibitions in state law, and in other states foreign interest in a possible acquisition would appear unlikely.

The paper concludes that reducing domestic restrictions on bank expansion would be desirable to promote competition and for supervisory reasons.

INTRODUCTION

The acquisition in recent years of large U.S. banks by foreign banks is symptomatic, in part, of the discriminatory effects of state and federal bank structure law and federal competitive policy.[1] This paper deals with the effect of domestic bank structure law and competitive policy upon potential foreign and domestic acquisition partners for large U.S. banks.[2] A state-by-state analysis of potential domestic acquisition partners for large banks is employed to demonstrate the effects of U.S. law and policy, including the prohibition of interstate banking expansion, state banking law restrictions and antitrust enforcement. That analysis, which is described fully in an appendix to this paper, is based on specific decision rules concerning the feasibility of particular combinations and alternative assumptions concerning the likelihood of denial on antitrust grounds. The analysis focuses throughout on acquisitions that may be desired or sought in order to strengthen the financial resources, management, or competitive position of the ten largest banks in each state.

RESTRICTIONS ON DOMESTIC ACQUISITIONS

The McFadden Act and the Douglas Amendment to the Bank Holding Company Act (BHCA), together with state branching and bank holding company laws, effectively preclude interstate acquisitions by U.S. banks and bank holding companies.[3] Antitrust standards incorporated in the BHCA and the Bank Merger Act limit U.S. bank expansion within their home states. Those standards reflect U.S. policy designed to preserve and promote competitive domestic banking markets. In some states, within-state acquisitions are limited further by laws prohibiting or limiting branching or multibank holding companies. Those restrictions on domestic bank expansion reflect policies intended, in part, to prevent undue concentration of economic power or to protect local banks.

Limitations on domestic banks run counter to bank stockholders' interests by reducing the number of eligible major buyers. They complicate bank regulators' efforts to find strong institutions capable of rescuing a troubled bank. The U.S. market also would be more attractive to foreign banks if geographical restraints on expansion were reduced or eliminated.

Liberalization of existing restraints would entail basic changes in U.S. law and policy regarding interstate operations of domestic banking operations and promotion of competition in U.S. banking markets.

FOREIGN BANK ADVANTAGES

Although U.S. banking organizations are barred, in practice, from acquiring banks across state lines, foreign banks with no existing deposit-taking operations in the United States, i.e., branches or subsidiary banks, are eligible to acquire a U.S. bank anywhere in the country, unless prohibited by state law. Moreover, subject to Federal Reserve regulations regarding "home state" designation,[4] even foreign banks that have U.S. branch or agency facilities potentially may acquire a bank in any state, subject again to state law limitations, by a one time only change of their home state.[5] Foreign banks that have an existing U.S. bank subsidiary are subject to the same limitation on out-of-state acquisitions that applies to U.S. banking organizations under the Douglas Amendment. Four foreign banks with grandfathered subsidiaries in more than one state[6] have a choice of home state designation, which may increase their options for possible future acquisitions. Indirect foreign acquisitions through merger of banks into existing U.S. subsidiaries outside the designated home state remain possible, but will be subject to special scrutiny by the Federal Reserve Board in connection with its regulation of foreign bank's interstate activities.[7]

Given the effective prohibition of interstate acquisitions by U.S. banking organizations, antitrust enforcement, and state limitations on multiple office banking, some of the largest U.S. banks acquired by foreign institutions were unavailable to a domestic bank purchaser. Antitrust considerations would probably have ruled out within-state acquisitions by institutions large enough to buy some of the banks involved, e.g., Union Bank and Marine Midland. The antitrust constraint may be overcome in a failing bank situation, under the failing company doctrine, but the BHCA prohibition on interstate acquisitions eliminates out-of-state buyers which might otherwise be available to buy a failing bank.[8] In states prohibiting branching and multibank holding companies, *all* domestic acquisitions may be ruled out, even if capable, willing domestic buyers are available and there are no competitive concerns. In just such a situation in Illinois, LaSalle National Bank was purchased by Algemene Bank Nederland in a divestiture stemming from the BHCA Amendments in 1970.

ANALYSIS OF LARGE BANK ACQUISITION PARTNERS

Prominent recent foreign takeovers of U.S. banks illustrate the limitations of U.S. law and policy on acquisitions by domestic institutions.

The full impact of restraints on domestic acquisitions is far-reaching. This is demonstrated by a state-by-state analysis involving a detailed count of feasible domestic acquisition partners for each of the top 10 banks in each state, the District of Columbia, and Puerto Rico. That analysis entailed a review of the statewide and local market positions of 514 banks,[9] and application of reasonable decision rules to determine how many in-state acquiring banks and bank holding companies would be available for each large bank in the event that financial difficulty or other circumstances short of failure created a need or desire for a merger or acquisition. Assumptions were made regarding the feasibility of particular acquirer/acquired pairs and the likelihood of antitrust action to disallow any given combination.

The decision rules and assumptions were necessarily general, and a certain amount of informed judgment was involved in applying them to specific cases. They are, after all, surrogates for a complex regulatory process that involves a detailed examination of many facts and subjective considerations which influence regulatory decisions in any actual case. The decision rules and assumptions, therefore, merely produce a test to give a rough picture of possible outcomes. Although the decision rules are generally conservative, as explained in the appendix, one point requires particular attention. It was assumed throughout that a top 10 bank would be absorbed only if it needed an acquisition partner to strengthen its financial or managerial resources or its competitive position. Thus, a key decision rule requires that the acquiring banking organization be twice the size of the acquired bank (in terms of deposits). Because of this decision rule, possible combinations among like-sized banks, which might be proposed and not ruled out by state law or antitrust considerations, are not reflected in the analysis. This factor affects the reported counts in a few states. On the other hand, the counts may be overstated because intangible factors, such as board or management incompatibility, which have been known to squelch otherwise "reasonable" combinations, are ignored throughout.

Separate counts, based on three different assumptions regarding antitrust enforcement, were made. Those assumptions were: (1) fairly conventional antitrust guidelines for horizontal acquisitions in a given market; (2) stricter antitrust standards based on the entrenchment and potential competition doctrines; and (3) no antitrust enforcement. The analysis, the underlying assumptions and the results are described more fully in the appendix.

On the basis of legal restrictions, the decision rules regarding feasibility and the first antitrust assumption, i.e., conventional antitrust analysis, *only 16* of the three largest banks in each state, the District of

Columbia, and Puerto Rico would have potential domestic acquisition partners, short of an actual failure or officially declared emergency. No domestic partner would be available for any of the four largest banks in 36 states, nor for any of the top 10 banks in eight states, including Indiana, Louisiana, New Jersey, Pennsylvania and Virginia.[10] States where domestic acquisition of any of the top four or top 10 banks would be ruled out are indicated in Table 1. In those states, acquisition of the largest banks could be accomplished *only* by a foreign institution, except in a failing bank situation.

Under the second assumption, antitrust policy based on the potential competition or entrenchment doctrines, the number of banks without potential domestic partners would be slightly higher. Because foreign acquiring banks often do not have established positions in domestic banking markets, antitrust enforcement based on the potential competition or entrenchment doctrines further favors foreign institutions as acquirers of large domestic banks.[11]

Table 1
States Where Top 4 and Top 10 Banks Would be
Unavailable for Domestic Acquisition[a]

No Acquisition Partners for Top 10 Banks	No Acquisition Partners for Top 4 Banks	
	States listed in Column 1 plus:	
Arkansas	California	Missouri
Indiana	Connecticut	Nebraska
Louisiana	Delaware	Nevada
New Jersey	District of Columbia	New Hampshire
North Dakota	Georgia	New York
Pennsylvania	Hawaii	North Carolina
Virginia	Illinois	Oklahoma
West Virginia	Kansas	Oregon
	Kentucky	South Carolina
	Maine	South Dakota
	Maryland	Tennessee
	Massachusetts	Texas
	Minnesota	Utah
	Mississippi	Vermont

Source: Appendix Table A-1.
[a] Based on decision rules about feasibility and antitrust action, described in the Appendix, and individual state bank structure laws.

IMPLICATION OF ANALYSIS OF
ACQUISITION PARTNERS

The foregoing indicates the pervasive and extreme restraints on domestic acquisitions. Clearly there are many situations in which only foreign banks would be eligible to make acquisitions intended to strengthen a domestic bank's financial, managerial, or overall competitive position, or to purchase troubled large banks in the United States.

Even foreign banks, however, could not rescue troubled banks in states that prohibit holding companies or foreign ownership of banks. The potential implications are far-reaching. In those states, at least the largest bank in each market has no potential corporate acquisition partner. Although individuals may have the financial resources required to acquire some of those banks, the prohibition of corporate ownership prevents pairing of troubled banks with those organizations that can best provide specialized financial and managerial resources.

The importance of antitrust considerations in limiting the number of available domestic partners for large banks should not be exaggerated. This is particularly true when the bank to be acquired is weak (but not failing) and requires financial or managerial assistance from a large institution. Analysis based on the assumption of no antitrust enforcement, i.e., assuming no concern whatever for anticompetitive factors, demonstrates that relative size considerations and state banking code restrictions have a significant limiting effect. Table 2 lists states where two or more of the top four banks would have no domestic acquirers based on those considerations alone.

The number of large banks which have no available domestic acquisition partners would be reduced substantially and the number of potential partners for others would be increased if the BHCA were amended to permit out-of-state acquisitions in emergency and failing bank situations. The benefits of interstate holding company acquisitions of troubled banks are implicit in the absence of several states from Table 2. In many cases, the potential acquisition partners were subsidiaries of out-of-state holding companies. Although in several cases the bank to be acquired was larger than the individual acquiring bank, the holding company's consolidated resources met the financial standards outlined for this study.[12] A review of the potential pairings of banks revealed that in 23 instances, in 12 states, the only acquisition partner for one of the four largest banks was a bank that satisfied the financial require-

Table 2
States Where Some of Top Four Banks Would be Unavailable for
Domestic Acquisition, Even with No Antitrust Enforcement

State	No. of Top 4 Banks With No Potential Acquirer	State	No. of Top 4 Banks With No Potential Acquirer
Alabama	2	Missouri	2
Alaska	2	Nebraska	2
Arkansas	4	New Hampshire	3
Connecticut	2	New Jersey	2
Delaware	2	New York	3
District of Columbia	2	North Carolina	3
Georgia	2	Ohio	2
Hawaii	2	Oklahoma	4
Illinois	2	Pennsylvania	3
Indiana	4	Rhode Island	3
Kansas	4	South Carolina	4
Kentucky	3	Tennessee	4
Louisiana	4	Texas	3
Maine	4	Vermont	4
Maryland	3	Virginia	3
Mississippi	3	West Virginia	4
		Puerto Rico	2

Source: Appendix and Table A-3.

ments for acquisition only through consolidation with its bank affiliates[13] (Table 3).

The state-by-state benefits of an amendment to the BHCA, however, would depend upon the nature of the exempted acquisitions. A uniform absolute size limit on such acquisitions, e.g., deposits of more

Table 3
Rank of Banks Whose Only Potential Acquirer is a Bank
Subsidiary of an Out-of-State Holding Company, By State

	Bank Rank			
	1	2	3	4
Arizona	X			
Colorado	X	X		
Idaho	X	X		
Montana	X	X	X	X
Nebraska	X		X	
Nevada		X		
New Mexico	X			
North Dakota		X	X	X
Oregon		X		
South Dakota	X	X		X
Utah	X			
Washington	X	X		

than $500 million, would leave without acquisition partners 28 large banks in 11 states, most of them in less affluent states.[14] Indeed, all of the top four banks in Arkansas, Maine, Vermont, and West Virginia would be without acquisition partners. Large banks from contiguous states may not acquire failing banks despite extended records of serving the affected markets as correspondents. Although that opportunity is available to foreign banks, their interest in entering states without important financial centers is doubtful. Foreign-acquired U.S. banks have been heavily concentrated in major money center locations to date and, in fact, there are no foreign bank subsidiaries, branches or other offices in the 11 states identified above. In those states, and others, the possibility even of a foreign takeover in an emergency situation may be only theoretical.

CONCLUSION

Loosening the restrictions on interstate holding company acquisitions of banks would provide opportunities for growth of stronger institutions and a means for rescue of troubled banks. Such acquisitions could be controlled in an orderly way through the regulatory process and subject to existing antitrust constraints. Permitting domestic interstate acquisition of troubled banks would be a constructive step toward eliminating the Douglas Amendment's discriminatory effect on United States banking organizations now reflected in a substantial number of foreign takeovers. Foreign banks' advantage in domestic acquisitions could be reduced or eliminated by imposing new restrictions on foreign takeovers. However, any such restrictions would be contrary to United States policy on international investment. Moreover, from a supervisory standpoint, reducing existing domestic restrictions is preferable. It would increase the number of potential buyers for troubled banks and, more generally, provide the benefit of fresh sources of capital, management expertise and competitive vigor.

APPENDIX

ESTIMATES OF POTENTIAL WITHIN-STATE ACQUIRERS FOR THE TEN LARGEST BANKS IN EACH STATE, D.C., AND PUERTO RICO

In order to estimate the number of potential acquirers for leading banks in each state, certain decision rules concerning the feasibility of particular combinations and assumptions about the likelihood of regulatory denial or antitrust action to thwart a particular combination were necessary. The decision rules and alternative antitrust assumptions, described below, were used to count the number of possible domestic acquirers of the largest banks in each state, subject to the additional constraints imposed by state banking law.

The specification of the decision rules regarding feasibility of particular combinations, and the application of those rules and alternative antitrust assumptions in particular cases necessarily involves a substantial amount of informed judgment. The exercise was intended only to produce a rough description of possible outcomes.

One decision rule requires particular attention. It is assumed throughout that a top 10 bank would be absorbed only if it needed strengthening, and the necessary strengthening was assumed to be available only from a larger banking organization. Specifically, the first rule requires that the acquiring organization be twice the size of the bank to be acquired. Thus, some combinations among like-sized banks, which might otherwise be possible, are ruled out. The count of feasible combinations in some states is sensitive to that rule. In general, however, the decision rules are considered to be quite conservative, as discussed below.

Feasible acquisitions for each bank were counted based on the following decision rules, in combination with alternative antitrust policy assumptions and subject to bank structure law constraints:

1. An acquirer with twice the deposits of the bank to be taken over has adequate financial resources to absorb (and bolster) the bank (and therefore gain regulatory approval).
2. At any time, only one bank subsidiary of a multibank holding company requires more financial support than the parent com-

pany and existing affiliates could provide, and severance of that bank from the system will not adversely affect either the bank or its affiliate banks.

3. All of a multibank holding company's subsidiaries' deposits can be consolidated to determine financial and managerial ability to undertake an acquisition (see rule 1). .

4. A multibank holding company or a bank in a statewide branching state with adequate resources as defined in rules 1 and 3, can absorb a bank located anywhere within the state, however remote from existing offices.

5. Unit banks located within the same city can be merged or consolidated, however remote the existing offices.

Those decision rules are generally conservative. That is, a count of potential in-state acquirers based on them will overstate the number of feasible combinations likely to arise in actual experience. The underlying assumptions, for example, do not reflect possible differences in business orientation and interests of the acquiring banks. Thus, a holding company which only operates rural banks is considered a possible acquirer of a regional money center bank, and a purely wholesale bank may be paired with a smaller, consumer-oriented suburban bank. The rules for determining feasible combinations also ignore important intangible considerations. For example, it is implicitly assumed that there are no problems in terms of management incompatibility.

Rule 2 dictates that only one subsidiary of a holding company can be in trouble, requiring spin-off/acquisition for support. In actuality, however, several or all affiliated banks in an organization could be in difficulty and require support at the same time from the same banking organization. In practice, holding company subsidiary banks are rarely as easily separated or unified as assumed in rules 2 and 3. Also, rules 4 and 5 disregard practical problems of geographical separation that would deter some otherwise feasible combinations.

Assumptions were necessary to evaluate the likelihood of antitrust action (or significantly adverse anticompetitive findings by the bank regulatory agency involved) to forestall a potential acquisition. It was assumed that a transaction would be disapproved, stopped (or never attempted) if:

(a) The transaction would result in control of over 20 percent of deposits in a given market;[15]

(b) The potential acquirer or the bank to be acquired is very large

Table A-1
Number of Potential Acquiring Institutions of Ten Largest Banks, By State
(December 31, 1978)

	Rank of Bank										No. with partners	No. w/two or more partners
	1	2	3	4	5	6	7	8	9	10		
Alabama			2*	2*		2	2	2	3	6	7	7
Alaska		2	1	1		1	3	3	4	5	8	5
Arizona			1	1		2	4	6	7	8	7	5
Arkansas											0	0
California						2**	2**	2**	2**	3**	5	5
Colorado	1**	1**	1*	1*	1	2	3	3	3	3	10	5
Connecticut								4	5	6	3	3
Delaware				*a*	3	3	2	5	5	5	6	6
Dist. of Col.					4	5	5	5	6	6	6	6
Florida		3	3	5	4	6	7	7	6	7	9	9
Georgia			2			3	2	4	3	4	6	6
Hawaii						1	2	5	*b*	*b*	3	2
Idaho			2	3		3	4	4	4	4	7	7
Illinois					2**	3*	3*	3	4	4	6	6
Indiana											0	0
Iowa		1	3	2	4	5	5	5	5	5	9	8
Kansas								1			1	0
Kentucky							1				1	0
Louisiana											0	0
Maine					1	2	1	1	3	2	6	3
Maryland						2	1	3	4	2	5	4
Massachusetts					5*	4	4	4	3	6	6	6
Michigan				3**	2**	4**	3*	3*	4*	4*	7	7
Minnesota					1	1	1	1	1	1	6	0
Mississippi										2	1	1
Missouri			1*	1*		2*	4	4	7	7	7	5
Montana	1	2	1	1	1	2	2	1	1	2	10	4
Nebraska						1				1	2	0
Nevada						2	2	7	*b*	*b*	3	3
New Hampshire					2	1	1		2	2	5	3

relative to other banks in the market and the other is a significant competitor in that market.[16]

Those guidelines for possible antitrust concerns, while perhaps somewhat stringent (and therefore tending to *understate* the number of permissible combinations) do not reflect the possibility of antitrust denial based on the entrenchment or potential competition doctrines.[17] An important offsetting factor is that many banks, deterred by the uncertainty, time and expense involved in antitrust litigation, may elect not to challenge a Justice Department suit, even though a defense might be successful in some cases. The prior notification requirements (in merger or holding company applications) and the automatic stay of the transaction when challenged under antitrust statutes tend to "favor" Justice Department suits to block mergers and holding company acquisitions

Table A-1 continued

					Rank of Bank					No. with partners	No. w/two or more partners
	1	2	3	4	5	6	7	8	9	10	
New Jersey											0	0
New Mexico				2	2	2	2	1			5	4
New York							2**	2**	3**	4**	4	4
North Carolina						3	2	1	1	1	5	2
North Dakota^c											0	0
Ohio				1**		2**	4*		1*	7*	5	3
Oklahoma					1	2	2		2	2	5	4
Oregon						3	2	3	3	4	5	5
Pennsylvania											0	0
Rhode Island				2	2	2	5	5	5	6	7	7
South Carolina						1	3	3	4	3	5	4
South Dakota^d								1			1	0
Tennessee						2*	3	2	3	4	5	5
Texas							4*	4*	3*	5*	4	4
Utah							1	2	3	5	4	3
Vermont					1	4	4	4	1	3	6	4
Virginia											0	0
Washington							1	2	3	4	4	3
West Virginia											0	0
Wisconsin				5	3	2	3	3	3	3	7	7
Wyoming		1	1	1	1	2	2	1	2	2	9	4
Puerto Rico			1	1	1	3	4	4	4	8	8	5

^aThe fourth largest bank in Delaware is state controlled. Accordingly, it is not considered a candidate for acquisition.

^bHawaii and Nevada each have only eight banks.

^cThe largest bank in North Dakota is state controlled. Accordingly, it is not considered a candidate for acquisition.

^dSouth Dakota now permits entry through *de novo* bank formation and through acquisition of existing banks by out-of-state bank holding companies, thereby providing potential acquisition partners for its largest banks.

*Acquiring institutions with over $1 billion in deposits and acquiring bank with over $500 million in deposits.

**Acquiring institution with over $2 billion in deposits and acquired with over $1 billion in deposits.

Note: Based on decision rules 1 through 5 regarding feasibility, conventional antitrust assumptions A and B, and state banking code restrictions.

of banks.

The results of the analysis are summarized in Tables A-1 and A-2.[18] Considering only the more conventional antitrust analysis (i.e., assumptions a and b in combination with bank structure law restrictions and decision rules 1 through 5), of the three largest banks in each of the 50 states, Puerto Rico, and the District of Columbia, short of an actual failure or officially declared emergency situation which would override anticompetitive concerns, *only 16* of the 155 banks[19] would have potential domestic partners. In 36 states, none of the four largest banks would have a potential partner, and in eight states, none would be available for any of the top 10 banks in the state.

Table A-2
Summary: Number of Domestic Partners for Top 10 Banks in Each State

Number of	Rank of Bank										
Partners	1	2	3	4	5	6	7	8	9	10	TOTAL
0	49	47	43	35	29	19	13	15	14	12	276
1	2	3	5	8	10	6	7	8	6	3	58
2		1	2	5	6	16	13	5	4	8	60
3		1	2	1	3	5	6	7	10	4	39
4					2	4	10	10	3	9	38
5				2	2	1	2	4	8	5	24
6						1	0	1	3	4	9
7							1	2	2	3	8
8										2	2
9											0

Note: Based on Table A-1.

Separate counts were made under assumptions of stricter antitrust standards, specified as follows:

(c) The potential acquirer is very large relative to banking organizations in the region or state, and the acquired bank is an established bank of significant size in its market.
(d) The acquired bank is very large relative to other banking organizations in its market, and the acquirer is very large relative to the acquired bank and to its market.

Those additional assumptions leave a slightly larger number of large banks without potential acquisition partners, and some others with fewer potential partners. In smaller states with more, generally relatively small banks, acquisition of the states' top ranked banks by subsidiaries of the very large out-of-state bank holding companies may raise more questions of antitrust violations. However, even under those conditions, the state-by-state *pattern* of large banks without potential partners follows that pattern resulting from the application of traditional antitrust standards.

The financial/managerial resources necessary to absorb large banks and banking structure laws are substantial barriers to acquisitions of large banks. A review of the three largest banks in each state reveals that 94 of the 155 would be without a domestic acquirer, even if antitrust enforcement was completely relaxed (see Table A-3). Of the top 10 banks in the 12 states in which none or only one had an acquirer under the initial assumptions (a and b) about antitrust enforcement,

Table A-3
Four Largest Banks, by State, Without Potential Acquirers Due to
Size and State Banking Code Restrictions
(December 31, 1978)

State	Bank Rank				State	Bank Rank			
	1	2	3	4		1	2	3	4
Alabama	X	X			Nebraska		X		X
Alaska	X	X			Nevada	X			
Arizona		X			New Hampshire	X	X	X	
Arkansas	X	X	X	X	New Jersey	X	X		
California	X				New Mexico				
Colorado					New York	X	X	X	
Connecticut	X	X			North Carolina	X	X	X	
Delaware	X	X			North Dakota	b			
Dist. of Co.	X	X		a	Ohio	X	X	c	
Florida	X				Oklahoma	X	X	X	
Georgia	X	X			Oregon	X			
Hawaii	X	X			Pennsylvania	X	X	X	
Idaho					Rhode Island	X	X	X	
Illinois	X	X			South Carolina	X	X	X	
Indiana	X	X	X	X	South Dakota			d	X
Iowa	X				Tennessee	X	X	X	X
Kansas	X	X	X	X	Texas	X	X	X	
Kentucky	X	X		X	Utah				
Louisiana	X	X	X	X	Vermont	X	X	X	X
Maine	X	X	X	X	Virginia	X	X	X	
Maryland	X	X	X	X	Washington				
Massachusetts	X				West Virginia	X	X	X	X
Michigan	X				Wisconsin	X			
Minnesota					Wyoming				
Mississippi	X	X	X	X	Puerto Rico	X	X		
Missouri	X	X			*No partner*	40	34	20	12
Montana					*With partner*	11	18	32	39

[a]The fourth largest bank in Delaware is state controlled. Accordingly, it is not considered a candidate for acquisition.

[b]The largest bank in North Dakota is state controlled. Accordingly, it is not considered a candidate for acquisition.

[c]As a result of the January 1, 1979, change in Ohio's branching code, and the subsequent mergers of the subsidiaries of some of the state's largest holding companies, three of the top four (the three largest) banks would be without potential domestic based acquirers.

[d]South Dakota now permits entry through *de novo* bank formation and through acquisition of existing banks by out-of-state bank holding companies, thereby providing potential acquisition partners for its largest bank.

Note: The determination of possible acquisitions given in this table is based on state banking law restrictions, decision rules 1 through 5, and the assumption that there is no antitrust enforcement.

75 of 119 banks would be without a potential acquirer even in the absence of antitrust enforcement.

The number of large banks without potential acquisition partners would be reduced substantially, and the number of potential partners for others would be increased if the BHCA and the Bank Merger Act were amended to permit out-of-state acquisitions of large banks and holding companies in emergency and failing bank situations. The state-by-state benefits of such amendments, however, depend upon the nature of the transactions exempted from the McFadden Act and Douglas Amendment to the BHCA, e.g., whether there would be a relative rank standard or an absolute size standard. Applying a $500 million deposit limit—a standard somewhat more stringent than that proposed by the Board of Governors in 1975—28 of the four largest banks in each state (206) would still be without partners (see Table A-4). Nineteen are located in states ranked in the lower one-third by family income, and include all of the four largest in Arkansas, Maine, Vermont and West Virginia.[20]

Different exemptions to the prohibition to interstate acquisition by bank holding companies based on other criteria would generate varied state-by-state benefits that, as long as the restraints remained effective, could be beneficial, or onerous, to bank customers and shareholders, depending upon population growth, industrial development, or merely political geography.

Table A-4
States Where Some of the Top Four Banks Would Not
Have Acquisition Partners, Even Permitting
Interstate Acquisitions of Banks with Over
$500 Million in Deposits
(December 31, 1978)

State	Bank Rank				State Rank Median Family Income (1975)
	1	2	3	4	
Alaska		X			1
Arkansas	X	X	X	X	49
Kansas		X	X	X	31
Kentucky				X	48
Maine	X	X	X	X	43
Mississippi			X		50
Nebraska		X		X	25
New Hampshire	X	X	X		24
South Dakota[a]			X[a]		41
Vermont	X	X	X	X	37
West Virginia	X	X	X	X	42
No Partner	5	8	8	7	28

[a] South Dakota now permits entry through *de novo* bank formation and through acquisition of existing banks by out-of-state bank holding companies, thereby providing potential acquisition partners for its largest banks.

FOOTNOTES

[1] Foreign banking corporations that acquire U.S. banks may have tax and other financial advantages–or disadvantages–relative to U.S. banking corporations. Those advantages, however, are different from the issues of banking market structure and competitive policy considered in this paper.

We recognize that foreign individuals–like individual American citizens–can acquire U.S. banks that may be unavailable in practice for purchase by domestic banking organizations. This can be beneficial if the rescue of a troubled bank is involved. However, the substantial resources required ordinarily precludes acquisitions of the largest banks by individuals.

[2] The identification of "acceptable," "possible," or "potential" acquisition partners is limited to the specific quantified conditions delineated below. It does not represent an appraisal of desire or suitability of management expertise, personalities, or other factors influencing decisions to merge/affiliate the paired institutions.

[3] Interstate expansion of full service banking by U.S. institutions could be effected if authorized by individual states. Proposals have been considered in New York and California (See "A Way for Banks to Jump State Lines," *Business Week*, January 21, 1980, p. 35.). Under revised banking statutes enacted in Maine in 1975, an out-of-state bank holding company may acquire a Maine bank if the privilege is reciprocated. Iowa now permits Northwest Bancorporation, Minneapolis, Minnesota, a multistate bank holding company that controlled banks in Iowa prior to passage of the BHCA to acquire additional banks in that state. Multistate bank holding companies in existence prior to passage of the BHCA of 1956 may expand by internal growth through *de novo* branching or by external growth through merging other banks into the "grandfathered" out-of-state banking subsidiaries, subject to state law and regulatory approval. In addition, South Dakota recently enacted legislation permitting, subject to certain restrictions, entry by out-of-state bank holding companies through acquisition of existing banks and through establishment of new banks. Under similar legislation in Delaware, out-of-state holding companies may establish *de novo* banks in that state. Provisions of the Delaware and South Dakota laws, however, dictate large scale operations and thereby limit such entry to the very largest institutions.

[4] See the Federal Reserve Board's interpretations on "Interstate Banking Restrictions for Foreign Banks," *Federal Register*, Vol. 45, No. 198, October 9, 1980, pp. 67056-9.

[5] Branch or agency operations grandfathered by the International Banking Act of 1978 (IBA) would not be affected by a foreign bank's acquisition of a subsidiary bank in a different state. However, future expansion of locations in the original state(s) would be limited if the state where the subsidiary is acquired is designated the home state.

[6] See "Confinement of Domestic Banking in the United States," *Bank Stock Quarterly*, M. A. Schapiro & Co., Inc., N.Y., October 1978, Tables III and IV, for lists of foreign bank multistate activities grandfathered by the BHCA and IBA.

[7] See Board of Governors, "Interstate Banking Restrictions. . . ."

[8] In the aftermath of the Franklin National Bank failure in 1974, the Board of Governors proposed legislation exempting takeovers of failing banks from the Douglas Amendment prohibition. That proposal was designed to permit out-of-state acquisitions of large banks and bank holding companies only, defined as those institutions with over $500 million in assets. See Statement by Robert C. Holland before the Subcommittee on Financial Institutions Supervision, Regulations and Insurance of the Committee on Banking, Currency and Housing, U.S. House of Representatives, July 16, 1975; and Statement by Robert C. Holland before Subcommittee on Financial Institutions of the Committee on Banking, Housing and Urban Affairs, U.S. Senate, July 22, 1975.

The Federal Financial Institutions Examination Council (FFIEC) recently proposed permitting out-of-state holding company acquisitions of a bank in receivership or a bank holding company with a bank in receivership if the bank's total assets are in excess of $1.5 billion or if the bank is one of the state's three largest insured banks. The proposal would also permit out-of-state acquisitions of failed insured thrift institutions which have assets in excess of $1 billion or which are among the three largest in the state. See the FFIEC proposal, release dated April 9, 1980; and *The American Banker*, April 14, 1980, p. 7.

[9] The study covered 514 banks, rather than 520: Two states (Hawaii and Nevada) had only eight commercial banks at the end of 1978, and one of the ten largest in two states (Delaware and North Dakota) was state owned. The anomalous statistics in the text, in which an odd number of banks results from an aggregation of an even number of banks, reflects the presence of North Dakota among the states where banks have few "acquisition partners."

[10] For detail, see Appendix Table A-1.

[11] See Steven J. Weiss, *Competitive Standards Applied to Foreign and Domestic Acquisitions of U.S. Banks*, Chapter 9, this book.

[12] See decision rules 1 and 3, and the accompanying text in the appendix.

[13] In a few cases, perhaps, consolidation of affiliates located in the same state alone would have met the financial conditions delineated in the appendix. However, we did not make separate counts based on limited, specific consolidation of banks that might be adopted for particular legal or managerial reasons.

[14] See Appendix Table A-4 and accompanying text.

[15] This is based on the landmark Phillipsburg decision standards on horizontal acquisitions. In that case, the resulting bank would have held 19 percent of assets and of demand deposits, 23 percent of total deposits and 27 percent of loans held by commercial banks in the Phillipsburg, New Jersey-Easton, Pennsylvania area. *United States* v. *Phillipsburg National Bank and Trust Company, et. al.* 26 L Ed. 2d 658, at 668.

[16] See Donald I. Baker, "Competition's Role in the Regulation of Banking," *The Bankers Magazine*, Summer 1971; and the Department of Justice, "Merger Guidelines," May 30, 1968, paragraphs 5-7, *et passim*. In markets in which the market shares of the four largest firms amount to less than 75 percent, the Department will ordinarily challenge acquisitions of firms accounting for 5 percent of the market by another with 5 percent; . . . 4 percent . . . by 10 percent; . . . 3 percent . . . by 15 percent; . . . 2 percent . . . by 20 percent; and . . . 1 percent . . . by 25 percent or more. These views also have influenced the willingness of the Board of Governors to approve acquisitions of banks by large holding companies. See, especially, the decision on an application by First International Bancshares, *Federal Reserve Bulletin*, January 1974, pp. 43-6. The apparent reversal of the position taken in that case is reviewed by Anne S. Weaver, "Bank Holding Companies: Competitive Issues and Policy," *Economic Perspectives*, Federal Reserve Bank of Chicago, September/October 1979.

[17] See "Merger Guidelines" paragraphs 18, 20 *et passim*. The guidelines specify, for example, that a merger between one of the most likely entrants and any firm with 25 percent or more of the market, or any firm with 10 percent or more in a market in which the four largest firms hold 75 percent, would be challenged. In our analysis, we grouped banks and holding companies with only nominal market positions in the targeted market with potential entrants. Although this is more liberal than the "Merger Guidelines" specify, it is consistent with the failure to challenge certain mergers and holding company acquisitions, whatever the rationale for the Department of Justice decision.

[18] The analysis is based on year-end 1978 data, which was the most recent at the time the analysis was undertaken. The nationwide results should not vary greatly from one year to another. However, changes in an individual state's banking structure code—a change from countywide to statewide branching, for example—could affect the count for that state materially.

Legislation permitting entry by out-of-state bank holding companies was recently enacted in South Dakota, subject to certain limitations, and similar legislation is being considered by other states. The South Dakota statute, of course, vitiates the analysis based on circumstances prevailing at the end of 1978. However, because of certain provisions in the new law, it appears unlikely to stimulate many out-of-state acquisitions.

[19] The largest bank in North Dakota is state-owned and is excluded from this count and the similar counts reported in subsequent paragraphs.

[20] Two (of four) Little Rock banks together list 13 banks in five states as correspondents. The resources of all 13 correspondents meet the assumed standards for acquiring two of the four; 12 for acquiring three; and 8 for acquiring all four. The comparisons for the other states are less dramatic. By quirk of geography, Maine banks would be without help even with a contiguous state exemption to the McFadden Act and Douglas Amendment.

## 9

COMPETITIVE STANDARDS APPLIED TO FOREIGN AND DOMESTIC ACQUISITIONS OF U.S. BANKS

STEVEN J. WEISS

SUMMARY

Competitive effects are a major factor in federal agencies' decisions on any bank acquisition, whether the acquirer is domestic or foreign. Some observers of large U.S. bank acquisitions by foreign banking organizations have claimed that competitive standards, as applied by U.S. regulators, unfairly favor foreign applicants. This paper reviews agency decisions, noting that benefits were often cited and competitive effects were only rarely an important factor. Two different concerns about ostensible advantages of foreign bank acquirers are then evaluated.

One concern voiced by U.S. critics is that domestic banks' within-state acquisitions may be denied on antitrust grounds because of agencies' considerations of potential or "probable future" competitive effects but that such considerations are not applied with equal force to foreign bank applications, suggesting a possible "double standard." Some critics have argued that foreign bank entry should be limited to *de novo* or foothold entry. The paper concludes that the allegation of unequal treatment is invalid. Rather, the existing positions in U.S. markets of foreign bank acquirers is objectively different from that of eligible (in-state) acquirers capable of taking over large domestic banks. To limit foreign banks' U.S. expansion to *de novo* or foothold entry would sacrifice potential gains and violate U.S. policy regarding international investment while offering no clear prospect of offsetting benefits.

The second question raised about regulatory treatment of competitive effects in foreign as opposed to domestic acquisitions concerns possible effects outside U.S. markets of large foreign takeovers. World-wide competitive effects are not generally taken into account in U.S. regulatory decisions on foreign banks' acquisitions of U. S. institutions. To do so would raise questions of extraterritoriality. The paper indicates that global competitive effects are unlikely to be significant and concludes that there appears to be little of immediate or serious consequence in the fact that U.S. policy on foreign acquisitions looks only at their effects on domestic markets.

INTRODUCTION

Competitive effects are a major factor in federal agencies' consideration of any bank merger or holding company acquisition, regardless of whether the acquiring banking organization is domestic or foreign. In terms of conventional competitive analysis, a spokesman for the Antitrust Division of the Justice Department explained that:

> Nationality of an acquiring banking institution will not affect the market structure of the market involved, the market shares of the parties to the merger, or the other objective criteria by which such transactions are analyzed. Likewise the more subjective criteria do not differ whether the acquiring institution is a domestic or foreign corporation. Thus, the standards and methodologies . . . apply equally to acquisitions by foreign or domestic institutions.[1]

Thus, "nationality is a neutral factor"[2] in the analysis, and is accorded no special weight in federal agency decisions on acquisitions and mergers.[3]

Some observers of recent takeovers of large U.S. banks by foreign banks have claimed that competitive standards, as applied by regulatory authorities to foreign acquisitions, unfairly favor foreign applicants, to the disadvantage of competing U.S. banking organizations. Two different concerns have been expressed, these are summarized briefly below and analyzed in the principal sections of this paper, following a brief review of federal agency evaluations of competitive factors in foreign bank acquisitions of U.S. banks.

Most foreign banks which have acquired U.S. banks are large by any standard, and some have acquired substantial U.S. institutions.[4] Acquisition opportunities for domestic banks and bank holding companies are severely limited, not only by legal restrictions on interstate expansion and within-state mergers and acquisitions, but also by application of antitrust standards designed to preserve and foster competition in the domestic banking industry.[5] Foreign takeovers of U.S. banks are typically "market extension" acquistions or mergers,[6] i.e., the foreign bank does not presently compete in the acquired bank's market, or the foreign bank has only a minimal competitive presence. In such situations, even if a large bank is the target, elimination of existing competition is not a major concern for the regulatory agencies. Similar proposals by large domestic banking organizations, however, have often been denied on the grounds that competition would be better served if the applicant organization expanded *de novo* or by foothold acquisition of a smaller bank. Some critics have charged that U.S. regulators have favored foreign bank acquisitions by not imposing the same requirements on large foreign institutions entering U.S. markets. That allegation is examined later in this paper.

A related question arises from the fact that large foreign banks compete with U.S. multinational banks not only in domestic markets, but also in foreign banking markets, and in the global financial arena generally. It has been argued that foreign institutions gain a competitive advantage in global markets by their ability to acquire large U.S. banks. The final section of this paper analyzes whether and to what extent worldwide competitive effects should be taken into account in U.S. regulatory decisions on foreign bank acquisition proposals.

REVIEW OF FEDERAL AGENCY DECISIONS

Thirty-six cases of foreign bank acquisitions of U.S. banks[7] were reviewed in order to assess federal regulatory agencies' analysis of the competitive effects of foreign bank takeovers. Nineteen of the transactions were direct acquisitions by a foreign banking organization, requiring approval by the Federal Reserve Board under the Bank Holding Company Act. The other seventeen were indirect acquisitions by foreign bank parents through mergers of U.S.-owned banks into established domestic subsidiary banks, requiring approval by the appropriate federal bank regulatory agency under the Bank Merger Act.[8] The Appendix lists some basic facts about the transactions that were reviewed.

Agency decisions on proposed acquisitions entail an evaluation of competitive effects and expected benefits to the convenience and needs of the affected communities as well as an assessment of how the proposal will affect the acquired bank's financial situation, managerial resources and future prospects. If anticompetitive effects are determined to be more than "slightly adverse," denial of a proposed transaction would be indicated unless the agency finds significant offsetting benefits from other factors.

Anticompetitive effects, whether elimination of present or potential competition or reduction of "probable future competition,"[9] were a significant concern in very few of the agency decisions on foreign bank acquisitions.[10] Many of the acquisitions were judged to be procompetitive, involving entry by strong banking organizations not previously established in the affected local or metropolitan markets.[11] Positive considerations with regard to statutory factors other than competition were noted in almost all cases (see Appendix).

The case that appears to have raised the most significant concerns about competitive effects is the acquisition of Union Bank, Los Angeles, by Standard Chartered Bank Limited. In its decision, the Federal Reserve Board examined the competitive effects with regard to Union Bank and Standard Chartered's existing California subsidiary, Chartered Bank of London.[12] The banks were, respectively, sixth and twenty-first largest in the state. The Board found that some existing competition between the banks would be eliminated in three metropolitan markets and considered the competitive effects to be "slightly adverse."[13] It concluded that the proposal would provide Union Bank "strong financial support, including $25 million in new capital." The decision details a number of "considerations relating to the convenience and needs of the communities to be served," which are judged to be "favorable" and to "outweigh the slightly adverse competitive effects" of the proposal.

In some of the merger cases, anticompetitive effects were noted because the foreign bank's subsidiary was located fairly close to the bank to be acquired. In the agencies' judgment, anticompetitive effects were mitigated, in several of these cases, by the fact that the existing foreign bank subsidiary was wholesale-oriented and was seeking to enter the retail market through merger.[14] In other merger cases, the fact that many larger and stronger competitors were present in the market was cited as a factor ameliorating minor anticompetitive concerns.[15]

Elimination of potential competition, or the likelihood that the foreign bank would enter the market by more procompetitive alternative means, either by a smaller acquisition or *de novo* expansion, only rarely appeared to be important considerations in the federal agencies' decisions. Some critics have argued that those considerations, which are sometimes critical in decisions on domestic applications, are not applied as rigorously by regulators to foreign bank acquisition proposals.

ALLEGED UNEQUAL APPLICATION OF
COMPETITIVE STANDARDS

Implying that a "double standard" has been at work in federal agency reviews of foreign takeovers of U.S. banks, Carol Greenwald, former Commissioner of Banks in the Commonwealth of Massachusetts, urged a congressional committee to "insist that the Justice Department and the bank regulatory authorities apply the same competitive test for large foreign and American banks."[16] Another observer asserted that U.S. banks' equality of opportunity for expansion was infringed by "more liberal attitudes of the American bank regulators toward foreign commercial bank takeovers."[17] Greenwald's basic concern about an allegedly unequal standard was expressed as follows:

> Competition ... [is] best served by welcoming foreign banks to establish *de novo* banks in American markets or in allowing them to make toehold acquisitions. This is the standard to which we hold large American banks; it makes no sense to me to distort that standard for foreign banks. [18]

De novo entry and "toehold" acquisitions have recently been endorsed, at least implicitly, by other critics of foreign takeovers as acceptable alternatives to large bank acquisitions.[19] Senator Proxmire, observing that the IBA established a basic framework of competitive equality, commented that:

> A basic question arises as to whether it is in the national interest for foreign banks to acquire large domestic banks or whether foreign banks should establish their presence here with *de novo* or toehold acquisitions. Such a strategy would promote competition in the United States and in the world market.[20]

PREFERENCE FOR PROCOMPETITIVE ENTRY BY
LARGE BANKING ORGANIZATIONS

Justice Department policy on bank acquisitions by large out-of-area institutions suggests that the entry of large banking organizations into a new market should be *de novo*, i.e., through newly chartered subsidiaries or branches, where permitted, or by "toehold" or foothold acquisitions. Donald I. Baker described the Justice Department policy as follows:

The Department has a more general goal in our merger program—to prevent the largest banks in a state from attaining a position of overwhelming statewide dominance by systematic acquisition of the leading banks in local markets. Our approach is to encourage such banks to expand into new local markets, but only by *de novo* branching or by "foothold" acquisitions of lesser banks in these local markets.[21]

To a certain degree the federal bank regulators have encouraged a similar acquisition philosophy. In a recent review of Federal Reserve Board policy, Anne S. Weaver noted that:

> . . . the Board is concerned with the probability that a holding company will enter a market by the most pro-competitive means. If, instead of acquiring a market leader, the organization enters by acquiring a foothold bank or better, by establishing a new bank, competition will be intensified. This is the thinking behind [the doctrine of] "probable future competition."[22]

Entry into new markets via a foothold acquisition in some instances may have certain procompetitive effects. The expansion of large banking organizations is most likely to be limited to foothold or *de novo* entry when the organization is among the largest in its state and is considered, among other things, to be a likely potential entrant into the market whose entry would substantially deconcentrate the market and have significant procompetitive effects. Acquisitions of leading banks in the market are variously described as anticompetitive or less procompetitive. That is the announced policy of the Federal Reserve Board and FDIC, but that policy has not been universally held or uniformly applied by the three federal bank regulatory agencies.[23]

Policy of the Office of the Comptroller of the Currency

The Office of the Comptroller of the Currency (OCC) has taken a somewhat different approach, which it believes more accurately reflects the state of antitrust law today, and recognizes the realities of the marketplace and the appropriate role of bank regulators. The OCC's position was formally stated in its decision on a recent New Jersey merger case, which contains the following comment:[24]

> Although one might describe an even more desirable scenario of transactions, the Bank Merger Act and the Clayton Act do not contem-

plate regulatory or judicial speculation to divine and shape the *optimal* banking structure in a given market. Such a standard, in our judgment, would be almost impossible to administer. The Clayton Act deals with reasonable probabilities, not ephemeral possibilities. Moreover, we believe that a requirement that every transaction be optimal in terms of future competition is inconsistent with the thrust of the antitrust laws whose object is to prevent substantial anticompetitive behavior. The transaction before us is procompetitive and will lead to immediate tangible enhancement of the structure and performance of the markets in question. Therefore, it is not illegal and should not be disapproved.

In its handling of merger cases, the OCC attempts to maximize the procompetitive effects of legal mergers, to produce beneficial results for banking in the affected communities. Regulatory flexibility inherent in the decision-making process may be used to achieve those ends. For example, merger transactions may be used as the occasion to increase the number of strong competitors in a given area by requiring divestitures by the merging banks; and other commitments which significantly serve the convenience and needs of the community may be extracted from the merging banks by the regulators as a condition to approval.

Competitive Tests Applied to Foreign Banks

The preference for procompetitive entry, as previously described, has been imposed in the context of large domestic banking organizations' applications for within-state market extension mergers or acquisitions. A regulatory decision to limit a domestic firm's expansion to *de novo* entry or foothold acquisition would be based on considerations of the firm's existing market position in the state, its record of past expansion, and its demonstrated competitive capabilities. When a foreign bank is not already present within a state, such considerations clearly do not apply with comparable force; the foreign bank's competitive position is objectively different from that of an eligible (in-state) domestic bank or bank holding company acquirer. Because domestic restrictions on multistate expansion preclude entry through acquisition of large banks by noncompeting domestic banking organizations headquartered in other states, no potential domestic acquirer can be comparably situated, in competitive terms.

If the foreign organization already has an established position in the domestic market, the U.S. regulatory authority must consider that fact, and the analysis is more complicated. How to weigh a foreign bank's existing presence in competitive analysis is a question that has been addressed most explicitly by the New York State Banking Department. The question was posed as follows in connection with a 1973 ruling on a proposed merger of the Long Island Trust Company into the existing New York subsidiary of the Barclays Bank group:

> At the heart of the issue [i.e., application of antitrust principles to foreign banks] is the question: Should the Barclays group be regarded solely as a '$289 million bank' representing only New York State assets or as a '$24 billion bank' representing total worldwide assets or as something in between?[25]

New York Bank Superintendent Albright enunciated two "general principles" to apply to foreign bank expansion within New York by merger or acquisition:

> (i) the size of a foreign bank should be discounted to take into account the fact that the bulk of its assets were outside the United States and (ii) for reasons of fairness, the foreign bank should be treated in the same manner as a New York State headquartered bank comparable to the adjusted size of the foreign bank. To do otherwise would result in an unfair "double standard" favoring foreign banks over U.S. banks.[26]

Barclay's proposed acquisition of Long Island Trust, analyzed on this basis, was denied by New York State largely on potential competition grounds.[27] Barclays' subsequent proposal to acquire First Westchester National Bank was approved on the basis of a competitive analysis carefully distinguishing a different set of facts.[28]

If there is a regulatory preference for *de novo* entry or foothold acquisition, a key factor in the competitive analysis of a market extension merger or acquisition is a determination of the likelihood of the acquiring bank's expansion into the market by those alternative means. Since such alternatives are almost always possible, careful regulatory judgment is required.

> ... Virtually all market extension acquisitions or mergers result in the elimination of some "potential competition." The difficult question is, when should the elimination of "potential competition" be regarded as a significant adverse competitive factor? The answer is necessarily a question of judgment, depending on such factors as the size and market strength of the bank to be acquired, the quality of competition in the market, the capacity of the applicant to enter the market through a

smaller acquisition or by *de novo* branching and whether or not such entry by alternative means is reasonably likely. In this respect, the problem is one of distinguishing between "reasonable expectations" and "remote possibilities."[29]

Such considerations formed the basis for the New York Superintendent's distinction between the two Barclays applications. On similar grounds, a realistic judgment must be made about foreign banks' likely interest in U.S. markets and the likelihood of foreign entry by *de novo* expansion or foothold acquisition before ruling out any particular acquisition or restricting acquisitions in general. Foreign banks have generally served large business customers through branches, agencies or *de novo* subsidiaries. Acquisition of an established domestic bank often signals a foreign bank's desire to penetrate more deeply into other sections of the domestic market, including retail banking,[30] in addition to their more traditional servicing of larger firms and internationally oriented customers. If foreign banks were limited to *de novo* or foothold entry, their initiatives in such nontraditional areas might be stifled, and the result would be merely to "sacrifice mergers or acquisitions which were from a competitive perspective either neutral or procompetitive."[31]

More importantly, a restrictive policy would deny benefits noted in many large-bank acquisitions in which foreign buyers provided new capital or managerial resources that would otherwise have been unavailable to the acquired bank, and new services were expected to benefit the affected community. In his study of foreign takeovers, Donald Jacobs, recognizing that such benefits can and do flow from the strong backing provided acquired U.S. institutions by foreign bank acquirers, concluded that:

> . . . the major impact of foreign bank purchases on the U.S. intermediation system will be to increase the intensity of competition in these markets. Even though I believe commercial banking markets are now, for the most part, highly competitive, additional competition brought by an enhanced capital position of some existing participants would seem to be socially desirable. I see no reason to argue that destructive competition will arise. Nor do I think American banks are so competitively weak they need protection from large foreign banks. Thus, I conclude *benign neglect* is the appropriate public policy toward foreign banks' purchase of U.S. banks.[32]

Conclusion

Most foreign acquisitions have involved banks that were either relatively small in their market or newly chartered by the acquiring firm.

It is true that in some cases foreign institutions have been able to acquire larger U.S. banks than could domestic banking organizations, and that ability does constitute an advantageous means of establishing or building a presence in U.S. markets.[33] That result is not inconsistent with equal application of a competitive standard to domestic and foreign bank acquisitions. The foreign bank positions in the U.S. market have been nonexistent or minimal relative to those of eligible (in-state) domestic bank or bank holding company acquirers which, because of their different competitive positions, might have been denied a similar acquisition on the grounds of potential competition or "probable future competition." Limiting foreign banks' U.S. expansion to *de novo* entry or foothold acquisition would sacrifice potential gains and offer no clear prospect of offsetting benefits. Moreover, any such policy would discriminate against foreign investment, representing a breach of the present U.S. policy of neutrality toward international capital flows.[34]

The second question raised about regulatory consideration of competitive effects in foreign versus domestic acquisitions concerns possible impacts outside U.S. markets of large foreign takeovers.

FAILURE OF U. S. POLICY TO CONSIDER GLOBAL COMPETITIVE EFFECTS

Recognizing that U.S. banks compete with large multinational rivals in foreign markets as well as in this country and in the global financial arena generally, Senator Heinz has suggested that "serious problems" are raised by "the unique anticompetitive effects" of foreign bank takeovers. He observed that

> A foreign bank can be a substantial competitor of its U.S. target bank even though the foreign bank has no offices in the U.S., or even if its offices here appear insignificant when measured by local deposits and assets.[35]

In an article written after Lloyds' acquisition of First Western Bank, an academic observer noted that

> The [Federal Reserve] Board has not yet publicly voiced concern over the possibility that the addition of significant United States arms to worldwide banking monoliths may raise the question of restraint of global competition. . .[36]

...it may well be asked how much longer the question of global impact of multinational bank establishment in the United States can or will be avoided by looking only at the questions raised by the Bank Holding Company Act.[37]

The issue posed here is: To what extent can or should worldwide competitive effects be taken into account in U.S. regulatory decisions on foreign banks' proposed acquisitions of U.S. financial institutions? Apart from considering the applicable standards in U.S. law, there is a question of how relevant or serious such global competitive effects actually may be.

The Bank Holding Company Act and Bank Merger Act direct the agencies to consider competitive effects in terms of domestic markets, i.e., "in any part of the United States," or "in any section of the country."[38] This language would appear to limit U.S. agencies' competitive analysis to domestic market effects. That has been the Federal Reserve Board's practice, which is also in keeping with its general policy on regulation of foreign bank holding companies.[39] Given the extraterritorial nature of the issue, it seems that any attempt to control "restraint of global banking competition" is inherently beyond the reach of any sovereign authority.[40]

In practice, U.S. regulators' evaluations of competitive effects of proposed foreign bank acquisitions have focused almost entirely on the local or metropolitan area market(s) involved. This is true of the competitive analysis of merger and acquisition applications generally. In its recent decisions on large foreign bank holding company acquisitions, the Federal Reserve Board has commented on competitive effects beyond the acquired bank's metropolitan market(s) or its home state. In its decision on the NatWest case, the Board noted that some competition in the national market would be eliminated.[41] With regard to Hongkong and Shanghai Banking Corporation's acquisition of Marine Midland Banks, Inc., the Board commented that the proposal would have significant effects in national and international markets, because of a strengthening of Marine Midland's competitive abilities.[42] The Board's recent decisions cite the acquiring organizations' global ranks and describe their worldwide operations, signalling an awareness of possible global competitive effects.

A particular proposal may have competitive effects in international financial markets, by either reducing or stimulating competition in overseas markets, by increasing concentration of banking resources worldwide, or by affecting global rankings, but at the same time may have no appreciable impact on U.S. markets. Under the present statutory language, an application probably could not be denied on such grounds even if the Board concluded that the worldwide competitive position of U.S. banks would be adversely affected. The Board has not indicated any concern about those matters and, in fact, it is hard to conceive of how any specific transaction would have an adverse competitive effect that is relevant to U.S. interests.

The worldwide standing of individual foreign banks may be enhanced by acquisition of large U.S. institutions, but the number of such cases remains small and their aggregate impact quite minor.[43]

Concentration of global banking resources is marginally increased by foreign banks' acquisitions of large U.S. financial institutions. However, even if that were a mandated concern of United States regulators, denial of specific applications or even a ban on foreign takeovers would hardly affect the overall trends, which are affected much more significantly by fundamental economic forces and policies of authorities in other countries.[44]

Finally, a foreign bank's acquisition of a U.S. bank with multinational operations may eliminate actual or potential competition between the two institutions in some foreign markets or competition between them for the business of substantial clients in the U.S. However, it would be difficult to argue that preservation of competition in foreign banking markets is a legitimate focus of U.S. policy or that reduction by one of the number of large bank competitors would have a significant effect in either the "national" U.S. market or international banking markets.

Conclusion

There appears to be little of immediate or serious consequence in the fact that United States policy on foreign acquisitions looks only at their effects on domestic markets. Although the law could be broadened to mandate consideration of global competitive effects, the practical impact of such a change would appear inconsequential or irrelevant to the practical scope of United States policy.

Acknowledgments

C. F. Muckenfuss III, Wm. Paul Smith and Thomas P. Vartanian provided helpful comments and material to improve earlier drafts of the paper and Mark Au assisted with the research.

FOOTNOTES

[1] Donald L. Flexner, Testimony before the Senate Committee on Banking, Housing, and Urban Affairs, in Hearings on *Edge Corporation Branching; Foreign Bank Takeovers; and International Banking Facilities*, 96th Cong., 1st Sess., July 23, 1979, p. 23.

[2] *Ibid.*

[3] For a discussion of the statutes governing acquisitions and mergers of U.S. banking organizations (Bank Holding Company Act, Bank Merger Act, and Change of Bank Control Act), see John E. Shockey and William B. Glidden, *Foreign-Controlled U.S. Banks: The Legal and Regulatory Environment*, OCC Staff Paper, 1980.

[4] See data in the Appendix to this paper.

[5] For an analysis of the impact of those restrictions on U.S. banking organizations' domestic acquisition opportunities, see Wm. Paul Smith and Steven J. Weiss, *Potential Acquisition Partners for Large U.S. Banks: Discriminatory Effects of Law and Policy*, OCC Staff Paper, 1980.

[6] Indirect acquisition of U.S. banks may be effected by merger of a U.S. bank into an existing U.S.-chartered bank subsidiary of a foreign banking institution.

[7] This review does not cover foreign acquisitions of newly established (*de novo*) banks, which constitute a significant proportion of foreign ownership of U.S. banks. See William A. Longbrake, Melanie Quinn and Judith A. Walter, *Foreign Ownership of U.S. Banks: Facts and Patterns*, OCC Staff Paper, 1980.

[8] The "appropriate" agency, which is determined by the charter status of the resulting bank, may be the Federal Deposit Insurance Corporation, Federal Reserve Board, or the Comptroller of the Currency.

[9] For a discussion of the potential competition and "probable future competition" doctrines, see Anne S. Weaver, "Bank Holding Companies: Competitive Issues and Policy," Federal Reserve Bank of Chicago, *Economic Perspectives*, September/October 1979.

[10] Anticompetitive concerns may be overriden in order to allow takeover or rescue of a failing or failed bank. A significant proportion of foreign-acquired U.S. banks have been weak or failing institutions. (See Longbrake, Quinn and Walter, *op. cit.*).

[11] For example, in its order approving the acquisition of First Western Bank and Trust by Lloyds Bank Ltd., the Board found that "the proposal may increase competition, as affiliation with Lloyds should make Bank a stronger and more vigorous competitor of other California banks in local banking markets throughout the state." *Federal Reserve Bulletin*, February 1974, p. 125.

[12] Federal Reserve Board order approving the acquisition of Union Bank by Standard Chartered Bank, Ltd., *Federal Reserve Bulletin*, April 1979, pp. 350-353.

[13] For a critical review of the Board's competitive analysis in this case, and the two other major large-bank acquisition cases (NatWest-NBNA and Hongkong and Shanghai-Marine Midland), see Dennis J. Lehr and Benton R. Hammond, "Regulating Foreign Acquisition of U.S. Banks: The CBCA and the BHCA," *Banking Law Journal*, vol. 90, no. 2, (February 1980), pp. 136-147.

[14] For example, in its decision approving the merger of the Mitsubishi Bank of California with Hacienda Bank, the FDIC observed that:

> Mitsubishi has specialized in commercial and international banking, establishing its offices in areas where such business may best be developed. Hacienda Bank, in contrast, has concentrated on retail banking and its primary trade areas are residential communities. (FDIC, *Annual Report*, 1976, p. 77).

[15] For example, in its decision approving the merger of Chartered Bank of London with Commercial and Farmers NB, the FDIC found that "while the proposed merger would eliminate some potential competition, in view of the proponents' relative sizes and the dominance of the relevant markets by a small number of institutions, this is not viewed as significant." (FDIC *Annual Report*, 1977, p. 106.)

[16] Testimony before the House Subcommittee on Commerce, Consumer and Monetary Af-

fairs, in Hearings on *The Operations of Federal Agencies in Monitoring, Reporting on, and Analyzing Foreign Investments in the United States (Part 4—Foreign Investments in U.S. Banks)*, 96th Cong., 1st Sess., July 31, 1979, p. 26.

[17] Douglas V. Austin, "Banking Structure Equality Sacrificed in the Name of Anti-trust," *American Banker*, No. 183, September 21, 1979, p. 4.

[18] Greenwald, *op. cit.*, p. 25.

[19] H. R. 5937, the "Foreign Bank Takeovers Study Act," introduced by Rep. Rosenthal on November 27, 1979, would exempt "toehold" acquisitions from a moratorium on foreign acquisitions of U.S. banks. The bill defines "toehold" to mean "a small position generally less than 20 percentum and not including any of the leading institutions in any market, as determined by the applicable Federal depository institution regulatory agency" (section 2(6)).

[20] Opening Remarks by Senator Proxmire, Senate Committee on Banking, Housing, and Urban Affairs, Hearings on *Edge Corporation Branching, Foreign Bank Takeovers; and International Banking Facilities*, 96th Cong., 1st Sess., July 16, 1979, p. 1.

[21] Donald I. Baker, "Competition's Role in the Regulation of Banking," *The Bankers Magazine*, Summer 1971, p. 79.

[22] Weaver, *op. cit.*, p. 20.

[23] Critics have argued that the administration of the Bank Merger Act by the three agencies has been characterized by a lack of uniform standards (See U.S. Senate, Committee on Governmental Affairs, *Study of Federal Regulation*, vol. V, "Regulatory Organization," December 1977, pp. 213-15).

[24] Decision of the Comptroller of the Currency on the Application of First National State Bank of Central Jersey, . . . (May 9, 1979), p. 23. See also the OCC brief filed in *U.S.* v. *First National State Bancorp, et al.* (D. N. J., Civil Action No. 79-1975).

[25] Recommendation of New York Superintendent of Banks, quoted in New York State Banking Department, "Application of Barclays Bank of New York for permission to merge First Westchester National Bank," January 8, 1974, p. 4 (cited hereinafter as "Westchester decision").

[26] *Ibid.* Superintendent Siebert, in her report on the proposed acquisition of Marine Midland by Hongkong and Shanghai Banking Corp. (HSBC) stated that ". . . HSBC must be considered for purposes of this application, not merely a $239 million bank (which represents the deposits of its New York City branches) but rather similar to the size of several of the major New York banks". "Report of the Superintendent of Banks of New York State on the Proposed Acquisition by the Hongkong and Shanghai Banking Corporation of Marine Midland Banks, Inc.," June 29, 1979, pp. 12-13.

[27] Westchester decision, p. 13. Ironically, in light of subsequent arguments that foreign banks enjoy an unfair advantage in acquiring U.S. banks, the decision was viewed with concern by some foreign observers as "denying fair treatment to foreign institutions seeking to enter the New York market" (*Ibid.*, p. 4). See also "NY Ruling Against Barclays Resented," *New York Times*, May 19, 1973, p. 49. *The Banker*, noting that acquisition opportunities are increasingly limited by regulatory authorities, commented that "It is becoming doubtful whether there are many attractive parts of the world, *even outside Long Island*, where a bank like Barclays would now be allowed to take over a considerable retail bank" ("Obstacle Course for Bankers," *The Banker*, June 1973, p. 611) [emphasis added].

[28] See Westchester decision. In its advisory report on competitive factors to the Federal Reserve Board, which approved the merger, the FDIC stated that:

> Both banks under present State law may branch *de novo* in Westchester County and throughout New York City. However, both banks are of relatively modest size in their markets and the intense competition of numerous alternatives for banking services available in these markets would render of slight competitive significance any elimination of potential *de novo* competition between them that might result from their proposed merger.

[29] Westchester decision, p. 12.

[30] See Judith A. Walter, *Foreign Acquisitions of U.S. Banks: Motives and Tactical Considerations*, OCC Staff Paper, 1980.

[31] Flexner, *op. cit.*, p. 39.

[32] Donald P. Jacobs, "Proposed Public Policy on the Purchase of American Banks," unpublished paper, Northwestern University, Graduate School of Management, p. 10.

[33] The advantage in terms of acquired market share should not be overstated, for it may dissipate through time. Empirical studies of domestic bank holding company acquisitions have demonstrated a tendency for large bank market shares to *decline* after acquisitions by an outside holding company; moreover, post-acquisition loss of market share tends to be larger in the case of acquisitions by the largest holding companies. See Bernard Shull, "Multiple-Office Banking and the Structure of Banking Markets: The New York and Virginia Experience," *Conference on Bank Structure and Competition*, Federal Reserve Bank of Chicago, 1972, and "The Structural Impact of Multiple-Office Banking in New York and Virginia," *Antitrust Bulletin*, vol. 23, Fall 1978; and James Burke, "Bank Holding Company Behavior and Structural Change," *Journal of Bank Research*, vol. 23, Spring 1978. Other studies, somewhat limited in their scope or method relative to those previously cited, have found no significant (systematic) impact of foothold acquisition on market structure (Stephen A. Rhoades, "The Impact of Foothold Acquisitions on Bank Market Structure," *Antitrust Bulletin*, vol. 22, Spring 1977, or no major changes in market shares of banks acquired by bank holding companies (Donald R. Fraser, "Holding Company Affiliation and Commercial Bank Market Share," *Antitrust Bulletin*, Winter 1978; and Lawrence G. Goldberg, "Bank Holding Company Acquisitions and Their Impact on Market Shares," *Journal of Money, Credit and Banking*, vol. 3, February 1976).

[34] See discussion and references cited in Steven J. Weiss, *A Critical Evaluation of Reciprocity in Foreign Bank Acquisitions*, OCC Staff Paper, 1980.

[35] Senator John Heinz III, "Foreign Takeovers of U.S. Banking—A Real Danger?,"*The Journal of the Institute for Socioeconomic Studies*, vol. 3 (Autumn 1979), p. 6.

[36] Cynthia Crawford Lichtenstein, "Foreign Participation in United States Banking: Regulatory Myths and Realities," *Boston College Industrial and Commercial Law Review*, vol. XV, no. 5 (May 1974), pp. 967-8. The author notes that the Board "has no mandate to consider such a problem" and suggests that the Lloyds case "conceivably . . . raises the issue . . . The combination presumably has some impact on some markets (if only on the multinational competition between Lloyds and Barclays)" (*Ibid.*, p. 968).

[37] *Ibid.*, p. 971. Similarly, Carol Greenwald asked, "In an increasingly interrelated world economy, should we have no concern about concentration in the world or in parts of the world larger than nations?" ("Let's Put a Hold on Foreign Take-overs of Our Banks," *The Bankers Magazine*, November/December, 1979, p. 52).

[38] A bill proposed by the Federal Financial Institutions Examination Council to provide for interstate domestic takeovers in extraordinary (emergency) situations contains broader language: an acquisition under the extraordinary procedures could be denied if it was believed to pose an adverse effect on "competition, or upon the concentration of financial resources in any state, region, or the nation" as a whole (Proposal dated April 9, 1980).

[39] See "Statement of Policy on Supervision and Regulation of Foreign Bank Holding Companies," Federal Reserve Board Release, February 23, 1979.

[40] Lichtenstein notes that "there is a form of multinational antitrust standard in Articles 85 and 86 of the Treaty of Rome, but the day when the Charter of the United Nations will be amended to provide for a review of the global competitive impact of multinational acquisitions seems a long way away" (*op. cit.*, p. 968, note 323).

[41] "NatWest also operates one branch office in the [NYC] market [where all but three of NBNA's 142 branches are located], which does not provide a full range of banking services to individuals, but rather offers commercial banking services to large national and international organizations. While NBNA also competes for commercial banking business on a national basis, the aggregate amount of NBNA and the NatWest branch of such commercial banking business in the country or in any other relevant area is not significant." (*Federal Reserve Bulletin*, April 1979, p. 358).

[42] "... the added support that would be provided under this proposal would permit [Marine Midland] to grow in a more orderly way and to become a more aggressive competitor, thereby benefiting the communities it serves ... the effect of this increased financial and competitive strength would be felt statewide, but it would also have a significant effect in national and international markets ...." (*Ibid.*, p. 355).

[43] See C. Stewart Goddin and Steven J. Weiss, *U. S. Banks' Loss of Global Standing*, OCC Staff Paper, 1980.

[44] *Ibid.*

APPENDIX

The tables in this Appendix present some summary information on acquisitions of U.S. banks by foreign banking organizations and bank regulatory agencies' decisions approving the acquisitions. The first table covers direct acquisitions by foreign banks and the second covers indirect acquisitions effected by merger of a bank into an existing foreign bank-controlled U.S. subsidiary bank.

The first four columns identify the acquiring foreign organizations and the acquired banks and show their size at the time of acquisition (measured by total assets or deposits). In the second table, this information is given for both the foreign banks and their existing U.S. subsidiaries that were involved in the transactions.

The next three columns contain notes based on the regulatory agencies' decisions indicating (1) presence of the acquiring organizations in the relevant market(s) of the acquired bank prior to the acquisition; (2) the agencies' judgments regarding competitive effects of the proposed acquisitions; and (3) positive effects noted by the agencies with regard to other factors besides competition, i.e., capital infusion, benefits to convenience and needs of the affected communities, and/or anticipated improvements in management or future prospects of the acquired bank.

For reference purposes, the last two columns give the dates of the decisions and citations.

Name and Nationality of Acquiring Bank or Bank Holding Company	Size of Acquiring Banking Organization [Assets (A) or Deposits (D) in $ billions]^a	Name of Acquired Bank or Bank Holding Company	Size of Acquiring Bank or Holding Company [Deposits $ millions
The Royal Trust Co., Canada	1.6 (A)	Inter National Bank of Miami	43
Lloyds Bank, Ltd., United Kingdom	13.4 (A) 12.4 (D)	First Western Bank & Trust Company	1.1 bill.
The Bank of Nova Scotia, Canada	12.1 (D)	Banco Mercantile de Puerto Rico	87
The Royal Trust Co., Canada	3.2 (A)	Lale Mabry State Bank	5.2
The Royal Trust Co., Canada	3.4 (A)	The First Bank of Gulfport	21.3
Banco de Santander, S. A., Spain	3.2 (D)	FNB of Puerto Rico	29.3
The Royal Trust Co., Canada	3.4 (A)	North Avenue NB	27
Banco Union, C. A., Venezuela	1.1 (A) 1.0 (D)	Union Chelsea NB	28
The Royal Trust Co., Canada	3.7 (A)	First Bank of Pembroke Pines	13.3
The Royal Trust Co., Canada	4.1 (A)	Baymeadows Bank	7.4
Banco Central, S. A., Spain	8.5 (A) 7.2 (D)	Banco Economias	199
Metropolitan Bank & Trust Co., Philippines	0.2 (D)	International Bank of California	4.4

Direct Acquisitions by Foreign Banking Organizations and United States Agency Decisions

Presence of Acquiring Firm in the Relevant Market(s)	Agency's Judgment Regarding Competitive Effects	Positive Effects Noted Regarding Other Factors[b]	Date and Citation of Agency Decision
None	May promote competition.	+ Capital + C & N	6/16/72 F. R. Bull., 7/72 pp. 665-66
None	Procompetitive.	+ Capital + Management + C & N	12/10/73 F. R. Bull., 2/74 pp. 125-26
4 branches ($80.5 mill. deposits)	Anticompetitive effects (outweighed by other factors)	+ Management + C & N + Future Prosp.	4/9/75 F. R. Bull., 5/75 pp. 309-10
None	No significant effects (foothold entry)	None	4/23/76 F. R. Bull., 5/76 pp. 453-54
None	No significant effects (foothold entry)	None	6/11/76 F. R. Bull., 7/76 pp. 623-24
Rep. ofcs.	Procompetitive (foothold entry)	+ Capital + Management + Future Prosp.	7/30/76 F. R. Bull., 8/76 pp. 690-91
None	Procompetitive (foothold entry)	+ Capital	10/29/76 F. R. Bull., 11/76 pp. 962-63
Agency	Procompetitive	+ Capital + C & N + Future Prosp.	12/31/76 F. R. Bull., 1/77 pp. 61-63
Subsidiary Banks ($80.3 mill. deposits)	No significant adverse effects.	+ C & N	2/7/77 F. R. Bull., 3/77 pp. 277-79
None	Procompetitive (foothold entry)	+ C & N	4/8/77 F. R. Bull., 5/77 pp. 498-99
None	Procompetitive	+ C & N + Future Prosp.	7/1/77 F. R. Bull., 8/77 pp. 841-42
Agency	Procompetitive	+ Management	8/10/77 F. R. Bull., 9/77 pp. 935-38

Name and Nationality of Acquiring Bank or Bank Holding Company	Size of Acquiring Banking Organization [Assets (A) or Deposits (D) in $ billions][a]	Name of Acquired Bank or Bank Holding Company	Size of Acquiring Bank or Holding Company [Deposits $ millions][a]
Banco Exterior de Espana, S. A., Spain	3.3 (A) 2.2 (D)	Century NB & Trust Co.	33
The Royal Trust Co., Canada	4.7 (A)	The American Bank of Orange County	9.7
Banco Nacional de Mexico, S. A., Mexico	2.1 (D)	Community Bank of San Jose	64.7
The Hongkong & Shanghai Banking Corp., Hong Kong	13.0 (D)	Marine Midland Banks, Inc.	7.0 bill.
National Westminster Bank, Ltd., United Kingdom	38.5 (A)	National Bank of North America	2.3 bill.
Standard Chartered Bank, Ltd., United Kingdom	18.0 (A)	Union Bank	4.0 bill.
Algemene Bank Nederland, N. V., Netherlands	38.0 (A)	La Salle National Bank	747.3

[a]Data from agency decisions; assets in $ billions where indicated.

[b]Notations in this column indicate cases where the agency decision specifically mentioned injections of capital of benefits to the convenience and needs (C & N) of the affected community, anticipated strengthening of the acquired bank's management or enhancement of its future prospects a factors that lent weight toward approval. In some cases, the acquired bank was failing or failed an "+ Future Prospects" indicates an emergency takeover.

Presence of Acquiring Firm in the Relevant Market(s)	Agency's Judgment Regarding Competitive Effects	Positive Effects Noted Regarding Other Factors[b]	Date and Citation of Agency Decision
None	No significant effects.	None	11/2/77 F. R. Bull., 5/78 pp. 1079
None	Procompetitive (foothold entry)	None	4/5/78 F. R. Bull., 5/78 pp. 404-05
None	No significant effects.	None	5/19/78 F. R. Bull., 6/78 pp. 488-89
2 Branches ($204 mill. deposits)	Slightly	+ Capital + C & N	3/16/79 F. R. Bull., 4/79 pp. 354-57
Branch	No significant effects.	+ Capital + C & N	3/16/79 F. R. Bull., 4/79 pp. 357-60
Subsidiary bank ($399 mill. deposits)	No significant effects.	+ Capital + C & N	3/16/79 F. R. Bull., 4/79 pp. 350-52
Branch ($28 mill. deposits)	No significant effects.	+ Capital	7/13/79 F. R. Bull., 8/79 pp. 658-59

Name and Nationality of Acquiring Bank (Name of U.S. Subsidiary)	Total Assets of Acquiring Bank[a] (Total Assets of U.S. Subsidiary)[a] ($ millions)	Name of Acquired Bank	Total Assets of Acquired Bank ($ millions)[c]
Canadian Imperial Bank of Commerce, Canada (California Canadian Bank)	$ 6,208[f] 73	Northern California National Bank	$ 8.5
Canadian Imperial Bank of Commerce, Canada (California Canadian Bank)	8,629 93	City Bank of San Diego	18.6
Barclays Bank, Ltd., United Kingdom (Barclays Bank of California)	15,137 66	First Valley Bank	48.1
Hongkong & Shanghai Banking Corp., Hong Kong (The Hongkong & Shanghai Banking Corp. of California)	3,713 91	Republic National Bank & Trust Company	25.1
Sanwa Bank, Ltd., Japan (The Sanwa Bank of California)	25,449 66	Charter Bank	27.6
Barclays Bank, Ltd., United Kingdom (Barclays Bank of New York)	28,302 48.5[b]	First Westchester National Bank	178[b]
Standard & Chartered Bank, Ltd., United Kingdom (Chartered Bank of London)	8,457 59	Liberty National Bank	101.4
Barclays Bank, Ltd., United Kingdom (Barclays Bank of California)	28,302 304	The County Bank	44.6
Consortium:		Franklin National Bank	3.6 bill.
Amsterdam-Rotterdam Bank, Netherlands	9,682		
Creditanstalk-Bankverein, Austria	4,049		
Deutsche Bank, A. E., West Germany	24,555		
Midland Bank, Ltd., United Kingdom	19,416		
Societe General de Banque, S. A., Belgium	9,064		
Societe Generale, France (European-American Bank & Trust Co.)	24,157 366		
Tokai Bank, Ltd., Japan (Centinela Bank)	21,040 28	Tokai Bank of California	44.8
Bank of Tokyo, Japan (The Bank of Tokyo of California)	23,712 917	Southern California First National Bank	884.1
Lloyds Bank, Ltd., United Kingdom (Lloyds Bank of California)	20,026 1,300	First State Bank of Northern California	63.1

Presence of Acquiring Bank[d] (and Existing Subsidiary) in Relevant Market(s)	Agency's Judgment Regarding Competitive Effects	Positive Effects Noted Regarding Other Factors[e]	Date and Citation of Agency Decision
None	No adverse effects.	+ Management + C & N	7/21/66 FDIC Ann. Rpt. '66 pp. 50-51
None	No adverse effects.	+ C & N	3/27/69 FDIC Ann. Rpt. '69 pp. 45-46
None	No adverse effects.	+ C & N	10/17/69 FDIC Ann. Rpt. '69 pp. 101-3
(Proximity of offices in one market.)	No significant effects.	+ C & N	11/10/70 FDIC Ann. Rpt. '70 pp. 107-09
(Proximity of offices in one market.)	Procompetitive	+ C & N + Future Prosp.	11/29/73 FDIC Ann. Rpt. '73 pp. 125-27
2 direct branches of parent bank [deposits of $159 mill.] (Offices in same market)	No significant effects.	+ C & N	4/24/74 Federal Register 5/21/74 Vol. 39, p. 115353
(Proximity of offices in one market.)	No significant effects.	+ C & N	5/31/74 FDIC Ann. Rpt. '74 pp. 79-81
(Slight proximity of offices in one market.)	No significant effects.	+ C & N	10/1/74 FDIC Ann. Rpt. '74 pp. 131-32
N/A	N/A	(Failed Bank)	10/8/74 FDIC Ann. Rpt. '74 p. 138
(Slight proximity of offices in one market.)	No adverse effects.	+ Management + Future Prosp.	7/11/75 FDIC Ann. Rpt. '75 pp. 73-75
(Proximity of offices in three markets.)	Minimal anti-competitive effects.	+ Capital/+ C & N + Management + Future Prosp.	7/25/75 FDIC Ann. Rpt. '75 pp. 77-81
N/A	N/A	(Failed bank)	5/22/76 FDIC Ann. Rpt. '76 p. 71

325

Name and Nationality of Acquiring Bank (Name of U.S. Subsidiary)	Total Assets of Acquiring Bank[a] (Total Assets of U.S. Subsidiary)[a] ($ millions)	Name of Acquired Bank	Total Assets of Acquired Bank ($ millions)[c]
Mitsubishi Bank, Ltd., Japan (The Mitsubishi Bank of California)	30,147 139	Hacienda Bank	56.9
Bank Leumi le Israel, Israel (Bank Leumi Trust Company of New York)	7,905 491	American Bank & Trust Company	267.7
Standard Chartered Bank, Ltd. United Kingdom (The Chartered Bank of London)	15,805 285	Commercial and Farmers National Bank	101.0
The Sanwa Bank, Ltd., Japan (Golden State Sanwa Bank)	40,251 250	Golden State Bank	132.0
Banco de Santander, S. A., Spain (Banco de Santander-Puerto Rico)	10,459 52	Banco Credito y Ahorro Ponceno	197.0

[a]The figures for total consolidated assets of the acquiring parent bank are derived from *The Banker* (London) annual listing of the "Top 300" commercial banks. With minor exceptions, the asset figu presented for each parent institution is as of the close of account date most nearly preceding the a quisition decision date.

[b]The asset figure for Canadian Imperial Bank was derived from *Polk's World Bank Director* March 1966 (143 ed.). The close of account date was 31 October, 1965. This substitution of sourc was necessitated by the fact that *The Banker* s listing of the "Top 300" did not commence until 197

[c]Figures as cited in agency decision; assets in $ billions where indicated.

[d]Deposits.

[e]Indicated here only when noted in agency decision.

[f]See explanatory note to previous table.

Presence of Acquiring Bank[d] (and Existing Subsidiary) in Relevant Market(s)	Agency's Judgment Regarding Competitive Effects	Positive Effects Noted Regarding Other Factors[e]	Date and Citation of Agency Decision
(Minimal proximity of offices.)	No significant effects.	None	6/25/76 FDIC Ann. Rpt. '76 pp. 76-77
N/A	N/A	(Failed bank)	9/15/76 FDIC Ann. Rpt. '76 p. 85
None	No significant effects.	+ C & N	11/21/77 FDIC Ann. Rpt. '77 pp. 105-06
(Proximity of offices in one market.)	No significant effects.	None	12/27/77 FDIC Ann. Rpt. '77 p. 108
N/A	N/A	(Failed bank)	3/31/78 FDIC Ann. Rpt. '78 p. 62

10

SUPERVISORY PERFORMANCE OF FOREIGN–CONTROLLED U.S. BANKING ORGANIZATIONS

JUDITH A. WALTER

SUMMARY

This paper presents the results of a review by experienced examiners of the performance and condition of 35 United States banks controlled by foreigners. Its purpose is to gain insight into the prudential aspects of foreign ownership of United States banking organizations.

The results of this review, which is almost totally reliant upon examination reports and correspondence files, shows that foreign ownership of United States banks has presented no problems significantly different nor greater than for United States banks as a whole.

Although the paper uses a four-part breakdown of the total sample into "pure" *de novo* foreign-owned banks, *de novo* foreign-owned banks that subsequently acquired United States banks, banks acquired by foreign banks and banks acquired by foreign individuals, it finds the distinction between foreign bank owners and foreign individual owners to be most worthy of note.

From a supervisory standpoint, the ownership of the 22 banks by foreign banking institutions appears to pose no special concerns since the United States banks possess sound balance sheets and conservative management. The paper also observes that after acquisition by foreign banks, prospects for existing United States banks have appeared better, according to examiners.

The 13 banks acquired by foreign individuals present a more mixed picture, ranging from sound, well-run institutions to some below average and requiring special supervisory attention. In general, it appears that when foreign individuals have acquired banks with supervisory problems, the overall ratings have not improved substantially even though there may be favorable trends in specific areas. Importantly, problems that are noted appear mostly to be carry-overs from previous United States owners and not generally related to the fact of foreign ownership.

METHODOLOGY

To gain insight into the prudential aspects of foreign ownership of United States banking organizations, experienced Comptroller of the Currency (OCC) examiners reviewed examination reports (and correspondence files when possible) of a sample of foreign-owned United States banks.

The sample consists of 35 banks[1] known to be foreign-controlled.[2] The majority of the sample banks are located in California, New York, and Florida. The foreign owners are from 17 countries: Europe and Canada (15 banks), Latin America (8 banks), Asia (9 banks) and other regions (3 banks).[3] The sample banks range in size from less than $10 million to approximately $4 billion (assets on December 30, 1979). Most cases of foreign ownership that were accomplished by acquisition in 1979 were eliminated from the sample because a post-acquisition examination had not yet been conducted.

This review focused on the supervisory performance from 1974 to the present. When judgments about a bank's condition prior to 1974 were important to the review, knowledgeable examiners in the field were consulted. In addition, examiners were contacted to gather pertinent, current information not yet included in examination files. Information developed during the review was summarized systematically for each bank. Composite ratings were recorded, along with ratings and/or brief narratives on management, assets, capital, earnings, and violations of law. For comparison, individual bank summaries were subsequently put into four groups: (1) "pure" *de novo* foreign owned banks; (2) *de novo* foreign-owned banks that subsequently acquired United States banks; (3) banks acquired by foreign banks; and (4) banks acquired by foreign individuals.

In attempting to determine the prudential characteristics of foreign-owned United States banks, reviewers relied on the quantitative measurements and qualitative judgments normally used by bank examiners in assessing the safety and soundness of a bank. For reports of examination, various ratios are computed to evaluate financial performance and operating condition. These are supplemented with evaluations of such factors as compliance with law, adequacy of internal controls, and management's ability to administer and plan for the future. All three federal commercial bank regulators now use a system of numerical ratings for five areas of bank performance—capital adequacy, asset quality, management/administration, earnings, liquidity. An overall, or composite, rating is derived from those ratings and other pertinent factors to reflect, as comprehensively as possible, a bank's general condition and soundness.

Ratings are based on a scale of one through five, in ascending order of supervisory concern. For the specific areas of performance, the numerical ratings and their shorthand descriptions are:

1   strong
2   satisfactory
3   fair (below average)
4   marginal
5   unsatisfactory

Composite ratings incorporate the whole complex of factors judged to have significant bearing on the overall condition and soundness of a bank. Briefly, the distinctions are:

1   Basically sound. Criticisms are minor. Banks in this group are more capable than others of withstanding the vagaries of business conditions.
2   Sound. Weaknesses are correctable and do not undermine the bank's basic stability.
3   Weak. A combination of financial and operational weakness, and/or lack of compliance with law or regulation may make the bank vulnerable to adverse business conditions.
4   Seriously weak. A high volume of serious weaknesses require effective action to avoid impairing the future viability of the bank.
5   Volume and severity of weaknesses require urgent attention to avoid regulatory intervention.

The primary purpose of the rating system is to identify banks requiring special supervisory attention and/or concern. Banks with a composite rating of 3 are considered to have deficiencies warranting extra attention but are not deemed to pose significant risks. Those with composite ratings of 4 or 5 are characterized by some seriously unsatisfactory conditions that carry a relatively high possibility of failure or insolvency, and, thus, require close supervisory attention.

The supervisory agencies include all banks rated 3, 4, or 5 in a centrally administered program of special supervisory attention. Thus, in reviewing examination reports and files for the 35 sample banks, special scrutiny was given to banks with composite ratings of 3 or lower. In particular, reviewers attempted to discern trends and noteworthy characteristics of each bank's condition that might be linked to, or reflect upon, its ownership.

OVERVIEW OF FINDINGS

The review indicated that 20 of the 22 banks established or acquired by foreign banks (those in the first three groups) are in sound condition, with composite ratings of 2 or 1 and few problems. The two remaining banks are currently rated 3. When a troubled or failing bank was acquired, in all but one case capital injections and/or stronger management provided by the parent bank have resulted in an improved condition. When stronger banks were acquired, favorable ratings have been maintained.

Acquisitions by individuals (the fourth group) are more difficult to summarize. The banks in that group are divided almost evenly between those now considered to be in sound condition (six banks with composite ratings of 1 or 2) and those felt to be relatively weak (seven banks with composite ratings of 3). None currently is in serious or near-failing condition. In general, it appears that when foriegn individuals have acquired banks with supervisory problems, the overall ratings have not improved substantially even though there may be favorable trends in specific areas. For most banks that were in satisfactory condition at the time of acquisition, favorable ratings have been maintained or slightly improved. There is only one instance of clear deterioration from a satisfactory condition following acquisition.

The problem of identifying affiliated businesses[4] appeared to be the only prudential concern more often associated with foreign-owned banks. Examiners cited this as a problem at four banks owned by individuals. Although in no case did they consider this a critical problem, reviewers did believe that it was less frequent in cases of domestic ownership. Apart from the difficulty of identifying affiliates, reviewers concluded that the 13 sample banks did not differ significantly from similarly rated banks with domestic owners.

In the sections that follow, each of the four groups of foreign ownership—"pure" *de novo* banks; *de novo* banks that subsequently made acquisitions; acquisitions by foreign banks; and acquisitions by foreign individuals—is considered separately. For each group, there are general observations and highlights of the reviewers' findings in specific areas.

"Pure" De Novo Banks

Of the eight pure *de novo* banks in the sample, two were established in the 1920s, one in the 1950s, and five in the early to mid-1970s. Generally, they share a wholesale and international orientation. Examiners characterized several as "essentially a branch" of the foreign parent bank. Each of these banks had a composite rating of 2 or 1. Senior management is provided on a rotational basis by the parent and, with one exception, management ratings are satisfactory and senior executives described as "knowledgeable," "professional," "competent," and/or "capable."

- Asset quality ratings for seven of the eight banks were in the two most favorable categories at the most recent examination, and this appears to have been true historically.
- Loan portfolios are typically comprised of a high volume of loans to United States subsidiaries of home country companies. Frequently a portion of those is purchased from the parent bank. For all but one of these banks, examiners have repeatedly noted loan concentrations[5] to home country customers and have made observations such as "[bank's] activities complement those of the worldwide group."
- Insider loans[6] are not a factor for these banks. Such activity was found in only one bank and it was in conformance with United States law and regulation and was not criticized by examiners.[7]
- Recent evaluations of earnings of these banks are a mixture of "fair" (three banks) and "satisfactory" (five banks). These banks generally have retained 100 percent of earnings; however, one commenced cash dividends in 1978.

- Three of the eight have the best ratings for capital adequacy; the other five are in the next highest rating category. Parent banks have "historically supplied capital when needed."

- There is no consistent pattern of serious violations of law[8] for any bank in this group.

- Internal controls are judged to be good for most of these banks.

Other than loan concentrations related to home country customers, the characteristics shared by pure *de novo* foreign owned banks appear to be mainly in the area of adjusting to United States banking practices. There are several instances, all associated with newly formed banks or a new rotation of senior officers, in which examiners commented on difficulties arising from "unfamiliarity with United States banking practices." A specific example was "weaknesses in documenting collateral in accordance with usual United States custom." In all such instances, there were no similar comments on the subsequent examination or there was evidence that problems pointed out were being corrected.

De Novo Foreign Owned Banks That
Subsequently Acquired U. S. Banks

There are nine banks in this group. Two were founded in the 1950s, five in the 1960s and two in the early 1970s. Those nine banks acquired 12 United States banks between 1969 and 1979. Of the 12 banks acquired, at the time of acquisition, four were in considerably less favorable condition (inadequate capital or higher level of classified assets) than the acquiring bank, and two were in very serious problem/failure status. Eight of the nine sample banks currently have composite ratings of 2 with the ninth rated 3.

In all but one case, the mergers appear to have been accomplished smoothly, with no lingering adverse effect on the resulting bank, regardless of condition of the bank it acquired. In the one exceptional case, the problems of the acquired bank were judged to be responsible, at least partially, for lowering the ratings of the resulting bank.

This group of banks generally resembles the pure *de novo* banks, except for a greater retail orientation, accomplished or augmented by the acquisitions they have made.

- Management is rated "strong" or "satisfactory" in eight of the nine cases. As with the pure *de novo* banks, senior management tends to be composed of career employees of the parent bank who are judged to be "thoroughly competent" or "capable" in most cases.

- Five of the banks are internationally oriented. In four of them, home country concentrations have been noted.

- Assets are rated "satisfactory" of "strong" in all cases, with a low level of classified assets, particularly in the more serious categories. In one instance, the examiner explicitly noted that the "low volume of classified assets results from prudent domestic loan policies."

- Insider loans are insignificant or minimal, and there are no recent incidences of classification of insider loans.

- Recent earnings ratings for six of the nine banks are no better than "fair" with the remainder "satisfactory" or "strong." Dividends either are not paid or are at a reasonable level in all but one case.

- Capital adequacy ratings are generally "satisfactory." The record indicates that parents have supplied capital when needed and, in four instances, acquisitions were accompanied by significant capital injections.

- As with *de novo* banks, there is no consistent pattern of violations of law.

- Internal controls for these banks are adequate to good.

- In two instances there were prior references to insufficient credit information on loans to customers of the parent bank. Those comments were not repeated at later examination dates.

The policies of most of these banks are consistently labeled "conservative." Like the *de novo* banks, most of these banks operate as "part of a worldwide banking chain," serving home country customers as a major part of their business and "relying on the parent's worldwide resources."

Acquisitions by Foreign Banks

This group consists of five banks acquired by foreign banks from 1974 through 1977. Two banks were in sound condition at the time of acquisition, one had a history of high management turnover and was undercapitalized, and two were acquired under emergency circumstances. In all cases, management control now rests with the foreign parent bank.

Four of the five now have composite ratings of 2 or 1. Since acquisition, the two emergency acquisitions have improved ratings overall and in several performance areas. In one case the composite rating has moved up to a 2 and in the other up to a 3.

- Asset quality is rated "satisfactory" in four cases. In the fifth case, although asset quality is given a "marginal" rating, most criticized assets "are a carryover from the bank [prior to acquisition]" and the examiner commented that "[new] formal loan policies have resulted in quality loans having been added to the bank's portfolio."

- An increase in international lending was observed in three banks. In one case, the reviewer noted that none of the international loans was criticized; in another, it was noted that "tough credit standards [were] instituted."

- Four of the five banks received "satisfactory" management ratings at the most recent examination; the management of the fifth was rated "fair." (In the last case, one of the two emergency acquisitions, the examiner noted that "management still involves two former directors, on a limited basis, and two former loan officers who were in positions of responsibility at the time of this [sic] failure of the former bank.")

- Insider loans in three banks decreased after acquisition. In four of the five banks no insider loans were classified at the most recent examination.

- Recent earnings ratings for the group are mixed. In three, earnings are "satisfactory" or "strong" with improvement shown in two; in the other two (both of the emergency acquisitions), earnings are still weak. Four of the five pay no dividend to the parent.

- Capital adequacy ratings are "satisfactory" or "strong" in all but one case, where the rating is "fair." Parents have made injections of capital in four cases; in the fifth, the bank was already well-capitalized.

- Violations of law noted in the most recent examination reports were technical or minor in all cases. In two cases, this is an improvement from pre-acquisition circumstances.

- Internal controls appear satisfactory and/or improving in all cases.

For each of the banks, reviewers commented that prospects appear better since acquisition. One examiner stated explicitly that "during the . . . period since its acquisition,. . . the bank has continued to operate in a generally autonomous manner while enjoying some direct and indirect benefits in the [parent's] group." For one of the banks acquired under emergency circumstances, the examiner recommended an upgraded rating about a year after acquisition, noting that "the depth of management expertise available through the [foreign parent bank] . . . mitigates the seriousness of the problems."

ACQUISITION BY FOREIGN INDIVIDUALS

The 13 acquisitions by foreign individuals include only two completed prior to 1975. Therefore, the historical record in most of the cases is relatively short. In the discussion that follows, the 13 banks in this group are divided into two sub-groups—those that were relatively weak at the time they were acquired (seven banks) and those that were sound when acquired (six banks).

Acquisitions of Weak Banks

Of the seven banks in this group, two were in serious difficulty when they were acquired and the rest had composite ratings of 3 or the equivalent. Six of them are currently rated 3, and the seventh has improved to 4 or slightly better. Examination report narratives, augmenting composite ratings, indicate that three of the banks have improved in condition since acquisition. Three others *appear* to be improving, but since the post-acquisition examinations were slightly less than a year ago, conclusions can only be preliminary. In the seventh case, the bank's condition is unchanged.

In all cases, a new chief executive officer was installed following acquisition. Nevertheless, management ratings have not improved. In two cases, although the new senior management has been judged "capable and experienced," mediocrity or weakness of middle management has lowered the management rating. In a case of quite recent acquisition, the bank's management rating went down because the new management, although "competent," does not yet "have a handle on the affairs of the bank." And in another of the recent acquisitions, although management is still rated "marginal," the reviewers stated that the "prior president was a cause of many of the [bank's] problems."

- Asset ratings range from "satisfactory" (two cases) through "fair" (three cases) to "marginal" (two cases). In four cases, asset quality has improved since acquisition. In two of these cases, this may be partly attributable to an improving local economy.

- In two cases, either actual increase in international lending or a strategy to engage in more international activity was noted.

- Insider loans are not considered a problem at any of the seven banks. In one case, it was noted that insider abuse had been a problem associated with the bank's previous domestic owner.

- Except for one bank with recent "satisfactory" earnings, the earnings ratings of this group ranged from "fair" to "unsatisfactory." All seven banks had earnings problems prior to acquisition. Three have shown improvement; in three there has been no change; the earnings rating has decreased in one. None of these banks is paying a dividend. In two cases, dividends are explicitly restricted by supervisory agencies.

- Capital adequacy is currently rated "satisfactory" for three of these banks. In two cases that is the direct result of significant capital injections made by the new owners. Three banks have capital adequacy ratings of "fair," and for two of these, examination narrative indicates that the capital base has improved, but not sufficiently to warrant a higher rating. In the remaining bank, the rating has improved from "unsatisfactory" to "marginal" as a result of capital injection by the new owner. Nevertheless, more is needed, and the reviewer noted that the most recent examination report expressed some doubt about the willingness and ability of the owner to make another needed infusion.

- Violations of law are, in all cases, judged by reviewers to be minor or technical.

- Internal controls were adequate or being improved in all but one case, where they had declined to an unsatisfactory condition under the new owner.

Overall assessments of weak banks acquired by foreign individuals tended to emphasize the continuing nature of problems carried over from the prior ownership. In two cases, reviewers judged the new owners to have had a beneficial impact on the acquired bank, e.g., "the [supervisory agency] is happy with the stability that the present owners have brought to an organization that was of serious concern . . . before the acquisition." In another case, there was some, but not unanimous, opinion that the problems of the bank were worse after the acquisition. For the four remaining banks, no clear judgments could be made about the effect of the ownership change. Certainly, for the most recent acquisitions, prospects are still somewhat difficult to determine.

Acquisitions of Sound Banks

Six cases of the banks acquired by individuals were in sound condition at the time of acquisition. In five of those cases, the sound condition has been maintained since acquisition. Because the sixth case appears to be extraordinary, it is discussed separately.

The one case of deterioration in condition under a foreign individual owner occurred during nine months of ownership which terminated when the acquirer defaulted on purchase agreements and/or loans to make purchase. During the nine months, classified loans increased, large loan losses caused a weakened condition, and serious violations of law were identified. In the judgment of the reviewers, there is "little doubt the ownership [by the individual] was a detriment."

Of the five remaining banks, four have composite ratings of 2 and one a composite of 1, maintaining the favorable pre-acquisition ratings.

- The five banks' management was rated "satisfactory." In at least one case, this represented an improvement. Management has been changed, with either a whole new senior management team or chief executive officer, in four cases. In the fifth case, the previous chief executive officer, described by the examiner as "good and effective," was retained by a new foreign owner who appears not to be active in the affairs of the bank.

- Asset quality is rated "satisfactory" in four cases and "strong" in one. Classified assets have shown a marked decrease in three banks. This may be partly attributable to an improved local economy.

- In two cases there has been a greater emphasis on international lending.

- In none of these cases are insider loans a problem.

- Earnings for the entire group were rated "satisfactory" at the most recent examination, and in two cases this represented an improvement. In two cases moderate cash dividends have been maintained and in one case only minimal stock dividends have been distributed. In the remaining two cases, the new owner has instituted a policy of retaining all earnings.

- Capital adequacy ratings were judged "satisfactory" in three cases and "strong" in two. In the latter two cases, capital injections have not been necessary. Among the other three, one owner has made capital injections to keep pace with asset growth and another owner has abolished dividends to build the bank's capital position.

- In no case were violations of law considered significant or harmful.

SUMMARY

From a supervisory standpoint, the ownership of 22 sample banks by foreign banking institutions appears to pose no special concerns. To the contrary, the group is characterized by sound balance sheets and conservative management. With loan portfolios that are internationally (and home country) oriented to some degree (more so for the wholesale-oriented *de novo* banks), these banks maintain asset quality ratings of "satisfactory" or "strong." Although they are not particularly good earners, the tendency to retain 100 percent of earnings and the parent banks' willingness to provide capital when needed result in strong capital positions. Especially for the *de novo* banks, policies of rotating senior management from elsewhere in the parent bank system have occasionally given rise to problems caused by lack of familiarity with United States banking practices. Such situations appear to have been rectified quickly, however, and the overall impression is that these banks are operated with careful attention to United States law and regulation.

The 13 sample banks acquired by foreign individuals present a mixed picture, ranging from sound and well-run institutions to ones whose conditions are below average and require some special supervisory attention. Senior management installed by foreign individual owners tend to be United States bankers. Not unexpectedly, their ratings as managers are closely correlated with those of the banks'—"satisfactory" for the six stronger banks in the group and "fair" for the seven weaker ones. In four of the 13 cases, the change in ownership has been accompanied by an increase in international lending. Asset quality is mixed, as are earnings. In most cases, and particularly for the recent acquisitions, the reviewers believe that asset and earnings problems noted at the most recent examination are a carry-over from the previous ownership.

Capital adequacy ratings for banks acquired by foreign individuals are generally better than ratings in other performance areas, frequently because of capital injected by the new owners. For 12 of the 13 cases, there is no record of abuse in the areas of insider loans or violations of the law. In the single exceptional case, deterioration in condition was a direct result of abuses linked to the owner.

Our reviewers gave special scrutiny to the six banks acquired by foreign individuals which had composite ratings of 3. They found that "the problems in these banks are generally not related to the fact that ownership is foreign. Indeed, there is little difference noted between these and most other . . . banks [being given extra supervisory attention]."

Overall, based on our sample, it does not appear that foreign ownership of United States banks has presented problems significantly different or greater than for United States banks as a whole.

Acknowledgments

Essential gathering and initial interpretation of data were carried out by Office of the Comptroller of the Currency examiners David Baer, Kathy Bedard, William Freeman, Robert Inskeep, Joseph Malott, Thomas McAllister, and John Mercer. Barbara Norris, Robert Inskeep, and John Mercer assisted in preliminary analysis; Patricia Zito offered valuable insights during the early drafting. Helpful comments on later drafts were made by Paul Homan, Robert Bench, Edmund Zito, Joseph Malott, and William Freeman.

FOOTNOTES

[1] A total of 102 banks have been identified as currently having foreign ownership of at least 25 percent.

Examination reports of 37 banks were actually reviewed; however reviews of examination reports for three banks acquired by the same individual and subsequently divested have been treated as a single observation.

[2] Control was defined as a minimum of 25 percent ownership. In one case, a bank with foreign ownership of more than 25 percent was eliminated from consideration because examiners advised that the foreign investor was not in a controlling position.

[3] When individuals from more than one country were involved in an acquisition, the nationality of the owner with the largest portion of equity was recorded.

[4] Examiners must be able to identify businesses affiliated with a bank and know the nature of the relationship in order to assess the effect of such affiliations on the soundness of the bank and ascertain compliance with laws (e.g., 12 USC 371(c)) covering such relationships.

[5] Loans that are apparently independent may, in some cases, depend on the same fundamental factor for repayment which, if it were to weaken, could adversely affect all of those loans. An example is loans to borrowers engaged in or dependent on a single industry. Similarly, loans to a foreign government, its agencies, and majority-owned or controlled enterprises may fall into the same category. Clusters of such loans that exceed 25 percent of a bank's capital are deemed "concentrations of credit." Concentrations may or may not be criticized by examiners, depending on the quality of the underlying loans and how well bank management identifies, analyzes and controls the concentration.

[6] Insider loans are those extended to directors and their stockholders (or their interests). If such loans are unjustified (i.e., are based excessively on the borrowers' position with the bank), the bank's lending policies are likely to be criticized by examiners.

[7] Criticized (or "classified") loans are those where there is or may be an interruption of repayment. The degree of potential or actual interruption is reflected in the four loan classifications, which range from "Other Loans Especially Mentioned" (potentially weak credits that, if not strengthened, could impair the bank's position in the future) to "Loss" (loans considered uncollectable and that should be written off).

[8] Evaluation of a bank's adherence to laws and regulations is an integral part of the examination procedure. Some violations of law are considered important, impairing the safety and soundness of a bank. Others are minor or technical in nature and do not seriously harm the bank or its customers. Patterns of consistent violation may signal circumstances that require further exploration and/or stronger remedial measures.

## 11

ANALYSIS OF CURRENT OPERATIONS OF FOREIGN–OWNED U.S. BANKS

ELLEN S. GOLDBERG

SUMMARY

This paper contrasts the 1979 performance and condition of a sample of 47 foreign-owned United States banks with United States-owned peer banks using selected balance sheet and income statement ratios. It also compares the foreign-owned banks with each other using the following four categories: banks acquired by foreign banks, banks acquired by foreign individuals, banks established *de novo* that have subsequently merged with other United States banks, and *de novo* banks which have not subsequently merged with other United States banks.

In the overall comparison of foreign-owned banks to United States peer banks the following observations were made about foreign-owned United States banks:

- In 1979, they had lower returns on assets and equity than their peers.
- Capital position as represented by the ratio of equity-to-assets was higher than their peers, with the greatest difference noted between the *de novo* banks without subsequent mergers and their peers.
- Commercial and industrial loans were on average a higher proportion of total loans, with the highest proportion found in the category of *de novo* United States banks that have not subsequently merged.
- Residential mortgages as a percentage of loans were lower than their peers.

- Ownership of state, county and municipal securities as a percentage of total securities was lower than their peers.
- Time deposits of $100,000 or more as a percentage of total assets was higher than their peers.

Among the foreign-owned United States banks, comparisons show that *de novo* banks which have not subsequently merged with United States banks tend to be wholesale and internationally oriented with high proportions of commercial and industrial loans, loans in foreign offices and purchased funds. *De novo* banks which subsequently merged, however, tend to look much more like their peers in balance sheet structure with a more retail orientation and little international activity. Banks acquired by foreign individuals and banks acquired by foreign banks have mixed characteristics when compared to peers.

METHODOLOGY

The purpose of this study is to determine whether and how the present structure and operations of foreign-owned banks differ from United States peer banks and from one another based on category of ownership. Data from 1979 are used to construct a variety of ratios to analyze differences in asset mix, liability mix, earnings performance, and capital structure.

To determine how the structure and performance of foreign-owned banks may differ from United States-owned peer banks, a sample of 47 banks of the 143 known foreign-owned banks was selected for study. These 143 banks consist of the 97 known United States commercial banks acquired by foreign interests[1] and the 46 known foreign-owned *de novo* United States banks.[2] Ninety-six foreign-owned banks were excluded from the sample for the following reasons:

- Forty-three banks which were acquired or established after year-end 1977 were excluded to ensure that the sample banks had at least two years under foreign ownership. Any less time under foreign control, it was felt, would not be sufficient for any policy changes of the new owners to be reflected in the banks' balance sheets.
- Eighteen banks which merged into existing foreign-owned banks

were consolidated and, in effect, disappeared through consolidation.

- Nine banks which were "problem" banks at the time of acquisition were eliminated. They were either failing banks or were deemed by the bank regulators to have serious problems at the time of acquisition. These banks were eliminated because it was felt that their inclusion would distort the results of the analysis.
- Nine acquired banks were omitted because foreign control was subsequently relinquished to American owners.
- Seventeen banks were excluded because of data availability problems. Seven of those were *de novo* banks which were not included in the sample because their existence was discovered after the sample was selected and analysis begun.

Because operations of foreign-owned banks may be significantly affected by the method by which foreign ownership is accomplished, the foreign-owned banks were analyzed in the following four categories:

Number of Banks	Categories
7	Banks acquired by foreign banks.
13	Banks acquired by foreign individuals.
19	Banks established *de novo* by foreign parent banks which have not subsequently merged with U.S. banks—"pure" *de novo* banks.
8	Banks established *de novo* by foreign parent banks which *have* subsequently merged with U.S. banks—"hybrid" *de novo* banks.
47	

A list of the sample foreign-owned banks is presented in Appendix A. The "hybrid" *de novo* bank mergers are detailed in Appendix B. Distribution of the sample by state, asset size, nationality of owners, and year of acquisition, merger or formation appear in Tables 1 through 4.

Eighteen ratios were calculated for the sample foreign-owned banks and compared to peer group averages computed by the National Bank Surveillance System (NBSS) of the Office of the Comptroller of the Currency.[3] Year-average 1979 figures were used throughout.[4] A description of the NBSS peer group classifications is presented in Appendix C, and a detailed list of the ratios examined appears in Appendix D.

The ratios examined were broken into three categories:

Table 1
Distribution by State

	B/BHC	Indiv.	"Pure" De Novo	"Hybrid" De Novo	Total
California	2	3	6	6	17
New York	1	1	10	2	14
Florida	4	6	–	–	10
Illinois	–	–	3	–	3
Louisiana	–	1	–	–	1
New Jersey	–	1	–	–	1
Texas	–	1	–	–	1
Total	7	13	19	8	47

Table 2
Distribution by Asset Size*

	B/BHC	Indiv.	"Pure" De Novo	"Hybrid" De Novo	Total
$ 1- 5 billion	1	1	2	1	5
$500-999 million	–	–	2	5	7
$300-499 million	–	1	2	–	3
$100-299 million	1	3	7	2	13
$ 40- 99 million	2	5	3	–	10
$ 25- 39 million	–	2	2	–	4
$ 10- 24 million	2	–	1	–	3
$ 0- 9 million	1	1	–	–	2
Total	7	13	19	8	47

*Asset size is as of December 31, 1978 because the current peer group assignments in the Office of the Comptroller of the Currency's National Bank Surveillance System (NBSS), which was used for the peer bank analysis, are on the basis of year-end 1978 asset size.

- *Asset Mix*—includes 1 to 4 family real estate loans, total personal loans to individuals, commercial and industrial loans, and loans in foreign offices, each as a percentage of total gross loans. The investment portfolio was analyzed by examining state, county and municipal securities as a percentage of total securities, securities held in foreign offices as a percentage of total securities, and total investment securities as a percentage of total assets.
- *Liability Mix*—includes demand deposits to total deposits; and demand deposits, savings deposits, time deposits of $100,000 or more, deposits in foreign offices (primarily Eurodollars), total deposits, and federal funds purchased and repurchase agreements, each as a percentage of total assets. Also, the loan-to-deposit ratio was analyzed.[5]

Table 3
Distribution by Nationality of Owners/Acquirers

	B/BHC	Indiv.	"Pure" De Novo	"Hybrid" De Novo	Total
U.K.	1	–	1	3	5
Spain	1	2	–	–	3
Other Europe	–	3	3	–	6
Japan	–	–	10	3	13
Other Asia	1	1	–	–	2
Latin America	–	5	1	1	7
Canada	4	–	3	1	8
Israel	–	–	1	–	1
Middle East	–	2	–	–	2
Total	7	13	19	8	47

Table 4
Distribution by Year of Acquisition, Merger or Formation

	B/BHC	Indiv.	"Pure" De Novo*	"Hybrid" De Novo*	Total
1920-29	–	–	4	–	4
1950-59	–	–	3	–	3
1960-69	–	–	1	1	2
1970	–	1	–	1	2
1971	–	–	2	–	2
1972	1	1	2	–	4
1973	–	2	1	–	3
1974	1	2	4	4	11
1975	–	1	–	1	2
1976	2	2	–	1	5
1977	3	4	2	–	9
Total	7	13	19	8	47

*For the "pure" *de novo* banks the year noted is the year of establishment, while for the "hybrid" *de novo* banks the year noted is the year of the first merger with a U.S. bank.

- *Earnings Performance and Capital Ratios*—includes return on assets, return on equity, and equity capital to total assets.

Data for each foreign-owned bank in the sample were compared with composite data from its NBSS peer group.[6] Group means were calculated for each ratio for the foreign-owned banks and compared to the NBSS peer group composite. This composite was calculated by weighting the NBSS peer group average by the number of foreign-owned banks in that NBSS peer group classification.[7] The comparison of the foreign-owned banks with a composite of peer banks avoids the problem of attempting to select individual peers and relies on a large group of peers to offset possible distortion caused by outliers. The NBSS peer groups are composed of banks with the same structure (unit or branch banks) and located in similar types of markets (urban versus rural). However, in these calculations the peer group average is not limited to geographically similar peers.

In addition to group means, the group medians were computed for each ratio. When there is a small sample size, the means can be greatly affected by extreme values for any one bank. In those cases, the median is a more appropriate measure to consider. Therefore, both means and medians were calculated for all the ratios for each of the four groups. Additional measures used were the number of non-zero values and the number of observations in which the foreign-owned bank ratio was higher than the peer group ratio.

BANKS ACQUIRED BY FOREIGN BANKS

The seven sample banks acquired by foreign banks are located in New York, California, and Florida. They range in asset size at the time of acquisition from $7.3 million to $1.3 billion, and six of the seven are currently below $300 million in assets. Four of the seven were acquired by Royal Trust Company of Canada and the other three were acquired by banks in the United Kingdom, Spain, and the Philippines. The seven sample banks were acquired between 1972 and 1977, with five of the seven acquisitions occurring in 1976 and 1977.

Seven general observations regarding the banks acquired by foreign banks can be made by examining the results of the sample means and medians in Table 5. It is evident that the banks acquired by foreign banks tended to have a somewhat lower proportion of 1 to 4 family real estate loans as a percentage of total loans and a similar proportion of personal loans to individuals as a percentage of total loans compared to their peers in 1979. The banks owned by foreign banks had, on average, a much lower proportion of total investments in state, county, and municipal securities (SCM's) and a lower proportion of assets invested in securities in 1979 than their peers. On the liability side, these banks generally had a higher proportion of demand deposits, a similar proportion of savings deposits, and a higher proportion of time deposits of $100,000 or more in 1979 than their peers. Finally, it appears that the

Table 5
Comparative Financial Data for U.S. Banks Acquired by Foreign Banks or Bank Holding Companies
Year Average 1979

	Mean		Median		No. of Foreign-Owned Banks > Peers	No. of Foreign-Owned Bank Non-Zeros	No. of Peer Bank Non-Zeros
	Foreign-Owned Banks	Peer Group Banks	Foreign-Owned Banks	Peer Group Banks			
ASSET MIX:							
Real Estate Loans 1-4 Family/Gross Loans	7.82	19.61	6.20	20.54	1/7	5	7
Personal Loans/Gross Loans	31.54	32.08	34.55	33.61	4/7	7	7
Commercial & Industrial Loans/Gross Loans	37.43	25.99	22.78	24.70	2/7	7	7
Loans in Foreign Offices/Gross Loans[a]	1.65	1.08	NM[b]	NM[b]	1/1	1	1
Gross Loans/Total Assets	55.18	54.15	54.82	54.30	3/7	7	7
State & Municipal Securities/Total Securities	12.47	38.90	13.97	44.96	0/7	6	7
Securities in Foreign Offices/Total Securities[a]	0	0	0	0	0/0	0	0
Investment Securities/Total Assets	15.68	24.18	16.81	24.89	0/7	7	7
LIABILITY MIX:							
Demand Deposits/Total Deposits	47.43	36.00	45.09	35.44	6/7	7	7
Demand Deposits/Total Assets	39.53	30.51	38.51	31.07	7/7	7	7
Savings Deposits/Total Assets	19.04	21.25	21.94	22.57	4/7	7	7
Time $100M + over/Total Assets	17.59	12.30	15.53	11.19	5/7	7	7
Deposits in Foreign Offices/Total Assets[a]	0.22	1.19	NM[b]	NM[b]	0/1	1	1
Total Deposits/Total Assets	84.18	84.77	85.67	87.08	3/7	7	7
Fed Funds & Repos/Total Assets	3.62	3.96	2.99	2.06	3/7	5	5
Net Loans/Total Deposits	62.83	63.39	62.37	61.70	3/7	7	7
EARNINGS AND CAPITAL RATIOS:							
Return on Assets	.51	.91	.49	.90	1/7	7	7
Return on Equity	7.81	12.28	8.50	12.99	2/7	7	7
Equity Capital/Total Assets	9.21	8.00	8.30	7.94	3/7	7	7

[a]Data available only for banks with $300 million or more in assets.
[b]Not meaningful.

return on assets and return on equity were somewhat lower than the peers on average in 1979. However, the mean and median equity capital ratios were generally higher among the banks acquired by foreign banks than their peers in 1979.

A detailed analysis of the banks acquired by foreign banks appears next, based on the data in Table 5.

Asset Mix

The average loan portfolio of the banks acquired by foreign banks is characterized as follows. The peer group averaged about three times more 1 to 4 family real estate loans in 1979 than these foreign-owned banks. Two of the seven foreign-acquired banks did not engage in this type of lending at any call date in 1979. However, the average proportion of personal loans to individuals was nearly equal for the banks acquired by foreign banks and for the peers. The banks acquired by foreign banks had a higher mean proportion of commercial and industrial (C & I) loans than the peers during 1979; however, the median proportion of C & I loans was slightly lower than the peers. The reason for this difference is that the foreign-acquired bank group mean was skewed higher due to one bank's particularly high ratio of C & I loans to total loans.

Data were available on loans in foreign offices only for banks with total assets of $300 million or more, leaving only one foreign-acquired bank in this group with data. No meaningful conclusion can be drawn from this one observation. Finally, the proportion of total loans to assets was on average approximately 55 percent for both the banks acquired by foreign banks and the peer banks.

Turning to the investment portfolio, the data in Table 5 indicate that the foreign-acquired banks' mean proportion of SCM's to total securities was less than one-third that of the peer banks in 1979, and the median difference between the two groups was even greater. It should be noted that factors such as the bank's tax position and local laws on the collateralization of public deposits by SCM's would have an influence on the foreign-owned banks' decision to purchase them.[8] The proportion of total investment securities to total assets for banks acquired by foreign banks was about ten percentage points lower than the peers in 1979, and none of the seven foreign-acquired banks had a higher proportion of investments to total assets than the peers.

Liability Mix

Table 5 indicates that the banks acquired by foreign banks' mean proportion of demand deposits to total assets was about ten percentage points higher than the peer banks. The mean proportion of savings deposits to total assets was nearly the same for both the foreign-acquired banks and the peers. The banks acquired by foreign banks' mean proportion of time deposits of $100,000 or more to total assets was five percentage points higher than their peers, with five out of the seven foreign-acquired banks having a higher proportion of large time deposits.

The mean proportion of federal funds purchased and repurchase agreements as a percentage of total assets was slightly lower for the foreign-acquired banks than for the peers, while the median proportion was higher, indicating that the foreign-acquired bank mean was influenced by a high value. In fact, two of the seven banks acquired by foreign banks did not participate in the fed funds or repo markets on any call date in 1979. Finally, the loan-to-deposit ratio was essentially the same for the banks acquired by foreign banks and the peers.

Earnings Performance and Capital Ratios

Return on assets for the banks acquired by foreign banks was, on average, about half that of the peer banks. Only one of the seven foreign-acquired banks had a higher return on assets than its peers. Likewise, the average return on equity of the foreign-acquired banks was much less than that of the peer banks in 1979 (7.81 percent and 12.28 percent, respectively). However, the equity capital ratio (equity capital to total assets) was stronger on average for the banks acquired by foreign banks than for the peers (9.21 percent and 8.00 percent, respectively).

BANKS ACQUIRED BY FOREIGN INDIVIDUALS

Ten of the thirteen banks acquired by foreign individuals are located in California, New York, and Florida, a concentration similar to that exhibited by the banks acquired by foreign banks. Ten of the thirteen foreign-owned banks are in the $25 to $300 million asset size range, with five of those ten in the $40 to $99 million asset size range. Greater detail and other characteristics of these banks are summarized in Tables 1 through 4.

Some general observations about the banks acquired by foreign individuals compared to their peers can be made using the 1979 data in Table 6. The banks acquired by foreign individuals had a somewhat lower proportion of their loan portfolios in 1 to 4 family real estate loans and personal loans than the peers. Also, the banks acquired by foreign individuals on average had a much lower proportion of their investment portfolios in SCM's than their peers, but had similar size portfolios. The liability mix of the banks acquired by foreign individuals compared to the peers is characterized by a somewhat higher proportion of demand deposits, a slightly lower proportion of savings deposits, and a higher proportion of large time deposits. The banks acquired by foreign individuals had on average a lower loan-to-deposit ratio than their peers in 1979. In addition, the return on assets, return on equity, and equity capital ratios were somewhat lower for the banks acquired by foreign individuals than their peers.

Asset Mix

As revealed in Table 6, the banks acquired by foreign individuals had on average one-third less 1 to 4 family real estate loans than their peers. The median proportion of personal loans to individuals as a percentage of total loans was about ten percentage points lower for the banks acquired by foreign individuals compared to the peers, while the median proportions of C & I loans were nearly the same for the two groups.

Turning to the investment portfolio, Table 6 indicates that the mean proportion of SCM's to total securities was three times higher for the peers than for the banks acquired by foreign individuals. This ratio was higher for the foreign-acquired banks than the peer banks in only two of the thirteen cases, while three of the thirteen foreign-acquired banks did not hold SCM's at any of the call dates in 1979. However, the banks acquired by foreign individuals had, on average, approximately the same proportion of investment securities as a percentage of total assets as the peer banks.

Table 6

Comparative Financial Data for U.S. Banks Acquired by Foreign Individuals
Year Average 1979

	Mean		Median		No. of Foreign-Owned Banks > Peers	No. of Foreign-Owned Bank Non-Zeros	No. of Peer Bank Non-Zeros
	Foreign-Owned Banks	Peer Group Banks	Foreign-Owned Banks	Peer Group Banks			
ASSET MIX:							
Real Estate Loans 1-4 Family/Gross Loans	14.29	21.75	16.74	21.14	4/13	13	13
Personal Loans/Gross Loans	28.96	31.50	23.47	32.50	4/13	13	13
Commercial & Industrial Loans/Gross Loans	30.27	24.99	22.48	23.30	6/13	13	13
Loans in Foreign Offices/Gross Loans[a]	1.30	0.33	NM[b]	NM[b]	1/2	1	2
Gross Loans/Total Assets	48.51	55.24	47.97	54.81	4/13	13	13
State & Municipal Securities/Total Securities	15.89	45.74	6.61	49.03	2/13	10	13
Securities in Foreign Offices /Total Securities[a]	0.18	0.05	NM[b]	NM[b]	1/2	1	1
Investment Securities/Total Assets	26.22	25.57	22.54	25.42	6/13	13	13
LIABILITY MIX:							
Demand Deposits/Total Deposits	42.31	34.64	41.30	35.17	10/13	13	13
Demand Deposits/Total Assets	36.41	29.89	34.06	30.14	11/13	13	13
Savings Deposits/Total Assets	19.66	23.63	21.06	23.30	3/13	13	13
Time $100M + over/Total Assets	19.07	11.47	17.47	10.61	9/13	13	13
Deposits in Foreign Offices/Total Assets[a]	0.56	0.37	NM[b]	NM[b]	1/2	1	2
Total Deposits/Total Assets	86.60	86.35	87.87	87.51	8/13	13	13
Fed Funds & Repos/Total Assets	3.33	3.22	2.50	2.29	5/13	10	13
Net Loans/Total Deposits	55.40	63.38	51.21	63.40	5/13	13	13
EARNINGS AND CAPITAL RATIOS:							
Return on Assets	.59	.94	.71	.96	4/13	13	13
Return on Equity	2.44	12.78	9.87	13.06	3/13	13	13
Equity Capital/Total Assets	7.52	7.56	6.54	7.54	4/13	13	13

[a]Data available only for banks with $300 million or more in assets.
[b]Not meaningful.

Liability Mix

The banks acquired by foreign individuals had a higher percentage of demand deposits to total assets than the peer banks. The proportion of savings deposits to total assets was slightly less for the banks acquired by foreign individuals than for the peers, while these foreign-acquired banks exhibited a much higher average proportion of time deposits of $100,000 or more to total assets than their peers (19.7 percent compared to 11.47 percent, respectively). The banks acquired by foreign individuals had a similar proportion of total deposits to total assets and federal funds purchased and repurchase agreements to total assets compared to the peers. However, the foreign-acquired bank group had a much lower average loan-to-deposit ratio in 1979 than the peer group (55.40 percent and 63.38 percent, respectively), indicating a higher potential for expansion of the loan portfolio among these foreign-acquired banks.

Earnings Performance and Capital Ratios

Because of the poor earnings performance in 1979, i.e., net losses, experienced by two of the thirteen banks acquired by foreign individuals, the group mean return on assets and return on equity were skewed lower. Therefore, the median return on assets and return on equity should be considered in this analysis. The median return on assets was lower for the foreign-acquired bank group than the peers (.71 percent and .96 percent, respectively), as was the return on equity (9.87 percent and 13.06 percent, respectively). The average equity capital ratios in 1979 were nearly equal for the banks acquired by foreign individuals and the peers (7.52 percent and 7.56 percent, respectively).

BANKS ESTABLISHED DE NOVO BY FOREIGN PARENT BANKS WHICH HAVE NOT SUBSEQUENTLY MERGED WITH U. S. BANKS—"PURE" DE NOVO BANKS

The nineteen pure *de novo* banks analyzed are all located in major financial centers, with ten located in New York, three in Chicago, and six in the cities of Los Angeles and San Francisco. The nineteen pure *de novo* banks range in asset size from $13 million to $3 billion. Seven of the nineteen banks are in the $100 to $299 million asset category, while the remaining twelve banks are distributed rather evenly among the various size categories. About half of the nineteen pure *de novo* banks are owned by banks in Japan. More detail on these characteristics of the nineteen banks and their dates of establishment are given in Tables 1 through 4.

The pure *de novo* banks are quite different in many respects from both their United States peers and from the other foreign-owned bank groups. The pure *de novo* banks tend to have a more wholesale orientation, which is evident by the higher proportion of commercial and industrial loans, the lower level of savings and demand deposits, and the greater reliance on large time deposits. In addition, the pure *de novo* banks generally have a much higher proportion of both loans and deposits in foreign offices, indicating a higher degree of international activity. Finally, they generally have better capitalization, as illustrated by the higher equity capital ratio. Detailed analysis of these differences appears below, based on the data in Table 7.

Asset Mix

The ratio of 1 to 4 family real estate loans to total loans for the pure *de novo* banks in 1979 was well below that of their peers. Six of the nineteen pure *de novo* banks did not engage in 1 to 4 family real estate lending at any call date in 1979. A lower proportion for the pure *de novo* banks compared to the peers was also exhibited for personal loans to individuals. However, the average proportion of commercial and industrial loans to total loans was much higher for the pure *de novo* banks (53.57 percent) compared to the peers (28.67 percent), and higher than levels noted earlier for foreign-acquired banks. Six pure *de novo* banks had data available on loans in foreign offices, and five of the six had such loans in 1979. The average proportion of loans in foreign offices to total loans was much higher for the pure *de novo* banks than for the peers (26.36 percent and 2.81 percent, respectively), indicating a higher degree of international activity among the pure *de novo* banks. These asset ratios tend to indicate the generally more wholesale nature of the pure *de novo* banks.

The average investment portfolio of the pure *de novo* banks had a lower proportion of SCM's to total securities (35.30 percent) than their peers (50.18 percent), but a higher proportion of these securities than

Table 7

Comparative Financial Data for U.S. Banks Established *De Novo* by Foreign Parent Banks—"Pure" *De Novo* Banks Year Average 1979

	Mean		Median		No. of Foreign-Owned Banks > Peers	No. of Foreign-Owned Bank Non-Zeros	No. of Peer Bank Non-Zeros
	Foreign-Owned Banks	Peer Group Banks	Foreign-Owned Banks	Peer Group Banks			
ASSET MIX:							
Real Estate Loans 1-4 Family/Gross Loans	4.18	18.43	5.94	17.36	2/19	13	19
Personal Loans/Gross Loans	6.86	28.61	1.38	26.43	0/19	15	19
Commercial & Industrial Loans/Gross Loans	53.57	28.67	50.57	32.04	16/19	18	19
Loans in Foreign Offices/Gross Loans[a]	26.36	2.81	31.59	2.75	5/6	5	6
Gross Loans/Total Assets	49.54	55.05	54.07	54.81	9/19	19	19
State & Municipal Securities/Total Securities	35.30	50.18	26.82	50.70	5/19	18	19
Securities in Foreign Offices/Total Securities[a]	8.48	0.61	4.27	0.71	5/6	5	5
Investment Securities/Total Assets	17.56	24.48	13.92	25.42	4/19	19	19
LIABILITY MIX:							
Demand Deposits/Total Deposits	29.16	35.45	21.81	35.31	6/19	18	19
Demand Deposits/Total Assets	23.86	29.97	17.95	29.89	5/19	18	19
Savings Deposits/Total Assets	5.88	20.69	4.15	19.20	1/19	18	19
Time $100M + over/Total Assets	36.49	14.23	31.07	15.45	17/19	19	19
Deposits in Foreign Offices/Total Assets[a]	26.45	3.15	31.88	3.12	5/6	5	6
Total Deposits/Total Assets	80.19	84.60	82.03	84.30	8/19	19	19
Fed Funds & Repos/Total Assets	1.65	4.87	0.42	5.10	3/19	14	19
Net Loans/Total Deposits	60.24	64.48	64.94	63.49	10/19	18	19
EARNINGS AND CAPITAL RATIOS:							
Return on Assets	.88	.96	.65	.96	5/19	19	19
Return on Equity	7.93	13.57	7.05	13.42	3/19	19	19
Equity Capital/Total Assets	12.41	7.08	9.08	7.26	11/19	19	19

[a]Data available only for banks with $300 million or more in assets.

either of the foreign-acquired bank groups. In addition, the pure *de novo* banks had a higher average proportion of securities held in foreign offices to total securities than the peers (8.48 percent and 0.61 percent, respectively).

Liability Mix

The pure *de novo* banks had, on average, lower proportions of both demand and savings deposits in 1979 compared to the peers, and also compared to both foreign-acquired bank groups. The proportion of savings deposits to total assets was particularly low in 1979 for the pure *de novo* banks (5.88 percent) compared to the peers (20.69 percent). In contrast, the average percentage of large time deposits to total assets was much higher for the pure *de novo* banks (36.49 percent) than the peers (14.23 percent), or the foreign-acquired banks. The six pure *de novo* banks with data available also had a much higher ratio of deposits in foreign offices, primarily Eurodollars, to total assets in 1979 compared to the peers (26.45 percent and 3.15 percent, respectively). These ratios point to the pure *de novo* banks' lack of a retail deposit base and the reliance on the money markets for funds. The pure *de novo* banks' average proportion of federal funds purchased and repurchase agreements to total assets was somewhat lower compared to the peers and to both foreign-acquired bank groups.

Earnings Performance and Capital Ratios

The average return on assets was slightly lower for the pure *de novo* banks in 1979 compared to their peers (.88 percent and .96 percent, respectively), but was generally higher than the banks acquired by foreign individuals or by foreign banks. The average return on equity was lower for the pure *de novo* banks (7.93 percent) compared to the peers (13.57 percent), primarily due to a higher proportion of capital rather than to lower earnings. The average ratio of equity capital to total assets was considerably higher for the pure *de novo* banks than the peers (12.41 percent and 7.08 percent, respectively).

BANKS ESTABLISHED DE NOVO BY FOREIGN PARENT BANKS WHICH HAVE SUBSEQUENTLY MERGED WITH U. S. BANKS—"HYBRID" DE NOVO BANKS

Six of the eight hybrid *de novo* banks are located in California and two in New York; five of the eight are in the $500 to $999 million asset size category; and three each are owned by banks in the United Kingdom and Japan. More detailed information on the eight hybrid *de novo* banks, including the year of their first merger, is presented in Tables 1 through 4 and Appendix B.

The data in Table 8 suggest several general observations regarding the hybrid *de novo* banks. First, in contrast to the pure *de novo* banks, it appears that the hybrid *de novo* banks bear a strong resemblance to their peers. This is true on the basis of both the loan portfolio and deposit structure. In fact, the only area of noticeable difference between the hybrid *de novo* banks and their peers is a somewhat higher proportion of large time deposits exhibited by the hybrid *de novo* banks. The mergers with United States banks were all made by these *de novo* banks in 1976 or before and the time period examined here is 1979. Therefore, even after having had at least three years for the *de novo* banks to influence or change the United States banks merged, these hybrid *de novo* banks are currently very similar to the peer banks.

The above observations might lead to the tentative conclusion that when foreign *de novo* banks merge with United States banks, they become more like their domestic peers by adding a more retail orientation (through increasing core deposits and increasing consumer-type loans) to the wholesale and international orientation of the pure *de novo* banks.

Asset Mix

The average proportion of 1 to 4 family real estate loans to total loans was slightly lower in 1979 for the hybrid *de novo* banks compared with their peers (13.24 percent and 17.14 percent, respectively). In addition, it should be noted that all eight hybrid *de novo* banks made 1 to 4 family real estate loans. The proportion of personal loans as a percentage of total loans was nearly the same for the hybrid *de novo* banks and their peers in 1979. The hybrid *de novo* banks had a slightly higher proportion of C & I loans to total loans than their peers (33.54 percent and 29.41 percent, respectively), but much lower than

Table 8
Comparative Financial Data for *De Novo* Banks Which Have Subsequently Merged With U.S. Banks—"Hybrid" *De Novo* Banks
Year Average 1979

	Mean		Median		No. of Foreign-Owned Banks > Peers	No. of Foreign-Owned Bank Non-Zeros	No. of Peer Bank Non-Zeros
	Foreign-Owned Banks	Peer Group Banks	Foreign-Owned Banks	Peer Group Banks			
ASSET MIX:							
Real Estate Loans 1-4 Family/Gross Loans	13.24	17.14	14.03	16.83	3/8	8	8
Personal Loans/Gross Loans	25.17	26.92	26.10	26.58	3/8	8	8
Commercial & Industrial Loans/Gross Loans	33.54	29.41	34.85	30.82	5/8	8	8
Loans in Foreign Offices/Gross Loans[a]	4.51	2.17	NM[b]	2.75	1/6	2	6
Gross Loans/Total Assets	64.40	55.49	69.77	55.15	6/8	8	8
State & Municipal Securities/Total Securities	37.78	50.55	37.24	50.70	2/8	8	8
Securities in Foreign Offices/Total Securities[a]	3.45	0.51	NM[b]	.71	1/6	1	4
Investment Securities/Total Assets	16.25	22.37	15.83	22.23	2/8	8	8
LIABILITY MIX:							
Demand Deposits/Total Deposits	33.40	35.89	36.57	36.49	3/8	8	8
Demand Deposits/Total Assets	28.54	30.44	30.55	29.89	3/8	8	8
Savings Deposits/Total Assets	14.41	19.12	16.06	18.04	3/8	8	8
Time $100M + over/Total Assets	29.80	15.64	26.10	14.58	7/8	8	8
Deposits in Foreign Offices/Total Assets[a]	4.54	2.45	NM[b]	3.12	1/6	1	6
Total Deposits/Total Assets	84.18	82.54	85.64	81.92	5/8	8	8
Fed Funds & Repos/Total Assets	3.30	6.76	2.01	7.41	1/8	8	8
Net Loans/Total Deposits	75.21	66.56	77.47	66.22	6/8	8	8
EARNINGS AND CAPITAL RATIOS:							
Return on Assets	.60	.89	.50	.88	1/8	8	8
Return on Equity	8.70	13.39	6.97	13.42	1/8	8	8
Equity Capital/Total Assets	6.72	6.49	6.73	6.33	4/8	8	8

[a]Data available only for banks with $300 million or more in assets.
[b]Not meaningful.

the pure *de novo* banks (53.57 percent). Only two of the six hybrid *de novo* banks with data available had loans in foreign offices and their proportion of these deposits to total assets was much lower in 1979 than the pure *de novo* banks (4.51 percent and 26.36 percent, respectively). These ratios indicate the less wholesale/international orientation of the hybrid *de novo* banks as compared to the pure *de novo* banks.

The hybrid *de novo* banks had a lower average proportion of SCM's as a percentage of total securities (37.78 percent) compared to the peers (50.55 percent), about the same as the pure *de novo* banks, but much higher than the foreign-acquired banks. Like the pure *de novo* banks, the hybrid *de novo* banks had a lower proportion of investment securities to total assets than their peers.

Liability Mix

The hybrid *de novo* banks exhibited a similar proportion of demand deposits to total assets compared to the peers, but a lower percentage of savings to total assets. However, the mean proportion of savings deposits to total assets was much greater in 1979 for the hybrid *de novo* banks (14.41 percent) than the pure *de novo* banks (5.88 percent), indicating their higher degree of consumer business. The hybrid *de novo* banks had a much higher proportion of large time deposits to total assets in 1979 than the peers (29.80 percent and 15.64 percent, respectively), but a lower proportion than the pure *de novo* bank average (36.49 percent), again pointing to their less reliance than the pure *de novo* banks on the money markets for sources of funds.

Unlike the pure *de novo* banks, the hybrid *de novo* banks did not have a high incidence or proportion of deposits in foreign offices (Eurodollars). The hybrid *de novo* banks had a lower average proportion of federal funds purchased and repurchase agreements to total assets in 1979 than their peers (3.30 percent and 6.76 percent, respectively).

The average loan-to-deposit ratio was higher in 1979 for the hybrid *de novo* banks (75.21 percent) than the peers (66.56 percent), the pure *de novo* banks (60.24 percent), and the banks acquired by foreign individuals or banks.

Earnings Performance and Capital Ratios

The average return on assets was lower for the hybrid *de novo* banks than their peers in 1979 (.60 percent compared to .89 percent, respectively), as was the return on equity (8.70 percent and 13.39 percent, respectively). The average equity capital ratio was approximately equal in 1979 for the hybrid *de novo* banks and the peers (6.72 percent and 6.49 percent, respectively).

SUMMARY OF FINDINGS

Certain attributes were found common to the foreign-owned banks in general compared to their peers and are described as follows:

- The average proportion of commercial and industrial loans to total loans was higher in 1979 in each of the four foreign-owned bank groups compared to their United States peers. The ratio was much higher for the pure *de novo* banks compared to the peers.
- Real estate loans (1 to 4 family) as a percentage of total loans was lower on average in 1979 in all four foreign-owned bank groups than the peers. The ratio was much lower than the peers among the pure *de novo* banks and the banks acquired by foreign banks.
- All four foreign-owned bank groups had lower proportions of SCM's to total securities than the peers. The ratio was much lower than the peers for the banks acquired by foreign banks and for the banks acquired by foreign individuals.
- The mean and median proportion of large time deposits to total assets was higher for each of the foreign-owned bank groups compared to their peers. This ratio was considerably higher than the peers for the banks acquired by foreign individuals, the pure *de novo* banks, and the hybrid *de novo* banks.
- All four foreign-owned bank groups had lower returns on assets and equity than their peers.

Some apparent differences between the pure *de novo* banks and the hybrid *de novo* banks emerge from the findings of this study. The pure *de novo* banks, as would be expected, tend to be wholesale and internationally oriented banks with high proportions of commercial and industrial loans, loans in foreign offices, and purchased funds. However, the *de novo* banks that subsequently merged with United States banks ("hybrid" *de novo* banks) look very different from the pure *de novo* banks, and are much more like their peers in balance sheet structure. The hybrid *de novo* have a more retail orientation, closely resembling their peers in proportions of 1 to 4 family real estate loans, personal loans to individuals, commercial and industrial loans, and demand deposits. Also, the hybrid *de novo* banks have very little international activity as represented by loans, securities, and deposits in foreign offices.

CONCLUSIONS

This analysis examined the foreign-owned banks acquired or established in 1977 or earlier and compared them to the composite National Bank Surveillance System peer group averages for the year 1979. The purpose of the analysis was to attempt to determine differences that may currently exist between the foreign-owned banks and their peers and among the different groups of foreign-owned banks. It should be noted that it cannot be concluded that any differences that exist are necessarily caused by foreign ownership.

Certain differences are apparent among the four foreign-owned bank groups, i.e., banks acquired by foreign banks or individuals, *de novo* banks that subsequently merged with other United States banks ("hybrid" *de novo* banks), and *de novo* banks that have not merged ("pure" *de novo* banks). In addition, several differences common to the foreign-owned banks in general compared to their peer banks were noted.

The foreign-owned banks that are most similar to their peers are the *de novo* banks that subsequently merged with United States banks ("hybrid" *de novo* banks). Those banks have a generally more retail orientation than the other foreign-owned banks, with 1 to 4 family real estate loans averaging about 15 percent of the loan portfolio, personal loans about 25 percent of the loan portfolio, and commercial and industrial loans about one-third of total loans in 1979. Their deposit structure is characterized as follows: the proportion of demand deposits to total assets averaged about 35 percent, savings deposits about 15 percent of total assets, and time deposits of $100,000 or more about 25 percent of total assets. The ratio of large time deposits is somewhat higher among these foreign-owned banks than their peers.

The "pure" *de novo* banks tend to be wholesale and internationally oriented. These banks generally have a higher proportion of commercial and industrial loans and loans in foreign offices compared to the domestic peers. They also have a lower proportion of demand and savings deposits, and a higher percentage of large time deposits in foreign offices than the peers.

Finally, the banks acquired by foreign banks and the banks acquired by foreign individuals exhibit mixed results when compared to the domestic peers. They tend to have, on average, somewhat lower proportions of 1 to 4 family real estate loans to total loans and SCM's to total securities compared to their peers. Their proportions of demand and large time deposits to total assets are generally higher than the peers, while the average ratios of personal loans to total loans, savings deposits to total assets, and federal funds purchased plus repurchase agreements to total assets are generally similar to the peers. Their returns on assets and equity are, on average, lower for these two foreign-acquired bank groups than for their domestic peers.

Acknowledgments

The author wishes to thank William A. Longbrake, Steven J. Weiss, and Judith A. Walter for their helpful comments and encouragement in preparing this paper.

FOOTNOTES

[1] William A. Longbrake, Melanie R. Quinn, and Judith A. Walter, *Foreign Ownership of U.S. Banks: Facts and Patterns*, OCC Staff Paper, 1980, p. 2 and footnote 3. The 97 known acquisitions include 92 acquisitions from 1970 through March 31, 1980 and 5 banks acquired before 1970.

[2] Longbrake, Quinn, and Walter, *op. cit.*, Appendix II. Because some *de novo* banks have merged with existing U.S. banks, some foreign-owned banks appear on both the foreign acquisition and *de novo* bank lists.

[3] The National Bank Surveillance System (NBSS) maintains supervisory and administrative systems, and prepares bank performance reports designed to serve as bank supervisory, examination, and management tools. Each bank in the system is placed into a peer group based on total asset size, whether it operates as a branch system or unit bank, and whether it is located in an urban or rural community. The peer group average for a particular ratio is the arithmetic mean of all such calculations for the group.

[4] Year-average figures were computed by adding the balance of the account on the quarterly Call Report at year-end 1978 to the balance at each quarter-end in 1979 and dividing by five.

[5] This ratio is not a measure of liability mix, but is used to assess the ability of a bank's deposits to support loan growth.

[6] The data for this study are Call Report figures obtained from:
1) The National Bank Surveillance System (NBSS) at the Office of the Comptroller of the Currency—provided peer bank averages and ratios from Bank Performance Reports (BPRs).

2) The FDIC computer data base.

Four of the 47 sample foreign-owned banks were acquired by Royal Trust Company of Canada. So as not to over-emphasize the behavior of Royal Trust Company in the analysis, the four banks were given the weight of one.

[7] For example, assume that there were five banks in the foreign-owned bank group, two of which were in the $1-5 billion asset size category (NBSS peer group 2) and three were in the $500 million-$1 billion asset size category with 3 or more full service branches (NBSS peer group 3); then the peer group average would be computed as follows: The NBSS peer group 2 average (137 banks) would be weighted twice, the NBSS peer group 3 average (79 banks) would be weighted three times, and the sum of these figures would be divided by five to result in a weighted average peer group mean. This would be compared to the average ratio for the five foreign-owned banks.

[8] Blair B. Hodgkins and Ellen S. Goldberg, *Effect of Foreign Acquisition on the Balance Sheet Structure and Earnings Performance of American Banks*, OCC Staff Paper, 1980 and James V. Houpt, "The Effect of Foreign-Acquisitions on the Performance of U.S. Banks," *Federal Reserve Bulletin*, July 1980.

APPENDIX

Appendix A
Banks Analyzed

Acquired By Foreign Banks

	NBSS Peer Group	State
Lloyds Bank of California	2	CA
Royal Trust Bank of Miami, N.A.	7	FL
Century National Bank & Trust Co.	10	NY
Royal Trust Bank of Palm Beach, N.A.	10	FL
Royal Trust Bank of Orlando	19	FL
Royal Trust Bank of Tampa	19	FL
International Bank of California	21	CA
(7 banks)		

Acquired By Foreign Individuals

	NBSS Peer Group	State
Bank of California, N.A.	2	CA
National American Bank of New Orleans	5	LA
Intercontinental Bank	7	FL
Security National Bank	7	CA
Republic National Bank of Miami	8	FL
Totalbank	9	FL
United Americas Bank	9	NY
Central National Bank of Miami	10	FL
Dadeland National Bank	10	FL
Main Bank of Houston	10	TX
Caribbean National Bank	13	FL
Security National Bank of New Jersey	13	NJ
Camino—California Bank	21	CA
(13 banks)		

"Pure" *De Novo* Banks

	NBSS Peer Group	State
Bank of Tokyo Trust Company	2	NY
Sumitomo Bank of California	2	CA
Industrial Bank of Japan	4	NY
J. Henry Schroder Bank & Trust Co.	4	NY
Atlantic Bank of New York	5	NY
Fuji Bank and Trust Company	6	NY
French Bank of California[a]	7	CA
Japan California Bank	7	CA
Banco di Roma (Chicago)	8	IL
Chicago-Tokyo Bank	8	IL
Daiwa Bank and Trust Company	8	NY
First Pacific Bank of Chicago	8	IL
Mitsui Bank of California	8	CA
Bank of the Orient	9	CA
Toronto Dominion Bank of California	9	CA
Banco de Bogota Trust Company	10	NY
Canadian Bank of Commerce Trust Co.	14	NY
Israel Discount Trust Company	14	NY
Bank of Montreal Trust Company	19	NY
(19 banks)		

"Hybrid" *De Novo* Banks

	NBSS Peer Group	State
Republic National Bank of New York	2	NY
Barclays Bank of New York	3	NY
Barclays Bank of California	4	CA
California Canadian Bank	4	CA
Chartered Bank of London, San Francisco[b]	4	CA
Golden State Sanwa Bank	4	CA
Mitsubishi Bank of California	7	CA
Tokai Bank of California	7	CA
(8 banks)		

[a]This bank was merged into Bank of the West in March 1980, after the period under analysis in this study.

[b]This bank was merged into Union Bank in January 1980, after the period under analysis in this study.

Appendix B
"Hybrid" *De Novo* Bank Mergers

Hybrid *De Novo* Bank	U.S. Bank Merged	Year of Merger
Republic National Bank of New York	Kings Lafayette Bank & Trust Co.	1974
Barclays Bank of New York	First Westchester National Bank	1974
Barclays Bank of California	First Valley Bank	1970
	County Bank of Santa Barbara	1974
California Canadian Bank	Northern California National Bank of San Mateo	1966
	City Bank of San Diego	1969
Chartered Bank of London, San Francisco	Liberty National Bank	1974
	Commercial & Farmers Bank of Oxnard	1977
Golden State Sanwa Bank	Charter Bank	1973
	Golden State Bank	1977
Mitsubishi Bank of California	Hacienda Bank	1976
Tokai Bank of California	Centinela Bank	1975

Appendix C
National Bank Surveillance System Peer Group Reference Table

Peer Group	Asset Range	No. Banks	Branch	Unit	Urban	Rural
1	Over $5 billion	27				
2	$1-$5 billion	137				
3	$500 million-$1 billion	79	x			
4	$500 million-$1 billion	55		x		
5	$300 million-$500 million	75	x			
6	$300 million-$500 million	69		x		
7	$100 million-$300 million	328	x			
8	$100 million-$300 million	223		x		
9	$40 million-$100 million	271	x		x	
10	$40 million-$100 million	341		x	x	
11	$40 million-$100 million	320	x			x
12	$40 million-$100 million	393		x		x
13	$25 million-$40 million	144	x		x	
14	$25 million-$40 million	167		x	x	
15	$25 million-$40 million	293	x			x
16	$25 million-$40 million	414		x		x
17	$20 million-$25 million	128		x		
18	$20 million-$25 million	369				x
19	$10 million-$20 million	303		x		
20	$10 million-$20 million	861				x
21	$0-$10 million	118		x		
22	$0-$10 million	472				x

An urban bank is located in a Standard Metropolitan Statistical Area (SMSA). A rural bank is not located in an SMSA. For Peer Groups 3 through 6, a branch bank maintains 3 or more branches while a unit bank maintains 2 or fewer branches. For Peer Groups 7 through 12 a branch bank maintains 2 or more branches while a unit bank maintains 1 branch or no branches. For Peer Groups 13-16, a branch bank maintains at least 1 branch, while a unit bank maintains no branches.

Appendix D
Ratios Examined

Asset Mix
   Real Estate Loans 1-to-4 Family/Total Gross Loans
   Loans to Individuals, Personal/Total Gross Loans
   Commercial and Industrial Loans/Total Gross Loans
   Loans in Foreign Offices/Total Gross Loans
   Gross Loans/Total Assets
   State, County, and Municipal Securities/Total Securities
   Securities Held in Foreign Offices/Total Securities
   Total Investment Securities/Total Assets

Liability Mix
   Demand Deposits/Total Deposits
   Demand Deposits/Total Assets
   Savings Deposits/Total Assets
   Time Deposits $100,000 or more/Total Assets
   Deposits in Foreign Offices/Total Assets
   Total Deposits/Total Assets
   Federal Funds Purchased and Repurchase Agreements/Total Assets
   Net Loans/Total Deposits[a]

Earnings Performance and Capital Ratios
   Return on Assets (Net Income/Total Assets)
   Return on Equity (Net Income/Total Equity Capital)
   Capital Ratio (Total Equity Capital/Total Assets)

---

[a]This ratio is not a measure of liability structure, but is used to assess the ability of a bank's deposits to support loan growth.

Appendix D (continued)

Ratio	Year	Foreign-Acquired Banks				Peer-Bank Groups				Number of Foreign-Acquired banks greater than Peer-Bank Groups
		Mean	Median	Standard Deviation	No. Nonzero	Mean	Median	Standard Deviation	No. Nonzero	
Return on Equity	2 years before acquisition	1.52	4.72	15.30	20	3.12	7.96	19.38	20	8
	1 year before acquisition	0.90	6.62	16.04	20	6.33	10.77	13.39	20	6
	1 year after acquisition	2.90	5.90	12.73	20	4.05	11.66	21.49	20	7
	2 years after acquisition	5.44	7.24	8.00	20	9.33	11.76	11.13	20	3
Equity Capital / Total Assets	2 years before acquisition	9.07	8.26	4.80	20	8.63	7.80	2.59	20	10
	1 year before acquisition	8.69	8.12	3.72	20	8.39	7.67	2.68	20	8
	1 year after acquisition	8.10	7.55	3.21	20	7.76	7.39	1.58	20	11
	2 years after acquisition	8.04	7.18	3.44	20	7.91	7.71	1.71	20	9

COMPARATIVE COST ANALYSIS OF FOREIGN-OWNED U.S. BANKS

ELLEN S. GOLDBERG

SUMMARY

This paper examines foreign-owned United States banks to determine if they enjoy any cost advantages from receipt of low cost or interest-free funds from their respective parent banks. With this goal, liability mix, interest cost and foreign assets, and liabilities of the foreign-owned United States banks are compared with United States-owned peer banks of similar size and location.

The paper finds that, in general, foreign-owned United States banks have a lower proportion of core deposits (demand, savings, time deposits under $100,000) and a higher proportion of purchased funds (time deposits of $100,000 or more, federal funds purchased, repurchase agreements, and other borrowings) than their domestically owned peers.

Foreign-owned United States banks are also found on average to have a higher total cost of interest-bearing deposits and a higher blended cost of all interest-bearing funds than their peers, but this higher cost is primarily because of the higher proportion of more costly purchased funds than core deposits in their funds mix rather than because of higher rates paid.

Given data constraints during the measurement period, the foreign-owned United States banks' actual involvement with their respective parent organizations had to be inferred. A simple comparison of balances with foreign banks or deposits of foreign banks, the titles of reported asset and liability items on United States bank balance sheets, was made with peer banks, but it was impossible to tell whether these balances or deposits were attributable in whole or in part to the foreign-owned bank's parent. The paper finds that foreign-owned banks have both a higher incidence and proportion of demand and time deposits of foreign banks (due to) than peers. They also have a higher proportion of balances with foreign banks (due from) than their domestically owned peers.

After many more observations about other differences among foreign-owned banks based on location, size and activity, the paper concludes that, ". . . on a total cost of funds basis, United States subsidiaries of foreign banks appear to have no comparative cost advantage over their domestic peers." Even with the higher proportions of foreign bank deposits in foreign-owned United States banks, the larger effects of the latter group's unfavorable and more costly liability mix more than outweigh any resulting, small compensatory effects.

INTRODUCTION

The purpose of this study is to determine whether United States subsidiaries of foreign banks enjoy a competitive cost advantage over domestically owned peer banks because the foreign parent may pass along interest-free or low cost funds to its United States subsidiary. Various ratios and interest rates were compiled from 1976 through mid-year 1979 in order to determine differences in liability mix, funds cost and international funds levels.

The data show that United States subsidiaries of foreign banks tend to have unfavorable liability mixes compared to those of their domestic peers, i.e., they exhibit a generally lower proportion of core deposits and a larger proportion of higher-cost purchased funds. That unfavorable liability mix leads to a generally higher total cost of funds.

This study concludes that, on a total cost of funds basis, there appears to be no comparative cost advantage for the United States subsidiaries of foreign banks. There is some indication that United States subsidiaries of foreign banks, particularly those established *de novo* which have not merged with United States banks, have a higher proportion of demand and time deposits of foreign banks than their United States peer banks. Even if those deposits were entirely interest-free deposits of the foreign parent, that would not offset the banks' unfavorable liability mix which results in a higher total cost of funds.

METHODOLOGY

The liability mix, cost of funds characteristics and international funds levels were examined for a sample of 16 United States subsidiaries of foreign banks for the period 1976 through 1979 and compared to domestic peer banks. Differences among the foreign-owned banks based on size, geographic location, and whether the subsidiaries merged with United States banks were also analyzed. Since the study was designed to determine possible comparative cost advantages of United States subsidiaries of foreign banks, the potential population was limited to the 74 United States banks known to be owned by foreign banks. These 74 banks consist of the 40 known acquisitions of United States commercial banks by foreign banks[1] and the 34 *de novo* subsidiaries of foreign banks.[2] The sample of 16 banks was chosen based on the following criteria:

- Only banks established or acquired/merged before December 31, 1976 were included to ensure that the sample banks had been under foreign ownership for several years. This eliminated twenty banks.
- Banks with fewer than two branches generally engage in operations that are purely wholesale, and it is difficult to find domestically owned peer banks for such banks. Thus, only banks with two or more full service branches were selected. This eliminated sixteen *de novo* banks.

The remainder of the banks were eliminated for the following reasons:

- Nineteen acquired banks were merged with *de novo* subsidiaries of foreign banks and, in effect, disappeared through consolidation.
- Three banks were omitted because foreign control was subsequently relinquished.

Table 1 presents characteristics of the 16 banks in the sample by type of ownership, geographic location, asset size, nationality of owner, and year of acquisition or formation. A list of the sample foreign-owned banks and their domestic peers is contained in Appendix A.

The following criteria were used for selecting domestically owned peers:

Table 1
Characteristics of the Sample Foreign-Owned Banks

Foreign-Owned Bank Name	Location	Type	Asset Size	Nationality of Ownership	Year[a]
Atlantic Bank of New York	New York	Pure *De Novo*[b]	$300-499 million	Greece	1926
Bank Leumi Trust Co. of New York	New York	Hybrid *De Novo*[c]	$1-5 billion	Israel	1976
Barclays Bank of California	California	Hybrid *De Novo*	$500-999 million	U.K.	1970
Barclays Bank of New York	New York	Hybrid *De Novo*	$500-999 million	U.K.	1974
California Canadian Bank	California	Hybrid *De Novo*	$500-999 million	Canada	1969
California First Bank	California	Hybrid *De Novo*	$1-5 billion	Japan	1975
Chartered Bank of London	California	Hybrid *De Novo*	$500-999 million	U.K.	1974
European-American Bank and Trust	New York	Hybrid *De Novo*	$1-5 billion	European banks	1974
French Bank of California	California	Pure *De Novo*	$100-299 million	France	1972
Golden State Sanwa Bank	California	Hybrid *De Novo*	$500-999 million	Japan	1974
Japan California Bank	California	Pure *De Novo*	$100-299 million	Japan	1974
Lloyds Bank California[d]	California	Hybrid Bank	$1-5 billion	U.K.	1974
Mitsubishi Bank of California	California	Hybrid *De Novo*	$100-299 million	Japan	1974
Republic National Bank of New York	New York	Hybrid *De Novo*	$1-5 billion	Japan	1976
Sumitomo Bank of California	California	Pure *De Novo*	$1-5 billion	Brazil	1974
Tokai Bank of California	California	Hybrid *De Novo*	$100-299 million	Japan	1952
				Japan	1975

[a]For the pure *de novo* banks, the year noted is the year established, while for the hybrid banks, it is the year of the first merger or acquisition of a U.S. bank.

[b]A pure *de novo* bank, for purposes of this analysis, is a bank established *de novo* in the U.S. by a foreign parent bank that has not merged with a U.S. bank.

[c]A hybrid *de novo* bank, for purposes of this analysis, is a bank established *de novo* in the U.S. by a foreign parent bank that *has* subsequently merged with a U.S. bank.

[d]Lloyds Group acquired First Western Bank and Trust in 1974 and changed the bank's name to Lloyds Bank California. Lloyds Bank California subsequently merged First State Bank of Northern California in 1976.

- They were in the same National Bank Surveillance System (NBSS) peer group as the foreign-owned banks.[3] (Appendix B describes the NBSS peer groups.)
- They were located in the same Standard Metropolitan Statistical Area (SMSA), state or region as the foreign-owned banks.

A series of ratios and interest rates were analyzed from 1976 through June 30, 1979[4] for the foreign-owned banks and compared to those of selected domestic peer banks and to peer group averages computed by the National Bank Surveillance System (NBSS).

The ratios and interest rates examined were broken into three categories: liability mix, interest rates, and due to and due from foreign banks. The first two, liability mix and interest rates, influence the cost of funds of the banks. The third is used as a possible indicator of the extent to which money may be passing between the foreign parent and the United States subsidiary. The three categories were defined as follows:

- *Liability Mix*—ratio of deposits in foreign offices (primarily Eurodollars), purchased funds, and core deposits, each as a percentage of total assets.
- *Interest Rates*—rates on deposits in foreign offices and on certificates of deposit (CDs) of $100,000 or more; the blended cost of all interest-bearing deposits,[5] and the blended or weighted average cost of all interest-bearing funds.[6]
- *Due To and Due From Foreign Banks*—deposits of banks in foreign countries (due to) as a percentage of total deposits, and balances with banks in foreign countries (due from) as a percentage of total cash and due from banks. (It was impossible to tell whether these deposits were exclusively the deposits of or balances with the foreign parent bank.)

Appendix C presents a list of the ratios and interest rates analyzed.

Data for the sample foreign-owned banks in the sample were compared with those for selected peer banks of similar size and location and with NBSS peer groups.[7] Sample means were calculated for each ratio for the composite of the foreign-owned banks in the sample, for the geographically similar peers, and for the NBSS peer group. The NBSS peer group composite was calculated by weighting the NBSS peer group average for a particular size class by the number of foreign-owned banks in that NBSS peer group classification.[8]

Composite means were calculated for the sample banks grouped by asset size, geographic location, and type of activity in the United States to ascertain if there were differences based on those attributes. Analyses were made of the differences in the ratios and rates of the foreign-owned banks compared to the geographically similar domestic peers and to the NBSS peer group average, including changes in the spreads among the groups over time, changes in the ratios themselves over time, and differences among the groups based on size, location, and activity in the United States.

FOREIGN-OWNED BANKS COMPARED TO GEOGRAPHICALLY SIMILAR PEERS

Liability Mix

As revealed in Table 2, the foreign-owned bank mean proportion of assets funded by core deposits, i.e., demand deposits, savings deposits, and time deposits of under $100,000, was consistently a quarter lower than the geographically similar peers, and this difference was highly statistically significant in each of the four years. Both the foreign-owned banks and the peers exhibited declining proportions of core deposits over time. The foreign-owned banks' mean ratio of purchased funds, i.e., time deposits of $100,000 or more, federal funds purchased, repurchase agreements, and other borrowings, as a percentage of total assets was nearly double that of geographically similar peers, and again the difference was highly statistically significant. Both groups had increasing proportions of purchased funds over the four years examined. For 12 of the 16 foreign-owned banks in the sample, data were available on deposits in foreign offices (primarily interest-bearing Eurodollars), and only half of those banks had foreign office deposits. Comparing the means of the foreign-owned banks with deposits in foreign offices to those of the peers with such deposits, reveals that, in 1976-79, foreign-owned banks averaged about three times as much as the peers, and these differences were statistically significant in each of the four years. It should be noted, however, that both the incidence and the proportion of foreign office deposits were rather low for both the foreign-owned bank group and the geographically similar peers. Both the foreign-owned banks and the geographically similar peers experienced an increasing proportion of deposits in foreign offices over the four year period.

Interest Rates

The mean rates the foreign-owned banks paid on large certificates of deposit (CDs) and on deposits in foreign offices (Eurodollars) during the four years were generally mixed in comparison to those paid by the geographically similar peers.[9] On a total cost of funds basis, it is noted that the weighted average cost of all interest-bearing deposits and the cost of all interest-bearing funds were about 80 basis points higher for the foreign-owned banks than for the geographically similar peers in 1978 and the first half of 1979, the two periods with the highest statistical difference. The generally higher cost of funds appears to be the result of the foreign-owned banks' lower proportion of core deposits and higher proportion of purchased funds, rather than higher rates paid on those funds.

Due to and Due From Foreign Banks

The volume of due to and due from foreign bank accounts does not necessarily point to the passing of funds between the foreign parent and the United States subsidiary; however, a higher level would tend to suggest some degree of passing of funds between parent and subsidiary. Table 2 reveals that the foreign-owned banks had more than 10 times the amount of demand deposits of foreign banks (due to foreign banks) as a percentage of total deposits than the geographically similar peers, with the difference being highly statistically significant. Also, the foreign-owned banks' proportion of time deposits of foreign banks as a percentage of total deposits averaged between 3 and 6 percent over the four-year period, while the geographically similar peers generally had no such deposits. Again the difference between the two groups of banks in this ratio was statistically significant. However, the proportions of these deposits to total deposits (3 to 4 percent for demand and 3 to 6 percent for time) are relatively low. Over the four years examined, foreign-owned banks experienced a slight decline in demand deposits of foreign banks as a percentage of total deposits and an increase in time deposits of foreign banks as a percentage of total deposits. Also, 14 of the 16 foreign-owned banks in the sample held demand deposits of foreign

Table 2

	Foreign-Owned Banks				
	1976[a]	1977[a]	1978[a]	6/30/79[a]	No. of Nonzeros
Liability Mix:					
Deposits in Foreign Offices/ Total Assets	10.79+	12.34#	12.73#	13.66+	6
Purchased Funds/ Total Assets[b]	26.85*	26.89*	30.21*	33.31*	16
Core Deposits/ Total Assets[c]	58.29*	57.76*	56.44*	52.60*	16
Interest Rates:					
Rate on Deposits in Foreign Offices	5.85	5.23	7.58	9.44	6
Rate on Large CDs— $100,000 or more	5.42	5.20+	7.28	9.50	16
Rate on All Interest- Bearing Deposits	5.43	5.38	6.69*	8.15+	16
Rate on All Interest- Bearing Funds	5.46	5.43	6.82*	8.36+	16

	12/31/75	12/31/76	12/31/77	12/31/78	No. of Nonzeros
Due to and Due from Foreign Banks:					
Deposits of Banks in Foreign Countries/ Total Deposits:					
Demand Deposits	3.93*	4.91*	3.29*	3.48*	14
Time Deposits	3.22+	3.24*	6.74+	6.64#	8
Balance with Foreign Banks/Total Cash and Due from Banks	12.80	13.14	11.80#	8.56	14

[a]Represents year average figures for 1976 through 1978 and year-to-date figures for 1979 through June 30, 1979 computed by adding the balance of the account on the Report of Condition of the Call Report at the preceding year-end to the balance at each subsequent reporting period (quarter) during the current year and dividing by the number of reporting periods.

[b]Purchased funds include time deposits of $100,000 or more, federal funds purchased, securities sold under agreements to repurchase, and other borrowings.

[c]Core deposits include demand deposits, savings deposits, time deposits under $100,000 and foreign office deposits.

N/A—not available.

Mean Ratios for All Banks Analyzed

	Geographically Similar Peers					NBSS Peer Group Composite			
1976[a]	1977[a]	1978[a]	6/30/79[a]	No. of Nonzeros	1976[a]	1977[a]	1978[a]	6/30/79[a]
2.88	3.12	3.76	5.21	3	2.15	2.79	2.90	3.38
16.49	14.58	19.01	22.44	16	20.16	19.98	22.72	24.60
74.80	77.09	72.52	68.81	16	70.48	71.34	68.28	65.73
5.76	5.76	7.74	9.14	5	7.35	5.86	8.28	9.90
7.11	7.79	7.00	9.95	16	5.87	5.75	7.47	9.71
5.40	5.38	5.82	7.44	16	5.46	5.48	6.20	7.28
5.49	5.60	6.00	7.56	16	5.28	5.34	6.23	7.17
12/31/75	12/31/76	12/31/77	12/31/78	No. of Nonzeros	12/31/75	12/31/76	12/31/77	12/31/78
0.30	0.29	0.29	0.32	7	N/A	N/A	N/A	N/A
0.02	0.00	0.13	0.01	2	N/A	N/A	N/A	N/A
2.31	2.79	0.75	1.40	9	N/A	N/A	N/A	N/A

The three symbols of *, #, and + indicate the levels of statistical significance of the difference between the foreign-owned banks and the geographically similar peers. Three statistical tests were computed: the Student's t-test, the Mann-Whitney U-test, and the Wilcoxon matched-pairs, singed-rank test (for a description of these tests see Blair B. Hodgkins and Ellen S. Goldberg, "Effect of Foreign Acquisition on the Balance Sheet Structure and Earnings Performance of American Banks," OCC Staff Paper, 1980-9). The levels of significance indicated in the table are those for the Wilcoxon matched-pairs, signed-rank test, which is the most restrictive of the three tests. In many cases, all three tests indicated levels of significance above 90 percent. The key to the symbols for levels of significance is as follows:

* significant at an α of 99%
# significant at an α of 95%
+ significant at an α of 90%

banks and eight held time deposits of foreign banks. By contrast, only seven of the 14 peer banks held demand deposits of foreign banks and only two held time deposits of foreign banks.

Balances with foreign banks (due from foreign banks) as a percentage of total cash and due from banks were generally higher for the foreign-owned banks than their geographically similar peers, with the difference significant in one of the four years. Such balances are usually associated with foreign exchange activity and would indicate a higher degree of international activity among the foreign-owned banks than among the domestically owned peers. Fourteen of the 16 foreign-owned banks had balances with foreign banks, while only nine of the 14 geographically similar peers had such balances during the period examined.

FOREIGN-OWNED BANKS COMPARED TO NBSS PEER GROUPS

Liability Mix

Some interesting observations arise upon comparison of the foreign-owned banks with a broad base of similar-size peer banks (i.e., NBSS peers). Table 2 shows that the NBSS peer group mean proportion of assets funded by purchased funds was somewhat higher than the geographically similar peers over the four-year period, but was still lower than the foreign-owned bank group mean. The foreign-owned banks, therefore, not only had a considerably higher proportion of purchased funds than geographically similar peers, but also had a generally higher proportion of purchased funds than banks of similar size, but not necessarily located in the same geographic area. Table 2 also reveals that the NBSS peer group mean ratio of deposits in foreign offices to total assets was slightly lower than the geographically similar peers during the four years, and was much lower than the foreign-owned bank mean.

Interest Rates

Although the foreign-owned banks, on average, had a higher proportion of both purchased funds and deposits in foreign offices compared to the NBSS peer groups, the rates they paid on foreign office deposits and certificates of deposit of $100,000 or more were, on average, somewhat lower. However, the weighted average cost of interest-bearing deposits and cost of interest-bearing funds were generally higher for the foreign-owned banks than their NBSS peers, probably because of their larger proportion of higher cost interest-bearing funds rather than the rates they paid on those funds.

COMPARISONS BASED ON GEOGRAPHIC LOCATION

Tables 3 and 4 show the sample means for California and New York banks, respectively. The foreign-owned banks are compared with the geographically similar peers. Observations based on the comparisons in Tables 3 and 4 follow.

Liability Mix

Ratios for the geographically similar peers in New York and California reflect differences between the states in the history of branch banking laws and thrift institution traditions, as well as their financial markets and economies. This is evident in the higher proportion of "money market" purchased funds and deposits in foreign offices (Eurodollars) exhibited by the New York peer banks in comparison to the California peer banks. The California peer banks tend to have a higher proportion of assets funded by core deposits (particularly savings deposits) than the New York peer banks. For the foreign-owned banks in California and New York, however, the proportion of assets funded by core deposits is higher for the New York foreign-owned banks than those in California. Also, the California foreign-owned banks had a somewhat higher mean proportion of purchased funds than the New York foreign-owned banks in three of the four years examined. Both the California and New York foreign-owned banks had, on average, a lower percentage of core deposits and a higher proportion of purchased funds than their geographically similar peers, and these differences were generally statistically significant. The New York foreign-owned banks, like their New York peers, had a higher mean proportion of deposits in foreign offices than the California foreign-owned banks and the California peers.

Table 3
Mean Ratios for California Banks

	Foreign-Owned Banks in California					Geographically Similar Peers				
	1976[a]	1977[a]	1978[a]	6/30/79[a]	No. of Nonzeros	1976[a]	1977[a]	1978[a]	6/30/79[a]	No. of Nonzeros
Liability Mix:										
Deposits in Foreign Offices/Total Assets	5.84	7.98*	7.00	4.95	3	1.44	1.98	2.08	2.19	1
Purchased Funds/Total Assets[b]	27.40*	26.46*	31.37*	36.52*	11	16.40	12.85	17.46	22.19	11
Core Deposits/Total Assets[c]	55.88*	55.75*	53.96*	47.84*	11	78.84	79.60	74.74	69.64	11
Interest Rates:										
Rate on Deposits in Foreign Offices	6.44	5.42	8.12	9.38	3	4.69	4.65	6.27	7.70	1
Rate on Large CDs–$100,000 or more	5.29	5.20#	7.19	9.30	11	7.89	8.93	7.07	10.06	11
Rate on All Interest-Bearing Deposits	5.39	5.34	6.66*	8.05#	11	5.47	5.41	5.94	7.11	11
Rate on All Interest-Bearing Funds	5.43	5.41	6.81*	8.32#	11	5.59	5.75	6.23	7.25	11

	12/31/75	12/31/76	12/31/77	12/31/78	No. of Nonzeros	12/31/75	12/31/76	12/31/77	12/31/78	No. of Nonzeros
Due to and Due From Foreign Banks:										
Deposits of Banks in Foreign Countries/Total Deposits:										
Demand Deposits	2.42*	1.73#	1.61#	1.07#	9	0.15	0.11	0.12	0.13	3
Time Deposits	5.83	3.78	7.89+	9.43	5	0.03	0.00	0.02	0.01	1
Balance with Foreign Banks/Total Cash and Due From Banks	4.74	6.03	4.13#	0.48	9	1.09	0.97	0.28	2.02	3

[a]Represents year average figures for 1976 through 1978 and year-to-date figures for 1979 through June 30, 1979 computed by adding the balance of the account on the Report of Condition of the Call Report at the preceding year-end to the balance at each subsequent reporting period (quarter) during the current year and dividing by the number of reporting periods.

[b]Purchased funds include time deposits of $100,000 or more, federal funds purchased, securities sold under agreements to repurchase, and other borrowings.

[c]Core deposits include demand deposits, savings deposits, time deposits under $100,000 and foreign office deposits.

Wilcoxon test levels of significance:

    * significant at an α of 99%
    # significant at an α of 95%
    + significant at an α of 90%

Table 4

Mean Ratios for New York Banks

	Foreign-Owned Banks in New York					Geographically Similar Peers				
	1976[a]	1977[a]	1978[a]	6/30/79[a]	No. of Nonzeros	1976[a]	1977[a]	1978[a]	6/30/79[a]	No. of Nonzeros
Liability Mix:										
Deposits in Foreign Offices/Total Assets	15.74	15.61	17.03	20.20	3	3.44	3.18	4.02	5.98	4
Purchased Funds/Total Assets[b]	25.63*	27.85+	27.67	26.26	5	16.68	18.40	22.43	22.98	5
Core Deposits/Total Assets[c]	63.57	62.14+	61.89	63.06	5	72.12	70.69	67.61	67.41	5
Interest Rates:										
Rate on Deposits in Foreign Offices	5.25	5.03	7.03	9.49	3	6.12	6.04	8.11	9.50	4
Rate on Large CDs–$100,000 or more	5.71	5.19	7.49	9.94	5	5.38	5.29	6.83	9.70	5
Rate on All Interest-Bearing Deposits	5.52+	5.46	6.74+	8.36	5	5.24	5.22	5.58	8.16	5
Rate on All Interest-Bearing Funds	5.52	5.46	6.85+	8.44	5	5.26	5.29	5.50	8.20	5
	12/31/75	12/31/76	12/31/77	12/31/78	No. of Nonzeros	12/31/75	12/31/76	12/31/77	12/31/78	No. of Nonzeros
Due to and Due From Foreign Banks:										
Deposits of Banks in Foreign Countries/Total Deposits:										
Demand Deposits	6.95+	11.26+	6.66+	7.80+	5	0.59	0.65	0.63	0.66	4
Time Deposits	0.61	2.53	5.30	1.06	3	0.00	0.00	0.28	0.00	1
Balance with Foreign Banks/Total Cash and Due From Banks	27.32	27.36	27.12	24.07	5	4.52	6.43	1.69	0.40	4

[a]Represents year average figures for 1976 through 1978 and year-to-date figures for 1979 through June 30, 1979 computed by adding the balance of the account on the Report of Condition of the Call Report at the preceding year-end to the balance at each subsequent reporting period (quarter) during the current year and dividing by the number of reporting periods.

[b]Purchased funds include time deposits of $100,000 or more, federal funds purchased, securities sold under agreements to repurchase, and other borrowings.

[c]Core deposits include demand deposits, savings deposits, time deposits under $100,000 and foreign office deposits.

Wilcoxon test levels of significance:

* significant at an α of 99%
# significant at an α of 95%
+ significant at an α of 90%

381

Interest Rates

The New York foreign-owned banks paid less, on average, for deposits in foreign offices than the New York peer banks from 1976 to 1978, but the differences were not statistically significant. The average rate on CD's of $100,000 or more was generally higher for the foreign-owned New York banks than for the New York peer banks. However, again primarily because of the liability mix, the New York foreign-owned banks had a higher cost of interest-bearing funds than the geographically similar peers. In 1978 and the first half of 1979, the California foreign-owned banks had, on average, a higher cost of interest-bearing deposits and funds than their geographically similar peers. On average, the New York foreign-owned banks had a somewhat higher cost of interest-bearing deposits and funds than the California foreign-owned banks.

Due To and Due From Foreign Banks

All five New York foreign-owned banks and nine of the 11 California foreign-owned banks held demand deposits of foreign banks. The New York foreign-owned banks had a higher proportion of such deposits than the California foreign-owned banks; however, the California foreign-owned banks, in general, had a somewhat higher proportion of foreign banks' time deposits than the New York foreign-owned banks. Few of the geographically similar peers held foreign bank demand and time deposits and the proportion held, if any, was quite small.

The foreign-owned banks in New York had much higher balances with foreign banks as a percentage of total cash and due from banks than the foreign-owned banks in California. This is in line with the higher degree of international activity exhibited by the New York banks. Both foreign-owned bank groups had a higher proportion of balances with foreign banks than their geographically similar peers.

COMPARISONS BASED ON ASSET SIZE[10]

Tables 5 through 7 present the means for the sample foreign-owned banks grouped according to asset size, compared to those for the geographically similar peers and the NBSS peer groups. The NBSS size categories relevant to this discussion are: the $1 to $5 billion asset size range (NBSS Peer Group 2), the $500 million to $1 billion asset size range (NBSS Peer Group 4), and the $100 to $300 million asset size range (NBSS Peer Group 7). Following are observations based on comparisons between foreign-owned banks and their peers in similar asset size groups.

Liability Mix

Among the foreign-owned banks it appears that the smaller the foreign-owned bank, the lower the proportion of core deposits and the higher the proportion of purchased funds. Only the largest foreign-owned banks, those in the $1 to $5 billion asset size category, have deposits in foreign offices (Eurodollars). Their proportion of these deposits to total assets is considerably higher than either the geographically similar peers or the NBSS peer group average, but all showed an increasing reliance on Eurodollars as a source of funds. Foreign-owned banks in each size class had lower proportions of core deposits and higher proportions of purchased funds compared to their geographically similar peers, and these differences were statistically significant for two of the three size classes. This is particularly evident in the $100 to $300 million asset size foreign-owned banks, which showed, for the first six months of 1979, an average proportion of purchased funds that exceeded the average proportion of core deposits.

Interest Rates

The foreign-owned banks do not exhibit any particular trend of higher or lower rates paid for large CDs and for deposits in foreign offices across asset size categories, or when compared with their geographically similar peers. However, Tables 5 through 7 show that the largest foreign-owned banks had a higher cost of interest-bearing deposits and funds than the smaller foreign-owned banks. An analysis of those tables reveals that the higher cost of funds is primarily due to the higher proportion of deposits in foreign offices (Eurodollars) exhibited by the larger foreign-owned banks. Foreign-owned banks in each size group had higher average costs of funds than either the geographically similar peers or the NBSS peer groups.

Table 5

	Foreign-Owned Banks in Peer Group 2[a]				
	1976[b]	1977[b]	1978[b]	6/30/79[b]	No. of Nonzeros
Liability Mix:					
Deposits in Foreign Offices/Total Assets	14.37*	14.40*	14.85*	15.94*	6
Purchased Funds/ Total Assets[c]	24.41*	25.19*	25.41*	24.82	6
Core Deposits/ Total Assets[d]	65.06+	64.53*	64.04+	64.42	6
Interest Rates:					
Rate on Deposits in Foreign Offices	5.85	5.22	7.58	9.44+	6
Rate on Large CDs— $100,000 or more	5.49	5.00	6.91	10.09+	6
Rate on All Interest- Bearing Deposits	5.64#	5.47+	6.72*	8.45*	6
Rate on All Interest- Bearing Funds	5.67*	5.51+	6.83*	8.47	6
	12/31/75	12/31/76	12/31/77	12/31/78	No. of Nonzeros
Due To and Due From Foreign Banks:					
Deposits of Banks in Foreign Countries/ Total Deposits:					
Demand Deposits	2.10#	3.45#	1.94+	2.61+	6
Time Deposits	0.60	2.36	5.29	0.35	3
Balance with Foreign Banks/Total Cash and Due From Banks	18.14	20.34	15.70	4.09	6

[a] Peer Group 2 includes banks with total assets of $1 to $5 billion as of December 31, 1978, as determined by the National Bank Surveillance System (NBSS) of the Office of the Comptroller of the Currency. The NBSS peer group 2 average included 138 banks as of June 30, 1979.

[b] Represents years average figures for 1976 through 1978 and year-to-date average figures for 1979 through June 30, 1979 computed by adding the balance of the account on the Report of Condition of the Call Report at the preceding year-end to the balance at each subsequent reporting period (quarter) during the current year and dividing by the number of reporting periods.

N/A—not available.

	Geographically Similar Peers					NBSS Peer Group Composite			
76^b	1977^b	1978^b	6/30/79^b	No. of Nonzeros		1976^b	1977^b	1978^b	6/30/79^b
3.35	3.27	3.99	5.71	4		3.73	3.93	4.25	4.68
18.18	17.64	22.28	23.03	6		23.94	24.13	27.50	29.67
72.03	73.11	68.69	67.85	6		66.73	66.85	63.26	60.56
5.70	5.73	7.66	8.73	4		6.53	5.75	7.85	9.49
5.59	5.35	6.68	9.57	6		5.73	5.49	7.50	9.89
5.30	5.21	6.06	7.18	6		5.46	5.43	6.34	7.63
5.30	5.24	6.25	7.72	6		5.40	5.45	6.59	7.93

31/75	12/31/76	12/31/77	12/31/78	No. of Nonzeros		12/31/75	12/31/76	12/31/77	12/31/78
0.44	0.47	0.52	0.56	5		N/A	N/A	N/A	N/A
0.03	0.00	0.30	0.02	2		N/A	N/A	N/A	N/A
3.74	5.52	1.45	2.49	6		N/A	N/A	N/A	N/A

^{c}Purchased funds include time deposits of $100,000 or more, federal funds purchased, securities sold under agreements to repurchase, and other borrowings.

^{d}Core deposits include demand deposits, savings deposits, time deposits under $100,000, and foreign office deposits.

Wilcoxon test levels of significance:
* significant at an a of 99%
# significant at an a of 95%
+ significant at an a of 90%

Table 6

	Foreign-Owned Banks in Peer Group 4[a]				
	1976[b]	1977[b]	1978[b]	6/30/79[b]	No. of Nonzeros
Liability Mix:					
Deposits in Foreign Offices/Total Assets	0.00	0.00	0.00	0.00	0
Purchased Funds/Total Assets[c]	25.32	24.69	29.70	35.65	4
Core Deposits/ Total Assets[d]	65.71	67.28	63.61	56.64	4
Interest Rates:					
Rate on Deposits in Foreign Offices	0.00	0.00	0.00	0.00	0
Rate on Large CDs— $100,000 or more	5.35+	6.25	7.18	9.57	4
Rate on All Interest-Bearing Deposits	5.18	5.32	6.54	7.85	4
Rate on All Interest-Bearing Funds	5.23	5.41	6.73	8.27	4

	12/31/75	12/31/76	12/31/77	12/31/78	No. of Nonzeros
Due To and Due From Foreign Banks:					
Deposits of Banks in Foreign Countries/ Total Deposits:					
Demand Deposits	1.92#	1.30+	1.33+	1.03+	3
Time Deposits	0.00	0.00	3.20	4.25	1
Balance with Foreign Banks/Total Cash and Due From Banks	1.45	1.82	1.23	0.55	3

[a]Peer Group 4 includes banks with total assets of $500 million to $1 billion as of December 31, 1978, and 2 or less full service branches, as determined by the National Bank Surveillance System (NBSS) of the Office of the Comptroller of the Currency. The NBSS peer Group 4 average included 50 banks as of June 30, 1979.

[b]Represents year average figures for 1976 through 1978 and year-to-date average figures for 1979 through June 30, 1979 computed by adding the balance of the account on the Report of Condition of the Call Report at the preceding year-end to the balance at each subsequent reporting period (quarter) during the current year and dividing by the number of reporting periods.

N/A—not available.

lean Ratios for Peer Group 4^d Banks (Assets of \$500 Million to \$1 Billion)

	Geographically Similar Peers					NBSS Peer Group Composite			
976^b	1977^b	1978^b	6/30/79^b	No. of Nonzeros	1976^b	1977^b	1978^b	6/30/79^b
.00	0.00	0.00	0.00	0	0.00	2.41	2.27	3.04
.85	12.89	17.64	24.61	4	24.67	24.33	27.45	29.12
.26	79.23	73.86	66.30	4	65.84	67.82	63.75	60.45
.00	0.00	0.00	0.00	0	8.71	5.80	8.87	10.79
.25	7.65	7.19	9.63	4	6.11	6.00	7.49	9.94
.71	5.53	6.06	7.35	4	5.45	5.50	6.42	7.75
.65	5.48	6.15	7.45	4	5.41	5.51	6.90	8.07
31/75	12/31/76	12/31/77	12/31/78	No. of Nonzeros	12/31/75	12/31/76	12/31/77	12/31/78
.17	0.15	0.15	0.10	2	N/A	N/A	N/A	N/A
.00	0.00	0.00	0.00	0	N/A	N/A	N/A	N/A
.21	2.01	0.55	0.50	2	N/A	N/A	N/A	N/A

^{c}Purchased funds include time deposits of \$100,000 or more, federal funds purchased, securities sold under agreements to repurchase, and other borrowings.

^{d}Core deposits include demand deposits, savings deposits, time deposits under \$100,000 and foreign office deposits.

Since the sample size was too small for the Wilcoxon test, the next most restrictive test, Mann-Whitney, was used. Levels of significance for Mann-Whitney are:

* significant at an a of 99%

\# significant at an a of 95%

+ significant at an a of 90%

Table 7

	Foreign-Owned Banks in Peer Group 7[a]				
	1976[b]	1977[b]	1978[b]	6/30/79[b]	No. of Nonzeros
Liability Mix:					
Deposits in Foreign Offices/Total Assets	N/A	N/A	N/A	N/A	N/A
Purchased Funds/ Total Assets[c]	30.39#	30.30+	36.67+	43.26#	4
Core Deposits/ Total Assets[d]	39.52#	35.46#	36.34#	28.21#	4
Interest Rates:					
Rate on Deposits in Foreign Offices	N/A	N/A	N/A	N/A	N/A
Rate on Large CDs— $100,000 or more	5.16	4.65#	7.92	8.68#	4
Rate on All Interest-Bearing Deposits	5.48	5.29#	6.92#	8.23#	4
Rate on All Interest-Bearing Funds	5.50+	5.39#	7.08	8.51#	4

	12/31/75	12/31/76	12/31/77	12/31/78	No. of Nonzeros
Due To and Due From Foreign Banks:					
Deposits of Banks in Foreign Countries/ Total Deposits:					
Demand Deposits	4.90#	3.40#	3.19#	2.12	3
Time Deposits	8.75	4.98#	8.88#	10.36	4
Balance with Foreign Banks/Total Cash and Due From Banks	0.65	0.88#	3.05#	0.18	3

[a]Peer Group 7 includes banks with total assets of between $100 and $300 million as of December 31, 1978 and 2 more full service branches, as determined by the National Bank Surveillance System (NBSS) of the Office of the Comptroller of the Currency. The NBSS peer group 7 average included 326 banks as of June 30, 1979.

[b]Represents year average figures for 1976 through 1978 and year-to-date average figures for 1979 through June 30, 1979 computed by adding the balance of the account on the Report of Condition of the Call Report at the preceding year-end to the balance at each subsequent reporting period (quarter) during the current year and dividing by the number of reporting periods.

N/A—not available.

	Geographically Similar Peers					NBSS Peer Group Composite		
976^b	1977^b	1978^b	6/30/79^b	No. of Nonzeros	1976^b	1977^b	1978^b	6/30/79^b
N/A	N/A	NA/	N/A	NA/	N/A	N/A	N/A	N/A
12.19	9.63	14.24	17.90	4	11.52	11.10	12.86	14.49
81.10	84.08	79.29	75.28	4	79.26	80.07	78.30	76.46
N/A	N/A	N/A	N/A	N/A	N/A	N/A	N/A	N/A
9.17	12.86	6.91	10.67	4	5.82	5.87	7.36	9.42
5.52	5.64	5.80	6.79	4	5.51	5.55	5.92	6.57
5.91	6.61	6.47	6.48	4	4.93	4.95	5.15	5.22
/31/75	12/31/76	12/31/77	12/31/78	No. of Nonzeros	12/31/75	12/31/76	12/31/77	12/31/78
0.00	0.00	0.00	0.00	0	N/A	N/A	N/A	N/A
0.00	0.00	0.00	0.00	0	N/A	N/A	N/A	N/A
0.00	0.00	0.00	0.00	0	N/A	N/A	N/A	N/A

^{c}Purchased funds include time deposits of \$100,000 or more, federal funds purchased, securities sold under agreements to repurchase, and other borrowings.

^{d}Core deposits include demand deposits, savings deposits, time deposits under \$100,000, and foreign office deposits.

Since the sample size was too small for the Wilcoxon test, the next most restrictive test, Mann-Whitney, was used. Levels of significance for Mann-Whitney are:

    * significant at an a of 99%
    # significant at an a of 95%
    + significant at an a of 90%

Due To and Due From Foreign Banks

The incidence of demand deposits of foreign banks (due to) was high in each size group of foreign-owned banks, particularly among the largest banks. All three size groups had a higher proportion of these deposits than the geographically similar peers. This was particularly evident for the smallest size group, where none of the peers had these deposits, but three of the four foreign-owned banks held between 2.12 and 4.90 percent of their total deposits in deposits of foreign banks over the four-year period. These smaller foreign-owned banks also had a higher incidence of time deposits of foreign banks and a higher proportion of such deposits to total deposits than the other two foreign-owned bank groups. The largest foreign-owned banks had the highest proportion of balances with foreign banks (due from foreign banks). Foreign-owned banks in the $1 to $5 billion and the $100 to $300 million asset category had higher proportions of due from foreign banks than their peers, while foreign-owned banks in the $500 million to $1 billion asset category had about the same proportion of such balances as their peers.

COMPARISONS BASED ON WHETHER THE FOREIGN-OWNED DE NOVO BANKS HAVE SUBSEQUENTLY MERGED WITH U. S. BANKS[11]

Table 8 compares the ratios and rates for the four banks in the sample established *de novo* that have *not* merged with United States banks, the "pure" *de novo* banks, with the twelve banks in the sample established *de novo* that *have* subsequently merged with United States banks, the "hybrid" *de novo* banks. The analysis was undertaken to determine whether *de novo* subsidiaries of foreign banks, once they merge with United States banks, change in liability structure or pay different interest rates on those liabilities.

Liability Mix

The "pure" *de novo* banks (all having two or more full service branches) had, on average, a lower proportion of assets funded by core deposits, and a higher proportion of assets funded by purchased funds

Table 8
Mean Ratios for "Pure"[a] and "Hybrid"[b] De Novo Banks

	"Pure" De Novo Banks[a]					"Hybrid" De Novo Banks[b]				
	1976[c]	1977[c]	1978[c]	6/30/79[c]	No. of Nonzeros	1976[c]	1977[c]	1978[c]	6/30/79[c]	No. of Nonzeros
Liability Mix:										
Deposits in Foreign Offices/Total Assets	5.99	5.17	3.95	3.44	2	14.85	15.21	16.24	17.76	5
Purchased Funds/Total Assets[d]	33.36	31.18	30.87	38.61	4	24.68	25.47	30.00	31.55	12
Core Deposits/Total Assets[e]	50.96	54.03	56.03	48.95	4	60.73	58.98	56.57	53.47	12
Interest Rates:										
Rate on Deposits in Foreign Offices	6.83	6.12	8.46	10.95	2	5.65	5.04	7.40	9.13	5
Rate on Large CDs–$100,000 or more	5.11	4.49	7.28	8.64	4	5.53	5.43	7.29	9.78	12
Rate on All Interest-Bearing Deposits	5.48	5.34	6.84	8.17	4	5.42	5.38	6.63	8.13	12
Rate on All Interest-Bearing Funds	5.44	5.40	6.95	8.32	4	5.46	5.43	6.78	8.36	12

	12/31/75	12/31/76	12/31/77	12/31/78	No. of Nonzeros	12/31/75	12/31/76	12/31/77	12/31/78	No. of Nonzeros
Due To and Due From Foreign Banks:										
Deposits of Banks in Foreign Countries/ Total Deposits:										
Demand Deposits	8.81	12.03	7.14	9.43	4	2.15	2.31	2.08	2.03	11
Time Deposits	4.33	2.78	4.00	3.29	3	0.40	2.19	8.93	6.65	5
Balance with Foreign Banks/Total Cash and Due From Banks	0.53	0.92	2.51	1.68	4	17.71	19.34	16.69	9.95	10

[a]"Pure" De Novo Banks is the term used to describe subsidiaries of foreign banks established *de novo* that have *not* merged with U.S. banks. The four "pure" de novo banks in this study are Atlantic Bank of New York, French Bank of California, Japan California Bank and Sumitomo Bank of California.

[b]"Hybrid" De Novo Banks is the term used to describe subsidiaries of foreign banks established *de novo* that *have* merged with U.S. banks.

[c]Represents year average figures for 1976 through 1978 and year-to-date average figures for 1979 through June 30, 1979 computed by adding the balance of the account on the Report of Condition of the Call Report at the preceding year-end to the balance at each subsequent reporting period (quarter) during the current year and dividing by the number of reporting periods.

[d]Purchased funds include time deposits of $100,000 or more, federal funds purchased, securities sold under agreements to repurchase, and other borrowings.

[e]Core deposits include demand deposits, savings deposits, time deposits under $100,000, and foreign office deposits.

than the "hybrid" *de novo* banks, indicating the more wholesale nature of even these sample "pure" *de novo* banks that have two or more branches. Among those banks for which data on deposits in foreign offices were available, two of the four "pure" *de novo* banks and 10 of the 12 "hybrid" *de novo* banks, both of the "pure" *de novo* banks had such deposits but only five of the 10 "hybrid" *de novo* banks had foreign office (primarily Eurodollar) deposits. The "hybrid" *de novo* banks had a higher proportion of such deposits.

Interest Rates

Table 8 indicates that, in general, during the period examined, the "pure" *de novo* banks paid higher rates for deposits in foreign offices and lower rates for large certificates of deposit than the "hybrid" *de novo* banks. On a total cost basis, the two groups had a fairly similar average cost of interest-bearing deposits and interest-bearing funds.

Due To and Due From Foreign Banks

The "pure" *de novo* banks had a much higher average proportion of demand deposits of foreign banks to total deposits than the "hybrid" *de novo* banks (ranging from 7.14 to 9.43 percent over the period as compared to 2.03 to 2.31 percent, respectively), perhaps indicating less need on the part of the "hybrid" *de novo* banks for such funds because of a stronger local deposit base. All four of the "pure" *de novo* banks and 11 of the 12 "hybrid" *de novo* banks had demand deposits of foreign banks. The proportion of time deposits of foreign banks to total deposits was somewhat mixed.

The "hybrid" *de novo* banks had, on average, a much higher proportion of balances with banks in foreign countries to total cash and due from banks than the "pure" *de novo* banks (9.95 to 19.34 percent compared to 0.53 to 2.51 percent, respectively). The trend among the "hybrid" *de novo* banks, however, appeared to be decreasing.

SUMMARY OF FINDINGS

This paper examined banks that are subsidiaries of foreign banks to determine if they have comparative cost advantages over domestic banks because of the ability of their parent banks to pass along to them interest-free or low-cost funds. The liability mix, interest cost, and international funds levels were analyzed and compared to domestically owned peers of similar size and location and to a broad base of similar size peers. Differences among the foreign-owned banks, based on geographic location, asset size, and activity within the United States were also analyzed.

The foreign-owned banks were found to share certain attributes compared to the geographically similar domestically owned peers and the NBSS peer groups:

- The foreign-owned banks had a generally lower proportion of core deposits (demand deposits, savings deposits, and time deposits under $100,000), and a higher proportion of purchased funds (time deposits of $100,000 or more, federal funds purchased, repurchase agreements, and other borrowings) than either the geographically similar peers or the NBSS peer groups.
- The foreign-owned banks tended to have a somewhat higher proportion of deposits in foreign offices (primarily Eurodollars) than either of the peer groups. However, such deposits generally represented only a small proportion of total deposits in the foreign-owned banks.
- The foreign-owned banks' average rates on deposits in foreign offices (Eurodollars) and on certificates of deposit of $100,000 or more were mixed when compared with the two peer groups.
- The foreign-owned banks had, on average, a higher total cost of interest-bearing deposits and a higher blended cost of all interest-bearing funds than either the geographically similar peers or the NBSS peer groups. This higher cost of funds was primarily due to the *lower proportion* of core deposits and higher proportion of more expensive purchased funds, rather than to higher rates paid for these deposits and funds.
- The foreign-owned banks had both a higher incidence and a higher proportion of demand and time deposits of foreign banks than the geographically similar peers. Although it is impossible to know from the data whether these are exclusively the deposits of the parent bank, the average proportion of such deposits was not a very large percentage of total deposits for the foreign-owned banks.

Differences among the foreign-owned banks based on geographic location, asset size, and activity within the United States are as follows:

- Although the California peer banks have a generally higher proportion of core deposits and a lower proportion of purchased funds than the New York peer banks, the foreign-owned banks in New York and California had similar proportions of core deposits, and the California foreign-owned banks had, on average, a higher proportion of purchased funds than the New York foreign-owned banks.
- The New York foreign-owned banks had a generally higher average cost of all interest-bearing deposits and funds than the California foreign-owned banks, primarily due to a higher proportion of deposits in foreign offices (Eurodollars).
- The New York foreign-owned banks generally exhibited a higher proportion of demand deposits of foreign banks than the California foreign-owned banks.
- In general, the data indicated that the smaller the foreign-owned banks, the lower the proportion of core deposits and the higher the proportion of purchased funds.
- The largest ($1 to $5 billion in assets) foreign-owned banks had a higher incidence and proportion of deposits in foreign offices (Eurodollar deposits) and a higher average cost of funds than the smaller foreign-owned banks.
- The foreign-owned banks did not differ in their proportion of demand deposits of foreign banks on the basis of asset size, but they did have higher proportions of such deposits than their geographically similar peers. However, the absolute proportion was not very high for the foreign-owned banks. The smallest ($100 to $300 million in assets) foreign-owned banks had a higher proportion of time deposits of foreign banks than the other size groups.
- The *de novo* subsidiaries of foreign banks that have not merged with United States banks had a generally lower proportion of core deposits and higher proportion of purchased funds than the *de novo* banks that have merged with United States banks.

CONCLUSIONS

In general, the United States subsidiaries of foreign banks had a lower proportion of core deposits and a higher proportion of more expensive purchased funds than their domestic peers. Also, the foreign-owned banks had, on average, a higher proportion of deposits in foreign offices (primarily Eurodollars) than the peers; however, the proportion of these deposits to total assets was generally not very high. There appeared to be no consistent pattern of higher or lower rates paid on deposits in foreign offices and large certificates of deposit for the foreign-owned banks compared to the peers. However, on a total cost of funds basis, the foreign-owned banks exhibited a higher blended cost of all interest-bearing deposits and all interest-bearing funds. This higher total cost of funds appears to be due primarily to liability mix, i.e., a higher proportion of more expensive purchased funds and a lower proportion of core deposits than the peer banks, rather than to higher interest rates paid on the interest-bearing funds.

It was also evident that the foreign-owned banks had a generally higher incidence and a higher proportion of demand and time deposits of foreign banks, although the proportions were quite small. It is not possible to know from the available data whether or not these are exclusively the deposits of the foreign parent bank.

On a total cost of funds basis, United States subsidiaries of foreign banks appear to have no comparative cost advantage over their domestic peers. Even if their higher proportion of foreign bank deposits were entirely interest-free deposits of their foreign parents, it would not offset their unfavorable liability mix.

Acknowledgments

The author wishes to thank William A. Longbrake, Steven J. Weiss, and Judith A. Walter for their valuable comments on methodology and presentation of findings. The author also wishes to thank Blair B. Hodgkins for assistance in conducting the statistical tests, David Dale for assistance in analyzing the data and Elizabeth A. Callaghan for assistance in preparing the data for analysis.

FOOTNOTES

[1] William A. Longbrake, Melanie R. Quinn, and Judith A. Walter, *Foreign Ownership of U.S. Banks: Facts and Patterns*, OCC Staff Paper, 1980, Table 4 and fn. 3. The 40 known acquisitions by foreign banks include 36 banks acquired from 1970 through March 31, 1980, and 4 banks acquired before 1970.

[2] Longbrake, Quinn, and Walter, *op. cit.*, Table 1 and Appendix II. The 34 *de novo* banks include only those established by foreign banks. One bank, Republic National Bank of New York, is a bank holding company which, in turn, is controlled by a foreign individual, Edmond Safra. Safra acquired Kings Lafayette Bank and Trust in 1974 and Flagship Bank of Adventura in 1978. Kings Lafayette was absorbed by Republic National Bank of New York (Safra's *de novo* bank) in 1974.

[3] The National Bank Surveillance System (NBSS) of the Office of the Comptroller of the Currency maintains supervisory and administrative systems, and prepares bank performance reports designed to serve as bank supervisory, examination, and management tools. Each bank in the system is placed in a peer group based on total asset size, whether it operates as a branch system or unit bank, and whether it is located in an urban or rural community. The peer group average for a particular ratio is the arithmetic mean of all such calculations for the group. See Appendix B for a description of the NBSS peer groups.

[4] The data collected were year-average figures for 1976 through 1978 and year-to-date average figures through June 30, 1979, computed by adding the balance of the account on the quarterly Call Report at the preceding year-end to the balance at each subsequent reporting period (quarter) during the current year and dividing by the number of reporting periods.

[5] The blended cost of all interest-bearing deposits is defined by NBSS as the sum of the interest expense on all time, savings and foreign office deposits divided by the average balance of these deposits.

[6] The blended cost of all interest-bearing funds is defined by NBSS as the sum of the interest expense on all time and savings deposits, foreign office deposits, borrowed money, subordinated notes and debentures, federal funds purchased and securities sold under agreements to repurchase (repurchase agreements) divided by the average amount of the liabilities or funds which generated those expenses.

[7] The data for this study are Call Report figures obtained from:

- The National Bank Surveillance System (NBSS) at the Office of the Comptroller of the Currency—provided peer bank averages and bank performance reports (BPRs).
- the FDIC computer data base.

Data limitations are described as follows:

- The quarterly Call Reports during the period under analysis did not provide for separating the deposits of (due to) and balances with (due from) the foreign parent banks from the deposits and balances of other foreign banks. As a substitute, this study analyzes the total due to and due from foreign bank accounts.
- Because only year-end rather than year-average figures were available for the due to and due from foreign bank accounts, year-end data for 1975 through 1978 were used to provide for a four-year analysis. Also, the NBSS did not provide peer bank composites for these accounts.
- Data were available on deposits in foreign offices (primarily interest-bearing Eurodollar deposits) only for banks with $300 million or more in total assets. Thus, data were not available for four of the 16 banks in the sample.

[8] For example, assume that there were five banks in the foreign-owned bank group, two of which were in the $1-5 billion asset size category (NBSS peer group 2) and three were in the $500 million-$1 billion asset size category with 3 or more full service branches (NBSS peer group 3); then the peer group average would be computed as follows: The NBSS peer group 2 average (137 banks) would be weighted twice, the NBSS peer group 3 average (79 banks) would be weighted three times, and the sum of these figures would be divided by five to result in a weighted average peer group mean. This would be compared to the average of the five foreign-owned banks.

[9] It is widely believed that foreign banks operating in the U.S. pay a premium for large domestic CD's over well-established U.S. banks, and "the amount of the premium usually reflects the length of time a foreign bank has been established in the U.S. market, and newer, less familiar banks pay a higher premium." (Judith A. Walter, *Foreign Acquisitions of U.S. Banks: Motives and Tactical Considerations*, OCC Staff Study, 1980, p. 13.) The sample banks in this study were all established or acquired in 1974 or earlier, with over half established before 1970, indicating that the sample banks were fairly well established by the time of this study. Further, 12 of the 16 banks in the sample merged with U.S. banks in 1976 or before, perhaps resulting in a reduction of the premium. (Walter, *op. cit.*, indicates that acquisition or merger of a U.S. bank may be a shortcut for reducing the premium.)

[10] Since the number of sample banks in the asset size groups is quite small (6 banks in the $1 to $5 billion category and 4 each in the $500 million to $1 billion and $100 to $300 million categories), the mean values may be affected by outliers.

[11] Since the number of sample banks in the *de novo* bank groups is quite small (4 "pure" *de novo* banks and 12 "hybrid" *de novo* banks), the mean values may be affected by outliers.

Banks Analyzed in the Comparative Cost Analysis

Foreign-Owned Banks	State	Peer Banks	State	NBSS Peer Group[a]
Bank Leumi Trust Co. of New York	NY	Manufactures & Traders Trust	NY	2
European-American Bank & Trust	NY	National Bank of North America	NY	2
Republic National Bank of New York	NY	United Jersey Bank	NJ	2
California First Bank	CA	Bank of Hawaii[b]	HI	2
Lloyds Bank of California	CA	City National Bank	CA	2
Sumitomo Bank of California	CA	First National Bank of Nevada[b]	NV	2
Barclays Bank of New York	NY	The National State Bank	NJ	3
Barclays Bank of California[c]	CA	Hibernia Bank	CA	4
California Canadian Bank	CA	Manufacturers Bank	CA	4
Chartered Bank of London[d]	CA	San Diego Trust & Savings Bank	CA	4
Golden State Sanwa Bank	CA			4
Atlantic Bank of New York	NY	Sterling National Bank	NY	5
French Bank of California[c,e]	CA	American National Bank	CA	7
Japan California Bank	CA	First National Bank of San Diego	CA	7
Mitsubishi Bank of California	CA	Valley National Bank	CA	7
Tokai Bank of California	CA			7

[a]Peer group banks were selected on the basis of asset size as of December 31, 1978, because the current peer group assignments in the National Bank Surveillance System (NBSS), which was used in the peer selection process, are on the basis of year-end 1978 asset size.

[b]Because there is only one non-foreign-acquired California bank in the $1-5 billion asset size range, the peer search was extended to the Office of the Comptroller of the Currency region.

[c]While there are four foreign-owned banks in this group, only three American-owned banks that met the asset size and geographic location criteria could be found.

[d]Chartered Bank of London, San Francisco was merged into Union Bank in January 1980, after the period under analysis in this study.

[e]French Bank of California was merged into Bank of the West in March 1980, after the period under analysis in this

National Bank Surveillance System Peer Group Reference Table

Peer Group	Asset Range	No. Banks	Branch[a]	Unit[a]	Urban[a]	Rural[a]
1	Over $5 billion	27				
2	$1-$5 billion	137				
3	$500 million-$1 billion	79	X			
4	$500 million-$1 billion	55		X		
5	$300 million-$500 million	75	X			
6	$300 million-$500 million	69		X		
7	$100 million-$300 million	328	X			
8	$100 million-$300 million	223		X		
9	$40 million-$100 million	271	X		X	
10	$40 million-$100 million	341		X	X	
11	$40 million-$100 million	320	X			X
12	$40 million-$100 million	393		X		X
13	$25 million-$40 million	144	X		X	
14	$25 million-$40 million	167		X	X	
15	$25 million-$40 million	293	X			X
16	$25 million-$40 million	414		X		X
17	$20 million-$25 million	128			X	
18	$20 million-$25 million	369				X
19	$10 million-$20 million	303			X	
20	$10 million-$20 million	861				X
21	$0-$10 million	118			X	
22	$0-$10 million	472				X

[a]An urban bank is located in a Standard Metropolitan Statistical Area (SMSA). A rural bank is not located in an SMSA. For Peer Groups 3 through 6, a branch bank maintains 3 or more branches while a unit bank maintains 2 or fewer branches. For Peer Groups 7 through 12 a branch bank maintains 2 or more branches while a unit bank maintains 1 branch or no branches. For Peer Groups 13-16, a branch bank maintains at least 1 branch, while a unit bank maintains no branches.

Appendix C
Ratios and Rates Examined

Liability Mix:
   Deposits in Foreign Offices/Total Assets
   Purchased Funds/Total Assets[a]
   Core Deposits/Total Assets[b]

Interest Rates:
   Rate on Deposits in Foreign Offices
   Rate on Large CDs–$100,000 or more
   Rate on All Interest-Bearing Deposits[c]
   Rate on All Interest-Bearing Funds[d]

Due To and Due From Foreign Banks:
   Deposits of Banks in Foreign Countries (Due To)/
      Total Deposits:

         Demand Deposits
         Time Deposits

   Balance with Banks in Foreign Countries (Due From)/
      Total Cash and Due From Banks

---

[a]Purchased funds include time deposits of $100,000 or more, federal funds purchased, repurchase agreements, and other borrowings.

[b]Core deposits include demand deposits, savings deposits, time deposits under $100,000, and foreign office deposits.

[c]Defined as interest on all time and savings deposits and on foreign deposits divided by the average balance of all time and savings deposits and interest-bearing foreign office deposits.

[d]Same as above plus federal funds purchased and repurchase agreements, other borrowings, and subordinated notes and debentures.

13

EFFECT OF FOREIGN ACQUISITION ON THE BALANCE SHEET STRUCTURE AND EARNINGS PERFORMANCE OF U.S. BANKS

BLAIR B. HODGKINS

ELLEN S. GOLDBERG

SUMMARY

This paper presents an analysis of a sample of foreign-acquired United States banks before and after acquisition in comparison to United States-owned peer banks. The study identifies differences between the two groups prior to and following acquisition as well as changes in the foreign-acquired banks which may be related to their acquisition by foreign interests.

The study finds that, prior to acquisition, foreign-acquired banks differ from American-owned peer banks in three areas:

- They have relatively lower proportions of residential real estate loans to total loans.
- They hold lower proportions of their investments in state, county and municipal securities (SCM's).
- They have lower earnings.

With their acquisition, foreign-acquired banks, relative to United States-owned peer banks, exhibit major changes in four areas:

- The composition of their consumer loan portfolios changes, with residential real estate loans increasing and personal loans decreasing as proportions of gross loans.

- Total securities as a percent of total assets declines. Also, holdings of SCM's as a proportion of total securities decline, reinforcing the phenomenon noted prior to acquisition.
- The deposit mix changes, with savings deposits declining and time deposits increasing.
- Earnings, as measured by both return on assets and return on equity, increase slightly.

After their acquisition, foreign-acquired banks differ from United States-owned banks in three areas:

- They have relatively smaller investment portfolios, and their investment portfolios contain relatively lesser amounts of SCM's.
- They have relatively higher levels of time deposits and relatively lower levels of savings deposits.
- Their earnings, while improved, remain lower than those of the peer banks.

The study states that while changes in balance sheet structure and earnings performance may accompany the acquisition of United States banks by foreign interests, it cannot be asserted that any of the changes observed in this analysis is attributable solely to *foreign* acquisition of the banks. The paper concludes that there is little evidence to indicate that foreign-acquired banks turn away from their local markets.

INTRODUCTION

Concern has been expressed that the takeover of a United States bank by foreign interests may result in a reorientation of the bank's activities to the detriment of its customers and the local economy in which it operates.[1] This study compares foreign-acquired United States banks before and after acquisition to nonacquired United States banks. The purpose is to identify changes in loan and investment portfolio composition, deposit structure, earnings performance and capital structure in the foreign-acquired banks which differ significantly from changes in United States-owned banks.

METHODOLOGY

A sample of 25 of the 97 known foreign-acquired banks[2] was selected for study.[3] The foreign-acquired banks included in the study are listed in Appendix A. Seventy-two foreign-acquired banks were not included in the sample for a variety of reasons.

- Forty-seven banks for which the necessary data were not available were excluded. Of these, 40 banks acquired after year-end 1977 were excluded because their relatively short time under foreign control reduces the likelihood that policy changes introduced by the new owners will be fully reflected in the banks' balance sheet figures. Also, seven banks acquired prior to 1970 were excluded because major changes in reporting requirements which occurred in 1969 severely limit the comparability of pre- and post-1969 data.
- Fourteen banks which merged into existing foreign-owned banks were excluded because they represent only a small proportion of the resulting banks' assets and liabilities, and this precludes any meaningful before-and-after analysis.
- Two banks which did not have 25 percent foreign ownership were not considered to be foreign controlled and were excluded from the study.
- Six banks which had failed or which had serious problems at the time of acquisition were excluded because it was felt that their inclusion would distort the analysis.
- Three foreign-acquired banks which later reverted to American ownership were excluded.

Each foreign-acquired bank was paired with a composite of five United States-owned peer banks. Groups of peer banks, rather than individual peer banks, were used to minimize potential distortion caused by outliers. Also, it was felt that selecting one bank as the most appropriate peer for a given foreign-acquired bank would be a difficult and somewhat arbitrary process.

Peer banks were selected on the basis of several criteria. The first was size, as measured by total assets. In most cases the size categories used were those of the Office of the Comptroller of the Currency's National Bank Surveillance System (NBSS). The NBSS size categories are given in Appendix B. Slightly different size categories were used in two cases because the relevant NBSS size categories did not contain five banks meeting the other peer-bank selection criteria. The second criterion was geographic location. In most cases it was possible to select peer banks of the appropriate size within the foreign-acquired bank's standard metropolitan statistical area (SMSA). In those cases where this was not possible, the geographical area was expanded to the state or region in which the foreign-acquired bank was located. The third criterion was bank type—unit or branch. The NBSS type classifications (see Appendix B) were used, and in nearly all cases it was possible to select five peers of the same type as a given foreign-acquired bank. The specific size, geographic and type criteria used to select peer banks for each foreign-acquired bank are presented in Appendix C. Finally, to avoid complicating and perhaps biasing the study, peer banks had to be free from any foreign ownership and could not have merged with or been consolidated into other institutions over the relevant time period.

Balance sheet and income statement data[4] for each foreign-acquired bank and its peer-group composite were compared over a four-year period—two years prior to acquisition, one year prior to acquisition, one year following acquisition and two years following acquisition. These paired observations were then separated into four groups, with all two-years-prior-to-acquisition observations in one group and so on.[5]

Several ratios were constructed from the data and were examined for each paired set of observations over the relevant four-year period. The ratios were divided into those related to asset structure, liability structure, earnings performance and capital structure. The specific ratios are presented in Table 1. The mean, standard deviation and median of the 20 observations were calculated for each ratio for each of the four years. The number of observations for which the foreign-acquired-bank ratio was greater than the corresponding peer-bank-group ratio was also calculated. These statistics are presented in Appendix D.

Three tests were used to determine whether statistically significant differences exist between foreign-acquired and United States-owned banks. The Gosset (Student's) t-test was used to determine whether the differences between the mean values of each ratio for the foreign-acquired banks and their peer-bank groups was significant. The null hypothesis tested in each case was that the difference in the mean value of the ratios for foreign-acquired banks and United States-owned banks was zero and the alternative hypothesis that the difference was not equal to zero:

Table 1
Ratios Examined

Asset Structure

Gross Loans as a percentage of Total Assets
Real Estate Loans (1-4 family) as a percentage of Gross Loans
Personal Loans as a percentage of Gross Loans
Commercial & Industrial Loans as a percentage of Gross Loans
Total Securities as a percentage of Total Assets
State, County & Municipal Securities as a percentage of Total Securities

Liability Structure

Total Deposits as a percentage of Total Assets
Demand Deposits as a percentage of Total Deposits
Savings Deposits as a percentage of Total Deposits
Time Deposits as a percentage of Total Deposits
Deposits in Foreign Offices as a percentage of Total Deposits
Federal Funds Purchased plus Repurchase Agreements as a percentage of Total Assets
Gross Loans as a percentage of Total Deposits[a]

Earnings Performance and Capital Structure

Net Income as a percentage of Total Assets (Return on Assets)
Net Income as a percentage of Equity Capital (Return on Equity)
Equity Capital as a percentage of Total Assets

[a]Although this ratio is not technically a measure of liability structure, it can be used to asses the ability of a bank's deposits to support loan growth.

$$H_0 : X_f - X_p = 0$$
$$H_1 : X_f - X_p = 0$$

where:

X_f = mean ratio value of foreign-acquired banks
X_p = mean ratio value of United States-owned banks.

Because there was no reason *a priori* to expect that any particular mean ratio values of one group of banks would exceed that of the other group, only two-tailed tests were performed.

Underlying the use of the t-test is the assumption that the values for each ratio used follow the normal distribution. The validity of this assumption for some of the ratios tested is doubtful. Therefore, two tests— the Mann-Whitney U-test and the Wilcoxon matched-pairs signed-rank test—which do not rely on any specific assumptions regarding the distribution of the values were also used. These tests are called nonparametric tests because they do not use any parameter of the distributions, such as the means or variances. Rather, they are directly concerned with the distribution of observed values.

In applying the Mann-Whitney test, all sample observations—in this case 20 for the foreign-acquired banks and 20 for the peer bank groups—are ranked as if they represent a single sample. The sum of the ranks associated with observations in each sample is computed. The U-statistic is calculated using the larger of the two sums and the number of observations in each sample, then compared to critical values obtained from a table to determine significance.

For the Wilcoxon matched-paris, signed-rank test, the values for one sample are subtracted from the corresponding values of the other sample, and the differences are ranked by absolute value. The sign (positive or negative) of each difference is applied to its rank, and each set of ranks is summed. The sum with the smaller absolute value is compared to critical values in a table to determine significance. For each of these tests, the null hypothesis is that the distributions of ratio values for foreign-acquired banks and for United States-owned banks are identical, and the alternative hypothesis is that the distributions are different.[6]

Asset Composition

The data on asset composition for the sample foreign-acquired banks and United States-owned peer-bank groups are presented in Table 2. They indicate that the two groups of banks do not differ significantly in the proportion of their assets used for lending either before or after acquisition, although the loan mix for each group does differ somewhat from that of the other. In the area of investments, foreign-acquired banks have lower proportions of total securities to total assets and state, county and municipal securities (SCM's) to total securities than do their peer banks, both before and after acquisition. Of particular note is the decline in the holdings of SCM's on the part of the foreign-acquired banks over the entire period studied.

Total Loans

The overall lending activity of the foreign-acquired banks compared to United States-owned peer banks was examined using the ratio of gross loans to total assets. The ratio is slightly higher for the foreign-acquired banks than for the peer banks for all four years, but not significantly so in any. Also, the slight increases in the ratios from two years before acquisition to two years after acquisition are roughly comparable for the two groups of banks. Therefore, it cannot be said that United States-owned banks and foreign-acquired banks differ significantly, either before or after acquisition, with respect to the proportion of total assets devoted to lending operations.

Consumer Loans

In examining the banks' consumer lending activities, two loan categories were used. The first was consumer real estate loans as measured by the ratio of 1-to-4-family real estate loans to gross loans. The foreign-acquired banks in the sample have a lower mean proportion of their gross loans in 1-to-4-family real estate loans than do their United States-owned peer banks both before and after acquisition, and as is shown in Table 2 these differences are statistically significant for the populations at no less than the 90 percent level through the first year after acquisition. The difference between the values of the ratio for the foreign-acquired banks and their peers is not significant in the second year after acquisition except under the Mann-Whitney test. While this ratio is quite stable for the peer banks, it increases over the four years for the foreign-acquired banks. Thus it appears that foreign-acquired banks, as a group, may increase their emphasis on consumer real estate lending after acquisition, although the level of their activity in this area remains below that of their peer banks two years after acquisition.

The second consumer loan category examined was personal loans, measured as a percentage of gross loans. While the mean ratio of personal loans to gross loans is higher for the sample foreign-acquired banks than for their peer banks for the two years before acquisition and one year after acquisition, it is not possible, based on the significance tests, to conclude that this pattern of differences exists for all foreign-acquired banks in comparison to United States-owned banks. However, the variability of the ratio for the foreign-acquired banks is in contrast to the stability for the United States-owned peer banks. The change in the differences between the mean values of the ratios for the two groups from two years before acquisition to two years after acquisition is statistically significant at the 90 percent level using a two-tailed t-test indicating that, relative to United States-owned banks, foreign-acquired banks reduce their emphasis on personal lending after acquisition.[7] This

Table 2
Asset Composition

	Foreign-Acquired Bank Mean $\bar{X}_f$	Peer-Bank Group Mean $\bar{X}_p$	Difference $\bar{X}_f - \bar{X}_p$	Level of Significance[a]		
				Gosset t-test	Mann-Whitney U-test	Wilcoxon Matched-Pairs Signed-Rank test
Gross Loans/Total Assets						
2 years before acquisition	48.44	47.76	0.68			
1 year before acquisition	51.91	50.09	1.82			
1 year after acquisition	51.79	51.43	0.36			
2 years after acquisition	51.71	50.68	1.03			
Real Estate Loans (1-4 fam.)/Gross Loans						
2 years before acquisition	9.24	16.55	(7.31)	95	90	90
1 year before acquisition	11.42	16.82	(5.40)	90	90	90
1 year after acquisition	10.18	16.42	(6.24)	95	95	90
2 years after acquisition	11.61	16.79	(5.18)		90	
Personal Loans/Gross Loans						
2 years before acquisition	33.41	30.30	3.11			
1 year before acquisition	34.04	30.04	4.00			
1 year after acquisition	32.58	29.54	3.04			

2 years after acquisition	28.74	30.13	(1.39)			
C & I Loans/Gross Loans						
2 years before acquisition	39.31	30.75	8.56			
1 year before acquisition	38.05	32.10	5.95			
1 year after acquisition	39.32	29.76	9.56	90		
2 years after acquisition	39.21	29.42	9.79	90		
Total Securities/Total Assets						
2 years before acquisition	28.73	30.39	(1.66)			
1 year before acquisition	25.63	29.19	(3.56)			
1 year after acquisition	23.39	28.81	(5.42)	95	90	95
2 years after acquisition	21.83	28.24	(6.41)	99	98	99
SCM Securities/Total Securities						
2 years before acquisition	27.21	40.31	(13.10)	99	98	99
1 year before acquisition	22.86	39.11	(16.25)	99	99	99
1 year after acquisition	21.06	41.28	(20.22)	99.9	99	99
2 years after acquisition	19.12	41.13	(22.01)	99.9	99	99

[a] Levels of significance below 90 percent are not shown.

reduction appears to be offset, at least in part, by the increase in 1-to-4-family real estate loans noted above.

Commercial Loans

The ratio of commercial and industrial (C & I) loans to gross loans was examined to measure any changes in commercial lending activity. The mean value of this ratio is substantially greater for the sample foreign-acquired banks than it is for the peer-bank groups for all four years, although the differences are statistically significant only under one of the three tests used. The mean value of the ratio is stable for the foreign-acquired banks while it declines slightly for the peer banks. The sample statistics appear to indicate that foreign-acquired banks, both before and after acquisition, generally have a higher proportion of their loan portfolios in C & I loans than do their United States-owned peer banks; however, the failure of the nonparametric tests to classify the observed sample differences as significant for the populations renders this a somewhat uncertain conclusion.

Investments

The ratios of total securities to total assets and state, county and municipal securities (SCM's) to total securities were examined in the comparison of the two groups of banks' investment activities. The mean value of the ratio of total securities to total assets is lower for the sample foreign-acquired banks than for their peers in each of the four years. The difference is not statistically significant two years before acquisition, but it becomes increasingly significant following acquisition even though the mean value of the ratio declines steadily for each group over the period studied. A two-tailed test of the change in the differences between the mean values of the ratios for the two groups from two years before acquisition to two years after acquisition, which indicates that the change is statistically significant at the 95 percent level, confirms that foreign-acquired banks generally reduce their total investments in securities as a percent of total assets following acquisitions relative to their United States-owned peer banks.

The data clearly show that foreign-acquired banks hold a lower proportion of their total investment portfolios in SCM's than do their United States-owned peers, both before and after acquisition. The mean value of the ratio for the peer banks varies within a relatively narrow range during the period studied, while that of the foreign-acquired banks declines steadily over the period. Thus, while it is clear that after acquisition foreign-acquired banks as a group reduce their holdings of SCM's, it is also apparent that the new owners do not initiate the policy of holding fewer SCM's. The reasons for the rather wide and highly significant differences between the two groups of banks cannot be determined with certainty. The generally lower profitability of the foreign-acquired banks relative to their United States-owned peer banks suggests that SCM's may be of less value for tax-reduction purposes to foreign-acquired banks, which often have been marginally profitable at acquisition. Also, holdings of SCM's are often related to deposits of state and local governments, and if for any reason foreign-acquired banks are less likely than United States-owned banks to be depositories of public funds, then their corresponding holdings of SCM's may be expected to represent a lower proportion of their securities portfolios than do those of the United States-owned banks.

The decline in holdings of SCM's by foreign-acquired banks in the sample from two years before acquisition to two years after acquisition accounts for just over half of the decline of the relative size of the total securities portfolio noted above. Thus it appears that after acquisition foreign-acquired banks reduce their holdings of securities other than SCM's as well as those of SCM's.

Liability Composition

The findings on liability composition for the foreign-acquired banks and the United States-owned peer banks appear in Table 3. The data indicate that before acquisition the two groups of banks are generally similar with respect to liability composition but that some changes in the deposit structure of foreign-acquired banks occur after acquisition which do not take place among United States-owned peer banks. Foreign-acquired banks generally experience declines in the ratio of savings deposits to total deposits and increases in the proportion of time deposits following acquisition, while United States-owned peer banks' ratios of savings and time deposits to total deposits remain stable. After acquisition, foreign-acquired banks' mean proportion of savings deposits is significantly lower than that of their peer banks, while their mean proportion of time deposits is higher than that of their peers. The data further suggest that no notable changes in the proportions of demand

Table 3
Liability Composition

	Foreign-Acquired Bank Mean $\bar{X}_f$	Peer-Bank Group Mean $\bar{X}_p$	Difference $\bar{X}_f - \bar{X}_p$	Level of Significance[a]		
				Gosset t-test	Mann-Whitney U-test	Wilcoxon Matched-Pairs Signed-Rank test
Total Deposits/Total Assets						
2 years before acquisition	83.98	87.41	(3.43)	90		
1 year before acquisition	85.04	88.15	(3.11)	90		90
1 year after acquisition	84.94	87.95	(3.01)	90		95
2 years after acquisition	85.64	87.46	(1.82)			
Demand Deposits/Total Deposits						
2 years before acquisition	47.41	46.90	0.51			
1 year before acquisition	46.97	46.21	0.76			
1 year after acquisition	48.17	45.93	2.24			
2 years after acquisition	44.72	46.75	(2.03)			
Savings Deposits/Total Deposits						
2 years before acquisition	23.89	28.04	(4.15)			
1 year before acquisition	25.64	28.78	(3.14)			
1 year after acquisition	22.87	29.10	(6.23)	98	95	98
2 years after acquisition	21.16	28.00	(6.84)	99	99	99

Time Deposits / Total Deposits						
2 years before acquisition	28.14	25.06	3.08			
1 year before acquisition	26.72	24.93	1.79			
1 year after acquisition	28.20	24.85	3.35	90		
2 years after acquisition	33.61	25.13	8.48	99.9	95	99
Deposits in Foreign Offices / Total Deposits						
2 years before acquisition	0.56	0.05	0.51			
1 year before acquisition	0.73	0.08	0.65			
1 year after acquisition	0.97	0.12	0.85			
2 years after acquisition	0.84	0.12	0.72			
Fed Funds Purchased plus RP's / Total Assets						
2 years before acquisition	3.93	1.31	2.62			
1 year before acquisition	3.75	1.61	2.14			
1 year after acquisition	4.10	2.25	1.85			
2 years after acquisition	3.40	2.01	1.39			
Gross Loans / Total Deposits						
2 years before acquisition	57.84	54.82	3.02			
1 year before acquisition	61.59	56.95	4.64			
1 year after acquisition	61.57	58.59	2.98			
2 years after acquisition	60.61	58.25	2.36			

[a] Levels of significance below 90 percent are not shown.

deposits to total deposits, total deposits to total assets, or federal funds purchased plus repurchase agreements to total assets occur for the foreign-acquired banks following acquisition.

Deposits

The overall deposit structure of the foreign-acquired banks compared to United States-owned peer banks was examined using the ratio of total deposits to total assets. The ratio is slightly lower for the foreign-acquired banks than it is for the peer banks in all four years. These differences are significant one year before and one year after acquisition, but the reasons for these differences are not clear. The ratio increases slightly for the foreign-acquired banks after acquisition, while it remains relatively stable for the peers.

Four ratios were used to analyze the composition of the banks' deposits. The first was demand deposits to total deposits. This ratio is relatively stable over the period examined for both the foreign-acquired banks and the peer banks, although the ratio does decline slightly for the foreign-acquired banks in the second year after acquisition. The ratio is generally higher for the foreign-acquired banks than it is for the peers, but the difference is not statistically significant in any of the four years.

The second deposit category examined was savings deposits, measured as a percentage of total deposits. The foreign-acquired banks have a lower mean proportion of savings deposits to total deposits than do the United States-owned peer banks both before and after acquisition, and these differences are statistically significant at no less than the 95 percent level following acquisition, as is shown in Table 3. Also of note is the fact that while this ratio is quite stable for the peer banks during the period examined, it exhibits a decline in the two years after acquisition for the foreign-acquired banks. These data tend to indicate a decreased reliance on savings deposits as a source of funds among foreign-acquired banks after acquisition compared to their United States-owned peers.

The third deposit ratio analyzed was time deposits to total deposits. The foreign-acquired banks' mean proportion of time deposits to total deposits is higher than that of the peers in each of the four years, and the difference is statistically significant in the second year after acquisition. Not only is the foreign-acquired banks' mean ratio of time deposits to total deposits higher than that of the peers in each of the years examined, but the ratio also increases in each of the two years after acquisition for the foreign-acquired banks, while it remains stable for the peers. These data suggest that foreign-acquired banks develop an increased reliance on time deposits, possibly large time deposits, after acquisition. Although the available data did not permit a break out of large time deposits ($100,000 or more), other research on how foreign-acquired banks currently differ from United States-owned peer banks indicates that foreign-acquired banks have a generally higher proportion of such money-market time deposits than do United States-owned peers.[8]

Another indicator of deposit structure analyzed was the ratio of deposits in foreign offices (primarily Eurodollar deposits[9]) to total deposits. Unfortunately, these data are available for only three of the twenty foreign-acquired banks because only banks with $300 million or more in total assets must report this information. Of the three foreign-acquired banks with data, two have deposits in foreign offices. Although the foreign-acquired banks' mean proportion of deposits in foreign offices to total deposits is higher than the peers' in each of the four years examined, none of the differences is statistically significant, and the mean proportions are quite small for both groups (less than one percent) in each of the four years. Therefore, it appears that foreign-acquired banks generally do not increase their reliance on foreign sources of deposits after acquisition. To analyze other sources of funds, the proportion of federal funds purchased plus securities sold under agreements to repurchase (RP's or repo's) as a percentage of total assets was examined. Although the mean ratio is higher for the foreign-acquired banks than it is for the peers in each of the four years, the difference is not statistically significant in any of the four years. The movement of the ratio is somewhat mixed for the foreign-acquired bank group over the four year period but is generally increasing for the peer banks.

Liquidity

The ratio used to assess liquidity and capacity for loan growth was the loan-to-deposit ratio. The mean loan-to-deposit ratio is slightly higher for the foreign-acquired banks than it is for the peers in each of the years examined, but the difference is not statistically significant in any of the four years. Each group exhibits a generally increasing trend over the four years. Thus, on balance, there appears to be little difference in liquidity between the two groups of banks.

Earnings Performance and Capital Structure

The figures on earnings and capital presented in Table 4 indicate that foreign-acquired banks, as a group, have somewhat lower earnings than do their peer banks, while their levels of capitalization are nearly equivalent. The decline in the mean values for return on assets (ROA) and return on equity (ROE) for the foreign-acquired banks prior to acquisition and the increase following acquisition appears to indicate that the new owners may have had some success in turning the banks around. However, because of the extremely wide variation in the individual ROA and ROE figures for the foreign-acquired banks, the differences over time are not statistically significant.

Earnings

The medians, as well as the means, for return on assets and return on equity are shown in Table 4 since the means may be distorted by extremely large negative values.[10] The mean ROA for the foreign-acquired banks is consistently lower than is that for the United States-owned peer banks, and the differences are statistically significant for the two years after acquisition. The medians present a similar picture. In terms of change over time, the mean and median ROA figures for the foreign-acquired banks appear to indicate an improvement in earnings performance, especially following acquisition. The mean ROA suggests a similar improvement on the part of the peer banks; however, the median appears to indicate relative stability, especially after the first year.

The statistics on ROE reinforce the somewhat cloudy picture presented by the ROA statistics. Foreign-acquired banks again appear to be poorer earners during all four years than their peers, but some apparent improvement is evident.

Capital

The mean ratio of equity capital to total assets for foreign-acquired banks is slightly greater than is that for United States-owned banks for all four years. However, none of these differences is statistically significant under any of the three tests used. The mean ratio declines for the foreign-acquired banks prior to acquisition and then stabilizes, while it declines and then increases slightly in the last year for the peer-group

Table 4
Earnings Performance and Capital Structure

	Means			Medians			Level of Significance[a]		
	Foreign-Acquired Bank $\bar{X}_f$	Peer-Bank Group $\bar{X}_p$	Difference $\bar{X}_f - \bar{X}_p$	Foreign-Acquired Bank $\bar{M}_f$	Peer-Bank Group $\bar{M}_p$	Difference $\bar{M}_f - \bar{M}_p$	Gosset t-test	Mann-Whitney U-test	Wilcoxon Matched Pairs Signed-Rank test
Return on Assets									
2 years before acquisition	0.17	0.40	(0.23)	0.34	0.70	(0.36)		90	
1 year before acquisition	0.09	0.41	(0.32)	0.36	0.80	(0.44)			
1 year after acquisition	0.10	0.47	(0.37)	0.38	0.82	(0.44)		95	90
2 years after acquisition	0.42	0.70	(0.28)	0.45	0.80	(0.35)		95	98
Return on Equity									
2 years before acquisition	1.52	3.12	(1.60)	4.71	7.96	(3.25)			
1 year before acquisition	0.90	6.33	(5.43)	6.62	10.77	(4.15)		98	
1 year after acquisition	2.90	4.05	(1.15)	5.90	11.66	(5.76)		95	
2 years after acquisition	5.44	9.33	(3.89)	7.24	11.76	(4.52)	90	99	98
Equity Capital									
Total Assets									
2 years before acquisition	9.07	8.63	0.44						
1 year before acquisition	8.69	8.39	0.30						
1 year after acquisition	8.10	7.76	0.34						
2 years after acquisition	8.04	7.91	0.13						

[a] Levels of significance below 90 percent are not shown.

417

banks. Based on these observations, it is not possible to assert that the two groups differ appreciably with respect to capital structure.

CONCLUSIONS

Certain conclusions may be drawn from the results of this study; however, it should be noted that this study uses a relatively small sample of foreign-acquired banks and covers a somewhat limited period of time. Because the majority of acquisitions of American banks by foreign interests has occurred since the mid-1970s, most foreign-acquired banks have limited experience under foreign ownership.

This analysis has shown that certain differences in balance sheet structure do exist between foreign-acquired banks and United States-owned peer banks, both before and after acquisition. In addition, it has shown that significant changes occur in the foreign-acquired banks during the first two years following acquisition.[11]

Prior to their acquisition, foreign-acquired banks are similar to their peer banks except for their relatively lower levels of consumer real estate loans, state, county and municipal securities holdings, and earnings. Following their acquisition, the foreign-acquired banks exhibit changes in four areas. First, there is an apparent shift in the mix of the consumer loan portfolio away from personal loans toward real estate loans. Second, holdings of SCM's in particular and securities in general show a marked decline. Third, there is a shift in the deposit mix of foreign-acquired banks, with a decline in savings deposits and an increase in time deposits. Finally, there is a moderate increase in the earnings of foreign-acquired banks.

After acquisition, the major differences between foreign-acquired banks and United States-owned banks are in the areas of investments, deposits and earnings. Foreign-acquired banks clearly have relatively smaller securities portfolios and hold relatively smaller amounts of SCM's than do their peer banks. However, it is not clear whether this results from the nationality of the banks' ownership, their low earnings, a combination of these factors, or an entirely different set of factors. Foreign-acquired banks also have relatively lower savings deposits and relatively higher time deposits than do their peers. While it was not possible to break out large time deposits (certificates of deposits of $100,000 or more), other studies[12] have indicated that foreign-acquired banks tend to be more dependent on purchased funds than do United States-owned banks, and it is likely that this tendency is a factor in the pattern observed in this study. Lastly, the earnings of foreign-acquired banks remain below those of their peer banks, although some improvement is evident.

Although after acquisition foreign-acquired banks and United States-owned banks differ in the important areas discussed above, there are many other areas in which they do not differ or in which they differ only marginally. The size of the loan portfolio, measured as a percentage of total assets, is similar for the two groups of banks. In the area of deposits, the two groups' levels of demand deposits to total deposits are not significantly different, while their levels of total deposits to total assets differ significantly only in the first year after acquisition. Also, their loan-to-deposit ratios are approximately equivalent. The two groups are alike with respect to deposits in foreign offices in that most of the banks in both groups do not have such deposits. Finally, the levels of capitalization for the two groups are very similar.

The results of this study of foreign-acquired banks and United States-owned peer banks indicate that the concerns that an American bank taken over by foreign interests will neglect its natural, local market and be reoriented toward international activity may be for the most part unfounded. Only in the area of investments is the behavior of foreign-acquired banks of the type which would be expected on the basis of such concerns. This behavior, however, represents a continuation of a trend noted in these banks prior to acquisition and, because of the generally lower profitability of foreign-acquired banks at the time of acquisition, may very well be motivated by sound business judgment. Moreover, none of the other observed changes can be characterized as representing neglect of their local markets on the part of the foreign-acquired banks. Finally, it cannot be said that any of the observed changes is in fact the result of the acquisition of these banks by foreign interests *per se*.

Acknowledgments

The authors wish to thank William A. Longbrake, Steven J. Weiss, and Judith A. Walter of the Office of the Comptroller of the Currency and James V. Houpt of the Board of Governors of the Federal Reserve System for their helpful comments on methodology and presentation of findings. They also wish to thank Margaret J. Smith, Thomas A. Loeffler, and David Dale for their advice and assistance in obtaining and analyzing the data and Mark B. Au for his assistance in preparing the data for analysis.

FOOTNOTES

[1] See, for example, Muriel Siebert, *Report of the Superintendent of Banks of New York State on the Proposed Acquisition by the Hongkong and Shanghai Banking Corp. of Marine Midland Banks, Inc.*, June 29, 1979, and Carol S. Greenwald, Testimony before the House Subcommittee on Commerce, Consumer and Monetary Affairs of the House Committee on Government Operations in Hearings on *The Operations of Federal Agencies in Monitoring, Reporting on, and Analyzing Foreign Investments in the United States (Part 4—Foreign Investments in U.S. Banks)*, 96th Cong., 1st sess., July 31 and August 1, 1979, p. 26.

[2] William A. Longbrake, Melanie R. Quinn, and Judith A. Walter, *Foreign Ownership of U.S. Banks: Facts and Patterns*, OCC Staff Paper, 1980, p. 2 and footnote 3; see Appendix I of that paper for the complete listing of known foreign acquisitions of U.S. banks.

[3] Seven of the 25 foreign-acquired banks in the sample were acquired by Royal Trust Company of Canada. In order to avoid overemphasizing the behavior of Royal Trust Company with respect to its acquired banks, the seven Royal Trust banks were given the weight of one bank in the analysis. Also, one bank, Century National Bank and Trust Company, was acquired by foreign interests in 1975 and sold to other foreign interests in 1977. Each transaction was considered to be a separate foreign acquisition for purposes of this study, and therefore this bank was counted twice in the study. These adjustments resulted in there being 20 rather than 25 sets of observations. The analysis was performed several times in order to assess the effect of combining the seven Royal Trust banks and including both acquisitions of Century National Bank and Trust Company. The results of those analyses are substantially similar to those presented here.

[4] The data for this study are from the Federal Reserve Board Micro Data Base, which consists of quarterly call report information on national banks, Federal Reserve System state member banks, and state nonmember banks insured by the Federal Deposit Insurance Corporation. All data are year end figures.

[5] James V. Houpt of the Board of Governors of the Federal Reserve System has approached this subject in his paper, "The Effect of Foreign-Acquisitions on the Performance of U.S. Banks," summarized in the *Federal Reserve Bulletin*, July 1980. Houpt's methodology, while similar to that used in this study, differs in several respects, most notably in that the effect of foreign acquisition on United States banks is analyzed in Houpt's study by using rates of change of various balance sheet and financial performance measures.

[6] The Mann-Whitney test and the Wilcoxon test differ in that the Wilcoxon test requires that the observations in one sample be correlated to observations in the other sample. The Wilcoxon test is therefore the more restrictive of the two tests. The Mann-Whitney test, on the other hand, is more likely to identify a significant difference between the two samples since it lacks this restriction. For a more complete explanation of these and other nonparametric methods, see Audrey Haber and Richard P. Runyon, *General Statistics*, Addison-Wesley Publishing Company, 1969, or Robert L. Winkler and William L. Hays, *Statistics: Probability, Inference, and Decision* (Second Edition), Holt, Rinehart and Winston, 1975.

[7] The null hypothesis tested was that the change in the differences between the mean values of the ratios for the two groups from two years before acquisition to two years after acquisition was zero, and the alternative hypothesis was that the change was not equal to zero:

$H_0: D_1 - D_2 = 0$

$H_1: D_1 - D_2 = 0$

Where:

$D_1 = X_f - X_p$

X_f = mean value of foreign-acquired banks two years before acquisition

X_p = mean value of peer banks two years before acquisition

$D_2 = X_f' - X_p'$

X_f' = mean value of foreign-acquired banks two years after acquisition

X_p' = mean value of peer banks two years after acquisition

[8] Ellen S. Goldberg, *Analysis of Current Operations of Foreign-Owned U. S. Banks*, OCC Staff Paper, 1980, and James V. Houpt, "The Effect of Foreign-Acquisitions on the Performance of U. S. Banks," summarized in *Federal Reserve Bulletin*, July 1980.

[9] Goldberg, *op. cit.*

[10] The Gosset (student's) t-test determines whether the differences between the *mean* values of each ratio for the two groups are significant; however, the two nonparametric tests used (Wilcoxon and Mann-Whitney) do not rely on either means or medians, but rather are concerned with the distribution of the observed values. Therefore, wide variations in the data which may distort the means do not impair the ability of these tests to detect significant differences between the two samples.

[11] Although there are differences between this study and Houpt's study (*op. cit.*) in methodology and in the specific items used to measure the effect of foreign acquisition on United States banks, the conclusions reached in this study are generally consistent with Houpt's earlier findings.

[12] Goldberg, *op. cit.*, and Houpt, *op. cit.*

Appendix A
Foreign-Acquired Banks Included in Sample

Name[a]	Location	Month & Year of Acquisition	Percent Foreign Ownership	Total Assets Prior to Acquisition ($000,000)
Republic National Bank of Miami	Miami, FL	10/70	61	24.9
The Bank of California, NA	San Francisco, CA	1973[b]	14[c]	2,564.7
Royal Trust Bank of Miami, NA (Inter National Bank of Miami)	Miami, FL	9/72	99	53.1
Security National Bank	Walnut Creek, CA	1/73	95	97.3
Intercontinental Bank (Bank of Miami Beach)	Miami, FL	6/73	61	62.4
United Americas Bank (Underwriters Bank & Trust Co.)	New York, NY	11/73	53	41.8
Lloyds Bank California (First Western Bank & Trust Co.)	Los Angeles, CA	1/74	99	1,349.7
National American Bank of New Orleans	New Orleans, LA	7/74	43	286.3
Century National Bank & Trust Co.	New York, NY	5/75	98	48.3
Totalbank	Miami, FL	6/75	25	11.4
Camino-California Bank	Palo Alto, CA	7/75	67	21.5
Royal Trust Bank of Tampa (Dale Mabry State Bank)	Tampa, FL	2/76	100	7.3
Royal Trust Bank of St. Petersburg (First Bank of Gulfport)	Gulfport, FL	7/76	100	19.8
Security National Bank of New Jersey	Newark, NJ	7/76	56	26.3
California Overseas Bank (Ahmanson Bank)	Los Angeles, CA	11/76	99	29.1

Royal Trust Bank of Palm Beach, NA (Worth Avenue National Bank)	Palm Beach, FL	11/76	95	27.7
Caribbean National Bank (Pan American Bank of Coral Gables, NA)	Coral Gables, FL	5/77	89	27.9
Royal Trust Bank of Broward City (First Bank of Pembroke Pines)	Pembroke Pines, FL	5/77	99	19.8
Royal Trust Bank of Jacksonville (Baymeadows Bank)	Jacksonville, FL	6/77	99	9.6
Central National Bank of Miami	Miami, FL	8/77	76	38.1
Main Bank of Houston	Houston, TX	9/77	69	93.3
Dadeland National Bank (Flagship National Bank of Dadeland)	Miami, FL	11/77	95	37.9
Century National Bank & Trust Co.	New York, NY	12/77	98	43.0
First National Bank of Greater Miami (First National Bank of Hialeah)	Hialeah, FL	12/77	80	138.9
International Bank of California	Los Angeles, CA	12/77	34	6.9
Royal Trust Bank of Orlando (American Bank of Orange County)	Orlando, FL	5/78[d]	98	7.6

[a] The name of the bank prior to acquisition is in parentheses if it differs from the current name.

[b] It is believed that the foreign interest which controls the Bank of California, NA, acquired a significant proportion of its shares prior to 1973; however, the nature of the reporting requirements at that time was such that the earliest ownership has been confirmed is 1973.

[c] The foreign interest with 14 percent ownership as of 1973 is the largest single shareholder in the Bank of California. Also, supposedly related business interests hold additional shares. Therefore, it is believed that the foreign interest has effective control of the bank, and the bank was consequently included in this study.

[d] The cut-off acquisition date for this study is year-end 1977. However, since the American Bank of Orange County was acquired by the Royal Trust Company of Canada, which had previous to this transaction acquired several other Florida banks, in the first half of 1978, it was felt that any changes instituted by the acquiring foreign interest would be reflected in the year-end 1978 balance sheet figures. This bank was therefore included in this study.

Appendix B
National Bank Surveillance System Peer Group Reference Table

Peer Group	Asset Range	Branch	Unit	Urban	Rural
1	Over $5 billion				
2	$1-$5 billion				
3	$500 million-$1 billion	X			
4	$500 million-$1 billion		X		
5	$300-$500 million	X			
6	$300-$500 million		X		
7	$100-$300 million	X			
8	$100-$300 million		X		
9	$40-$100 million	X		X	
10	$40-$100 million		X	X	
11	$40-$100 million	X			X
12	$40-$100 million		X		X
13	$25-$40 million	X		X	
14	$25-$40 million		X	X	
15	$25-$40 million	X			X
16	$25-$40 million		X		X
17	$20-$25 million			X	
18	$20-$25 million				X
19	$10-$20 million			X	
20	$10-$20 million				X
21	$00-$10 million			X	
22	$00-$10 million				X

An urban bank is located in an SMSA. A rural bank is not located in an SMSA. For Peer Groups 3 through 6, a branch bank maintains 3 or more branches while a unit bank maintains 1 or 2 branches. For Peer Groups 7 through 12, a branch bank maintains 2 or more branches while a unit bank maintains 1 branch or no branches. For Peer Group 13 through 16, a branch bank maintains at least 1 branch, while a unit bank maintains no branches.

Appendix C
Peer Bank Selection Criteria

Foreign-Acquired Bank		Peer-Bank Selection Criteria	
Name	Total Assets[a] as of 12/31/78 ($000,000)	Asset Size Limits[a] ($000,000)	Location	Type[b]
Republic National Bank of Miami	217.3	100–300	Miami SMSA	Unit
The Bank of California, NA	3,248.3	1,000–5,000	CA, OR, WA	Branch
Royal Trust Bank of Miami, NA	135.9	100–300	Miami SMSA	Branch
Security National Bank	211.2	100–300	CA	Branch
Intercontinental Bank	251.2	100–300	Miami SMSA	Branch
United Americas Bank	48.9	40–100	New York SMSA[c]	Branch
Lloyds Bank California	2,110.6	1,000–5,000	CA, OR, WA	Branch
National American Bank of New Orleans	337.3	300–500	LA	Unit
Century National Bank & Trust Co.	79.3	40–100	New York SMSA[d]	Branch
Totalbank	78.2	40–100	Miami SMSA	Branch
Camino-California Bank	8.4	0–15	CA	Urban
Royal Trust Bank of Tampa	12.7	10–20	Tampa-St. Petersburg SMSA	Urban
Royal Trust Bank of St. Petersburg	31.6	25–40	Tampa-St. Petersburg SMSA	Urban
Security National Bank of New Jersey	38.7	40–100	Newark SMSA	Branch
California Overseas Bank	81.8	40–100	CA	Branch
Royal Trust Bank of Palm Beach, NA	40.5	40–100	West Palm Beach- Boca Raton SMSA	Unit
Caribbean National Bank	28.8	25–40	Miami SMSA	Unit
Royal Trust Bank of Broward City	38.3	25–40	Ft. Lauderdale- Hollywood SMSA	Branch
Royal Trust Bank of Jacksonville	13.9	10–20	Jacksonville SMSA	Urban
Central National Bank of Miami	53.5	40–100	Miami SMSA	Unit
Main Bank of Houston	63.4	40–100	Houston SMSA	Unit
Dadeland National Bank	44.9	25–40	Miami SMSA	Unit
Century National Bank & Trust Co.	79.3	40–100	New York SMSA	Unit
First National Bank of Greater Miami	185.8	100–300	Miami SMSA	Branch
International Bank of California	7.4	0–10	CA	Urban
Royal Trust Bank of Orlando	17.8	10–25	Jacksonville SMSA	Urban

[a] Peer group banks were selected on the basis of asset size as of December 31, 1978, because the current peer group assignments in the NBSS, which was used in the peer selection process, are on the basis of year-end 1978 asset size.

[b] See Appendix B for an explanation of type classification.

[c] The New York SMSA includes Bergen County, New Jersey, where two of the five peer banks are located.

[d] The New York SMSA includes Bergen County, New Jersey, where three of the five peer banks are located.

Appendix D
Supplementary Statistics, By Year, For Foreign-Acquired Banks and Peer-Bank Groups

Ratio	Year	Foreign-Acquired Banks				Peer-Bank Groups				Number of Foreign-Acquired Banks greater than Peer-Bank Groups
		Mean	Median	Standard Deviation	No. Nonzero	Mean	Median	Standard Deviation	No. Nonzero	
Gross Loans / Total Assets	2 years before acquisition	48.44	47.75	11.70	20	47.76	48.44	5.64	20	10
	1 year before acquisition	51.91	51.55	12.29	20	50.09	50.54	6.15	20	10
	1 year after acquisition	51.79	55.31	12.39	20	51.43	51.88	6.99	20	11
	2 years after acquisition	51.71	51.83	9.82	20	50.68	51.04	6.92	20	10
Real Estate Loans (1-4 family) / Gross Loans	2 years before acquisition	9.24	8.23	7.80	17	16.55	12.51	10.28	20	7
	1 year before acquisition	11.42	10.13	9.41	17	16.82	13.51	9.15	20	7
	1 year after acquisition	10.18	7.95	8.95	17	16.42	13.08	9.33	20	7
	2 years after acquisition	11.61	7.05	11.20	17	16.79	14.33	8.50	20	7
Personal Loans / Gross Loans	2 years before acquisition	33.41	30.03	20.04	20	30.30	29.50	8.52	20	9
	1 year before acquisition	34.04	30.68	18.73	20	30.04	28.16	8.43	20	11
	1 year after acquisition	32.58	30.44	18.88	20	29.54	28.13	8.14	20	12
	2 years after acquisition	28.74	27.83	18.17	20	30.13	28.24	7.81	20	9

	2 years before acquisition	1 year before acquisition	1 year after acquisition	2 years after acquisition								
C & I Loans / Gross Loans												
2 years before acquisition	39.31	37.01	21.91	20	30.75	29.55	8.60	20	11
1 year before acquisition	38.05	31.83	20.74	20	32.10	33.36	11.23	20	11
1 year after acquisition	39.32	29.65	24.05	20	29.76	27.83	9.23	20	12
2 years after acquisition	39.21	29.05	23.98	20	29.42	28.46	9.51	20	9
Total Securities / Total Assets												
2 years before acquisition	28.73	27.80	11.77	20	30.39	30.92	6.49	20	9
1 year before acquisition	25.63	23.85	12.13	20	29.19	29.52	7.32	20	8
1 year after acquisition	23.39	22.50	10.85	20	28.81	29.19	7.49	20	5
2 years after acquisition	21.83	20.74	10.21	20	28.24	28.54	6.97	20	3
State, County & Municipal Securities / Total Securities												
2 years before acquisition	27.21	28.35	16.12	17	40.31	47.05	17.81	18	4
1 year before acquisition	22.86	21.40	17.78	17	39.11	43.38	18.75	18	2
1 year after acquisition	21.06	21.28	18.49	16	41.28	43.74	17.73	19	4
2 years after acquisition	19.12	18.44	17.75	15	41.13	45.51	18.90	18	4
Total Deposits / Total Assets												
2 years before acquisition	83.98	85.43	7.86	20	87.41	87.76	2.78	20	8
1 year before acquisition	85.04	87.08	8.05	20	88.15	89.43	2.92	20	8
1 year after acquisition	84.94	88.17	8.08	20	87.95	89.41	3.47	20	6
2 years after acquisition	85.64	86.66	6.38	20	87.46	88.44	3.28	20	8

Appendix D (continued)

Ratio	Year	Foreign-Acquired Banks				Peer-Bank Groups				Number of Foreign-Acquired Banks greater than Peer-Bank Groups
		Mean	Median	Standard Deviation	No. Nonzero	Mean	Median	Standard Deviation	No. Nonzero	
Demand Deposits / Total Deposits	2 years before acquisition	47.41	44.47	9.14	20	46.90	45.81	6.12	20	8
	1 year before acquisition	46.97	45.53	6.98	20	46.21	44.51	5.31	20	12
	1 year after acquisition	48.17	44.51	11.04	20	45.93	43.79	5.42	20	10
	2 years after acquisition	44.72	43.68	10.94	20	46.75	46.07	5.62	20	6
Savings Deposits / Total Deposits	2 years before acquisition	23.89	23.22	10.72	20	28.04	28.65	6.85	20	9
	1 year before acquisition	25.64	24.90	11.21	20	28.78	29.02	6.93	20	10
	1 year after acquisition	22.87	24.44	9.36	20	29.10	29.24	6.67	20	6
	2 years after acquisition	21.16	23.19	8.15	20	28.00	26.91	6.06	20	5
Time Deposits / Total Deposits	2 years before acquisition	28.14	27.16	12.25	20	25.06	24.22	6.44	20	10
	1 year before acquisition	26.72	25.51	10.63	20	24.93	24.99	6.67	20	10
	1 year after acquisition	28.20	23.36	11.76	20	24.85	23.61	6.99	20	11
	2 years after acquisition	33.61	31.24	12.22	20	25.13	24.28	7.11	20	16

Deposits in Foreign Offices	2 years before acquisition	0.56	0.00	2.42	1	0.05	0.00	0.16	2	1
	1 year before acquisition	0.73	0.00	3.19	1	0.08	0.00	0.24	2	1
	1 year after acquisition	0.97	0.00	3.44	2	0.12	0.00	0.35	2	2
	2 years after acquisition	0.84	0.00	3.01	2	0.12	0.00	0.35	2	2
Total Deposits										
Federal Funds Purchased plus RP's	2 years before acquisition	3.93	0.00	6.67	9	1.31	0.49	1.87	14	7
	1 year before acquisition	3.75	0.05	6.27	10	1.61	0.35	2.45	12	7
	1 year after acquisition	4.10	0.88	6.28	12	2.25	0.50	3.28	16	9
	2 years after acquisition	3.40	1.30	4.71	13	2.01	0.71	3.10	14	7
Total Assets										
Gross Loans	2 years before acquisition	57.84	57.44	13.63	20	54.82	54.46	7.04	20	12
	1 year before acquisition	61.59	60.49	15.27	20	56.95	57.81	7.51	20	11
	1 year after acquisition	61.57	61.52	15.73	20	58.59	59.11	8.04	20	13
	2 years after acquisition	60.61	63.65	11.47	20	58.25	59.52	8.04	20	12
Total Deposits										
Return on Assets	2 years before acquisition	0.17	0.34	0.78	20	0.40	0.70	1.13	20	6
	1 year before acquisition	0.09	0.36	1.22	20	0.41	0.80	1.17	20	6
	1 year after acquisition	0.10	0.38	1.01	20	0.47	0.82	1.22	20	6
	2 years after acquisition	0.42	0.45	0.57	20	0.70	0.80	0.98	20	6

Appendix D (continued)

Ratio	Year	Foreign-Acquired Banks				Peer-Bank Groups				Number of Foreign-Acquired Banks greater than Peer-Bank Groups
		Mean	Median	Standard Deviation	No. Nonzero	Mean	Median	Standard Deviation	No. Nonzero	
Return on Equity	2 years before acquisition	1.52	4.72	15.30	20	3.12	7.96	19.38	20	8
	1 year before acquisition	0.90	6.62	16.04	20	6.33	10.77	13.39	20	6
	1 year after acquisition	2.90	5.90	12.73	20	4.05	11.66	21.49	20	7
	2 years after acquisition	5.44	7.24	8.00	20	9.33	11.76	11.13	20	3
Equity Capital / Total Assets	2 years before acquisition	9.07	8.26	4.80	20	8.63	7.80	2.59	20	10
	1 year before acquisition	8.69	8.12	3.72	20	8.39	7.67	2.68	20	8
	1 year after acquisition	8.10	7.55	3.21	20	7.76	7.39	1.58	20	11
	2 years after acquisition	8.04	7.18	3.44	20	7.91	7.71	1.71	20	9

PRICES PAID BY FOREIGN INTERESTS TO ACQUIRE U.S. BANKS

THOMAS A. LOEFFLER

WILLIAM A. LONGBRAKE

SUMMARY

This study of prices paid by foreign interests to acquire U.S. banks reviews the factors affecting acquisition motives and valuation and examines the evidence pertaining to the prices paid by foreign investors to acquire U.S. banks. Two primary motives for the acquisition of U.S. banks by foreign interests are postulated. Foreign interests may perceive the opportunity to enhance the profitability of the target U.S. bank and/or may be seeking to realize the benefits of diversification by entry into the U.S. banking market. In the former case, prices paid by foreign investors should be comparable to prices paid by domestic banks assuming the existence of domestic competitive alternatives. The latter motivation implies a premium in excess of a domestic competitive alternative as the foreign interest achieves initial penetration of the U.S. banking market.

The evidence indicates that foreign interests have paid acquisition premiums for U.S. banks in excess of the premiums paid in domestic acquisitions. The ratio of acquisition price to book value was computed for a sample of foreign acquisitions and compared to the same ratio for domestic acquisitions. Bank size, location, and date of acquisition were held constant in the sampling procedure. The results indicate a statistically significant relationship of acquisition price to book value for foreign acquisitions in excess of comparable domestic acquisitions. This evidence suggests that the hypothesis of diversification premiums is warranted. It further suggests that in the absence of a diversification motive, foreign acquisitions would be priced comparably to domestic acquisitions except where structural obstacles precluded the possibility of competing bids from potential domestic acquirers.

INTRODUCTION

An issue raised by the foreign acquisitions phenomenon is how prices paid by foreign entities to acquire equity interests in American banks compare with prices paid by domestic investors to acquire equity interests in similarly situated U.S. banks. This paper describes the factors that affect acquisition prices and discusses, in general terms, differences in the relative importance placed on certain of the factors by domestic and foreign acquirers that may lead to differences in acquisition prices. To determine whether such differences in acquisition values exist, data from a sample of 37 domestic and 25 foreign acquisitions of U.S. banks with less than $215 million in total assets, which were consummated during the period 1974-78, are analyzed.[1]

FACTORS INFLUENCING ACQUISITION PRICES

Several factors affect the prices investors, including foreign entities, are willing to pay to acquire a U.S. bank. Richard Brealey, in a study of firms from various industries that were growing through acquisition, identified several purported benefits that encouraged the firms to pay premiums to acquire the stock of other firms. These included:[2]

- the combined company could earn a higher return on capital by reduction in competition, the ability to achieve economies of scale, and higher utilization of existing capacity.
- the combined company could more effectively use exceptionally able management.
- the stock of the acquired firm was undervalued by the market, allowing the acquiring firm to benefit from underpriced assets.
- combined operations insured the total company against the effect of a set-back in any single sector.

- the addition of better management at the acquired firm would result in higher earnings.

While these benefits applied to both industrial companies and banks, Thomas Piper, in a study of bank acquisitions, enumerated several additional benefits for banks which included:[3]

- at times disparities exist in the market valuation between large banks and small banks, allowing large banks to acquire the assets of small banks and have the market value them higher.
- increased profitability through changes in portfolio management, such as shifting the target bank's portfolio from Treasury securities to tax-exempt securities, raise the after-tax return.
- larger banks could operate on lower levels of capital than the smaller bank.

Additional incentives for foreign banks to acquire American banks include:[4]

- the size of the U.S. economy and the perceived growth potential of U.S. banking markets.
- the potential for international risk diversification accentuated by the political and economic stability of the U.S.
- the acquisition of dollar-based operations stemming from the role of the dollar as the world's major trading and reserve currency and from the uncertainties about the continuing supply of Eurodollars.

Rather than achieving these objectives through establishing a *de novo* presence in the U.S., foreign banks have apparently been induced to acquire existing U.S. banks due to the cost and delay in establishing such a presence through the *de novo* route.

Generalizing the motivations suggested by these studies,[5] foreign acquisitions of U.S. banks may be attributed to:[6]

1. the perception of foreign entities that a U.S. bank's profitability could be enhanced by the infusion of additional capital and/or managerial resources, and/or
2. a diversification potential that exists from foreign entry into the U.S. banking market.

The perception of enhanced profitability, of course, would be common to both foreign and domestic acquirers. Different acquisition values would be placed on target banks only if expectations were divergent or if the domestic market structure prevented acquisition by U.S. banks. Foreign entities may place higher premiums on the acquisition of U.S. banks if these entities overestimate the potential for enhanced profitability due to unfamiliarity with the U.S. banking market.[7] An undervaluation of this potential would, in the absence of structural obstacles to domestic acquisition, generally, be bid away by other domestic banks. Given such structural obstacles as exist in the U.S., however, foreign entities may be able to acquire U.S. banks at a price below a competitive alternative due to the limitations on acquisitions by domestic banks. This would be especially pertinent to the acquisition of large U.S. banks or U.S. banks of any size in unit banking states. Thus, an unfamiliarity with U.S. banking operations may lead to higher acquisition prices offered by foreign entities than otherwise warranted, while structural or size limitations on acquisitions by other domestic banks may permit acquisition by foreign entities at lower prices.

The diversification potential of acquisitions of U.S. banks by foreign entities should result in a generally higher valuation being placed on a target U.S. bank by the foreign entity. Such a premium would be most pronounced in the initial acquisition of a U.S. bank by a foreign entity and decline in importance thereafter. This diversification potential of gaining entry to the U.S. banking market would not require an additional perception on the part of the foreign entity that it would enhance the profitability of the U.S. bank. The value of this diversification would include the relationship of the U.S. bank's earnings to that of the foreign entity, the stability and depth of funding sources, and the potential for more profitable lending and investment opportunities. This diversification value should lead to systematically higher acquisition prices being offered by foreign entities for the acquisition of U.S. banks in relation to those that would be offered by other U.S. banks.

ACQUISITION PRICES AND PREMIUMS

The best indicator of the value which investors place on the acquisition of a U.S. bank is the premium they are willing to pay over current market value. The presumption is that an investor in a domestic bank would not be willing to sell the stock of the bank to any other investor, domestic or foreign, unless the offer was at a premium over market value.[8] However, the stock of most acquired banks is closely held and is traded infrequently. In such instances, a market value frequently does not exist, and as a matter of convenience, the book value is commonly used as a reference basis for forming a judgment as to the value of the stock.[9] Book value, of course, is not generally a very good indicator of future prospects. However, the book value may be used as a starting point. The premium paid over book value will depend on the value the potential acquirer places on the kinds of factors listed above.

Analysis of data on industrial and bank acquisitions has been undertaken several times in the past two decades. For example, Brealey finds that the acquiring firms pay premiums over the market value averaging approximately 25 percent.[10] Piper, in his study of bank acquisitions, found that over the 21-year period from 1946 to 1967 the premium paid over market value averaged 125 percent for 19 banks. However, the median for this group of banks was only 25 percent.[11] The premium paid over book value averaged 28 percent for 51 banks; the median value was 18 percent.

Price-to-book-value ratios for domestic bank stocks acquired by foreign individuals are contained in Table 1. Table 2 presents prices paid for the stock of U.S. banks by foreign banks and bank holding companies in relation to both book value and market value. The data in Tables 1 and 2 have been derived from a variety of sources and may not, in all instances, be entirely comparable. Nevertheless, the data are sufficiently reliable for general assessment of magnitudes and trends.

There are eleven banks in Table 2 for which there are both price-to-market value and price-to-book value data. The average ratio of price-to-market value for these banks is 1.94; the average ratio of price-to-book value is 2.07. The premium of 94 percent over market value in these banks is somewhat less than the 125 percent premium over market value in the Piper study. However, it is somewhat greater than the 69 percent premium over market value for five financial firms acquired by American companies.[12]

Looking only at the ratio of price-to-book value, the 20 U.S. banks in Table 2 acquired by foreign banks or bank holding companies have an average price-to-book value ratio of 2.10. The average ratio for price-to-book value for 22 U.S. banks acquired by foreign individuals shown in Table 1 is 1.85. These average premiums of 110 percent and 85 percent are somewhat larger than the premium of 74 percent over book value paid by American banks and bank holding companies to acquire 20 domestic banks during 1979.[13] However, these figures may not be strictly comparable since the foreign acquisitions in Tables 1 and 2 took

Table 1
Acquisitions by Foreign Individuals[1]

Bank Acquired	Nationality of Acquirer	Completion Date of Transaction	Total Assets Prior to Transaction ($ millions)	Ratio of Price to Book Value
Security NB	Saudi Arabia	01-10-73	$ 97.3	3.737
Banco Mercantile de Puerto Rico	Canada	06-09-75	99.2	1.230
*Ahmanson Bank	Philippines	11-08-76	25.9	1.301
*Flagship NB of Dadeland	Spain, Costa Rica, El Salvador	03-15-77	37.9	2.173
*First Bk. of Pembroke Pines	Canada	05-07-77	19.8	2.000
*Pan American Bk. of Coral Gables, N.A.	Venezuela	05-12-77	27.9	2.155
*Central NB of Miami	Colombia	08-10-77	38.1	2.440
*Main Bank of Houston	Saudi Arabia	09-06-77	93.3	1.250
*First NB Hialeah	Venezuela	12-15-77	138.9	1.660
*Northside Bank of Miami	Cuba	12-21-78	11.4	2.240
*Dania Bank	Venezuela	04-11-78	126.3	1.472
*Pan American NB of East L.A.	Indonesia	04-78	30.4	1.838
*National Bank of Georgia	Saudi Arabia	06-28-78	388.9	1.340
*Biscayne Bank[2]	Portugal	06-78, 11-78	13.1	3.050
*Peoples Bank	Saudi Arabia	07-21-78	33.6	2.418
Main Bank of Houston[3]	Saudi Arabia	07-21-78	68.4	1.350
*Western Bank	Syria	07-24-78	152.6	1.565
Coolidge Bank and Trust Co.	U.K.	11-09-78	140.0	1.460
Metropolitan Bank	Syria	01-03-79	20.8	1.690
First City NB of Jacksonville	Netherlands & Canada	02-14-79	8.2	1.790
American Bank of Commerce	Canada	03-09-79	8.0	1.090
Hemisphere NB	Argentina	12-05-79	21.0	1.370

*Banks used in "Comparison of Domestic and Foreign Bank Acquisitions," Table 4.

[1] Data unavailable for some banks within acquisition category.

[2] Figures shown are averages of figures for the two acquisition dates listed.

[3] Second acquisition of a majority of bank stock by foreign individual.

Table 2
Acquisitions by Foreign Banks and Holding Companies[1]

Bank Acquired	Acquired By	Completion Date of Transaction	Bank Assets Prior to Transaction ($ millions)	Ratio of Price to Market Value	Ratio of Price to Book Value
Florida Banks					
*American Bank of Orange County	Royal Trust Co.	12-05-78	$ 7.6	1.27	1.714
Inter National of Miami	Royal Trust Co.	09-02-72	51.1	3.25	3.136
*Dale Mabry Savings Bank	Royal Trust Co.	02-25-76	7.3	n/a	2.000
First of Gulfport	Royal Trust Co.	07-22-76	24.3	1.58	n/a
*Worth Avenue	Royal Trust Co.	11-29-76	27.7	1.57	2.192
*BayMeadows	Royal Trust Co.	06-22-77	9.6	2.00	2.007
California Banks	*Japanese Banks*				
*Centinela Bank	Tokai California	07-11-75	$ 31.2	2.00	2.016
So. Cal FNB	Bank of Tokyo of California	10-01-75	889.2	n/a	1.828
*Golden State	Sanwa California	12-27-77	144.7	n/a	2.089
*Hacienda Bank	Mitsubishi Calif.	02-09-76	55.6	1.25	2.697
California Banks	*U.K. Banks*				
First Western	Lloyds Bank, Ltd.	01-16-74	$ 1,333.6	n/a	1.790
*Liberty National	Chartered Bank of London, SF	07-01-74	101.4	n/a	2.937
*County Bank Santa Barbara	Barclays of Calif.	10-01-74	48.1	n/a	2.884
*Commercial & Farmers Bank of Oxnard	Chartered Bank of London, SF	12-16-77	79.6	n/a	2.331
Union Bank	Standard Chartered	04-17-79	5,183.1	1.59	1.814
	Other Foreign Banks				
Banks					
*First Westchester	Barclays of N.Y.	06-01-74	$ 214.2	2.13	2.189
*Community Bank of San Jose	Ammex Holding	06-30-78	72.5	n/a	1.601
NB of North America	NatWest	04-16-79	4,326.0	n/a	1.730
LaSalle National	Algemene Bank	08-14-79	925.7	1.97	1.880
Bank of the West	French Bank Ca.	03-18-80	589.3	2.31	2.250
Marine Midland	Hongkong and Shanghai	03-04-80	15,690.9	2.00	.900

*Banks used in "Comparison of Domestic and Foreign Bank Acquisitions" Table 4.
[1] Data unavailable for some banks within acquisition category.

place over the period 1971 to 1980. Also, there is no assurance that there is comparability on the basis of bank size or bank condition. As a result, a sample of domestically acquired banks was developed to obtain comparability to the extent feasible. This sample is shown in Table 3.

Initial selection of the sample of U.S. banks acquired by foreign interests was based on the availability of purchase price data. Cases in which the acquisition was related to serious supervisory problems or where the acquired bank had failed were eliminated. In the case of U.S. banks acquired by foreign banks or bank holding companies, only going-concern acquisitions were considered; purchase and assumption transactions were excluded. Price data were collected from a variety of sources including newspaper clippings, Moody's *Bank and Finance Manual*, Comptroller of the Currency and Federal Deposit Insurance Corporation merger files, and bank holding company acquisition filings with the Federal Reserve.

The domestic sample of acquired banks was developed from mergers and bank holding company acquisitions of separately owned and managed banks from 1974 through 1978. Price data for few foreign acquired U.S. banks were available prior to 1974 and, so, no data for comparable domestic acquisitions were collected for the earlier period.

Because most of the domestic mergers involved stock exchanges, availability of purchase price data was limited. Cash value of stock as stated in the merger agreement, whether for full or fractional shares, was found for 26 banks. Of those 26 banks, three with serious supervisory problems were eliminated. Table 3 shows data for the remaining 23. These 23 banks ranged in size, in terms of total assets at the time of acquisition, from $4.5 million to $177.3 million.

Due to a geographic bias among the foreign acquisitions, the sample of domestic bank mergers was augmented by a sample drawn from domestic bank holding company acquisitions. The 25 foreign acquisitions were almost exclusively located in three states—California, Florida, and Texas—states which can readily be characterized as high growth areas. The sample of domestic mergers, however, is drawn from throughout the U.S. and may thus exhibit, on average, a lower growth potential with a correspondingly less attractive acquisition value. Therefore, a sample of domestic bank holding company acquisitions, drawn from the states of Florida and Texas, was constructed conforming to the criteria in terms of size and date of acquisition described above. This sample of 14 domestic bank holding company acquisitions is also presented in Table 3. These 14 banks ranged in size from $5.8 million to $150.6 million in total assets.

Because no large banks were included in the domestic sample, the largest foreign acquired U.S. bank included in the sample had $214 million in total assets at the time of acquisition.

The final sample for comparison of domestic and foreign bank acquisitions in terms of prices paid relative to book value consisted of 62 small- to medium-sized banks—12 acquired by foreign banks or bank holding companies, 13 acquired by foreign individuals, and 37 acquired by domestic banks or bank holding companies—which were free of serious supervisory problems at the time of acquisition. In addition, the sample was limited to acquisitions made in the years 1974 through 1978.

A comparison of domestic and foreign acquisitions is presented in Table 4. The average price-to-book-value ratio for the 12 banks acquired by foreign banks or bank holding companies is 2.22. The ratio for the 13 banks acquired by foreign individuals is 1.97. However, data were available for banks acquired by foreign individuals only for the years 1976, 1977 and 1978. The eight banks acquired over these same three years by foreign banks or bank holding companies had a ratio of price-to-book value equaling 2.08, not much different from the 1.97. Furthermore, the median values for the two groups of banks are 2.14 for banks acquired by foreign banks or bank holding companies and 2.00 for banks acquired by foreign individuals.

In contrast, the average price-to-book value ratio for the 37 domestic acquisitions was 1.48 and the median was 1.44. When all the foreign acquired banks are grouped together, the average price-to-book value ratio for the 25 banks is 2.09 and the median is 2.09. The average size in terms of total assets of U.S. banks acquired by foreign interests was $61.7 million, compared to an average size for domestic acquisitions of $44.6 million. Although the average size for the foreign-acquired banks is somewhat greater, the medians are quite close—$37.9 million for the foreign-acquired banks and $36.9 million for the domestically-acquired banks.

The sample is less well balanced in terms of location. The foreign-acquired banks include 12 in Florida, 9 in California, 3 in Texas and 1 in New York. The domestically-acquired banks include 8 in Florida, 2 in California, 6 in Texas, 1 in New York and 20 in other states. However, as can be seen in Table 4, the two samples of banks are relatively well distributed with respect to year of acquisition.

The difference between the average price to book value ratios for foreign and domestic acquisitions is .616 (2.089-1.483). While it appears that foreign interests have been willing to pay substantial premiums rel-

Table 3

Domestic Bank Mergers and Bank Holding Company Acquisitions, 1974-1978

Bank Acquired	Bank Acquiring	Completion Date of Transaction	Bank Assets Prior ($ millions)	Ratio of Price to Book Value
Mergers				
Peoples Bk. & Tr. Co. of Fairfax, VA	Dominion NB, Baileys Crossroads, VA	04-01-74	$ 19.5	.956
Bellman-Wall NB, Wall Twp., NJ	The First Jersey NB, Jersey City	08-02-74	57.0	2.296
Beach City Banking Co., Beach City, OH	The United NB & Tr. Co., Canton, OH	11-01-74	10.3	.424
Deep River Bk. & Tr. Co., Deep River, OH	Community Banking Co., N. Bradford, OH	11-30-74	12.8	1.364
Motherlode Bk., Placerville, CA	Security Pacific NB, Los Angeles, CA	06-29-75	86.9	2.488
State Bk. Co., Massilon, OH	1st NB of Canton, Canton, OH	10-31-75	23.5	1.588
Merchants NB of St. Johnsburg, VT	1st NB of Springfield, VT	06-30-76	93.7	1.731
Guaranty Bk., Canby, OR	Bk. of Oregon, Woodlawn, OR	07-01-76	7.7	1.711
Hardwick Tr. Co., Hardwick, VT	The Merchants Bk., Burlington, VT	09-30-76	7.1	1.404
Fairfax Co. NB, Seven Corners, VA	Virginia NB, Norfolk, VA	11-12-76	62.5	1.320
Odensburg Tr. Co., Odensburg, NY	Oneida NB & Tr. Co. of Central NY, Oneida, NY	11-19-76	31.8	1.168
Atlantic St. Bk., Pt. Pleasant, NJ	Citizens St. Bk. of NJ	12-15-76	10.5	1.294
Bk. of North Lake, North Lake, WI	Valley Bk of Hartford, Hartford, WI	12-26-76	62.1	1.396
Potomac Bk. & Tr. Co., Fairfax, VA	Dominion NB, Fairfax, VA	03-04-77	38.7	.462
2nd NB of Richmond, Richmond, VA	Metropolitan NB, Richmond, VA	03-25-77	35.0	1.315
Lafayette Bk. & Tr. Co., Fayetteville, NC	Southern NB of Lumberton, NC	04-01-77	11.4	1.223
New Franken Bk., New Franken, WI	Peoples Marine Bk., Green Bay, WI	04-30-77	11.2	1.109
Potomac NB, Potomac, MD	Commerce Bk. & Tr. Co. of MD, Bethesda, MD	09-01-77	39.2	2.171
The 1st NB of Orange City, Orange, CA	Wells Fargo Bk., NA, San Fran., CA	05-06-78	177.3	2.358

Bank Acquired	Bank Holding Company	Date of Board Approval[1]	Bank Assets ($ millions)[2]	Ratio of Price to Book Value[3]
The Trotwood Bk., Trotwood, OH	The Central Tr. Co. of Montgomery City, NA Dayton, OH	05-04-78	39.9	1.625
The Pittsfield NB, Pittsfield, NB	Concord NB	06-29-78	4.5	.966
City Bank of Troy, Troy, MO	Peoples Bk. of Hawk Point, Hawk Point, MO	06-30-78	5.3	1.564
Farmers & Merchants St. Bk of Merrill, MI	Frankenmuth Bk. & Tr., Frankenmuth, MI	09-30-78	92.1	1.154

Bank Holding Company Acquisitions

Florida

American Bk. of Ft. Myers	Ellis Bkng. Corp.	01-15-76	$ 14.8	1.506
North Port Bk., North Port	Ellis Bkng. Corp.	03-03-76	14.0	0.796
Security NB, Ft. Myers	Exchange Bancorp.	10-04-76	55.0	1.700
First NB, Sebring	Florida Bancshares	06-29-77	36.9	1.213
Amelia Island Bank, Fernandina Bch.	Barnett Bks.	09-28-77	5.8	1.250
The Vanderbilt Bank, Naples	Exchange Bancorp	09-22-78	15.0	1.719
Peoples State Bank, New Port Richey	Barnett Bks.	10-27-78	71.7	2.000
The National Bank of Cape Coral	Flordia National Banks	10-05-78	36.9	1.583

Texas

Beaumont State Bank	First International	02-28-77	$ 55.0	1.999
East Dallas Bk., Dallas	First City Bancorp.	03-07-77	29.0	1.602
Ridglea Bank, Fort Worth	Republic of Texas Corp.	03-17-78	104.5	1.528
Bexar County NB, San Antonio	Republic of Texas Corp.	06-16-78	150.6	1.435
Guaranty NB, Houston	National Bancshares	06-27-78	45.9	1.720
City National Bank, Fort Worth	Republic of Texas Corp.	10-10-78	74.2	1.750

[1] Federal Reserve Board action date as listed in the *Federal Reserve Bulletin*, various issues.
[2] Assets as of quarterly reporting date following Federal Reserve Board approval.
[3] Book value as of quarterly reporting date following Federal Reserve Board approval.

Table 4

Comparison of Domestic and Foreign Acquisitions

| | Foreign | | | | | | Domestic | | |
| | Banks | | | Individuals | | | | | |
Year	Number	Price/Book Value	Average Assets	Number	Price/Book Value	Average Assets	Number	Price/Book Value	Average Assets
1974	3	2.67	$119.6				4	1.26	$24.9
1975	1	2.02	31.2				2	2.04	55.2
1976	3	2.30	30.2	1	1.30	$25.9	10	1.40	35.9
1977	3	2.14	78.0	6	1.95	59.3	9	1.37	29.1
1978	2	1.66	40.0	6	2.10	61.2	12	1.62	68.2
	12	2.22	$ 66.2	13	1.97	$57.6	37	1.48	$44.6
Median		2.14	$ 49.4		2.00	$33.6		1.44	$36.9

| | Foreign | | Domestic | |
	Price/Book Value	Avg. Assets	Price/Book Value	Avg. Assets
Average	2.09	$61.7	1.48	$44.6
Median	2.09	37.9	1.44	36.9

442

ative to domestic acquisitions, it is important to make sure that the difference is not due to other factors such as the location of the acquired bank and the year of the transaction. This requires controlling for the influence of time and location on the price-to-book value ratio. This was accomplished through application of multiple regression techniques in which the price-to-book value ratio was the dependent variable and a series of binary variables for nationality of acquirer (foreign or domestic), year (1974-75, 1976, 1977 or 1978), and location (Florida, California, Texas or all other states) are the explanatory variables. These variables are defined in Table 5. In the regression, the constant term is the average price-to-book value ratio for banks in states other than Florida, California and Texas that were purchased in 1976 by domestic acquirers. The average is 1.266, as can be seen in Regression 1 in Table 6. To obtain the average ratio for banks with different characteristics, say foreign acquisitions in Florida during 1976, simply add the coefficients of the relevant variables to the constant term; in this case, add .318 for Florida and .367 for foreign acquisition to 1.266 to obtain 1.951. This same procedure can be used to determine average ratios for banks with other characteristics.

Regression 1 in Table 6 indicates that the average difference between the price-to-book value ratios for domestic and foreign acquisitions, controlling for time and location, is .367 rather than .616 when time

Table 5
Variable List

Variable	Definition
FORACQ	= 1 if foreign acquisition = 0 if domestic acquisition
CAL	= 1 if acquisition of bank in California = 0 otherwise
FLA	= 1 if acquisition of bank in Florida = 0 otherwise
TEX	= 1 if acquisition of bank in Texas = 0 otherwise
YEAR 74-75	= 1 if acquisition during 1974-75 = 0 otherwise
YEAR 77	= 1 if acquisition during 1977 = 0 otherwise
YEAR 78	= 1 if acquisition during 1978 = 0 otherwise

Table 6
Regressions on Acquisition Premiums in Domestic and Foreign Acquisitions
(Dependent Variable = Acquisition Price/Book Value)

Variable	Regression 1			Regression 2		
	Coefficient		t-statistic	Coefficient		t-statistic
CONSTANT	1.266		–	1.366		–
FORACQ	0.367		2.043	0.606		2.988
CAL	0.531		2.574			
FLA	0.318		1.843			
TEX	0.241		1.184			
YEAR 74-75	0.289		1.462			
YEAR 77	0.024		0.378	0.070		0.283
YEAR 78	0.089		0.534	0.256		1.124
R^2		0.4006			0.4481	
F		5.156			4.331	
N		62			20	

and location were not considered. The premium of .367, though smaller, is statistically significant. The results also support the hypothesis that higher premiums are paid in growth states such as California, Florida and Texas. Premiums were higher during 1974-75 than in later years.

There was a sufficient number of foreign (12) and domestic (8) acquisitions in Florida to reestimate the regression for just those banks. According to the results shown in Regression 2 in Table 6, foreign interests paid an average premium of .606 for the 12 banks they acquired relative to the price-to-book value ratio of the 8 domestically-acquired banks. Thus, Regression 1, which covers acquisitions in all states, understates the premium foreign interests paid in Florida. There were insufficient numbers of foreign *and* domestic acquisitions in any other state to develop reliable statistics by focusing only on acquisitions in a single state.

CONCLUSION

Acquisition prices offered by foreign interests for U.S. banks have generally been higher than those paid by domestic banks as measured by the price-to-book value ratio. Several motivations have induced foreign entities to acquire U.S. banks including the potential for enhancing the profitability of the U.S. bank and the diversification value. While this diversification value, including market penetration, ought to result systematically in higher acquisition prices being offered by foreign entities for initial entry into the U.S. banking market, structural characteristics of the regulation of U.S. banks preventing acquisition by other domestic entities may permit foreign entities to acquire U.S. banks at less than competitive prices. Until such diversification opportunities are exhausted by acquisition of a U.S. bank, foreign entities have an incentive to offer higher prices for U.S. banks than would be warranted by other domestic investors. Thereafter, only the existence of structural obstacles to acquisitions by domestic entities would permit foreign entities to acquire U.S. banks at prices below comparable domestic transactions.

Acknowledgments

Diane Page assisted in the research and Judith A. Walter, Steven J. Weiss and Robert Baer made helpful comments on earlier drafts.

FOOTNOTES

[1] The foreign acquisition of U.S. banks has also raised an issue of equitable treatment for U.S. investors of acquired banks. The issue implies that investors in the stock of U.S. banks may not realize a value commensurate with the risk and return characteristics of the acquired bank. This assertion implicitly entails an assumption either that the market mechanism by which security prices of American corporations are valued is defective or that competitive alternatives to acquisition by other domestic banks are absent. If either of these assumptions is warranted, the resulting inequitable treatment of U.S. investors would be attributed to a deficiency in the American market system rather than the presence of foreign investors.

[2] Ricahrd Brealey, *Security Prices in a Competitive Market*, MIT Press, 1974, pp. 49-51.

[3] Thomas Piper, *The Economics of Bank Acquisition by Registered Bank Holding Companies*, Federal Reserve Bank of Boston, 1971, chap. IV.

[4] Judith A. Walter, "Foreign Acquisitions of U.S. Banks: Motives and Factual Considerations," *OCC Staff Paper*, June 1980.

[5] Several commentators on foreign acquisitions have proposed that depressed U.S. bank stock prices have contributed to the motivation of foreign entities to acquire U.S. banks. This phenomenon, by itself, would not explain these foreign acquisitions in the absence of the two motivations described above. For a fuller treatment of this issue see Walter, *ibid.*, pp. 14-19.

[6] Of these two motivations, only the first, enhanced profitability, is necessarily related to foreign acquisition of existing U.S. banks. The diversification motive could also be accomplished through the *de novo* bank alternative. The higher costs entailed in organizing a new bank would, however, generally result in foreign acquisition of existing U.S. banks.

[7] An additional source of valuation disparities could arise from the risk/return/valuation preferences of foreign entities. If foreign entities are less risk averse than U.S. domestic entities, the foreign entities would place a higher value on any given rate of return regardless of the potential for profitability enhancement. Differences in planning horizons could also contribute to valuation disparities between foreign and domestic entities.

[8] Offers of foreign entities to acquire equity interests in U.S. banks are normally made in cash. Because foreign banks are not subject to the same public disclosure requirements as American banks and because few foreign bank stocks are traded in active markets readily accessible to U.S. investors, it may be difficult for stockholders to judge the fairness of an offer to exchange shares of a foreign institution for those of a domestic bank. The circumstances under which such a situation might arise, however, are probably quite rare. Stockholders of closely held banks could reject offers if they did not feel capable of assessing their value. For banks which are widely held by the public, foreign entities would be unlikely to present offers of exchange that would be difficult to assess because investors would most likely be unreceptive and defeat the proposed acquisition.

[9] Investment bankers assert that because foreign acquisition bids are generally keyed to book value, market values are largely irrelevant to foreign acquirers. When stocks are selling at a discount to book value, it follows that an acquisition bid above book value will be at an even higher premium relative to market value.

[10] Brealey, *op. cit.*

[11] Piper, p. 198. Piper noted that between the first and second halves of the 21-year period, bank stock prices had declined considerably below book value.

[12] Dwight B. Crane, Paul W. Marshall, and Kenneth E. Lanham, "Foreign Bank Acquisition of American Banks," Report to the Office of the Comptroller of the Currency, November 1979.

[13] *Ibid.*, p. b-7.

THE CO
BALANCE
DOMESTIC AN[
BANKS I[

STEVEN J. WEISS

SUMMARY

This paper analyzes various differences between domestic and foreign banks that affect their relative competitive advantages in the U.S. market. The sources of possible foreign bank advantages which have drawn the most concern of U.S. bankers and policy makers are (1) foreign banks' advantages in multistate operations; (2) the broader range of nonbank activities and investments authorized for foreign compared to domestic banks; and (3) differences in regulatory burden and degree of home country government support. Those topics are examined, together with a review of regulatory changes and anecdotal evidence on competition between domestic and foreign banks in the U.S. It is concluded that in spite of differences in regulatory treatment, their U.S. operations are not affected by any major imbalance in competitive opportunity.

Foreign banks have advantages in multistate operations because of "grandfathered" facilities established before restrictions imposed by the International Banking Act of 1978, their ability to change "home state," and the opportunity to establish "limited" branch facilities, but those differences do not appear so consequential as to justify any new constraints on foreign bank expansion.

Foreign banks are able to engage in a broader range of nonbanking activities and to hold investments in nonfinancial enterprises that would in some cases be impermissible for U.S. banking operations. U.S. policy has been formulated to accommodate such differences in a way that

gn bank activity in the domestic market without creating
imbalance of competitive opportunity.

ms of home country supervisory advantages, particularly effec-
apital requirements and government support, comparative advan-
e is difficult to assess because of differences in accounting practices
and other factors. Overall, the largest U.S. banks, those most intensively
involved in competition with foreign multinational banks, do not appear, in general, to suffer significant disadvantage in the overall balance
of capital requirements and other regulatory factors.

INTRODUCTION

Foreign acquisitions of U.S. banks have raised concerns about the
competitive position and opportunities of U.S. banking organizations
vis-a-vis foreign banks. A U.S. banker testifed that ". . . foreign banks
operating in this country do have the leverage advantage, the funding
advantage, the locational advantage, and we are seriously impaired;"[1]
a prominent foreign bank spokesman conceded that ". . . many foreign
banking institutions do not have the same constraints domestic banks
have in terms of return on capital, return on assets or capital adequacy
ratios."[2] Various foreign bank advantages may affect their competition
with U.S. banks in one or more tiers of banking markets, i.e., the global
international banking arena, the domestic U.S. financial market, or specific metropolitan (local) banking markets within the U.S.

The purpose of this paper is to evaluate the balance of competitive
opportunity between domestic and foreign banks in their U.S. operations. The analysis considers foreign banks' operations through branches, agencies, and other forms, including bank subsidiaries established *de
novo* or through acquisition of established U.S. banks.[3] Specific competitive advantages that foreign banks or foreign-owned U.S. banks may
enjoy relative to U.S.-owned rivals are examined in turn. The possible
sources of advantage analyzed in this paper are (1) differences in ability
to conduct multistate operations within the U.S.; (2) broader powers
and permissible investments of foreign banks, including affiliations with
securities firms and other nonbanking businesses; and (3) different
(lighter) regulatory burdens which, in combination with support from
home-country governments, may translate into financial advantages.
Analyzing the impact of any single factor which may give one group of

institutions some competitive advantage over others is extremely difficult because of the complexity of laws, regulations, practices and relationships between banks and governments in different countries. Nonetheless, this paper identifies options for dealing with certain instances of competitive imbalance and recommends a course of action, where appropriate. The paper concludes with some general observations about overall regulatory and competitive balance.

IMPACT OF THE INTERNATIONAL BANKING ACT OF 1978

It is important to bear in mind that the competitive position of foreign banks in U.S. markets is significantly affected by the International Banking Act of 1978 (IBA)[4]. Some important changes have not yet been fully implemented, and the full impact of other recent changes on foreign banks will be discernible only with the passage of time. As Comptroller of the Currency John G. Heimann recently observed:

> ... The ultimate impact on the competitive balance will depend on how foreign banks respond to new conditions and new opportunities, the reactions of their domestic rivals, and any further changes in U.S. laws and regulations that may be brought about by the dynamic unfolding of events.[5]

In its overall impact, the IBA reduced or eliminated advantages that previously applied to foreign branches and agencies operating in the U.S. as opposed to subsidiaries. Donald Jacobs has observed that some of the foreign banks involved in the large recent takeovers had previously established branches here, and

> Clearly, the major interest in purchase came after the elements of constraints included in the IBA were known to the managements of foreign banks. This suggests that the IBA did reduce the operating advantages of branches over chartering *de novo* or purchasing an existing bank.[6]

According to Serge Bellanger, then Chairman of the Institute of Foreign Bankers, a trend toward foreign bank subsidiary operations would be in keeping with Congressional design:

Throughout the IBA hearings, there was recurring recognition that foreign banks had certain advantages over domestic banks because of their
ability under the laws of certain states to establish branches and, to a
lesser extent, agencies. It was widely accepted, however, that entry into
the U.S. through subsidiaries avoided such competitive advantages. The
deliberate effect of IBA has been to encourage foreign bank entry
through subsidiaries, which are more readily treated the same as domestic banks.[7]

Thus, to the extent that foreign banks operate in the U.S. through subsidiaries, whether *de novo* or via acquisition, competitive differences
tend to be reduced.

MULTISTATE OPERATIONS OF FOREIGN BANKS

In testimony during 1979, a U.S. banker summarized the advantages
of foreign banks in multistate operations as follows:

Notwithstanding the IBA's goal of equitable treatment, there still remain areas where foreign banks enjoy competitive advantages over U.S.
banks, most notably in interstate banking privileges. For example, foreign banks are the only full-service commercial banking institutions in
the United States that continue to have the ability to establish branch
and agency offices in more than one state. Further, foreign banks are
the only banking institutions in the United States that can acquire a
large domestic bank in one state *and* establish branch and agency offices
in other states. Essentially, foreign banks are the only banking institutions in the U.S. that can operate free from the major restrictions of the
McFadden Act and Douglas Amendment to the Bank Holding Company
Act.

While the IBA was supposed to put U.S. and foreign banks on a more
equal competitive footing, the generous grandfathering under the Act
and the great freedom allowed in home state selection do not appear to
impose major restraints. In fact, . . . the IBA seems to have spurred major bank acquisitions by foreign banks.[8]

To the extent that foreign banks do retain advantages in multistate operations, it is important to assess the significance of the remaining differences between U.S. and foreign bank opportunities for multistate
operations, and it is appropriate to consider whether further changes in
U.S. laws and regulations are desirable.

Foreign banks' ability to operate full service branches in more than one state was widely cited in the debates leading to the IBA, as a major competitive advantage of foreign banks. Even though foreign branches are not permitted in a large number of states,[9] large foreign banking organizations were able to establish broad interstate networks through various combinations of branches, agencies, and subsidiary banks. The real significance of this advantage has been questioned by some observers. Franklin R. Edwards and Jack Zwick concluded that foreign banks' multistate branch operations did not pose a serious competitive threat to U.S. banks.[10] They noted that large U.S. banks, through loan production offices, offices of nonbank affiliates and Edge Act and Agreement Corporations, are able to establish multistate organizations for virtually all banking services except retail deposit-taking. Stephen A. Rhoades has described "the broader geographic spread of domestic multibank holding companies through their nonbank subsidiaries" which "the expansion of foreign banks in the United States has not matched. . . ."[11] Rhoades documents how U.S. bank holding companies expanded rapidly during the 1970s into new nonbank activities authorized by the Federal Reserve Board after the 1970 amendments to the Bank Holding Company Act. Holding company expansion has occurred

> . . . through either *de novo* entry or acquisition of existing firms. The most extensive acquisition activity has been directed toward local market, consumer-oriented industries; thus bank holding companies have acquired many of the largest mortgage banking firms in the country and a significant number of sizable consumer finance companies. . . . The extensive national coverage achieved in this manner is illustrated by the fact that Citicorp has 229 consumer finance offices and mortgage outlets in 55 cities. Moreover, including loan production offices and Edge Act corporations, Citicorp now has about 400 offices in 38 states and the District of Columbia; Bank of America has 350 offices in 41 states; and Manufacturers Hanover Trust Company has 190 offices in 10 states.[12]

Donald Jacobs observed that, given the types of business usually sought by foreign banks, i.e., borrowing and foreign exchange needs of large and intermediate corporate clients, the multistate advantage may not be material, because the market for those services is essentially national in scope.[13] Jacobs noted, however, that his argument assumed that foreign branches were established to serve the needs of large and medium-sized companies.[14]

Foreign banks' current advantages in multistate operations are the result of three statutory or regulatory factors. First, substantial multi-state facilities were "grandfathered" by the IBA. Second, foreign banks enjoy greater locational flexibility than their domestic counterparts because of their ability to change their "home state" designation. Third, foreign banks are able to establish "limited" branches outside their home states.

"Grandfathered" Multistate Facilities

One of the most important provisions of the IBA limited *new* full-service deposit-taking facilities of foreign banks to a single "home" state. In the interest of fairness, section 5 of the IBA contains a grandfather clause which permits the continued operation of foreign-owned multistate deposit-taking facilities that were established, or for which permission to operate had been sought, on or before July 27, 1978. Foreign-owned interstate operations on that date were already quite extensive.[15] The substantial grandfathering, therefore, perpetuates a locational advantage[16] that domestic institutions cannot quite match, although they can come close by utilizing alternative devices.[17] Serge Bellanger commented that the IBA "has practically no significant impact on the expansion of foreign bank operations in the United States. Virtually every major bank in the world was set up in this country before the July 27, 1978, grandfathering date."[18] Appendix A to this paper is a table summarizing the latest available information on grandfathered deposit-taking facilities of major foreign banks. It shows that at least 40 of the 50 largest non-U.S. banking organizations have grandfathered facilities, and 26 have grandfathered facilities in at least two states. The grandfathering reflects a deliberate decision by Congress and there have been no serious proposals to reverse it.

Change of "Home" State

Under the Federal Reserve Board's "home state" ruling[19] many foreign banks retain options for establishing multistate operations beyond those already grandfathered by the IBA. Foreign banks are permitted a one-time change in their designated home state designation. Thus, foreign banks with existing branches or agencies in one or more states can redesignate their home state and establish new full-service branches or acquire a bank in a state where they are not presently represented, subject to certain restrictions and limitations.[20] The regulation perpetuates, even for institutions with established U.S. deposit-taking facilities, foreign banks' relative advantage as potential acquirers of domestic institutions: "The possibility of future bank acquisitions could be an important factor influencing a foreign bank's choice of home state, in addition to the factor of being able to establish full-service branches only in the home state."[21] The regulation extends to foreign organizations an extra measure of locational flexibility.[22]

"Limited" Branch Facilities

The IBA provides for a foreign bank's establishment of "limited" branches outside its designated home state. The deposit-taking powers of "limited" branches are restricted in the same manner as Edge Act corporations, i.e., they can only accept deposits from nonresidents or deposits arising principally from international trade or banking transactions. The IBA mandated regulatory changes designed to facilitate the establishment of Edge Act corporations by both domestic and foreign banking organizations. "Limited" branches constitute an alternative form of interstate expansion that is available only to foreign banks. Unlike Edge Act facilities, whose loans must be related to international trade or business, "limited" branches are empowered to extend commercial loans for domestic purposes. The Senate Report accompanying the IBA acknowledged this difference:

> This lending ability is a privilege not extended to United States banks under United States law, but it is not a significant advantage for foreign banks, since U.S. banks have many other ways of soliciting and competing for domestic loan business.[23]

Thus, although this option is clearly more attractive for foreign banks than Edge Act facilities,[24] it does not constitute a substantial competitive imbalance.

Conclusions on Multistate Operations

Foreign banks do enjoy several advantages in locational flexibility and interstate expansion potential relative to domestic banking organizations. *Bank Stock Quarterly* commented on the IBA's grandfather provisions as follows:

> The concept of equitable national treatment in the area of interstate activities surely loses meaning when so great a number of large organizations enjoy the advantages of multistate operations which are denied to all others. If multistate operation is acceptable for 39 banking organizations with presence in 26 states, one cannot justly deny such opportunities to their competitors. Only the opposite tack, extending the expansion powers of American banking companies now artificially enclosed within state borders, can justify the claim of equitable treatment.[25]

The case for liberalizing domestic banks' geographic expansion opportunities is strengthened by the differential advantages, no matter how slight, accorded to foreign banks through establishment of limited branches and the option to change home states. An alternative approach to reducing this competitive imbalance, i.e., tightening restrictions imposed on foreign banks, would be an anticompetitive move and one which, in the opinion of many observers, would represent a step backward and away from the practical realities of bank competition in the U.S. today.[26]

BROADER SCOPE OF FOREIGN BANK POWERS, PERMISSSIBLE INVESTMENTS AND AFFILIATIONS

Some critics of foreign takeovers of large U.S. banks have raised concerns about foreign banks' direct and indirect involvement in nonbanking business, activities, and affiliations that are not generally authorized for domestic banks and bank holding companies. Representative Rosenthal pointed out that:

> ... the Federal Reserve now permits U.S. banks to be bought by foreign holding companies with big multinational conglomerate involvement in manufacturing, mining, trade, shipping et cetera ... when our domestic bank holding companies are not permitted the same involvement in other industries.[27]

Senator Heinz expressed his concern about possible competitive disadvantage for U.S. banks as follows:

> Because the major American banks are increasingly dependent on the banking business of foreign and multinational customers, the present ability of foreign bank holding companies to retain and establish affiliations with a broad variety of non-banking business is certain to have a profound effect on banking competition in the United States if such foreign organizations are permitted to acquire major U.S. banks. In fact, those major U.S. banks which are not affiliated through a foreign parent company with important non-banking enterprises will be at a serious competitive disadvantage . . .[28]

Banks in many foreign countries are permitted a considerably broader range of activities, investments and affiliations in "nonbanking" areas than is permitted to domestic banking organizations under U.S. law.

In many foreign countries, close ties between banks and nonbank enterprises have been traditionally permitted or even actively encouraged. Banks in some countries are allowed to hold, and do hold, direct equity investments in nonbanking companies. Even where direct equity holdings are limited, banks may have indirect equity interests through affiliations with investment or merchant banks or relationships, other than equity holdings, with nonbanking concerns. Relationships with industry may take the form of interlocking directorships, cross-ownership or less formal traditional ties among groups of companies. Moreover, banks in many countries engage in nonbanking activities that would be proscribed by U.S. law and policy.[29]

This section examines the questions of whether and to what extent foreign banks may have competitive advantages in their U.S. operations because of their broader powers and affiliations with nonbanking enterprises.

Nonbanking activities and investments of foreign banks raise regulatory issues that have commanded the special attention of the U.S. Congress[30] and bank supervisory autorities.[31] Policy makers have also addressed the possible competitive impacts of such nonbank relationships on the operations of U.S. banks, both in the United States and overseas, and have dealt with the matter essentially by focusing on relationships having practical consequences within the domestic marketplace and by allowing U.S. banks' overseas nonbanking activities to be governed, in part, by host country policies.[32] Given the broad differences in national policies which exist, further steps by the U.S. Government in the direction of equalizing U.S. and foreign involvement in nonbanking areas would entail either extraterritorial extension of U.S. standards or fundamental revision of U.S. domestic banking policies.

U.S. Law and Policy

U.S. law has required a clear separation of banking and the securities business since 1933 (the Glass-Steagall Act) and, since passage of the Bank Holding Company Act of 1956 (BHCA), has strictly limited the scope of bank holding companies' nonbanking activities.[33]

Foreign bank holding company activities in the U.S. have been subject to essentially the same separation of banking and nonbanking activities, according to essentially the same standards, although overseas nonbanking operations and interests may be exempted from the non-banking prohibitions of U.S. law.[34] When a foreign bank applies for permission to acquire a U.S. bank and, thereby, become a foreign bank holding company, the Federal Reserve Board takes account of its related overseas nonbanking interests and activities,[35] focusing particularly on any existing nonbank operations in the U.S. As a condition of approval, foreign bank holding companies have been required to divest securities affiliates[36] or other nonbank companies[37] whose activities in the U.S. are inconsistent with restrictions imposed on domestic banks.

The IBA imposed those same requirements on foreign banks that operate in the U.S. through branches or agencies.[38] Before the IBA, foreign banks that had U.S. branches or agencies but not bank subsidiaries were not subject to the nonbanking prohibitions of the BHCA. Their previously established nonbanking activities and affiliated operations in the U.S., most notably securities affiliates,[39] were grandfathered by the IBA, subject to certain limitations.[40]

The treatment of foreign banks' U.S. securities affiliates was the subject of extensive deliberation in Congressional hearings leading up to the IBA.[41] Since the securities business is a normal part of the banking business in many countries,[42] foreign banks' establishment of U.S. securities affiliates is not surprising. Moreover, as several observers have noted, such affiliates were established partly in response to U.S. banks' and brokerage firms' competitive initiatives in securities markets abroad.[43] Concern about possible retaliation against U.S. interests overseas supported the grandfather provision in the IBA.[44] The New York Clearing House banks, which compete most directly with the foreign banks that have securities affiliates, voiced no objection to the grandfathering of the limited number of existing securities affiliates.[45] The Congress gave particular consideration to the important role played by foreign bank securities affiliates in regional stock exchanges and in channeling foreign investment funds into the U.S. market.[46] U.S. securities affiliates of foreign banks are not numerous, nor do they conduct a substantial proportion of overall domestic securities business (see data in Appendix B).

U.S. policy concerning foreign banks' overseas involvement with nonbank enterprise has sought to accommodate differences between U.S. and other nations' laws and practices so that foreign banks may compete in the U.S. on an equitable basis, while at the same time preserving the separation of banking and commerce in the U.S. The policy has been designed, in essence, to insulate the U.S. market from the combination of banking and commerce permitted overseas and to minimize possible competitive disadvantages to U.S. banks stemming from foreign banks' involvement with commercial enterprise. The Bank Holding Company Act was amended in 1966, 1970, and again in 1978—as part of the IBA—to permit foreign bank participation in U.S. banking markets on a basis consistent with those objectives.[47]

Neither the Congress nor the Federal Reserve Board has attempted to restrict foreign banks' overseas operations or investments to make them conform with U.S. domestic requirements. Instead, Congress deliberately provided that foreign nonbanking activities and investments of foreign banking organizations may be exempt from the nonbanking prohibitions of U.S. law. The Federal Reserve Board has implemented regulations to carry out the Congressional policy. Federal Reserve Board Governor Henry C. Wallich summarized the Board's position as follows:

> The Board generally supports the concept that activities of an essentially foreign character should not be disturbed by U.S. laws and regulations unless they directly and significantly impact U.S. institutions and policies. Relationships between foreign banks and nonbanking activities in foreign counties affect the structure and functioning of foreign economies and financial markets, which are not the responsibility of the U.S. Government or its bank supervisory agencies. So long as those foreign relationships do not do violence to the objectives of the Bank Holding Company Act relating to the structure and conduct of banking in this country, it is sensible public policy in today's world to make an accommodation to the realities of the way in which international banking is conducted.[48]

The present U.S. policy does not appear to pose a threat to the sep-

aration of banking and commerce in the U.S. Foreign banking organizations do have possible advantages because of their more extensive
involvement with nonbanking enterprise, e.g. greater diversification and
growth potential on a global level. However, the limitations on their
nonbank activities or investments in the U.S. minimize their possible
competitive advantages vis-a-vis domestic institutions in U.S. markets.

Possible Domestic Competitive Effects[49]

U.S. banks' domestic operations could be affected in several ways by
foreign banks' involvement with nonbanking enterprise overseas.

First, if foreign nonbank companies operating in the U.S. tend to
channel their banking business to related foreign-owned banks in this
country, U.S. banks are denied an opportunity to gain domestic business. Present laws and regulations preclude domestic operations of direct
commercial affiliates and prohibit preferential credit extension to exempt nonbank companies. Nonetheless, home country ties may be in-
formal and relationships may exist even though no clear determination
of control is warranted.[50] Some foreign corporations undoubtedly follow such home country ties in establishing bank relationships, but such
a tendency is little different from the normal business practices of multinational companies, which gravitate toward home country banks
whether or not any relationships exist. Some concentration of loans to
home country multinational corporations has been noted by bank examiners, particularly in the loan portfolios of foreign-owned banks that
were established *de novo* and whose activities typically complement
those of the worldwide group.[51] In the same way, U.S. banks' overseas
activities are heavily oriented to serving the needs of U.S.-based multinationals. As transnational banking competition intensifies, however,
traditional home country loyalties are tending to weaken or break
down.[52]

It has also been argued that affiliated nonbank companies could
channel funds to foreign-owned banks at below market rates or borrow
funds at noncompetitive rates, thereby indirectly subsidizing the foreign-
owned banks' U.S. operations. If that occurred, the foreign-owned
banks would have an advantage in competing for other business not affected by such nonmarket behavior. Such activity is not unknown
among multinational corporations. There is, of necessity, a compensa-

tory loss to the nonbank firms whose nonmarket transactions indirectly subsidize the foreign-owned banks. Such activity tends, therefore, to be self-limiting. Indirect evidence discussed in the next section of this paper suggests that this type of cross-subsidy is not an extensive practice. Analysis of foreign-owned U.S. banks' financial performance shows that they tend to have a higher overall cost of funds than geographically similar domestically owned peers.[53] Foreign-owned U.S. banks were also found to be less profitable, on average, than their peers.[54]

Finally, it is conceivable that foreign banks' ability to offer abroad, directly or through affiliates, services which U.S. institutions are unable to provide here could attract a certain amount of business from U.S. multinational firms at the expense of domestic banks. That possibility is limited by the fact that U.S. banks could respond to most substantial challenges through activities of their own overseas, where they have greater freedom to engage in nonbanking activities. There is no evidence that U.S. banks have been seriously hurt by foreign banks' ability to offer a broader range of services in other markets. On the whole, there is no reason to believe that U.S. banks are adversely affected because foreign banks own nonfinancial enterprises outside the U.S. Present U.S. policy constitutes a reasonable adjustment to the realities of multinational banking and the different laws and practices prevalent in other nations.

Conclusion on Nonbanking Activities and Investments

The competitive balance between domestic and foreign banks in the U.S. is not significantly affected by differences in overseas nonbanking activities and investments. The U.S. domestic policy of separating banking and commerce has produced compromises in U.S. regulation of both foreign banking organizations' overseas involvement with nonbank enterprise and U.S. banks' activities abroad. If, as a condition of entry, foreign banks' overseas operations and holdings were required fully to conform with U.S. domestic policies, many, if not most, major foreign banks would be disqualified from establishing facilities in the U.S. Imposing such a requirement would constitute extraterritorial application of U.S. standards, which would appear not only impractical but also inadvisable. Achievement of perfect regulatory equality would in effect screen out many foreign entrants, sacrificing benefits of foreign competition, expertise and capital in U.S. financial markets. Retaliation by foreign governments would likely follow, to the clear detriment of U.S. commercial interests. An alternative approach to achieving a better competitive balance would be to reconsider the traditional limitations on U.S. banking organizations' nonbanking activities. That course of action, although perhaps appropriate on other grounds, does not appear justified simply on the basis of any U.S. bank disadvantages in domestic competition with foreign rivals.

REGULATORY FINANCIAL ADVANTAGES AND SUPPORT BY HOME GOVERNMENT

Many observers of foreign bank competitive behavior in U.S. markets have alluded to foreign banks' apparent cost advantages. A U.S. banker noted that

> . . . there has been no clear resolution of the question as to what capital-to-assets ratio is appropriate. The pressures to which U.S. banks have been subject . . . impose real constraints on asset growth because of the necessity to constantly increase capital to preserve this ratio. Many foreign banks are relatively free from these same constraints, and are, therefore, able to leverage themselves more highly. In our view, this is a distinct advantage competitively for foreign banks.[55]

An article in *Dun's Review* concluded that

> The foreign banks are able to offer better rates than U.S. banks because they are more highly leveraged and are accustomed to working with lower profit margins and smaller spreads, ...[56]

In his study on "Foreign Banks in the United States," Noel Delaney reported that

> . . . both U.S. and foreign bankers have pointed to the State-owned French and Italian banks as being aggressive price cutters. With no annual meetings or dividend requirements, and with unlimited capital from their governments, these banks are said to largely ignore the profitability of their loan terms.[57]

Concerns about foreign banks' possible comparative cost advantages seem to arise from observations of apparent rate cutting, a phenomenon which can have different meanings. It may indicate a business decision to sacrifice profit in order to gain market share, a time-honored competitive practice. Such a decision may appeal to new market entrants, particularly if they lack other powerful competitive weapons. In some situations, apparent rate-cutting may stem from differences in loan pricing techniques, e.g., setting rates on some basis other than the "prime" convention. Rate-cutting may reflect real underlying financial advantages attributable to supervisory differences in capital requirements, differing profit objectives, and direct or indirect subsidization by the home country government. To the extent that such factors give some foreign banks advantages, questions arise as to whether and how such advantages may be transferred to a foreign-owned U.S. subsidiary and how they may be affected by regulatory changes currently being implemented or proposed.

Government Regulation and Support

For supervisory purposes, most countries impose capital requirements on their banks. Most industrialized nations impose legally fixed capital ratios.[58] In the U.S. and the U.K. there are no legal requirements, but supervisors do monitor capital levels carefully and through a variety of objective and subjective criteria determine adequate capital levels for individual institutions on a case-by-case basis. Leverage is a concern to bank supervisors in all countries, but some tolerate lower capital ratios than others.

Governments may support their domestic banks in a variety of ways, e.g., by providing central bank clearing, discount and lender-of-last-resort facilities; by establishing deposit insurance arrangements; by depositing public funds in banks; and by enacting any number of protective laws and regulations.[59]

Whether banks' capital levels are set by law, regulation, or supervisory jawboning (and affected in varying degrees by market discipline), results are uneven and can affect the competitive balance. The ratios used to judge capital adequacy for supervisory purposes relate capital to total assets or to risk assets.[60] Although established as a measure of protecting solvency, the ratios have an impact on banks' competitive abilities. For example, if one bank is more highly leveraged than another, i.e. if its percentage of capital to assets is lower, it can undercut its competitor on loan pricing and still earn the same rate of return on capital.

Impact of Regulatory Differences

It is widely believed that U.S. banks face more stringent capital requirements than foreign banks. The conclusion, therefore, is drawn that U.S. banks are competitively disadvantaged. However, as an across-the-board proposition, that is not clearly supported by data for recent years, nor is it supported by the fact that U.S. banks have greatly expanded their operations overseas and have been strong competitors in foreign markets. Available international comparisons indicate that capital ratios for major U.S. banks fall somewhere in the middle when compared to those of the largest banks in other countries.

Comparing capital ratios across countries is a statistical exercise fraught with perils. There are substantial differences among countries in accounting conventions and disclosure requirements, not the least of which is the existence of "hidden" or "inner" reserves of banks in some countries.[61] In spite of the many problems involved in such comparisons, summary data on capital ratios for the largest banks in the world, for 1972-3 and 1977-8, are presented in Table 1.[62] It is conventional to compare ratios of the world's major banking institutions, which compete on a global basis, rather than national averages, which reflect banks of all sizes and types. Table 1 is based on figures for the world's "Top 300" (according to annual rankings by *The Banker*), most of which are significant competitors in international banking markets.

The U.S. figures do appear to be at the high end of the international spectrum, but patterns are less clear when underlying differences and discrepancies in the data are taken into account. Accounting differences may have a very significant impact in certain cases. Thus, because Swiss, Italian, Japanese and some other banks hold "hidden," or "inner," non-published reserves, the published ratios are "probably considerably lower than reality."[63] If an adjustment were possible, the large Swiss banks' ratios might be revealed as the highest.[64]

The individual bank data indicate some wide differences among banks from a given country. Among the largest Japanese banks, the

Table 1
Ratios of Capital to Deposits, Largest World Banks by
Country, Selected Years
(Ratios Expressed as Percentages)

	1972	1973	1977	1978
United States				
Median	7.4	7.0	6.8	6.7
Upper Quarter	8.6	8.2	7.9	7.7
Lower Quarter	6.0	6.0	5.4	5.6
Japan				
Median	5.2	4.9	4.6	4.3
Upper Quarter	5.8	5.8	5.4	5.4
Lower Quarter	3.7	3.6	3.2	3.0
United Kingdom				
Median	6.6	7.3	5.8	6.8
Upper Quarter	7.4	8.4	6.5	7.9
Lower Quarter	4.3	3.9	4.8	6.2
France				
Median	3.1	2.9	2.6	2.4
Upper Quarter	5.2	3.8	4.0	3.5
Lower Quarter	1.4	1.1	1.8	1.6
Germany				
Median	3.6	3.6	3.6	3.3
Upper Quarter	4.4	4.1	4.3	4.0
Lower Quarter	3.4	3.2	2.6	2.7
Italy				
Median	1.7	2.0	3.1	3.5
Upper Quarter	3.0	2.7	4.2	4.5
Lower Quarter	1.2	1.1	2.3	2.3
Switzerland				
Median	5.6	5.7	6.3	6.6
Netherlands				
Median	4.1	3.6	3.1	3.8
Canada				
Median	3.8	3.3	3.2	3.5
Other Developed Countries				
Median	5.8	5.7	6.6	6.4
Upper Quarter	7.7	7.3	10.2	8.3
Lower Quarter	4.6	4.3	4.5	3.8
Less Developed Countries				
Median	6.4	6.2	6.1	5.4
Upper Quarter	8.6	9.2	8.6	6.5
Lower Quarter	4.6	4.6	4.4	4.2

Note:

Ratios are calculated from data published by *The Banker*. The median and upper and lower quartile figures are derived from the ratios for individual banks from each country, or group of countries, appearing among the "Top 300" world banks as ranked by *The Banker*. Because of year-to-year changes in the composition of the "Top 300," the number of banks included for each country or group varies. See the sources for explanation of the data and compositional changes.

Sources

Figures for 1972 and 1973 are from Ian Peacock, "The Squeeze on Capital Ratios," *The Banker*, June 1975, Table 1, p. 667. Figures for 1977 and 1978, were calculated from data published in *The Banker's* annual "Top 300" listing (June 1978 and June 1979, respectively).

ratio ranged from less than 4 percent to more than 20 percent. Three of the largest French banks, which are state-owned, have ratios of only around one percent, a situation which has prevailed throughout the 1970s.[65] Ratios for private banks in France, however, are more in line with other large banks' figures. Among the largest U.S. banks, there is a strong tendency for the very largest to have the lowest ratios[66] —a tendency which appears in some other countries as well, though the pattern elsewhere is not so dramatic as in the U.S. The 1978 median ratio for the U.S., 6.7 percent, is based on figures for the 56 largest banking organizations; the ratio is 5.0 percent for the top 10 alone, and 4.5 percent for the top five.

Overall, the data indicate lower capital ratios for *some* foreign bank competitors of U.S. banks, although the difference is less for the largest, money center banks than for all U.S. banks. The differences between U.S. and foreign banks would be reduced, generally, if capital and reserves of banks in all foreign countries were fully disclosed. The widest spread appears vis-a-vis the French banks, where the clear government support of the large nationalized banks is an important factor. Anticipated government backing, whether direct or tacit, is a significant determinant of the actual capital ratios that a bank can maintain.[67]

Some foreign banks, particularly those which are state-owned, may receive direct or indirect subsidies or may accept lower targets for return on equity than are typical for U.S. banks or would be acceptable to U.S. regulators or financial markets. As a major or controlling shareholder, the home government may be willing to give subsidies or accept lower profits in order to foster other objectives. In either case, U.S. branches or agencies of a foreign bank could have a pricing advantage over domestic rivals or over operations of banks from other countries. The actual extent of such behavior is not clearly known. With regard to the nationalized French banks, for example, it has been noted that they were legally established as commercial enterprises, "expected to behave like private banks, and they do."[68] Nonetheless, in connection with recent moves to partially denationalize the three largest French banks, Finance Minister Rene Monory commented that they will ". . . behave differently when some 25 percent of their capital is privately owned and quoted on the stock exchange."[69]

To the extent that some foreign banks have greater leverage or lower profitability targets than U.S. banks, their branches or agencies would have some direct competitive advantage in the U.S. market. A U.S. *subsidiary* of a foreign bank, however, could only benefit indirectly because U.S. subsidiaries of foreign banks are subject to the same capital requirements as comparable domestically owned banks; and U.S. regulators could, and would, demand corrective action if the subsidiary's earnings or capital were unsatisfactory.

A foreign parent bank could pass through to the U.S. subsidiary the benefit of its high leverage by placing interest-free deposits or accepting a below market rate. The same technique could be used to transmit the benefits from a home government subsidy. Such transactions are nearly impossible to detect from financial statements or call reports. An analysis of data for a sample of U.S. subsidiaries of foreign banks and comparably situated, domestically owned banks of similar size revealed that the foreign bank subsidiaries had, on average, a higher overall cost of funds.[70] The difference arises primarily because they hold a higher proportion of purchased funds and a lower proportion of core deposits than domestically owned peers. U.S. subsidiaries of foreign banks were found to have higher proportions of foreign bank deposits than their peers. Such deposits could not be identified as originating from the foreign parent bank. The amounts were small, in any case, and would not significantly offset the differences in liability mix, even if all were deposited at below market rates.[71]

Impact of Regulatory Changes

The relative financial advantages of foreign and domestic banks in the U.S. will be affected by regulatory changes implemented as a result of the IBA and by policies now being proposed or implemented by foreign governments.

Undoubtedly the most significant and immediate effects will come from new, post-IBA regulatory requirements imposed on foreign branches and agencies. Federal Reserve Board regulations establish reserve requirements, effective on September 4, 1980, which will eliminate perhaps the most critical advantage formerly enjoyed by foreign banks.[72] Funding costs of foreign branches engaged in "retail" business, defined as accepting deposits of less than $100,000, will be increased further by the requirement of FDIC insurance, subject to certain exemptions.[73] Wholesale-oriented foreign branches and agencies will be able to avoid FDIC insurance and thus maintain a marginal advantage over domestic competitors.[74] The new reserve requirements are expected to have a substantial impact on foreign banks' cost of funds. In fact, for-

eign bankers have argued that their operations will be put at a net disadvantage by the new regulatory requirements.[75]

To the extent that foreign bank operations in the U.S. benefit from
regulatory advantages in their home countries, those differences appear
likely to diminish over time as international supervisory standards con-
verge. One potentially important movement is toward imposition of
controls on the consolidated balance sheets of foreign multinational
banks, *i.e.*, taking into account their overseas as well as domestic operations in determining capital requirements. That approach, which has
been used by regulators in the U.S. for some time, is uncommon elsewhere. However, it is "already used by the Dutch, is now being adopted
by the Swiss, . . . will soon also be put into practice by the Bank of
England"[76] and has been actively supported by West German supervisory authorities.[77] Movement by foreign authorities toward regulation
on a consolidated basis will increase their overall capital requirements
and reduce differentials in capital ratios between U.S. and foreign multinational banks.[78] French authorities have ordered the large nationalized banks to increase substantially their capital ratios to levels closer
to those of their European competitors.[79] That change alone, when and
if accomplished, would reduce perhaps the major current disparity
among banks in the international competitive arena.

Conclusions on Supervisory Advantages and Government Support

Some foreign banks do appear to have advantages relative to other
multinational bank competitors because of regulatory differences, especially lower capital requirements, and various forms of home government support. Post-IBA changes in U.S. requirements are expected to
eliminate significant financial advantages that foreign banks' U.S. branch
and agency operations formerly experienced. Recent or prospective
regulatory changes in other countries should contribute to a further
diminution of existing regulatory differences.

OVERALL REGULATORY AND COMPETITIVE BALANCE

Many factors affect the relative competitive abilities of U.S. and foreign banks. Differences in regulatory burdens are inevitable and clear

conclusions about their overall impact are elusive, particularly because conditions change over time.

The dramatic increase in foreign bank activity in the U.S. provides some good examples and anecdotal evidence of shifting relative advantages. New entrants had incentives to shave prices to gain market share. One of their effective moves was to price, below prime, based on a spread over LIBOR (the London interbank offered rate), an unconventional approach for the U.S. market until relatively recently. U.S. banks responded quickly, however, and the advantage proved somewhat transitory, as well as sensitive to swings in LIBOR.[80]

Some advantages experienced by new entrants into a market may be only short term in nature, such as aggressive pricing, the flexibility of small staffs, the ability to concentrate on the upper tier of the whole-sale market, and close ties to home country multinational corporations.[81]

> In order to continue growing . . . [foreign banks] will need to expand their operations, which will add to their costs and squeeze margins. Also, to the extent that any excessive rate-shaving has occurred, market forces can be counted on to exert a self-correcting effect.[82]

Aggressive pricing alone may gain some business, but as competition intensifies, other factors become increasingly important. As Chase Manhattan noted in its 1978 annual report, "the quality of a bank's non-credit services can prove to be the cutting edge."[83] According to some reports, foreign banks have been somewhat hampered as a result.[84] Because of their wholesale and international orientation, many foreign banks are likely to retain a competitive advantage over all but the largest domestic banks for certain types of business.

A foreign banker observed that "Every bank active in its native environment has enormous advantages over any foreign bank invading its territory."[85] Those advantages include a familiar name, good contacts and sources of funds. Foreign banks usually have to pay more for funds, "not because they are less reliable than their American counterparts but just because they have funny names and that can worry some corporate officials."[86] Foreign institutions have generally paid a premium of 30 to 40 basis points[87] on commercial paper, certificates of deposit and banker's acceptances. A number of foreign banks have been working deliberately to make themselves better known and so reduce the premium.[88] It seems reasonable to expect that the premium will shrink with the passage of time, at least for the larger foreign banks.

In their competitive response to the foreign bank "invasion" here, U.S. banks have sought the business of foreign multinational corpora-

tions. Although many foreign banks originally followed those companies to this country, a Swiss banker observed that they are now finding it
increasingly difficult to lend to them because the corporations want to
establish solid credit with domestic institutions.[89] An official of a Japanese bank's New York branch reportedly conceded that U.S. banks are
"grabbing our market."[90]

The foregoing anecdotes illustrate how difficult it is to make any definitive statement regarding the balance of regulatory and competitive
advantages in a given setting. Generally, U.S. banks are subject to a
broader array of regulatory burdens than their rivals in the global arena,
but that doesn't necessarily affect their overseas operations directly.[91]
Competitive advantages derive from a host of factors, some of which
may outweigh those resulting from differences in capital or other regulatory requirements that can be seen in the growing domestic and international presence of banks, notwithstanding their relatively high capital
requirements. It can also be seen in the competitive success enjoyed by
U.S. banks in penetrating markets overseas, even in nations where they
are subjected to differentially burdensome requirements.[92]

CONCLUSION

Within the U.S. market, some differential treatment of foreign bank
operations arose out of IBA grandfathering, and new statutory requirements and their implementing regulations. Further adjustments of the
competitive balance with respect to multistate operations and nonbanking interests could be obtained either by imposing new restrictions on
foreign banks or by liberalizing restrictions on domestic institutions.
The latter approach appears preferable because it would enhance overall
competitive opportunities and market performance; however, there do
not appear to be such serious inequities that there is a compelling need
for change solely on the basis of the competitive balance between domestic and foreign banks. Financial advantages of foreign branches and
agencies will be reduced significantly by new requirements stemming
from the IBA. Regulatory trends outside the U.S., moreover, appear to
favor gradual lessening of international regulatory differences. Recent
developments within the U.S. and anecdotal evidence suggest that the
competitive balance between domestic and foreign banks, however imperfect, is not seriously out of line.

Acknowledgements

Judith A. Walter contributed important material for two sections of the paper. Nancy Lowther and Melanie Quinn assisted in the research for this paper, and Stephen Wood provided substantial help in documentation and revision of earlier drafts. Helpful comments on previous versions of the paper were given by C. Stewart Goddin, Robert R. Bench and Charles E. Lord and Neal M. Soss of the Office of the Comptroller of the Currency, and James V. Houpt of the Federal Reserve Board.

FOOTNOTES

[1] Statement of Richard Thomas, President, First Chicago Corp., in Hearings before the Senate Committee on Banking, Housing, and Urban Affairs on *Edge Corporation Branching; Foreign Bank Takeovers; and International Banking Facilities*, 96th Cong., 1st sess., July 16 and 20, 1979, p. 344.

[2] Serge Bellanger, "The New Order of Banking: an 'Across the Border' Concept?" Address to the New York State Bankers Association, June 18, 1979, quoted in the *American Banker*, August 9, 1979, p. 5.

[3] With regard to acquisitions, it has been argued that U.S. banking organizations are unfairly denied opportunities equivalent to those enjoyed by their foreign rivals and that they are disadvantaged in three ways: foreign banks can acquire large U.S. institutions that are foreclosed, in practice, to domestic banking organizations; U.S. institutions are unable to purchase large banks abroad; and competitive standards applied by U.S. regulatory authorities unfairly favor proposed acquisitions by foreign banks. Those concerns are examined elsewhere. See Wm. Paul Smith and Steven J. Weiss, *Potential Acquisition Partners for Large U.S. Banks: The Discriminatory Effects of Law and Policy*, OCC Staff Paper, 1980; Steven J. Wess, *A Critical Evaluation of Reciprocity in Foreign Bank Acquisitions*, OCC Staff Paper, 1980; and, Steven J. Weiss, *Competitive Standards Applied to Foreign and Domestic Acquisitions of U.S. Banks*, OCC Staff Paper, 1980. Other research has found that the impact of foreign acquisitions on U.S. banks' global competitive position has been minimal. See C. Stewart Goddin and Steven J. Weiss, *U.S. Banks' Loss of Global Standing*, OCC Staff Paper, 1980.

[4] For discussion of the IBA's provisions and implementation, see Sydney J. Key and James M. Brundy, "Implementation of the International Banking Act," *Federal Reserve Bulletin*, October 1979, pp. 785-96; Michael J. Feinman, "National Treatment of Foreign Banks Operating in the United States: The International Banking Act of 1978," *Law and Policy in International Business*, Vol. 11, No. 3 (1979), pp. 1109-49; and *The International Banking Act of 1978*, A Report by the Board of Governors of the Federal Reserve System, September 1980.

[5] John G. Heimann, U.S. Comptroller of the Currency, "Impact of the International Banking Act of 1978 on Foreign Bank Competition in the United States," Address to the Consular Law Society of New York, March 26, 1980, p. 7.

[6] Donald P. Jacobs, "Proposed Public Policy on the Purchase of American Banks," unpublished paper, Northwestern University, Graduate School of Management, p. 7. Jacobs noted,

however, that if government-owned or -sponsored banks have significant advantages in terms of capital [see discussion below], those banks "would continue to have a bias toward operating through branches rather than chartering a bank *de novo* or purchasing an existing bank."

[7] Statement of Serge Bellanger, Chairman, Institute of Foreign Bankers, in Hearings before the Senate Committee on Banking, Housing, and Urban Affairs on *Edge Corporation Branching . . .*, p. 210.

[8] Thomas, *op. cit.*, p. 306. Mr. Thomas indicated in his testimony that his purpose was

> . . . not to urge further restrictions on foreign banks but rather to encourage this Committee to take a hard look at the McFadden Act and Douglas Amendment *in light* of the privileges which Congress has given foreign banks.

[9] See William B. Glidden and John E. Shockey, "U.S. Branches and Agencies of Foreign Banks: A Comparison of the Federal and State Chartering Options," *University of Illinois Law Forum*, Volume 1980, No. 1, pp. 65-90.

[10] Franklin R. Edwards and Jack Zwick, "Activities and Regulatory Issues—Foreign Banks in the United States," *Columbia Journal of World Business*, Spring 1975, pp. 64-5.

[11] Stephen A. Rhoades, "The Competitive Effects of Interstate Banking," *Federal Reserve Bulletin*, January 1980, p. 3.

[12] *Ibid.* Tables 3 and 4 in Rhoades' article display the record since 1971 of bank holding company acquisitions of nonbanking firms, by activity, and *de novo* entry into nonbanking activities (*Ibid.* p. 4).

[13] Jacobs, *op. cit.* pp. 3-4. Jacobs concluded: ". . . I would argue that in the past the concern about the foreign branch location advantage was a real issue; with the passage of years it was becoming near myth. In the not too distant future, if this situation was allowed to continue, it would produce no material advantage" (p. 4).

[14] *Ibid.* p. 4. While Jacobs' assumption appears valid for multinational banks' overseas activities in general, there is evidence of some banks' increasing interest in entering retail markets outside their home country, especially through subsidiaries. See Judith A. Walter, *Foreign Acquisitions of U.S. Banks: Motives and Timing Factors*, OCC Staff Paper, 1980; and Michael Lafferty, "Gains at the Retail End," *Financial Times*, May 27, 1980, p. XXII.

[15] Lists of foreign banking organizations with grandfathered multistate banking operations were presented in M. A. Schapiro & Co., "Confinement of Domestic Banking in the United States," *Bank Stock Quarterly*, October 1978, pp. 6 and 9. See also Appendix A. Domestic multistate operations were grandfathered with the passage of the Bank Holding Company Act of 1956.

[16] The ability of foreign banks to offer full banking services in multiple locations across the country is seen as an advantage in serving large corporate clients. Also, some bankers have argued that foreign banks' multistate facilities give them an advantage of operations in multiple time zones (see Neil J. Pinsky, "Implications of the International Banking Act of 1978 for Competition in Banking," *Issues in Bank Regulation*, Autumn 1979, p. 18).

[17] The IBA-mandated liberalization of Edge Act Corporation regulations increases interstate options of both domestic and foreign banks.

[18] Serge Bellanger, "The Operational Implications of the International Banking Act of 1978—or—The New Rules." Remarks to the International Banking Conference of the American Bankers' Association held in New York, January 28, 1980, p. 3.

[19] See the Federal Reserve Board's final ruling on Regulation K, 12 CFR Part 211. "International Banking Operations; Interstate Banking Restrictions for Foreign Banks," *Federal Register*, Vol. 45, no. 198, October 9, 1980, pp. 67056-67059.

[20] If a bank were to change its home state it would be required to roll back the activities of any nongrandfathered facilities in its prior home state to include only those activities permissible for Edge Act Corporations. See John E. Shockey and William B. Glidden, *Foreign-Controlled U.S. Banks: The Legal and Regulatory Environment*, OCC Staff Paper, 1980, p. 8 and accompanying notes; and Stanley F. Farrar, Allen L. Raiken and Leo Clarke, "Choice of Home

State Under the International Banking Act of 1978," *University of Illinois Law Forum*, Vol. 1980, No. 1, pp. 91-110.

[21] Key and Brundy, *op. cit.*, p. 793.

[22] Foreign banks' options for future acquisitions in the U.S. are extensive, even without the possibility of changing home state designations. Based on their existing U.S. operations, and taking account of the Douglas Amendment limitation on holding company bank subsidiaries to a single state, for the purpose of prospective acquisitions, 45 of the top 50 non-U.S. banks could declare New York as their home state, 18 could designate Illinois and 23 California. Those numbers involve substantial double counting due to the facts that many of the banks now have an apparent choice of home state (reflecting grandfathered multistate facilities) and others, with no U.S. operations, are unrestricted. (See data in Appendix A.)

[23] U.S. Congress, Senate Committee on Banking, Housing and Urban Affairs, *International Banking Act of 1978*, Report no. 95-1073 to accompany H.R. 10899, 95th Cong., 2nd sess., 1978, p. 11. Proposed revisions of Edge Act corporation regulations would move U.S. banks a step closer to parity.

[24] See Lord O'Brien, "United States Sets Boundaries for International Banks," *The Banker*, December 1978, p. 16. Lord O'Brien observes that limited branches would enable most foreign banks to undertake, outside their home states, most business that they would ordinarily seek, and that the funding limitation is "not by any means an intolerable restriction."

[25] M. A. Schapiro & Co., *op cit.*, p. 8.

[26] U.S. Comptroller of the Currency John G. Heimann, affirming that view, stated that "[T]he clearly desirable couse of action . . . is to begin freeing up geographic constraints . . ." on U.S. banks. (Heimann, *op. cit.*, p. 9.)

[27] U.S. Congress, House, Rep. Benjamin Rosenthal speaking on H.R. 5937, *Foreign Bank Takeovers Study Act*, November 27, 1979, *Congressional Record*, p. H11218.

[28] Senator John Heinz III, "Foreign Takeovers of U.S. Banking—A Real Danger?," *The Journal of the Institute for Socioeconomic Studies*, vol. 3 (Autumn 1979), p. 6.

[29] See Henry S. Terrell, "Activities Permitted to Commercial Banks in Selected Foreign Countries," Study Paper No. 4, Foreign Operations Task Force, Board of Governors of the Federal Reserve System, n.d.; Dimitri Vittas, ed., *Banking Systems Abroad* (London: Inter-Bank Research Organisation, 1978); Inter-Bank Research Organisation, *The Regulation of Banks in the Member States of the EEC* (London: Inter-Bank Research Organisation, 1978); and *Who Owns What in World Banking, 1979-80* (London: The Banker Research Unit, 1980).

[30] As described below, Congress amended the Bank Holding Company Act in 1966, 1970, and 1978 in order to accommodate foreign banks' overseas nonbanking interests. See discussion in statement by Henry C. Wallich, Member, Board of Governors of the Federal Reserve System in hearings before a Subcommittee of the House Committee on Government Operations on *Foreign Acquisitions of U.S. Banks and the Non-Banking Activities of Foreign Bank Holding Companies*, 96th Cong., 2nd sess. at 373-410 (1980); and Shockey and Glidden, *op. cit.*

[31] See Federal Reserve Board's reporting requirements for foreign banks in *Federal Register*, Vol. 46, no. 29, February 12, 1981, pp. 12110-12142 for F.R. Y-7, F.R. 2068, and F.R. Y-8(f); proposed redefinition of foreign bank holding companies for regulatory purposes in "Nonbanking Activities of Foreign Bank Holding Companies and Foreign Banks," *Federal Register*, Vol. 45, May 7, 1980, pp. 30082-86; and discussion in Wallich, *op. cit.*, and *Foreign Acquisitions of United States Banks*, A Study by the Staff of the Federal Reserve Board, June 30, 1980.

[32] Under section 4(c)(13) of the BHCA and sections 25 and 25(a) of the Federal Reserve Act, the Federal Reserve Board is authorized to allow banks and bank holding companies to invest in any foreign company which does no business in the U.S., if the Board deems that investment to be in the public interest. See discussion in Edwards and Zwick, *op. cit.*, p. 70. The Board, as a matter of policy, however, has not permitted U.S. banking organizations to acquire, controlling interests in foreign nonfinancial businesses (Wallich, *op. cit.*).

[33] The 1970 BHCA Amendments gave the Federal Reserve Board authority to extend by regulation the scope of permissible nonbanking activities but maintained a requirement that

such activities be closely related to banking. Federal or state laws circumscribe activities, of banks or their direct subsidiaries, that are not considered incidental to banking.

[34] The exemptions are provided for in sections 2(h) and 4(c)(9) of the BHCA; see Wallich, *op. cit.* for a discussion of these exemptions and the Federal Reserve Board's regulatory actions under section 4(c)(9). Amendments in 1970 extended coverage of the BHCA to one-bank holding companies for the first time, including some foreign banking organizations. That change necessitated certain exemptions from the general nonbanking prohibitions for foreign bank holding companies, in part in order to accommodate foreign bank interests in the U.S. and to avoid possible retaliation against U.S. banks' overseas interests by foreign governments (see Cynthia Crawford Lichtenstein, "Foreign Participation in United States Banking: Regulatory Myths and Realities," *Boston College Industrial and Commercial Law Review*, vol. XV, no. 5 (May 1974), pp. 924-6 and 935 and citations therein).

[35] The Federal Reserve Board's first action under regulatory amendments implementing section 4(c)(9) of the BHCA involved applications by three Japanese banks to acquire *de novo* banks. The Board's approach was discussed in a press release dated December 2, 1971; see also the Board's orders, and Governor Brimmer's dissent, published in the *Federal Reserve Bulletin*, January 1972, pp. 49-53.

[36] See, for example, Federal Reserve Board Order approving the application of Banco di Roma, S.P.A., (*Federal Reserve Bulletin*, October 1972, pp. 940-1).

[37] See, for example, Federal Reserve Board Order approving the application of Lloyds Bank Limited (*Federal Reserve Bulletin*, February 1974, pp. 139-142).

[38] See Key and Brundy, *op. cit.*, p. 793.

[39] For a discussion of foreign banks' U.S. securities affiliates, see Edwards and Zwick, *op. cit.*, pp. 62-3; Francis A. Lees, *Foreign Banking and Investment in the United States: Issues and Alternatives* (New York: John Wiley and Sons, 1976), pp. 80-90, 114, 118-120; and James C. Baker and Jacobus T. Severiens, "Assessing U.S. Controls Over Foreign Investment Firms," *Burroughs Clearing House*, May 1978.

[40] Nonbanking activities undertaken by September 17, 1978, the date the IBA was enacted, may be retained until December 31, 1985. After December 31, 1985, those nonbanking activities undertaken by July 26, 1978, may be continued unless the Board of Governors determines that termination of permission for those activities "is necessary to prevent undue concentration of resources, decreased or unfair competition, conflicts of interest, or unsound banking practices" (IBA, Section 8c).

[41] See, generally, testimony on H.R. 7325, *International Banking Act of 1977*, during Hearings before a subcommittee of the House Committee on Banking, Finance and Urban Affairs, 95th Cong., 1st sess. July 12, 13 and 19, 1977.

[42] See Vittas, *op. cit.*; Fred H. Klopstock, "A New Stage in the Evolution of International Banking," *International Review of the History of Banking*, No. 6-1973, p. 19; and Francis A. Lees, *op. cit.*, pp. 80-84.

[43] See Edwards and Zwick, *op. cit.*, p. 62; and Baker and Severiens, *op. cit.*, pp. 47, 49.

[44] See testimony of Hon. Stephen S. Gardner, Vice Chairman, Board of Governors of the Federal Reserve System, during Hearings before a subcommittee of the House Committee on Banking, Finance and Urban Affairs on H.R. 7325, *International Banking Act of 1977*, 95th Cong., 1st sess., July 12, 1977, p. 159.

[45] See statement of John F. Lee, Executive Vice President, New York Clearing House Association, during Hearings before a subcommittee of the House Committee on Banking, Finance and Urban Affairs on H.R. 7325, *International Banking Act of 1977*, July 13, 1977, p. 295.

[46] In his comments on HR 13876, IBA of 1976, to Rep. Henry Reuss, Chairman, House Committee on Banking, Currency and Housing, Senator Frank Moss of Utah warned that the elimination of foreign-owned securities affiliates from regional stock exchanges would make these markets less competitive relative to the New York Stock Exchange in terms of retail trading activity, market making and the quality of the various markets. He pointed out that in 1975 Congress had adopted a policy of opening up membership in U.S. securities exchanges to foreign firms and noted that although the number of foreign members on the various regional ex-

changes is small, "they are significant . . . eliminating even a few of them could be expected to reduce order flow significantly and to decrease competition drastically." (Letters from Moss to Reuss, July 16, 1976, Hearing on H.R. 7325, *International Banking Act of 1977, op. cit.*, pp. 418-423.) See also the testimony of James E. Dowd, President of the Boston Stock Exchange, Inc.; and Hart Perry, President of SoGen-Swiss International Corp. during the Hearings, pp. 388-444.

[47] See discussion and references cited in footnote 34.

[48] Wallich, *op. cit.*

[49] The following paragraphs are largely taken from testimony by John G. Heimann, U.S. Comptroller of the Currency, in hearings before the Subcommittee of the House Committee on Government Operations on *Foreign Acquisitions of U.S. Banks and the Non-Banking Activities of Foreign Bank Holding Companies*, 96th Cong., 2nd sess. at 273-362 (1980).

[50] See discussion of Japanese cases in Federal Reserve Board orders cited in footnote 35.

[51] See Judith A. Walter, *Supervisory Performance of Foreign-Controlled U.S. Banking Organizations*, OCC Staff Paper, 1980.

[52] Anecdotal evidence supporting this point, with respect to competition within the U.S. market, is discussed in the last section of this paper.

[53] See Ellen S. Goldberg, *Comparative Cost Analysis of Foreign-Owned U.S. Banks*, OCC Staff Paper, 1980.

[54] See Blair B. Hodgkins and Ellen S. Goldberg, *Effect of Foreign Acquisition on the Balance Sheet Structure and Earnings Performance of American Banks*, OCC Staff Paper, 1980. The foreign-owned sample used in this analysis excludes weak or failed banks acquired by foreigners, in order to avoid distortions of the results. See also James V. Houpt, "The Effect of Foreign Acquisitions on the Performance of U.S. Banks," Federal Reserve Board Staff Study, summarized in *Federal Reserve Bulletin*, July 1980.

[55] Statement of John J. Duffy, Executive Vice President, Security Pacific National Bank, in Hearings before the Senate Banking Housing, and Urban Affairs Committee on *Edge Corporation Branching; . . .*, p. 262.

[56] Lynn Adkins, "Foreign Banking's U.S. Invasion," *Dun's Review*, February 1978, p. 78.

[57] Noel Delaney, Foreign Banks in the United States," Memorandum, L. F. Rothschild, Unterberg, Towbin (January 1, 1979), pp. 10-11. Delaney reported that "Although this point appears theoretically consistent, . . ." he had "found no evidence to support it" (p. 11). (No other source of empirical evidence was discovered in the research for this paper.)

[58] For a review of capital requirements in 42 countries, see Brock Short, "Capital Requirements for Commercial Banks," *IMF Staff Papers*, September 1978, pp. 559-62. See also Inter-Bank Research Organisation, *The Regulation of Banks in the Member States of the EEC, op. cit.* For a careful discussion of conceptual and measurement problems in international comparisons, see Pierre Jaans, Comissioner of Banks in Luxembourg, "Measuring Capital and Liquidity Adequacy for International Banking Business," Record of Proceedings, International Conference of Banking Supervisors, London, July 5-6, 1979, pp. 24-30.

[59] With regard to government support of U.S. banks, an important factor is the virtually comprehensive federal deposit insurance system, which protects the majority of depositors, and, more generally, U.S. regulators' perceived willingness to rescue a failing or failed bank rather than close it, especially if the bank is large. Some bankers have argued that since "deposit insurance provides adequate coverage . . . there is no need for double protection by requiring capital on top of insurance" (Yair E. Orgler and Benjamin Wolkowitz, *Bank Capital* (New York: Van Nostrand Reinhold, 1976), p. 116). Empirical studies have demonstrated a tendency for U.S. bankers to substitute deposit insurance for equity capital (See John Mingo, "Regulatory Influence on Bank Capital Investment," *Journal of Finance*, September 1975, pp. 1111-1121).

[60] In some cases, ratios may also be defined in relation to deposits. A study of 14 industrialized countries for the Committee on Banking Regulations and Supervisory Practices, sponsored by the Bank for International Settlements, indicates that some countries compare capital to total assets, others compare capital to risk assets. The U.S., U.K., Canada and Ireland use both ratios. (Study entitled "Consolidation of banks' balance sheets: aggregation of risk-bearing as-

sets as a method of supervising bank solvency," 1978).

[61] For a discussion of inner reserves and other accounting and disclosure matters, see Testimony of John G. Heimann, *op. cit.*, Appendix A, and Barry Rile, "Financial Information–Reluctance to Reveal All," *Financial Times*, May 28, 1980, p. xxxix.

[62] See note to Table 1 for a description of the data. To the maximum extent possible, individual institutions' figures were obtained by the source (*The Banker*) on a consolidated basis for the banking organizations in the "Top 300" list. It should be noted, in contrast, that in many countries capital requirements are imposed on individual banks, therefore in some cases not taking into account overseas operations that are conducted through subsidiaries. The U.S. figures in the table are for bank holding companies, consolidated. Ratios for the lead banks are somewhat higher due to double leveraging (See Gregory Boczar and Samuel H. Talley, "Bank Holding Company Double Leveraging," Presented at the Eastern Finance Association Meetings, Washington, D.C., November 1978; and Fred W. DeBussey, "Double Leveraging in Bank Holding Companies," *Bankers Magazine*, March/April 1978, pp. 86-90).

[63] Ian Peacock, "The Squeeze on Capital Ratios," *The Banker*, June 1975, p. 667. Peacock notes that ". . . during 1974, when banks were seen to be under pressure to improve their operating ratios, the Italian and large Japanese banks released additional reserves. As balance sheet totals remained relatively stable, operating ratios improved dramatically" (*loc. cit.*)

[64] Swiss bankers are reportedly concerned about "the squeeze being placed on them by Switzerland's high capital requirements . . . [which] are higher than those in other countries." (Peter Montagnon, "Bankers Foresee Accelerating Decline," *Financial Times*, April 29, 1980, p. VI.

[65] Vittas, *op. cit.*, p. 121.

[66] During testimony on the condition of the banking system before the Senate Committee on Banking, Housing, and Urban Affairs on May 21, 1980, John G. Heimann, U.S. Comptroller of the Currency, noted that equity ratios are not uniform among all national banks. As the table below reveals, larger U.S. banks are characterized by *lower* equity capital to asset ratios relative to their smaller bank counterparts. National banks with assets less than $1 billion increased their capital ratios over the 1978-79 period while the larger banks with assets over $1 billion experienced a decline, from a ratio of 4.70 percent at year-end 1978 to 4.63 percent at the end of 1979.

Equity Capital of National Banks by Size
(Dollar Amounts in Millions)

	Total Equity		Equity as % of Assets	
Asset Size Class	1978	1979	1978	1979
Less than $100 million	$ 9,371	$ 9,703	7.83	8.07
$100 million to $1 billion	11,479	12,279	6.76	6.89
More than $1 billion	28,349	32,315	4.70	4.63
Ten largest	14,966	16,669	4.13	4.02

[67] Peacock cites the U.K. clearing banks as obvious cases where banks benefit from "the comfort of the effective backing of the central bank" (*op. cit.*, p. 669). He points out that the value of anticipated home government support clearly depends on the credit of the government itself and notes that "Even the largest banks in some developing countries have to maintain comparatively high capital ratios."

[68] See David A. Alhadeff, *Competition and Controls in Banking: A Study of the Regulation of Bank Competition in Italy, France and England* (Berkeley: Univ. of California Press, 1968), p. 102. Vittas, *op. cit.*, makes similar statements regarding the state-owned banks in France (pp. 96, 100 and 123) and Italy (pp. 140, 160).

[69] Quoted in Paul Lewis, "France to Sell Part of Public Holdings," *New York Times*, March 31, 1980, p. D5. Mr. Monory argued "that giving private investors a bigger stake . . . encourages efficiency and makes them better able to conduct business in countries with strong free-market economies . . . ."

[70] For full detail of the analysis, see Goldberg, *op. cit*. The sample used in the analysis includes U.S. banks owned by foreign banks for which data are available for at least three years. The period of analysis is 1976 through 6/30/79. None of the banks is government owned.

[71] U.S. subsidiaries of foreign banks may also gain relative to domestic peers if the parent bank is satisfied with a relatively modest dividend payout. Available evidence indicates some tendency for foreign acquirers to reduce or eliminate dividends, which has the effect of strengthening the bank's capital position. (See Judith A. Walter, *Supervisory Performance of Foreign-Controlled U.S. Banking Organizations*, OCC Staff Paper, 1980.)

[72] For the text of the Federal Reserve Board's reserve requirement regulations for U.S. branches and agencies of foreign banks see *Federal Register*, Vol. 45, No. 59, March 25, 1980, pp. 19216-21.

[73] State-chartered branches are not required to have FDIC insurance in states that do not require coverage for state banks that accept deposits from the general public. Otherwise, a branch may be exempted if the FDIC determines on the basis of size and nature of its deposits that a branch is not engaged in retail business, if its deposits are limited to certain exempt categories and other deposits less than $100,000 do not amount to more than 4 percent of the branch's total deposits. The FDIC's final rule was published on June 28, 1979. See 12 CFR, 346 Foreign Banks.

[74] Pinsky, *op. cit*., p. 3.

[75] See Institute of Foreign Bankers, position paper filed with the Federal Reserve Board re Proposed Regulations Implementing Section 7 of the International Banking Act of 1978 (Docket No. R-0238), November 23, 1979.

[76] Peter Conoboy and Dimitri Vittas, "The Regulatory Framework—Supervisors in Close Consultation," *Financial Times*, May 27, 1980, p. XXXVIII.

[77] See David Marsh, "Controls—Consensus in Favour of Cautious Line," *Financial Times*, February 20, 1980, p. viii, and Hugo Colje, "Bank Supervision on a Consolidated Basis," *The Banker*, June 1980, pp. 29-34.

[78] It would appear likely that Swiss and British multinational banks would then clearly have higher ratios than the largest U.S. multinational, even without allowing for hidden reserves, as discussed earlier.

[79] See Paul Lewis, *op. cit*., p. D1 and Terry Dodsworth, "French State Sector—A Foothold for the Private Shareholder," *Financial Times*, February 12, 1980, p. 19. Reportedly, the denationalization move was motivated in past by the need to increase capital in the face of the French government's reluctance to appropriate additional funds for the state-owned banks. For further discussion, see Vivian Lewis, "France's Nationalized Banks—A Whiff of Re-privatisation," *The Banker*, July 1980, pp. 43-48.

[80] See Chris Welles, "Bankers, Bankers Everywhere—But How Much Business Are They Getting?" *Institutional Investor*, September 1977, pp. 131, 135.

[81] See Harry Taylor, Vice Chairman, Manufacturers Hanover Trust, "The U.S. is No Pot of Gold for Foreign Banks," *Institutional Investor*, October 1979, p. 13. Taylor notes that U.S. banks used to enjoy similar advantages overseas. For some observations on how foreign banks might be expected to adjust their operations to the post-IBA regulatory requirements see Bellanger, "The Operational Implications . . .," pp. 3-4.

[82] Heimann, "Impact of the International Banking Act," p. 7.

[83] See Frank Vogl, "Global Competition in Banking Gives Treasurers Wider Choices," *Financier*, July 1979, p. 15.

[84] See, for example, Larry Gurwin, "Marketing: The Courtship of U.S. Companies," *Institutional Investor*, September 1978, p. 142.

[85] See Bror V. Ingvarson, President, Nordic American Banking Corporation, "Foreign Competition With The Small-Medium U.S. Bank," *American Banker*, March 23, 1979, p. 16.

[86] Adkins, *op. cit.*, p. 78.

[87] Bellanger, "The Operational Implications . . . ," p. 4.

[88] "It has been noted that the better established foreign banking offices in New York pay lower rates than do the more recent entrants" (Pinsky, *op. cit.*, p. 23). In an attempt to help the saleability of their commercial paper issues in the U.S. market, certain foreign banking organizations have recently applied for, and received, evaluations of their debt instruments from various rating services. Since late 1978, Standard and Poors has reviewed and rated the commercial paper offerings of 12 foreign banks. During the same period fewer than half that number of U.S. banks sought their rating. It is likely that foreign banks believe such independent appraisals from respected domestic services will help lower the premiums they must pay on borrowed funds by increasing public confidence and by generating greater name recognition throughout the market.

[89] William T. Mundt, Assistant Vice President of Swiss Bank Corporation, quoted in *Washington Financial Reports*, No. 26, August 2, 1979, p. A-39.

[90] Welles, *op. cit.*, p. 122.

[91] German bankers argued vigorously that they suffer regulatory disadvantages compared to U.S. banks overseas, *e.g.* in their London operations, due to home country requirements (New York interview, November 1979).

[92] See, generally, U.S. Department of the Treasury, *Report to Congress on Foreign Government Treatment of U.S. Commercial Banking Organizations*, 1979. As a case in point, it is noted that U.S. banks are eager to establish branch operations in Mexico (p. 19), notwithstanding the differential restrictions imposed on foreign banks there (Ch. 21).

Appendix A
50 Largest Foreign Banks' U.S. Banking Operations

World Rank	Bank Name	Country	Deposits US $ Billions 12/31/79	Presence in U.S. NY	CA	IL	Other States
2	Banque Nationale de Paris	France	86	B	S		
3	Credit Agricole Mutuel	France	86			B*	
4	Deutsche Bank	Germany	85	B*, A		B	
5	Credit Lyonnais	France	81	B			
6	Societe Generale	France	77	B*, A			
8	Dresdner Bank	Germany	66	B		B	
9	National Westminster Bk, Ltd.	U.K.	59	B, S*		B	
10	Barclays Bank, Ltd.	U.K.	59	B, S	S	B	Pennsylvania B, Mass. B
11	Westdeutsche Landesbank Girozentrale	Germany	57	B			
12	Commerzbank	Germany	55	B		B	
13	Dai-Ichi Kangyo Bank, Ltd.	Japan	52	B		S	
15	Norinchukin Bk.	Japan	48				
16	Fuji Bank, Ltd.	Japan	48	S			
17	Sumitomo Bank, Ltd.	Japan	47	B	S	B	Washington B
18	Bayerische Landesbank Girozentrale	Germany	46	B			
19	Bayerische Vereinsbank	Germany	45				
20	Mitsubishi Bank, Ltd.	Japan	45	B	S	B	
21	Sanwa Bank, Ltd.	Japan	44	B	S	B	
22	Rabobank Nederland	Netherlands	44				
23	Industrial Bank of Japan, Ltd.	Japan	42	S			
24	Bayerische Hypotheken- und Wechsel-Bank	Germany	41	B			
25	Algemene Bank Nederland	Netherlands	40	B		B, S*	Pennsylvania B*
26	Midland Bank, Ltd.	U.K.	40	A			
27	Banca Nazionale del Lavoro	Italy	40	B			

Appendix A (continued)

World Rank	Bank Name	Country	Deposits US $ Billions 12/31/79	Presence in U.S.			Other States
				NY	CA	IL	
28	Royal Bank of Canada	Canada	39	S			Oregon B*
29	Amsterdam-Rotterdam Bank	Netherlands	39	A			
30	Swiss Bank Corp.	Switzerland	38	B		B	
32	Union Bank of Switzerland	Switzerland	37	B		B	
33	Lloyds Bank, Ltd.	U.K.	36	B	S	B	Pennsylvania B
34	Canadian Imperial Bank of Commerce	Canada	35	S	S		Oregon B / Washington B
35	Long-Term Credit Bank of Japan, Ltd.	Japan	35	B			
36	Banca Commerciale Italiana	Italy	34	B		B	
37	Bank of Tokyo, Ltd.	Japan	33	S	S		Oregon B / Washington B
38	Tokai Bank, Ltd.	Japan	32	B			
39	Credit Suisse	Switzerland	30	B	S		
41	Societe Generale de Banque	Belgium	30	A			
42	Mitsui Bank, Ltd.	Japan	30	B	S		Washington B
43	Taiyo Kobe Bank, Ltd.	Japan	30	B			Washington B
45	Mitsubishi Trust & Banking Corp.	Japan	30	B	S	B	

478

								State	
47	28	Bank of Montreal	Canada		S			Washington	B
48	28	Sumitomo Trust & Banking Co., Ltd.	Japan	B	S	B			
49	27	Daiwa Bank, Ltd.	Japan	S	S			Mass.	B
50	27	Bank of Nova Scotia	Canada	S				Oregon	B*
								Washington	B
51	26	Mitsui Trust & Banking Co., Ltd.	Japan	B		S		Washington	B
52	26	Bank fuer Gemeinwirtschaft	Germany	B					
53	26	Credito Italiano	Italy	B					
54	25	Standard Chartered Bank, Ltd.	U.K.	B		S	B	Washington	B
55	24	Hessische Landesbank-Girozentrale	Germany						
56	24	Banco de Roma	Italy	B			B, S		
58	24	Monte dei Paschi di Siena	Italy						

Sources: *American Banker,* "500 Largest Banks in the World," July 25, 1980. Commercial banks are ranked annually by deposits. "Structure Data" from the Federal Reserve 886 Foreign Financial File as of December 1979.

Symbols:

B—a U.S. branch banking operation of the foreign parent bank which will apparently be grandfathered under the provisions of the International Banking Act of 1978.

S—a U.S. subsidiary banking operation of the foreign parent bank which will apparently be grandfathered under the provisions of the International Banking Act of 1978.

A—foreign parent bank participation in the European American Bank which purchased Franklin National Bank in 1974.

*—banking operation of the foreign parent bank in the U.S. which had not been established as of the IBA grandfathering date (7-27-78). Final determinations as per grandfather status have not been made as of this writing.

Appendix B

Foreign Banks with U.S. Securities Affiliates in the United States (12-31-79)[a]

Foreign Bank[b]	Domicile of Foreign Bank	U.S. Securities Affiliates	Total Capitalization of Securities Affiliate[c]	
			12-31-79 ($000)	Rank Among the Top 250
Algemene Bank Nederland NV	Netherlands	ABD Securities Corp.	6,744.8	98
Amsterdam-Rotterdam Bank	Netherlands	SoGen-Swiss International Corp.	n.a.	n.a.
Banco Ambrosiano	Italy	Ultrafin International Corp.	5,206.0	117
Banco de Credito Argentino	Argentina	Argentine Banking Corp.	n.a.	n.a.
Banco de Galicia Y Buenos Aires	Argentina	Argentine Banking Corp.	n.a.	n.a.
Banco di Roma	Italy	Europartners Securities Corp.	8,337.0	85
Banco Espanol del Rio de la Plata, Ltd.	Argentina	Argentine Banking Corp.	n.a.	n.a.
Banco Ganadero Argentino S.A.	Argentina	Argentine Banking Corp.	n.a.	n.a.
Bank Hapoalim B.M.	Israel	Ampal Investment Co.	n.a.	n.a.
Bank Julius Baer & Co., Ltd.	Switzerland	Baer Securities Corp.	873.1	235
Bank Leu, Ltd.	Switzerland	Europartners Securities Corp.	8,337.0	85
Bank Leumi le Israel B.M.	Israel	Leumi Securities Corp.	n.a.	n.a.
Bank of Tokyo, Ltd.	Japan	Nomura Securities International, Inc.	15,485.7	50
Banque Bruxelles Lambert	Belgium	ABD Securities Corp.	6,744.8	98
Banque de L'Indochine et de Suez	France	Suez American Corp.	n.a.	n.a.
Banque Nationale de Paris	France	French American Capital Corp.	n.a.	n.a.
Banque Rothschild	France	New Count Securities Corp.	9,206.2	80
Bayerische Hypotheken und Wechsel-Bank	W. Germany	ABD Securities Corp.	6,744.8	98
Berlinger Handels-und Frankfurter Bank	W. Germany	BHF Securities Corp	n.a.	n.a.
Bremar Holdings, Ltd.	United Kingdom	Bremar Holdings Corp.	n.a.	n.a.
Charterhouse Group, Ltd.	United Kingdom	Charterhouse Group International, Inc.	n.a.	n.a.
Commerzbank AG.	W. Germany	Europartners Securities Corp.	8,337.0	85

Bank	Country	U.S. Affiliate		
Compagnie de Financiere de Paris et des Pays-Bas	France	A. G. Becker & Co., Inc.		
		Becker Securities Corp.		
		Warburg Paribas Becker, Inc.		
		The Becker Warburg Paribas Group, Inc. and Subsidiaries	80,747.0	16
Credit Lyonnais	France	Europartners Securities Corp.	8,337.0	85
Credit Suisse	Switzerland	SoGen-Swiss International Corp.	n.a.	n.a.
		Swiss American Securities, Inc.	10,869.3	70
Dai-Ichi Kangyo Bank, Ltd.	Japan	Yamaichi International (America) Inc.	7,500.0	95
Daiwa Bank, Ltd.	Japan	New Japan Securities International, Inc.	1,818.0	187
		Nomura Securities International, Inc.	15,485.7	50
Deutsche Bank, A.G.	W. Germany	Atlantic Capital Corp.	10,136.0	76
Dresdner Bank	W. Germany	ABD Securities Corp.	6,744.8	98
Robert Fleming & Co., Ltd.	United Kingdom	Robert Fleming, Inc.	3,319.5	152
Fuji Bank, Ltd.	Japan	Nikko Securities International, Inc.	6,208.0	106
		Yamaichi International (America) Inc.	7,500.0	95
Hill Samuel & Co., Ltd.	United Kingdom	Hill Samuel Securities Corp.	n.a.	n.a.
Industrial Bank of Japan, Ltd.	Japan	Daiwa Securities (America), Inc.	11,365.8	68
		New Japan Securities International, Inc.	1,818.0	187
		Nikko Securities International, Inc.	6,208.0	106
		Yamaichi International (America) Inc.	7,500.0	95
Kleinwort Benson Ltd.	United Kingdom	Kleinwort Benson, Inc.	1,636.0	200
Long-Term Credit Bank of Japan	Japan	Daiwa Securities (America), Inc.	11,365.8	68
Mitsubishi Bank, Ltd.	Japan	Nikko Securities International	6,208.0	106
		Yamaichi International (America) Inc.	7,500.0	95
Mitsui Bank, Ltd.	Japan	Nomura Securities International, Inc.	15,485.7	50

Appendix B (continued)

Foreign Bank[b]	Domicile of Foreign Bank	U.S. Securities Affiliates	Total Capitalization of Securities Affiliate[c]	
			12-31-79 ($000)	Rank Among the Top 250
Nordic Bank, Ltd.[d]	United Kingdom	Europartners Securities Corp.	8,337.0	85
Pierson, Heldring & Pierson	Netherlands	New Court Securities Corp.	9,206.2	80
N. M. Rothschild & Sons	United Kingdom	New Court Securities Corp.	9,206.2	80
Sanwa Bank, Ltd.	Japan	New Japan Securities International, Inc.	1,818.0	187
Schroders, Ltd.	United Kingdom	Nomura Securities International, Inc.	15,485.7	50
		Schroder Naess & Thomas Division	n.a.	n.a.
Skandinaviska Enskilda Banken	Sweden	Scandinavian Securities Corp.	n.a.	n.a.
Societe Generale	France	SoGen-Swiss International Corp.	n.a.	n.a.
Societe Generale Alsacienne de Banque	France	SoGen-Swiss International Corp.	n.a.	n.a.
Societe Generale de Banque	Belgium	SoGen-Swiss International Corp.	n.a.	n.a.
Sumitomo Trust & Banking Co., Ltd.	Japan	Daiwa Securities (America), Inc.	11,365.8	68
		New Japan Securities International, Inc.	1,818.0	187
Swiss Bank Corp.	Switzerland	Basle Securities Corp.	n.a.	n.a.
Swiss Credit Bank	Switzerland	First Boston, Inc.	122,254.3	10
Tokai Bank, Ltd.	Japan	Nikko Securities International, Inc.	6,208.0	106
Union Bank of Switzerland	Switzerland	UBS Securities, Inc.	n.a.	n.a.
S.G. Warburg & Co., Ltd.	United Kingdom	A. G. Becker & Co., Inc.		
		Becker Securities Corp.		
		Warburg Paribas Becker, Inc.		
		The Becker Warburg Paribas Group, Inc. and Subsidiaries	80,747.0	16
Yasuda Trust & Banking Co., Ltd.	Japan	Daiwa Securities (America), Inc.	11,365.8	68

Notes: U.S. securities affiliates of foreign banks comprise a very small segment of the American securities market. Of the 32 foreign bank securities firms listed above, only 16 companies rank among the top 250 securities firms in terms of total capital. The combined assets of these 16 foreign-owned securities companies represent only about half that of the largest domestically-owned securities firm, Merrill Lynch.

[a] Sources: *American Banker* (3-14-80); *Institutional Investor* (9-70); and *CDE Stock Ownership Directory* (1980).

[b] Includes foreign commercial banks, merchant banks, and investment banks.

[c] Source: *1980 Investment Banker Broker Directory.*

[d] Nordic Bank Ltd. is jointly owned by: Den Norske Creditbank (Norway); Kansallis-Osake Pankki (Finland); Svenska Handelsbanken (Sweden).

SELECTED BIBLIOGRAPHY

Compiled By
DIANE PAGE

FOREIGN BANKING IN THE U.S. AND RELATED TOPICS OF INTERNATIONAL BANKING

This listing includes current sources on the topic of foreign banking activities in the United States and related aspects of the larger topic of international banking. The bibliography contains, but is not limited to, all major works consulted in the development of the text.

Adkins, Lynn. "Foreign Banking's U.S. Invasion." *Dun's Review*, February 1978, pp. 76-78.

Alhadeff, David A. *Competition and Controls in Banking: A Study of the Regulation of Bank Competition in Italy, France, and England*. Berkeley: University of California Press, 1968.

Aliber, Robert Z. "International Banking Growth and Regulation." *Columbia Journal of World Business*, Winter 1975, pp. 9-15.

American Bar Association. *A Guide to Foreign Investment Under United States Law*. Committee to Study Foreign Investment in the United States of the Section of Corporate Banking and Business Law of the American Bar Association. Allan R. Roth, project coordinator. New York: Law & Business, Inc., 1979.

Anderson, Gerald H. "Current Developments in the Regulation of International Banking." Federal Reserve Bank of Cleveland *Economic Review*, January 1980, pp. 1-15.

Association of Bank Holding Companies. "Classification of State Laws Affecting the Corporate Acquisition of Bank Stock." *Bank Holding Company Facts*, Spring 1979, pp. 30-31.

Austin, Douglas V. "Banking Structure Equality Sacrificed in the Name of Antitrust." *American Banker*, September 21, 1979.

Baker, Donald I. "Competition's Role in the Regulation of Banking." *The Bankers Magazine*, (Boston) Summer 1971, pp. 75-82.

Baker, James C. *International Bank Regulation*. New York: Praeger, 1978.

———. "Nationwide Branch Banking: The Edge Act Corporation and Other Methods." *Issues in Bank Regulation*, Summer 1977, pp. 31-36.

Baker, James C. and Severiens, Jacobus T. "Assessing U.S. Controls Over Foreign Investment Firms." *Burroughs Clearing House*, vol. 62, May 1978, pp. 20, 45-60.

The Bankers' Almanac and Yearbook 1978-79. West Sussex, England: Thomas Skinner Directories, 1979.

Battey, Phil. "Fed Proposes Foreign Interstate Curbs." *American Banker*, October 25, 1979.

Bellanger, Serge, "The New Order of Banking: An 'Across the Border' Concept?" Address before the New York State Banker's Association, Lake Placid, New York, June 18, 1979. Quoted in "International Banking Act to Spur Interstate Branching." *American Banker*, August 9, 1979.

——. "The Operational Implications of the International Banking Act of 1978, or the New Rules." Remarks to the International Banking Conference of the American Bankers Association, New York, January 28, 1980.

Bennett, Robert A. "Competition From Foreign Institutions Felt." *New York Times*, April 10, 1979.

——. "Foreigner's Takeovers Irk Banks." *New York Times*, March 12, 1979.

——. "New York's New Foreign Bankers." *New York Times*, July 8, 1978.

Bergsten, C. Fred. *American Multinationals and American Interest*. Washington, D.C.: Brookings Institute, 1978.

Blandon, Michael. "American Grandfathers." *Financial Times*, November 6, 1978.

Blunden, George. "International Cooperation in Banking Supervision" *Bank of England Quarterly Bulletin*, vol. 17, September 1977, pp. 325-329.

——. "The Supervision of the UK Banking System." *Bank of England Quarterly Bulletin*, vol. 15, June 1975, pp. 188-194.

Brealey, Richard. *Security Prices in a Competitive Market*. Cambridge: MIT Press, 1974.

Brouillette, Geoff. "Foreign Subsidiaries are Fastest Growing Segment of California Banking." *American Banker*, July 30, 1975.

Burke, James. "Bank Holding Company Behavior and Structural Change." *Journal of Bank Research*, vol. 9, Spring 1978, pp. 43-52.

Burr, Rosemary. "The Changing World of Foreign Banks." *The Banker*, April 1978, pp. 45-47.

California. State of California Banking Department. *Report on Foreign Banking Matters of the Superintendent of Banks*. By Donald E. Pearson, April 1974.

Canada. Canadian Finance Minister. *White Paper on the Revision of Canadian Banking Legislation*. August 1976.

Cassidy, Robert F. "The International Banking Act's Cost Impact on Foreign Banks." *American Banker*, March 23, 1979.

Cates, David C. "Foreign Banks are Cracking the Facade of U.S. Banking." *Fortune*, August 28, 1978, pp. 95-99.

Christelow, Dorothy B. "National Policies Toward Foreign Direct Investment." Federal Reserve Bank of New York *Quarterly Review*, vol. 14, Winter 1979-80, pp. 21-32.

Colje, Hugo. "Bank Supervision on a Consolidated Basis." *The Banker* (London), June 1979, pp. 29-34.

"Competing Onshore. International Banking: A Survey." *The Economist*, March 31, 1979, after p. 46.

Connelly, Julie. "Citicorp's Global Money Grab." *Institutional Investor*, September 1978, pp. 63-64.

Conoboy, Peter and Vittas, Dimitri. "The Regulatory Framework—Supervisors in Close Consultation." *Financial Times*, May 27, 1980.

Cotta, Alain. "Savings Banks Expand Internationally." *The Banker* (London), July 1978, pp. 89-90.

"Cracks In Glass-Steagall?" *Forbes*, September 15, 1975, pp. 58-59.

Dahl, Frederick R. "International Operations of U.S. Banks: Growth and Public Policy Implications." *Law and Contemporary Problems*, vol. 32, Winter 1976, pp. 100-130.

Delaney, Noel. *Report on Foreign Banks in the United States*. New York: L. F. Rothschild, Unterberg, Towbin, January 1979.

Dizard, John. "The Bittersweet Future of Foreign Banks in Canada." *Institutional Investor* (International Edition), February 1980, pp. 61-67.

Dodsworth, Terry. "French State Sector—A Foothold for the Private Shareholder." *Financial Times*, February 12, 1980.

Dreyer, H. Peter. "Dutch Welcome Foreign Banks." *Journal of Commerce*, March 14, 1980.

"Editorial—Thinking the Unthinkable." *American Banker*, April 24, 1980.

Eldred, Thomas P., III. "Foreign Retail Banking Experiences Slow Growth in the U.S." *American Banker*, March 23, 1979.

"Examining the Growth of Foreign Banking." *Burroughs Clearinghouse*, July 1979, pp. 11-ff.

Farrar, Stanley F.; Raiher, Allan L.; and Clarke, Leo. "Choice of Home State Under the International Banking Act of 1978." *University of Illinois Law Forum*, vol. 1980, no. 1, pp. 91-110.

Feinman, Michael J. "National Treatment of Foreign Banks Operating in the United States: The International Banking Act of 1978." *Law and Policy in International Business*, vol. 11, 1979, pp. 1109-1149.

Field, Peter. "Biting into the Big Apple." *Euromoney*, June 1978, pp. 49-57.

Fleming, Stewart. "The Big U.S. Banks Turn to The Neglected Back Yard." *Financial Times*, January 12, 1979.

"The Foreign Bankers Are Coming." *New York Times*, February 22, 1979.

"Foreign Banks Law Delay Criticized." *Financial Times*, June 22, 1978.

"Foreign Investors—America's New Immigrants." *It's Your Business*. Produced by the U.S. Chamber of Commerce. Program no. 11. November 18, 1979.

Fraser, Donald R. "Holding Company Affiliation and Commercial Bank Holding Market Share." *Antitrust Bulletin*, vol. 23, Winter 1978, pp. 825-835.

Fraser, Robert D. *International Banking and Finance*. 4th ed. Washington, D.C.: R & H Publishers, 1978.

Gabrielle, Marco A. "Foreign Bank Entry into U.S. Reflects Today's Realities." *American Banker*, March 23, 1979.

Glassman, Cynthia and Eisenbeis, Robert A. "Bank Holding Companies and Concentration of Banking and Financial Resources." In *The Bank Holding Company Movement to 1978: A Compendium*, pp. 209-261. Robert A. Eisenbeis, study director. Washington, D.C.: Board of Governors of the Federal Reserve System, 1978.

Glidden, William B. and Shockey, John E. "U.S. Branches and Agencies of Foreign Banks: A Comparison of the Federal and State Chartering Options." *The University of Illinois Law Forum*, vol. 1980, no. 1, pp. 65-90.

Goddin, C. Stewart and Weiss, Steven J. *U.S. Banks' Loss of Global Standing*. Office of the Comptroller of the Currency Staff Paper, Washington, D.C., 1980.

Goldberg, Ellen S. *Analysis of Current Operations of Foreign-Owned U.S. Banks*. Office of the Comptroller of the Currency Staff Paper, Washington, D.C., 1980.

——. *Comparative Cost Analysis of Foreign-Owned U.S. Banks*. Office of the Comptroller of the Currency Staff Paper, Washington, D.C., 1980.

Goldberg, Lawrence G. "Bank Holding Company Acquisitions and Their Impact on Market Shares." *Journal of Money, Credit and Banking*, vol. 8, February 1976, pp. 127-130.

Golembe Associates, Inc. "Memorandum Re: Foreign Banking Activities in the United States." *Golembe Reports*, vol. 1979-6.

Greenwald, Carol S. "Let's Put a Hold on Foreign Take-overs of Our Banks." *The Bankers Magazine* (Boston), November-December 1979, pp. 49-54.

Greer, Phillip and Kandel, Myron. "New Study Discounts Threat of Foreign Banks in the U.S." *New York Post*, November 6, 1977.

Gruber, William. "Foreign Banks Are Growing Force in Chicago Market." *Chicago Tribune*, August 22, 1979.

Gurwin, Larry. "Marketing: The Courtship of U.S. Companies." *Institutional Investor*, September 1978, pp. 129-144.

Hablutzel, Philip and Lutz, Carol R. "The Foreign Bank in the United States After the International Banking Act of 1978: The New Dual System." *Banking Law Journal*, vol. 96, February 1979, pp. 133-153.

Hall, William and Lafferty, Michael. "The Reasons for Going In." *Financial Times*, March 19, 1979.

Harrigan, Susan. "Miami Is Prospering Aided By Latin Money, Illegal-Drug Business." *Wall Street Journal*, November 28, 1979.

"Hassling Over Bank Takeovers." *The Journal of Commerce*, July 10, 1979.

Heimann, John G. "Impact of the International Banking Act of 1978 on Foreign Bank Competition in the United States." Address to Consular Law Society of New York, March 26, 1980.

Heinz, H. John, III. "Foreign Takeover of U.S. Banking—A Real Danger?" *Journal of the Institute for Socioeconomic Studies*, vol. IV, Autumn 1979, pp. 1-9.

"Here Come Foreign Banks Again." *Business Week*, June 26, 1978, pp. 78-86.

Hertel, Frederick C. "Effects of the IBA on Foreign and U.S. Banks." *American Banker*, March 23, 1979.

Hodgkins, Blair B. and Goldberg, Ellen S. *Effect of Foreign Acquisition on the Balance Sheet Structure and Earnings Performance of American Banks*. Office of the Comptroller of the Currency Staff Paper. Washington, D.C., 1980.

Horvitz, Paul. "How to Discourage Foreign Takeovers." *American Banker*, August 13, 1979.

Houpt, James V. "The Effect of Foreign Acquisitions on the Performance of U.S. Banks." Board of Governors of the Federal Reserve System Staff Study, summarized in "Foreign Ownership and the Performance of U.S. Banks." *Federal Reserve Bulletin*, July 1980, pp. 543-544.

Hutton, H. R. "The Regulation of Foreign Banks—A European Viewpoint." *Columbia Journal of World Business*, Winter 1975, pp. 109-114.

Ingvarson, Bror V. "Foreign Competition With the Small Medium U.S. Bank," *American Banker*, March 23, 1979.

Institute of Foreign Bankers. Position paper filed with the Federal Reserve Board re Proposed Regulations Implementing Section 7 of the International Banking Act of 1978 (Docket No. R-0238). November 23, 1979.

International Banking Operations in the United States. Corporate Law and Practice, Course Handbook series; 313. Peter Hornbostel, chairman. New York: Practising Law Institute, 1979.

"Invasion Fleet." *Economist*, April 15, 1978, pp. 123-124.

Jaans, Pierre. "Measuring Capital Liquidity Adequacy for International Banking Business." *Record of Proceedings*. International Conference of Banking Supervisors, London, July 5-6, 1979, pp. 24-30.

Jacobs, Donald P. "Foreign Takeovers Spurred By Obsolete Merger Laws." *American Banker*, August 16, 1979.

——. "Proposed Public Policy on the Purchase of American Banks." Unpublished Paper, 1979. Graduate School of Management, Northwestern University, Evanston, Illinois.

Jacobs, Klaas Peter. "The Development of International and Multinational Banking in Europe." *Columbia Journal of World Business*, Winter 1975, pp. 33-39.

Janssen, Richard F. and Herman, Tom. "Outcome of Foreign Bids for U.S. Banks Put in Doubt by New Interest in Congress." *Wall Street Journal*, March 5, 1979.

"Japanese Banks Move for Internationalization." *The Oriental Economist*, November 1976, pp. 6-10.

Kelly, Janet. *Bankers and Borders: The Case of American Banks in Britain*. Cambridge: Ballinger Publishing Co., 1977.

Key, Sydney J. and Brundy, James M. "Implementation of the International Banking Act." *Federal Reserve Bulletin*, October 1979, pp. 785-796.

Klopstock, Fred H. "A New Stage in the Evolution of International Banking." *International Review of the History of Banking*, no. 6, 1973, pp. 14-21.

Kraar, Louis. "Hongkong's Beleaguered Financial Fortress." *Fortune*, May 1976. pp. 86-ff.

Kvasnicka, Joseph G. "International Banking Part II." Federal Reserve Bank of Chicago *Business Conditions*, March 1976, pp. 3-11.

Lafferty, Michael. "Gains at the Retail End." *Financial Times*, May 27, 1980.

Lees, Francis A. *Foreign Banking and Investment in the United States: Issues and Alternatives*. New York: John Wiley and Sons, 1976.

Lehr, Dennis J. and Hammond, Benton R. "Regulating Foreign Acquisition of U.S. Banks: The CBCA and the BHCA." *Banking Law Journal*, vol. 90, February 1980, pp. 136-147.

Lewis, Paul. "France to Sell Part of Public Holdings." *New York Times*, March 31, 1980.

Lewis, Vivian. "France's Nationalized Banks—A Whiff of Re-privatisation." *The Banker* (London), July 1980, pp. 43-48.

Lichtenstein, Cynthia Crawford. "Foreign Participation in United States Banking: Regulatory Myths and Realities." *Boston College Industrial and Commercial Law Review*, vol. 15, May 1974, pp. 924-ff.

"Location, Tax Benefits Helping Miami Become Latin Banking Center." *American Banker*, January 17, 1978.

Longbrake, William A.; Quinn, Melanie R.; and Walter, Judith A. *Foreign Ownership of U.S. Banks: Facts and Patterns*. Office of the Comptroller of the Currency Staff Paper. Washington, D.C., 1980.

McConnel, C. Edward. "The Impact of International Banking Activities on Bank Performance." Address before the American Bankers Association International Banking Conference, "Strategies for the Eighties," New York, January 19, 1979.

"McEnteer Sees Difficulty for Foreign Banks in Pa." *American Banker*, March 28, 1979.

McKeating, Mike. "The Bitter Battle for Marine Bank." *Buffalo News*, September 30, 1979.

Malcolm, Andrew H. "Canadian Banks Heading South." *New York Times*, December 4, 1979.

"Marine Midland Charter Fought." *Evening Star* (Washington, D.C.), October 24, 1979.

"Marine Midland May Go National; Foreign Banks Advised to Avoid Retail Operations." *Washington Financial Reports*, July 2, 1979. Washington, D.C.: The Bureau of National Affairs, 1979.

Marsh, David. "Controls—Concensus in Favour of Cautious Line." *Financial Times*, February 20, 1980.

Mastropasqua, Salvatore. *The Banking Systems in the Countries of the EEC: Institutional and Structural Aspects*. Alphen aan den Rijn, Netherlands: Sijthoff and Noordhoff International Publishers, 1978.

Mattera, Anthony F. "International Activities of U.S. Banks (As of December 31, 1978)." *American Banker*, March 23, 1979.

Mayer, Martin. *The Bankers*. New York: Weybright and Talley, 1974.

Melitz, Jacques. *The French Financial System: Mechanisms and Propositions for Reform*. Paper prepared for the Conference on the Political Economy of

France, American Enterprise Institute for Public Research. Washington, D.C., May 29-31, 1980.

Metz, Robert. "Banks As Lure to Foreign Bids." *New York Times*, April 16, 1979.

Miller, Judith. "Foreign-Bought Banks Found to Aid Consumers." *New York Times*, July 31, 1979.

Miller, Richard B. "Brimmer on Banking—Moving Into the Eighties." *The Bankers' Magazine*, September-October 1979, pp. 26-34.

Mingo, John. "Regulatory Influence on Bank Capital Investment." *Journal of Finance*, September 1975, pp. 1111-1121.

Mixson, Paul. "The Red Herring of Foreign Banks." *United States Banker*, October 1978, pp. 40-42.

Montagnon, Peter. "Bankers Foresee Accelerating Decline," *Financial Times*, April 29, 1980.

Morrison, Ian and Vittas, Dimitri. "The Structure of Banking Systems Abroad." *The Magazine of Bank Administration*, August 1979, pp. 42-46.

Mundheim, Robert H. and Helenick, David W. "American Attitudes Toward Foreign Direct Investment In the United States." Remarks at the Southwestern Legal Foundation Symposium on Securities Regulation, Dallas, Texas, April 20, 1979.

"New Focus on International Services." *Morgan Guaranty Survey*, May 1980, pp. 10-14.

"N.Y. Ruling Against Barclays Resented." *New York Times*, May 19, 1973.

New York. State of New York Banking Department. *Annual Report of the Superintendent of Banks*. George C. Van Tuyl, Jr., Superintendent. Albany, 1913.

New York. State of New York Banking Department. Letter of Recommendation of the Superintendent of Banks to the Banking Board regarding the application of Barclays Bank of New York for permission to merge First Westchester National Bank. Presented by Harry W. Albright. January 8, 1974.

New York. Superintendent of Banks of New York State. *Report on the Proposed Acquisition by the Hongkong and Shanghai Banking Corporation of Marine Midland Banks, Inc.* Muriel Siebert, Superintendent. June 28, 1979.

"The 1978 Global Banking Report." *Institutional Investor*, June 1978, pp. 133-ff.

O'Brien, Lord. "United States Sets the Boundaries for Foreign Banks," *The Banker* (London), December 1978, pp. 15-19.

Orgler, Yair E. and Wolkowitz, Benjamin. *Bank Capital*. New York: Van Nostrand Reinhold, 1976.

Osborn, Neil. "Will Foreign Takeovers of U.S. Banks Be Stopped?" *Institutional Investor*, September 1978, pp. 157-168.

Page, Diane and Soss, Neal M. *Some Evidence on Transnational Banking Structure*. Office of the Comptroller of the Currency Staff Paper, Washington, D.C., 1980.

Payment Systems, Inc. *Foreign Banks: A New Competitive Force in the U.S.* White Paper. Atlanta: Payment Systems, Inc., October 1979.

Peacock, Ian. "The Squeeze on Capital Ratios." *The Banker* (London), June 1975, pp. 667-673.

Phelps, Clyde William. *The Foreign Expansion of American Banks*. New York: Ronald Press, 1927; reprinted ed., New York: Arno Press, 1976.

Pinsky, Neil J. "Implications of the International Banking Act of 1978 for Competition in Banking." *Issues In Bank Regulation*, Autumn 1979, pp. 16-24.

Piper, Thomas. *The Economics of Bank Acquisition by Registered Bank Holding Companies*. Research Report no. 48. Federal Reserve Bank of Boston, 1971.

Porter, Sylvia. "Foreign Bank Takeover Veil Is Lifted." *Evening Star* (Washington, D.C.), August 9, 1979.

"The Regulation of Foreign Banks in U.S." *New York Times*, July 25, 1978.

Reimnitz, Jurgen. "German Banks Follow German Investment." *Euromoney*, June 1978, p. 91.

Revell, Jack. *The British Financial System*. New York: Harper and Row, 1973.

Rhoades, Stephen A. "The Impact of Foothold Acquisitions on Bank Market Structure." *Antitrust Bulletin*, vol. 22, Spring 1977, pp. 119-129.

Rile, Barry. "Financial Information—Reluctance to Reveal All." *Financial Times*, May 28, 1980.

Rosenthal, Benjamin. Representative Rosenthal speaking on the Foreign Bank Takeover Study Act, H.R. 5937, 96th Cong., 1st sess., 1979. *Congressional*

Rothstein, David L. "Deterrents to Retail Involvement for Foreign Branches." *American Banker*, March 23, 1979.

Roussakis, E.N. "The Internationalization of U.S. Commercial Banks." *The Magazine of Bank Administration*. Part 1, October 1979, pp. 24-30. Part 2, November 1979, pp. 8-10.

M. A. Schapiro & Co., Inc. "Confinement of Domestic Banking in the United States: The Coming of Nationwide Banking." *Bank Stock Quarterly*, October 1978. pp. 6-ff.

——. "Unequal Opportunity: Growth of Domestic Banks Constricted." *Bank Stock Quarterly*, May 1978, pp. 1-ff.

Severeins, Jacobus T. "Assessing Foreign Bank Acquisitions." *Burroughs Clearing House*, February 1980, p. 18.

Shay, Jerome W. "Interstate Banking Restrictions of the International Banking and Bank Holding Company Acts." *Banking Law Journal*, vol. 97, June-July, 1980, pp. 524-556.

Shockey, John E. and Glidden, William B. *Foreign-Controlled U.S. Banks: The Legal and Regulatory Environment*. Office of the Comptroller of the Currency Staff Paper. Washington, D.C., 1980.

Short, Brock K. "Capital Requirements for Commercial Banks: A Survey of the Issues." *International Monetary Fund Staff Papers*, vol. 25, September 1978, pp. 528-563.

Shull, Bernard. "The Structural Impact of Multiple Office Banking in New York and Virginia." *Antitrust Bulletin*, vol. 23, Fall 1978, pp. 511-551.

Siebert, Muriel. Speech before the American Banker's Association Correspondent Banking Conference, San Francisco, November 19, 1979.

——. Statement before the Assembly Committee on Finance, Insurance and Commerce of the California Legislature, Sacramento, November 19, 1979.

Sinclair, Helen and Krossel, Martin. "Reciprocity: A Tough Game." *The Canadian Banker and ICB Review*, vol. 85, October 1978, pp. 10-15.

Skigen, Patricia and Fitzsimmons, John D. "The Impact of the International Banking Act of 1978 on Foreign Banks and Their Domestic and Foreign Affiliates." *The Business Lawyer*, vol. 35, November 1979, pp. 55-82.

Smith, William Paul and Weiss, Steven J., *Potential Acquisition Partners for Large U.S. Banks: The Discriminatory Effects of Law and Policy*. Comptroller of the Currency Staff Paper. Washington, D.C., 1980.

Stearns, Craig B. "Designing and Implementing An Acquisition Program: The Role of the Investment Banker." Presented at the Law and Business Seminar sponsored by the Legal Times of Washington and Law and Business, Inc., Washington, D.C., January 4-5, 1980.

Steuber, Ursel. *International Banking: The Foreign Activities of the Banks of the Principal Industrial Countries*. Leyden, Netherlands: A. W. Sijthoff, 1976.

Stove, Vincent W. "Australia Firm on Bank Policy." *Journal of Commerce*, June 5, 1979.

Taylor, Harry. "The U.S. Is No Pot of Gold for Foreign Banks." Speech before the 12th International Banking Meeting, Esteponez, Spain, June 1979. Published in *Institutional Investor* (International Edition), October 1979, p. 13.

Terrell, Henry S. *Activities Permitted to Commercial Banks in Selected Foreign Countries*. Foreign Operations Task Force Study Paper no. 4. Washington, D.C.: Board of Governors of the Federal Reserve System.

Terrell, Henry S. and Key, Sydney J. "The Growth of Foreign Banking in the United States: An Analytical Survey." In *Key Issues in International Banking*. Proceedings of Federal Reserve Bank of Boston Conference no. 18, Melvin Village, New Hampshire, October 6, 1977.

Terrell, Henry S. and Key, Sydney J. *U.S. Offices of Foreign Banks: The Recent Experience*. International Finance Discussion Papers, no. 124. Washington, D.C.: Board of Governors of the Federal Reserve System, September 1978.

Terrell, Henry S. and Leimon, John. "The U.S. Activities of Foreign-Owned Banking Organizations." *Columbia Journal of World Business*, Winter 1975, pp. 87-97.

"Tex Bill Signed Giving Regulator Tighter Rein on Ownership Changes." *American Banker*, May 22, 1977.

"Texas Regulators Study Closely Bank Acquisition Bids Involving Foreigners." *American Banker*, July 11, 1978.

Theobald, Thomas C. "Different Marketing Strategies Needed in Doing Business With Foreign Companies." *American Banker*, December 11, 1979.

"There are Happy Marriages." *Euromoney*, March 1980, p. 72.

Thorn, Philip; Lack, Jean; and Eistob, Mayo, eds. *Who Owns What in World Banking*. London: The Banker Research Unit of the Financial Times, Ltd., 1980.

"The Threat of Foreign Banking." *New York Times*, July 22, 1979.

"Top 300 Survey. Obstacle Course for Bankers." *The Banker* (London), June 1973, p. 611.

"The United Kingdom: A Country Risk Profile." *Citicorp Financial Review*, 2nd Qtr. 1979, pp. 31-36.

U.K. Bank of England. "Banking Mergers and Participations." Press notice issued November 16, 1972. Printed in *Bank of England Quarterly Bulletin*, December 1972, p. 452.

"U.S. Acquisitions: Springboard for Growth" in U.K. Banking VI, *Financial Times*, September 19, 1978.

U.S. Board of Governors of the Federal Reserve System. Press Release dated December 2, 1971. Approval of applications by three Japanese banks to become bank holding companies through acquisition of new non-member insured banks. Orders with Governor Brimmer's dissenting opinion published in *Federal Reserve Bulletin*, January 1972, pp. 49-53.

U.S. Board of Governors of the Federal Reserve System. Press Release dated February 23, 1979. Statement of Policy on Supervision and Regulation of Foreign Bank Holding Companies.

U.S. Congress. House. Committee on Banking, Currency, and Housing. *Financial Institutions and The Nation's Economy*. Compendium of papers prepared for the FINE Study. 94th Cong., 1st sess., 1975.

U.S. Congress. House. Committee on Banking, Currency, and Housing. *Financial Institutions and the Nation's Economy, "discussion principles." Hearings before the Subcommittee on Financial Institutions Supervision, Regulation, and Insurance*. 94th cong., 1st and 2nd sess., 1975-1976.

U.S. Congress. House. Committee on Banking, Finance and Urban Affairs. *International Banking Act of 1977. Hearings before the Subcommittee on Financial Institutions Supervision, Regulation, and Insurance on H.R. 7325*. 95th Cong., 1st sess., 1977.

U.S. Congress. House. Committee on Government Operations. *Foreign Acquisitions of U.S. Banks and the Nonbanking Activities of Foreign Bank Holding Companies. Hearing before the Subcommittee on Commerce, Consumer and Monetary Affairs*. 96th Cong., 2nd sess., 1980.

U.S. Congress. House. Committee on Government Operations. *Operations of Federal Agencies in Monitoring, Reporting On, and Analyzing Foreign Investment in the United States. Hearings before the Subcommittee on Commerce, Consumer and Monetary Affairs*. 95th Cong., 2nd sess.—96th Cong., 1st sess., 1978-1979.

U.S. Congress. Joint Economic Committee. *Foreign Banking in the United States*. By Jack Zwick. Economic Policies and Practices Series, Joint Committee Print, Study Paper 9. Washington, D.C.: U.S. Government Printing Office, 1966.

U.S. Congress. Senate. Committee on Banking, Housing, and Urban Affairs. *Edge Corporation Branching, Foreign Bank Takeovers and International Banking Facilities, Hearing*. 96th Cong., 1st sess., 1979.

U.S. Congress. Senate. Committee on Banking, Housing and Urban Affairs. *Foreign Bank Act of 1975. Hearings before the Subcommittee on Financial Institutions on S.958.* 94th Cong., 2nd sess., 1976.

U.S. Congress. Senate. Committee on Banking, Housing and Urban Affairs. *Foreign Takeovers of United States Banks.* A Study by the Staff of the Federal Reserve Board. 96th Cong., 2nd sess., July 1980.

U.S. Congress. Senate. Committee on Banking, Housing, and Urban Affairs. *International Banking Act of 1978. Hearing before the Subcommittee on Financial Institutions on H.R. 10899.* 95th Cong., 2nd sess., 1978.

U.S. Congress. Senate. Committee on Banking, Housing and Urban Affairs. *International Banking Act of 1978.* S. Rept. no. 95-1073 to accompany H.R. 10899, 95th Cong., 2nd sess., 1978.

U.S. Department of the Treasury. *Report to Congress on Foreign Government Treatment of U.S. Commercial Banking Organizations.* Washington, D.C.: Department of the Treasury, 1979.

U.S. Department of the Treasury. "U.S. Government Policy on Direct Investment." Policy Statement dated July 6, 1977.

U.S. General Accounting Office. *Considerable Increase in Foreign Banking in the United States Since 1972.* Report by the Comptroller General of the United States. Washington, D.C.: U.S. Government Printing Office, 1979.

U.S. General Accounting Office. *Despite Positive Effects, Further Foreign Acquisitions of U.S. Banks Should Be Limited Until Policy Conflicts Are Fully Addressed.* Washington, D.C.: Government Printing Office, 1980.

Utley, F. B. III. "Foreign Banks' Affiliation with United States Broker-Dealers: The Statutory Language and Assumptions of the Bank Holding Company Act." *Law and Policy in International Business*, vol. 7, 1975, pp. 1-56.

Vernon, Raymond, *Storm Over the Multinationals: The Real Issues.* Boston: Harvard University Press, 1977.

Vittas, Dimitri. "Public Ownership in Banking: A Survey of Seven Countries." *Issues in Bank Regulation*, vol. 2, Autumn 1978, pp. 7-22.

——. *The Regulation of Banks in the Member States of the EEC.* Alphen aan den Rijn, Netherlands: Sijthoff & Noordhoff, 1978.

——, ed. *Banking Systems Abroad.* London: Inter-Bank Research Organisation, April 1978.

Vogl, Frank. "Global Competition in Banking Gives Treasurers Wider Choices." *Financier*, July 1979, pp. 14-18.

Volcker, Paul A. "Treatment of Foreign Banks in the United States: Dilemmas and Opportunities." Federal Reserve Bank of New York *Quarterly Review*, Summer 1979, pp. 1-5.

Wallich, Henry C. "Developments In International Banking." Address before the Association of Foreign Banks. Berne, Switzerland, June 15, 1979.

Walter, Judith A. *Foreign Acquisition of U.S. Banks: Motives and Tactical Considerations.* Office of the Comptroller of the Currency Staff Paper. Washington, D.C., 1980.

——. *Supervisory Performance of Foreign-Controlled U.S. Banking Organizations.*

Office of the Comptroller of the Currency Staff Paper. Washington, D.C., 1980.

Walter, Judith A. and Weiss, Steven J. "An Evaluation of the Foreign Acquisition Issue." *Issues in Bank Regulation*, vol. 4, Winter 1981, pp. 3-9.

"A Way for Banks to Jump State Lines." *Business Week*, January 21, 1980, pp. 35-38.

Weaver, Anne S. "Bank Holding Companies: Competitive Issues and Policy." Federal Reserve Bank of Chicago *Economic Perspectives*, September/October 1979, pp. 15-23.

Weigold, C. Frederick. "Foreign Bids Seen Continuing." *American Banker*, July 3, 1979.

Weigold, C. Frederick. "International Banking Act Seen Spur to For. Acquisitions of U.S. Banks." *American Banker*, January 22, 1979.

——. "New Fed Disclosure Plan Worries Foreign Bankers." *American Banker*, November 26, 1979.

——. "Some Big Foreign Banks Weighing U.S. Bank Purchases." *American Banker*, May 10, 1978.

——. "Spaniards Look at Chicago Bank; Foreign Bids Seen Continuing." *American Banker*, July 3, 1979.

Weiss, Steven J. *The Competitive Balance Between Domestic and Foreign Banks in the U.S.* Office of the Comptroller of the Currency Staff Paper. Washington, D.C., 1980.

——. *Competitive Standards Applied to Foreign and Domestic Acquisitions of U.S. Banks*. Office of the Comptroller of the Currency Staff Paper. Washington, D.C., 1980. Article based on this paper forthcoming in the *Antitrust Bulletin*.

——. *A Critical Evaluation of Reciprocity in Foreign Bank Acquisitions*. Office of the Comptroller of the Currency Staff Paper. Washington, D.C., 1980.

——. "National Policies on Foreign Acquisitions of Banks." *The Bankers Magazine* (Boston), vol. 164, January-February 1981, pp. 25-29.

Welles, Chris. "Bankers, Bankers Everywhere—But How Much Business Are They Getting?" *Institutional Investor*, September 1977, pp. 115-136.

Wels, Alena and Conners, Tom. "Siebert Wary on Bank Takeovers." *The Journal of Commerce*, March 19, 1979.

"Why British Banks Are Storming U.S." *American Banker*, March 29, 1979.

Wilkins, Mira. *Foreign Enterprise in Florida*. Gainesville, Florida: University Presses of Florida, 1979.

Zwick, Jack and Edwards, Franklin R. "Activities and Regulatory Issues: Foreign Banks in the United States." *Columbia Journal of World Business*, Spring 1975, pp. 58-74.

Acknowledgments

Mark Au and Elizabeth A. Callaghan assisted in the compilation of the bibliography.